LONGMAN
PREPARATION COURSE
FOR THE
TOEFL® TEST

NEXT GENERATION
iBT

DEBORAH PHILLIPS

TOEFL® is the registered trademark of Educational Testing Service (ETS).
This publication is not endorsed or approved by ETS.

Longman

Longman Preparation Course for the TOEFL Test: iBT

Pearson Education, 10 Bank Street, White Plains, NY 10606

Editorial director: Pam Fishman
Project manager: Margo Grant
Development editor: Angela Castro, Jennifer Ademec
Vice President, director of design and production: Rhea Banker
Executive managing editor: Linda Moser
Project editor: Helen B. Ambrosio
Production coordinator: Melissa Leyva
Director of manufacturing: Patrice Fraccio
Senior manufacturing buyer: Nancy Flaggman
Cover design: Elizabeth Carlson, Barbara Sabella
CD-ROM project manager: Evelyn Fella
CD-ROM development editor: Lisa Hutchins
Text design adaptation: Page Designs International, Inc.
Text composition: Page Designs International, Inc.
Text photography: Hutchings Photography, Pearson Learning Group
Additional photograph credits: male professor on page 128 et al. © F64/ Photodisc Green/ Getty Images; Female professor on page 143 et al. © Patrick Clark/ Photodisc Green/ Getty Images; female professor on page 148 et al. © Emanuele Taroni/ Photodisc Green/ Getty Images; female professor on page 150 et al. © Photodisc Collection/ Getty Images; male professor on page 152 et al. © Doug Menuez/ Photodisc Green/ Getty Images; groundhogs on page 152 © CORBIS; bear on page 152 © CORBIS; male professor on page 154 et al. © Photodisc Blue/ Getty images; man and woman on page 349 et al. © Keith Brofsky/ Photodisc Green/ Getty Images; James Cook on page 432 © CORBIS; Kamehameha on page 432 © CORBIS; Liliuokalani on page 432 © CORBIS; Three-Mile Island on page 434 © Lef Skoogfors/CORBIS; female professor on page 232 et al. © Photodisc Blue/ Getty Images; Blue Grotto Cave on page 469 © Mimmo Jidice/CORBIS; Lava Bed National Monument on page 469 © David Muench/CORBIS; Carlsbad Caverns on page 496 © Adam Woolfitt/CORBIS.

Library of Congress Cataloging-in-Publication Data

Phillips, Deborah
  Longman preparation course for the TOEFL test : iBT /
Deborah Phillips.
     p. cm.
  ISBN 0-13-193290-X (pbk. : with CD-ROM and answer key) — ISBN
0-13-195051-7 (pbk. : with answer key) — ISBN 0-13-192341-2 (pbk. : with
CD-ROM and without answer key)
  1. English language—Textbooks for foreign speakers. 2. Test of English
as a foreign language—Study guides. 3. English language—Examinations—
Study guides. I. Title: Preparation course for the TOEFL test. II. Title.
  PE1128.P46176 2005
  428'.0076—dc22

                                        2005011430

Printed in the United States of America
3 4 5 6 7 8 9 10—CRK—10 09 08 07 06

CONTENTS

SECTION FOUR: WRITING

MINI-TESTS

INTRODUCTION

ABOUT THIS COURSE

PURPOSE OF THE COURSE

This course is intended to prepare students for the *iBT (internet-Based TOEFL)* test. It is based on the most up-to-date information available on the *iBT*.

   Longman Preparation Course for the TOEFL Test: Next Generation iBT can be used in a variety of ways, depending on the needs of the reader:

- It can be used as the primary classroom text in a course emphasizing preparation for the *iBT* TOEFL test.
- It can be used as a supplementary text in a more general ESL/EFL course.
- Along with its companion audio program, it can be used as a tool for individualized study by students preparing for the *iBT* TOEFL test outside of the ESL/EFL classroom.

WHAT IS IN THE BOOK

The book contains a variety of materials that together provide a comprehensive TOEFL preparation course:

- **Diagnostic Pre-Tests** for each section of the *iBT* TOEFL test (Reading, Listening, Speaking, Writing) measure students' level of performance and allow students to determine specific areas of weakness.
- **Language Skills** for each section of the test provide students with a thorough understanding of the language skills that are regularly tested on the *iBT* TOEFL test.
- **Test-Taking Strategies** for each section of the test provide students with clearly defined steps to maximize their performance on the test.
- **Exercises** provide practice of one or more skills in a non-TOEFL format.
- **TOEFL Exercises** provide practice of one or more skills in a TOEFL format.
- **TOEFL Review Exercises** provide practice of all of the skills taught up to that point in a TOEFL format.
- **TOEFL Post-Tests** for each section of the test measure the progress that students have made after working through the skills and strategies in the text.
- Eight **Mini-Tests** allow students to simulate the experience of taking actual tests using shorter versions (approximately 1.5 hours each) of the test.
- Two **Complete Tests** allow students to simulate the experience of taking actual tests using full-length versions (approximately 3.5 hours each) of the test.
- **Scoring Information** allows students to determine their approximate TOEFL scores on the Pre-Tests, Post-Tests, Mini-Tests, and Complete Tests.
- **Self Assessment Checklists** allow students to monitor their progress in specific language skills on the Pre-Tests, Post-Tests, Mini-Tests, and Complete Tests so that they can determine which skills have been mastered and which skills require further study.

WHAT IS ON THE CD-ROM

The CD-ROM, with 700 test items, includes a variety of materials that contribute to an effective preparation program for the *iBT* TOEFL test.

- An **Overview** describes the features of the CD-ROM.
- **Skills Practice** for each of the sections (Reading, Listening, Speaking, Writing) provide students with the opportunity to review and master each of the language skills on the test.
- Eight **Mini-Tests** allow students to simulate the experience of taking actual tests using shorter versions (approximately 1.5 hours each) of the test.
- Two **Complete Tests** allow students to simulate the experience of taking actual tests using full-length versions (approximately 3.5 hours each) of the test.
- **Answers** and **Explanations** for all skills practice and test items allow students to understand their errors and learn from their mistakes.
- **Skill Reports** relate the test items on the CD-ROM to the language skills presented in the book.
- **Results Reports** enable students to record and print out charts that monitor their progress on all skills practice and test items.

The following chart describes the contents of the CD-ROM:

	SKILLS PRACTICE		TESTS	
READING	Skills 1–2	39 questions	Mini-Test 1	13 questions
	Skills 3–4	33 questions	Mini-Test 2	13 questions
	Skills 5–6	39 questions	Mini-Test 3	13 questions
	Skills 7–8	33 questions	Mini-Test 4	13 questions
	Skills 9–10	15 questions	Mini-Test 5	13 questions
			Mini-Test 6	13 questions
			Mini-Test 7	13 questions
			Mini-Test 8	13 questions
			Complete Test 1	39 questions
			Complete Test 2	39 questions
LISTENING	Skills 1–2	20 questions	Mini-Test 1	11 questions
	Skills 3–4	18 questions	Mini-Test 2	11 questions
	Skills 5–6	15 questions	Mini-Test 3	11 questions
			Mini-Test 4	11 questions
			Mini-Test 5	11 questions
			Mini-Test 6	11 questions
			Mini-Test 7	11 questions
			Mini-Test 8	11 questions
			Complete Test 1	34 questions
			Complete Test 2	34 questions

SPEAKING	Skills 1–2 Skills 3–4 Skills 5–8 Skills 9–12 Skills 13–15 Skills 16–18	3 questions 3 questions 3 questions 3 questions 3 questions 3 questions	Mini-Test 1 Mini-Test 2 Mini-Test 3 Mini-Test 4 Mini-Test 5 Mini-Test 6 Mini-Test 7 Mini-Test 8	3 questions 3 questions 3 questions 3 questions 3 questions 3 questions 3 questions 3 questions
			Complete Test 1 Complete Test 2	6 questions 6 questions
WRITING	Skills 1–7 Skills 8–14	29 questions 50 questions	Mini-Test 1 Mini-Test 2 Mini-Test 3 Mini-Test 4 Mini-Test 5 Mini-Test 6 Mini-Test 7 Mini-Test 8	1 question 1 question 1 question 1 question 1 question 1 question 1 question 1 question
			Complete Test 1 Complete Test 2	2 questions 2 questions

WHAT IS ON THE AUDIO RECORDINGS

The recording program that can be purchased to accompany this book includes all of the recorded materials from the Listening, Writing, and Speaking sections and the Mini-Tests and Complete Tests. This program is available on either audio CDs or audio cassettes.

OTHER AVAILABLE MATERIALS

Longman publishes a full suite of materials for TOEFL preparation: materials for the paper test, for the computer-based CBT, and for the internet-based iBT, at both intermediate and advanced levels. Please contact Longman's website at www.longman.com for a complete list of TOEFL products.

ABOUT THE
iBT VERSION OF THE TOEFL TEST _____

OVERVIEW OF THE iBT TOEFL TEST

The *iBT* TOEFL test is a test to measure the English proficiency and academic skills of nonnative speakers of English. It is required primarily by English-language colleges and universities. Additionally, institutions such as government agencies, businesses, or scholarship programs may require this test.

DESCRIPTION OF THE iBT TOEFL TEST

The *iBT* version of the TOEFL test currently has the following four sections:

- The Reading section consists of three long passages and questions about the passages. The passages are on academic topics; they are the kind of material that might be found in an undergraduate university textbook. Students answer questions about main ideas, details, inferences, sentence restatements, sentence insertion, vocabulary, function, and overall ideas.
- The Listening section consists of six long passages and questions about the passages. The passages consist of two student conversations and four academic lectures or discussions. The questions ask the students to determine main ideas, details, function, stance, inferences, and overall organization.
- The Speaking section consists of six tasks, two independent tasks and four integrated tasks. In the two independent tasks, students must answer opinion questions about some aspect of academic life. In two integrated reading, listening, and speaking tasks, students must read a passage, listen to a passage, and speak about how the ideas in the two passages are related. In two integrated listening and speaking tasks, students must listen to long passages and then summarize and offer opinions on the information in the passages.
- The Writing section consists of two tasks, one integrated task and one independent task. In the integrated task, students must read an academic passage, listen to an academic passage, and write about how the ideas in the two passages are related. In the independent task, students must write a personal essay.

The probable format of an *iBT* TOEFL test is outlined in the following chart:

	iBT	APPROXIMATE TIME
READING	3 passages and 39 questions	60 minutes
LISTENING	6 passages and 34 questions	50 minutes
SPEAKING	6 tasks and 6 questions	20 minutes
WRITING	2 tasks and 2 questions	55 minutes

It should be noted that at least one of the sections of the test will include extra, uncounted material. Educational Testing Service (ETS) includes extra material to try out material for future tests. If you are given a longer section, you must work hard on all of the materials because you do not know which material counts and which material is extra. (If there are four reading passages instead of three, three of the passages will count and one of the passages will not be counted. It is possible that the uncounted passage could be any of the four passages.)

REGISTRATION FOR THE TEST

It is important to understand the following information about registration for the TOEFL test:

- The first step in the registration process is to obtain a copy of the *TOEFL Information Bulletin*. This bulletin can be obtained by downloading it or ordering it from the TOEFL website at www.toefl.org.
- From the bulletin, it is possible to determine when and where the *iBT* version of the TOEFL test will be given.
- Procedures for completing the registration form and submitting it are listed in the *TOEFL Information Bulletin*. These procedures must be followed exactly.

HOW THE TEST IS SCORED

Students should keep the following information in mind about the scoring of the *iBT* version of the TOEFL test:

- The *iBT* version of the TOEFL test is scored on a scale of 0 to 120 points.
- Each of the four sections (Reading, Listening, Speaking, and Writing) receives a scaled score from 0 to 30. The scaled scores from the four sections are added together to determine the overall score.
- Speaking is initially given a score of 0 to 4, and writing is initially given a score of 0 to 5. These scores are converted to scaled scores of 0 to 30. Criteria for the 0 to 5 writing scores and 0 to 4 speaking scores are included on pages 538–541.
- After students complete the Pre-Tests, Post-Tests, Mini-Tests, and Complete Tests in the book, it is possible for them to estimate their scaled scores. A description of how to estimate the scaled scores of the various sections is included on page 543.
- After students complete the Mini-Tests and Complete Tests on the CD-ROM, scaled scores will be provided.

TO THE STUDENTS

HOW TO PREPARE FOR THE iBT VERSION OF THE TEST

The *iBT* TOEFL test is a standardized test of English and academic skills. To do well on this test, you should therefore work in these areas to improve your score:

- You must work to improve your knowledge of the English *language skills* that are covered on the *iBT* TOEFL test.
- You must work to improve your knowledge of the *academic skills* that are covered on the *iBT* TOEFL test.
- You must understand the *test-taking strategies* that are appropriate for the *iBT* TOEFL test.
- You must take *practice tests* with the focus of applying your knowledge of the appropriate language skills and test-taking strategies.

This book can familiarize you with the English language skills, academic skills, and test-taking strategies necessary for the *iBT* TOEFL test, and it can also provide you with a considerable amount of test practice. A huge amount of additional practice of the English language skills, academic skills, test-taking strategies, and tests for the *iBT* TOEFL test is found on the CD-ROM.

HOW TO USE THIS BOOK

This book provides a variety of materials to help you prepare for the *iBT* TOEFL test. Following these steps can help you to get the most out of this book:

- Take the Diagnostic Pre-Test at the beginning of each section. When you take the Pre-Test, try to reproduce the conditions and time pressure of a real TOEFL test.
  - (A) Take each section of the test without interruption.
  - (B) Time yourself for each section so that you can experience the time pressure that exists on an actual TOEFL test.
  - (C) Play the listening recording one time only during the test. (You may play it more times when you are reviewing the test.)
- After you complete the Reading or Listening Pre-Test, you should score it, diagnose your answers, and record your results.
  - (A) Determine your TOEFL scaled score using the Scoring Information on pages 535–543.
  - (B) Complete the appropriate parts of the Skills Charts on pages 544–545 to determine which language skills you have mastered and which need further study.
  - (C) Record your results on the Progress Chart on page 554.
- After you complete the Speaking or Writing Pre-Test, you should evaluate it and determine your score.
  - (A) Complete the Self-Assessment Checklists on pages 546–553 to diagnose your responses.
  - (B) Determine your estimated scaled score using the Scoring information on pages 542–543.

- Work through the presentations and exercises for each section, paying particular attention to the skills that caused you problems in a Pre-Test. Each time that you complete a TOEFL-format exercise, try to simulate the conditions and time pressure of a real TOEFL test.

  (A) For reading questions, allow yourself one-and-a-half minutes for one question. (For example, if a reading passage has ten questions, you should allow yourself fifteen minutes to read the passage and answer the ten questions.)

  (B) For listening questions, play the recording one time only during the exercise. Do not stop the recording between the questions.

  (C) For speaking, allow yourself 15 to 20 seconds to prepare your response and 45 to 60 seconds to give your response.

  (D) For writing, allow yourself 20 minutes to write an integrated writing response and 30 minutes to write an independent writing response.

- When further practice on a specific point is included in an Appendix, a note in the text directs you to this practice. Complete the Appendix exercises on a specific point when the text directs you to those exercises and the point is an area that you need to improve.

- When you have completed all the skills exercises for a section, take the Post-Test for that section. Follow the directions above to reproduce the conditions and time pressure of a real TOEFL test. After you complete the Post-Test, follow the directions above to score it, diagnose your answers, and record your results.

- As you work through the course material, periodically schedule Mini-Tests and Complete Tests. There are eight Mini-Tests and two Complete Tests in the book. As you take each of the tests, follow the directions above to reproduce the conditions and time pressure of a real TOEFL test. After you finish each test, follow the directions above to score it, diagnose your answers, and record your results.

HOW TO USE THE CD-ROM

The CD-ROM provides additional practice of the language skills and *iBT*-version tests to supplement the language skills and tests in the book. The material on the CD-ROM is completely different from the material in the book to provide the maximum amount of practice. Following these steps can help you get the most out of the CD-ROM.

- After you have completed the language skills in the book, you should complete the related Skills Practice exercises on the CD-ROM.

	AFTER THIS IN THE BOOK	COMPLETE THIS ON THE CD-ROM
READING	Vocabulary and Reference Sentences Details Inferences Reading to Learn	Vocabulary and Reference Sentences Details Inferences Reading to Learn
LISTENING	Basic Comprehension Pragmatic Understanding Connecting Information	Basic Comprehension Pragmatic Understanding Connecting Information

	AFTER THIS IN THE BOOK	**COMPLETE THIS ON THE CD-ROM**
SPEAKING	Independent Tasks Integrated Tasks (Reading and Listening) Integrated Tasks (Listening)	Independent Tasks Integrated Tasks (Reading and Listening) Integrated Tasks (Listening)
WRITING	Integrated Task Independent Task	Integrated Tasks Independent Tasks

- Work slowly and carefully through the Reading and Listening Skills Practice exercises. These exercises are not timed but are instead designed to be done in a methodical and thoughtful way.
  - (A) Answer a question on the CD-ROM using the skills and strategies that you have learned in the book.
  - (B) Use the *Check Answer* button to determine whether the answer to that question is correct or incorrect.
  - (C) If your answer is incorrect, reconsider the question, and choose a different answer.
  - (D) Use the *Check Answer* button to check your new response.
  - (E) When you are satisfied that you have figured out as much as you can on your own, use the *Explain Answer* button to see an explanation.
  - (F) Then move on to the next question, and repeat this process.

- Work slowly and carefully through the Speaking and Writing Skills Practice exercises. These exercises are not timed but are instead designed to be done in a methodical and thoughtful way.
  - (A) Complete a speaking or writing task using the skills and strategies that you have learned in the book. Take good notes as you work on a task.
  - (B) Play back your spoken response in Speaking or review your written response in Writing.
  - (C) Use the *Sample Notes* button to compare your notes to the sample notes provided on the CD-ROM.
  - (D) Use the *Sample Answer* button to see an example of a good answer and to compare your response to this answer.
  - (E) Complete the *Self-Assessment Checklist* to evaluate how well you completed your response.

- As you work your way through the Skills Practice exercises, monitor your progress on the charts included in the program.
  - (A) The *Results Reports* include a list of each of the exercises that you have completed and how well you have done on each of the exercises. (If you do an exercise more than once, the results of each attempt will be listed. In Speaking, only the final attempt will be saved.) You can print the Results Reports if you would like to keep them in a notebook.
  - (B) The *Skill Reports* include a list of each of the language skills in the book, how many questions related to each language skill you have answered, and what percentage of the questions you have answered correctly. In this way, you can see clearly which language skills you have mastered and which language skills require further work. You can print the Skill Reports if you would like to keep them in a notebook.

- Use the Mini-Tests and Complete Tests on the CD-ROM periodically throughout the course to determine how well you have learned to apply the language skills and test-taking strategies presented in the course. The CD-ROM includes eight Mini-Tests and two Complete Tests.

- Take the tests in a manner that is as close as possible to the actual testing environment. Choose a time when you can work on a section without interruption.

- Work straight through each test section. The *Check Answer, Explain Answer, Sample Notes,* and *Sample Answer* buttons are not available during test sections.

- After you complete a Reading or Listening test section, do the following:

    (A) Follow the directions to go to the *Results Report* for the test that you have just completed. A TOEFL equivalent score is given in the upper right corner of the *Results Report* for the test that you just completed.

    (B) In the *Results Report,* see which questions you answered correctly and incorrectly, and see which language skills were tested in each question. Print the *Results Report* if you would like to keep it in a notebook.

    (C) In the *Results Report,* review each question by double-clicking on a particular question. When you double-click on a question in the *Results Report,* you can see the question, the answer that you chose, the correct answer, and the *Explain Answer* button. You may click on the *Explain Answer* button to see an explanation.

    (D) Return to the *Results Report* for a particular test whenever you would like by entering through the *Results* button on the Main Menu. You do not need to review a test section immediately but may instead wait to review the test section.

- After you complete a Speaking or Writing test section, do the following:

    (A) Complete the *Self-Assessment Checklist* as directed. (You must complete the *Self-Assessment Checklist* to receive an estimated score.)

    (B) Play back your spoken response in Speaking or review your written response in Writing.

    (C) Use the *Sample Notes* button to compare your notes to the sample notes provided on the CD-ROM.

    (D) Use the *Sample Answer* button to see an example of a good answer and to compare your response to this answer.

TO THE TEACHER

HOW TO GET THE MOST OUT OF THE SKILLS EXERCISES IN THE BOOK

The skills exercises are a vital part of the TOEFL preparation process presented in this book. Maximum benefit can be obtained from the exercises if the students are properly prepared for the exercises and if the exercises are carefully reviewed after completion.

- Be sure that the students have a clear idea of the appropriate skills and strategies involved in each exercise. Before beginning each exercise, review the skills and strategies that are used in that exercise. Then, when you review the exercises, reinforce the skills and strategies that can be used to determine the correct answers.
- As you review the exercises, be sure to discuss each answer, the incorrect answers as well as the correct answers. Discuss how students can determine that each correct answer is correct and each incorrect answer is incorrect.
- The exercises are designed to be completed in class rather than assigned as homework. The exercises are short and take very little time to complete, particularly since it is important to keep students under time pressure while they are working on the exercises. Considerably more time should be spent in reviewing exercises than in actually doing them.

HOW TO GET THE MOST OUT OF THE TESTS IN THE BOOK

There are four different types of tests in this book: Pre-Tests, Post-Tests, Mini-Tests, and Complete Tests. When the tests are given, it is important that the test conditions be as similar to actual TOEFL test conditions as possible; each section of the test should be given without interruption and under the time pressure of the actual test. Giving the speaking tests in the book presents a unique problem because the students need to respond individually during the tests. Various ways of giving speaking tests are possible; you will need to determine the best way to give the speaking tests for your situation. Here are some suggestions:

- You can have the students come in individually and respond to the questions as the teacher listens to the responses and evaluates them.
- You can have a room set up where students come in individually to take a speaking test and record his or her responses on a cassette recorder. Then either the student or the teacher will need to evaluate the responses.
- You can have a room set up where students come in in groups of four to take a speaking test and record the responses on four cassette recorders, one in each corner of the room. Then either the students or the teacher will need to evaluate the responses.
- You can have the students sit down in an audio lab or computer lab where they can record their responses on the system or on cassette recorders. Then either the students or the teacher will need to evaluate the responses.

Review of the tests should emphasize the function served by each of these different types of tests:

- While reviewing the Pre-Tests, you should encourage students to determine the areas where they require further practice.
- While reviewing the Post-Tests, you should emphasize the language skills and strategies involved in determining the correct answer to each question.
- While reviewing the Mini-Tests, you should review the language skills and test-taking strategies that are applicable to the tests.

- While reviewing the Complete Tests, you should emphasize the overall strategies for the Complete Tests and review the variety of individual language skills and strategies taught throughout the course.

HOW TO GET THE MOST OUT OF THE CD-ROM

The CD-ROM is designed to supplement the practice that is contained in the book and to provide an alternate modality for preparation for the *iBT* TOEFL test. Here are some ideas to consider as you decide how to incorporate the CD-ROM into your course:

- The CD-ROM is closely coordinated with the book and is intended to provide further practice of the skills and strategies that are presented in the book. This means that the overall organization of the CD-ROM parallels the organization of the book but that the exercise material and test items on the CD-ROM are different from those found in the book. It can thus be quite effective to teach and practice the language skills and strategies in the book and then use the CD-ROM for further practice and assignments.

- The CD-ROM can be used in a computer lab during class time (if you are lucky enough to have access to a computer lab during class time), but it does not need to be used in this way. It can also be quite effective to use the book during class time and to make assignments from the CD-ROM for the students to complete outside of class, either in the school computer lab or on their personal computers. Either method works quite well.

- The CD-ROM contains a Skills Practice section, eight Mini-Tests, and two Complete Tests. In the Skills Practice section, the students can practice and assess their mastery of specific skills. In the Mini-Tests and Complete Tests, the students can see how well they are able to apply their knowledge of the language skills and test-taking strategies to test sections.

- The CD-ROM scores the Skills Practice exercises and the test sections in different ways. The Skills Practice exercises are given a score that shows the percentage correct. The test sections are given TOEFL equivalent scores.

- The CD-ROM contains printable *Skill Reports* and *Results Reports* so that you can easily and efficiently keep track of your students' progress. You may want to ask your students to print the *Results Report* after they complete each exercise or test and compile the *Results Reports* in a notebook; you can then ask the students to turn in their notebooks periodically so that you can easily check that the assignments have been completed and monitor the progress that the students are making.

- The speaking tasks can be reviewed by the students immediately after the students have completed them. Each speaking task is also saved and can be accessed through the Results Menu, though only the most recent version of each speaking task is saved. The speaking tasks can also be saved to a disk and submitted to the teacher. (You could also have the students record their responses on a cassette recorder as they complete a test instead of having them record their responses on the computer. Then you could have the students turn in their cassettes for review instead of turning in computer disks.)

- The writing tasks can be printed when they are written so that they can be reviewed and analyzed. Each of the writing tasks is also automatically saved and can be accessed through the Results Menu. It is also possible for students to copy their writing tasks into a word processing program so that they can make changes, corrections, and improvements to their writing tasks.

HOW MUCH TIME TO SPEND ON THE MATERIAL

You may have questions about how much time it takes to complete the materials in this course. The numbers in the following chart indicate approximately how many hours it takes to complete the material[1]:

	BOOK		CD-ROM	
READING SKILLS	Pre-Test	2		
	Skills 1–2	8	Skills 1–2	2
	Skills 3–4	8	Skills 3–4	2
	Skills 5–6	8	Skills 5–6	2
	Skills 7–8	8	Skills 7–8	2
	Skills 9–10	8	Skills 9–10	1
	Post-Test	2		
LISTENING SKILLS	Pre-Test	1		
	Skills 1–2	6	Skills 1–2	2
	Skills 3–4	6	Skills 3–4	2
	Skills 5–6	6	Skills 5–6	2
	Post-Test	1		
SPEAKING SKILLS	Pre-Test	2		
	Skills 1–4	5	Skills 1–4	2
	Skills 5–8	5	Skills 5–8	2
	Skills 9–12	5	Skills 9–12	2
	Skills 13–15	4	Skills 13–15	2
	Skills 16–18	4	Skills 16–18	2
	Post-Test	2		
WRITING SKILLS	Pre-Test	2		
	Skills 1–7	12	Skills 1–7	3
	Skills 8–14	12	Skills 8–14	4
	Post-Test	2		
MINI-TEST 1	Reading	1	Reading	1
	Listening	1	Listening	1
	Speaking	1	Speaking	1
	Writing	1	Writing	1
MINI-TEST 2	Reading	1	Reading	1
	Listening	1	Listening	1
	Speaking	1	Speaking	1
	Writing	1	Writing	1

---

[1] The numbers related to the book indicate approximately how much class time it takes to introduce the material, complete the exercises, and review the exercises. The numbers related to the CD-ROM indicate approximately how much time it takes to complete the exercise and review it.

MINI-TEST 3	Reading Listening Speaking Writing	1 1 1 1	Reading Listening Speaking Writing	1 1 1 1
MINI-TEST 4	Reading Listening Speaking Writing	1 1 1 1	Reading Listening Speaking Writing	1 1 1 1
MINI-TEST 5	Reading Listening Speaking Writing	1 1 1 1	Reading Listening Speaking Writing	1 1 1 1
MINI-TEST 6	Reading Listening Speaking Writing	1 1 1 1	Reading Listening Speaking Writing	1 1 1 1
MINI-TEST 7	Reading Listening Speaking Writing	1 1 1 1	Reading Listening Speaking Writing	1 1 1 1
MINI-TEST 8	Reading Listening Speaking Writing	1 1 1 1	Reading Listening Speaking Writing	1 1 1 1
COMPLETE TEST 1	Reading Listening Speaking Writing	2 2 2 2	Reading Listening Speaking Writing	2 2 2 2
COMPLETE TEST 2	Reading Listening Speaking Writing	2 2 2 2	Reading Listening Speaking Writing	2 2 2 2
APPENDIX	Appendix A Appendix B Appendix C	6 6 21		
		200 hours		**80 hours**

HOW TO DIVIDE THE MATERIAL

You may need to divide the materials in this course so that they can be used over a number of sessions. The following is one suggested way to divide the materials into two sessions:

SESSION 1	BOOK		CD-ROM	
READING SKILLS	Pre-Test	2		
	Skills 1–2	8	Skills 1–2	2
	Skills 3–4	8	Skills 3–4	2
	Skills 5–6	8	Skills 5–6	2
LISTENING SKILLS	Pre-Test	1		
	Skills 1–2	6	Skills 1–2	2
	Skills 3–4	6	Skills 3–4	2
SPEAKING SKILLS	Pre-Test	2		
	Skills 1–4	5	Skills 1–4	2
	Skills 5–8	5	Skills 5–8	2
WRITING SKILLS	Pre-Test	2		
	Skills 1–7	12	Skills 1–7	3
MINI-TEST 1	Reading	1	Reading	1
	Listening	1	Listening	1
	Speaking	1	Speaking	1
	Writing	1	Writing	1
MINI-TEST 2	Reading	1	Reading	1
	Listening	1	Listening	1
	Speaking	1	Speaking	1
	Writing	1	Writing	1
MINI-TEST 3	Reading	1	Reading	1
	Listening	1	Listening	1
	Speaking	1	Speaking	1
	Writing	1	Writing	1
MINI-TEST 4	Reading	1	Reading	1
	Listening	1	Listening	1
	Speaking	1	Speaking	1
	Writing	1	Writing	1
COMPLETE TEST 1	Reading	2	Reading	2
	Listening	2	Listening	2
	Speaking	2	Speaking	2
	Writing	2	Writing	2
APPENDIX	Appendix A	6		
	Appendix B	6		
		101 hours		**41 hours**

SESSION 2	BOOK		CD-ROM	
READING SKILLS	Skills 7–8 Skills 9–10 Post-Test	8 8 2	Skills 7–8 Skills 9–10	2 1
LISTENING SKILLS	Skills 5–6 Post-Test	6 1	Skills 5–6	2
SPEAKING SKILLS	Skills 9–12 Skills 13–15 Skills 16–18 Post-Test	5 4 4 2	Skills 9–12 Skills 13–15 Skills 16–18	2 2 2
WRITING SKILLS	Skills 8–14 Post-Test	12 2	Skills 8–14	4
MINI-TEST 5	Reading Listening Speaking Writing	1 1 1 1	Reading Listening Speaking Writing	1 1 1 1
MINI-TEST 6	Reading Listening Speaking Writing	1 1 1 1	Reading Listening Speaking Writing	1 1 1 1
MINI-TEST 7	Reading Listening Speaking Writing	1 1 1 1	Reading Listening Speaking Writing	1 1 1 1
MINI-TEST 8	Reading Listening Speaking Writing	1 1 1 1	Reading Listening Speaking Writing	1 1 1 1
COMPLETE TEST 2	Reading Listening Speaking Writing	2 2 2 2	Reading Listening Speaking Writing	2 2 2 2
APPENDIX	Appendix C	21		
		99 hours		**39 hours**

The following is a suggested way to divide the materials into three sessions:

SESSION 1	BOOK		CD-ROM	
READING SKILLS	Pre-Test	2		
	Skills 1–2	8	Skills 1–2	2
	Skills 3–4	8	Skills 3–4	2
LISTENING SKILLS	Pre-Test	1		
	Skills 1–2	6	Skills 1–2	2
SPEAKING SKILLS	Pre-Test	2		
	Skills 1–4	5	Skills 1–4	2
MINI-TEST 1	Reading	1	Reading	1
	Listening	1	Listening	1
	Speaking	1	Speaking	1
	Writing	1	Writing	1
MINI-TEST 2	Reading	1	Reading	1
	Listening	1	Listening	1
	Speaking	1	Speaking	1
	Writing	1	Writing	1
MINI-TEST 3	Reading	1	Reading	1
	Listening	1	Listening	1
	Speaking	1	Speaking	1
	Writing	1	Writing	1
APPENDIX	Appendix C	21		
		65 hours		**20 hours**

SESSION 2	BOOK		CD-ROM	
READING SKILLS	Skills 5–6	8	Skills 5–6	2
	Skills 7–8	8	Skills 7–8	2
LISTENING SKILLS	Skills 3–4	6	Skills 3–4	2
SPEAKING SKILLS	Skills 5–8	5	Skills 5–8	2
	Skills 9–12	5	Skills 9–12	2
WRITING SKILLS	Pre-Test	2		
	Skills 1–7	12	Skills 1–7	3
MINI-TEST 4	Reading	1	Reading	1
	Listening	1	Listening	1
	Speaking	1	Speaking	1
	Writing	1	Writing	1
MINI-TEST 5	Reading	1	Reading	1
	Listening	1	Listening	1
	Speaking	1	Speaking	1
	Writing	1	Writing	1
COMPLETE TEST 1	Reading	2	Reading	2
	Listening	2	Listening	2
	Speaking	2	Speaking	2
	Writing	2	Writing	2
APPENDIX	Appendix A	6		
		68 hours		**29 hours**

SESSION 3	BOOK		CD-ROM	
READING SKILLS	Skills 9–10	8	Skills 9–10	1
	Post-Test	2		
LISTENING SKILLS	Skills 5–6	6	Skills 5–6	2
	Post-Test	1		
SPEAKING SKILLS	Skills 13–15	4	Skills 13–15	2
	Skills 16–18	4	Skills 16–18	2
	Post-Test	2		
WRITING SKILLS	Skills 8–14	12	Skills 8–14	4
	Post-Test	2		
MINI-TEST 6	Reading	1	Reading	1
	Listening	1	Listening	1
	Speaking	1	Speaking	1
	Writing	1	Writing	1
MINI-TEST 7	Reading	1	Reading	1
	Listening	1	Listening	1
	Speaking	1	Speaking	1
	Writing	1	Writing	1
MINI-TEST 8	Reading	1	Reading	1
	Listening	1	Listening	1
	Speaking	1	Speaking	1
	Writing	1	Writing	1
COMPLETE TEST 2	Reading	2	Reading	2
	Listening	2	Listening	2
	Speaking	2	Speaking	2
	Writing	2	Writing	2
APPENDIX	Appendix B	6		
		67 hours		**31 hours**

READING

READING DIAGNOSTIC PRE-TEST

30 minutes

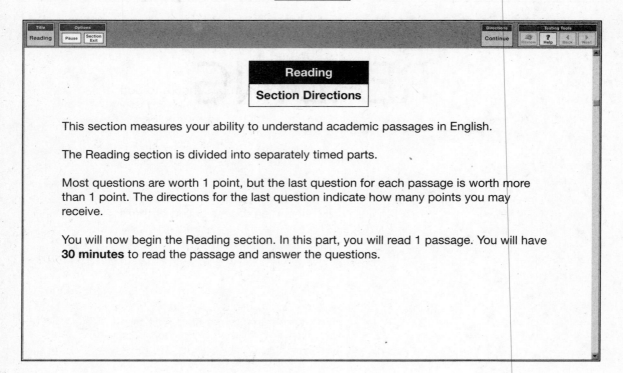

Reading

Section Directions

This section measures your ability to understand academic passages in English.

The Reading section is divided into separately timed parts.

Most questions are worth 1 point, but the last question for each passage is worth more than 1 point. The directions for the last question indicate how many points you may receive.

You will now begin the Reading section. In this part, you will read 1 passage. You will have **30 minutes** to read the passage and answer the questions.

Read the passage.

$\boxed{\text{30 minutes}}$

Paragraph

Aggression

1   Aggressive behavior is any behavior that is intended to cause injury, pain, suffering, damage, or destruction. While aggressive behavior is often thought of as purely physical, verbal attacks such as screaming and shouting or belittling and humiliating comments aimed at causing harm and suffering can also be a type of aggression. What is key to the definition of aggression is that whenever harm is inflicted, be it physical or verbal, it is intentional.

2   Questions about the causes of aggression have long been of concern to both social and biological scientists. Theories about the causes of aggression cover a broad spectrum, ranging from those with biological or instinctive emphases to those that portray aggression as a learned behavior.

3   Numerous theories are based on the idea that aggression is an inherent and natural human instinct. Aggression has been explained as an instinct that is directed externally toward others in a process called **displacement**, and it has been noted that aggressive impulses that are not channeled toward a specific person or group may be expressed indirectly through socially acceptable activities such as sports and competition in a process called **catharsis**. Biological, or instinctive, theories of aggression have also been put forth by **ethologists**, who study the behavior of animals in their natural environments. A number of ethologists have, based upon their observations of animals, supported the view that aggression is an innate instinct common to humans.

4   Two different schools of thought exist among those who view aggression as instinct. One group holds the view that aggression can build up spontaneously, with or without outside provocation, and violent behavior will thus result, perhaps as a result of little or no provocation. Another suggests that aggression is indeed an instinctive response but that, rather than occurring spontaneously and without provocation, it is a direct response to provocation from an outside source.

5   In contrast to instinct theories, social learning theories view aggression as a learned behavior. This approach focuses on the effect that role models and reinforcement of behavior have on the acquisition of aggressive behavior. Research has shown that aggressive behavior can be learned through a combination of modeling and positive reinforcement of the aggressive behavior and that children are influenced by the combined forces of observing aggressive behavior in parents, peers, or fictional role models and of noting either positive reinforcement for the aggressive behavior or, minimally, a lack of negative reinforcement for the behavior. While research has provided evidence that the behavior of a live model is more influential than that of a fictional model, fictional models of aggressive behavior such as those seen in movies and on television, do still have an impact on behavior. On-screen deaths or acts of violent behavior in certain television programs or movies can be counted in the tens, or hundreds, or even thousands; while some have argued that this sort of fictional violence does not in and of itself cause violence and may even have a beneficial cathartic effect, studies have shown correlations between viewing of violence and incidences of aggressive behavior in both childhood and adolescence. Studies have also shown that it is not just the modeling of aggressive behavior in either its real-life or fictional form that correlates with increased acts of violence in youths; a critical factor in increasing aggressive behaviors is the reinforcement of the behavior. If the aggressive role model is rewarded rather than punished for violent behavior, that behavior is more likely to be seen as positive and is thus more likely to be imitated.

Refer to this version of the passage to answer the questions that follow.

Paragraph

Aggression

1 Aggressive behavior is any behavior that is intended to cause injury, pain, suffering, damage, or destruction. While aggressive behavior is often thought of as purely physical, verbal attacks such as screaming and shouting or belittling and humiliating comments aimed at causing harm and suffering can also be a type of aggression. What is key to the definition of aggression is that whenever harm is inflicted, be it physical or verbal, it is intentional.

2 Questions about the causes of aggression have long been of concern to both social and biological scientists. Theories about the causes of aggression cover a broad spectrum, ranging from those with biological or instinctive emphases to those that portray aggression as a learned behavior.

3 Numerous theories are based on the idea that aggression is an inherent and natural human instinct. **8A** Aggression has been explained as an instinct that is directed externally toward others in a process called **displacement**, and it has been noted that aggressive impulses that are not channeled toward a specific person or group may be expressed indirectly through socially acceptable activities such as sports and competition in a process called **catharsis**. **8B** Biological, or instinctive, theories of aggression have also been put forth by **ethologists**, who study the behavior of animals in their natural environments. **8C** A number of ethologists have, based upon their observations of animals, supported the view that aggression is an innate instinct common to humans. **8D**

4 Two different schools of thought exist among those who view aggression as instinct. One group holds the view that aggression can build up spontaneously, with or without outside provocation, and violent behavior will thus result, perhaps as a result of little or no provocation. Another suggests that aggression is indeed an instinctive response but that, rather than occurring spontaneously and without provocation, it is a direct response to provocation from an outside source.

5 In contrast to instinct theories, social learning theories view aggression as a learned behavior. This approach focuses on the effect that role models and reinforcement of behavior have on the acquisition of aggressive behavior. Research has shown that aggressive behavior can be learned through a combination of modeling and positive reinforcement of the aggressive behavior and that children are influenced by the combined forces of observing aggressive behavior in parents, peers, or fictional role models and of noting either positive reinforcement for the aggressive behavior or, minimally, a lack of negative reinforcement for the behavior. While research has provided evidence that the behavior of a live model is more influential than that of a fictional model, fictional models of aggressive behavior such as those seen in movies and on television, do still have an impact on behavior. **18A** On-screen deaths or acts of violent behavior in certain television programs or movies can be counted in the tens, or hundreds, or even thousands; while some have argued that this sort of fictional violence does not in and of itself cause violence and may even have a beneficial cathartic effect, studies have shown correlations between viewing of violence and incidences of aggressive behavior in both childhood and adolescence. **18B** Studies have also shown that it is not just the modeling of aggressive behavior in either its real-life or fictional form that correlates with increased acts of violence in youths; a critical factor in increasing aggressive behaviors is the reinforcement of the behavior. **18C** If the aggressive role model is rewarded rather than punished for violent behavior, that behavior is more likely to be seen as positive and is thus more likely to be imitated. **18D**

Questions

1. Which of the following is NOT defined as aggressive behavior?
   - Ⓐ Inflicting pain accidentally
   - Ⓑ Making insulting remarks
   - Ⓒ Destroying property
   - Ⓓ Trying unsuccessfully to injure someone

2. The author mentions belittling and humiliating comments in paragraph 1 in order to
   - Ⓐ demonstrate how serious the problem of aggression is
   - Ⓑ clarify the difference between intentional and unintentional aggression
   - Ⓒ provide examples of verbal aggression
   - Ⓓ illustrate the nature of physical aggression

3. The word intentional in paragraph 1 is closest in meaning to
   - Ⓐ deliberate
   - Ⓑ estimated
   - Ⓒ forbidden
   - Ⓓ intermittent

4. Which of the sentences below expresses the essential information in the highlighted sentence in paragraph 2? *Incorrect* choices change the meaning in important ways or leave out essential information.
   - Ⓐ Biological theories of aggression emphasize its instinctive nature.
   - Ⓑ Theories that consider aggression biological are more accepted than those that consider it learned.
   - Ⓒ Various theories about aggression attribute it to either natural or learned causes.
   - Ⓓ Various theories try to compare the idea that aggression is biological with the idea that it is learned.

5. According to paragraph 3, displacement is
   - Ⓐ internally directed aggression
   - Ⓑ a modeled type of aggression
   - Ⓒ aggression that is unintentional
   - Ⓓ aggression that is directed outward

6. It can be inferred from paragraph 3 that catharsis
   - Ⓐ is a positive process
   - Ⓑ involves channeling aggression internally
   - Ⓒ is studied by ethologists
   - Ⓓ should be negatively reinforced

7. An ethologist would be most likely to study
   - Ⓐ learned catharsis in a certain species of monkey
   - Ⓑ the evolution of a certain type of fish
   - Ⓒ the bone structure of a certain type of dinosaur
   - Ⓓ the manner in which a certain male lion fights other male lions

8. Look at the four squares [■] that indicate where the following sentence can be added to paragraph 3.

   One may, for example, release aggression by joining a football team or a debate team or even a cooking competition.

   Click on a square [■] to add the sentence to the passage.

9. The phrase schools of thought in paragraph 4 is closest in meaning to
   - Ⓐ institutions of higher learning
   - Ⓑ lessons to improve behavior
   - Ⓒ methods of instruction
   - Ⓓ sets of shared beliefs

10. It is NOT mentioned in paragraph 4 that some believe that instinctive aggression may occur
    - Ⓐ without being provoked
    - Ⓑ in order to cause provocation
    - Ⓒ in response to minor provocation
    - Ⓓ in response to strong provocation

11. The word it in paragraph 4 refers to
    - Ⓐ aggression
    - Ⓑ an instinctive response
    - Ⓒ provocation
    - Ⓓ a direct response

12. The author begins paragraph 5 with the expression In contrast to instinct theories in order to

  Ⓐ introduce the instinct theories that will be presented in paragraph 5

  Ⓑ indicate that paragraph 5 will present two contrasting theories

  Ⓒ contrast instinctive theories of aggression with biological theories of aggression

  Ⓓ provide a transition to the idea that will be presented in paragraph 5

13. Which of the sentences below expresses the essential information in the highlighted sentence in paragraph 5? *Incorrect* choices change the meaning in important ways or leave out essential information.

  Ⓐ Research on aggression has shown that the best way to combat aggression is to model appropriate behavior and positively reinforce non-aggressive behavior.

  Ⓑ Children learn to behave aggressively by witnessing aggressive behavior that is rewarded or is at least not punished.

  Ⓒ When aggressive behavior is combined with modeling, it takes positive reinforcement to disrupt this type of behavior.

  Ⓓ Children will model aggressive behavior even in circumstances when the aggressive behavior is negatively reinforced.

14. The word that in paragraph 5 refers to

  Ⓐ research

  Ⓑ evidence

  Ⓒ the behavior

  Ⓓ a live model

15. What is stated in paragraph 5 about the modeling of aggressive behavior?

  Ⓐ Fictional models are as likely to cause aggressive behavior as are live models.

  Ⓑ Little correlation has been found between viewing of aggressive behavior on television and acting aggressively.

  Ⓒ Aggression in works of fiction may cause aggressive behavior.

  Ⓓ Aggression in society has an effect on the type of violence in movies and on television.

16. The phrase in and of itself in paragraph 5 is closest in meaning to

  Ⓐ internally

  Ⓑ single-handedly

  Ⓒ genuinely

  Ⓓ semi-privately

17. The word critical in paragraph 5 could best be replaced by

  Ⓐ negative

  Ⓑ considerate

  Ⓒ crucial

  Ⓓ studied

18. Look at the four squares [■] that indicate where the following sentence can be added to paragraph 5.

  Thus, it is more common for a youth to imitate aggressors who have been rewarded than those who have been punished.

  Click on a square [■] to add the sentence to the passage.

19.

Directions:	Select the appropriate sentences from the answer choices, and match them to the theories to which they relate. TWO of the answer choices will not be used. ***This question is worth 3 points.***
theories attributing aggression to instinct	• •
theories attributing aggression to learned behaviors	• •

Answer Choices (choose 4 to complete the chart):

(1) Aggression occurs in response to rewards for aggressive behavior.

(2) Aggression occurs without outside provocation.

(3) Aggression occurs in order to provoke confrontations.

(4) Aggression occurs in response to observed behavior.

(5) Aggression occurs in response to negative reinforcement of aggressive behavior.

(6) Aggression occurs as a natural response to provocation.

20.

Directions:	An introductory sentence or a brief summary of the passage is provided below. Complete the summary by selecting the FOUR answer choices that express the most important ideas in the passage. Some sentences do not belong in the summary because they express ideas that are not presented in the passage or are minor ideas in the passage. ***This question is worth 4 points.***

The passage discusses causes of aggression.
•
•
•
•

Answer Choices (choose 4 to complete the chart):

(1) Aggression may be learned behavior that occurs in order to model aggression from others.

(2) Aggression may be instinctive behavior that occurs without provocation.

(3) Aggression may be learned behavior that occurs in response to observed behavior.

(4) Aggression may be instinctive behavior that occurs in order to provoke others.

(5) Aggression may be learned behavior that occurs in response to rewards for aggressive behavior.

(6) Aggression may be instinctive behavior that occurs in response to provocation.

Turn to the chart on page 544, and circle the numbers of the questions that you missed.

READING OVERVIEW

The first section on the *iBT* TOEFL test is the Reading section. This section consists of three passages, each followed by a number of questions. All of the questions accompanying a passage are worth one point each, except for the last question in the set, which is worth more than one point. You have 20 minutes to complete the first passage and 40 minutes to complete the second and third passages.

- The **passages** are lengthy readings (600 to 700 words each) on academic topics.
- The **questions** may ask about vocabulary, pronoun reference, the meanings of sentences, where sentences can be inserted, stated and unstated details, inferences, rhetorical purpose, and overall organization of ideas.

The following strategies can help you in the Reading section.

STRATEGIES FOR READING

1. **Be familiar with the directions.** The directions on every test are the same, so it is not necessary to spend time reading the directions carefully when you take the test. You should be completely familiar with the directions before the day of the test.

2. **Dismiss the directions as soon as they come up.** You should already be familiar with the directions, so you can click on Continue as soon as it appears and use your time on the passages and questions.

3. **Do not worry if a reading passage is on a topic that is not familiar to you.** All of the information that you need to answer the questions is included in the passages. You do not need any background knowledge to answer the questions.

4. **Do not spend too much time reading the passages.** You do not have time to read each passage in depth, and it is quite possible to answer the questions correctly without first reading the passages in depth.

5. **Skim each passage to determine the main idea and overall organization of ideas in the passage.** You do not need to understand every detail in each passage to answer the questions correctly. It is therefore a waste of time to read each passage with the intent of understanding every single detail before you try to answer the questions.

6. **Look at each question to determine what type of question it is.** The type of question tells you how to proceed to answer the question.
   - For *vocabulary questions,* the targeted word will be highlighted in the passage. Find the highlighted word, and read the context around it.
   - For *reference questions,* the targeted word will be highlighted in the passage. Find the targeted word, and read the context preceding the highlighted word.
   - For *sentence insertion questions,* there will be darkened squares indicating where the sentence might be inserted. Read the context around the darkened squares carefully.

- For *sentence restatement questions,* the targeted sentence will be highlighted in the passage. Read the highlighted sentence carefully. It may also be helpful to read the context around the highlighted sentence.
- For *detail questions, unstated detail questions,* and *inference questions,* choose a key word in the question, and skim for the key word (or a related idea) in order in the passage. Read the part of the passage around the key word (or related idea).
- For *rhetorical purpose questions,* the targeted word or phrase will be highlighted in the passage. Read the highlighted word or phrase and the context around it to determine the rhetorical purpose.
- For *overall ideas questions,* focus on the main ideas rather than details of the passages. The main ideas are most likely explained in the introductory paragraph and at the beginning or end of each supporting paragraph.

7. **Choose the best answer to each question.** You may be certain of a particular answer, or you may eliminate any definitely incorrect answers and choose from among the remaining answers.

8. **Do not spend too much time on a question you are completely unsure of.** If you do not know the answer to a question, simply guess and go on. You can return to this question later (while you are still working on the same passage) if you have time.

9. **Monitor the time carefully on the title bar of the computer screen.** The title bar indicates the time remaining in the section, the total number of questions in the section, and the number of the question that you are working on.

10. **Guess to complete the section before time is up.** It can only increase your score to guess the answers to questions that you do not have time to complete. (Points are not subtracted for incorrect answers.)

READING SKILLS

VOCABULARY AND REFERENCE

Reading Skill 1: UNDERSTAND VOCABULARY FROM CONTEXT

In the Reading section of the *iBT* TOEFL test, you may be asked to determine the meaning of a word or phrase. It may be a difficult word or phrase that you have never seen before, or it may be an easier-looking word or phrase that has a number of varied meanings. In any of these cases, the passage will probably give you a clear indication of what the word or phrase means. Look at an example of a difficult word that perhaps you have never seen before; in this example, the context helps you to understand the meaning of the unknown word.

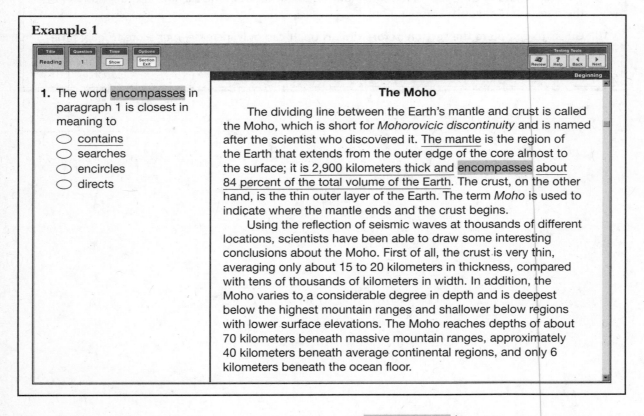

Example 1

Title: Reading | Question: 1 | Time: Show | Options: Section Exit | Testing Tools: Review Help Back Next

Beginning

1. The word encompasses in paragraph 1 is closest in meaning to
   ○ contains
   ○ searches
   ○ encircles
   ○ directs

The Moho

The dividing line between the Earth's mantle and crust is called the Moho, which is short for *Mohorovicic discontinuity* and is named after the scientist who discovered it. The mantle is the region of the Earth that extends from the outer edge of the core almost to the surface; it is 2,900 kilometers thick and encompasses about 84 percent of the total volume of the Earth. The crust, on the other hand, is the thin outer layer of the Earth. The term *Moho* is used to indicate where the mantle ends and the crust begins.

Using the reflection of seismic waves at thousands of different locations, scientists have been able to draw some interesting conclusions about the Moho. First of all, the crust is very thin, averaging only about 15 to 20 kilometers in thickness, compared with tens of thousands of kilometers in width. In addition, the Moho varies to a considerable degree in depth and is deepest below the highest mountain ranges and shallower below regions with lower surface elevations. The Moho reaches depths of about 70 kilometers beneath massive mountain ranges, approximately 40 kilometers beneath average continental regions, and only 6 kilometers beneath the ocean floor.

This question asks about the meaning of the word encompasses. In this question, you are not expected to know the meaning of this word. Instead, you should see in the context that *the mantle . . . is 2,900 kilometers thick and encompasses about 84 percent of the total volume of the Earth.* From this context, you can determine that *encompasses* is closest in meaning to *contains*. To answer this question, you should click on the first answer.

Next, look at an example of a word that you often see in everyday English. In this type of question, you should *not* give the normal, everyday meaning of the word; instead, a secondary meaning is being tested, so you must study the context to determine the meaning of the word in this situation.

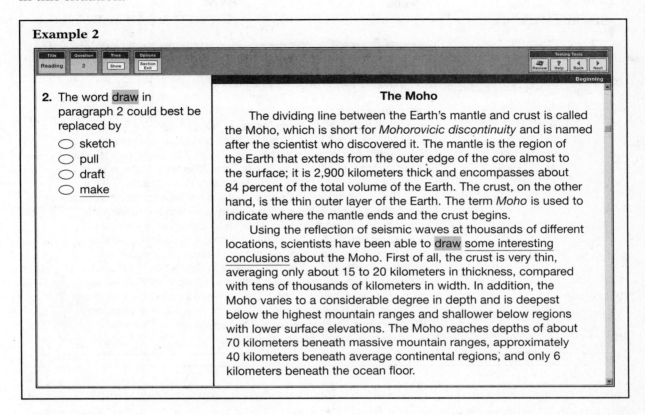

In this question, you are asked to choose a word that could replace draw. You should understand that *draw* is a normal, everyday word that is not being used in its normal, everyday way. To answer this type of question, you must see which answer best fits into the context in the passage. It does not make sense to talk about being able to *sketch, pull,* or *draft some interesting conclusions,* but it does make sense to *make some interesting conclusions.* To answer this question, you should click on the last answer.

Finally, look at an example of a phrase that perhaps you do not know; in this example, the context again helps you to understand the meaning of the unknown phrase.

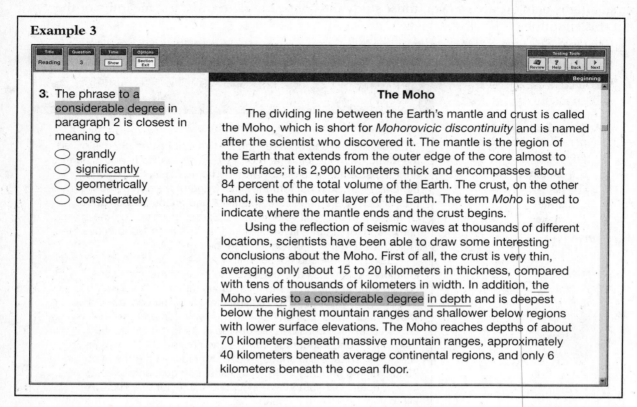

Example 3

3. The phrase to a considerable degree in paragraph 2 is closest in meaning to
   ○ grandly
   ○ significantly
   ○ geometrically
   ○ considerately

The Moho

The dividing line between the Earth's mantle and crust is called the Moho, which is short for *Mohorovicic discontinuity* and is named after the scientist who discovered it. The mantle is the region of the Earth that extends from the outer edge of the core almost to the surface; it is 2,900 kilometers thick and encompasses about 84 percent of the total volume of the Earth. The crust, on the other hand, is the thin outer layer of the Earth. The term *Moho* is used to indicate where the mantle ends and the crust begins.

Using the reflection of seismic waves at thousands of different locations, scientists have been able to draw some interesting conclusions about the Moho. First of all, the crust is very thin, averaging only about 15 to 20 kilometers in thickness, compared with tens of thousands of kilometers in width. In addition, the Moho varies to a considerable degree in depth and is deepest below the highest mountain ranges and shallower below regions with lower surface elevations. The Moho reaches depths of about 70 kilometers beneath massive mountain ranges, approximately 40 kilometers beneath average continental regions, and only 6 kilometers beneath the ocean floor.

This question asks about the meaning of the phrase to a considerable degree. In this question, you are again expected to determine from the context what the phrase means. The passage states that *the Moho varies to a considerable degree in depth*. From this context, you can determine that *to a considerable degree* is closest in meaning to *significantly*. To answer this question, you should click on the second answer.

The following chart outlines the key information that you should remember about questions testing vocabulary in context.

QUESTIONS ABOUT VOCABULARY IN CONTEXT	
HOW TO IDENTIFY THE QUESTION	The word (or phrase) X **is closest in meaning to . . .** The word (or phrase) X **could best be replaced by . . .**
WHERE TO FIND THE ANSWER	Information to help you to understand the meaning of an unknown word or phrase can often be found in the context surrounding the word or phrase.
HOW TO ANSWER THE QUESTION	1. Find the word or phrase in the passage. 2. Read the sentence that contains the word or phrase carefully. 3. Look for context clues to help you to understand the meaning. 4. Choose the answer that the context indicates.

READING EXERCISE 1: Study each of the passages, and choose the best answers to the questions that follow.

PASSAGE ONE (Questions 1–5)

Paragraph

Smog

1   The oxidation of exhaust gases is one of the primary sources of the world's pollution. The brown haze that is poised over some of the world's largest cities is properly called *photochemical smog*; it results from chemical reactions that take place in the air, using the energy of sunlight. The production of smog begins when gases are created in the cylinders of vehicle engines. It is there that oxygen and nitrogen gas combine as the fuel burns to form nitric oxide (NO), a colorless gas. The nitric oxide is forced out into the air through the vehicle tailpipe along with other gases.

2   When the gas reaches the air, it comes into contact with available oxygen from the atmosphere and combines with the oxygen to produce nitrogen dioxide (NO_2), which is a gas with a brownish hue. This nitrogen dioxide plays a role in the formation of acid rain in wetter or more humid climates and tends to decompose back into nitric oxide as it releases an oxygen atom from each molecule; the released oxygen atoms quickly combine with oxygen (O_2) molecules to form ozone (O_3). The brownish colored nitrogen dioxide is partially responsible for the brown color in smoggy air; the ozone is the toxic substance that causes irritation to eyes.

1. The word poised in paragraph 1 is closest in meaning to
   - (A) interacting
   - (B) sitting
   - (C) blowing
   - (D) poisoning

2. The phrase take place in paragraph 1 is closest in meaning to
   - (A) position themselves
   - (B) put
   - (C) are seated
   - (D) occur

3. The word forced in paragraph 1 could best be replaced by
   - (A) obliged
   - (B) required
   - (C) pushed
   - (D) commanded

4. The word hue in paragraph 2 is closest in meaning to
   - (A) color
   - (B) odor
   - (C) thickness
   - (D) smoke

5. The phrase plays a role in in paragraph 2 is closest in meaning to
   - (A) makes fun of
   - (B) serves a function in
   - (C) acts the part of
   - (D) moves about in

Autism

Autism is a developmental disorder that is characterized by severe behavioral abnormalities across all primary areas of functioning. Its onset is often early; it generally makes itself known by the age of two and one-half. It is not a single disease entity but is instead a syndrome defined by patterns and characteristics of behavior; it, therefore, most likely has multiple etiologies rather than a single causative factor. Autism is not fully understood and thus is controversial with respect to diagnosis, etiology, and treatment strategies.

6. The word primary in the passage could best be replaced by
   - Ⓐ elementary
   - Ⓑ main
   - Ⓒ introductory
   - Ⓓ primitive

7. The word onset in the passage is closest in meaning to
   - Ⓐ placement
   - Ⓑ arrangement
   - Ⓒ support
   - Ⓓ beginning

8. The word syndrome in the passage is closest in meaning to
   - Ⓐ concurrent set of symptoms
   - Ⓑ feeling of euphoria
   - Ⓒ mental breakdown
   - Ⓓ repetitive task

9. The word etiologies in the passage is closest in meaning to
   - Ⓐ symptoms
   - Ⓑ patterns
   - Ⓒ causes
   - Ⓓ onsets

10. The phrase with respect to in the passage could best be replaced by
    - Ⓐ with dignity toward
    - Ⓑ in regard to
    - Ⓒ irrespective of
    - Ⓓ out of politeness for

PASSAGE THREE *(Questions 11–15)*

Parasitic Plants

1   Parasitic plants are plants that survive by using food produced by host plants rather than by producing their own food from the Sun's energy. Because they do not need sunlight to survive, parasitic plants are generally found in umbrageous areas rather than in areas exposed to direct sunlight. Parasitic plants attach themselves to host plants, often to the stems or roots, by means of haustoria, which the parasite uses to make its way into the food channels of the host plant and absorb the nutrients that it needs to survive from the host plant.

2   The world's heaviest flower, a species of rafflesia, is a parasite that flourishes among, and lives off of, the roots of jungle vines. Each of these ponderous blooms can weigh up to 15 pounds (7 kg) and can measure up to 3 feet (1m) across.

11. The word umbrageous in paragraph 1 is closest in meaning to

Ⓐ moist
Ⓑ well lit
Ⓒ shaded
Ⓓ buried

12. Haustoria in paragraph 1 are most likely

Ⓐ offshoots from the parasite
Ⓑ seeds of the host plant
Ⓒ fruits from the host plant
Ⓓ food for the parasite

13. The phrase make its way into in paragraph 1 is closest in meaning to

Ⓐ develop
Ⓑ penetrate
Ⓒ outline
Ⓓ eat

14. The word ponderous in paragraph 2 is closest in meaning to

Ⓐ smelly
Ⓑ hidden
Ⓒ mature
Ⓓ heavy

15. The word across in paragraph 2 could best be replaced by

Ⓐ in diameter
Ⓑ on the other side
Ⓒ at a distance
Ⓓ inside and out

PASSAGE FOUR *(Questions 16–24)*

Paragraph

Edna Ferber

1   Edna Ferber (1887–1968) was a popular American novelist in the first half of the twentieth century. She embarked on her career by working as a newspaper reporter in Wisconsin and soon began writing novels. Her first novel, *Dawn O'Hara, the Girl Who Laughed,* was published in 1911, when she was only twenty-four years old.

2   Her big break came with the novel *So Big* (1924), which was awarded the Pulitzer Prize in Literature. The main conflict in the novel is between a mother who places a high value on hard work and honor and a son who repudiates his mother's values, instead preferring the easier path to fortune and celebrity. Like many of Ferber's novels, this novel features a tenacious female protagonist with strong character who struggles to deal with ethical dilemmas about the importance of status and money.

3   Probably the best known of Ferber's novels was *Show Boat* (1926), which tells the story of a Southern woman married to a charismatic but irresponsible man who leaves her with a daughter she must take great pains to support. In 1927, the novel was made into a musical that has endured to the present.

4   Other well-known novels by Ferber include *Cimarron* (1930) and *Giant* (1952), both of which were made into movies. These were epic novels about the settlement and growth of the West, centering on strong female lead characters who marry men lacking the same strength of character.

16. The phrase embarked on in paragraph 1 is closest in meaning to

  Ⓐ took a trip to
  Ⓑ started out on
  Ⓒ improved upon
  Ⓓ had an opinion about

17. The word break in paragraph 2 could best be replaced by

  Ⓐ rupture
  Ⓑ revelation
  Ⓒ opportunity
  Ⓓ rest

18. The word places in paragraph 2 could best be replaced by

  Ⓐ locates
  Ⓑ puts
  Ⓒ recites
  Ⓓ positions

19. The word repudiates in paragraph 2 is closest in meaning to

  Ⓐ refuses to accept
  Ⓑ lives up to
  Ⓒ tries to understand
  Ⓓ makes the best of

20. The word protagonist in paragraph 2 is closest in meaning to

  Ⓐ arch enemy
  Ⓑ voracious reader
  Ⓒ skilled worker
  Ⓓ lead character

21. The phrase take great pains in paragraph 3 is closest in meaning to

  Ⓐ work diligently
  Ⓑ recognize hurtfully
  Ⓒ accept unequivocally
  Ⓓ hurt agonizingly

22. The word endured in paragraph 3 is closest in meaning to

  Ⓐ lasted
  Ⓑ tested
  Ⓒ waited
  Ⓓ limited

23. The word epic in paragraph 4 could best be replaced by

  Ⓐ lengthy narrative
  Ⓑ detailed non-fictional
  Ⓒ emotionally romantic
  Ⓓ rousing Western

24. The phrase centering on in paragraph 4
could best be replaced by

(A) circling around
(B) pointing to
(C) focusing on
(D) arranging for

Reading Skill 2: RECOGNIZE REFERENTS

In the Reading section of the *iBT* TOEFL test, you may be asked to determine the referent for a particular pronoun or adjective (the noun to which a pronoun or adjective refers). You may be asked to find the referent for a variety of words, perhaps for a third person subject pronoun (*he, she, it, they*), a third person object pronoun (*him, her, it, them*), a relative pronoun (*who, which, that*), a third person possessive adjective (*his, her, its, their*), a third person possessive pronoun (*his, hers, theirs*), a demonstrative pronoun or adjective (*this, that, these, those*), or for a quantifier (*one, some, a few, many*). A referent generally precedes the pronoun or adjective in the passage; thus, to answer this type of question, you should study the context around the pronoun or adjective carefully and look for a referent that agrees with the noun or pronoun in front of the pronoun or adjective. Look at an example of a question that asks for the referent of the subject pronoun *it*.

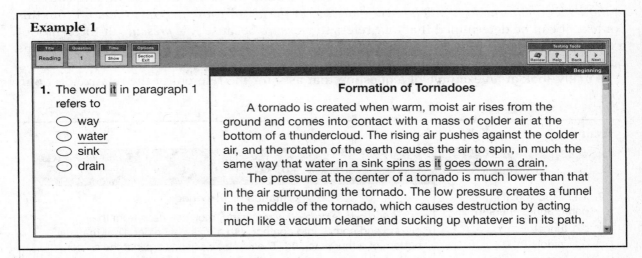

Example 1

1. The word it in paragraph 1 refers to	**Formation of Tornadoes**
○ way	A tornado is created when warm, moist air rises from the ground and comes into contact with a mass of colder air at the bottom of a thundercloud. The rising air pushes against the colder air, and the rotation of the earth causes the air to spin, in much the same way that <u>water in a sink spins as</u> it <u>goes down a drain</u>.
○ <u>water</u>	
○ sink	
○ drain	
	The pressure at the center of a tornado is much lower than that in the air surrounding the tornado. The low pressure creates a funnel in the middle of the tornado, which causes destruction by acting much like a vacuum cleaner and sucking up whatever is in its path.

In this example, you are asked to find the referent for the subject pronoun it. You should study the context around the singular pronoun *it* and look for a singular noun in front of *it* that fits into the context. The context around the pronoun states that *water in a sink spins as it goes down a drain*. From this context, it can be determined that *it* refers to *water* because it is *water* that *goes down a drain*. To answer this question, you should click on the second answer.

Now, look at an example of a question that asks for the referent of the demonstrative pronoun *that*.

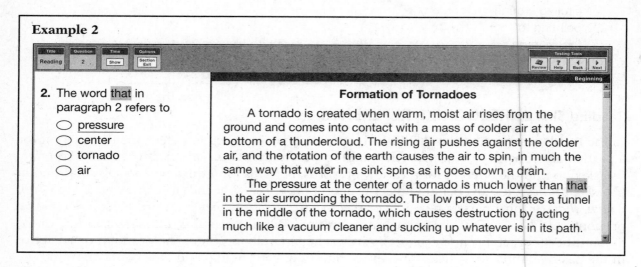

Example 2

| Title | Question | Time | Options | | Testing Tools |
| Reading | 2 | Show | Section Exit | | Review Help Back Next |

Beginning

2. The word that in paragraph 2 refers to
- ○ pressure
- ○ center
- ○ tornado
- ○ air

Formation of Tornadoes

A tornado is created when warm, moist air rises from the ground and comes into contact with a mass of colder air at the bottom of a thundercloud. The rising air pushes against the colder air, and the rotation of the earth causes the air to spin, in much the same way that water in a sink spins as it goes down a drain.

The pressure at the center of a tornado is much lower than that in the air surrounding the tornado. The low pressure creates a funnel in the middle of the tornado, which causes destruction by acting much like a vacuum cleaner and sucking up whatever is in its path.

In this example, you are asked to find the referent for the demonstrative pronoun that. You should study the context around the singular pronoun *that* and look for a singular noun in front of *that* that fits into the context. The context around the pronoun states that *the pressure at the center of a tornado is much lower than that in the air surrounding the tornado.* From this context, it can be determined that *that* refers to *pressure* because it is *pressure* at the center of a tornado that is much lower than *pressure* in the air surrounding the tornado. To answer this question, you should click on the first answer.

Finally, look at an example of a question that asks for the referent of the relative pronoun *which*.

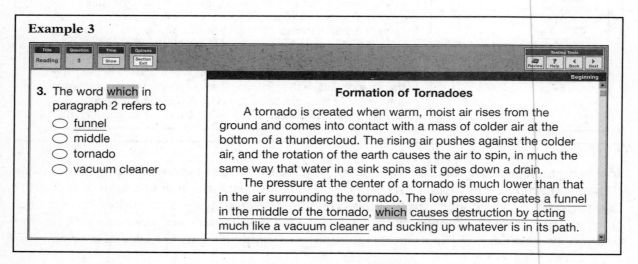

Example 3

| Title | Question | Time | Options | | Testing Tools |
| Reading | 3 | Show | Section Exit | | Review Help Back Next |

Beginning

3. The word which in paragraph 2 refers to
- ○ funnel
- ○ middle
- ○ tornado
- ○ vacuum cleaner

Formation of Tornadoes

A tornado is created when warm, moist air rises from the ground and comes into contact with a mass of colder air at the bottom of a thundercloud. The rising air pushes against the colder air, and the rotation of the earth causes the air to spin, in much the same way that water in a sink spins as it goes down a drain.

The pressure at the center of a tornado is much lower than that in the air surrounding the tornado. The low pressure creates a funnel in the middle of the tornado, which causes destruction by acting much like a vacuum cleaner and sucking up whatever is in its path.

In this example, you are asked to find the referent for the relative pronoun which. You should study the context around the relative pronoun *which* and look for a noun in front of *which* that fits into the context. The context around the pronoun mentions *a funnel in the middle of the tornado, which causes destruction by acting much like a vacuum cleaner.* From this context, it can be determined that *which* refers to *funnel* because it is a *funnel* that causes destruction by acting like a vacuum cleaner. To answer this question, you should click on the first answer.

The following chart outlines the key information that you should remember about questions testing referents.

QUESTIONS ABOUT REFERENTS	
HOW TO IDENTIFY THE QUESTION	The word X **refers** to . . .
WHERE TO FIND THE ANSWER	The pronoun or adjective is highlighted in the passage. The referent is generally in front of the highlighted word.
HOW TO ANSWER THE QUESTION	1. Locate the highlighted pronoun or adjective. 2. Look *before* the highlighted word for nouns that agree with the highlighted word. 3. Try each of the nouns in the context around the highlighted word. 4. Eliminate any definitely wrong answers, and choose the best answer from the remaining choices.

READING EXERCISE 2: Study each of the passages, and choose the best answers to the questions that follow.

PASSAGE ONE (Questions 1–4)

Animal Congregation

Many types of animals combine the advantages of family association with those conferred by membership in still larger groups. Bees congregate in hives; some fish move in schools; ants gather in mounds; wolves live in packs; deer associate in herds. The main

Line advantage of membership in a mass community is the safety that it provides. A large group
(5) of prey may be easier for a predator to find at any given point than is a small one, and a predator may think twice before taking on such a group; if a predator does decide to challenge a large group, it may merely encounter a confusing mass of moving bodies and possibly may not succeed in its primary goal.

1. The word those in the passage refers to
   Ⓐ types
   Ⓑ animals
   Ⓒ advantages
   Ⓓ groups

2. The word it in line 4 refers to
   Ⓐ advantage
   Ⓑ membership
   Ⓒ community
   Ⓓ safety

3. The word one in the passage refers to
   Ⓐ group
   Ⓑ prey
   Ⓒ predator
   Ⓓ point

4. The word it in line 7 refers to
   Ⓐ predator
   Ⓑ group
   Ⓒ mass
   Ⓓ goal

PASSAGE TWO (Questions 5–9)

Chromium Compounds

Paragraph

1   Most chromium compounds have brightly colored hues, and as a result they are widely used as coloring agents, or pigments, in paints. In addition to having a pleasing color, a paint must protect the surface to which it is applied and be easy to apply in a thin, uniform coat.

2   All paints consist of two parts. One is a powder of solid particles that is the source of the color and the opaqueness and is known as the pigment. The other, called the binder, is the liquid into which the pigment is blended. The binder used in some paints is made from oily solvents such as those derived from petroleum resources. When applied, these solvents evaporate, leaving deposits of pigment on the surface.

5. The word they in paragraph 1 refers to
- Ⓐ chromium compounds
- Ⓑ brightly colored hues
- Ⓒ coloring agents
- Ⓓ pigments

6. The word it in paragraph 1 refers to
- Ⓐ a pleasing color
- Ⓑ a paint
- Ⓒ the surface
- Ⓓ a thin, uniform coat

7. The word that in paragraph 2 refers to
- Ⓐ a powder
- Ⓑ solid particles
- Ⓒ the source
- Ⓓ the color

8. The word which in paragraph 2 refers to
- Ⓐ powder
- Ⓑ paint
- Ⓒ liquid
- Ⓓ pigment

9. The word those in paragraph 2 refers to
- Ⓐ some paints
- Ⓑ oily solvents
- Ⓒ petroleum resources
- Ⓓ deposits of pigment

PASSAGE THREE *(Questions 10–13)*

New World Epidemics

A huge loss of life resulted from the introduction of Old World diseases into the Americas in the early sixteenth century. The inhabitants of the Americas were separated from Asia, Africa, and Europe by rising oceans following the Ice Ages, and, as a result, they were isolated by means of this watery barrier from numerous virulent epidemic diseases that had developed across the ocean, such as measles, smallpox, pneumonia, and malaria. Pre-Columbian Americans had a relatively disease-free environment but also lacked the antibodies needed to protect them from bacteria and viruses brought to America by European explorers and colonists. A devastating outbreak of disease that strikes for the first time against a completely unprotected population is known as a virgin soil epidemic. Virgin soil epidemics contributed to an unbelievable decline in the population of native inhabitants of the Americas, one that has been estimated at as much as an 80 percent decrease of the native population in the centuries following the arrival of Europeans in the Americas.

10. The word they in the passage refers to
  - Ⓐ the inhabitants
  - Ⓑ epidemic diseases
  - Ⓒ rising oceans
  - Ⓓ the Ice Ages

11. The word that in the passage refers to
  - Ⓐ a disease-free environment
  - Ⓑ this watery barrier
  - Ⓒ virulent epidemic diseases
  - Ⓓ the ocean

12. The word them in the passage refers to
  - Ⓐ pre-Columbian Americans
  - Ⓑ the antibodies
  - Ⓒ bacteria and viruses
  - Ⓓ European explorers and colonists

13. The word one in the passage refers to
  - Ⓐ a virgin soil epidemic
  - Ⓑ an unbelievable decline
  - Ⓒ the population of native inhabitants
  - Ⓓ the arrival of Europeans

Horatio Alger, Jr.

Paragraph

1   Horatio Alger, Jr. (1832–1899) was the author of more than 100 books for boys in the second half of the nineteenth century that focused on the theme of success coming to those who work hard to achieve it. The son of a minister, Alger came from a prominent Massachusetts family. He graduated with honors from Harvard in 1852 and graduated from the Cambridge Divinity School eight years later. He served as a minister for a short time before moving to New York City in 1866 to devote his time to writing inspirational books for boys.

2   In many of his books, he wrote about the poor and homeless children of the slums of New York City, seeing them as unfortunate pawns of society who, if only given the opportunity, could improve their lot. A general plotline that he followed often was of a poor boy who managed to achieve a respectable and successful life by working hard and taking advantage of opportunities presented. Though his writing style was characterized by simplicity and repetition, it was well received by his target audience; his books were enormously popular, selling millions of copies well into the first few decades of the twentieth century.

14. The word that in paragraph 1 refers to
  Ⓐ author
  Ⓑ books
  Ⓒ boys
  Ⓓ half

15. The word it in paragraph 1 refers to
  Ⓐ the second half
  Ⓑ the nineteenth century
  Ⓒ 100
  Ⓓ success

16. The word them in paragraph 2 refers to
  Ⓐ books
  Ⓑ children
  Ⓒ slums
  Ⓓ pawns

17. The word who in paragraph 2 refers to
  Ⓐ slums
  Ⓑ society
  Ⓒ pawns
  Ⓓ opportunity

18. The word it in paragraph 2 refers to
  Ⓐ style
  Ⓑ simplicity
  Ⓒ repetition
  Ⓓ audience

READING EXERCISE (Skills 1–2): Read the passage.

Coral Colonies

1   Coral colonies require a series of complicated events and circumstances to develop into the characteristically intricate reef structures for which they are known. These events and circumstances involve physical and chemical processes as well as delicate interactions among various animals and plants for coral colonies to thrive.

2   The basic element in the development of coralline reef structures is a group of animals from the *Anthozoa* class, called stony corals, that is closely related to jellyfish and sea anemones. These small polyps (the individual animals that make up the coral reef), which are for the most part only a fraction of an inch in length, live in colonies made up of an immeasurable number of polyps clustered together. Each individual polyp obtains calcium from the seawater where it lives to create a skeleton around the lower part of its body, and the polyps attach themselves both to the living tissue and to the external skeletons of other polyps. Many polyps tend to retreat inside of their skeletons during hours of daylight and then stretch partially outside of their skeletons during hours of darkness to feed on minute plankton from the water around them. The mouth at the top of each body is surrounded by rings of tentacles used to grab onto food, and these rings of tentacles make the polyps look like flowers with rings of clustered petals; because of this, biologists for years thought that corals were plants rather than animals.

3   Once these coralline structures are established, they reproduce very quickly. They build in upward and outward directions to create a fringe of living coral surrounding the skeletal remnants of once-living coral. That coralline structures are commonplace in tropical waters around the world is due to the fact that they reproduce so quickly rather than the fact that they are hardy life-forms easily able to withstand external forces of nature. They cannot survive in water that is too dirty, and they need water that is at least 72° F (or 22° C) to exist, so they are formed only in waters ranging from 30° north to 30° south of the equator. They need a significant amount of sunlight, so they live only within an area between the surface of the ocean and a few meters beneath it. In addition, they require specific types of microscopic algae for their existence, and their skeletal shells are delicate in nature and are easily damaged or fragmented. They are also prey to other sea animals such as sponges and clams that bore into their skeletal structures and weaken them.

4   Coral colonies cannot build reef structures without considerable assistance. The many openings in and among the skeletons must be filled in and cemented together by material from around the colonies. The filling material often consists of fine sediments created either from the borings and waste of other animals around the coral or from the skeletons, shells, and remnants of dead plants and animals. The material that is used to cement the coral reefs comes from algae and other microscopic forms of seaweed.

5   An additional part of the process of reef formation is the ongoing compaction and cementation that occurs throughout the process. Because of the soluble and delicate nature of the material from which coral is created, the relatively unstable crystals of corals and shells break down over time and are then rearranged as a more stable form of limestone.

6   The coralline structures that are created through these complicated processes are extremely variable in form. They may, for example, be treelike and branching, or they may have more rounded and compact shapes. What they share in common, however, is the extraordinary variety of plant and animal life-forms that are a necessary part of the ongoing process of their formation.

GLOSSARY
polyps: simple sea animals with tube-shaped bodies

Refer to this version of the passage to answer the questions that follow.

Coral Colonies

1   Coral colonies require a series of complicated events and circumstances to develop into the characteristically intricate reef structures for which they are known. These events and circumstances involve physical and chemical processes as well as delicate interactions among various animals and plants for coral colonies to thrive.

2   The basic element in the development of coralline reef structures is a group of animals from the *Anthozoa* class, called stony corals, that is closely related to jellyfish and sea anemones. These small polyps (the individual animals that make up the coral reef), which are for the most part only a fraction of an inch in length, live in colonies made up of an immeasurable number of polyps clustered together. Each individual polyp obtains calcium from the seawater where it lives to create a skeleton around the lower part of its body, and the polyps attach themselves both to the living tissue and to the external skeletons of other polyps. Many polyps tend to retreat inside of their skeletons during hours of daylight and then stretch partially outside of their skeletons during hours of darkness to feed on minute plankton from the water around them. The mouth at the top of each body is surrounded by rings of tentacles used to grab onto food, and these rings of tentacles make the polyps look like flowers with rings of clustered petals; because of this, biologists for years thought that corals were plants rather than animals.

3   Once these coralline structures are established, they reproduce very quickly. They build in upward and outward directions to create a fringe of living coral surrounding the skeletal remnants of once-living coral. That coralline structures are commonplace in tropical waters around the world is due to the fact that they reproduce so quickly rather than the fact that they are hardy life-forms easily able to withstand external forces of nature. They cannot survive in water that is too dirty, and they need water that is at least 72° F (or 22° C) to exist, so they are formed only in waters ranging from 30° north to 30° south of the equator. They need a significant amount of sunlight, so they live only within an area between the surface of the ocean and a few meters beneath it. In addition, they require specific types of microscopic algae for their existence, and their skeletal shells are delicate in nature and are easily damaged or fragmented. They are also prey to other sea animals such as sponges and clams that bore into their skeletal structures and weaken them.

4   Coral colonies cannot build reef structures without considerable assistance. The many openings in and among the skeletons must be filled in and cemented together by material from around the colonies. The filling material often consists of fine sediments created either from the borings and waste of other animals around the coral or from the skeletons, shells, and remnants of dead plants and animals. The material that is used to cement the coral reefs comes from algae and other microscopic forms of seaweed.

5   An additional part of the process of reef formation is the ongoing compaction and cementation that occurs throughout the process. Because of the soluble and delicate nature of the material from which coral is created, the relatively unstable crystals of corals and shells break down over time and are then rearranged as a more stable form of limestone.

6   The coralline structures that are created through these complicated processes are extremely variable in form. They may, for example, be treelike and branching, or they may have more rounded and compact shapes. What they share in common, however, is the extraordinary variety of plant and animal life-forms that are a necessary part of the ongoing process of their formation.

GLOSSARY
polyps: simple sea animals with tube-shaped bodies

Questions

1. The word they in paragraph 1 refers to
   A coral colonies
   B events and circumstances
   C intricate reef structures
   D chemical processes

2. The word that in paragraph 2 refers to
   A the basic element
   B the development of coralline reef structures
   C a group of animals
   D the *Anthozoa* class

3. The phrase an immeasurable number in paragraph 2 is closest in meaning to
   A an exact integer
   B a huge quantity
   C a surprising total
   D a changing sum

4. The word minute in paragraph 2 could best be replaced by
   A tiny
   B light
   C timely
   D soft

5. The phrase once-living in paragraph 3 is closest in meaning to
   A aging
   B dead
   C growing
   D solitary

6. The word hardy in paragraph 3 is closest in meaning to
   A difficult
   B fragile
   C scarce
   D rugged

7. The word They in paragraph 3 refers to
   A coralline structures
   B upward and outward directions
   C skeletal remnants
   D external forces of nature

8. The word them in paragraph 3 refers to
   A sea animals
   B sponges and clams
   C skeletal structures
   D many openings

9. The word borings in paragraph 4 is closest in meaning to
   A dull pieces
   B strange creations
   C living beings
   D powdery remnants

10. The word ongoing in paragraph 5 is closest in meaning to
    A mobile
    B continuous
    C increasing
    D periodic

11. The phrase break down in paragraph 5 is closest in meaning to
    A cease functioning
    B interrupt
    C descend
    D decompose

12. The word that in paragraph 6 refers to
    A variety
    B life-forms
    C part
    D process

13. The word their in paragraph 6 refers to
    A coralline structures
    B complicated processes
    C rounded and more compact shapes
    D plant and animal life-forms

SENTENCES

Reading Skill 3: SIMPLIFY MEANINGS OF SENTENCES

In the Reading section of the *iBT* TOEFL test, you may be asked to simplify the meaning of a long and complex sentence. In this type of question, you must choose the one answer that is closest to the meaning of a sentence that is highlighted in the passage. Look at an example from the TOEFL test that asks how to simplify the meaning of a highlighted sentence.

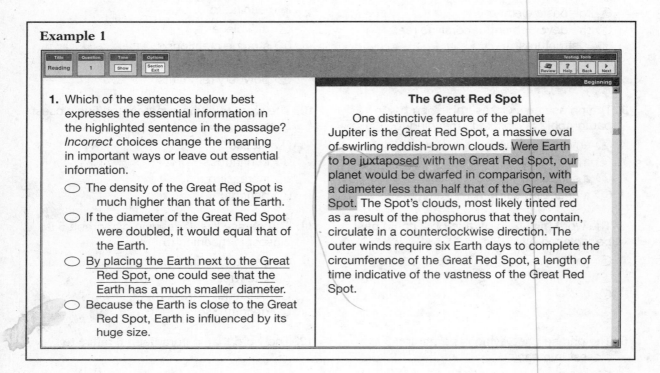

Example 1

1. Which of the sentences below best expresses the essential information in the highlighted sentence in the passage? *Incorrect* choices change the meaning in important ways or leave out essential information.

- ○ The density of the Great Red Spot is much higher than that of the Earth.
- ○ If the diameter of the Great Red Spot were doubled, it would equal that of the Earth.
- ○ By placing the Earth next to the Great Red Spot, one could see that the Earth has a much smaller diameter.
- ○ Because the Earth is close to the Great Red Spot, Earth is influenced by its huge size.

The Great Red Spot

One distinctive feature of the planet Jupiter is the Great Red Spot, a massive oval of swirling reddish-brown clouds. Were Earth to be juxtaposed with the Great Red Spot, our planet would be dwarfed in comparison, with a diameter less than half that of the Great Red Spot. The Spot's clouds, most likely tinted red as a result of the phosphorus that they contain, circulate in a counterclockwise direction. The outer winds require six Earth days to complete the circumference of the Great Red Spot, a length of time indicative of the vastness of the Great Red Spot.

This question asks about the essential meaning of a complex sentence. To answer this question, you should break the complex sentence down into parts. The first part of the sentence says *were Earth to be juxtaposed with the Great Red Spot,* which means *by placing the Earth next to the Great Red Spot.* The next part of the sentence states that *our planet would be dwarfed in comparison, with a diameter less than half that of the Great Red Spot,* which means that *the Earth has a much smaller diameter.* To answer this question, you should click on the third answer.

Now look at another example that asks how to simplify the meaning of a highlighted sentence.

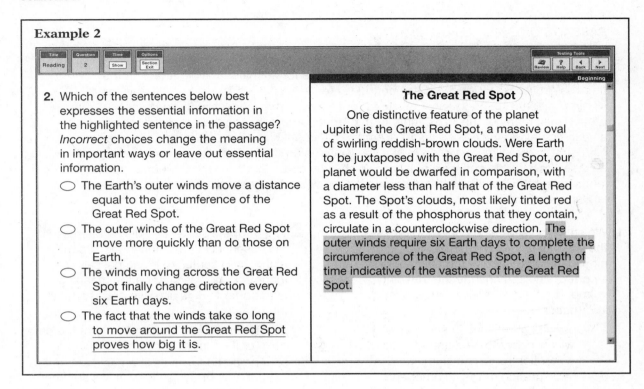

Example 2

2. Which of the sentences below best expresses the essential information in the highlighted sentence in the passage? *Incorrect* choices change the meaning in important ways or leave out essential information.

○ The Earth's outer winds move a distance equal to the circumference of the Great Red Spot.

○ The outer winds of the Great Red Spot move more quickly than do those on Earth.

○ The winds moving across the Great Red Spot finally change direction every six Earth days.

○ The fact that the winds take so long to move around the Great Red Spot proves how big it is.

The Great Red Spot

One distinctive feature of the planet Jupiter is the Great Red Spot, a massive oval of swirling reddish-brown clouds. Were Earth to be juxtaposed with the Great Red Spot, our planet would be dwarfed in comparison, with a diameter less than half that of the Great Red Spot. The Spot's clouds, most likely tinted red as a result of the phosphorus that they contain, circulate in a counterclockwise direction. The outer winds require six Earth days to complete the circumference of the Great Red Spot, a length of time indicative of the vastness of the Great Red Spot.

This question asks about the essential information in the highlighted sentence. To answer this question, you should break the highlighted sentence down into meaningful parts. The first part of the highlighted sentence states that *the outer winds require six Earth days to complete the circumference of the Great Red Spot,* which means that *the winds take so long to move around the Great Red Spot.* The second part of the highlighted sentence states that this is *a length of time indicative of the vastness of the Great Red Spot,* which means that this *proves how big it is.* To answer this question, you should click on the last answer.

The following chart outlines the key information that you should remember about questions testing the simplified meanings of sentences.

QUESTIONS ABOUT SIMPLIFYING THE MEANINGS OF SENTENCES	
HOW TO IDENTIFY THE QUESTION	Which of the **sentences below** best expresses the **essential information . . . ?**
WHERE TO FIND THE ANSWER	The targeted sentence is highlighted in the passage. Information to answer the question is in the highlighted sentence and may also be in the context around the highlighted sentence.
HOW TO ANSWER THE QUESTION	1. Study the highlighted sentence carefully. 2. Break the sentence down into meaningful parts by looking for punctuation and transition expressions. 3. If the highlighted sentence makes references to information outside of the highlighted sentence, read the context around the highlighted sentence. 4. Study the answer choices, and eliminate definitely wrong answers. 5. Choose the best answer from the remaining choices.

camouflage = wii)

READING EXERCISE 3: Study each of the passages, and choose the best answers to the questions that follow.

PASSAGE ONE *(Questions 1–2)*

Camouflage (wii))

Camouflage is one of the most effective ways for animals to avoid attack in the treeless Arctic. However, the summer and winter landscapes there are so diverse that a single protective coloring scheme would, of course, prove ineffective in one season or the other. Thus, many of the inhabitants of the Arctic tundra change their camouflage twice a year. The arctic fox is a clear-cut example of this phenomenon; it sports a brownish-gray coat in the summer which then turns white as cold weather sets in, and the process reverses itself in the springtime. Its brownish-gray coat blends in with the barren tundra landscape in the months without snow, and the white coat naturally blends in with the landscape of the frozen wintertime tundra.

1. Which of the sentences below expresses the essential information in the first highlighted sentence in the passage? *Incorrect* choices change the meaning in important ways or leave out essential information.

   Ⓐ Opposite conditions in summer and in winter necessitate different protective coloration for Arctic animals.

   Ⓑ The coloration of the summer and winter landscapes in the Arctic fails to protect the Arctic tundra.

   Ⓒ In a single season, protective coloring schemes are ineffective in the treeless Arctic.

   Ⓓ For many animals, a single protective coloring scheme effectively protects them during summer and winter months.

2. Which of the sentences below expresses the essential information in the second highlighted sentence in the passage? *Incorrect* choices change the meaning in important ways or leave out essential information.

   Ⓐ The arctic fox is unusual in that the color of its coat changes for no reason.

   Ⓑ The arctic fox lives in an environment that is brownish gray in the summer and white in the winter.

   Ⓒ It is a phenomenon that the coat of the arctic fox turns white in the springtime and gray in the fall.

   Ⓓ The arctic fox demonstrates that protective coloration can change during different seasons.

PASSAGE TWO *(Questions 3–6)*

Post-it® Notes

Paragraph

1   Post-it® Notes were invented in the 1970s at the 3M company in Minnesota quite by accident. Researchers at 3M were working on developing different types of adhesives, and one particularly weak adhesive, a compound of acrylate copolymer microspheres, was developed. Employees at 3M were asked if they could think of a use for a weak adhesive which, provided it did not get dirty, could be reused. One suggestion was that it could be applied to a piece of paper to use as a bookmark that would stay in place in a book. Another use was found when the product was attached to a report that was to be sent to a colleague with a request for comments on the report; the colleague made his comments on the paper attached to the report and returned the report. The idea for Post-it Notes was born.

2   It was decided within the company that there would be a test launch of the product in 1977 in four American cities. Sales of this innovative product in test cities were less than stellar, most likely because the product, while innovative, was also quite unfamiliar. A final attempt was then made in the city of Boise to introduce the product. In this attempt, 3M salesmen gave demonstrations of the product in offices throughout Boise and gave away free samples of the product. When the salesmen returned a week later to the offices where the product had been demonstrated and given away, a huge percentage of the office workers, having noted how useful the simple little product could be, were interested in purchasing it. Over time, 3M came to understand the huge potential of this new product, and over the next few decades more than 400 varieties of Post-it products—in different colors, shapes, and sizes—have been developed.

3. Which of the sentences below expresses the essential information in the first highlighted sentence in paragraph 1? *Incorrect* choices change the meaning in important ways or leave out essential information.

  Ⓐ Of the many adhesives that were being developed at 3M, one was not a particularly strong adhesive.

  Ⓑ Researchers at 3M spent many years trying to develop a really weak adhesive.

  Ⓒ Numerous weak adhesives resulted from a program to develop the strongest adhesive of all.

  Ⓓ Researchers were assigned to develop different types of uses for acrylate copolymer microspheres.

4. Which of the sentences below expresses the essential information in the second highlighted sentence in paragraph 1? *Incorrect* choices change the meaning in important ways or leave out essential information.

  Ⓐ The 3M company suggested applying for a patent on the product in a report prepared by a colleague.

  Ⓑ One unexpectedly-discovered use for the adhesive was in sending and receiving notes attached to documents.

  Ⓒ A note was attached to a report asking for suggestions for uses of one of 3M's products.

  Ⓓ A colleague who developed the new product kept notes with suggestions by other workers.

Summer and winter landscapes are different.

If the camouflage color stays the same, it either won't work in the summer or it won't work in the winter

5. Which of the sentences below expresses the essential information in the first highlighted sentence in paragraph 2? *Incorrect* choices change the meaning in important ways or leave out essential information.

Ⓐ The 3M company was unfamiliar with the process of using test cities to introduce innovative products.

Ⓑ Sales of the product soared even though the product was quite unfamiliar to most customers.

Ⓒ The new product did not sell well because potential customers did not understand it.

Ⓓ After selling the product for a while, the company understood that the product was not innovative enough.

6. Which of the sentences below expresses the essential information in the second highlighted sentence in paragraph 2? *Incorrect* choices change the meaning in important ways or leave out essential information.

Ⓐ The company immediately understood the potential of the product and began to develop it further.

Ⓑ The company worked overtime to develop its new product, initially creating numerous varieties to make it successful.

Ⓒ The company initially introduced 400 varieties of the product and then watched for decades as sales improved.

Ⓓ It took some time for the company to understand how important its new product was and how many variations were possible.

The Pulitzer Prize

Paragraph

1   The Pulitzer Prize came about as part of an attempt by newspaperman Joseph Pulitzer to upgrade the profession of journalism. Pulitzer, the owner of the *New York World* and the *St. Louis Post-Dispatch,* made a proposal in 1903 to Columbia University to make a $2 million bequest to the university for the dual purposes of establishing a school of journalism at the university and also establishing prizes for exceptional work in journalism and other fields. However, the university did not initially respond as one might expect to such a seemingly generous offer.

2   Interestingly, Columbia University was not immediately amenable to the proposal by Pulitzer inasmuch as journalism was not held in high regard in general and Pulitzer's papers were more known for their sensationalization of the news than for the high quality of the journalism. The trustees of the university were not at all sure that they wanted a school of journalism because newspaper reporting was considered more of a trade than a profession at the time and they did not want to decrease the academic prestige of their institution. It took years of discussions and negotiations before the terms for the establishment of the school of journalism and the prizes bearing Pulitzer's name were agreed upon, and it was not actually until the year after Pulitzer's death in 1911 that construction began on the building to house Columbia's new school of journalism. The school of journalism opened in 1913, and the first prizes were awarded in 1917, for work done the previous year.

3   The method for selecting Pulitzer Prize winners and the categories for prizes have changed slightly over the years. Today, 21 different awards are given in three different areas, with the majority of awards going to journalists; 14 of the 21 awards are from various aspects of journalism (i.e., news reporting, feature writing, cartoons, and photography), 6 awards are given in letters (in fiction, nonfiction, history, drama, poetry, and biography), and 1 award in music. Columbia University appoints nominating juries comprised of experts in each field, and the nominating juries submit these nominations for each category to the Pulitzer Prize Board, which makes the final decisions and awards the prizes.

7. Which of the sentences below expresses the essential information in the highlighted sentence in paragraph 1? *Incorrect* choices change the meaning in important ways or leave out essential information.

   Ⓐ Joseph Pulitzer generously offered to donate a large sum of money to Columbia University for two specific purposes.

   Ⓑ In 1903, an attempt was made by Joseph Pulitzer to halt the movement of the school of journalism and the journalism prizes from Columbia University.

   Ⓒ Joseph Pulitzer requested that Columbia University donate a large sum of money to the *New York World* and the *St. Louis Post-Dispatch* for the purpose of establishing journalism scholarships and prizes.

   Ⓓ In 1903, Joseph Pulitzer decided to give up his position as head of two newspapers to take over the department of journalism at Columbia University.

8. Which of the sentences below expresses the essential information in the first highlighted sentence in paragraph 2? *Incorrect* choices change the meaning in important ways or leave out essential information.

   Ⓐ The university immediately appreciated Pulitzer's proposal, agreeing completely with Pulitzer as to the need for high-quality journalism.

   Ⓑ University officials were unhappy when they read a sensationalized version of Pulitzer's proposal in one of Pulitzer's newspapers.

   Ⓒ Initially, the university was not interested in working with Pulitzer because they did not have a high opinion of newspapers in general and Pulitzer's in particular.

   Ⓓ The Pulitzer papers did not have a high regard for what was being taught in Columbia University's school of journalism.

9. Which of the sentences below expresses the essential information in the second highlighted sentence in paragraph 2? *Incorrect* choices change the meaning in important ways or leave out essential information.

Ⓐ There were long discussions about the names that could be used in the new school of journalism and the journalism prizes, and these discussions proved quite harmful to Pulitzer.

Ⓑ It took quite some time for Pulitzer and Columbia University to reach an agreement, and the agreement was not actually implemented until after Pulitzer's death.

Ⓒ University officials spent years discussing what the new journalism building would look like and finally came to a decision about it in 1911.

Ⓓ Pulitzer's death caused university officials to rethink their decision on a school of journalism and to decide that it was a good idea to have one.

10. Which of the sentences below expresses the essential information in the highlighted sentence in paragraph 3? *Incorrect* choices change the meaning in important ways or leave out essential information.

Ⓐ The 21 awards are divided equally among journalism, letters, and music.

Ⓑ Three different awards are given to journalists, while the others are given to artists and musicians.

Ⓒ Most awards are given in three different areas of journalism, while the rest are given in letters and music.

Ⓓ Two-thirds of the awards are for journalism, while the other third goes to other fields.

PASSAGE FOUR *(Questions 11–14)*

Competition and Cooperation

Paragraph
1

Explanations of the interrelationship between competition and cooperation have evolved over time. Early research into competition and cooperation defined each of them in terms of the distribution of rewards related to each. Competition was defined as a situation in which rewards are distributed unequally on the basis of performance; cooperation, on the other hand, was defined as a situation in which rewards are distributed equally on the basis of mutual interactive behavior among individuals. By this definition, a competitive situation requires at least one competitor to fail for each competitor that wins, while a cooperative situation offers a reward only if all members of the group receive it.

2

Researchers have found definitions of competition and cooperation based upon rewards inadequate primarily because definitions of these two concepts based upon rewards depict them as opposites. In current understanding, competition is not viewed as the opposite of cooperation; instead, cooperation is viewed as an integral component of competition. Cooperation is necessary among team members, perhaps in a sporting event or in a political race, in order to win the competition; it is equally important to understand that cooperation is of great importance between teams, in that same sporting event or political race, inasmuch as the opposing teams need to be in agreement as to the basic ground rules of the game or election in order to compete.

3

Interestingly, the word *competition* is derived from a Latin verb which means "to seek together." An understanding of the derivation of the word *competition* supports the understanding that cooperation, rather than evoking a characteristic at the opposite extreme of human nature from competition, is in reality a necessary factor in competition.

11. Which of the sentences below expresses the essential information in the highlighted sentence in paragraph 1? *Incorrect* choices change the meaning in important ways or leave out essential information.

Ⓐ Unequal rewards for competition should be distributed equally to achieve cooperation.

Ⓑ Earlier definitions of competition and cooperation described them in basically the same way.

Ⓒ Competition and cooperation were seen as opposites, with rewards distributed equally to those who competed and unequally to those who cooperated.

Ⓓ Competition was defined in terms of unequal distribution of rewards and cooperation in terms of equal distribution of rewards.

12. Which of the sentences below expresses the essential information in the first highlighted sentence in paragraph 2? *Incorrect* choices change the meaning in important ways or leave out essential information.

Ⓐ It does not work well to define competition and cooperation in terms of rewards because definitions of this type incorrectly indicate that the two are opposites.

Ⓑ Researchers tend to define competition and cooperation on the basis of rewards because this shows how the two differ.

Ⓒ Researchers are looking for ways to define cooperation and competition in terms of rewards but have so far not been able to come up with definitions.

Ⓓ Research has shown that the optimal definitions of competition and cooperation are those indicating that the two are opposites.

13. Which of the sentences below expresses the essential information in the second highlighted sentence in paragraph 2? *Incorrect* choices change the meaning in important ways or leave out essential information.

Ⓐ Because sports and politics are so competitive, participants may appear to be cooperating but are not really doing so.

Ⓑ In a number of contexts, cooperation is necessary both among team members and between opposing teams.

Ⓒ When cooperation exists in contests such as games and elections, competition naturally decreases.

Ⓓ In sports, cooperation is necessary among team members but should not take place between opposing teams.

14. Which of the sentences below expresses the essential information in the highlighted sentence in paragraph 3? *Incorrect* choices change the meaning in important ways or leave out essential information.

Ⓐ The derivation of the word *competition* indicates that competition and cooperation are clearly opposing forces.

Ⓑ The derivation of the word *competition* shows us that competition is necessary for cooperation to succeed.

Ⓒ The derivation of the word *competition* demonstrates that cooperation is an integral part of competition.

Ⓓ The derivation of the word *competition* leads to the conclusion that cooperation cannot exist without competition.

Reading Skill 4: INSERT SENTENCES INTO THE PASSAGE

In the Reading section of the *iBT* TOEFL test, you may be asked to determine where to insert a sentence into a passage. In this type of question, you must click on one of a number of squares in a passage to indicate that the sentence should be inserted in that position. Look at an example from the TOEFL test that asks where to insert a particular sentence.

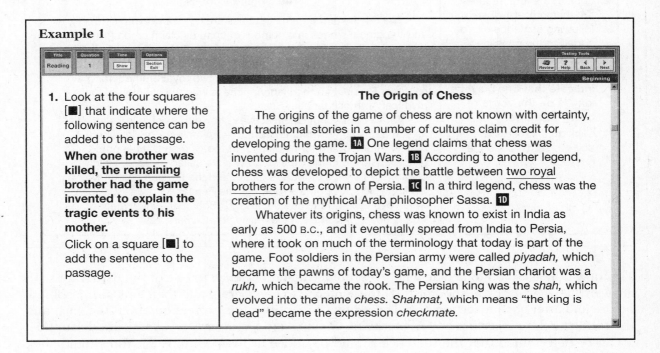

Example 1

1. Look at the four squares [■] that indicate where the following sentence can be added to the passage.

   When one brother was killed, the remaining brother had the game invented to explain the tragic events to his mother.

   Click on a square [■] to add the sentence to the passage.

The Origin of Chess

The origins of the game of chess are not known with certainty, and traditional stories in a number of cultures claim credit for developing the game. **1A** One legend claims that chess was invented during the Trojan Wars. **1B** According to another legend, chess was developed to depict the battle between two royal brothers for the crown of Persia. **1C** In a third legend, chess was the creation of the mythical Arab philosopher Sassa. **1D**

Whatever its origins, chess was known to exist in India as early as 500 B.C., and it eventually spread from India to Persia, where it took on much of the terminology that today is part of the game. Foot soldiers in the Persian army were called *piyadah,* which became the pawns of today's game, and the Persian chariot was a *rukh,* which became the rook. The Persian king was the *shah,* which evolved into the name *chess. Shahmat,* which means "the king is dead" became the expression *checkmate.*

This question asks you to decide where a sentence could be *added* to one of the paragraphs. To answer this question, you should study the sentence to be inserted and then look at the context before and after each insertion box. The sentence mentions *one brother* and *the remaining brother,* and the context before insertion box **1C** mentions *two royal brothers.* From this, it can be determined that the sentence should be added at insertion box **1C**. You should click on **1C** to answer this question.

Now look at another example that asks where to insert a particular sentence.

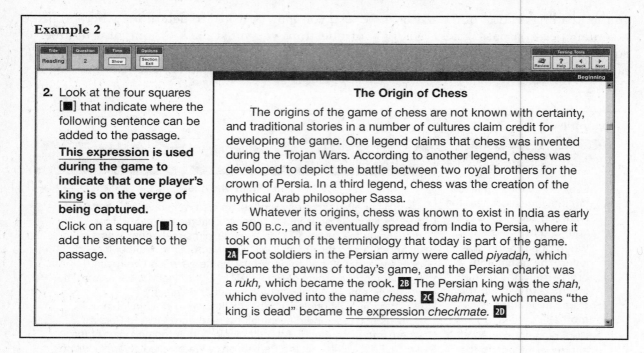

Example 2

2. Look at the four squares [■] that indicate where the following sentence can be added to the passage.

   This expression is used during the game to indicate that one player's king is on the verge of being captured.

   Click on a square [■] to add the sentence to the passage.

The Origin of Chess

The origins of the game of chess are not known with certainty, and traditional stories in a number of cultures claim credit for developing the game. One legend claims that chess was invented during the Trojan Wars. According to another legend, chess was developed to depict the battle between two royal brothers for the crown of Persia. In a third legend, chess was the creation of the mythical Arab philosopher Sassa.

Whatever its origins, chess was known to exist in India as early as 500 B.C., and it eventually spread from India to Persia, where it took on much of the terminology that today is part of the game. **2A** Foot soldiers in the Persian army were called *piyadah,* which became the pawns of today's game, and the Persian chariot was a *rukh,* which became the rook. **2B** The Persian king was the *shah,* which evolved into the name *chess.* **2C** *Shahmat,* which means "the king is dead" became the expression *checkmate.* **2D**

This question asks you to decide where a sentence could be *added* to one of the paragraphs. To answer this question, you should study the sentence to be inserted and then look at the context before and after each insertion box. The sentence mentions *this expression* about the *king,* and the context before insertion box **2D** mentions the *king* and *the expression checkmate.* From this, it can be determined that the sentence should be added at insertion box **2D**. You should click on **2D** to answer this question.

The following chart outlines the key information that you should remember about questions testing vocabulary in context.

QUESTIONS ABOUT INSERTING INFORMATION	
HOW TO IDENTIFY THE QUESTION	Look at the **four squares [■]** . . .
WHERE TO FIND THE ANSWER	The places where the sentence may be inserted are marked in the passage.
HOW TO ANSWER THE QUESTION	1. Look at the sentence to be inserted for any key words or ideas at the beginning or the end of the sentence. 2. Read the context before and after the insertion squares for any ideas that relate to the sentence to be inserted. 3. Choose the insertion square that is most related to the sentence to be inserted.

READING EXERCISE 4: Study each of the passages, and choose the best answers to the questions that follow.

PASSAGE ONE (Questions 1–2)

Popcorn

Paragraph

1   **1A** One method of popping corn involved skewering an ear of corn on a stick and roasting it until the kernels popped off the ear. **1B** Corn was also popped by first cutting the kernels off the cob, throwing them into a fire, and gathering them as they popped out of the fire. **1C** In a final method for popping corn, sand and unpopped kernels of corn were mixed together in a cooking pot and heated until the corn popped to the surface of the sand in the pot. **1D**

2   **2A** This traditional Native American dish was quite a novelty to newcomers to the Americas. **2B** Columbus and his sailors found natives in the West Indies wearing popcorn necklaces, and explorer Hernando Cortés described the use of popcorn amulets in the religious ceremonies of the Aztecs. **2C** According to legendary descriptions of the celebratory meal, Quadequina, the brother of Chief Massasoit, contributed several deerskin bags of popcorn to the celebration. **2D**

1. Look at the four squares [■] that indicate where the following sentence can be added to the first paragraph of the passage.

   Native Americans have been popping corn for at least 5,000 years, using a variety of different methods.

   Click on a square [■] to add the sentence to the passage.

2. Look at the four squares [■] that indicate where the following sentence can be added to the second paragraph of the passage.

   A century after these early explorers, the Pilgrims at Plymouth may have been introduced to popcorn at the first Thanksgiving dinner.

   Click on a square [■] to add the sentence to the passage.

Paragraph

Lions

1 ■**3A** Something unusual about lions is that they hunt in groups. ■**3B** Group hunting is beneficial to lions because it means that much larger prey can be captured by the lions. ■**3C** It also means that individual lions expend much less energy during a hunt. ■**3D**

2 There is a standard pattern to the process of hunting in groups. ■**4A** The process is initiated by a single female, who stations herself at a raised elevation to serve as a lookout to spot potential prey. ■**4B** When prey is spotted, a group of young lionesses advances on the herd and pushes the herd in the direction of a different lioness who has hidden herself downwind. ■**4C** It is up to this concealed female to choose the weakest member of the herd for the kill. ■**4D**

3 ■**5A** As can be seen from this description of the process, it is the females rather than the male or males in the pride that take part in the kill. ■**5B** The younger and stronger females are the ones who go on the attack. ■**5C** While the females are on the attack, the males stay behind to protect the rest of the pride from attack by predators such as hyenas. ■**5D**

3. Look at the four squares [■] that indicate where the following sentence can be added to the first paragraph of the passage.

   Other cats do not.

   Click on a square [■] to add the sentence to the passage.

4. Look at the four squares [■] that indicate where the following sentence can be added to the second paragraph of the passage.

   This is usually accomplished by knocking the prey to the ground and breaking its neck.

   Click on a square [■] to add the sentence to the passage.

5. Look at the four squares [■] that indicate where the following sentence can be added to the third paragraph of the passage.

   Thus, the males have a defensive rather than an offensive role.

   Click on a square [■] to add the sentence to the passage.

PASSAGE THREE *(Questions 6–7)*

Accidental Inventions

Paragraph

1   A number of products that we commonly use today were developed quite by accident. Two of many possible examples of this concept are the leotard and the Popsicle, each of which came about when an insightful person recognized a potential benefit in a negative situation.

2   The first of these accidental inventions is the leotard, a close-fitting, one-piece garment worn today by dancers, gymnasts, and acrobats, among others. **6A** In 1828, a circus performer named Nelson Hower was faced with the prospect of missing his performance because his costume was at the cleaners. **6B** Instead of canceling his part of the show, he decided to perform in his long underwear. **6C** Soon, other circus performers began performing the same way. **6D** When popular acrobat Jules Leotard adopted the style, it became known as the leotard.

3   **7A** Another product invented by chance was the Popsicle. **7B** In 1905, eleven-year-old Frank Epperson stirred up a drink of fruit-flavored powder and soda water and then mistakenly left the drink, with the spoon in it, out on the back porch overnight. **7C** As the temperature dropped that night, the soda water froze around the spoon, creating a tasty treat. **7D** Years later, remembering how enjoyable the treat had been, Epperson went into business producing Popsicles.

6. Look at the four squares [■] that indicate where the following sentence can be added to the second paragraph of the passage.

They enjoyed the comfort of performing in underwear rather than costumes.

Click on a square [■] to add the sentence to the passage.

7. Look at the four squares [■] that indicate where the following sentence can be added to the third paragraph of the passage.

It was a taste sensation that stayed on his mind.

Click on a square [■] to add the sentence to the passage.

PASSAGE FOUR *(Questions 8–9)*

Uranium

Paragraph

1   Uranium, a radioactive metal named after the planet Uranus, is a primary source of energy in nuclear power plants and certain nuclear weapons. It occurs naturally in three different isotopes, which differ in their facility in undergoing nuclear fission.

2   **8A** The three naturally occurring isotopes of uranium are U-234, U-235, and U-238. **8B** Each of these isotopes has the same atomic number of 92, which is the number of protons in the nucleus. **8C** However, each has a different number of neutrons and thus has a different atomic mass, which is the sum of the number of protons and neutrons. **8D**

3   Of these three naturally occurring isotopes of uranium, U-238 is by far the most common, while U-235 is the most capable of undergoing nuclear fission. **9A** More than 99 percent of all naturally occurring uranium is U-238, while U-234 and U-235 each makes up less than 1 percent. **9B** Nuclear fission can occur when a U-235 nucleus is struck by a neutron, and the nucleus splits, releasing energy and releasing two or more neutrons. **9C** However, nuclear fission rarely involves a U-238 or a U-234 nucleus because it is unusual for either of these nuclei to break apart when struck by a neutron. **9D**

8. Look at the four squares [■] that indicate where the following sentence can be added to the second paragraph of the passage.

   U-234 has 92 protons and 142 neutrons for an atomic mass of 234, U-235 has 92 protons and 143 neutrons for a total of 235, and U-238 has 92 protons and 146 neutrons for a total of 238.

   Click on a square [■] to add the sentence to the passage.

9. Look at the four squares [■] that indicate where the following sentence can be added to the third paragraph of the passage.

   These neutrons can create a chain reaction by causing other U-235 nuclei to break up.

   Click on a square [■] to add the sentence to the passage.

READING EXERCISE (Skills 3–4): Read the passage.

<table>
<tr><td>Paragraph</td><td style="text-align:center">

Theodore Dreiser

</td></tr>
</table>

Paragraph

Theodore Dreiser

1   Theodore Dreiser, the American author best known for the novel *Sister Carrie* (1912), introduced a powerful style of writing that had a profound influence on the writers that followed him, from Steinbeck to Fitzgerald and Hemingway. It was in *Sister Carrie* that Theodore Dreiser created a fictional account that laid bare the harsh reality of life in the big city and in which Dreiser established himself as the architect of a new genre.

2   Dreiser was born in 1871 into a large family whose fortunes had in the recent past taken a dramatic turn for the worse. Before Theodore's birth, his father had built up a successful factory business only to lose it to a fire. The family was rather abruptly thrust into poverty, and Theodore spent his youth moving from place to place in the Midwest as the family tried desperately to reestablish itself financially. He left home at the age of sixteen. After earning some money, he spent a year at Indiana University but left school and returned to Chicago, yearning for the glamour and excitement that it offered. At the age of twenty-two, he began work as a reporter for a small newspaper in Chicago, the *Daily Globe,* and later worked on newspapers in Pittsburgh, Cleveland, Saint Louis, and New York City. In his work as a reporter, he was witness to the seamier side of life and was responsible for recording events that befell the less fortunate in the city, the beggars, the alcoholics, the prostitutes, and the working poor.

3   Dreiser first tried his hand at fiction by writing short stories rather than novels, and the first four short stories that he wrote were published. Based on this, he was encouraged to write a novel that would accurately depict the harsh life of the city, and the novel *Sister Carrie* was the result of his effort. This novel chronicles the life of Carrie Meeber, a small-town girl who goes to Chicago in a quest for fame and fortune. As Carrie progresses from factory worker to Broadway star by manipulating anyone in her path, Dreiser sends a clear message about the tragedy of life that is devoted purely to the quest for money.

4   *Sister Carrie,* unfortunately for Dreiser, did not achieve immediate success. The novel was accepted for publication by Doubleday, but Dreiser was immediately asked to make major revisions to the novel. When Dreiser refused to make the revisions, Doubleday published only a limited number of copies of the book and refused to promote or advertise it. Published in limited release and without the backing of the company, the novel was a dismal failure, selling fewer than 500 copies.

5   After the failure of the novel that was so meaningful to him, Dreiser suffered a nervous breakdown; he was depressed, stricken with severe headaches, and unable to sleep for days on end. Having sunk to a point where he was considering suicide, he was sent by his brother to a sanatorium in White Plains, New York, where he eventually recovered. After leaving the sanatorium, he took a position as an editor for Butterick's. He was successful in this position, and was eventually able to purchase a one-third interest in a new publishing company, B. W. Dodge, which republished Dreiser's novel *Sister Carrie.* This new release of the novel proved considerably more successful than the first release had been. In its first year, the reissued version of *Sister Carrie* sold 4,500 copies, with strong reviews, and the next year it sold more than 10,000 copies. The recognition that accompanied the success of the novel was based not only on the power of the description of the perils of urban life but also on the new trend in literature that Dreiser was credited with establishing.

Refer to this version of the passage to answer the questions that follow.

Theodore Dreiser

Paragraph

1   **1A** Theodore Dreiser, the American author best known for the novel *Sister Carrie* (1912), introduced a powerful style of writing that had a profound influence on the writers that followed him, from Steinbeck to Fitzgerald and Hemingway. **1B** It was in *Sister Carrie* that Theodore Dreiser created a fictional account that laid bare the harsh reality of life in the big city and in which Dreiser established himself as the architect of a new genre. **1C**

2   Dreiser was born in 1871 into a large family whose fortunes had in the recent past taken a dramatic turn for the worse. Before Theodore's birth, his father had built up a successful factory business only to lose it to a fire. **4A** The family was rather abruptly thrust into poverty, and Theodore spent his youth moving from place to place in the Midwest as the family tried desperately to reestablish itself financially. **4B** He left home at the age of sixteen. **4C** After earning some money, he spent a year at Indiana University but left school and returned to Chicago, yearning for the glamour and excitement that it offered. **4D** At the age of twenty-two, he began work as a reporter for a small newspaper in Chicago, the *Daily Globe,* and later worked on newspapers in Pittsburgh, Cleveland, Saint Louis, and New York City. In his work as a reporter, he was witness to the seamier side of life and was responsible for recording events that befell the less fortunate in the city, the beggars, the alcoholics, the prostitutes, and the working poor.

3   **5A** Dreiser first tried his hand at fiction by writing short stories rather than novels, and the first four short stories that he wrote were published. **5B** Based on this, he was encouraged to write a novel that would accurately depict the harsh life of the city, and the novel *Sister Carrie* was the result of his effort. **5C** This novel chronicles the life of Carrie Meeber, a small-town girl who goes to Chicago in a quest for fame and fortune. **5D** As Carrie progresses from factory worker to Broadway star by manipulating anyone in her path, Dreiser sends a clear message about the tragedy of life that is devoted purely to the quest for money.

4   *Sister Carrie,* unfortunately for Dreiser, did not achieve immediate success. **7A** The novel was accepted for publication by Doubleday, but Dreiser was immediately asked to make major revisions to the novel. **7B** When Dreiser refused to make the revisions, Doubleday published only a limited number of copies of the book and refused to promote or advertise it. **7C** Published in limited release and without the backing of the company, the novel was a dismal failure, selling fewer than 500 copies. **7D**

5   After the failure of the novel that was so meaningful to him, Dreiser suffered a nervous breakdown; he was depressed, stricken with severe headaches, and unable to sleep for days on end. Having sunk to a point where he was considering suicide, he was sent by his brother to a sanatorium in White Plains, New York, where he eventually recovered. **10A** After leaving the sanatorium, he took a position as an editor for Butterick's. **10B** He was successful in this position, and was eventually able to purchase a one-third interest in a new publishing company, B. W. Dodge, which republished Dreiser's novel *Sister Carrie.* **10C** This new release of the novel proved considerably more successful than the first release had been. **10D** In its first year, the reissued version of *Sister Carrie* sold 4,500 copies, with strong reviews, and the next year it sold more than 10,000 copies. The recognition that accompanied the success of the novel was based not only on the power of the description of the perils of urban life but also on the new trend in literature that Dreiser was credited with establishing.

Questions

1. Look at the three squares [■] that indicate where the following sentence can be added to paragraph 1.

   This forceful first novel set a new path for American novels at the turn of the last century.

   Click on a square [■] to add the sentence to the passage.

2. Which of the sentences below expresses the essential information in the first highlighted sentence in paragraph 2? *Incorrect* choices change the meaning in important ways or leave out essential information.

   Ⓐ Dreiser's family had formerly been rich before it had become poor.

   Ⓑ Dreiser was, unfortunately, born into an overly dramatic family.

   Ⓒ The fortunes of Dreiser's family had recently increased.

   Ⓓ Members of Dreiser's family suffered from the serious effects of a disease.

3. Which of the sentences below expresses the essential information in the second highlighted sentence in paragraph 2? *Incorrect* choices change the meaning in important ways or leave out essential information.

   Ⓐ Dreiser served as a witness in a number of trials that involved beggars, alcoholics, and prostitutes.

   Ⓑ Dreiser observed and wrote about the poorer classes as part of his newspaper job.

   Ⓒ In New York City, during Dreiser's time, there were many people who were less fortunate than Dreiser.

   Ⓓ Dreiser's work involved working with beggars, alcoholics, and prostitutes.

4. Look at the four squares [■] that indicate where the following sentence can be added to paragraph 2.

   At this young age, he moved alone to Chicago and supported himself by taking odd jobs.

   Click on a square [■] to add the sentence to the passage.

5. Look at the four squares [■] that indicate where the following sentence can be added to paragraph 3.

   It was rather unusual for a novice writer to achieve so much so quickly.

   Click on a square [■] to add the sentence to the passage.

6. Which of the sentences below expresses the essential information in the highlighted sentence in paragraph 3? *Incorrect* choices change the meaning in important ways or leave out essential information.

   Ⓐ Dreiser devoted his life primarily to trying to become rich.

   Ⓑ In Dreiser's novel, Carrie succeeds by moving from a low-level job to stardom.

   Ⓒ Dreiser used one of his characters to demonstrate the negative aspects of lust for money.

   Ⓓ Dreiser tried to warn Carrie that she was taking the wrong path in life.

7. Look at the four squares [■] that indicate where the following sentence can be added to paragraph 4.

   These changes were intended to tone down some of the starker and more scandalous descriptions.

   Click on a square [■] to add the sentence to the passage.

8. Which of the sentences below expresses the essential information in the first highlighted sentence in paragraph 5? *Incorrect* choices change the meaning in important ways or leave out essential information.

   Ⓐ Dreiser recovered from an attempted suicide at a sanatorium.

   Ⓑ Dreiser's brother went to a sanatorium after attempting suicide.

   Ⓒ After being sent to a sanatorium, Dreiser considered committing suicide.

   Ⓓ Dreiser's brother stepped in to help Dreiser after Dreiser became depressed.

9. Which of the sentences below expresses the essential information in the second highlighted sentence in paragraph 5? *Incorrect* choices change the meaning in important ways or leave out essential information.

Ⓐ In Dreiser's novels, he recognized the power of urban life and new trends that existed in it.

Ⓑ The success of Dreiser's novel went unrecognized because it represented such a new trend in literature.

Ⓒ Dreiser credited his urban upbringing and literary background for the success that his novel achieved.

Ⓓ Dreiser achieved acclaim because his writing was so powerful and because he established a new trend.

10. Look at the four squares [■] that indicate where the following sentence can be added to paragraph 5.

This company was one that published magazines to promote sewing and the sale of clothing patterns.

Click on a square [■] to add the sentence to the passage.

READING REVIEW EXERCISE (Skills 1–4): Read the passage.

Paragraph

Pulsars

1   There is still much for astronomers to learn about pulsars. Based on what is known, the term **pulsar** is used to describe the phenomenon of short, precisely timed radio bursts that are emitted from somewhere in space. Though all is not known about pulsars, they are now believed in reality to emanate from spinning **neutron stars**, highly reduced cores of collapsed stars that are theorized to exist.

2   Pulsars were discovered in 1967, when Jocelyn Bell, a graduate student at Cambridge University, noticed an unusual pattern on a chart from a radio telescope. What made this pattern unusual was that, unlike other radio signals from celestial objects, this series of pulses had a highly regular period of 1.33730119 seconds. Because day after day the pulses came from the same place among the stars, Cambridge researchers came to the conclusion that they could not have come from a local source such as an Earth satellite.

3   A name was needed for this newly discovered phenomenon. The possibility that the signals were coming from a distant civilization was considered, and at that point the idea of naming the phenomenon L.G.M. (short for Little Green Men) was raised. However, after researchers had found three more regularly pulsing objects in other parts of the sky over the next few weeks, the name pulsar was selected instead of L.G.M.

4   As more and more pulsars were found, astronomers engaged in debates over their nature. It was determined that a pulsar could not be a star inasmuch as a normal star is too big to pulse so fast. The question was also raised as to whether a pulsar might be a white dwarf star, a dying star that has collapsed to approximately the size of the Earth and is slowly cooling off. However, this idea was also rejected because the fastest pulsar known at the time pulsed around thirty times per second and a white dwarf, which is the smallest known type of star, would not hold together if it were to spin that fast.

5   The final conclusion among astronomers was that only a neutron star, which is theorized to be the remaining core of a collapsed star that has been reduced to a highly dense radius of only around 10 kilometers, was small enough to be a pulsar. Further evidence of the link between pulsars and neutron stars was found in 1968, when a pulsar was found in the middle of the Crab Nebula. The Crab Nebula is what remains of the supernova of the year 1054, and inasmuch as it has been theorized that neutron stars sometimes remain following supernova explosions, it is believed that the pulsar coming from the Crab Nebula is evidently just such a neutron star.

6   The generally accepted theory for pulsars is the **lighthouse theory**, which is based upon a consideration of the theoretical properties of neutron stars and the observed properties of pulsars. According to the lighthouse theory, a spinning neutron star emits beams of radiation that sweep through the sky, and when one of the beams passes over the Earth, it is detectable on Earth. It is known as the lighthouse theory because the emissions from neutron stars are similar to the pulses of light emitted from lighthouses as they sweep over the ocean; the name lighthouse is therefore actually more appropriate than the name pulsar.

Refer to this version of the passage to answer the questions that follow.

Pulsars

1   There is still much for astronomers to learn about pulsars. Based on what is known, the term **pulsar** is used to describe the phenomenon of short, precisely timed radio bursts that are emitted from somewhere in space. Though all is not known about pulsars, they are now believed in reality to emanate from spinning **neutron stars**, highly reduced cores of collapsed stars that are theorized to exist.

2   Pulsars were discovered in 1967, when Jocelyn Bell, a graduate student at Cambridge University, noticed an unusual pattern on a chart from a radio telescope. What made this pattern unusual was that, unlike other radio signals from celestial objects, this series of pulses had a highly regular period of 1.33730119 seconds. Because day after day the pulses came from the same place among the stars, Cambridge researchers came to the conclusion that they could not have come from a local source such as an Earth satellite.

3   **5A** A name was needed for this newly discovered phenomenon. **5B** The possibility that the signals were coming from a distant civilization was considered, and at that point the idea of naming the phenomenon L.G.M. (short for Little Green Men) was raised. **5C** However, after researchers had found three more regularly pulsing objects in other parts of the sky over the next few weeks, the name pulsar was selected instead of L.G.M. **5D**

4   As more and more pulsars were found, astronomers engaged in debates over their nature. It was determined that a pulsar could not be a star inasmuch as a normal star is too big to pulse so fast. The question was also raised as to whether a pulsar might be a white dwarf star, a dying star that has collapsed to approximately the size of the Earth and is slowly cooling off. However, this idea was also rejected because the fastest pulsar known at the time pulsed around thirty times per second and a white dwarf, which is the smallest known type of star, would not hold together if it were to spin that fast.

5   The final conclusion among astronomers was that only a neutron star, which is theorized to be the remaining core of a collapsed star that has been reduced to a highly dense radius of only around 10 kilometers, was small enough to be a pulsar. Further evidence of the link between pulsars and neutron stars was found in 1968, when a pulsar was found in the middle of the Crab Nebula. The Crab Nebula is what remains of the supernova of the year 1054, and inasmuch as it has been theorized that neutron stars sometimes remain following supernova explosions, it is believed that the pulsar coming from the Crab Nebula is evidently just such a neutron star.

6   **13A** The generally accepted theory for pulsars is the **lighthouse theory**, which is based upon a consideration of the theoretical properties of neutron stars and the observed properties of pulsars. **13B** According to the lighthouse theory, a spinning neutron star emits beams of radiation that sweep through the sky, and when one of the beams passes over the Earth, it is detectable on Earth. **13C** It is known as the lighthouse theory because the emissions from neutron stars are similar to the pulses of light emitted from lighthouses as they sweep over the ocean; the name lighthouse is therefore actually more appropriate than the name pulsar. **13D**

Questions

1. The phrase emanate from in paragraph 1 is closest in meaning to
   Ⓐ develop from
   Ⓑ revolve around
   Ⓒ wander away from
   Ⓓ receive directions from

2. Which of the sentences below expresses the essential information in the highlighted sentence in paragraph 2? *Incorrect* choices change the meaning in important ways or leave out essential information.
   Ⓐ It was unusual for researchers to hear patterns from space.
   Ⓑ It was unusual for celestial objects to emit radio signals.
   Ⓒ It was unusual that the pattern of the pulsars was so regular.
   Ⓓ It was unusual that the period of pulses was only slightly more than a second in length.

3. The word they in paragraph 2 refers to
   Ⓐ day after day
   Ⓑ the pulses
   Ⓒ the stars
   Ⓓ Cambridge researchers

4. The word raised in paragraph 3 could best be replaced by
   Ⓐ lifted
   Ⓑ suggested
   Ⓒ discovered
   Ⓓ elevated

5. Look at the four squares [■] that indicate where the following sentence can be added to paragraph 3.

   This name was selected because it indicates a regularly pulsing radio source.

   Click on a square [■] to add the sentence to the passage.

6. The phrase engaged in in paragraph 4 could best be replaced by
   Ⓐ became attached to
   Ⓑ were disappointed in
   Ⓒ made promises about
   Ⓓ took part in

7. The word their in paragraph 4 refers to
   Ⓐ weeks
   Ⓑ pulsars
   Ⓒ astronomers
   Ⓓ details

8. Which of the sentences below expresses the essential information in the highlighted sentence in paragraph 4? *Incorrect* choices change the meaning in important ways or leave out essential information.
   Ⓐ Pulsars could not be white dwarfs because the frequency of the pulsars is too high.
   Ⓑ Pulsars cannot spin very fast because they will fall apart if they spin fast.
   Ⓒ White dwarfs cannot be dying stars because they cannot pulse at around thirty times per second.
   Ⓓ White dwarfs cannot contain pulsars because white dwarfs spin much faster than pulsars.

9. The word Further in paragraph 5 is closest in meaning to
   Ⓐ distant
   Ⓑ irrelevant
   Ⓒ additional
   Ⓓ unreliable

10. Which of the sentences below expresses the essential information in the highlighted sentence in paragraph 5? *Incorrect* choices change the meaning in important ways or leave out essential information.
   Ⓐ It is believed that the supernova of 1054 created the Crab Nebula, which contains a pulsing neutron star.
   Ⓑ It is believed that a pulsar created the Crab Nebula, which exploded in a supernova in 1054.
   Ⓒ It is believed that a neutron star exploded in the supernova of 1054, creating the Crab Nebula.
   Ⓓ It is believed that the Crab Nebula is a pulsar that is on the verge of becoming a supernova.

11. The word properties in paragraph 6 is closest in meaning to

Ⓐ lands

Ⓑ characteristics

Ⓒ masses

Ⓓ surroundings

12. The word it in paragraph 6 refers to

Ⓐ a spinning neutron star

Ⓑ the sky

Ⓒ one of the beams

Ⓓ the Earth

13. Look at the four squares [■] that indicate where the following sentence can be added to paragraph 6.

The periodic flashing of pulsars is related to rotation rather than pulsing, so the name pulsar is actually not very accurate.

Click on a square [■] to add the sentence to the passage.

DETILS

Reading Skill 5: FIND FACTUAL INFORMATION

In the Reading section of the *iBT* TOEFL test, you may be asked questions about factual information. The answers to these multiple-choice questions are often restatements of what is given in the passage. This means that the correct answer often expresses the same idea as what is written in the passage but that the words are not exactly the same. The answers to these questions are generally given in order in the passage, and the questions generally indicate which paragraph contains the answers, so the answers are not too difficult to locate. Look at an example of a factual information question.

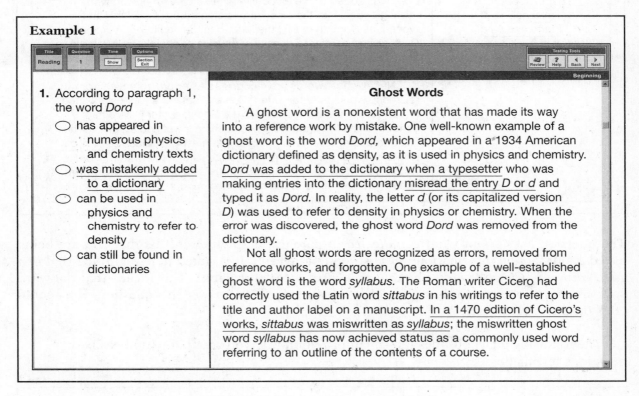

Example 1

Title: Reading Question: 1 Time: Show Options: Section Exit Testing Tools: Review Help Back Next Beginning

1. According to paragraph 1, the word *Dord*
   - ○ has appeared in numerous physics and chemistry texts
   - ○ was mistakenly added to a dictionary
   - ○ can be used in physics and chemistry to refer to density
   - ○ can still be found in dictionaries

Ghost Words

A ghost word is a nonexistent word that has made its way into a reference work by mistake. One well-known example of a ghost word is the word *Dord,* which appeared in a 1934 American dictionary defined as density, as it is used in physics and chemistry. *Dord* was added to the dictionary when a typesetter who was making entries into the dictionary misread the entry *D* or *d* and typed it as *Dord.* In reality, the letter *d* (or its capitalized version *D*) was used to refer to density in physics or chemistry. When the error was discovered, the ghost word *Dord* was removed from the dictionary.

Not all ghost words are recognized as errors, removed from reference works, and forgotten. One example of a well-established ghost word is the word *syllabus.* The Roman writer Cicero had correctly used the Latin word *sittabus* in his writings to refer to the title and author label on a manuscript. In a 1470 edition of Cicero's works, *sittabus* was miswritten as *syllabus*; the miswritten ghost word *syllabus* has now achieved status as a commonly used word referring to an outline of the contents of a course.

The question asks you to answer a question *according to paragraph 1,* which means that the correct answer is factual information from the first paragraph. It is stated in the first paragraph that *Dord was added to the dictionary when a typesetter . . . misread the entry* D *or* d. This means that the word *Dord* was mistakenly added to a dictionary. To answer this question, you should click on the second answer.

Now look at another example of a factual information question.

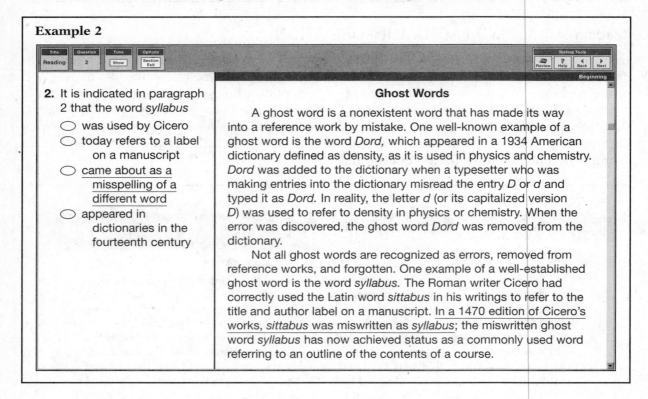

Example 2

2. It is indicated in paragraph 2 that the word *syllabus*
- ○ was used by Cicero
- ○ today refers to a label on a manuscript
- ○ came about as a misspelling of a different word
- ○ appeared in dictionaries in the fourteenth century

Ghost Words

A ghost word is a nonexistent word that has made its way into a reference work by mistake. One well-known example of a ghost word is the word *Dord,* which appeared in a 1934 American dictionary defined as density, as it is used in physics and chemistry. *Dord* was added to the dictionary when a typesetter who was making entries into the dictionary misread the entry *D* or *d* and typed it as *Dord*. In reality, the letter *d* (or its capitalized version *D*) was used to refer to density in physics or chemistry. When the error was discovered, the ghost word *Dord* was removed from the dictionary.

Not all ghost words are recognized as errors, removed from reference works, and forgotten. One example of a well-established ghost word is the word *syllabus*. The Roman writer Cicero had correctly used the Latin word *sittabus* in his writings to refer to the title and author label on a manuscript. In a 1470 edition of Cicero's works, *sittabus* was miswritten as *syllabus*; the miswritten ghost word *syllabus* has now achieved status as a commonly used word referring to an outline of the contents of a course.

The question asks about what is *indicated* in paragraph 2, which means that you are being asked about factual information in the second paragraph. It is stated in paragraph 2 that *in a 1470 edition of Cicero's works,* sittabus *was miswritten as* syllabus. This means that the word *syllabus* came about as a misspelling of a different word. To answer this question, you should click on the third answer.

The following chart outlines the key information that you should remember about questions testing details.

QUESTIONS ABOUT FACTUAL DETAILS	
HOW TO IDENTIFY THE QUESTION	**According to** paragraph X . . . It is **stated** in paragraph X . . . It is **indicated** in paragraph X . . . It is **mentioned** in paragraph X . . .
WHERE TO FIND THE ANSWER	These answers are generally found in order in the passage, and the paragraph where the answer is found is generally indicated in the question.
HOW TO ANSWER THE QUESTION	1. Choose a key word or idea in the question. 2. Skim the appropriate paragraph for the key word or idea. 3. Read the sentence that contains the key word or idea carefully. 4. Eliminate any definitely wrong answers, and choose the best answer from the remaining choices.

READING EXERCISE 5: Study each of the passages and choose the best answers to the questions that follow.

PASSAGE ONE (Questions 1–5)

Paragraph

Lake Baikal

1   Crescent-shaped Lake Baikal, in Siberia, is only the ninth largest lake in area at 385 miles (620 km) in length and 46 miles (74 km) in width, yet it is easily the largest body of fresh water in the world. It holds one-fifth of the world's total fresh water, which is more than the total of all the water in the five Great Lakes; it holds so much fresh water in spite of its less-than-impressive area because it is by far the world's deepest lake. The average depth of the lake is 1,312 feet (400 meters) below sea level, and the Olkhon Crevice, the lowest known point, is more than 5,250 feet (1,600 meters) deep.

2   Lake Baikal, which today is located near the center of the Asian peninsula, is most likely the world's oldest lake. It began forming 25 million years ago as Asia started splitting apart in a series of great faults. The Baikal Valley dropped away, eventually filling with water and creating the deepest of the world's lakes.

1. What is stated in paragraph 1 about the shape of Lake Baikal?

  Ⓐ It is wider than it is long.
  Ⓑ It is circular in shape.
  Ⓒ Its width is one-half of its length.
  Ⓓ It is shaped like a new moon.

2. It is indicated in paragraph 1 that the area of Lake Baikal

  Ⓐ is less than the area of eight other lakes
  Ⓑ is one-ninth the area of Siberia
  Ⓒ is greater than the area of any other freshwater lake
  Ⓓ is equal to the area of the five Great Lakes

3. According to paragraph 1, Lake Baikal

  Ⓐ holds one-fifth of the world's water
  Ⓑ holds five times the water of the Great Lakes
  Ⓒ holds one-ninth of the world's water
  Ⓓ holds 20 percent of the world's fresh water

4. According to paragraph 1, the Olkhon Crevice is

  Ⓐ outside of Lake Baikal
  Ⓑ 400 meters below sea level
  Ⓒ the deepest part of Lake Baikal
  Ⓓ 5,000 meters deep

5. It is mentioned in paragraph 2 that Lake Baikal

  Ⓐ is not as old as some other lakes
  Ⓑ formed when sections of the Earth were moving away from each other
  Ⓒ was fully formed 25 million years ago
  Ⓓ is today located on the edge of the Asian peninsula

Paragraph

The Postage Stamp

1   The postage stamp has been around for only a relatively short period of time. The use of stamps for postage was first proposed in England in 1837, when Sir Rowland Hill published a pamphlet entitled "Post Office Reform: Its Importance and Practicability" to put forth the ideas that postal rates should not be based on the distance that a letter or package travels but should instead be based on the weight of the letter or package and that fees for postal services should be collected in advance of the delivery, rather than after, through the use of postage stamps.

2   The ideas proposed by Hill went into effect in England almost immediately, and other countries soon followed suit. The first English stamp, which featured a portrait of then Queen Victoria, was printed in 1840. This stamp, the "penny black," came in sheets that needed to be separated with scissors and provided enough postage for a letter weighing 14 grams or less to any destination. In 1843, Brazil was the next nation to produce national postage stamps, and various areas in what is today Switzerland also produced postage stamps later in the same year. Postage stamps in five- and ten-cent denominations were first approved by the U.S. Congress in 1847, and by 1860 postage stamps were being issued in more than 90 governmental jurisdictions worldwide.

6. According to paragraph 1, postage stamps were first suggested
   - Ⓐ in the first half of the eighteenth century
   - Ⓑ in the second half of the eighteenth century
   - Ⓒ in the first half of the nineteenth century
   - Ⓓ in the second half of the nineteenth century

7. It is indicated in paragraph 1 that Sir Rowland Hill believed that postage fees
   - Ⓐ should be paid by the sender
   - Ⓑ should be related to distance
   - Ⓒ should have nothing to do with how heavy a package is
   - Ⓓ should be collected after the package is delivered

8. What is stated in paragraph 2 about the first English postage stamp?
   - Ⓐ It was designed by Queen Victoria.
   - Ⓑ It contained a drawing of a black penny.
   - Ⓒ It was produced in sheets of 14 stamps.
   - Ⓓ It could be used to send a lightweight letter.

9. According to paragraph 2, Brazil introduced postage stamps
   - Ⓐ before England
   - Ⓑ before Switzerland
   - Ⓒ after the United States
   - Ⓓ after Switzerland

10. It is mentioned in paragraph 2 that in 1847
    - Ⓐ postage stamps were in use in 90 different countries
    - Ⓑ it cost fifteen cents to mail a letter in the United States
    - Ⓒ two different denominations of postage stamps were introduced in the United States
    - Ⓓ the U.S. Congress introduced the "penny black" stamp

PASSAGE THREE *(Questions 11–15)*

The Clovis Culture

1   Archeologists have found sites all over North America that contain similar tools dating from a period about 12,000 years ago. The culture that developed these tools has been named Clovis after the site near Clovis, New Mexico, where the first tools of this sort were discovered in 1932. The tools are quite sophisticated and are unlike any tools that have been found in the Old World.

2   In the years since the first tools of this sort were discovered in New Mexico, archeologists have discovered Clovis tools in areas ranging from Mexico to Montana in the United States and Nova Scotia in Canada. All of the Clovis finds date from approximately the same period, a fact which suggests that the Clovis spread rapidly throughout the North American continent.

3   From the evidence that has been discovered, archeologists have concluded that the Clovis were a mobile culture. They traveled in groups of 40 to 50 individuals, migrating seasonally and returning to the same hunting camps each year. Their population increased rapidly as they spread out over the continent, and they were quite possibly motivated to develop their sophisticated hunting tools to feed their rapidly expanding populace.

11. What is stated in paragraph 1 about Clovis tools?

  Ⓐ They date from around 10,000 B.C.

  Ⓑ They have been in use for 12,000 years.

  Ⓒ They have been found at only one location.

  Ⓓ They were discovered by archeologists hundreds of years ago.

12. According to paragraph 1, the town of Clovis

  Ⓐ is in Mexico

  Ⓑ was founded in 1932

  Ⓒ is where all members of the Clovis culture lived

  Ⓓ is where the first remnants of an ancient culture were found

13. It is indicated in paragraph 1 that the tools found near Clovis, New Mexico, were

  Ⓐ very rudimentary

  Ⓑ similar to others found prior to 1932

  Ⓒ rather advanced

  Ⓓ similar to some found in Africa and Europe

14. According to paragraph 2, what conclusion have archeologists drawn from the Clovis finds?

  Ⓐ That the Clovis tended to remain in one place

  Ⓑ That the Clovis expanded relatively quickly

  Ⓒ That the Clovis lived throughout the world

  Ⓓ That the Clovis were a seafaring culture

15. It is mentioned in paragraph 3 that it is believed that the Clovis

  Ⓐ lived in familial groups of four or five people

  Ⓑ had a relatively stable population

  Ⓒ lived only in New Mexico

  Ⓓ spent summers and winters in different places

PASSAGE FOUR *(Questions 16–22)*

Brown Dwarfs

1   A brown dwarf is a celestial body that has never quite become a star. A typical brown dwarf has a mass that is 8 percent or less than that of the Sun. The mass of a brown dwarf is too small to generate the internal temperatures capable of igniting the nuclear burning of hydrogen to release energy and light.

2   A brown dwarf contracts at a steady rate, and after it has contracted as much as possible, a process that takes about 1 million years, it begins to cool off. Its emission of light diminishes with the decrease in its internal temperature, and after a period of 2 to 3 billion years, its emission of light is so weak that it can be difficult to observe from Earth.

3   Because of these characteristics of a brown dwarf, it can be easily distinguished from stars in different stages of formation. A brown dwarf is quite distinctive because its surface temperature is relatively cool and because its internal composition—approximately 75 percent hydrogen—has remained essentially the same as it was when first formed. A white dwarf, in contrast, has gone through a long period when it burns hydrogen, followed by another long period in which it burns the helium created by the burning of hydrogen and ends up with a core that consists mostly of oxygen and carbon with a thin layer of hydrogen surrounding the core.

4   It is not always as easy, however, to distinguish brown dwarfs from large planets. Though planets are not formed in the same way as brown dwarfs, they may in their current state have some of the same characteristics as a brown dwarf. The planet Jupiter, for example, is the largest planet in our solar system with a mass 317 times that of our planet and resembles a brown dwarf in that it radiates energy based on its internal energy. It is the mechanism by which they were formed that distinguishes a high-mass planet such as Jupiter from a low-mass brown dwarf.

16. It is stated in the passage that the mass of an average brown dwarf

   Ⓐ is smaller than the mass of the Sun

   Ⓑ generates an extremely high internal temperature

   Ⓒ is capable of igniting nuclear burning

   Ⓓ causes the release of considerable energy and light

17. According to paragraph 2, a brown dwarf cools off

   Ⓐ within the first million years of its existence

   Ⓑ after its contraction is complete

   Ⓒ at the same time that it contracts

   Ⓓ in order to begin contracting

18. What is stated in paragraph 2 about a brown dwarf that has cooled off for several million years?

   Ⓐ Its weak light makes it difficult to see from Earth.

   Ⓑ It no longer emits light.

   Ⓒ Its weak light has begun the process of restrengthening.

   Ⓓ Scientists are unable to study it.

19. It is indicated in paragraph 3 that

   Ⓐ the amount of hydrogen in a brown dwarf has increased dramatically

   Ⓑ a brown dwarf had far more hydrogen when it first formed

   Ⓒ three-quarters of the core of a brown dwarf is hydrogen

   Ⓓ the internal composition of a brown dwarf is always changing

20. According to paragraph 3, a white dwarf

   Ⓐ is approximately 75 percent hydrogen

   Ⓑ still burns a considerable amount of hydrogen

   Ⓒ creates hydrogen from helium

   Ⓓ no longer has a predominantly hydrogen core

21. What is mentioned in paragraph 4 about brown dwarfs?

(A) They are quite different from large planets.

(B) They are formed in the same way as large planets.

(C) They can share some similarities with large planets.

(D) They have nothing in common with large planets.

22. It is indicated in paragraph 4 that Jupiter

(A) radiates far less energy than a brown dwarf

(B) is a brown dwarf

(C) formed in the same way as a brown dwarf

(D) is in at least one respect similar to a brown dwarf

Reading Skill 6: UNDERSTAND NEGATIVE FACTS

In the Reading section of the *iBT* TOEFL test, you will sometimes be asked to find an answer that is *not stated*, or *not mentioned*, or *not true* in the passage. This type of question really means that three of the answers are *stated, mentioned,* or *true* in the passage, while one answer is not.

You should note that there are two kinds of answers to this type of question: (1) there are three answers that are true and one that is *not true* according to the passage, or (2) there are three true answers and one that is *not stated or mentioned* in the passage. Look at an example that asks you to find the one answer that is *not true*.

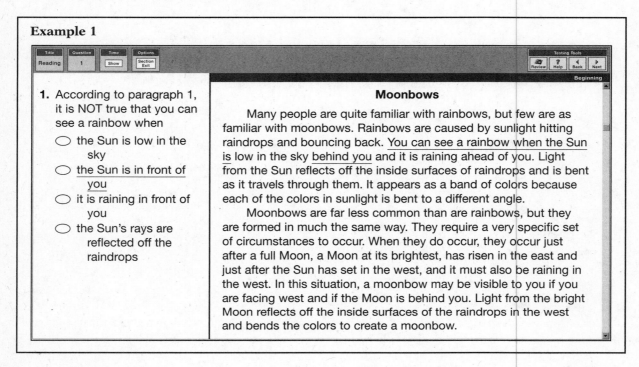

Example 1

Title	Question	Time	Options		Testing Tools
Reading	1	Show	Section Exit		Review Help Back Next

Beginning

1. According to paragraph 1, it is NOT true that you can see a rainbow when
   ○ the Sun is low in the sky
   ○ the Sun is in front of you
   ○ it is raining in front of you
   ○ the Sun's rays are reflected off the raindrops

Moonbows

Many people are quite familiar with rainbows, but few are as familiar with moonbows. Rainbows are caused by sunlight hitting raindrops and bouncing back. You can see a rainbow when the Sun is low in the sky behind you and it is raining ahead of you. Light from the Sun reflects off the inside surfaces of raindrops and is bent as it travels through them. It appears as a band of colors because each of the colors in sunlight is bent to a different angle.

Moonbows are far less common than are rainbows, but they are formed in much the same way. They require a very specific set of circumstances to occur. When they do occur, they occur just after a full Moon, a Moon at its brightest, has risen in the east and just after the Sun has set in the west, and it must also be raining in the west. In this situation, a moonbow may be visible to you if you are facing west and if the Moon is behind you. Light from the bright Moon reflects off the inside surfaces of the raindrops in the west and bends the colors to create a moonbow.

This question asks you to determine which of the answers is NOT true according to the information in the first paragraph. This means that three of the answers are true according to the passage, and one is not true. To answer this type of question, you must find the one answer that is not true according to the information in the first paragraph. It is stated in the first paragraph that *you can see a rainbow when the Sun is . . . behind you*. This means that it is NOT true that you can see a rainbow when *the Sun is in front of you*. To answer this question, you should click on the second answer.

The next example asks you to find the one answer that is *not mentioned*.

Example 2

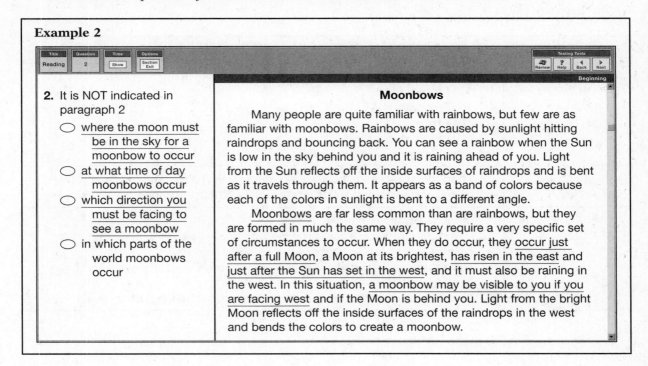

This question asks you to determine which of the answers is NOT indicated in the second paragraph. This means that three of the answers are indicated in the second paragraph, and one is not indicated. To answer this type of question, you must find the three answers that are indicated in the paragraph and then choose the remaining answer as the correct answer. The passage states that *moonbows . . . occur just after a full Moon . . . has risen in the east,* which indicates *where the Moon must be in the sky for a moonbow to occur* in the first answer. The passage states that *moonbows . . . occur . . . just after the Sun has set in the west,* which indicates *at what time of day moonbows occur* in the second answer. The passage states that *a moonbow may be visible to you if you are facing west,* which indicates *which direction you must be facing to see a moonbow* in the third answer. The last answer is the one that is NOT indicated in the passage and is therefore the best answer to this question. To answer this question, you should click on the last answer.

The following chart outlines the key information that you should remember about questions testing negative facts.

QUESTIONS ABOUT NEGATIVE FACTS		
HOW TO IDENTIFY THE QUESTION	It is **NOT stated** . . . It is **NOT mentioned** . . . It is **NOT discussed** . . . It is **NOT true** . . . It is **NOT indicated** . . . All of the following are **true EXCEPT** . . .	
WHERE TO FIND THE ANSWER	These answers are generally found in order in the passage, and the paragraph where the answer is found is generally indicated in the question.	
HOW TO ANSWER THE QUESTION	1. Choose a key word in the question. 2. Scan the appropriate place in the passage for the key word (or related idea). 3. Read the sentence that contains the key word carefully. 4. Look for the answers that are definitely true according to the passage. Eliminate those answers. 5. Choose the answer that is not true or not discussed in the passage.	

READING EXERCISE 6: Study each of the passages, and choose the best answers to the questions that follow.

PASSAGE ONE *(Questions 1–5)*

Flatfish

Members of the flatfish family, sand dabs and flounders, have an evolutionary advantage over many colorfully decorated ocean neighbors in that they are able to adapt their body coloration to different environments. These aquatic chameleons have flattened bodies that are well-suited to life along the ocean floor in the shallower areas of the continental shelf that they inhabit. They also have remarkably sensitive color vision that registers the subtlest gradations on the sea bottom and in the sea life around them. Information about the coloration of the environment is carried through the nervous system to chromatophores, which are pigment-carrying skin cells. These chromatophores are able to accurately reproduce not only the colors but also the texture of the ocean floor. Each time that a sand dab or flounder finds itself in a new environment, the pattern on the body of the fish adapts to fit in with the color and texture around it.

1. It is NOT stated in the passage that sand dabs
   A are a type of flatfish
   B are in the same family as flounders
   C have evolved
   D are colorfully decorated

2. According to the passages, it is NOT true that sand dabs and flounders
   A have flattened bodies
   B live along the ocean floor
   C live in the deepest part of the ocean
   D live along the continental shelf

3. All of the following are stated about the vision of sand dabs and flounders EXCEPT that they are
   A overly sensitive to light
   B able to see colors
   C able to see the sea bottom
   D aware of their surroundings

4. It is NOT true that chromatophores
   A are skin cells
   B carry pigment
   C adapt to surrounding colors
   D change the ocean floor

5. It is NOT mentioned in the passage that sand dabs and flounders
   A move to new environments
   B adapt their behavior
   C can change color
   D adapt to textures around them

Paragraph

Limestone Caves

1   Limestone caves can be spectacular structures filled with giant stalactites and stalagmites. These caves are formed when rainwater, which is a weak acid, dissolves calcite, or lime, out of limestone. Over time, the lime-laden water drips down into cracks, enlarging them into caves. Some of the lime is then redeposited to form stalactites and stalagmites.

2   Stalactites, which grow down from cave ceilings, are formed in limestone caves when groundwater containing dissolved lime drips from the roof of the cave and leaves a thin deposit as it evaporates. Stalactites generally grow only a fraction of an inch each year, but over time a considerable number may grow to be several yards long. In cases where the supply of water is seasonal, they may actually have growth rings resembling those on tree trunks that indicate how old the stalactites are.

3   Stalagmites are formed on the floor of a limestone cave where water containing dissolved lime has dripped either from the cave ceiling or from a stalactite above. They develop in the same way as stalactites, when water containing dissolved limestone evaporates. In some limestone caves with mature limestone development, stalactites and stalagmites grow together, creating limestone pillars that stretch from the cave floor to the cave ceiling.

6. It is indicated in paragraph 1 that all of the following are part of the process of forming limestone caves EXCEPT that

  Ⓐ rainwater dissolves lime from limestone
  Ⓑ the lime-filled water seeps into breaks in the ground
  Ⓒ the lime in the water evaporates
  Ⓓ the cracks in the ground develop into caves

7. According to paragraph 2, it is NOT true that stalactites

  Ⓐ enlarge cave ceilings
  Ⓑ are found in limestone caves
  Ⓒ grow in a downward direction
  Ⓓ grow quite slowly

8. It is NOT mentioned in paragraph 2

  Ⓐ how long stalactites may grow
  Ⓑ how the age of a stalactite is determined
  Ⓒ what one of the effects of a limited water supply is
  Ⓓ what causes stalactites to disappear

9. According to paragraph 3, stalagmites are NOT formed

  Ⓐ on cave floors
  Ⓑ from lime dissolved in water
  Ⓒ above stalactites
  Ⓓ as water containing lime evaporates

10. It is NOT indicated in paragraph 3 that limestone pillars

  Ⓐ result when a stalactite and a stalagmite grow together
  Ⓑ are attached to both the floor and the ceiling of a cave
  Ⓒ are relatively aged limestone formations
  Ⓓ are more durable than stalactites and stalagmites

PASSAGE THREE *(Questions 11–15)*

Wrigley's Chewing Gum

Paragraph

1   Wrigley's chewing gum was actually developed as a premium to be given away with other products rather than as a primary product for sale. As a teenager, William Wrigley Jr. was working for his father in Chicago selling soap that had been manufactured in his father's factory. The soap was not very popular with merchants because it was priced at five cents, and this selling price did not leave a good profit margin for the merchants. Wrigley convinced his father to raise the price to ten cents and to give away cheap umbrellas as a premium for the merchants. This worked successfully, confirming to Wrigley that the use of premiums was an effective sales tool.

2   Wrigley then established his own company; in his company he was selling soap as a wholesaler, giving baking soda away as a premium, and using a cookbook to promote each deal. Over time, the baking soda and cookbook became more popular than the soap, so Wrigley began a new operation selling baking soda. He began hunting for a new premium item to give away with sales of baking soda; he soon decided on chewing gum. Once again, when Wrigley realized that demand for the premium was stronger than the demand for the original product, he created the Wm. Wrigley Jr. Company to produce and sell chewing gum.

3   Wrigley started out with two brands of gum, Vassar and Lotta Gum, and soon introduced Juicy Fruit and Spearment. The latter two brands grew in popularity, while the first two were phased out. Juicy Fruit and Spearment are two of Wrigley's main brands to this day.

11. It is NOT indicated in paragraph 1 that young William was working

- Ⓐ in Chicago
- Ⓑ for his father
- Ⓒ as a soap salesman
- Ⓓ in his father's factory

12. According to paragraph 1, it is NOT true that the soap that young Wrigley was selling

- Ⓐ was originally well-liked
- Ⓑ was originally priced at five cents
- Ⓒ originally provided little profit for merchants
- Ⓓ eventually became more popular with merchants

13. According to paragraph 2, it is NOT true that, when Wrigley first founded his own company, he was

- Ⓐ selling soap
- Ⓑ selling chewing gum
- Ⓒ giving away cookbooks
- Ⓓ using baking soda as a premium

14. It is NOT mentioned in paragraph 2 that Wrigley later

- Ⓐ sold baking soda
- Ⓑ used chewing gun as a premium to sell baking soda
- Ⓒ sold chewing gum
- Ⓓ used baking soda as a premium to sell chewing gum

15. According to paragraph 3, the Wm. Wrigley Jr. Company did all of the following EXCEPT

- Ⓐ begin with two brands of gum
- Ⓑ add new brands to the original two
- Ⓒ phase out the last two brands
- Ⓓ phase out the first two brands

PASSAGE FOUR *(Questions 16–22)*

Dissociative Identity Disorder

Paragraph

1   Dissociative identity disorder is a psychological condition in which a person's identity dissociates, or fragments, thereby creating distinct independent identities within one individual. Each separate personality can be distinct from the other personalities in a number of ways, including posture, manner of moving, tone and pitch of voice, gestures, facial expressions, and use of language. A person suffering from dissociative identity disorder may have a large number of independent personalities or perhaps only two or three.

2   Two stories of actual women suffering from dissociative identity disorder have been extensively recounted in books and films that are familiar to the public. One of them is the story of a woman with 22 separate personalities known as Eve. In the 1950s, a book by Corbett Thigpen and a motion picture starring Joanne Woodward, each of which was titled *The Three Faces of Eve,* presented her story; the title referred to 3 faces, when the woman known as Eve actually experienced 22 different personalities, because only 3 of the personalities could exist at one time. Two decades later, Carolyn Sizemore, Eve's 22nd personality, wrote about her experiences in a book entitled *I'm Eve.* The second well-known story of a woman suffering from dissociative personality disorder is the story of Sybil, a woman whose 16 distinct personalities emerged over a period of 40 years. A book describing Sybil's experiences was written by Flora Rheta Schreiber and was published in 1973; a motion picture based on the book and starring Sally Field followed.

16. It is NOT stated in paragraph 1 that someone suffering from dissociative identity disorder has

ⓐ a psychological condition
ⓑ a fragmented identity
ⓒ a number of independent identities
ⓓ some violent and some nonviolent identities

17. It is indicated in paragraph 1 that distinct personalities can differ in all of the following ways EXCEPT

ⓐ manner of dressing
ⓑ manner of moving
ⓒ manner of speaking
ⓓ manner of gesturing

18. It is indicated in paragraph 2 that it is NOT true that Eve

ⓐ suffered from dissociative identity disorder
ⓑ starred in the movie about her life
ⓒ had 22 distinct personalities
ⓓ had only 3 distinct personalities at any one time

19. It is NOT stated in paragraph 2 that *The Three Faces of Eve*

ⓐ was based on the life of a real woman
ⓑ was the title of a book
ⓒ was the title of a movie
ⓓ was made into a movie in 1950

20. All of the following are mentioned in paragraph 2 about Carolyn Sizemore EXCEPT that she

ⓐ wrote *I'm Eve*
ⓑ was one of Eve's personalities
ⓒ wrote a book in the 1970s
ⓓ was familiar with all 22 personalities

21. According to paragraph 2, it is NOT true that Sybil

ⓐ was a real person
ⓑ suffered from dissociative identity disorder
ⓒ developed all her personalities over 16 years
ⓓ developed 16 distinctive personalities over a long period of time

22. It is NOT indicated in paragraph 2 that the book describing Sybil's experiences

ⓐ took 40 years to write
ⓑ was written by Flora Rheta Schreiber
ⓒ appeared in the 1970s
ⓓ was made into a movie

READING EXERCISE (Skills 5–6): Study the passage, and choose the best answers to the questions that follow.

John Muir

Paragraph

1   John Muir (1838–1914), a Scottish immigrant to the United States, is today recognized for his vital contributions in the area of environmental protection and conservation of the wilderness. As such, he is often referred to as the unofficial "Father of National Parks."

2   Muir came to his role as an environmentalist in a rather circuitous way. Born in Dunbar, Scotland, Muir came to the United States with his family at the age of eleven. The family settled on a Wisconsin farm, where Muir was educated at home rather than in public school because his father felt that participation in an education in a public school would violate his strict religious code. Young Muir did read considerably at home and also developed some interesting mechanical devices by whittling them from wood; when some of his inventions were put on display at a state fair, they were noted by officials from the University of Wisconsin, and Muir was invited to attend the university in spite of his lack of formal education. He left the university after two and a half years; later, while working in a carriage factory, he suffered an injury to his eye. His vision did recover, but following the accident he decided that he wanted to spend his life studying the beauty of the natural world rather than endangering his health working in a factory. He set out on a 1,000-mile walk south to the Gulf of Mexico, and from there he made his way to Yosemite, California, lured by a travel brochure highlighting the natural beauty of Yosemite.

3   He arrived in California in 1868, at the age of thirty, and once there, he took a number of odd jobs to support himself, working as a laborer, a sheepherder, and—after he had become familiar with the wilderness area—a guide. He also began a writing campaign to encourage public support for the preservation of the wilderness, particularly the area around Yosemite. He married in 1880, and for the years that followed he was more involved in family life and in running the ranch given to him and his wife by her parents than in preservation of the environment.

4   He had been away from the environmentalist movement for some time when, in 1889, he was asked by an editor of the magazine *The Century* to write some articles in support of the preservation of Yosemite. The editor, well aware of Muir's talent as a writer and his efforts in the 1870s to support the conservation of Yosemite, took Muir camping to areas of Yosemite that Muir had not seen for years, areas that had been spoiled through uncontrolled development. Because of the experience of this trip, Muir agreed to write two articles in support of the institution of a National Parks system in the United States with Yosemite as the first park to be so designated. These two articles in *The Century* initiated the Yosemite National Park campaign.

5   The campaign was indeed successful. The law creating Yosemite National Park was enacted in 1890, and three additional national parks were created soon after. A year later, a bill known as the Enabling Act was passed; this was a bill that gave U.S. presidents the right to reserve lands for preservation by the U.S. government. Pleased by this success but keenly aware of the need to continue the effort to preserve wilderness areas from undisciplined development, Muir established an organization in 1892, the Sierra Club, with the expressed goal of protecting the wilderness, particularly the area of the Sierra Nevada mountain range where Yosemite is located.

6   From then until his death in 1914, Muir worked assiduously on his writing in an effort to build recognition of the need for environmental protection. His writings from this period include *The Mountains of California* (1894), *Our National Parks* (1901), *My First Summer in the Sierra* (1911), and *My Boyhood and Youth* (1913).

7   A century later, the results of what John Muir was instrumental in initiating are remarkable. The National Park Service is now responsible for more than 350 parks, rivers, seashores, and preserves; more than 250 million people visit these parks each year, and the Sierra Club has more than 650,000 members.

Questions

1. According to paragraph 1, Muir was born
   - (A) in the first half of the eighteenth century
   - (B) in the second half of the eighteenth century
   - (C) in the first half of the nineteenth century
   - (D) in the second half of the nineteenth century

2. It is stated in paragraph 1 that Muir is known for
   - (A) his contributions to immigration reform
   - (B) his explorations of the wilderness
   - (C) his efforts to maintain natural areas
   - (D) his extensive studies of the national parks

3. It is indicated in paragraph 2 that Muir's early education
   - (A) was conducted at home
   - (B) took place in a religious school
   - (C) violated his father's wishes
   - (D) was in a public school

4. It is NOT mentioned in paragraph 2 that Muir
   - (A) whittled with wood
   - (B) was taught how to whittle by his father
   - (C) whittled mechanical devices
   - (D) was admitted to the university because of his whittling

5. According to paragraph 2, after Muir left the university, it is NOT true that he
   - (A) took a job in a factory
   - (B) suffered an unhealable injury
   - (C) made a decision to quit his job
   - (D) embarked on a long walking tour

6. All of the following are mentioned in paragraph 3 as jobs that Muir held EXCEPT
   - (A) a laborer
   - (B) an animal tender
   - (C) a wilderness guide
   - (D) a travel writer

7. It is stated in paragraph 3 that in the years after 1880, Muir
   - (A) took some odd jobs
   - (B) devoted a lot of time to his family
   - (C) gave his wife's parents a ranch
   - (D) spent most of his time preserving the environment

8. It is NOT mentioned in paragraph 4 that Muir
   - (A) had been uninvolved with environmentalists for a period of time
   - (B) was contacted by an editor for *The Century*
   - (C) worked as an editor for *The Century*
   - (D) wrote two articles for *The Century*

9. The camping trip that is discussed in paragraph 4
   - (A) occurred in the 1870s
   - (B) led Muir to areas that he had never before seen
   - (C) took place in areas that were in their natural state
   - (D) helped to convince Muir to write the articles

10. It is stated in paragraph 5 that the Enabling Act
    - (A) allowed the president to set aside lands to conserve them
    - (B) became law in 1890
    - (C) called for the establishment of the first three national parks
    - (D) preserved lands for government use

11. According to paragraph 5, it is NOT true that the Sierra Club was founded
    - (A) after the passage of the Enabling Act
    - (B) by John Muir
    - (C) before the turn of the century
    - (D) to move Yosemite to the Sierra Nevada

12. It is mentioned in paragraph 6 that, for the last decades of his life, Muir

Ⓐ spent a considerable amount of time in Yosemite

Ⓑ wrote a number of new laws

Ⓒ changed his mind on the need for environmental protection

Ⓓ devoted himself to increasing public awareness of the environment

13. It is NOT indicated in paragraph 7 that early in the twenty-first century

Ⓐ hundreds of locations are part of the National Park Service

Ⓑ numerous parks, rivers, seashores, and preserves are being developed

Ⓒ a quarter of a billion people visit these parks each year

Ⓓ more than a half a million people belong to the Sierra Club

READING REVIEW EXERCISE (Skills 1–6): Read the passage.

Paragraph

Caretaker Speech

1   Children learn to construct language from those around them. Until about the age of three, children tend to learn to develop their language by modeling the speech of their parents, but from that time on, peers have a growing influence as models for language development in children. It is easy to observe that, when adults and older children interact with younger children, they tend to modify their language to improve communication with younger children, and this modified language is called **caretaker speech**.

2   Caretaker speech is used often quite unconsciously; few people actually study how to modify language when speaking to young children but, instead, without thinking, find ways to reduce the complexity of language in order to communicate effectively with young children. A caretaker will unconsciously speak in one way with adults and in a very different way with young children. Caretaker speech tends to be slower speech with short, simple words and sentences which are said in a higher-pitched voice with exaggerated inflections and many repetitions of essential information. It is not limited to what is commonly called baby talk, which generally refers to the use of simplified, repeated syllable expressions such as *ma-ma, boo-boo, bye-bye, wa-wa,* but also includes the simplified sentence structures repeated in sing-song inflections.

3   Caretaker speech serves the very important function of allowing young children to acquire language more easily. The higher-pitched voice and the exaggerated inflections tend to focus the small child on what the caretaker is saying, the simplified words and sentences make it easier for the small child to begin to comprehend, and the repetitions reinforce the child's developing understanding. Then, as a child's speech develops, caretakers tend to adjust their language in response to the improved language skills, again quite unconsciously. Parents and older children regularly adjust their speech to a level that is slightly above that of a younger child; without studied recognition of what they are doing, these caretakers will speak in one way to a one-year-old and in a progressively more complex way as the child reaches the age of two or three.

4   An important point to note is that the function covered by caretaker speech, that of assisting a child to acquire language in small and simple steps, is an unconsciously used but extremely important part of the process of language acquisition and as such is quite universal. Studying cultures where children do not acquire language through caretaker speech is difficult because such cultures are difficult to find. The question of why caretaker speech is universal is not clearly understood; instead proponents on either side of the nature vs. nurture debate argue over whether caretaker speech is a natural function or a learned one. Those who believe that caretaker speech is a natural and inherent function in humans believe that it is human nature for children to acquire language and for those around them to encourage their language acquisition naturally; the presence of a child is itself a natural stimulus that increases the rate of caretaker speech among those present. In contrast, those who believe that caretaker speech develops through nurturing rather than nature argue that a person who is attempting to communicate with a child will learn by trying out different ways of communicating to determine which is the most effective from the reactions to the communication attempts; a parent might, for example, learn to use speech with exaggerated inflections with a small child because the exaggerated inflections do a better job of attracting the child's attention than do more subtle inflections. Whether caretaker speech results from nature or nurture, it does play an important and universal role in chid language acquisition.

Refer to this version of the passage to answer the questions that follow.

Caretaker Speech

Paragraph

1 Children learn to construct language from those around them. Until about the age of three, children tend to learn to develop their language by modeling the speech of their parents, but from that time on, peers have a growing influence as models for language development in children. It is easy to observe that, when adults and older children interact with younger children, they tend to modify their language to improve communication with younger children, and this modified language is called **caretaker speech**.

2 Caretaker speech is used often quite unconsciously; few people actually study how to modify language when speaking to young children but, instead, without thinking, find ways to reduce the complexity of language in order to communicate effectively with young children. **5A** A caretaker will unconsciously speak in one way with adults and in a very different way with young children. **5B** Caretaker speech tends to be slower speech with short, simple words and sentences which are said in a higher-pitched voice with exaggerated inflections and many repetitions of essential information. **5C** It is not limited to what is commonly called baby talk, which generally refers to the use of simplified, repeated syllable expressions such as *ma-ma, boo-boo, bye-bye, wa-wa,* but also includes the simplified sentence structures repeated in sing-song inflections. **5D**

3 Caretaker speech serves the very important function of allowing young children to acquire language more easily. The higher-pitched voice and the exaggerated inflections tend to focus the small child on what the caretaker is saying, the simplified words and sentences make it easier for the small child to begin to comprehend, and the repetitions reinforce the child's developing understanding. Then, as a child's speech develops, caretakers tend to adjust their language in response to the improved language skills, again quite unconsciously. Parents and older children regularly adjust their speech to a level that is slightly above that of a younger child; without studied recognition of what they are doing, these caretakers will speak in one way to a one-year-old and in a progressively more complex way as the child reaches the age of two or three.

4 **13A** An important point to note is that the function covered by caretaker speech, that of assisting a child to acquire language in small and simple steps, is an unconsciously used but extremely important part of the process of language acquisition and as such is quite universal. **13B** Studying cultures where children do not acquire language through caretaker speech is difficult because such cultures are difficult to find. **13C** The question of why caretaker speech is universal is not clearly understood; instead proponents on either side of the nature vs. nurture debate argue over whether caretaker speech is a natural function or a learned one. **13D** Those who believe that caretaker speech is a natural and inherent function in humans believe that it is human nature for children to acquire language and for those around them to encourage their language acquisition naturally; the presence of a child is itself a natural stimulus that increases the rate of caretaker speech among those present. In contrast, those who believe that caretaker speech develops through nurturing rather than nature argue that a person who is attempting to communicate with a child will learn by trying out different ways of communicating to determine which is the most effective from the reactions to the communication attempts; a parent might, for example, learn to use speech with exaggerated inflections with a small child because the exaggerated inflections do a better job of attracting the child's attention than do more subtle inflections. Whether caretaker speech results from nature or nurture, it does play an important and universal role in child language acquisition.

Questions

1. According to paragraph 1, children over the age of three
   - (A) learn little language from those around them
   - (B) are no longer influenced by the language of their parents
   - (C) are influenced more and more by those closer to their own age
   - (D) first begin to respond to caretaker speech

2. The word modeling in paragraph 1 could best be replaced by
   - (A) demonstrating
   - (B) mimicking
   - (C) building
   - (D) designing

3. Which of the sentences below expresses the essential information in the highlighted sentence in paragraph 2? *Incorrect* choices change the meaning in important ways or leave out essential information.
   - (A) Most people are quite aware of the use of caretaker speech because of thorough study and research about it.
   - (B) The unconscious use of caretaker speech involves a reduction in the complexity of language, while the conscious use of caretaker speech involves an increase in complexity.
   - (C) Young children tend to use caretaker speech quite unconsciously in order to reduce the complexity of their thoughts to language that they can express.
   - (D) People generally seem to be able to adapt their language to the level of a child's language without thinking consciously about it.

4. The word It in paragraph 2 refers to
   - (A) caretaker speech
   - (B) a higher-pitched voice
   - (C) essential information
   - (D) baby talk

5. Look at the four squares [■] that indicate where the following sentence can be added to paragraph 2.

   Examples of these are expressions such as "Say bye-bye" or "Where's da-da?"

   Click on a square [■] to add the sentence to the passage.

6. All of the following are mentioned in paragraph 3 as characteristics of caretaker speech EXCEPT
   - (A) overemphasized inflections
   - (B) the use of rhyming sounds
   - (C) the tendency to repeat oneself
   - (D) the use of easier words and structures

7. It is indicated in paragraph 3 that parents tend to
   - (A) speak in basically the same way to a one-year-old and a three-year-old
   - (B) use language that is far above the language level of a child
   - (C) speak in a progressively less complex way as a child matures
   - (D) modify their speech according to the language development of a child

8. The word reaches in paragraph 3 could best be replaced by
   - (A) holds on to
   - (B) takes charge of
   - (C) arrives at
   - (D) extends out to

9. The word that in paragraph 4 refers to
   - (A) an important point
   - (B) the function
   - (C) caretaker speech
   - (D) a child

10. Which of the sentences below expresses the essential information in the highlighted sentence in paragraph 4? *Incorrect* choices change the meaning in important ways or leave out essential information.

Ⓐ People who believe in nature over nurture feel that adults or older children who are around younger children will naturally make changes in their language.

Ⓑ Caretaker speech is one of many natural functions that are used to stimulate young children to develop more rapidly.

Ⓒ The natural human tendency to acquire language makes caretaker speech unimportant in improving the rate of language acquisition by children.

Ⓓ It is human nature for children to develop the use of caretaker speech in order to take part effectively in conversations around them.

11. According to paragraph 4, it is NOT expected that someone who believes in nurture over nature

Ⓐ would believe that caretaker speech is more of a learned style of language than a natural one

Ⓑ would use different styles of caretaker speech with children in response to what is working best

Ⓒ would learn to use different styles of caretaker speech with different children

Ⓓ would use less caretaker speech than do those who believe in nature over nurture

12. The phrase trying out in paragraph 4 is closest in meaning to

Ⓐ experimenting with

Ⓑ bringing about

Ⓒ throwing away

Ⓓ taking over

13. Look at the four squares [■] that indicate where the following sentence can be added to paragraph 4.

It is not merely a device used by English-speaking parents.

Click on a square [■] to add the sentence to the passage.

INFERENCES

Reading Skill 7: MAKE INFERENCES FROM STATED FACTS

In the Reading section of the *iBT* TOEFL test, you may sometimes be asked to answer a multiple-choice question by drawing a conclusion from a specific detail or details in the passage. Questions of this type contain the words *implied, inferred, likely,* or *probably* to let you know that the answer to the question is not directly stated. In this type of question, it is important to understand that you do not need to "pull the answer out of thin air." Instead, some information will be given in the passage, and you will draw a conclusion from that information. Look at an example of an inference question.

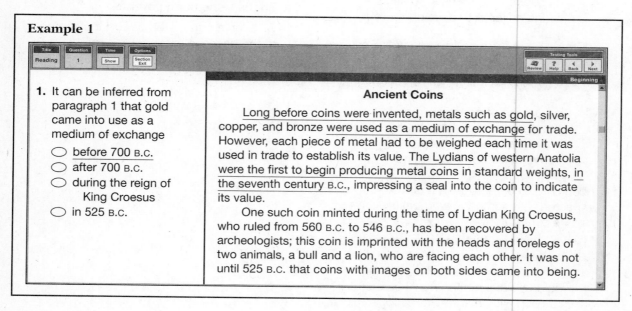

Example 1

1. It can be inferred from paragraph 1 that gold came into use as a medium of exchange

○ before 700 B.C.
○ after 700 B.C.
○ during the reign of King Croesus
○ in 525 B.C.

Ancient Coins

Long before coins were invented, metals such as gold, silver, copper, and bronze were used as a medium of exchange for trade. However, each piece of metal had to be weighed each time it was used in trade to establish its value. The Lydians of western Anatolia were the first to begin producing metal coins in standard weights, in the seventh century B.C., impressing a seal into the coin to indicate its value.

One such coin minted during the time of Lydian King Croesus, who ruled from 560 B.C. to 546 B.C., has been recovered by archeologists; this coin is imprinted with the heads and forelegs of two animals, a bull and a lion, who are facing each other. It was not until 525 B.C. that coins with images on both sides came into being.

In this example, you are asked to infer when gold came into use as a medium of exchange based upon stated information in the first paragraph. To answer this question, you should refer to the information about gold in the passage and draw a conclusion from that information. The passage states that *long before coins were invented, metals such as gold . . . were used as a medium of exchange* and that *the Lydians . . . were the first to begin producing metal coins . . . in the seventh century* B.C. From this context, it can be determined that gold came into use as a medium of exchange *before 700* B.C. To answer this question, you should click on the first answer.

Now, look at another example of an inference question.

Example 2

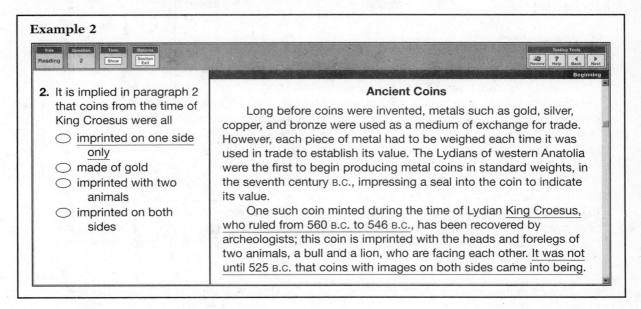

In this example, you are asked to determine what is implied about coins from the time of King Croesus, based upon stated information in the second paragraph. To answer this question, you should refer to the information about coins and King Croesus in the second paragraph. The passage mentions *King Croesus, who ruled from 560 B.C. to 546 B.C.* and that *it was not until 525 B.C. that coins with images on both sides came into being.* From this context, it can be determined that coins from the time of King Croesus were all *imprinted on one side only.* To answer this question, you should click on the first answer.

The following chart outlines the key information that you should remember about questions testing inferences.

QUESTIONS ABOUT INFERENCES FROM STATED FACTS	
HOW TO IDENTIFY THE QUESTION	It is **implied** in paragraph X . . . It can be **inferred** from paragraph X . . . It is most **likely** that . . . What **probably** happened . . . ?
WHERE TO FIND THE ANSWER	The answers to these questions are generally found in order in the passage.
HOW TO ANSWER THE QUESTION	1. Choose a key word or phrase in the question. 2. Scan the passage for the key word or phrase (or related idea). 3. Carefully read the sentence that contains the key word or phrase.

READING EXERCISE 7: Study each of the passages, and choose the best answers to the questions that follow.

PASSAGE One (Questions 1–4)

Tiger Moths

One of the most beautiful of the more than 100,000 known species in the order *Lepidoptera* are the tiger moths, moths known for the striking appeal of their distinctive coloration. This type of moth is covered with highly conspicuous orange-and-black or yellow-and-black patterns of spots and stripes. Such boldly patterned color combinations are commonplace in the animal world, serving the function of forewarning potential predators of unpleasant tastes and smells. This is unquestionably the function served by the striking coloration of the garden tiger moth, which is quite visually attractive but is also poisonous to predators. Certain glands in the garden tiger moth produce strong toxins that circulate throughout the insect's bloodstream, while other glands secrete bubbles that produce a noxious warning smell. The tiger moth, indeed, is a clear example of a concept that many predators intuitively understand, that creatures with the brightest coloration are often the least suitable to eat.

1. It is implied in the passage about the order *Lepidoptera* that
   - Ⓐ all members of the order are moths
   - Ⓑ there may be more than 100,000 species in this order
   - Ⓒ all members of the order are brightly colored
   - Ⓓ there are most likely fewer than 100,000 species in this order

2. It can be inferred from the passage that the tiger moth was so named because
   - Ⓐ its coloration resembles that of a tiger
   - Ⓑ it is a ferocious predator, like the tiger
   - Ⓒ its habitat is the same as the tiger's
   - Ⓓ it is a member of the same scientific classification as the tiger

3. What would most likely happen to a predator that wanted to eat a tiger moth?
   - Ⓐ The predator would be unable to catch it.
   - Ⓑ The predator would capture it by poisoning it.
   - Ⓒ The predator would be unable to find it.
   - Ⓓ The predator would back away from it.

4. Which of the following would a predator be most likely to attack successfully?
   - Ⓐ A purple and orange moth
   - Ⓑ A green and blue moth
   - Ⓒ A brown and grey moth
   - Ⓓ A red and yellow moth

PASSAGE TWO *(Questions 5–8)*

The Cambrian Explosion

Paragraph

1
Many of the major phyla of animals arose during the Cambrian period, in what is called the Cambrian Explosion. Prior to the Cambrian period, simple one-celled organisms had slowly evolved into primitive multicellular creatures. Then, in a relatively rapid explosion during the period from 540 million years ago to 500 million years ago, there was a period of astonishing diversification in which quickly developing organisms became widely distributed and formed complex communities.

2
One theoretical explanation for the rapid diversification that occurred during the Cambrian period is known as the theory of polar wander. According to this theory, the rapid diversification occurred because of an unusually rapid reorganization of the Earth's crust during the Cambrian period. This rapid change in the Earth's crust initiated evolutionary change inasmuch as change in the environment serves to trigger evolutionary change.

5. It can be inferred from paragraph 1 that
   - Ⓐ some major phyla developed during periods other than the Cambrian period
   - Ⓑ many other phyla of animals became extinct during the Cambrian Explosion
   - Ⓒ descriptions of various animal phyla were created during the Cambrian period
   - Ⓓ the major phyla of animals that came about during the Cambrian period died out in the Cambrian Explosion

6. It can be determined from paragraph 1 that the Cambrian Explosion most likely lasted
   - Ⓐ 40 million years
   - Ⓑ 450 million years
   - Ⓒ 500 million years
   - Ⓓ 540 million years

7. It is implied in paragraph 2 that
   - Ⓐ only one theory to explain the rapid diversification has been proposed
   - Ⓑ the polar wander explanation is accepted by all scientists
   - Ⓒ the theory of polar wander fails to adequately explain the rapid diversification
   - Ⓓ the theory of polar wander is not the only theory to explain the rapid diversification

8. It can be inferred from paragraph 2 that one basis of the theory of polar wander is that
   - Ⓐ relatively little change in the Earth's crust took place during the Cambrian period
   - Ⓑ rapid diversification was unable to take place because of the changes in the Earth's crust
   - Ⓒ the Earth's crust changed more slowly in other periods
   - Ⓓ evolutionary change is unrelated to changes in the environment

PASSAGE THREE *(Questions 9–13)*

The Golden Age of Comics

1   The period from the late 1930s to the middle 1940s is known as the Golden Age of comic books. The modern comic book came about in the early 1930s in the United States as a giveaway premium to promote the sales of a whole range of household products such as cereal and cleansers. The comic books, which were printed in bright colors to attract the attention of potential customers, proved so popular that some publishers decided to produce comic books that would come out on a monthly basis and would sell for a dime each. Though comic strips had been reproduced in publications prior to this time, the *Famous Funnies* comic book, which was started in 1934, marked the first occasion that a serialized book of comics was attempted.

2   Early comic books reprinted already existing comic strips and comics based on known characters; however, publishers soon began introducing original characters developed specifically for comic books. Superman was introduced in *Action Comics* in 1938, and Batman was introduced a year later. The tremendous success of these superhero comic books led to the development of numerous comic books on a variety of topics, though superhero comic books predominated. Astonishingly, by 1945 approximately 160 different comic books were being published in the United States each month, and 90 percent of U.S. children were said to read comic books on a regular basis.

9. It can be inferred from paragraph 1 that, at the beginning of the 1930s, comic books most likely cost
   - Ⓐ nothing
   - Ⓑ 5 cents
   - Ⓒ 10 cents
   - Ⓓ 25 cents

10. Comic books would least likely have been used to promote
   - Ⓐ soap
   - Ⓑ cookies
   - Ⓒ jewelry
   - Ⓓ bread

11. It is implied in the passage that *Famous Funnies*
   - Ⓐ was a promotional item
   - Ⓑ appeared in a magazine
   - Ⓒ had been produced prior to 1934
   - Ⓓ was published on a regular basis

12. From the information in paragraph 2, it appears that Superman most likely
   - Ⓐ was introduced sometime after Batman
   - Ⓑ was a character that first appeared in a comic book
   - Ⓒ first appeared in *Famous Funnies*
   - Ⓓ first appeared in a promotional comic strip

13. It is implied in paragraph 2 that it is surprising that
   - Ⓐ comic strips were more popular than comic books
   - Ⓑ superheroes were not too popular
   - Ⓒ 90 percent of U.S. children did not read comics
   - Ⓓ comic books developed so quickly

PASSAGE FOUR (Questions 14–19)

The Filibuster

Paragraph

1 The term *filibuster* has been in use since the mid-nineteenth century to describe the tactic of delaying legislative action in order to prevent the passage of a bill. The word comes from the Dutch *freebooter,* or pirate, and most likely developed from the idea that someone conducting a filibuster is trying to steal away the opportunity that proponents of a bill have to make it successful.

2 In the earlier history of the U.S. Congress, filibusters were used in both the House of Representatives and in the Senate, but they are now much more a part of the culture of the Senate than of the House. Because the House is a much larger body than is the Senate, the House now has rules which greatly limit the amount of time that each member may speak, which effectively serves to eliminate the filibuster as a mechanism for delaying legislation in the House.

3 In the Senate, the smaller of the two bodies, there are now rules that can constrain but not totally eliminate filibusters. The Senate adopted its first cloture rule in 1917, a rule which requires a vote of two-thirds of the Senate to limit debate to one hour on each side. The rule was changed in 1975 and now requires a vote of three-fifths of the members to invoke cloture in most situations.

4 The longest filibuster on record occurred in 1957, when Senator Strom Thurmond of South Carolina wanted to delay voting on civil rights legislation. The filibuster was conducted for twenty-four hours and 18 minutes on August 28 and 29, when Thurmond held the floor of the Senate by lecturing on the law and reading from court decisions and newspaper columns. It was his hope that this filibuster would rally opponents of civil rights legislation; however, two weeks after the filibuster, the Civil Rights Act of 1957 passed.

---

14. It can be inferred from the information in paragraph 1 that around 1800

- Ⓐ the first filibuster took place
- Ⓑ legislative action was never delayed
- Ⓒ the term *filibuster* was not in use in the U.S. Congress
- Ⓓ the Dutch introduced the term *freebooter*

15. It can be determined from paragraph 1 that a *freebooter* was most likely someone who

- Ⓐ served in the Senate
- Ⓑ robbed passing ships
- Ⓒ enacted legislation
- Ⓓ served in the Dutch government

16. It is implied in paragraph 2 that, in its early years, the House

- Ⓐ had no rules against filibusters
- Ⓑ had few filibusters
- Ⓒ had fewer filibusters than the Senate
- Ⓓ had the longest filibuster on record

17. Based on the information in paragraph 3, a vote of cloture would most likely be used to

- Ⓐ initiate filibusters
- Ⓑ break filibusters
- Ⓒ extend filibusters
- Ⓓ encourage filibusters

18. It can be inferred from the information in paragraph 3 that the 1975 rule change

- Ⓐ increased the number of people needed to vote for cloture
- Ⓑ made it easier to limit a filibuster
- Ⓒ covered all types of Senate votes
- Ⓓ decreased the number of people in the Senate

19. It is implied in paragraph 4 that Senator Thurmond was opposed to

- Ⓐ filibusters
- Ⓑ lecturing on the law
- Ⓒ speaking in the Senate
- Ⓓ the Civil Rights Act of 1957

Reading Skill 8: INFER RHETORICAL PURPOSE

In the Reading section of the *iBT* TOEFL test, you may be asked to explain why the author includes certain words, phrases, or sentences in a passage. The highlighted words, phrases, or sentences are included by the author to improve the rhetoric, or overall presentation of ideas, of the passage. You must decide which of four multiple-choice answers best explains why the author chose to include the highlighted information. Because you are asked about the rhetorical purpose for a certain piece of information, you must look at how the highlighted information fits into the overall presentation of ideas in the passage rather than only looking at the highlighted information itself.

Look at an example of a question that asks you to determine the rhetorical purpose of a particular phrase.

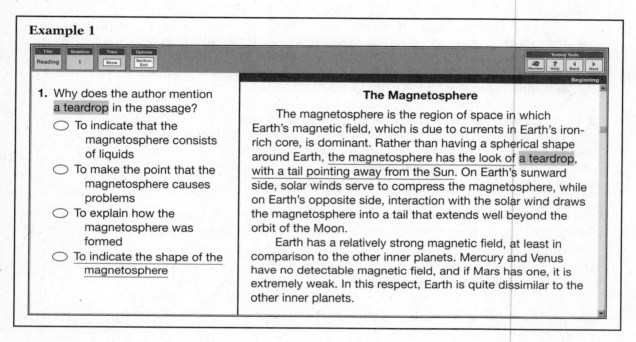

In this question, you are asked to explain why the author mentions *a teardrop* in the passage. To answer this question, you must look at the information around *a teardrop* to see how it fits into the ideas around it. The author states that *the magnetosphere has the look of a teardrop, with a tail pointing away from the Sun*. From this, it can be determined that the author mentions *a teardrop* in order *to indicate the shape of the magnetosphere*. To answer this question, you should click on the last answer.

Now look at another example, one that asks you about the rhetorical purpose of certain words in the passage.

Example 2

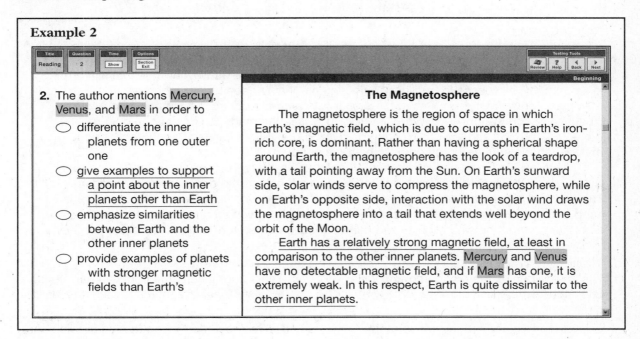

2. The author mentions Mercury, Venus, and Mars in order to
○ differentiate the inner planets from one outer one
○ give examples to support a point about the inner planets other than Earth
○ emphasize similarities between Earth and the other inner planets
○ provide examples of planets with stronger magnetic fields than Earth's

The Magnetosphere

The magnetosphere is the region of space in which Earth's magnetic field, which is due to currents in Earth's iron-rich core, is dominant. Rather than having a spherical shape around Earth, the magnetosphere has the look of a teardrop, with a tail pointing away from the Sun. On Earth's sunward side, solar winds serve to compress the magnetosphere, while on Earth's opposite side, interaction with the solar wind draws the magnetosphere into a tail that extends well beyond the orbit of the Moon.

Earth has a relatively strong magnetic field, at least in comparison to the other inner planets. Mercury and Venus have no detectable magnetic field, and if Mars has one, it is extremely weak. In this respect, Earth is quite dissimilar to the other inner planets.

In this question, you are asked to explain why the author mentions *Mercury, Venus,* and *Mars* in the passage. To answer this question, you must look at the information around *Mercury, Venus,* and *Mars* in the passage. The author states that *Earth has a relatively strong magnetic field, at least in comparison to the other inner planets* and that *Earth is quite dissimilar to the other inner planets.* From this, it can be determined that the author's purpose in mentioning *Mercury, Venus,* and *Mars* is to *give examples to support a point about the inner planets other than Earth.* To answer this question, you should click on the second answer.

The following chart outlines the key information that you should remember about questions testing rhetorical purpose.

QUESTIONS ABOUT RHETORICAL PURPOSE	
HOW TO IDENTIFY THE QUESTION	**Why** does the author . . . The author mentions X **in order to . . .**
WHERE TO FIND THE ANSWER	The targeted information is highlighted in the passage.
HOW TO ANSWER THE QUESTION	1. Study the highlighted information carefully. 2. Study the context around the highlighted information, and ask yourself how the highlighted information is related to the context around it. 3. Draw a conclusion about the purpose of the highlighted information. 4. Read the answer choices, and eliminate any definitely wrong answers. 5. Choose the best answer from the remaining choices.

READING EXERCISE 8: Study each of the passages, and choose the best answers to the questions that follow.

PASSAGE ONE *(Questions 1–4)*

Paragraph

Xerography

1   One more familiar use of electrochemistry that has made its way into the mainstream is xerography, a process for replicating documents that is dependent on photoconductive materials. A photoconductive material is an insulator in the dark but becomes a conductor when exposed to bright light. When a photocopy is being made, an image of a document is projected onto the surface of a rotating drum, and bright light causes the photoconductive material on the surface of the drum to become conductive.

2   As a result of the conductivity, the drum loses its charge in the lighted areas, and toner (small grains to which dry ink adheres) attaches itself only to the darker parts of the image. The grains are then carried to a sheet of paper and fused with heat. When a laser printer is used, the image is projected by means of a laser beam, which creates a brighter light and a greater contrast between lighter and darker areas and therefore results in sharper printed images.

1. The author begins the first paragraph with One more familiar use of electrochemistry in order to
   Ⓐ explain that xerography is one of the less familiar uses of electrochemistry
   Ⓑ make it clear that electrochemistry requires photoconductive materials
   Ⓒ show that xerography is the only known use for electrochemistry
   Ⓓ indicate that other less familiar uses have already been discussed

2. Why does the author explain that A photoconductive material is an insulator in the dark but becomes a conductor when exposed to bright light?
   Ⓐ It gives an explanation of a property that is necessary for xerography.
   Ⓑ It indicates that bright light is required for insulation to take place.
   Ⓒ It gives one example of a successful xerographic process.
   Ⓓ It explains the role of insulation in xerography.

3. The author places the phrase small grains to which dry ink adheres in parentheses in order to
   Ⓐ provide information that contradicts the previous statement
   Ⓑ provide another example of conductivity
   Ⓒ provide further detail information about toner
   Ⓓ provide an alternate explanation for the effectiveness of toner

4. Why is a laser printer mentioned?
   Ⓐ It is an alternative to xerography.
   Ⓑ It is a way of duplicating without using electrochemistry.
   Ⓒ It is a second example of xerography.
   Ⓓ It is a less effective type of xerography than is a photocopier.

PASSAGE TWO *(Questions 5–9)*

Paragraph

Demographic Change

1   By the end of the 1920s, American society had undergone a long and historic demographic change. Since the 1870s, the country had been moving from a more rural mode that was based on high birthrates—as high as 50 births annually per thousand people in the early nineteenth century—to a more metropolitan mode. Prior to the 1870s, the population of the country was increasing by about a third every decade; however, by the end of the 1920s, a radical about-face had taken place.

2   One major factor to affect the demographics of the country during this period was a dramatic decrease in birthrates. The trend during this era was more pronounced in urban areas but also had an effect in rural areas. As a result of the trend toward smaller families, particularly in cities, the birthrate was down to 27.7 births annually per thousand women by 1920 and had dropped even further—to 21.3 births annually per thousand women—by 1930.

3   At the same time, the deathrate, too, was falling. Urban living led to better sanitation, refrigeration, and water purification; it also resulted in better medical care as doctors and hospitals were more readily available. Most likely as a result of these factors, there were only eleven deaths per thousand annually by the early 1920s, which was half the rate of the 1880s.

5. Why does the author include the phrase as high as 50 births annually per thousand people in the early nineteenth century in paragraph 1?

   Ⓐ To show that metropolitan areas of the country had higher birthrates than rural areas

   Ⓑ To provide statistical evidence of the elevated birthrate in the 1870s

   Ⓒ To quantify what had happened with the American population in the previous century

   Ⓓ To argue against the belief that the demographics of the country had changed

6. The author uses the word however in paragraph 1 in order

   Ⓐ to make it clear that an extreme change had taken place

   Ⓑ to emphasize how tremendously the population was increasing

   Ⓒ to point out an alternate explanation for the change

   Ⓓ to indicate a difference of opinion with other demographers

7. The author includes the word too in paragraph 3

   Ⓐ to indicate that both the birthrate and the deathrate were holding steady

   Ⓑ to show that the rural mode was similar to the metropolitan mode

   Ⓒ to clarify the explanation that population trends before and after 1870 were similar

   Ⓓ to emphasize that paragraph 3 discusses a second factor in the demographic change

8. Why does the author mention better medical care in paragraph 3?

   Ⓐ It helps to explain why the birthrate is increasing.

   Ⓑ It is an example of a factor that contributed to the improved birthrate.

   Ⓒ It helps to explain why the deathrate is increasing.

   Ⓓ It is an example of a factor that contributed to the improved deathrate.

9. The author includes the expression Most likely in paragraph 3 to show

Ⓐ that the data about the average number of deaths was not verified

Ⓑ that doctors and hospitals may not have actually been more available

Ⓒ that other factors may have contributed to the decreasing deathrate

Ⓓ that the deathrate may not have decreased as much as stated

PASSAGE THREE (Questions 10–14)

Paragraph

The Hubble Telescope

1   The Hubble telescope was launched into space with great fanfare on April 25, 1990. Although there are many powerful telescopes at various locations on Earth, the Hubble telescope was expected to be able to provide considerably better information because it would be able to operate from the vacuum of space, without interference from the Earth's atmosphere. By launching the Hubble telescope into space, NASA was, in essence, placing an observatory above the Earth's atmosphere.

2   Unfortunately, the Hubble telescope was initially delayed in relaying its first pictures back from space due to a simple mathematical miscalculation. The Hubble telescope relies upon certain stars to orient its observations, and astronomers working on the pointing instructions for the telescope used charts created in 1950, with adjustments for the movements of the stars in the ensuing period. In making these adjustments, however, astronomers added the amount of the adjustment rather than subtracting it—a simple checkbook-balancing error. The adjustment was a change of only half a degree, but by adding half a degree rather than subtracting it, the telescope's aim was misdirected by millions of miles.

10. Why does the author mention many powerful telescopes at various locations on Earth in paragraph 1?

Ⓐ To emphasize the need for telescopes at various locations on Earth

Ⓑ To show that the Hubble telescope was different from existing telescopes

Ⓒ To indicate how the atmosphere improves the quality of information from space

Ⓓ To emphasize the similarities between the Hubble telescope and other telescopes

11. The author uses the phrase in essence in paragraph 2 in order to indicate that the information that follows the phrase

Ⓐ provides a simplified description of a previously stated situation

Ⓑ indicates the cause of a previously stated effect

Ⓒ provides further details about a previously stated main idea

Ⓓ indicates the classification to which previously stated examples belong

12. Why does the author begin paragraph 2 with Unfortunately?

Ⓐ It indicates that NASA has been unhappy with all of Hubble's photographs.

Ⓑ It shows that NASA's plan to use stars to orient the Hubble telescope was misguided.

Ⓒ It emphasizes the need to have telescopes on Earth.

Ⓓ It indicates that high expectations were not initially met.

13. The author mentions a simple checkbook-balancing error in paragraph 2 in order to suggest that

Ⓐ the astronomers must have difficulties with their checkbooks

Ⓑ the adjustment made by the astronomers should have been more than half a degree

Ⓒ a more balanced approach was needed when making adjustments

Ⓓ the mistake made by the astronomers was a simple, everyday error

14. Why does the author mention the detail millions of miles in paragraph 2?

Ⓐ It reinforces the idea that the mistake had a huge effect.

Ⓑ It emphasizes the wide range of the Hubble telescope.

Ⓒ It demonstrates that the Hubble telescope travels long distances.

Ⓓ It helps the reader to understand how powerful the Hubble telescope is.

PASSAGE FOUR *(Questions 15–19)*

Territoriality

Paragraph

1   In many species, members of the species exhibit aggressive behavior toward one another, often with a focus on territoriality, the fight for exclusive control of a particular area. The level of violence in territorial aggression varies widely from species to species, though few species fight other members of the species to death and instead rely on non-lethal contests for control of territory that involves noise-making maneuvers such as roaring or hissing or aggressive posturing or gestures.

2   Most bird species are known to be territorial to some degree, though the territorial behaviors exhibited by most species are limited to singing contests, which can go on for days, or threatening postures with wings lifted or extended. The swan, on the other hand, is quite unlike other birds in this respect. The swan may seem particularly elegant and serene as it glides across the surface of a lake; however, male swans are, in reality, quite territorial and will fight other male swans for the exclusive use of a lake no matter how large the lake is. Males will engage in ferocious contests, with their necks entwined as they attempt to cause mortal injury to each other.

15. Why does the author include the fight for exclusive control of a particular area in paragraph 1?

Ⓐ It presents an argument against a previously stated point.

Ⓑ It provides a definition of a previously stated term.

Ⓒ It presents a second area of focus of aggressive behavior.

Ⓓ It introduces a new idea to be further developed in the paragraph.

16. The author uses the word instead in paragraph 2 to show that the information that follows

Ⓐ contradicts what precedes it

Ⓑ expands upon what precedes it

Ⓒ provides an example of what precedes it

Ⓓ explains an effect of what precedes it

17. Why does the author mention singing contests in paragraph 2?

Ⓐ To demonstrate that birds create beautiful sounds

Ⓑ To provide an example of unusual behavior by birds

Ⓒ To show how violently aggressive some bird behavior is

Ⓓ To demonstrate that some types of territorial behaviors are not very aggressive

18. The author discusses the swan in paragraph 2 to provide an example of

Ⓐ a bird that makes threatening postures with its wings

Ⓑ a bird whose territorial behavior is extremely aggressive

Ⓒ non-lethal contests for control of territory

Ⓓ the limited aggressive behavior generally exhibited by birds

19. The author mentions their necks entwined in paragraph 2 in order

Ⓐ to indicate that swans are really rather affectionate

Ⓑ to emphasize how long swans' necks are

Ⓒ to make the point that the swans are only pretending to hurt one another

Ⓓ to create a mental image for the reader of fighting swans

READING EXERCISE (Skills 7–8): Read the passage.

Ella Deloria

1   In was not until her posthumous novel *Waterlily* was published in 1988 that Ella C. Deloria became known for her literary ability in addition to her already-established reputation in the academic arena of linguistics and ethnology. During her lifetime, she was recognized for the linguistic ability and cultural sensitivity that went into the production of a collection of traditional short stories entitled *Dakota Texts* (1932). After her death, her versions of a number of longer traditional stories and the novel *Waterlily* were published; with the publication of *Waterlily* came the recognition of her true literary ability and the awareness that it was the strength of her literary ability, in addition to her linguistic expertise and her deep cultural understanding, that had made her versions of traditional stories so compelling.

2   Ella Cara Deloria was born into a Nakota-speaking family in 1889; however, she grew up among the Lakota people in North Dakota, where her father was a leader in the Episcopal Church. Her father, the son of a traditional Nakota medicine man, valued both the cultural traditions of his family and those of the country of his citizenship. As a result, Deloria primarily spoke Nakota at home and Lakota when she was out in the community, and she was well versed there in the cultural traditions of her Sioux ancestors (with a complex kinship structure in which all of a child's father's brothers are also considered fathers, all of a child's mother's sisters are also considered mothers, and all of the children of all these mothers and fathers are considered siblings). Her education, however, was in English, at the Episcopalian Saint Elizabeth Mission School and the All Saints School. After high school, she attended Oberlin College in Ohio for one year, and then she transferred to Columbia University to study linguistics under Franz Boas, the founder of American Indian linguistics.

3   After graduating from Columbia, she was encouraged by Boas to collect and record traditional Lakota stories. She was in a unique position to take on this task because of her fluency in the Lakota language as well as in English, her understanding from childhood of the complexities and subtleties of Lakota culture, and her linguistic training from Columbia. The result of her research was the *Dakota Texts,* a bilingual collection of 64 short stories. To create this remarkable work, Deloria was able to elicit stories from venerable Sioux elders, without need for translators and with an awareness of appropriately respectful behavior. She listened to the stories as numerous generations had before her, and then, unlike previous generations, recorded them in writing—initially in Lakota and later in English. She transcribed them essentially as they were told but with her own understanding of the nuances of what was being told.

4   In addition to the shorter stories that were published in *Dakota Texts,* Deloria spent 1937 working on transcribing a number of longer and more complicated texts, which were not published until after her death. "Iron Hawk: Oglala Culture Hero" (1993) presents the diverse elements of the culture-hero genre; "The Buffalo People" (1994) focuses on the importance of tribal education in building character; "A Sioux Captive" (1994) tells the story of a Lakota woman who rescued her husband from the Crow; "The Prairie Dogs" (1994) describes the sense of hope offered by the Sioux warrior-society ceremonies and dances.

5   Her novel *Waterlily,* which was first published 40 years after it was completed and 17 years after her death, reflects her true literary talent as well as her accumulated understanding of traditional culture and customs. The novel recounts the fictional story of the difficult life of the title character, with a horrendous childhood experience as witness to a deadly enemy raid and a first marriage terminated by the untimely death of her husband in a smallpox epidemic, and comes to a close with the hopeful expectations of an impending second marriage. At the same time, it presents a masterful account of life in a nineteenth-century Sioux community with its detailed descriptions of interpersonal relationships and attitudes, everyday tasks and routines, and special ceremonies and celebrations.

GLOSSARY

The *Lakota, Nakota,* and *Dakota* are related groups of people who are part of the Sioux nation.

Refer to this version of the passage to answer the questions that follow.

Ella Deloria

Paragraph

1   In was not until her posthumous novel *Waterlily* was published in 1988 that Ella C. Deloria became known for her literary ability in addition to her already-established reputation in the academic arena of linguistics and ethnology. During her lifetime, she was recognized for the linguistic ability and cultural sensitivity that went into the production of a collection of traditional short stories entitled *Dakota Texts* (1932). After her death, her versions of a number of longer traditional stories and the novel *Waterlily* were published; with the publication of *Waterlily* came the recognition of her true literary ability and the awareness that it was the strength of her literary ability, in addition to her linguistic expertise and her deep cultural understanding, that had made her versions of traditional stories so compelling.

2   Ella Cara Deloria was born into a Nakota-speaking family in 1889; however, she grew up among the Lakota people in North Dakota, where her father was a leader in the Episcopal Church. Her father, the son of a traditional Nakota medicine man, valued both the cultural traditions of his family and those of the country of his citizenship. As a result, Deloria primarily spoke Nakota at home and Lakota when she was out in the community, and she was well versed there in the cultural traditions of her Sioux ancestors (with a complex kinship structure in which all of a child's father's brothers are also considered fathers, all of a child's mother's sisters are also considered mothers, and all of the children of all these mothers and fathers are considered siblings). Her education, however, was in English, at the Episcopalian Saint Elizabeth Mission School and the All Saints School. After high school, she attended Oberlin College in Ohio for one year, and then she transferred to Columbia University to study linguistics under Franz Boas, the founder of American Indian linguistics.

3   After graduating from Columbia, she was encouraged by Boas to collect and record traditional Lakota stories. She was in a unique position to take on this task because of her fluency in the Lakota language as well as in English, her understanding from childhood of the complexities and subtleties of Lakota culture, and her linguistic training from Columbia. The result of her research was the *Dakota Texts,* a bilingual collection of 64 short stories. To create this remarkable work, Deloria was able to elicit stories from venerable Sioux elders, without need for translators and with an awareness of appropriately respectful behavior. She listened to the stories as numerous generations had before her, and then, unlike previous generations, recorded them in writing—initially in Lakota and later in English. She transcribed them essentially as they were told but with her own understanding of the nuances of what was being told.

4   In addition to the shorter stories that were published in *Dakota Texts,* Deloria spent 1937 working on transcribing a number of longer and more complicated texts, which were not published until after her death. "Iron Hawk: Oglala Culture Hero" (1993) presents the diverse elements of the culture-hero genre; "The Buffalo People" (1994) focuses on the importance of tribal education in building character; "A Sioux Captive" (1994) tells the story of a Lakota woman who rescued her husband from the Crow; "The Prairie Dogs" (1994) describes the sense of hope offered by the Sioux warrior-society ceremonies and dances.

5   Her novel *Waterlily,* which was first published 40 years after it was completed and 17 years after her death, reflects her true literary talent as well as her accumulated understanding of traditional culture and customs. The novel recounts the fictional story of the difficult life of the title character, with a horrendous childhood experience as witness to a deadly enemy raid and a first marriage terminated by the untimely death of her husband in a smallpox epidemic, and comes to a close with the hopeful expectations of an impending second marriage. At the same time, it presents a masterful account of life in a nineteenth-century Sioux community with its detailed descriptions of interpersonal relationships and attitudes, everyday tasks and routines, and special ceremonies and celebrations.

GLOSSARY

The *Lakota, Nakota,* and *Dakota* are related groups of people that are part of the Sioux nation.

Questions

1. It can be inferred from paragraph 1 that, while she was alive, Ella Deloria
   - Ⓐ did little to make use of her education in linguistics
   - Ⓑ achieved acclaim more for her transcriptions than for her novel
   - Ⓒ was the published author of a number of types of fiction and nonfiction
   - Ⓓ was recognized for the literary maturity of her novel

2. Why does the author use the word however in paragraph 2?
   - Ⓐ To emphasize that she was born in an earlier century
   - Ⓑ To clarify the differences between the Lakota and the Dakota
   - Ⓒ To show that she was raised in a different environment from the one where she was born
   - Ⓓ To demonstrate that she was very different from other members of her family

3. Why does the author include the information with a complex kinship structure in which all of a child's father's brothers are also considered fathers, all of a child's mother's sisters are also considered mothers, and all of the children of all these mothers and fathers are considered siblings in parentheses?
   - Ⓐ To provide details to emphasize how the Nakota and the Lakota differed
   - Ⓑ To introduce the idea that Deloria's education in English was completely different from her home life
   - Ⓒ To provide an alternate explanation for Deloria's use of Nakota at home and Lakota in the community
   - Ⓓ To provide an example of one cultural tradition of the Sioux

4. Why does the author begin paragraph 3 with After graduating from Columbia?
   - Ⓐ To indicate that paragraph 3 follows paragraph 2 in chronological order
   - Ⓑ To clarify that paragraph 3 describes Deloria's education at Columbia
   - Ⓒ To recognize the importance of education throughout Deloria's life
   - Ⓓ To demonstrate that paragraph 3 provides examples of a concept presented in paragraph 2

5. It is implied in paragraph 3 that *Dakota Texts* was written
   - Ⓐ only in English
   - Ⓑ only in Dakota
   - Ⓒ in Dakota and Lakota
   - Ⓓ in Lakota and English

6. Why does the author mention an awareness of appropriately respectful behavior in paragraph 3?
   - Ⓐ To show one way that Deloria was qualified to elicit stories from Sioux elders
   - Ⓑ To show that Deloria's linguistic training had been effective
   - Ⓒ To show the difference between Deloria's transcriptions and her novel
   - Ⓓ To show why Deloria needed to work with a translator

7. It can be inferred from paragraph 4 that "Iron Hawk: Oglala Culture Hero" was published
   - Ⓐ in the same year that it was written
   - Ⓑ just prior to Deloria's death
   - Ⓒ long after it was transcribed
   - Ⓓ long before *Waterlily* was published

8. Why does the author discuss "The Prairie Dogs" in paragraph 4?
   - Ⓐ It was written by Deloria.
   - Ⓑ It describes Deloria's own life story.
   - Ⓒ It provides insight into rituals and dances.
   - Ⓓ It was one of the earliest short stories that Deloria transcribed.

9. It can be inferred from the passage that *Waterlily* was completed

Ⓐ in 1937
Ⓑ in 1948
Ⓒ in 1954
Ⓓ in 1988

10. Why does the author mention the untimely death of her husband in a smallpox epidemic in paragraph 5?

Ⓐ It provides a harsh example of Waterlily's difficult life.
Ⓑ It provides evidence of the historical existence of Waterlily.
Ⓒ It demonstrates how unusual Waterlily's life in a nineteenth-century Sioux community was.
Ⓓ It reinforces the overall message of hopelessness of *Waterlily*.

READING REVIEW EXERCISE (Skills 1–8): Read the passage.

Paragraph

Early Autos

1   America's passion for the automobile developed rather quickly in the beginning of the twentieth century. At the turn of that century, there were few automobiles, or horseless carriages, as they were called at the time, and those that existed were considered frivolous playthings of the rich. They were rather fragile machines that sputtered and smoked and broke down often; they were expensive toys that could not be counted on to get one where one needed to go; they could only be afforded by the wealthy class, who could afford both the expensive upkeep and the inherent delays that resulted from the use of a machine that tended to break down time and again. These early automobiles required repairs so frequently both because their engineering was at an immature stage and because roads were unpaved and often in poor condition. Then, when breakdowns occurred, there were no services such as roadside gas stations or tow trucks to assist drivers needing help in their predicament. Drivers of horse-drawn carriages considered the horseless mode of transportation foolhardy, preferring instead to rely on their four-legged "engines," which they considered a tremendously more dependable and cost-effective means of getting around.

2   Automobiles in the beginning of the twentieth century were quite unlike today's models. Many of them were electric cars, even though the electric models had quite a limited range and needed to be recharged frequently at electric charging stations; many others were powered by steam, though it was often required that drivers of steam cars be certified steam engineers due to the dangers inherent in operating a steam-powered machine. The early automobiles also lacked much emphasis on body design; in fact, they were often little more than benches on wheels, though by the end of the first decade of the century they had progressed to leather-upholstered chairs or sofas on thin wheels that absorbed little of the incessant pounding associated with the movement of these machines.

3   In spite of the rather rough and undeveloped nature of these early horseless carriages, something about them grabbed people's imagination, and their use increased rapidly, though not always smoothly. In the first decade of the last century, roads were shared by the horse-drawn and horseless variety of carriages, a situation that was rife with problems and required strict measures to control the incidents and accidents that resulted when two such different modes of transportation were used in close proximity. New York City, for example, banned horseless vehicles from Central Park early in the century because they had been involved in so many accidents, often causing injury or death; then, in 1904, New York state felt that it was necessary to control automobile traffic by placing speed limits of 20 miles per hour in open areas, 15 miles per hour in villages, and 10 miles per hour in cities or areas of congestion. However, the measures taken were less a means of limiting use of the automobile and more a way of controlling the effects of an invention whose use increased dramatically in a relatively short period of time. Under 5,000 automobiles were sold in the United States for a total cost of approximately $5 million in 1900, while considerably more cars, 181,000, were sold for $215 million in 1910, and by the middle of the 1920s, automobile manufacturing had become the top industry in the United States and accounted for 6 percent of the manufacturing in the country.

Refer to this version of the passage to answer the questions that follow.

Early Autos

Paragraph

1   America's passion for the automobile developed rather quickly in the beginning of the twentieth century. At the turn of that century, there were few automobiles, or horseless carriages, as they were called at the time, and those that existed were considered frivolous playthings of the rich. **5A** They were rather fragile machines that sputtered and smoked and broke down often; they were expensive toys that could not be counted on to get one where one needed to go; they could only be afforded by the wealthy class, who could afford both the expensive upkeep and the inherent delays that resulted from the use of a machine that tended to break down time and again. **5B** These early automobiles required repairs so frequently both because their engineering was at an immature stage and because roads were unpaved and often in poor condition. **5C** Then, when breakdowns occurred, there were no services such as roadside gas stations or tow trucks to assist drivers needing help in their predicament. **5D** Drivers of horse-drawn carriages considered the horseless mode of transportation foolhardy, preferring instead to rely on their four-legged "engines," which they considered a tremendously more dependable and cost-effective means of getting around.

2   Automobiles in the beginning of the twentieth century were quite unlike today's models. Many of them were electric cars, even though the electric models had quite a limited range and needed to be recharged frequently at electric charging stations; many others were powered by steam, though it was often required that drivers of steam cars be certified steam engineers due to the dangers inherent in operating a steam-powered machine. The early automobiles also lacked much emphasis on body design; in fact, they were often little more than benches on wheels, though by the end of the first decade of the century they had progressed to leather-upholstered chairs or sofas on thin wheels that absorbed little of the incessant pounding associated with the movement of these machines.

3   In spite of the rather rough and undeveloped nature of these early horseless carriages, something about them grabbed people's imagination, and their use increased rapidly, though not always smoothly. In the first decade of the last century, roads were shared by the horse-drawn and horseless variety of carriages, a situation that was rife with problems and required strict measures to control the incidents and accidents that resulted when two such different modes of transportation were used in close proximity. New York City, for example, banned horseless vehicles from Central Park early in the century because they had been involved in so many accidents, often causing injury or death; then, in 1904, New York state felt that it was necessary to control automobile traffic by placing speed limits of 20 miles per hour in open areas, 15 miles per hour in villages, and 10 miles per hour in cities or areas of congestion. However, the measures taken were less a means of limiting use of the automobile and more a way of controlling the effects of an invention whose use increased dramatically in a relatively short period of time. Under 5,000 automobiles were sold in the United States for a total cost of approximately $5 million in 1900, while considerably more cars, 181,000, were sold for $215 million in 1910, and by the middle of the 1920s, automobile manufacturing had become the top industry in the United States and accounted for 6 percent of the manufacturing in the country.

Questions

1. Based on the information in paragraph 1, who would have been most likely to own a car in 1900?
   - Ⓐ A skilled laborer
   - Ⓑ A successful investor
   - Ⓒ A scholarship student
   - Ⓓ A rural farmer

2. The word frivolous in paragraph 1 is closest in meaning to
   - Ⓐ trivial
   - Ⓑ delicate
   - Ⓒ essential
   - Ⓓ natural

3. It is indicated in paragraph 1 that it was necessary to repair early autos because of
   - Ⓐ the elaborate engines
   - Ⓑ the lack of roads
   - Ⓒ the immature drivers
   - Ⓓ the rough roads

4. The author refers to four-legged engines in paragraph 1 in order to indicate that
   - Ⓐ early autos had little more than an engine and wheels
   - Ⓑ it was foolish to travel on a four-legged animal
   - Ⓒ horses were an effective mode of transportation
   - Ⓓ automobile engines were evaluated in terms of their horsepower

5. Look at the four squares [■] that indicate where the following sentence can be added to paragraph 1.

   These horrendous road conditions forced drivers to use their automobiles on grooved, rutted, and bumpy roads.

   Click on a square [■] to add the sentence to the passage.

6. The phrase many others in paragraph 2 refers to
   - Ⓐ automobiles in the beginning of the twentieth century
   - Ⓑ today's models
   - Ⓒ electric models
   - Ⓓ electric charging stations

7. It is stated in paragraph 2 that the owners of steam-powered cars
   - Ⓐ sometimes had to demonstrate knowledge of steam engineering
   - Ⓑ had to hire drivers to operate their cars
   - Ⓒ often had to take their automobiles to charging stations
   - Ⓓ were often in danger because of the limited range of their automobiles

8. Why does the author mention benches on wheels in paragraph 2?
   - Ⓐ To show how remarkably automobile design had progressed
   - Ⓑ To show that car designs of the time were neither complex nor comfortable
   - Ⓒ To indicate that early automobiles had upholstered chairs or sofas
   - Ⓓ To emphasize how the early automobiles were designed to absorb the pounding of the machine on the road

9. The word incessant in paragraph 2 is closest in meaning to
   - Ⓐ heavy
   - Ⓑ bothersome
   - Ⓒ jolting
   - Ⓓ continual

10. The phrase rife with in paragraph 3 could be replaced by
    - Ⓐ full of
    - Ⓑ surrounded by
    - Ⓒ dangerous due to
    - Ⓓ occurring as a result of

11. It can be inferred from paragraph 3 that the government of New York state believed that
    - Ⓐ all horseless vehicles should be banned from all public parks
    - Ⓑ strict speed limits should be placed on horse-drawn carriages
    - Ⓒ horseless and horse-drawn vehicles should not travel on the same roads
    - Ⓓ it was safer for cars to travel faster where there was less traffic and fewer people

12. Which of the sentences below expresses the essential information in the highlighted sentence in paragraph 3? *Incorrect* choices change the meaning in important ways or leave out essential information.

(A) It was necessary to take a measured approach in dealing with inventions such as the automobile.

(B) The various laws were needed because the use of automobiles grew so fast.

(C) The dramatic look of the automobile changed considerably over a short period of time.

(D) It was important to lawmakers to discover the causes of the problems relating to automobiles.

13. According to paragraph 3, it is NOT true that

(A) the total cost of the automobiles sold in the United States in 1900 was around $5 million

(B) sales of cars increased by more than 175,000 from 1900 to 1910

(C) automobile manufacturing was the top U.S. industry in 1920

(D) automobile manufacturing represented more than 5 percent of total U.S. manufacturing by 1925

READING TO LEARN

Reading Skill 9: SELECT SUMMARY INFORMATION

In the Reading section of the *iBT* TOEFL test, you may be asked to complete a summary chart in which the overall topic is given and you must determine the major supporting ideas. Because this is a more complex type of question, it is worth more than a multiple-choice question; each question of this type will indicate how many points the question is worth.

To complete this type of question successfully, you must be able to recognize the rhetorical pattern of the information in the passage (i.e. compare and contrast, cause and effect, argument supported by reasons), including the major ideas and the critical supporting information. Look at an example of a question that asks you to select summary information.

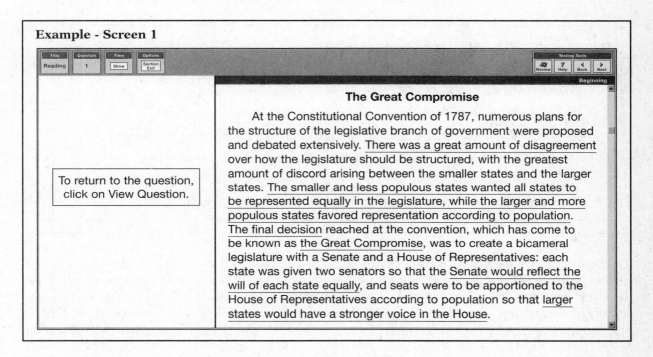

Example - Screen 1

To return to the question, click on View Question.

The Great Compromise

At the Constitutional Convention of 1787, numerous plans for the structure of the legislative branch of government were proposed and debated extensively. There was a great amount of disagreement over how the legislature should be structured, with the greatest amount of discord arising between the smaller states and the larger states. The smaller and less populous states wanted all states to be represented equally in the legislature, while the larger and more populous states favored representation according to population. The final decision reached at the convention, which has come to be known as the Great Compromise, was to create a bicameral legislature with a Senate and a House of Representatives: each state was given two senators so that the Senate would reflect the will of each state equally, and seats were to be apportioned to the House of Representatives according to population so that larger states would have a stronger voice in the House.

The passage is included on one screen, and the question is included on a different screen. You can click back and forth between the question and the passage while you are answering this type of question.

Example - Screen 2

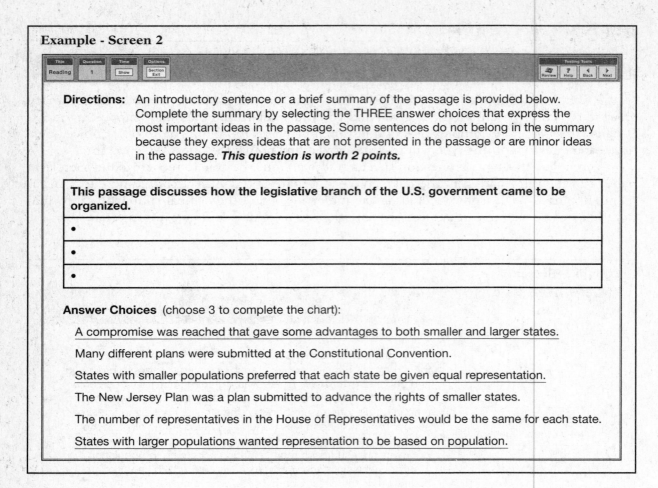

Directions: An introductory sentence or a brief summary of the passage is provided below. Complete the summary by selecting the THREE answer choices that express the most important ideas in the passage. Some sentences do not belong in the summary because they express ideas that are not presented in the passage or are minor ideas in the passage. *This question is worth 2 points.*

> **This passage discusses how the legislative branch of the U.S. government came to be organized.**
> -
> -
> -

Answer Choices (choose 3 to complete the chart):

A compromise was reached that gave some advantages to both smaller and larger states.

Many different plans were submitted at the Constitutional Convention.

States with smaller populations preferred that each state be given equal representation.

The New Jersey Plan was a plan submitted to advance the rights of smaller states.

The number of representatives in the House of Representatives would be the same for each state.

States with larger populations wanted representation to be based on population.

The three correct answer choices should be selected because they summarize the major points in the passage. The passage states that *there was a great amount of disagreement,* that the disagreement was that *the smaller and less populous states wanted all states to be represented equally in the legislature, while the larger and more populous states favored representation according to population,* and that *the final decision . . . was . . . the Great Compromise,* in which *the Senate would reflect the will of each state equally* and *the larger states would have a stronger voice in the House.* From this, it can be determined that the most important factors in the passage are that *states with smaller populations preferred that each state be given equal representation,* that *states with larger populations wanted representation to be based on population,* and that *a compromise was reached that gave some advantages to both smaller and larger states.*

The remaining answer choices are not part of the solution for a variety of reasons. The statement that *many different plans were submitted at the Constitutional Convention* is mentioned in the passage but is *not a major factor* in support of the topic. The statement that *the New Jersey Plan was a plan submitted to advance the rights of smaller states* is not discussed in the passage. The statement that *the number of representatives in the House of Representatives would be the same for each state* is not true according to the passage, which states that *seats were to be apportioned in the House of Representatives according to population so that larger states would have a stronger voice in the House.*

The following chart outlines the key information that you should remember about answering summary information questions.

QUESTIONS ABOUT SUMMARY INFORMATION	
HOW TO IDENTIFY THE QUESTION	A summary information chart is given.
WHERE TO FIND THE ANSWER	Because the answer demonstrates an understanding of the major points and critical supporting information, the information needed to answer the question is found throughout the passage.
HOW TO ANSWER THE QUESTION	1. Read the topic stated in the summary chart carefully. 2. Read the passage, focusing on the main ideas as they relate to the topic stated in the summary chart. 3. Read each answer choice, evaluating whether it is *true* information according to the passage, *false* information according to the passage, or *not discussed* in the passage. 4. Eliminate any answers that are *false* or *not discussed*. 5. For each statement that is *true* according to the passage, evaluate whether it is a *major factor* related to the topic or is a *minor detail*. 6. Select the answers that are true and are major factors as your responses. 7. Partial credit is possible, and your answers may be in any order.

READING EXERCISE 9: An introductory sentence or a brief summary of each passage is provided below each passage. Complete the summary by selecting the answer choices that express the most important ideas in the passage. Some sentences do not belong in the summary because they express ideas that are not presented in the passage or are minor ideas in the passage.

PASSAGE ONE *(Question 1)*

Island Plant Life

Islands are geographical formations that are completely surrounded by water, yet many islands are covered with a rich assortment of plant life. It may seem surprising that so much plant life exists on many islands, yet there are surprisingly simple explanations as to how the vegetation has been able to establish itself there. Some islands were formerly attached to larger bodies of land, while others were created on their own. Islands that were created when flooding or rising water levels cut them off from their neighbors often still have the plant life that they had before they were cut off. In cases where islands formed out of the ocean, they may have plant life from neighboring lands even though they were never actually attached to the neighboring lands. Winds carry many seeds to islands; some plants produce extremely light seeds that can float thousands of feet above the Earth and then drift down to islands where they can sprout and develop. Birds also carry seeds to islands; as birds move over open stretches of water, they can serve as the transportation system to spread seeds from place to place.

This passage discusses the ways that plant life is able to develop on islands.
•
•
•

Answer Choices (choose 3 to complete the chart):

(1) Some seeds are able to float great distances in the air.

(2) Some plant life existed before islands were cut off from larger bodies of land.

(3) Some islands have many different varieties of plants.

(4) Birds sometimes carry seeds to islands.

(5) Some islands were created when rising water cut them off from larger bodies of land.

(6) Some plant seeds are carried to islands by the wind.

Paragraph

Ben and Jerry

1   All successful businesses are not established and run in the same way, with formal business plans, traditional organizational structures, and a strong focus on profits. Ben Cohen and Jerry Greenfield, the entrepreneurs responsible for the highly successful ice cream business that bears their names, were businessmen with a rather unconventional approach.

2   They were rather unconventional from the start, not choosing to begin their careers by attending one of the elite business schools but instead choosing to take a five-dollar correspondence course from Pennsylvania State University. They had little financial backing to start their business, so they had to cut corners wherever they could; the only location they could afford for the startup of their business was a gas station that they converted to ice cream production. Though this start-up was rather unconventional, they were strongly committed to creating the best ice cream possible, and this commitment to the quality of their product eventually led to considerable success.

3   Even though they became extremely successful, they did not convert to a more conventional style of doing business. In an era where companies were measured on every penny of profit that they managed to squeeze out, Ben and Jerry had a strong belief that business should give back to the community; thus, they donated 7.5 percent of their pretax profit to social causes that they believed in. They also lacked the emphasis on executive salary and benefits packages that so preoccupy other corporations, opting instead for a five-to-one policy in which the salary of the employee receiving the highest pay could never be more than five times the salary of the employee receiving the lowest pay.

This passage discusses Ben and Jerry's unconventional company.
•
•
•

Answer Choices (choose 3 to complete the chart):

(1) They each had a personal commitment to social causes.

(2) They began their business with little background and investment.

(3) They believed strongly in producing a very high-quality product.

(4) They had a salary structure that limits the salaries of high-level executives.

(5) They set aside a noteworthy portion of their profits for social causes.

(6) They borrowed several thousand dollars from friends to start their business.

PASSAGE THREE (Question 3)

Paragraph

The Bald Eagle

1   When the bald eagle became the national symbol of the United States in 1782, soon after the country was born, it is estimated that there were as many as 75,000 nesting pairs in North America. By the early 1960s, however, the number of nesting pairs had been reduced to only around 450.

2   The demise of the bald eagle is generally attributed to the effects of the pesticide DDT (dichloro-diphenyl-trichloroethane). This pesticide was used to kill insects harmful to agriculture, thereby increasing agricultural production. One unintended negative result of the use of DDT was that, while it did get rid of the undesirable insects, it also made its way along the food chain into fish, a favorite food source of the bald eagle.

3   The bald eagle is now protected by federal laws. It was originally protected by the Bald Eagle Act of 1940 and later by the Endangered Species Act of 1973. However, it is not just the laws directly related to endangered species that aided in the resurgence of the bald eagle; its resurgence has also been widely attributed to the banning of DDT in 1972. Today there are more than 5,000 pairs of bald eagles, a tenfold increase over the low point of 450, and the bird was removed from the list of endangered species in July, 1999.

This passage discusses radical shifts in population that the bald eagle has undergone.
•
•
•
•

Answer Choices (choose 4 to complete the chart):

(1) The numbers of bald eagles were greatly reduced, at least in part due to the effects of a pesticide.

(2) The legislation has had a positive effect on the number of bald eagles.

(3) The bald eagle was named as the national symbol of the United States in the late eighteenth century.

(4) Early in the history of the United States, there were huge numbers of bald eagles.

(5) Two different pieces of legislation that affected the bald eagle were enacted 33 years apart.

(6) The federal government enacted legislation specifically designed to protect the bald eagle as well as to outlaw the pesticide DDT.

Modernism in Art

Paragraph

1   A proliferation of varying styles characterized the world of American art and architecture in the period between 1880 and the outbreak of World War II in 1939. In spite of the fact that these various styles often had little in common with each other, they are traditionally clustered under the label of **modernism**. It is thus rather difficult to give a precise definition of modernism, one that encompasses all the characteristics of the artists and architects who are commonly grouped under this label. What modernists do have in common is that their work contains at least one of two characteristics of modernism.

2   One fundamental characteristic of modernism is a demonstration of progressive innovation. In general, a modernist is someone who tries to develop an individual style by adding to or improving upon the style of immediate predecessors. The modernist belief was in starting with the ideas of the mainstream movement and then innovating from the mainstream to improve upon the ideas of predecessors rather than in breaking away from the mainstream to create something entirely new. However, because there were varying ideas on what constituted the mainstream and because the potential innovations emanating from the mainstream were infinite, modernism under this definition could take a myriad of directions.

3   A second fundamental characteristic of modernism was the belief that art could and should reflect the reality of modern life and would not, for example, focus on the lives of society's most privileged members or on otherworld entities such as angels and sprites. Though there was agreement among modernists as to the need for art to reflect modern life, there was far less agreement on what actually constituted modern life. Thus, modern artists and architects reflect very different aspects of modern life in their works.

Though modernism in art shares certain characteristics, these characteristics can be difficult to define precisely.
•
•
•
•

Answer Choices (choose 4 to complete the chart):

(1) A reflection of the reality of modern life is one aspect of modernism.

(2) There is no universal agreement as to exactly what makes up modern life.

(3) Modernism is a highly individualistic style of art.

(4) Modernism in art must improve upon the style of the mainstream.

(5) There were many different styles of American art in the early twentieth century.

(6) It can be difficult to define what the mainstream is.

Reading Skill 10: COMPLETE SCHEMATIC TABLES

In the Reading section of the *iBT* TOEFL test, you may be asked to complete a schematic table that outlines the key information from a passage. Because this is a more complex type of question, it is worth more than a multiple-choice question; each question of this type will indicate how many points the question is worth.

To complete this type of question successfully, you must be able to recognize overall organization of the information in the passage, including the major points and the critical supporting information. Look at an example of a question that asks you to complete a schematic table.

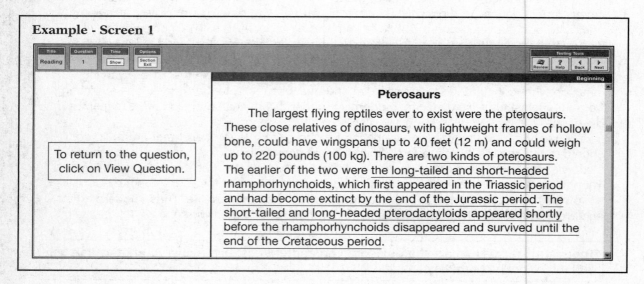

Example - Screen 1

Pterosaurs

The largest flying reptiles ever to exist were the pterosaurs. These close relatives of dinosaurs, with lightweight frames of hollow bone, could have wingspans up to 40 feet (12 m) and could weigh up to 220 pounds (100 kg). There are two kinds of pterosaurs. The earlier of the two were the long-tailed and short-headed rhamphorhynchoids, which first appeared in the Triassic period and had become extinct by the end of the Jurassic period. The short-tailed and long-headed pterodactyloids appeared shortly before the rhamphorhynchoids disappeared and survived until the end of the Cretaceous period.

To return to the question, click on View Question.

The passage is included on one screen, and the question is included on a different screen. You can click back and forth between the question and the passage while you are answering this type of question.

Example - Screen 2

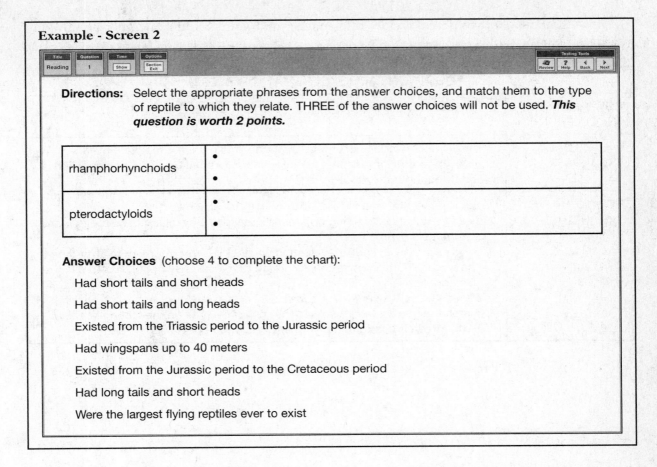

Directions: Select the appropriate phrases from the answer choices, and match them to the type of reptile to which they relate. THREE of the answer choices will not be used. ***This question is worth 2 points.***

rhamphorhynchoids	•
	•
pterodactyloids	•
	•

Answer Choices (choose 4 to complete the chart):

Had short tails and short heads

Had short tails and long heads

Existed from the Triassic period to the Jurassic period

Had wingspans up to 40 meters

Existed from the Jurassic period to the Cretaceous period

Had long tails and short heads

Were the largest flying reptiles ever to exist

The passage discusses *two kinds of pterosaurs*. One is *the long-tailed and short-headed rhamphorhynchoids, which first appeared in the Triassic period and had become extinct by the end of the Jurassic period.* From this, it can be determined that the rhamphorhynchoids *had long tails and short heads* and that they *existed from the Triassic period to the Jurassic period,* so these are the two correct answers that describe rhamphorhynchoids.

The passage goes on to state that *the short-tailed and long-headed pterodactyloids appeared shortly before the rhamphorhynchoids disappeared and survived until the end of the Cretaceous period.* From this, and from the information about rhamphorhynchoids, it can be determined that pterodactyloids *had short tails and long heads* and *existed from the Jurassic period to the Cretaceous period.*

The remaining answer choices are not a part of the correct solution. The description that they *had short tails and short heads* does not describe either of the types of pterosaurs described in the passage. The description that they *had wingspans up to 40 meters* is incorrect because the passage states that they *could have wingspans up to 40 feet (12 m).* The description that they *were the largest flying reptiles ever to exist* describes pterosaurs in general and is not a factor that differentiates rhamphorhynchoids and pterodactyloids.

The following chart outlines the key information that you should remember about completing schematic tables.

QUESTIONS ABOUT SCHEMATIC TABLES		
HOW TO IDENTIFY THE QUESTION	A schematic table is given.	
WHERE TO FIND THE ANSWER	Because the answer demonstrates an understanding of the major points and critical supporting information, the information needed to answer the question is found throughout the passage.	
HOW TO ANSWER THE QUESTION	1. Look at the information that is provided in the schematic table. 2. Read the passage, focusing on the main ideas as they relate to the topics in the schematic table. 3. Read each answer choice, evaluating whether it is *true* information according to the passage, *false* information according to the passage, or *not discussed* in the passage. 4. Eliminate any answers that are *false* or *not discussed*. 5. Match the *true* answer choices to the correct category in the schematic table. 6. Partial credit is possible, and your answers may appear in any order.	

READING EXERCISE 10: Study each passage, and complete the summary table that follows by matching the answer choice to its appropriate position in the table. Some answer choices do not belong in the table because they express ideas that are not presented in the passage or are minor ideas in the passage.

PASSAGE ONE (Question 1)

Sand Dunes

Paragraph

1   Sandy deserts contain enormous volumes of sand eroded from mountains and carried to the deserts by wind or water. The huge quantities of sand that make up sandy deserts are blown about into dunes of various shapes.

2   Ridge dunes form where there are large amounts of sand, generally in the interiors of deserts, and winds blow in one direction. Under these conditions, parallel ridges of sand, known as transverse dunes, form at right angles to the wind.

3   When the direction of the wind changes so that it comes from different directions, star-shaped dunes form from the massive amounts of sand in desert interiors. Star-shaped dunes are relatively stable dunes that reach incredible heights, up to 80 meters high in some deserts, and are quite common in massive deserts such as the Sahara.

4   Crescent dunes form on the edges of deserts where there is less sand and where the winds blow mainly in one direction. These dunes, which are also known as barchan dunes are less stable than star-shaped dunes and can shift as much as 20 meters per year as winds blow over the outer curves of the crescent in the direction of the pointed ends.

Directions:	Select the appropriate sentences from the answer choices, and match them to the critical information about the sand dunes to which they relate. THREE of the answer choices will not be used. ***This question is worth 3 points.***
amount of sand	• •
direction of winds	• •

Answer Choices (choose 4 to complete the chart):

(1) Ridge and crescent dunes form where the winds blow from one direction.

(2) Crescent dunes are also known as barchan dunes.

(3) Star-shaped dunes form where the winds blow from different directions.

(4) Transverse dunes are created parallel to the wind.

(5) Ridge and star dunes form where there is a lot of sand.

(6) Star-shaped dunes are more stable than crescent dunes.

(7) Crescent dunes form where there is less sand.

PASSAGE TWO *(Question 2)*

A Surprising Connection

1   It can be quite surprising to understand that the words *buckaroo* and *vaccine* are actually derived from the same source inasmuch as a buckaroo is a casual way of identifying a cowboy and a vaccine is a substance that can be used to prevent disease.

2   The word *buckaroo* might not be easily recognizable at first as a borrowing into English of the Spanish word *vaquero,* which in Spanish refers to a cowboy. The initial letter *v* in Spanish is pronounced with two lips rather than the pronunciation with the upper front teeth and lower lip of an English *v* and can sound more like the letter *b* than the letter *v* to an English speaker; thus, the English variation of the Spanish word begins with a *b* rather than a *v.* The English word also begins with the syllable *buck,* which is somewhat similar in sound to the first syllable of the Spanish word and is also an easily identifiable word itself in English.

3   The Spanish word *vaquero* comes from *vacca,* the Latin word for "cow." Another word from the same Latin source is *vaccine.* In the late eighteenth century, the English physician Edward Jenner discovered that inoculation with a form of cowpox was effective in preventing the dreaded disease smallpox. French chemist Louis Pasteur, who was himself experimenting with a number of varieties of inoculation, used the word *vaccination* for preventative inoculation in general and the word *vaccine* for the substance inoculated in honor of Jenner's earlier contribution to the development of vaccines.

Directions:	Select the appropriate phrases from the answer choices and match them to the pairs of words to which they relate. TWO of the answer choices will not be used. ***This question is worth 4 points.***	
buckaroo and ***vaquero***	• •	
buckaroo and ***vaccine***	• •	
vacca and ***vaccine***	• •	

Answer Choices (choose 6 to complete the chart):

(1) Are from different languages (Latin and English)

(2) Have the same meaning

(3) Are both Spanish words

(4) Refer to different things (an animal and a substance)

(5) Are found in the same language

(6) Have meanings referring to preventative medicine

(7) Are used in different languages (Spanish and English)

(8) Have different meanings (a person and a substance)

Paragraph

Carnivorous Plants

1   Unlike the majority of plants that create their nourishment from sunlight, such as the flowering hyacinth or the leafy choleus or the garden-variety dandelion, a limited number of plants are able to enhance their diet by fortifying it with insects and other small animals to supplement the food that they have produced from sunlight. These carnivorous plants can be categorized as those without moving traps that lure their intended victims and then trap them on a sticky surface or drown them in a pool of fluid and those with active traps—moving parts that ensnare prey.

2   Butterworts are harmless-looking plants with circles of flat and sticky leaves. If an insect is unfortunate enough to land on one of the seemingly inviting leaves, it sticks to the surface of the leaf and eventually dies and is digested by the plant.

3   The pitcher plant is a plant that is shaped like a pitcher and has fluid at the bottom. Insects are attracted to the pitcher plant by a nectar around the rim of the pitcher opening; when an insect lands on the rim, it cannot maintain its balance on the slippery surface of the rim and falls into the opening and drowns in the fluid.

4   Bladderworts are water plants with traps on their leaves that resemble tiny bubbles. A small animal may swim by the plant, totally oblivious to the danger posed by the harmless-looking bladderwort. If the small animal comes too close to the plant, the bubbles open without warning and the animal is pulled inside the plant and digested.

5   Probably the best known of the carnivorous plants is the Venus flytrap. This plant features unusual leaf tips that look like an inviting place for an insect to rest and offers the enticement of promised food. If an unwary ladybug or dragonfly settles on the leaves of the Venus flytrap, the two leaves suddenly snap shut, trapping the insect and creating a delicious meal for the plant.

Directions: Select the appropriate phrases from the answer choices, and match them to the type of carniverous plant to which they relate. TWO of the answer choices will not be used. ***This question is worth 3 points.***	
those with active traps	• •
those with inactive traps	• •

Answer Choices (choose 4 to complete the chart):

(1) Butterworts

(2) Bladderworts

(3) Dragonflies

(4) Pitcher plants

(5) Venus flytraps

(6) Dandelions

PASSAGE FOUR *(Question 4)*

William Faulkner

1   Author William Faulkner is today recognized as one of America's greatest writers on the basis of a body of novels that so convincingly portray the culture of the South in the years following the Civil War, with its citizens overcome by grief and defeat and trying to cling to old values while struggling to take their place in a changing world. The acclaim that today is Faulkner's, however, was slow in coming.

2   Though Faulkner was praised by some critics and reviewers during the first part of his career, his novels did not sell well and he was considered a fairly marginal author. For the first few decades of his career, he made his living writing magazine articles and working as a screenwriter rather than as a novelist. Throughout this period, he continued to write, though his novels, sometimes noted for the stirring portrait that they presented of life in the post-Civil War South, were generally relegated to the category of strictly regional writing and were not widely appreciated.

3   Beginning in 1946, Faulkner's career took an unexpected and dramatic turn as Faulkner came to be recognized as considerably more than a regional writer. *The Portable Faulkner* was published in that year by Viking Press; two years later he was elected to the prestigious National Academy of Arts and Letters; he was awarded the Nobel Prize for literature in 1949. Over the next decade, his work was recognized in various ways, including a National Book Award and two Pulitzer Prizes, and he became a novelist in residence at the University of Virginia. His success led to a degree of affluence that enabled him to take up the life of a southern gentleman, including horseback riding and fox hunting. Ironically, he died as a result of an accident related to these gentlemanly pursuits, succumbing as a result of injuries suffered during a fall from a horse.

Directions: Select the appropriate phrases from the answer choices, and match them to the phase of William Faulkner's career to which they relate. TWO of the answer choices will not be used. *This question is worth 3 points.*	
Faulkner in the first phase of his career	• • •
Faulkner in the second phase of his career	• • •

Answer Choices (choose 6 to complete the chart):

(1) Was considered one of America's greatest writers

(2) Received a small amount of critical acclaim

(3) Died as a result of a horseback-riding incident

(4) Received numerous awards and acclaim

(5) Was considered merely a regional writer

(6) Wrote novels about various American regions

(7) Made his living as a novelist

(8) Made his living with writing other than novels

READING EXERCISE (Skills 9–10): Study the passage, and choose the best answers to the questions that follow.

Species

1   Millions of different species exist on the earth. These millions of species, which have evolved over billions of years, are the result of two distinct but simultaneously occurring processes: the processes of **speciation** and **extinction**.

2   One of the processes that affects the number of species on earth is **speciation**, which results when one species diverges into two distinct species as a result of disparate natural selection in separate environments. Geographic isolation is one common mechanism that fosters speciation; speciation as a result of geographic isolation occurs when two populations of a species become separated for long periods of time into areas with different environmental conditions. After the two populations are separated, they evolve independently; if this divergence continues long enough, members of the two distinct populations eventually become so different genetically that they are two distinct species rather than one. The process of speciation may occur within hundreds of years for organisms that reproduce rapidly, but for most species the process of speciation can take thousands to millions of years. One example of speciation is the early fox, which over time evolved into two distinct species, the gray fox and the arctic fox. The early fox separated into populations which evolved differently in response to very different environments as the populations moved in different directions, one to colder northern climates and the other to warmer southern climates. The northern population adapted to cold weather by developing heavier fur, shorter ears, noses, and legs, and white fur to camouflage itself in the snow. The southern population adapted to warmer weather by developing lighter fur and longer ears, noses, and legs and keeping its darker fur for better camouflage protection.

3   Another of the processes that affects the number of species on earth is **extinction**, which refers to the situation in which a species ceases to exist. When environmental conditions change, a species needs to adapt to the new environmental conditions, or it may become extinct. Extinction of a species is not a rare occurrence but is instead a rather commonplace one: it has, in fact, been estimated that more than 99 percent of the species that have ever existed have become extinct. Extinction may occur when a species fails to adapt to evolving environmental conditions in a limited area, a process known as background extinction. In contrast, a broader and more abrupt extinction, known as mass extinction, may come about as a result of a catastrophic event or global climatic change. When such a catastrophic event or global climatic change occurs, some species are able to adapt to the new environment, while those that are unable to adapt become extinct. From geological and fossil evidence, it appears that at least five great mass extinctions have occurred; the last mass extinction occurred approximately 65 million years ago, when the dinosaurs became extinct after 140 million years of existence on earth, marking the end of the Mesozoic Era and the beginning of the Cenozoic Era.

4   The fact that millions of species are in existence today is evidence that speciation has clearly kept well ahead of extinction. In spite of the fact that there have been numerous periods of mass extinction, there is clear evidence that periods of mass extinction have been followed by periods of dramatic increases in new species to fill the void created by the mass extinctions, though it may take 10 million years or more following a mass extinction for biological diversity to be rebuilt through speciation. When the dinosaurs disappeared 65 million years ago, for example, the evolution and speciation of mammals increased spectacularly over the millions of years that ensued.

1.

Directions:	An introductory sentence or a brief summary of the passage is provided below. Complete the summary by selecting the THREE answer choices that express the most important ideas in the passage. Some sentences do not belong in the summary because they express ideas that are not presented in the passage or are minor ideas in the passage. *This question is worth 2 points.*

This passage discusses processes affecting the development of millions of species.
•
•
•

Answer Choices (choose 3 to complete the chart):

(1) Though numerous species have become extinct, far more new species have developed than have been lost.

(2) Only 1 percent of the species that have existed have become extinct.

(3) A single species can develop into distinct species through a process called speciation.

(4) The gray fox and the arctic fox separated into different species early in their development.

(5) Social isolation is a major factor that influences the degree of speciation.

(6) Numerous species become extinct when they fail to adapt to evolving conditions or fail to survive a cataclysmic event.

2.

Directions:	Select the appropriate phrases from the answer choices, and match them to the process of extinction to which they relate. TWO of the answer choices will not be used. *This question is worth 4 points.*

speciation	• •
extinction	• • •

Answer Choices (choose 6 to complete the chart):

(1) Can result from failure to adapt to changing environments

(2) Results in the creation of new species

(3) Results in the merging of different species

(4) Can result from failure to adjust to a cataclysmic event

(5) Can result from separation of populations

(6) Can result from the commingling of different species

(7) Results in the disappearance of a species

READING REVIEW EXERCISE (Skills 1–10): Read the passage.

Paragraph

Decisions

1   In a theoretical model of **decision making**, a decision is defined as the process of selecting one option from among a group of options for implementation. Decisions are formed by a **decision maker**, the one who actually chooses the final option, in conjunction with a **decision unit**, all of those in the organization around the decision maker who take part in the process. In this theoretical model, the members of the decision unit react to an unidentified problem by studying the problem, determining the objectives of the organization, formulating options, evaluating the strengths and weaknesses of each of the options, and reaching a conclusion. Many different factors can have an effect on the decision, including the nature of the problem itself, external forces exerting an influence on the organization, the internal dynamics of the decision unit, and the personality of the decision maker.

2   During recent years, decision making has been studied systematically by drawing from such diverse areas of study as psychology, sociology, business, government, history, mathematics, and statistics. Analyses of decisions often emphasize one of three principal conceptual perspectives (though often the approach that is actually employed is somewhat eclectic).

3   In the oldest of the three approaches, decisions are made by a **rational actor**, who makes a particular decision directly and purposefully in response to a specific threat from the external environment. It is assumed that this rational actor has clear objectives in mind, develops numerous reasonable options, considers the advantages and disadvantages of each option carefully, chooses the best option after careful analysis, and then proceeds to implement it fully. A variation of the rational actor model is a decision maker who is a **satisfier**, one who selects the first satisfactory option rather than continuing the decision-making process until the optimal decision has been reached.

4   A second perspective places an emphasis on the impact of routines on decisions within organizations. It demonstrates how organizational structures and routines such as standard operating procedures tend to limit the decision-making process in a variety of ways, perhaps by restricting the information available to the decision unit, by restricting the breadth of options among which the decision unit may choose, or by inhibiting the ability of the organization to implement the decision quickly and effectively once it has been taken. Pre-planned routines and standard operating procedures are essential to coordinate the efforts of large numbers of people in massive organizations. However, these same routines and procedures can also have an inhibiting effect on the ability of the organization to arrive at optimal decisions and implement them efficiently. In this sort of decision-making process, organizations tend to take not the optimal decision but the decision that best fits within the permitted operating parameters outlined by the organization.

5   A third conceptual perspective emphasizes the internal dynamics of the decision unit and the extent to which decisions are based on political forces within the organization. This perspective demonstrates how bargaining among individuals who have different interests and motives and varying levels of power in the decision unit leads to eventual compromise that is not the preferred choice of any of the members of the decision unit.

6   Each of these three perspectives on the decision-making process demonstrates a different point of view on decision making, a different lens through which the decision-making process can be observed. It is safe to say that decision making in most organizations shows marked influences from each perspective; i.e., an organization strives to get as close as possible to the rational model in its decisions, yet the internal routines and dynamics of the organization come into play in the decision.

Refer to this version of the passage to answer the following questions.

Paragraph | **Decisions**

1   In a theoretical model of **decision making**, a decision is defined as the process of selecting one option from among a group of options for implementation. **4A** Decisions are formed by a **decision maker**, the one who actually chooses the final option, in conjunction with a **decision unit**, all of those in the organization around the decision maker who take part in the process. **4B** In this theoretical model, the members of the decision unit react to an unidentified problem by studying the problem, determining the objectives of the organization, formulating options, evaluating the strengths and weaknesses of each of the options, and reaching a conclusion. **4C** Many different factors can have an effect on the decision, including the nature of the problem itself, external forces exerting an influence on the organization, the internal dynamics of the decision unit, and the personality of the decision maker. **4D**

2   During recent years, decision making has been studied systematically by drawing from such diverse areas of study as psychology, sociology, business, government, history, mathematics, and statistics. Analyses of decisions often emphasize one of three principal conceptual perspectives (though often the approach that is actually employed is somewhat eclectic).

3   In the oldest of the three approaches, decisions are made by a **rational actor**, who makes a particular decision directly and purposefully in response to a specific threat from the external environment. It is assumed that this rational actor has clear objectives in mind, develops numerous reasonable options, considers the advantages and disadvantages of each option carefully, chooses the best option after careful analysis, and then proceeds to implement it fully. A variation of the rational actor model is a decision maker who is a **satisfier**, one who selects the first satisfactory option rather than continuing the decision-making process until the optimal decision has been reached.

4   A second perspective places an emphasis on the impact of routines on decisions within organizations. It demonstrates how organizational structures and routines such as standard operating procedures tend to limit the decision-making process in a variety of ways, perhaps by restricting the information available to the decision unit, by restricting the breadth of options among which the decision unit may choose, or by inhibiting the ability of the organization to implement the decision quickly and effectively once it has been taken. Pre-planned routines and standard operating procedures are essential to coordinate the efforts of large numbers of people in massive organizations. However, these same routines and procedures can also have an inhibiting effect on the ability of the organization to arrive at optimal decisions and implement them efficiently. In this sort of decision-making process, organizations tend to take not the optimal decision but the decision that best fits within the permitted operating parameters outlined by the organization.

5   A third conceptual perspective emphasizes the internal dynamics of the decision unit and the extent to which decisions are based on political forces within the organization. This perspective demonstrates how bargaining among individuals who have different interests and motives and varying levels of power in the decision unit leads to eventual compromise that is not the preferred choice of any of the members of the decision unit.

6   Each of these three perspectives on the decision-making process demonstrates a different point of view on decision making, a different lens through which the decision-making process can be observed. It is safe to say that decision making in most organizations shows marked influences from each perspective; i.e., an organization strives to get as close as possible to the rational model in its decisions, yet the internal routines and dynamics of the organization come into play in the decision.

Questions

1. It can be inferred from the information in paragraph 1 that the theoretical decision-making process
   - (A) involves only the decision maker
   - (B) requires the contemplation of numerous options
   - (C) is made without the decision unit
   - (D) does not work in real situations

2. The phrase in conjunction with in paragraph 1 could best be replaced by
   - (A) along with
   - (B) tied to
   - (C) apart from
   - (D) connected to

3. All of the following are listed in paragraph 1 as having an effect on decisions EXCEPT
   - (A) evaluation of the problem
   - (B) focus on objectives
   - (C) generation of options
   - (D) open-ended discussions

4. Look at the four squares [■] that indicate where the following sentence can be added to the passage.

   Additionally, when a decision must be made in a crisis situation, both stress and the speed at which events are progressing can have an effect, often a negative one, on the decision process.

   Click on a square [■] to add the sentence to the passage.

5. The word eclectic in paragraph 2 is closest in meaning to
   - (A) bizarre
   - (B) personal
   - (C) mixed
   - (D) organized

6. It can be inferred from paragraph 3 that a rational actor would be least likely to
   - (A) deal with a specific threat
   - (B) work in a random fashion
   - (C) ponder various options
   - (D) consider disadvantages of options

7. The word it in paragraph 3 refers to
   - (A) each option
   - (B) the best option
   - (C) careful analysis
   - (D) variation

8. Why does the author mention a **satisfier, one who selects the first satisfactory option rather than continuing the decision-making process until the optimal decision has been reached** in paragraph 3?
   - (A) A satisfier shows contrasting behavior to a rational actor.
   - (B) A satisfier exhibits more common behavior than a rational actor.
   - (C) A satisfier is the predecessor of a rational actor.
   - (D) A satisfier shares some characteristics with a rational actor.

9. The word places in paragraph 4 could best be replaced by
   - (A) locates
   - (B) puts
   - (C) finds
   - (D) sets

10. Which of the sentences below expresses the essential information in the highlighted sentence in paragraph 4? *Incorrect* choices change the meaning in important ways or leave out essential information.
    - (A) Set routines within organizations tend to constrain decisions.
    - (B) The restriction of information limits the number of options in a decision.
    - (C) Organizations need to set up strict procedures to maximize the effectiveness of decisions.
    - (D) Procedures are needed to ensure that decisions are implemented quickly and effectively.

11. The word dynamics in paragraph 5 is closest in meaning to

Ⓐ explosions
Ⓑ emotions
Ⓒ philosophies
Ⓓ interactions

12. According to paragraph 5, what is the end result of political bargaining within an organization?

Ⓐ No decision is ever reached.
Ⓑ Differing interests and motives are changed.
Ⓒ No one is completely satisfied with the final outcome.
Ⓓ The members of the decision unit leave the unit.

13.

Directions:	An introductory sentence or a brief summary of the passage is provided below. Complete the summary by selecting the THREE answer choices that express the most important ideas in the passage. Some sentences do not belong in the summary because they express ideas that are not presented in the passage or are minor ideas in the passage. ***This question is worth 2 points.***

This passage presents different models for analyzing the process of decision making.
•
•
•

Answer Choices (choose 3 to complete the chart):

(1) One model looks at how satisfied all participants are after a given decision has been made.

(2) One model looks at how organizational structure and procedures influence a decision and how much a decision has been limited by these procedures.

(3) One model looks at how much a decision-making process has been manipulated and limited by factions within the organization.

(4) One model looks at how rational actors are able to work within organizational structures and routines to achieve optimal solutions.

(5) One model looks at how the decision-making process differs in diverse areas such as psychology, sociology, business, government, history, mathematics, and statistics.

(6) One model looks at how well a decision maker has analyzed a problem and possible solutions to achieve the optimal solution.

READING POST-TEST

30 minutes

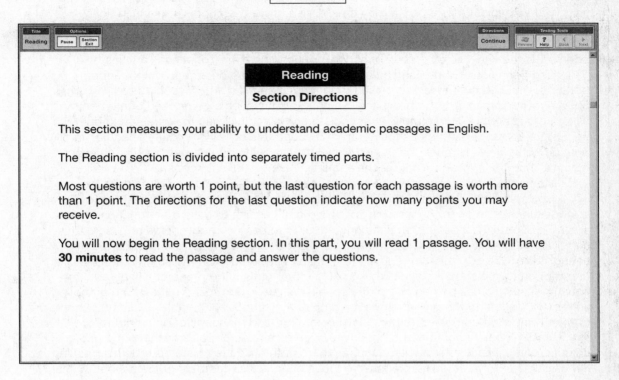

Reading
Section Directions

This section measures your ability to understand academic passages in English.

The Reading section is divided into separately timed parts.

Most questions are worth 1 point, but the last question for each passage is worth more than 1 point. The directions for the last question indicate how many points you may receive.

You will now begin the Reading section. In this part, you will read 1 passage. You will have **30 minutes** to read the passage and answer the questions.

Read the passage.

30 minutes

Aquatic Schools

Paragraph

1   Many species of fish, particularly smaller fish, travel in schools, moving in tight formations, often with the precision of the most highly disciplined military unit on parade. Some move in synchronized hordes, while others move in starkly geometric forms. In addition to the varieties of shapes of schools of fish, there are countless varieties of schooling behaviors. Some fish coalesce into schools and then spread out in random patterns, while others move into close formations at specific times, such as feeding times, but are more spread out at other times. Some move in schools composed of members of all age groups, while others move in schools predominantly when they are young but take up a more solitary existence as they mature. Though this behavior is quite a regular, familiar phenomenon, there is much that is not completely known about it, particularly the exact function that it serves and what mechanisms fish use to make it happen.

2   Numerous hypotheses have been proposed and tested concerning the purpose of schooling behavior in fish. Schooling certainly promotes the survival of the species, but questions arise as to the way the schooling enables fish to have a better chance of surviving. Certainly, the fact that fish congregate together in schools helps to ensure their survival in that schooling provides numerous types of protection for the members of the school. One form of protection derives from the sheer numbers in the school. When a predator attacks a school containing a huge number of fish, the predator will be able to consume only a small percentage of the school. Whereas some of the members of the school will be lost to the predator, the majority of the school will be able to survive. Another form of protection comes from the special coloration and markings of different types of fish. Certain types of coloration or markings such as stripes or patterns in vibrant and shiny colors create a visual effect when huge numbers of the fish are clustered together, making it more difficult for a potential predator to focus on specific members of the school. A final form of protection comes from a special sense that fish possess, a sense that is enhanced when fish swim in schools. This special sense is related to a set of lateral line organs that consist of rows of pores leading to fluid-filled canals. These organs are sensitive to minute vibrations in the water. The thousands of sets of those special organs in a school of fish together can prove very effective in warning the school about an approaching threat.

3   It is also unclear exactly how fish manage to maintain their tight formations. Sight seems to play a role in the ability of fish to move in schools, and some scientists believe that, at least in some species, sight may play the principal role. However, many experiments indicate that more than sight is involved. Some fish school quite well in the dark or in murky water where visibility is extremely limited. This indicates that senses other than eyesight must be involved in enabling the schooling behavior. The lateral line system most likely plays a significant role in the ability of fish to school. Because these lateral line organs are sensitive to the most minute vibrations and currents, this organ system may be used by fish to detect movements among members of their school even when eyesight is limited or unavailable.

Refer to this version of the passage to answer the questions that follow.

Aquatic Schools

Paragraph

1   Many species of fish, particularly smaller fish, travel in schools, moving in tight formations often with the precision of the most highly disciplined military unit on parade. **5A** Some move in synchronized hordes, while others move in starkly geometric forms. **5B** In addition to the varieties of shapes of schools of fish, there are countless varieties of schooling behaviors. **5C** Some fish coalesce into schools and then spread out in random patterns, while others move into close formations at specific times, such as feeding times, but are more spread out at other times. **5D** Some move in schools composed of members of all age groups, while others move in schools predominantly when they are young but take up a more solitary existence as they mature. Though this behavior is quite a regular, familiar phenomenon, there is much that is not completely known about it, particularly the exact function that it serves and what mechanisms fish use to make it happen.

2   Numerous hypotheses have been proposed and tested concerning the purpose of schooling behavior in fish. Schooling certainly promotes the survival of the species, but questions arise as to the way the schooling enables fish to have a better chance of surviving. Certainly, the fact that fish congregate together in schools helps to ensure their survival in that schooling provides numerous types of protection for the members of the school. One form of protection derives from the sheer numbers in the school. When a predator attacks a school containing a huge number of fish, the predator will be able to consume only a small percentage of the school. Whereas some of the members of the school will be lost to the predator, the majority of the school will be able to survive. Another form of protection comes from the special coloration and markings of different types of fish. Certain types of coloration or markings such as stripes or patterns in vibrant and shiny colors create a visual effect when huge numbers of the fish are clustered together, making it more difficult for a potential predator to focus on specific members of the school. A final form of protection comes from a special sense that fish possess, a sense that is enhanced when fish swim in schools. This special sense is related to a set of lateral line organs that consist of rows of pores leading to fluid-filled canals. These organs are sensitive to minute vibrations in the water. The thousands of sets of those special organs in a school of fish together can prove very effective in warning the school about an approaching threat.

3   **16A** It is also unclear exactly how fish manage to maintain their tight formations. **16B** Sight seems to play a role in the ability of fish to move in schools, and some scientists believe that, at least in some species, sight may play the principal role. **16C** However, many experiments indicate that more than sight is involved. Some fish school quite well in the dark or in murky water where visibility is extremely limited. **16D** This indicates that senses other than eyesight must be involved in enabling the schooling behavior. The lateral line system most likely plays a significant role in the ability of fish to school. Because these lateral line organs are sensitive to the most minute vibrations and currents, this organ system may be used by fish to detect movements among members of their school even when eyesight is limited or unavailable.

Questions

1. The author mentions the most highly disciplined military unit on parade in paragraph 1 in order to
   - A describe the aggressive nature of a school of fish
   - B provide an example of a way that military units travel
   - C create a mental image of the movement of a school of fish
   - D contrast the movement of a military unit with that of a school of fish

2. The word hordes in paragraph 1 is closest in meaning to
   - A shapes
   - B masses
   - C pairs
   - D patterns

3. All of the following are stated in paragraph 1 about schooling EXCEPT that
   - A it is quite common
   - B it can involve large numbers of fish
   - C it can involve a number of different fish behaviors
   - D it is fully understood

4. Which fish would be least likely to be in a school?
   - A A large, older fish
   - B A smaller, colorful fish
   - C A young, hungry fish
   - D A tiny, shiny fish

5. Look at the four squares [■] that indicate where the following sentence can be added to paragraph 1.

   These may take the shape, for example, of wedges, triangles, spheres, or ovals.

   Click on a square [■] to add the sentence to the passage.

6. The word it in paragraph 1 refers to
   - A existence
   - B behavior
   - C fish
   - D function

7. Which of the sentences below expresses the essential information in the first highlighted sentence in paragraph 2? *Incorrect* choices change the meaning in important ways or leave out essential information.
   - A After an attack, the fish that survive tend to move into schools.
   - B The survival of fish depends upon their ability to bring new members into the school.
   - C Many facts about the way that fish congregate in schools have been studied.
   - D Fish travel in schools to protect themselves in various ways.

8. The phrase sheer numbers in paragraph 2 could best be replaced by
   - A solitude
   - B interlude
   - C multitude
   - D similitude

9. It can be inferred from the passage that, when a predator attacks,
   - A it cannot possibly consume all members of a school if the school is large enough
   - B it rarely manages to catch any fish that are part of a school
   - C it is usually successful in wiping out the entire school
   - D it attacks only schools that lack sense organs

10. It is stated in paragraph 2 that
    - A fish in schools rarely have distinct markings
    - B schooling fish tend to have muted coloration
    - C the effect of coloration is multiplied when fish are massed together
    - D the bright coloration makes it easier for predators to spot fish

11. The word minute in paragraph 2 is closest in meaning to
   Ⓐ timely
   Ⓑ tiny
   Ⓒ careful
   Ⓓ instant

12. Which of the sentences below expresses the essential information in the second highlighted sentence in paragraph 2? *Incorrect* choices change the meaning in important ways or leave out essential information.
   Ⓐ There are thousands of ways that special organs warn fish about a predator.
   Ⓑ When the fish in a school work together, they can use their sense organs to scare off any approaching threat.
   Ⓒ The fish in a large school use their lateral line organs to send out warnings of the arrival of the school.
   Ⓓ Because so many fish are in a school, all of their sense organs work well together to provide warnings.

13. The author begins paragraph 3 with It is also unclear in order to indicate that
   Ⓐ contradictory information is about to be presented
   Ⓑ it is necessary to clarify a previously made point
   Ⓒ a second issue is about to be presented
   Ⓓ it is unclear how a problem can be resolved

14. According to paragraph 3,
   Ⓐ fish cannot see well
   Ⓑ sight is the only sense used by fish to remain in schools
   Ⓒ not all fish use sight to remain in schools
   Ⓓ fish can see quite well in the dark

15. The word murky in paragraph 3 is closest in meaning to
   Ⓐ cloudy
   Ⓑ warm
   Ⓒ clear
   Ⓓ deep

16. Look at the four squares [■] that indicate where the following sentence can be added to paragraph 3.

   The purpose of schooling behavior is not the only aspect of schooling that is not fully understood.

   Click on a square [■] to add the sentence to the passage.

17. The word This in paragraph 3 refers to the ability of fish to
   Ⓐ see well in dark water
   Ⓑ stay in schools when they cannot see well
   Ⓒ swim in water where the visibility is low
   Ⓓ use their sight to stay in schools

18. It is NOT stated in the passage that the lateral line system
   Ⓐ contains lines of pores
   Ⓑ can detect movement in the water
   Ⓒ quite possibly helps fish to remain in schools
   Ⓓ in fish is similar to sense organs in other animals

19.

Directions: An introductory sentence or a brief summary of the passage is provided below. Complete the summary by selecting the TWO answer choices that express the most important ideas in the passage. Some sentences do not belong in the summary because they express ideas that are not presented in the passage or are minor ideas in the passage. *This question is worth 3 points.*
This passage discusses schooling behavior in certain fish.
•
•

Answer Choices (choose 2 to complete the chart):

(1) Fish most likely move in schools in various types of water.

(2) Fish may move in schools by using various senses.

(3) Fish may move in schools at various times of the day or night.

(4) Fish most likely move in schools in various ways.

20.

Directions: Select the appropriate sentences from the answer choices, and match them to the hypotheses to which they relate. TWO of the answer choices will not be used. *This question is worth 4 points.*	
hypotheses related to purpose	• • •
hypotheses related to manner	• •

Answer Choices (choose 5 to complete the chart):

(1) Coloration provides protection.

(2) Lateral sense organs enable some fish to school.

(3) Sight provides protection.

(4) Coloration enables some fish to move.

(5) Large numbers provide protection.

(6) Sight enables some fish to school.

(7) Lateral sense organs provide protection.

Turn to the chart on page 544, and circle the numbers of the questions that you missed.

SECTION TWO

LISTENING

LISTENING DIAGNOSTIC PRE-TEST

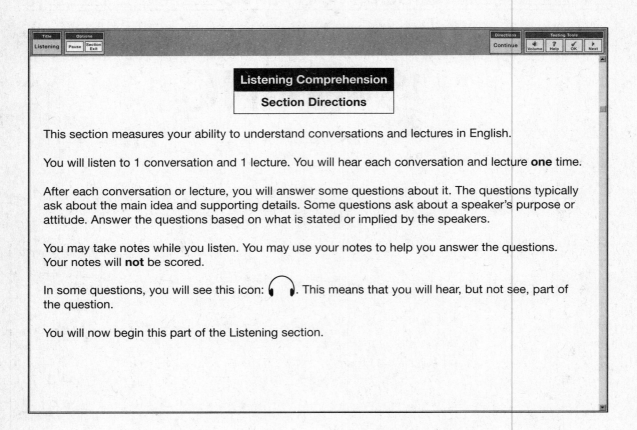

Listening Comprehension

Section Directions

This section measures your ability to understand conversations and lectures in English.

You will listen to 1 conversation and 1 lecture. You will hear each conversation and lecture **one** time.

After each conversation or lecture, you will answer some questions about it. The questions typically ask about the main idea and supporting details. Some questions ask about a speaker's purpose or attitude. Answer the questions based on what is stated or implied by the speakers.

You may take notes while you listen. You may use your notes to help you answer the questions. Your notes will **not** be scored.

In some questions, you will see this icon: 🎧. This means that you will hear, but not see, part of the question.

You will now begin this part of the Listening section.

Questions 1–6

Listen to a discussion between a student
and an advisor.

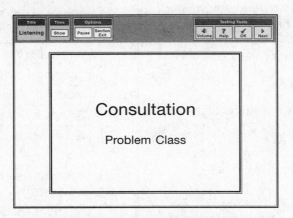

1. Why does the advisor want to talk with the student?

   Ⓐ To commend him on his work habits
   Ⓑ To discuss a deficiency in one class
   Ⓒ To discuss what his history professor is teaching
   Ⓓ To talk about each of the student's classes

2. What problems does the student have?

   Click on 2 answers.

   Ⓐ He is not doing well in any of his classes.
   Ⓑ His history teacher gives unfair assignments.
   Ⓒ He is not in class all the time.
   Ⓓ He does not understand what is being tested.

3. Listen again to part of the passage. Then answer the question. 🎧

   What does the advisor mean when she says this: 🎧

   Ⓐ "I do not believe what you just said."
   Ⓑ "What you just said is funny."
   Ⓒ "Your response is not acceptable."
   Ⓓ "Can you please repeat what you just said?"

4. How does the advisor seem to feel about the student's responses?

   Ⓐ She thinks he is not telling the truth.
   Ⓑ She seems to believe his excuses are weak.
   Ⓒ She seems to accept what he says.
   Ⓓ She thinks what he says is amusing.

5. Does the advisor recommend each of these?

For each answer, click in the YES or NO column.		
	YES	NO
Getting up in time for class		
Sitting in the back of the classroom		
Speaking more in class		
Finding out what is covered on the exams		
Taking careful notes		

6. What can be concluded from the conversation?

   Ⓐ There are good reasons that the student's grades are low.
   Ⓑ History class is too hard a class for this student.
   Ⓒ The advisor expects too much from the student.
   Ⓓ The student should really consider taking a different course.

Questions 7–12

Listen as an instructor leads a discussion of some material from a psychology class.

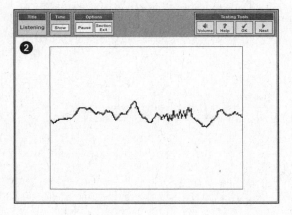

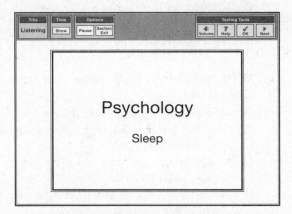

7. What does the instructor mainly want to get across in the discussion?

(A) The types of brain wave patterns that humans experience in sleep

(B) How much rest humans and other animals require

(C) How human sleep differs from the sleep of other animals

(D) The characteristics of sleep in all types of living beings

8. What happens during human sleep?

Click on 2 answers.

A Muscles become relaxed.

B The rate of breathing increases.

C The heart rate decreases.

D Brain waves stop.

9. What does the instructor mean when he says this:

(A) "Let's review the material we just covered."

(B) "Let's slow down because we're going too fast."

(C) "Let's take a break and start the class again in a while."

(D) "Let's move on to the next topic."

10. How long are the periods of dreaming for each of these groups of animals?

For each item, click in the correct column.

	No period of dreaming	Brief periods of dreaming	Longer periods of dreaming
Fish			
Mammals			
Birds			

11. How does the professor seem to feel about the students' responses?

(A) Surprised

(B) Unsure

(C) Satisfied

(D) Overwhelmed

12. What conclusion can be drawn from the discussion?

(A) All animals dream during their sleep.

(B) Humans are the only animals that dream in their sleep.

(C) Most animals do not have changes in brain waves during their sleep.

(D) Mammals seem to dream in their sleep, while other animals do not.

Turn to the chart on page 545, and circle the numbers of the questions that you missed.

LISTENING OVERVIEW

The second section on the *iBT* TOEFL test is the Listening section. This section consists of six passages, each followed by five or six questions. You may take notes as you listen to the passages and use your notes as you answer the questions.

- The **passages** are set in an academic environment. There are 2-to 3-minute conversations that take place outside of the classroom and 4-to 5-minute lectures that take place inside the classroom. The Listening section is divided into two parts, and each part of the Listening section contains one conversation and two lectures. The conversations are followed by five questions each, and the lectures are followed by six questions each.

- The **questions** may ask about main ideas and details, the speaker's function or stance, the organization of ideas, and inferences based on the passage.

The following strategies can help you in the Listening section.

STRATEGIES FOR LISTENING

1. **Be familiar with the directions.** The directions on every test are the same, so it is not necessary to spend time reading the directions carefully when you take the test. You should be completely familiar with the directions before the day of the test.

2. **Dismiss the directions as soon as they come up.** You should already be familiar with the directions, so you can click on `Continue` as soon as it appears and use your time on the passages and questions.

3. **Do not worry if a listening passage is on a topic that is not familiar to you.** All of the information that you need to answer the questions is included in the passages. You do not need any background knowledge to answer the questions.

4. **Listen carefully to the passage.** You will hear the passages one time only. You may not repeat the passages during the test.

5. **Use the visuals to help you to understand the passages.** Each passage begins with a photograph showing the setting (such as a classroom or a campus office) and the person or people who are speaking. There may be other visuals (such as a diagram, a drawing, or a blackboard with important terminology) to help you to understand the content of the passage.

6. **Take careful notes as you listen to the spoken material.** You should focus on the main points and key supporting material. Do not try to write down everything you hear. Do not write down too many unnecessary details.

7. **Look at each question to determine what type of question it is.** The type of question tells you how to proceed to answer the question.
   - For *gist questions,* listen carefully to the beginning of the passage to develop an initial idea about the gist of the passage. Then, as you listen to the rest of the passage, adjust your idea about the gist of the passage as you listen to what the speakers are saying.
   - For *detail questions,* listen carefully to the details in the passage. Then look for an answer that restates the information from the passage.

- For *function questions,* listen carefully to what the speaker says in the part of the passage that is repeated. Then draw a conclusion about why the speaker says it.
- For *stance questions,* listen carefully to what the speaker says in the part of the passage that is repeated. Then draw a conclusion about what the speaker feels.
- For *organization questions,* listen carefully to each of the points in the passage and consider how these points are organized. Then look for an answer that shows the organization of the points.
- For *relationship questions,* listen carefully to each of the points in the passage and consider how these points might be related. Then look for an answer that shows how the points are related.

8. **Choose the best answer to each question.** You may be certain of a particular answer, or you may eliminate any definitely incorrect answers and choose from among the remaining answers.

9. **Think carefully about a question before you answer it.** You may not return to a question later in the test. You have only one opportunity to answer a given question.

10. **Do not spend too much time on a question you are unsure of.** If you truly do not know the answer to a question, simply guess and go on.

11. **Monitor the time carefully on the title bar of the computer screen.** The title bar indicates the time remaining in the section, the total number of questions in the section, and the number of the question that you are working on.

12. **Guess to complete the section before time is up.** It can only increase your score to guess the answers to questions that you do not have time to complete. (Points are not subtracted for incorrect answers.)

LISTENING SKILLS

The following skills will help you to implement these strategies in the Listening section of the *iBT* TOEFL test.

BASIC COMPREHENSION

Basic comprehension questions are related to what is stated in the passage. These questions may ask about the overall **gist** (the main idea or overall topic), or they may ask about specific **details** in the passage.

Listening Skill 1: UNDERSTAND THE GIST

Gist questions are questions that ask about the overall ideas of a passage as a whole. They may ask what the *subject, topic,* or *main idea* of a passage is. They may also ask what overall *purpose* the passage serves. It is important to understand that the gist of a passage may be directly stated in the passage, or you may have to synthesize (bring together) information from different parts of the passage to understand the overall gist. Look at an example of a part of a listening passage.

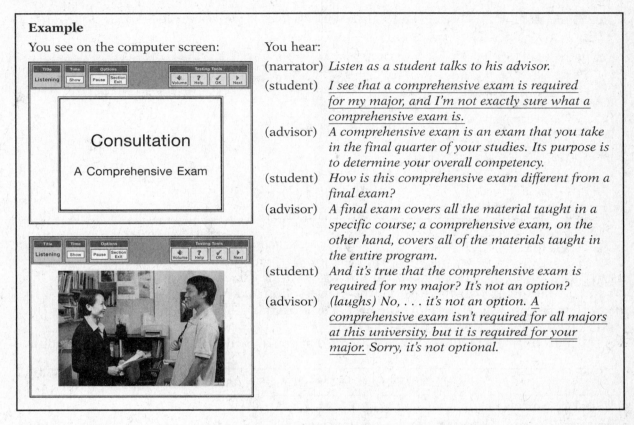

Example

You see on the computer screen:

You hear:

(narrator) *Listen as a student talks to his advisor.*

(student) *I see that a comprehensive exam is required for my major, and I'm not exactly sure what a comprehensive exam is.*

(advisor) *A comprehensive exam is an exam that you take in the final quarter of your studies. Its purpose is to determine your overall competency.*

(student) *How is this comprehensive exam different from a final exam?*

(advisor) *A final exam covers all the material taught in a specific course; a comprehensive exam, on the other hand, covers all of the materials taught in the entire program.*

(student) *And it's true that the comprehensive exam is required for my major? It's not an option?*

(advisor) *(laughs) No, . . . it's not an option. A comprehensive exam isn't required for all majors at this university, but it is required for your major. Sorry, it's not optional.*

After you listen to the conversation, the question and answer choices appear on the computer screen as the narrator states the question. This is a gist question that asks about the purpose of the passage.

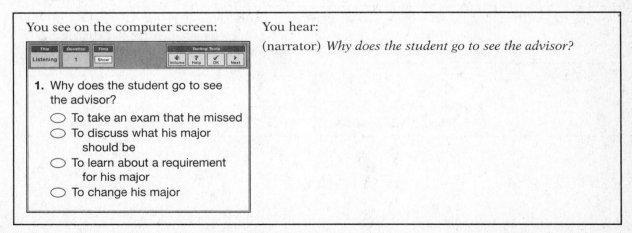

You see on the computer screen:

You hear:

(narrator) *Why does the student go to see the advisor?*

1. Why does the student go to see the advisor?
- ○ To take an exam that he missed
- ○ To discuss what his major should be
- ○ To learn about a requirement for his major
- ○ To change his major

In the conversation, the student says *I see that a comprehensive exam is required for my major, and I'm not exactly sure what a comprehensive exam is.* From this, it can be determined that the student goes to see his advisor in order *to learn about a requirement for his major.* The third answer is therefore the best answer to this question.

Now look at an example of another type of gist question. This gist question asks about the overall topic of the passage.

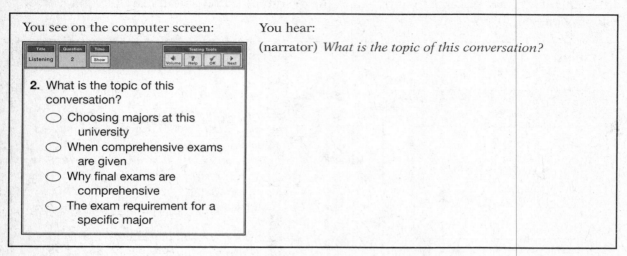

You see on the computer screen:

You hear:

(narrator) *What is the topic of this conversation?*

2. What is the topic of this conversation?
- ○ Choosing majors at this university
- ○ When comprehensive exams are given
- ○ Why final exams are comprehensive
- ○ The exam requirement for a specific major

In the conversation, the student says *I see that a comprehensive exam is required for my major, and I'm not exactly sure what a comprehensive exam is,* and the professor says *a comprehensive exam isn't required for all majors at this university, but it is required for <u>your</u> major.* From this, it can be determined that the topic of the conversation is *the exam requirement for a specific major.* The last answer is therefore the best answer to this question.

The following chart outlines the key points that you should remember about gist questions.

QUESTIONS ABOUT THE GIST OF A PASSAGE	
HOW TO IDENTIFY THE QUESTION	What is the **subject** of the passage? What is the **topic** of the passage? What is the **main idea** of the passage? What is the **purpose** of the passage? **Why** . . . in the passage?
WHERE TO FIND THE ANSWER	Information to help you understand the gist may be directly stated at the beginning of the passage. It may also be necessary for you to draw a conclusion about the gist based upon information provided throughout the passage.
HOW TO ANSWER THE QUESTION	1. Listen carefully to the beginning of the passage to develop an initial idea about the gist of the passage. 2. Then, as you listen to the rest of the passage, adjust your idea of the gist of the passage as you consider what the speakers are saying.

LISTENING EXERCISE 1: Listen to each passage and the questions that follow. Then choose the best answers to the questions.

PASSAGE ONE *(Questions 1–2)*

Listen to a conversation between a student and a professor.

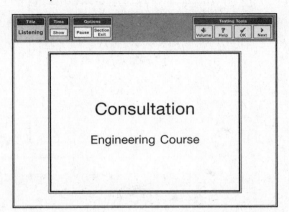

PASSAGE TWO *(Questions 3–4)*

Listen as a student visits a university office.

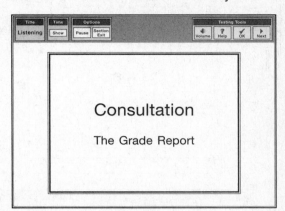

1. Why does the student go to see the professor?
   Ⓐ To ask the professor for a form
   Ⓑ To find out what will be taught
   Ⓒ To get a signature on a form
   Ⓓ To ask a question about some course material

2. What does the student want to do?
   Ⓐ Repeat a course
   Ⓑ Sign a form
   Ⓒ Find out his grade
   Ⓓ Learn about a course

3. Why does the student go to the office?
   Ⓐ To learn about a university policy
   Ⓑ To find a solution for a problem
   Ⓒ To file a form before the deadline
   Ⓓ To ask when something will happen

4. What is the topic of the conversation?
   Ⓐ Using the computer system
   Ⓑ Filing a change of address form
   Ⓒ Learning when grades will be sent out
   Ⓓ Finding a missing document

PASSAGE THREE (Questions 5–6)

Listen to some students having a discussion.

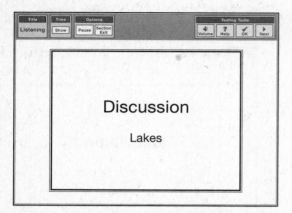

5. What are the students discussing?
   Ⓐ Various ways that major lakes formed
   Ⓑ The world's largest body of water
   Ⓒ Where various lakes are located
   Ⓓ Lakes that formed in the same way

6. Why are the students discussing this material?
   Ⓐ They have just seen a presentation about it.
   Ⓑ They are preparing for an exam on it.
   Ⓒ They must present it to their classmates.
   Ⓓ They are writing a research paper.

PASSAGE FOUR (Questions 7–8)

Listen as a professor leads a class discussion.

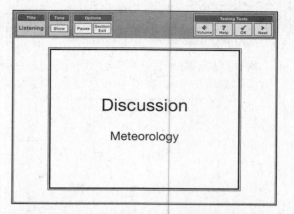

7. What is the topic of this discussion?
   Ⓐ Two contrasting theories on storms
   Ⓑ The function of centripetal force in storms
   Ⓒ The history of meteorology
   Ⓓ Like theories by two different scientists

8. Why is this topic being discussed?
   Ⓐ It was introduced by the professor.
   Ⓑ It was on an exam the students took.
   Ⓒ It was assigned to the students for homework.
   Ⓓ It was brought up by a student.

Listening Skill 2: UNDERSTAND THE DETAILS

Detail questions ask you about specific pieces of information that are stated in a passage. As you listen to each passage, you should focus on the details from the passage because questions about details quite commonly accompany the passages. Multiple-choice questions are used to test details, and these multiple-choice questions may have one correct answer or two correct answers. Look at an example of part of a passage.

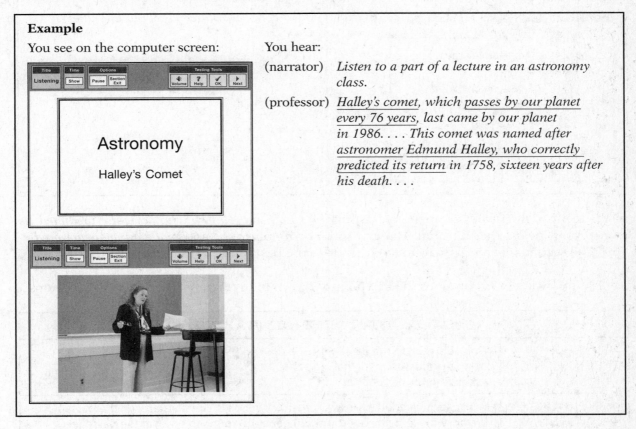

Example

You see on the computer screen:

You hear:

(narrator) *Listen to a part of a lecture in an astronomy class.*

(professor) *Halley's comet, which passes by our planet every 76 years, last came by our planet in 1986. . . . This comet was named after astronomer Edmund Halley, who correctly predicted its return in 1758, sixteen years after his death. . . .*

After you listen to the conversation, the first question and answer choices appear on the computer screen as the narrator states the question. This is a detail question with one correct answer.

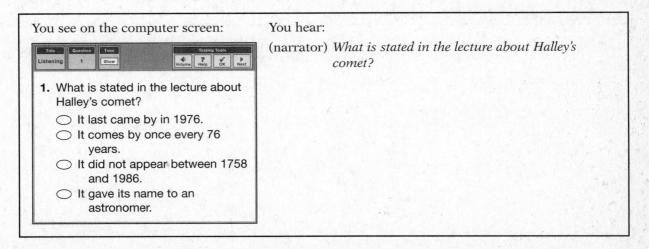

You see on the computer screen:

You hear:

(narrator) *What is stated in the lecture about Halley's comet?*

1. What is stated in the lecture about Halley's comet?
   ○ It last came by in 1976.
   ○ It comes by once every 76 years.
   ○ It did not appear between 1758 and 1986.
   ○ It gave its name to an astronomer.

In the lecture, the professor states that *Halley's comet . . . passes by our planet every 76 years.* This means that *it comes by once every 76 years.* The second answer is therefore the best answer to this question.

Now look at another example of a multiple-choice question about a direct detail. This question has two correct answers.

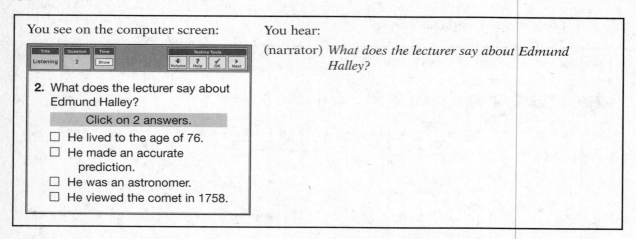

In the lecture, the professor mentions *astronomer Edmund Halley, who correctly predicted its return.* This means that Edmund Halley *was an astronomer . . .* and *made an accurate prediction.* The second and third answers are therefore the best answers to this question.

The following chart outlines the key points you should remember about detail questions.

QUESTIONS ABOUT THE DETAILS IN A PASSAGE	
HOW TO IDENTIFY THE QUESTION	What is **stated** in the passage . . . ? What is **indicated** in the passage . . . ? **According to** the speaker, . . . ?
WHERE TO FIND THE ANSWER(S)	Information needed to answer detail questions is directly stated in the passage. The answers to detail questions are generally found in order in the passage.
HOW TO ANSWER THE QUESTION	1. Listen carefully to the details in the passage. 2. Look for an answer that restates the information from the passage. 3. Eliminate the definitely wrong answers and choose the best answers from the remaining choices.

LISTENING EXERCISE 2: Listen to each passage and the questions that follow. Then choose the best answers to the questions.

PASSAGE ONE *(Questions 1–6)*

Listen as a student talks to an office worker on campus.

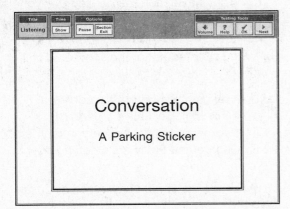

1. What is the student's situation?

Ⓐ She wants to buy another parking sticker.

Ⓑ She needs to pay a parking ticket.

Ⓒ She is trying to get her first parking sticker.

Ⓓ She would like to get a credit card.

2. How is the student going to pay?

Ⓐ With cash

Ⓑ With a check

Ⓒ With a credit card

Ⓓ With a debit card

3. What does the student NOT need to do?

Ⓐ Complete a form

Ⓑ Show identification

Ⓒ Pay a fee

Ⓓ Bring her car

4. Where does the sticker go?

Click on 2 answers.

Ａ On the front window

Ｂ On the back window

Ｃ On the right side

Ｄ On the left side

5. What is stated about parking on campus?

Ⓐ Students may not park in colored areas.

Ⓑ Campus parking areas are distinguished by color.

Ⓒ Areas marked with colors are not for parking.

Ⓓ Parking stickers are marked with different colors.

6. Who parks in which areas?

Click on 2 answers.

Ａ Students use blue parking areas.

Ｂ Faculty and staff use blue parking areas.

Ｃ Students use yellow parking areas.

Ｄ Faculty and staff use yellow parking areas.

PASSAGE TWO (Questions 7–11)

Listen to a discussion by some students who are taking a drama class.

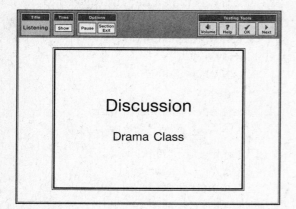

7. When is the students' performance?

  Ⓐ In three days

  Ⓑ In ten days

  Ⓒ In a few weeks

  Ⓓ In three months

8. Which of these is NOT a character in the scene?

  Ⓐ Emily

  Ⓑ George

  Ⓒ Thornton Wilder

  Ⓓ The Stage Manager

9. How familiar are the students with their lines?

  Ⓐ They have not even looked at their lines.

  Ⓑ They have read over their lines.

  Ⓒ They have each memorized their own lines.

  Ⓓ They have each memorized everyone's lines.

10. What is stated about the scene?

Click on 2 answers.

  Ⓐ It takes place before a wedding.

  Ⓑ It takes place during a wedding.

  Ⓒ George and Emily are getting married.

  Ⓓ George and Emily are wedding guests.

11. What are the students going to discuss next?

Click on 2 answers.

  Ⓐ Other plays

  Ⓑ Costumes

  Ⓒ Characters

  Ⓓ Props

PASSAGE THREE (Questions 12–17)

Listen to a lecture in an education class.

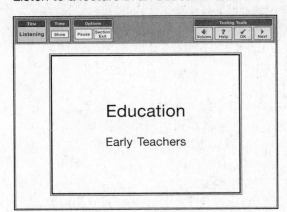

12. Who is listening to the lecture?

   Ⓐ Experienced teachers
   Ⓑ Students of American history
   Ⓒ School administrators
   Ⓓ Future teachers

13. The rules discussed in the lecture relate to what period of time?

   Ⓐ Late in the eighteenth century
   Ⓑ Early in the nineteenth century
   Ⓒ Early in the twentieth century
   Ⓓ Late in the twentieth century

14. What is stated in the lecture about the rules for teachers?

   Click on 2 answers.

   Ⓐ They were quite strict.
   Ⓑ They were established by the teachers themselves.
   Ⓒ They were not just about behavior at school.
   Ⓓ They were considered quite humorous by the teachers.

15. What rules about clothing are discussed in the lecture?

   Click on 2 answers.

   Ⓐ The style of trousers
   Ⓑ The color of cloth
   Ⓒ The length of the skirts
   Ⓓ The type of material

16. What were teachers required to do in the evening?

   Ⓐ Be in school
   Ⓑ Stay home
   Ⓒ Attend meetings
   Ⓓ Leave town

17. Where were teachers forbidden to go?

   Click on 2 answers.

   Ⓐ To stores
   Ⓑ To bars
   Ⓒ To friends' houses
   Ⓓ To ice cream shops

PASSAGE FOUR *(Questions 18–23)*

Listen to a discussion by some students taking a geology class.

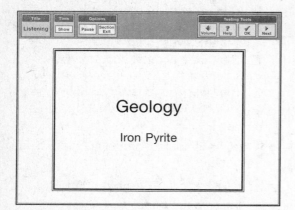

18. In what way is iron pyrite similar to gold?

- Ⓐ In color
- Ⓑ In shape
- Ⓒ In composition
- Ⓓ In reaction to heat

19. Why is iron pyrite called fool's gold?

- Ⓐ Some foolish people wasted time looking for it.
- Ⓑ Some foolish people thought that it was gold.
- Ⓒ Some foolish people preferred it to gold.
- Ⓓ Some foolish people gave it away.

20. What is iron pyrite composed of?

Click on 2 answers.

- Ⓐ Gold
- Ⓑ Sulfur
- Ⓒ Sparks
- Ⓓ Iron

21. How does iron pyrite react to heat?

Click on 2 answers.

- Ⓐ It creates smoke.
- Ⓑ It emits a bad smell.
- Ⓒ It becomes golden.
- Ⓓ It develops a shine.

22. Where did the word *pyrite* come from?

- Ⓐ From a Latin word meaning "gold"
- Ⓑ From a Latin word meaning "fire"
- Ⓒ From a Greek word meaning "iron"
- Ⓓ From a Greek word meaning "fire"

23. How did some ancient cultures use iron pyrite?

- Ⓐ To create gold
- Ⓑ To heat gold
- Ⓒ To start fires
- Ⓓ To reduce odors

LISTENING REVIEW EXERCISE (Skills 1–2): Listen to the passage and the questions that follow. Then choose the best answers to the questions.

Questions 1–7

Listen to a conversation between a student and a professor.

Consultation

Anthropology Paper

1. Why does the student go to see the professor?
   Ⓐ To take a test he has missed
   Ⓑ To get permission to write about a particular topic
   Ⓒ To ask a question about material from the course text
   Ⓓ To ask why certain material has been assigned

2. What is the topic of the paper he wants to write?
   Ⓐ The use of stars in navigation
   Ⓑ Various positions in the Roman military
   Ⓒ The importance of astronomy in ancient Rome
   Ⓓ A method of determining the roles for certain soldiers

3. Why were Roman soldiers asked to count the stars in the Big Dipper?
   Ⓐ To determine if they could use the stars to navigate
   Ⓑ To determine if they were knowledgeable about constellations
   Ⓒ To determine if they could see well at long distances
   Ⓓ To determine if they could count

4. Which of the following is NOT true?

   Ⓐ The Big Dipper is part of a binary star.

   Ⓑ Mizar is part of the Big Dipper.

   Ⓒ Alcor is part of a binary star.

   Ⓓ The Big Dipper contains a number of stars.

5. What two statements describe possible outcomes from the Roman eyesight test?

> Click on 2 answers.

   Ⓐ A soldier would fight as an archer.

   Ⓑ A soldier would fight on horseback.

   Ⓒ A soldier would become an officer.

   Ⓓ A soldier would fight on the front lines.

6. How does the term "survival of the fittest" relate to the test that the student describes?

   Ⓐ The soldiers in the best physical shape tended to survive in battles.

   Ⓑ The soldiers with better eyesight would fight from less dangerous positions.

   Ⓒ The fittest Romans were not in the military and therefore tended to survive.

   Ⓓ Those who could not see Alcor did not survive the Roman military tests.

7. What does the professor finally decide?

> Click on 2 answers.

   Ⓐ That the topic is not related to anthropology

   Ⓑ That the student should not use the topic for his paper

   Ⓒ That the student should concentrate on the concept of survival of the fittest

   Ⓓ That it is possible to use this topic for the paper

PRAGMATIC UNDERSTANDING

Pragmatic understanding questions ask about the more subtle understanding of spoken English than the main ideas and details that are part of basic comprehension. These questions may test the speaker's **function**, or purpose, in saying something. They may also ask about the speaker's **stance**, or attitude, toward a particular subject.

Listening Skill 3: UNDERSTAND THE FUNCTION

In the Listening part of the test, you may be asked about the speaker's function, or purpose, in saying something. This type of question asks you to understand not just what the speaker said but *why* the speaker said it. You may be asked, for example, to determine that a speaker said something in order to apologize, explain, clarify a point, change a topic, indicate a change of opinion, or suggest a new action. To answer this type of question, you must listen to what is said in a particular context and draw a conclusion about the speaker's purpose in saying it. Look at an example of a part of a listening passage.

Example

You see on the computer screen:

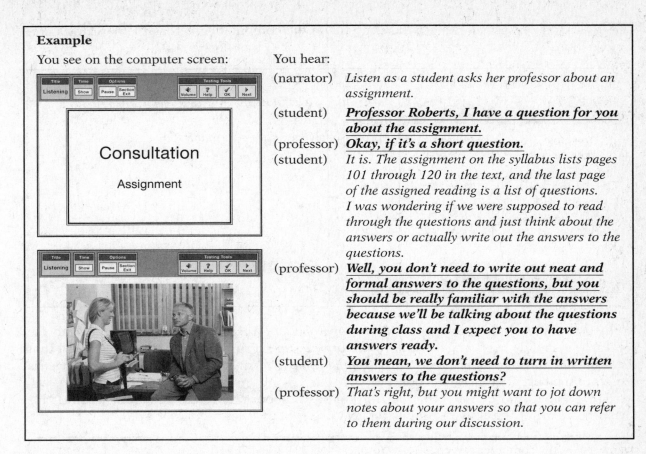

You hear:

(narrator) *Listen as a student asks her professor about an assignment.*

(student) ***Professor Roberts, I have a question for you about the assignment.***

(professor) ***Okay, if it's a short question.***

(student) *It is. The assignment on the syllabus lists pages 101 through 120 in the text, and the last page of the assigned reading is a list of questions. I was wondering if we were supposed to read through the questions and just think about the answers or actually write out the answers to the questions.*

(professor) ***Well, you don't need to write out neat and formal answers to the questions, but you should be really familiar with the answers because we'll be talking about the questions during class and I expect you to have answers ready.***

(student) ***You mean, we don't need to turn in written answers to the questions?***

(professor) *That's right, but you might want to jot down notes about your answers so that you can refer to them during our discussion.*

After you listen to the conversation, a function question asks about the speaker's purpose in saying something. To start this question, a part of the conversation is replayed.

You see on the computer screen:

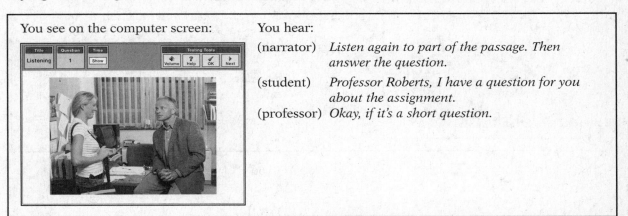

You hear:

(narrator) *Listen again to part of the passage. Then answer the question.*

(student) *Professor Roberts, I have a question for you about the assignment.*

(professor) *Okay, if it's a short question.*

The question and answer choices then appear on the computer screen as the narrator states the question.

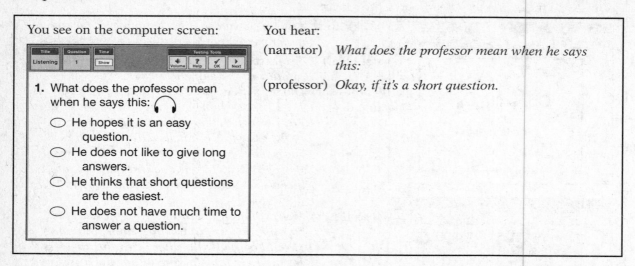

You see on the computer screen:

1. What does the professor mean when he says this:

○ He hopes it is an easy question.
○ He does not like to give long answers.
○ He thinks that short questions are the easiest.
○ He does not have much time to answer a question.

You hear:

(narrator) *What does the professor mean when he says this:*

(professor) *Okay, if it's a short question.*

In the conversation, the student says *Professor Roberts, I have a question for you . . .* and the professor responds by saying *okay, if it's a short question.* From this, it can be concluded that the professor means that *he does not have much time to answer a question.* The last answer is therefore the best answer to this question.

Now look at an example of a question that asks about a different function. To start this question, a part of the conversation is replayed.

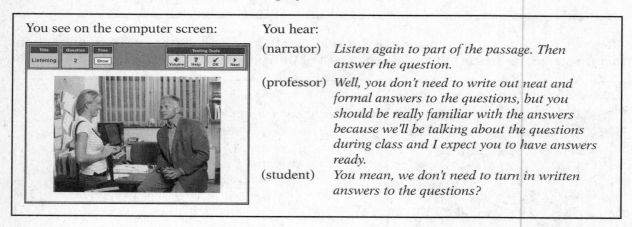

You see on the computer screen:

You hear:

(narrator) *Listen again to part of the passage. Then answer the question.*

(professor) *Well, you don't need to write out neat and formal answers to the questions, but you should be really familiar with the answers because we'll be talking about the questions during class and I expect you to have answers ready.*

(student) *You mean, we don't need to turn in written answers to the questions?*

The question and answer choices then appear on the computer screen as the narrator states the question.

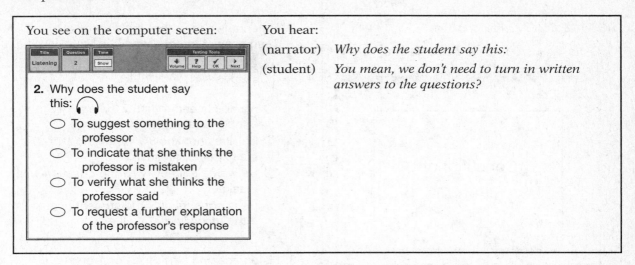

You see on the computer screen:	You hear:
	(narrator) *Why does the student say this:*
	(student) *You mean, we don't need to turn in written answers to the questions?*

In the conversation, the professor says *well, you don't need to write out neat and formal answers to the questions, but you should be familiar with the answers,* and the student responds by saying *you mean, we don't need to turn in written answers to the questions?* From this, it can be concluded that the student said this *to verify what she thinks the professor said.* The third answer is therefore the best answer to this question.

The following chart outlines the key points that you should remember about function questions.

QUESTIONS ABOUT FUNCTION	
HOW TO IDENTIFY THE QUESTION	**Listen again** to part of the passage. **Why** does the speaker say this?
WHERE TO FIND THE ANSWER	The part of the passage that indicates what the speakers says will be replayed for you.
HOW TO ANSWER	1. Listen carefully to *what* the speaker says in the part of the passage that is repeated. 2. Draw a conclusion about *why* the speaker says it.

LISTENING EXERCISE 3: Listen to each passage and the questions that follow. Then choose the best answers to the questions.

PASSAGE ONE *(Questions 1–4)*

Listen as a student talks to a librarian.

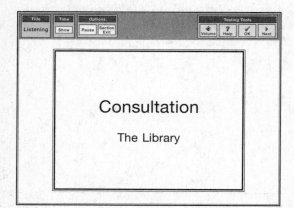

1. Listen again to part of the conversation. Then answer the question. 🎧

   Why does the librarian say this: 🎧

   Ⓐ To show that he is busy with someone else
   Ⓑ To indicate that he is ready to help
   Ⓒ To question why the student is there
   Ⓓ To demonstrate that he is bothered by the question

2. Listen again to part of the conversation. Then answer the question. 🎧

   What does the librarian mean when he says this: 🎧

   Ⓐ He does need to know the age of the magazine.
   Ⓑ He does not know why the student asked the question.
   Ⓒ He wants to know why the question was asked.
   Ⓓ He is not sure why the student needs the magazine.

3. Listen again to part of the conversation. Then answer the question. 🎧

   Why does the student say this: 🎧

   Ⓐ She does not remember what she just said.
   Ⓑ She realizes that she has just interrupted the professor.
   Ⓒ She recognizes that she has just said something incorrect.
   Ⓓ She does not understand what the librarian just said.

4. Listen again to part of the conversation. Then answer the question. 🎧

   What does the librarian mean when he says this: 🎧

   Ⓐ His services are free of charge.
   Ⓑ He has a lot of free time.
   Ⓒ He wants the student to feel relaxed.
   Ⓓ He is always eager to help.

PASSAGE TWO *(Questions 5–9)*

Listen to two students having a conversation.

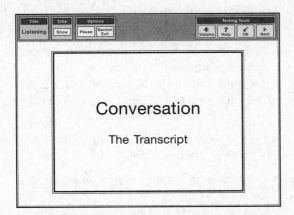

5. Listen again to part of the conversation. Then answer the question. 🎧

Why does the man say this: 🎧

- Ⓐ To show that he knows all the answers
- Ⓑ To show that it is not hard for her to ask a question
- Ⓒ To show that he always asks a lot of questions
- Ⓓ To show that he is happy to help her

6. Listen again to part of the conversation. Then answer the question. 🎧

What does the man mean when he says this: 🎧

- Ⓐ The question is a difficult one to handle.
- Ⓑ He can answer the question easily.
- Ⓒ He knows how to apply for a scholarship.
- Ⓓ He will take care of the transcript for her.

7. Listen again to part of the conversation. Then answer the question. 🎧

What does the woman mean when she says this: 🎧

- Ⓐ It sounds hard to do.
- Ⓑ She does not think she can do it.
- Ⓒ That sounds too easy.
- Ⓓ She can do it all herself.

8. Listen again to part of the conversation. Then answer the question. 🎧

Why does the man say this: 🎧

- Ⓐ To suggest that it is not likely that she will get what she wants
- Ⓑ To show that he thinks she will be lucky
- Ⓒ To state that she can always depend on him
- Ⓓ To imply that it will not take longer than a week

9. Listen again to part of the conversation. Then answer the question. 🎧

What does the man imply when he says this: 🎧

- Ⓐ The registrar's office is closing soon.
- Ⓑ It is best not to waste any time.
- Ⓒ The registrar will be able to tell her about the scholarship.
- Ⓓ He will go to the registrar's office in her place.

PASSAGE THREE (Questions 10–13)

Listen to a group of students discussing information from a zoology class.

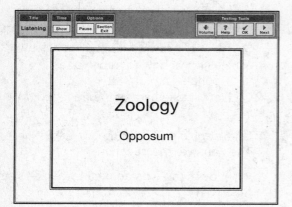

Zoology

Opposum

10. Listen again to part of the discussion. Then answer the question.

What does the woman mean when she says this:

- (A) She thinks that none of them knows what it is.
- (B) She is surprised that she knows what it is.
- (C) She does not need to know what it is.
- (D) She does not know what it is but thinks she should.

11. Listen again to part of the discussion. Then answer the question.

Why does the man say this:

- (A) To show that the woman's statement is not completely correct
- (B) To indicate that he is not completely sure of the answer
- (C) To encourage the woman to try again
- (D) To urge the woman to be more precise

12. Listen again to part of the discussion. Then answer the question.

What does the man mean when he says this:

- (A) "It's not clear."
- (B) "You're mistaken."
- (C) "That's right."
- (D) "It's your idea."

13. Listen again to part of the discussion. Then answer the question.

Why does the man say this:

- (A) To show that he is in a hurry
- (B) To show that he is reconsidering his answer
- (C) To show that he needs to rest
- (D) To show that he is sure of his response

PASSAGE FOUR *(Questions 14–19)*

Listen to a discussion in an astronomy class.

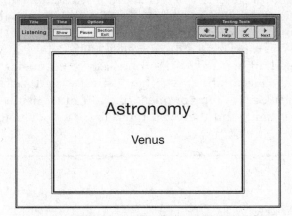

14. Listen again to part of the discussion. Then answer the question.

Why does the professor say this:

Ⓐ She wants to show that the answer is not correct.
Ⓑ She would prefer an answer from a different student.
Ⓒ She wants the student to change her answer.
Ⓓ She would prefer a more definite response.

15. Listen again to part of the discussion. Then answer the question.

What does the professor mean when she says this:

Ⓐ The student should try to be more logical.
Ⓑ The student should explain his answer further.
Ⓒ The student's answer is not correct.
Ⓓ The student should listen more carefully.

16. Listen again to part of the discussion. Then answer the question.

What does the professor mean when she says this:

Ⓐ The students should know the answer.
Ⓑ She is preparing to review something from a previous lesson.
Ⓒ There is no need to discuss this now.
Ⓓ She is in a hurry to finish the lecture.

17. Listen again to part of the discussion. Then answer the question.

Why does the professor say this:

Ⓐ To indicate that she is not sure of the answer
Ⓑ To suggest an answer to a question that she just asked
Ⓒ To propose an alternate explanation to one just presented
Ⓓ To encourage the students to explain why her suggestion is not accurate

18. Listen again to part of the discussion. Then answer the question.

Why does the professor say this:

Ⓐ To show that she wants more information
Ⓑ To change the question that she wants answered
Ⓒ To call on a different student for an answer
Ⓓ To correct something that she just said

19. Listen again to part of the discussion. Then answer the question.

What does the student mean when he says this:

Ⓐ He needs more time to think of the answer.
Ⓑ He wants the professor to call on someone else.
Ⓒ He thinks he answered too quickly.
Ⓓ He wants to change his answer.

Listening Skill 4: UNDERSTAND THE SPEAKER'S STANCE

In the Listening part of the test, you may be asked questions about the speaker's stance, or attitude. This type of question asks you how the speaker seems to feel about a particular topic. Often the speaker does not say directly how he or she feels; instead, you must understand the speaker's attitude from a combination of the words the speaker says, the context in which the words are said, and the way the words are said. You may, for example, be asked to determine if the speaker feels positive or negative, happy or sad, impressed or unimpressed, or enthusiastic or bored about a particular topic. You may also be asked about whether a speaker is doubtful or certain about what he or she is saying. To answer this type of question, you must listen to what is said in a particular context and how it is said, and then you must draw a conclusion about the speaker's stance, or attitude.

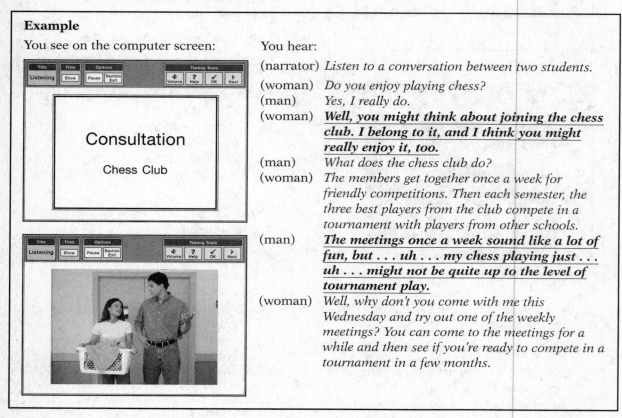

Example

You see on the computer screen:

You hear:

(narrator) *Listen to a conversation between two students.*

(woman) *Do you enjoy playing chess?*

(man) *Yes, I really do.*

(woman) ***Well, you might think about joining the chess club. I belong to it, and I think you might really enjoy it, too.***

(man) *What does the chess club do?*

(woman) *The members get together once a week for friendly competitions. Then each semester, the three best players from the club compete in a tournament with players from other schools.*

(man) ***The meetings once a week sound like a lot of fun, but . . . uh . . . my chess playing just . . . uh . . . might not be quite up to the level of tournament play.***

(woman) *Well, why don't you come with me this Wednesday and try out one of the weekly meetings? You can come to the meetings for a while and then see if you're ready to compete in a tournament in a few months.*

After you listen to the conversation, the question and answer choices appear on the computer screen as the narrator states the question. This is a stance question that asks about the speaker's attitude. To start this question, a part of the conversation is replayed.

You see on the computer screen:

You hear:

(narrator) *Listen again to part of the conversation. Then answer the question.*

(woman) *Do you enjoy playing chess?*

(man) *Yes, I really do.*

(woman) *Well, you might think about joining the chess club. I belong to it, and I think you might really enjoy it, too.*

(narrator) *How does the woman seem to feel about the chess club?*

The question and answer choices then appear on the computer screen as the narrator states the question.

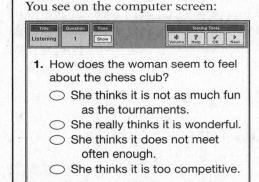

You see on the computer screen:

You hear:

(narrator) *How does the woman seem to feel about the chess club?*

1. How does the woman seem to feel about the chess club?

- ○ She thinks it is not as much fun as the tournaments.
- ○ She really thinks it is wonderful.
- ○ She thinks it does not meet often enough.
- ○ She thinks it is too competitive.

In the conversation, the woman says *well, you might think about joining the chess club. I belong to it, and I think you might really enjoy it, too.* From this, it can be determined that *she really thinks it is wonderful.* The second answer is therefore the best answer to this question.

Now look at an example of a different type of question that asks about the speaker's attitude.

You see on the computer screen:

You hear:

(narrator) *Listen again to part of the conversation. Then answer the question.*

(man) *The meetings once a week sound like a lot of fun, but . . . uh . . . my chess playing just . . . uh . . . might not be <u>quite</u> up to the level of tournament play.*

The question and answer choices then appear on the computer screen as the narrator states the question.

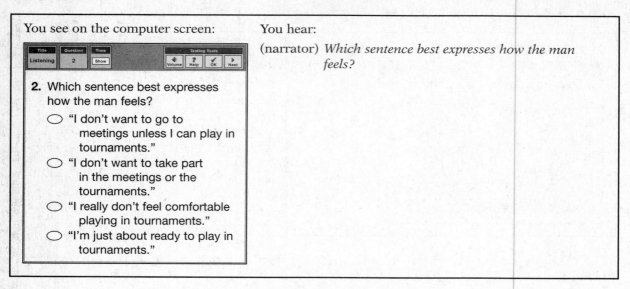

In the conversation, the man says *the meetings once a week sound like a lot of fun, but . . . uh . . . my chess playing just . . . uh . . . might not be quite up to the level of tournament play.* From this, it can be determined that the man would most likely enjoy going to the meetings but would not feel comfortable playing in tournaments. The third answer is therefore the best answer to this question.

The following chart outlines the key points that you should remember about questions on the speaker's stance.

QUESTIONS ABOUT THE SPEAKER'S STANCE	
HOW TO IDENTIFY THE QUESTION	**Listen again** to part of the passage. What is the **attitude, opinion, point of view** of the speaker? Select the sentence that best expresses how the speaker **feels**. What does the speaker **mean?**
WHERE TO FIND THE ANSWER	The part of the passage that indicates what the speaker says will be replayed for you.
HOW TO ANSWER THE QUESTION	1. Listen carefully to *what* the speaker says in the part of the passage that is repeated. 2. Draw a conclusion about *how* the speaker *feels*.

LISTENING EXERCISE 4: Listen to each passage and the questions that follow. Then choose the best answers to the questions.

PASSAGE ONE *(Questions 1–2)*

Listen as an advisor discusses a student's course load with the student.

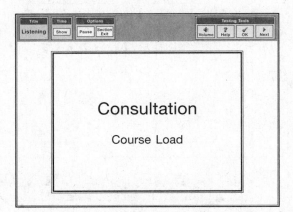

1. Listen again to part of the discussion. Then answer the question.

   How does the student seem to feel about taking the maximum number of courses?

   Ⓐ It is too much work.
   Ⓑ It is the best thing to do.
   Ⓒ It is only done when necessary.
   Ⓓ It is required in graduate school.

2. Listen again to part of the discussion. Then answer the question.

   Which sentence best expresses what the advisor might say to the student?

   Ⓐ "You really need to work harder in your classes."
   Ⓑ "Graduate schools prefer students who take a lot of classes."
   Ⓒ "You should do better work in fewer classes."
   Ⓓ "It's important for you to take more classes."

PASSAGE TWO *(Questions 3–4)*

Listen to a conversation between two students.

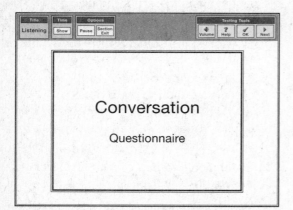

3. Listen again to part of the conversation. Then answer the question.

   How does the man seem to feel about the assignment?

   Ⓐ It will be interesting.
   Ⓑ It will be worth the effort.
   Ⓒ It will be impossible to do.
   Ⓓ It will take a lot of effort.

4. Listen again to part of the conversation. Then answer the question.

   Which sentence best expresses how the woman feels about the assignment?

   Ⓐ This assignment will be enjoyable.
   Ⓑ It will be so hard to do this assignment correctly.
   Ⓒ The assignment will take too much time.
   Ⓓ It will be enjoyable to respond to the survey questions.

PASSAGE THREE *(Questions 5–6)*

Listen to a lecture in a course on Native American studies.

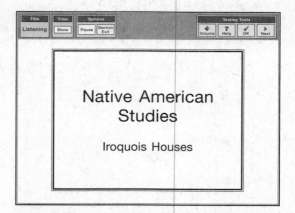

5. Listen again to part of the lecture. Then answer the question.

   How does the professor seem to feel about the design of the Iroquois village?

   Ⓐ It is too simple.
   Ⓑ It is remarkably effective.
   Ⓒ It is overly embellished.
   Ⓓ It is unnatural.

6. Listen again to part of the lecture. Then answer the question.

   Which sentence best expresses how the student seems to feel about the assignment?

   Ⓐ "This sounds like a very creative assignment."
   Ⓑ "It always helps to do your best."
   Ⓒ "This is too complicated to do."
   Ⓓ "This isn't one of my specialties."

PASSAGE FOUR *(Questions 7–8)*

Listen to a discussion by two students taking a meteorology class.

Meteorology

Hail

7. Listen again to part of the discussion. Then answer the question.

How does the man seem to feel about the topic in the beginning of the conversation?

(A) It is easy for him to explain.

(B) He finds it very interesting.

(C) He does not like it.

(D) It does not make sense to him.

8. Listen again to part of the discussion. Then answer the question.

Which sentence best expresses how the man feels at the end of the conversation?

(A) "I can't believe I need to know this!"

(B) "I actually think I understand this!"

(C) "This is impossible for me to understand!"

(D) "I'm sure I already understood this!"

LISTENING EXERCISE (Skills 3–4): Listen to the passage and the questions that follow. Then choose the best answers to the questions.

Questions 1–6

Listen to a discussion in an American history class.

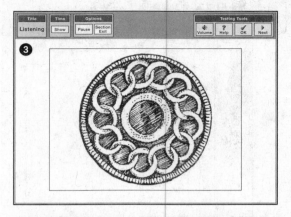

1. Listen again to part of the discussion. Then answer the question.

   How does the professor seem to feel when she says this:

   Ⓐ Satisfied
   Ⓑ Curious
   Ⓒ Tired
   Ⓓ Frustrated

2. Listen again to part of the discussion. Then answer the question.

   Why does the professor say this:

   Ⓐ Because she wants the students to disagree with her
   Ⓑ Because she is trying to confuse the students
   Ⓒ Because she thinks that the students do not know the answer
   Ⓓ Because she believes that this information is correct

3. Listen again to part of the discussion. Then answer the question.

Why does the professor say this:

Ⓐ She is feeling sorry for Sam.
Ⓑ Sam does not seem to know the answer.
Ⓒ Sam's classmates should try to be more helpful.
Ⓓ She thinks Sam has done enough, and she wants to give someone else a chance.

4. Listen again to part of the discussion. Then answer the question.

Why does the professor say this:

Ⓐ To show that she is uncertain
Ⓑ To change the subject
Ⓒ To suggest that she forgot what she said
Ⓓ To correct herself

5. Listen again to part of the discussion. Then answer the question.

How does the professor seem to feel when she says this:

Ⓐ It was good that the young country issued coins.
Ⓑ These words represent the unity of the young country.
Ⓒ The first coin was really the only one the country needed.
Ⓓ The first coin played an important role in unifying the colonies.

6. Listen again to part of the discussion. Then answer the question.

What might the professor say?

Ⓐ "Better preparation is important."
Ⓑ "Quizzes are an important part of this class."
Ⓒ "It's easier to give quizzes than to lecture."
Ⓓ "You're obviously quite prepared for the quiz."

LISTENING REVIEW EXERCISE (Skills 1–4): Listen to the passage and the questions that follow. Then choose the best answers to the questions.

Questions 1–8

Listen to a lecture in a zoology class.

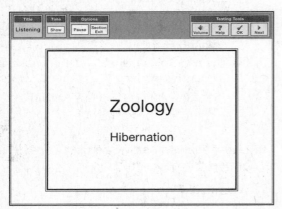

groundhogs

1. Listen again to part of the lecture. Then answer the question.

   What does the professor mean when he says this:
   - (A) The students are late to class.
   - (B) The students are quite calm.
   - (C) The students must stay after class.
   - (D) The students are too noisy.

2. What is the topic of the talk?
   - (A) Why the groundhog hibernates
   - (B) Which folktales relate to hibernation
   - (C) How various animals hibernate
   - (D) Where animals hibernate

3. What is NOT mentioned by the professor as a way that various types of animals prepare for the cold weather?
   - (A) Some build warmer dens or nests.
   - (B) Some head to southern climates.
   - (C) Some increase their activity.
   - (D) Some hibernate, at least partially.

4. Listen again to part of the lecture. Then answer the question.

   How does the professor seem to feel about the ability of the groundhog to predict the end of winter when he says this:
   - (A) He believes in it.
   - (B) He's shocked by it.
   - (C) He's enthusiastic about it.
   - (D) He's unimpressed by it.

5. Which is NOT a good hibernator?
   - (A) A groundhog
   - (B) A squirrel
   - (C) A bat
   - (D) A bear

6. Listen again to part of the lecture. Then answer the question.

   Why does the professor say this:
   - (A) To indicate that Tom should have asked that question earlier
   - (B) To show that hibernation should have been defined earlier
   - (C) To state that the lecture should have been started earlier
   - (D) To indicate that the question had already been answered

7. What happens to body temperature and heart rate during hibernation?

   Click on 2 answers.
   - (A) Body temperature increases.
   - (B) Body temperature decreases.
   - (C) Heart rate increases.
   - (D) Heart rate decreases.

8. What part of the bear most likely warms up first from hibernation?
   - (A) The head
   - (B) The paws
   - (C) The chest
   - (D) The tail

CONNECTING INFORMATION

Questions about connecting information involve a number of ideas rather than a single idea. These questions may ask about the **organization** of the ideas or about the **relationships** between or among ideas.

Listening Skill 5: UNDERSTAND THE ORGANIZATION

Organization questions are questions that ask about how the ideas in the passage are organized. They may ask specifically about how information is organized, or they may ask you to fill out a chart that shows the organization. It is important to understand that this type of question is based on an understanding of the main points and how they are organized rather than on a single point. Look at an example.

Example

You see on the computer screen:

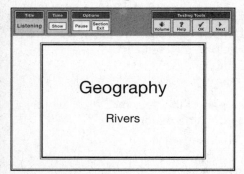

You hear:

(narrator) *Listen to a part of a lecture in a geography class.*

(professor) *Today, I'll be talking about the major rivers of the world. The four longest are the Nile, the Amazon, the Mississippi, and the Yangtze.*

The Nile River in Africa is the longest, at 4,145 miles in length. It flows north from the equator to empty into the Mediterranean and irrigates more than a million acres of land.

The Amazon River in South America is slightly shorter than the Nile at just over 4,000 miles in length. Though it is the world's second longest river, it carries more water than any other river.

Asia also has a massive river system. The Yangtze River in China is Asia's longest at 3,436 miles. Because the mountains at its source are at such a high altitude, the Yangtze flows more rapidly than other major rivers for most of its length.

The Mississippi River is the best-known river system in North America, and it's the United States' chief inland waterway. However, it's not the longest river in North America; the Missouri River, at 2,340 miles in length, is slightly longer than the Mississippi.

After you listen to the conversation, the first question and answer choices appear on the computer screen as the narrator states the question. This is a multiple-choice question that asks about the organization of the information in the passage.

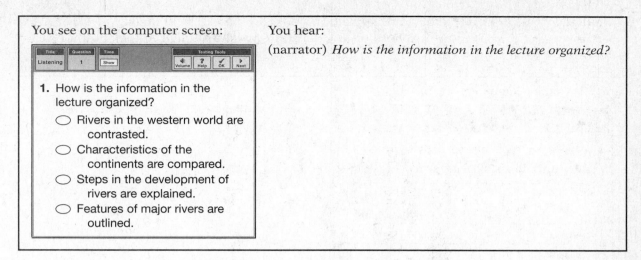

In the lecture, the professor says *today, I'll be talking about the major rivers of the world,* that *the Nile River in Africa is the longest, at 4,145 miles in length,* that *the Amazon River in South America is . . . over 4,000 miles in length,* that *the Yangtze River in China is Asia's longest at 3,436 miles,* and that *the Missouri River, at 2,340 miles in length, is slightly longer than the Mississippi.* From this, it can be determined that the organization of the information in the lecture is that *features of major rivers are outlined.* The last answer is therefore the best answer to this question.

Now look at an example of an organization question that asks what is included in the passage. To answer this question, you must click in the correct column for each term.

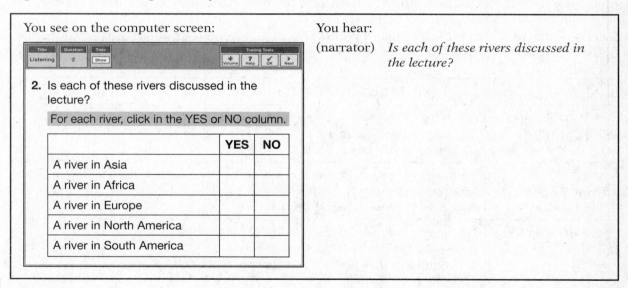

In the lecture, the professor mentions *the Nile River in Africa, . . . the Amazon River in South America, . . . the Yangtze River in China . . . Asia's longest, . . .* and *the Mississippi River . . . the best-known river system in North America.* From this, it can be determined that you should click in the YES columns for *a river in Asia, a river in Africa, a river in North America,* and *a river in South America.* You should click in the NO column for *a river in Europe.*

Now look at an example of an organization question that asks the length of each of the rivers discussed in the lecture. To answer this question, you must click in the correct box for each of the rivers.

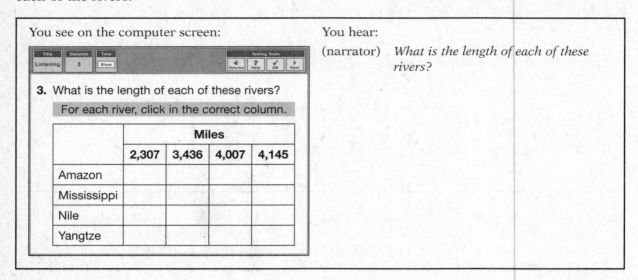

In the lecture, the professor says *the Nile River in Africa is the longest, at 4,145 miles in length,* that *the Amazon River in South America is . . . over 4,000 miles in length,* that *the Yangtze River in China is Asia's longest at 3,436 miles,* and that *the Missouri River, at 2,340 miles in length, is slightly longer than the Mississippi.* From this, it can be determined that the *Amazon* is *4,007* miles, the *Mississippi* is *2,307* miles, the *Nile* is *4,145* miles, and the *Yangtze* is *3,436* miles.

The following chart outlines the key points you should remember about organization questions.

QUESTIONS ABOUT THE ORGANIZATION	
HOW TO IDENTIFY THE QUESTION	How is the information in the passage **organized?** Click in the correct **column . . .** Click in the correct **box . . .**
WHERE TO FIND THE ANSWER	Information to answer organization questions is not directly stated in the passage. It is necessary to understand the main points and draw a conclusion based on the main points to answer the question.
HOW TO ANSWER THE QUESTION	1. Listen carefully to each of the points in the passage. 2. Consider how these points are organized. 3. Look for an answer that shows the organization of the points. 4. Eliminate the definitely wrong answers, and choose the best answer from the remaining choices.

LISTENING EXERCISE 5: Listen to each passage and the questions that follow. Then choose the best answers to the questions.

PASSAGE ONE *(Questions 1–3)*

Listen to a lecture in a biology class.

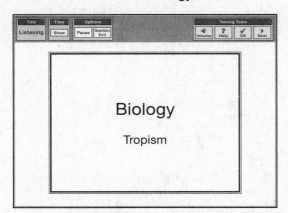

1. How is the information in the passage organized?

Ⓐ Various types of plants are explained.

Ⓑ Various ways that plants respond to stimuli are classified.

Ⓒ Various plants that survive in different environments are described.

Ⓓ Various areas where plants grow best are outlined.

2. Is each of these kinds of tropism described in the passage?

For each item, click in the YES or NO column.		
	YES	NO
The way plants respond to water		
The way plants respond to cold		
The way plants respond to geography		
The way plants respond to gravity		
The way plants respond to height		
The way plants respond to light		

3. What is each of these types of tropism?

For each item, click in the correct column.			
	Phototropism	**Geotropism**	**Hydrotropism**
A response to light			
A response to water			
A response to gravity			

PASSAGE TWO (Questions 4–6)

Listen to a lecture in an archeology class.

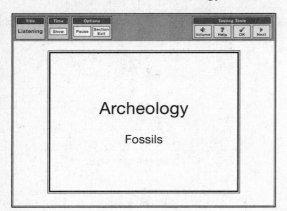

4. How is the information in the passage organized?

   Ⓐ The steps in a process are outlined.
   Ⓑ Various types of fossils are classified.
   Ⓒ The history of a particular fossil is described.
   Ⓓ The formation of plant and animal fossils is contrasted.

5. The professor explains the steps in the process of animal fossil formation. Put these steps in order.

For each step in the process, click in the correct column.				
	STEP 1	STEP 2	STEP 3	STEP 4
Hard tissues become buried.				
The animal dies.				
Minerals replace the bones.				
Soft tissues decompose.				

6. Indicate whether each of these steps occurs as an animal becomes a fossil.

For each statement, click in the YES or NO column.		
	YES	NO
After an animal dies, its hard tissues decompose.		
Layers of sediment cover the remains of a dead animal.		
Minerals from the bones dissolve in groundwater.		
Hard tissue is replaced by minerals.		
Earth movements cause the fossils to move.		

PASSAGE THREE (Questions 7–9)

Listen to a discussion by a group of students taking a law class.

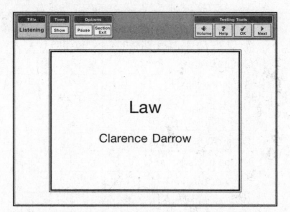

7. How do the students organize their discussion?

    Ⓐ They contrast cases by different defense lawyers.

    Ⓑ They explain how a lawyer defended his clients.

    Ⓒ They talk about examples of different types of cases.

    Ⓓ They discuss a lawyer's cases in chronological order.

8. Do the students discuss each of these cases in which Darrow participated?

For each case, click in the YES or NO column.		
	YES	**NO**
A case involving a railway union president		
A case involving coal miners having an accident		
A case involving the murder of a teenager		
A case involving a high-school biology teacher		
A case involving the owner of some monkeys		

9. The students discuss a number of cases in which Clarence Darrow was involved. What was each of these cases about?

For each case, click in the correct column.

	Railroad strike	Evolution in the classroom	Murder trial
The Scopes case			
The Loeb-Leopold case			
The Debs case			

PASSAGE FOUR (Questions 10–14)

Listen to a discussion in a physiology class.

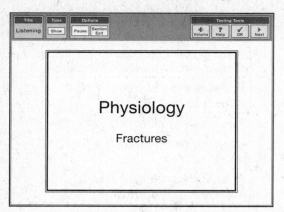

10. How is the information in the discussion organized?

Ⓐ Simple and compound fractures are contrasted.

Ⓑ Various types of fractures are classified according to the number of breaks.

Ⓒ Different ways that bones can break are described.

Ⓓ Medical conditions are categorized according to seriousness.

11. What does each type of fracture describe?

For each type of fracture, click in the correct column.			
	Describes amount of damage	Describes number of breaks	Describes neither
Simple fracture			
Single fracture			
Compound fracture			
Complex fracture			
Double fracture			
Multiple fracture			
Greenstick fracture			

12. How can each type of fracture be described?

For each type of fracture, click in the correct column.			
	Partial fracture	Complete fracture with no broken skin	Complete fracture with broken skin
Simple fracture			
Compound fracture			
Greenstick fracture			

13. How many breaks does each type of fracture have?

For each type of fracture, click in the correct column.			
	One break	Two breaks	Numerous breaks
Single fracture			
Double fracture			
Multiple fracture			

14. How serious is each type of fracture?

For each type of fracture, click in the correct column.			
	Less serious	Serious	More serious
Simple fracture			
Compound fracture			
Greenstick fracture			

Listening Skill 6: UNDERSTAND RELATIONSHIPS

Relationship questions ask you to recognize how different ideas or pieces of information in the passage are related. As you listen to a passage, you should listen to the different ideas that are presented and focus on how the ideas are interrelated. You may, for example, be asked to draw a conclusion, predict an outcome, make an inference, recognize a sequence, or determine the cause for a certain effect. It is important to understand that the answer to this type of question is based upon a number of ideas or pieces of information from the passage rather than on a single detail. Look at an example.

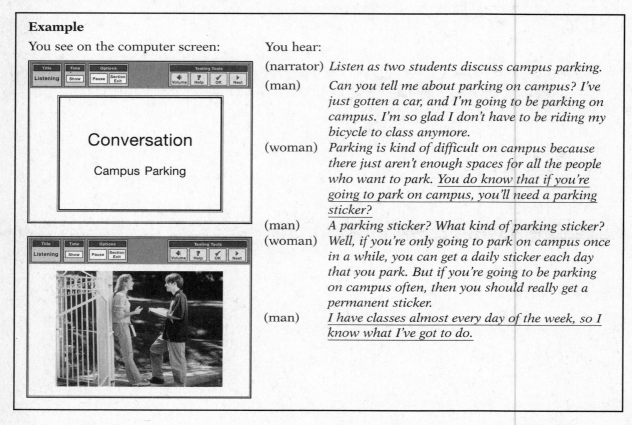

Example

You see on the computer screen:

Conversation

Campus Parking

You hear:

(narrator) *Listen as two students discuss campus parking.*

(man) *Can you tell me about parking on campus? I've just gotten a car, and I'm going to be parking on campus. I'm so glad I don't have to be riding my bicycle to class anymore.*

(woman) *Parking is kind of difficult on campus because there just aren't enough spaces for all the people who want to park. You do know that if you're going to park on campus, you'll need a parking sticker?*

(man) *A parking sticker? What kind of parking sticker?*

(woman) *Well, if you're only going to park on campus once in a while, you can get a daily sticker each day that you park. But if you're going to be parking on campus often, then you should really get a permanent sticker.*

(man) *I have classes almost every day of the week, so I know what I've got to do.*

After you listen to the conversation, a question and answer choices appear on the computer screen as the narrator states the question. This is a relationship question that asks you to predict an outcome.

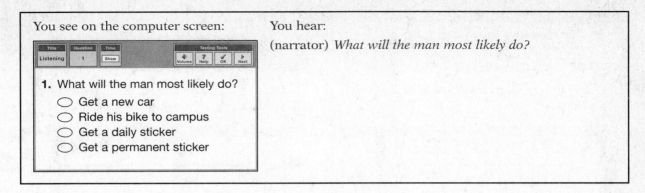

In the lecture, the woman says *you do know that if you're going to park on campus, you'll need a parking sticker* and *if you're going to be parking on campus often, then you should really get a permanent sticker,* and the man replies *I have classes almost every day of the week, so I know what I've got to do.* It can be inferred from this that the man will most likely *get a permanent sticker.* The last answer is therefore the best answer to this question.

The following chart outlines the key points you should remember about detail questions.

QUESTIONS ABOUT RELATIONSHIPS	
HOW TO IDENTIFY THE QUESTION	What is most **likely . . . ?** What is **implied . . . ?** What can be **inferred . . . ?**
WHERE TO FIND THE ANSWER	Information to answer relationship questions is *not* directly stated in the passage. It is necessary to understand the main points and draw a conclusion based on the main points to answer the question.
HOW TO ANSWER THE QUESTION	1. Listen carefully to each of the points in the passage. 2. Consider how these points might be related. 3. Look for an answer that shows how the points are related. 4. Eliminate the definitely wrong answers, and choose the best answer from the remaining choices.

LISTENING EXERCISE 6: Listen to each passage and the questions that follow. Then choose the best answers to the questions.

PASSAGE ONE *(Questions 1–2)*

Listen as a student asks her advisor about a placement test.

PASSAGE TWO *(Questions 3–4)*

Listen as a student meets with his professor to discuss a term paper he is writing.

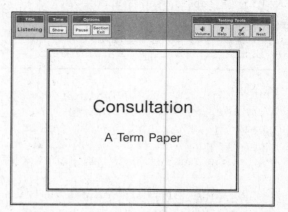

1. What is implied about the math placement test?

   Ⓐ It is really difficult.

   Ⓑ It is required for all students.

   Ⓒ The advisor does not recommend it.

   Ⓓ Not all students take it.

2. What is the student most likely going to do?

   Ⓐ Try to score well on the test

   Ⓑ Take the beginning math class

   Ⓒ Speak to a different advisor

   Ⓓ Skip the placement test

3. How was this meeting most likely initiated?

   Ⓐ The student requested the meeting.

   Ⓑ The student stopped by the office for an unscheduled meeting.

   Ⓒ The meeting happened by chance.

   Ⓓ The professor asked the student to come.

4. What is the professor's overall assessment of the outline?

   Ⓐ There is no room for improvement.

   Ⓑ It is not as good as it could be.

   Ⓒ Nothing about it is right.

   Ⓓ It is too organized.

PASSAGE THREE (Questions 5–6)

Listen to a lecture in a botany class.

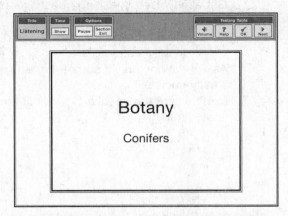

5. What does the professor imply about conifers in the lecture?

Ⓐ The vast majority of the world's trees are conifers.

Ⓑ One reason for the long survival of conifers is their ability to survive drought.

Ⓒ All conifers have needle-shaped leaves.

Ⓓ Some conifers have flowers instead of cones.

6. What are the students most likely supposed to do for the next class?

Ⓐ Outline the material in Chapter 23

Ⓑ Discuss the questions in the text

Ⓒ Turn in written answers to questions

Ⓓ Prepare a written assignment about conifers

PASSAGE FOUR (Questions 7–9)

Listen as a professor talks to a group of students in an economics class.

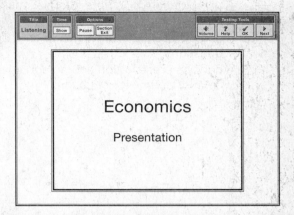

7. What topic would be most acceptable to the professor?

Ⓐ An in-depth analysis of the theoretical model of diminishing returns

Ⓑ A detailed comparison of the theoretical model of diminishing returns and a theoretical model of diminishing marginal utility

Ⓒ An analysis of the failure of National Bank based on the theoretical model of diminishing returns

Ⓓ A detailed comparison of the failure of National Bank and the failure of Independence Bank

8. Which would most likely get a good grade?

Ⓐ A presentation so thorough and long that there are no questions

Ⓑ A presentation full of lots of questions for the audience

Ⓒ A short presentation with lots of time for questions

Ⓓ A concise presentation and an equal amount of time for questions

9. Which of the following would the professor most likely say?

Ⓐ "Get as involved in asking questions as you can."

Ⓑ "Take all the time you want asking and answering questions."

Ⓒ "Ask questions only if something is really unclear."

Ⓓ "Don't waste the speaker's time with too many questions."

LISTENING EXERCISE (Skills 5–6): Listen to the passage and the questions that follow. Then choose the best answers to the questions.

Questions 1–7

Listen to a discussion about a history course.

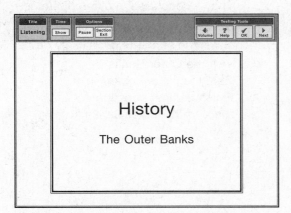

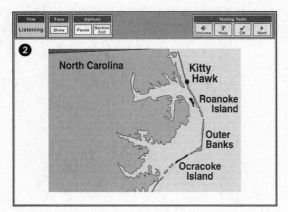

1. What does the discussion focus on?
   - Ⓐ Historical events at three locations
   - Ⓑ A century-by-century history of an area
   - Ⓒ Various ways the Wright brothers proved influential
   - Ⓓ Three different study questions

2. How are the locations presented?
   - Ⓐ In spatial order from south to north
   - Ⓑ In order of importance
   - Ⓒ In the order suggested by the professor
   - Ⓓ In chronological order

3. When did these people live?

For each person or people, click in the correct column.			
	16th century	18th century	20th century
Blackbeard			
Wright brothers			
Lost colonists			

4. With what people are these locations associated?

For each location, click in the correct column.			
	Blackbeard	Wright brothers	Lost colonists
Roanoke Island			
Ocracoke Island			
Kitty Hawk			

5. Do the students discuss these places?

For each place, click in the YES or NO column.		
	YES	NO
A place where a ship was lost		
A place where a colony was established		
A place used as a pirate's hideout		
A place that was attacked by pirates		
A place where there is an airport		
A place where an event in aviation history took place		

6. What can be inferred from the passage about the events selected by the students?

Ⓐ They all involved famous people.
Ⓑ They were not all positive events.
Ⓒ They all took place within the last century.
Ⓓ They all occurred in different states.

7. What will the students most likely do next?

Ⓐ Visit the Outer Banks
Ⓑ Take the history exam
Ⓒ Finish the last question
Ⓓ Discuss the Outer Banks further

LISTENING REVIEW EXERCISE (Skills 1–6): Listen to the passage and the questions that follow. Then choose the best answers to the questions.

Questions 1–6

Listen to a lecture in a botany class.

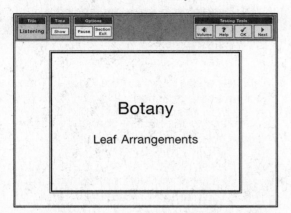

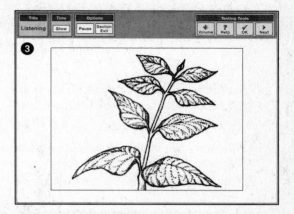

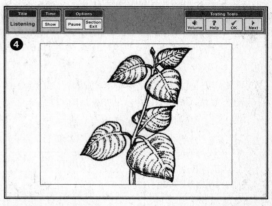

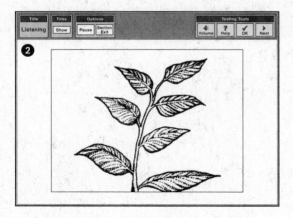

1. Why is the professor discussing leaf arrangements with the students?

   Ⓐ To prepare them for an assignment
   Ⓑ To prepare them for an exam
   Ⓒ To review a completed assignment
   Ⓓ To review an exam that was given

2. What points does the professor want to make about leaf arrangements on plants?

   Click on 2 answers.

   Ⓐ Leaves always appear in even-numbered patterns.
   Ⓑ Leaf arrangements are generally quite orderly.
   Ⓒ Leaves tend to be arranged far away from nodes.
   Ⓓ Leaves tend to be arranged in ways that maximize the light that reaches them.

3. With what type of leaf arrangements are these node patterns associated?

   For each node pattern, click in the correct column.

	Opposite	Alternate	Whorled
One leaf per node			
Two leaves per node			
Three leaves per node			

4. How common are these types of leaf arrangements?

   For each phrase, click in the correct column.

	Opposite	Alternate	Whorled
Least common			
Neither most nor least common			
Most common			

5. What does the professor say about the botanical garden?

   Click on 2 answers.

   Ⓐ It belongs to the university.
   Ⓑ It has quite a limited number of plants.
   Ⓒ The plants in it are not labeled.
   Ⓓ It has examples of all three leaf structures.

6. Listen again to part of the lecture. Then answer the question.

   What does the professor mean when he says this:

   Ⓐ "Class is not over yet."
   Ⓑ "I have something more to say."
   Ⓒ "You need to be careful."
   Ⓓ "Please help me out with this."

LISTENING POST-TEST

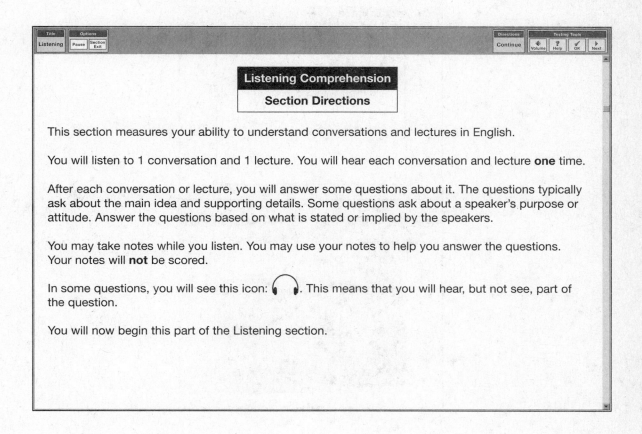

Listening Comprehension

Section Directions

This section measures your ability to understand conversations and lectures in English.

You will listen to 1 conversation and 1 lecture. You will hear each conversation and lecture **one** time.

After each conversation or lecture, you will answer some questions about it. The questions typically ask about the main idea and supporting details. Some questions ask about a speaker's purpose or attitude. Answer the questions based on what is stated or implied by the speakers.

You may take notes while you listen. You may use your notes to help you answer the questions. Your notes will **not** be scored.

In some questions, you will see this icon: 🎧. This means that you will hear, but not see, part of the question.

You will now begin this part of the Listening section.

Questions 1–6

Listen to a conversation between a student and a professor.

1. Why is the student talking with the professor?

  Ⓐ To explain why she missed a class
  Ⓑ To clarify an assignment he gave in class
  Ⓒ To find out which composer she should choose
  Ⓓ To let the professor know what she thinks of the assignment

2. Listen again to part of the passage. Then answer the question. 🎧

  Why does the professor say this: 🎧

  Ⓐ He wants to find out what the student already knows.
  Ⓑ He is not sure exactly what the project is.
  Ⓒ He would like to know which class the student is talking about.
  Ⓓ He does not remember what he said in class.

3. Is each of these part of the assignment?

For each item, click in the YES or NO column.	YES	NO
Learning about the life of a composer the professor has selected		
Studying the writing style of a composer		
Performing a composition written by a certain composer		
Writing a piece of music in the style of a composer		

4. What does the student say about a composer for her project?

Click on 2 answers.

  Ⓐ She has already selected one.
  Ⓑ She would like to choose a different one.
  Ⓒ It is not one that was covered in class.
  Ⓓ She has already done some research on one.

5. How does the student seem to feel about the assignment?

  Ⓐ It seems quite boring and unreasonable.
  Ⓑ She thinks it will be extremely easy.
  Ⓒ It seems interesting but challenging to her.
  Ⓓ She seems quite unconcerned about it.

6. What conclusion can be drawn about the assignment?

  Ⓐ It requires students to develop their own style of music.
  Ⓑ It will most likely result in very similar projects from students.
  Ⓒ It is something that can be completed quickly and easily.
  Ⓓ It involves both research and production from students.

Questions 7–12

Listen as an instructor leads a discussion of some material from a geography class.

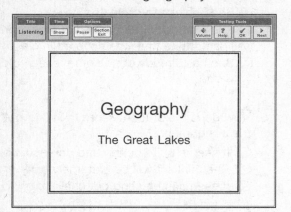

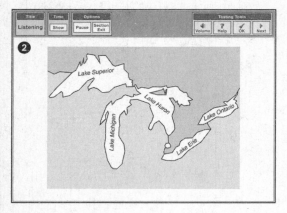

7. What is the instructor's main point?

Ⓐ That there are reasons to support the idea that Lake Superior is not the largest of the Great Lakes

Ⓑ That certain arguments support traditional ideas about the Great Lakes

Ⓒ That there are reasons to support the idea that Lake Michigan and Lake Huron are acting as two distinct lakes

Ⓓ That scientific data demonstrate that the Great Lakes are actually one large lake

8. Why does the instructor say this:

Ⓐ To confirm that the answer the students believe is really correct

Ⓑ To trick the students into thinking that it is a really easy question

Ⓒ To encourage the students to answer quickly

Ⓓ To show that the answer the students believe is correct is not

9. Which of the Great Lakes has traditionally been considered the largest?

Ⓐ Lake Michigan
Ⓑ Lake Superior
Ⓒ Lake Ontario
Ⓓ Lake Huron

10. Listen again to part of the passage. Then answer the question.

How does the professor seem to feel about the student's response?

Ⓐ It needs further explanation.
Ⓑ Nothing was correct in it.
Ⓒ It was exceptional.
Ⓓ He hopes the other students can do better.

11. What is true about Lakes Michigan and Huron?

For each statement, click in the YES or NO column.		
	YES	NO
Their elevation is the same.		
The flow of water between them can go back and forth.		
They are each individually larger than Lake Superior.		
They are each 3 to 5 miles wide.		

12. What can be inferred from the discussion?

Ⓐ That a common conception is not necessarily scientifically accurate

Ⓑ That two lakes can never act as one

Ⓒ That Lake Superior is inarguably the world's largest freshwater lake

Ⓓ That traditional beliefs are never wrong

Turn to the chart on page 545, and circle the numbers of the questions that you missed.

SECTION THREE

SPEAKING

SPEAKING DIAGNOSTIC PRE-TEST

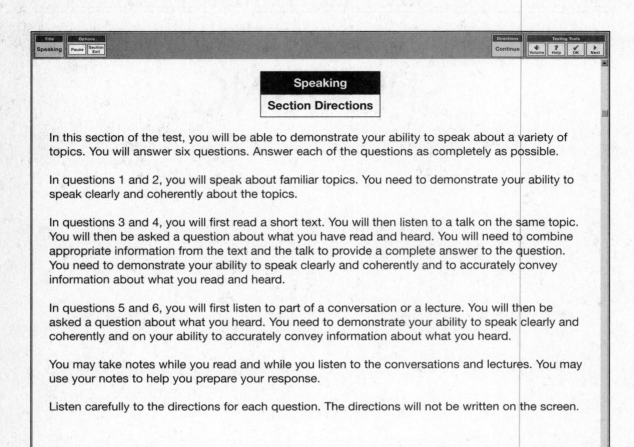

Speaking

Section Directions

In this section of the test, you will be able to demonstrate your ability to speak about a variety of topics. You will answer six questions. Answer each of the questions as completely as possible.

In questions 1 and 2, you will speak about familiar topics. You need to demonstrate your ability to speak clearly and coherently about the topics.

In questions 3 and 4, you will first read a short text. You will then listen to a talk on the same topic. You will then be asked a question about what you have read and heard. You will need to combine appropriate information from the text and the talk to provide a complete answer to the question. You need to demonstrate your ability to speak clearly and coherently and to accurately convey information about what you read and heard.

In questions 5 and 6, you will first listen to part of a conversation or a lecture. You will then be asked a question about what you heard. You need to demonstrate your ability to speak clearly and coherently and on your ability to accurately convey information about what you heard.

You may take notes while you read and while you listen to the conversations and lectures. You may use your notes to help you prepare your response.

Listen carefully to the directions for each question. The directions will not be written on the screen.

Questions 1–6

Question 1
Read the question. On a piece of paper, take notes on the main points of a response. Then respond to the question.

> What are the characteristics of a good teacher? Use reasons and examples to support your response.

Question 2
Read the question. On a piece of paper, take notes on the main points of a response. Then respond to the question.

> Would you prefer to take a vacation in the mountains or at the ocean? Use reasons to support your response.

Question 3

Read the passage. On a piece of paper, take notes on the main points of the reading passage.

Notice from the humanities department

Because so many students have been registering for classes in the Humanities Department for which they have not fulfilled the prerequisites, the faculty committee of the Humanities Department has decided that a new policy will go into effect for the coming semester. This new policy, which was instituted by a unanimous vote of the faculty committee of the Humanities Department, is that all students who want to register in courses other than introductory courses in the Humanities Department must obtain signatures from their advisors before registering in these courses. It is the responsibility of advisors to determine if students have completed appropriate prerequisites before authorizing enrollment in courses.

Listen to the passage. On a piece of paper, take notes on the main points of the listening passage.

Now answer the following question:

How does the students' conversation add to the information included in the notice?

Question 4

Read the passage. On a piece of paper, take notes on the main points of the reading passage.

Nonverbal communication is any kind of communication that takes place without the use of words. It can refer to facial expressions such as smiling or frowning; it can refer to movements of the head such as nodding the head to show agreement or shaking it to show disagreement; it can refer to hand gestures such as offering the hand to shake in greeting or waving the hand to say "hello" or "good-bye." Nonverbal communication can also refer to a whole host of other ways of communicating without words inasmuch as nonverbal communication is limited only by exclusion: it is any type of communication *without* words. Communication is verbal if words are used; it is nonverbal if words are not used.

Listen to the passage. On a piece of paper, take notes on the main points of the listening passage.

Now answer the following question:

How does the professor supplement the information included in the reading?

Question 5

Listen to the passage. On a piece of paper, take notes on the main points of the listening passage.

Now answer the following question:

> What does the man suggest the woman should do to deal with the problem she is having?

Question 6

Listen to the passage. On a piece of paper, take notes on the main points of the listening passage.

Now answer the following question:

> What points does the professor make about echolocation?

After you have completed this test, fill in the chart on pages 546–551.

SPEAKING OVERVIEW

The third section on the *iBT* TOEFL test is the Speaking section. This section consists of six tasks: two independent tasks and four integrated tasks. Two of the integrated tasks combine reading and listening with speaking, and the other two integrated tasks combine listening with speaking. To complete these tasks, you will speak into a microphone and your responses will be recorded on the computer.

- The two **independent** tasks each consist of a question to be answered. The ideas in your responses come from your personal experience rather than from material that is given to you.

- The two **reading, listening, and speaking integrated** tasks each consist of a reading passage, a listening passage, and a question that asks how the ideas in the two passages are related.

- The two **listening and speaking integrated** tasks each consist of a longer listening passage and a question that asks you to summarize key points of the passage.

Because these kinds of tasks are different, there are different strategies for each kind. The following strategies can help you on the independent tasks in the Speaking section.

STRATEGIES FOR AN INDEPENDENT SPEAKING TASK

1. **Be familiar with the directions.** The directions on every test are the same, so it is not necessary to spend time reading the directions carefully when you take the test. You should be completely familiar with the directions before the day of the test.

2. **Dismiss the directions as soon as they come up.** You should already be familiar with the directions, so you can click on Continue as soon as it appears and use your time on the passages and questions.

3. **Read the question carefully, and answer the question exactly as it is asked.** You will be given some time at the beginning of the task to be sure that you understand the question and what the question is asking you to do.

4. **Organize your response very clearly.** You should have a topic statement and supporting details.

5. **Use transitions to make your response cohesive.** Your response is easier to understand if you show how the ideas in your response are related.

6. **Stick to vocabulary, sentence structures, and grammatical points that you know.** This is not the best time to try out new words, structures, or grammar points.

7. **Speak slowly and distinctly.** It is better to speak clearly so that you can be understood than to race through your response so that you will be able to say more.

8. **Monitor the time carefully on the title bar of the computer screen.** The title bar indicates how much time you have to complete your response.

The following strategies can help you on the reading, listening, and speaking integrated tasks in the Speaking section.

STRATEGIES FOR AN INTEGRATED SPEAKING TASK
(Reading, Listening, and Speaking)

1. **Be familiar with the directions.** The directions on every test are the same, so it is not necessary to spend time reading the directions carefully when you take the test. You should be completely familiar with the directions before the day of the test.

2. **Dismiss the directions as soon as they come up.** You should already be familiar with the directions, so you can click on ⏹ Continue as soon as it appears and use your time on the passages and questions.

3. **Do not worry if the material in the integrated task is on a topic that is not familiar to you.** All of the information that you need to plan your response is included in the passages. You do not need any background knowledge to answer the questions.

4. **Read the reading passage carefully.** You will have only a limited time to read the passage.

5. **Take careful notes as you read the passage.** You should focus on the main points and key supporting material. Do not try to write down everything you read. Do not write down too many unnecessary details.

6. **Listen carefully to the passage.** You will hear the passage one time only. You may not hear the passage again.

7. **Take careful notes as you listen to the spoken material.** You should focus on the main points and key supporting material. Do not try to write down everything you hear. Do not write down too many unnecessary details.

8. **Organize your response very clearly.** You should have an overall topic statement that shows the relationship between the reading passage and the listening passage. You should also discuss the reading passage and the listening passage.

9. **Use transitions to make your response cohesive.** Your response is easier to understand if you show how the ideas in your response are related.

10. **Stick to vocabulary, sentence structures, and grammatical points that you know.** This is not the best time to try out new words, structures, or grammar points.

11. **Speak slowly and distinctly.** It is better to speak clearly so that you can be understood than to race through your response so that you can say more.

12. **Monitor the time carefully on the title bar of the computer screen.** The title bar indicates how much time you have to complete your response.

The following strategies can help you on the listening and speaking integrated tasks in the Speaking section.

STRATEGIES FOR AN INTEGRATED SPEAKING TASK
(Listening and Speaking)

---

1. **Be familiar with the directions.** The directions on every test are the same, so it is not necessary to spend time reading the directions carefully when you take the test. You should be completely familiar with the directions before the day of the test.

2. **Dismiss the directions as soon as they come up.** You should already be familiar with the directions, so you can click on `Continue` as soon as it appears and use your time on the passages and questions.

3. **Do not worry if the material in the integrated task is on a topic that is not familiar to you.** All of the information that you need to plan your response is included in the passages. You do not need any background knowledge to answer the questions.

4. **Listen carefully to the passage.** You will hear the passage one time only. You may not hear the passage again.

5. **Take careful notes as you listen to the spoken material.** You should focus on the main points and key supporting material. Do not try to write down everything you hear. Do not write down too many unnecessary details.

6. **Organize your response very clearly.** You should have an overall topic statement that states the main point of the passage and details that support the main point.

7. **Use transitions to make your response cohesive.** Your response is easier to understand if you show how the ideas in your response are related.

8. **Stick to vocabulary, sentence structures, and grammatical points that you know.** This is not the best time to try out new words, structures, or grammar points.

9. **Speak slowly and distinctly.** It is better to speak clearly so that you can be understood than to race through your response so that you can say more.

10. **Monitor the time carefully on the title bar of the computer screen.** The title bar indicates how much time you have to complete your response.

SPEAKING SKILLS

The following skills will help you to implement these strategies in the Speaking section of the *iBT* TOEFL test.

INDEPENDENT TASKS

There are two independent speaking tasks. These two independent speaking tasks are a free-choice response and a paired-choice response.

Speaking Skill 1: PLAN THE FREE-CHOICE RESPONSE

The first and most important step in the independent free-choice task in the Speaking section of the *iBT* TOEFL test is to decode the question to determine what the intended outline is. Independent free-choice questions generally give clear clues about how your answer should be constructed. It is important to follow the clues that are given in the topic when you are planning your answer. You will probably not be given too much credit for a response that does not cover the question in the way that is intended. Study the following question.

Question

Where would you like to be professionally in ten years? Use details to support your response.

As you read this topic, you should quickly determine that you should state clearly *where you would like to be professionally in ten years* and support that statement with details. You will have a little bit of time before you speak to plan your ideas. Study the following plan for the response to the question.

TOPIC STATEMENT: I would like to own my own business

SUPPORT: how I will work toward owning my business
(details):
- will get master's in business (entrepreneurship)
- will work in company while planning my business
- will start my own business when I am ready

In this plan, there is a topic statement about owning my own business and supporting details about the steps I will take to work toward this goal.

The following chart outlines the key information that you should remember about planning the response.

PLANNING THE RESPONSE	
HOW TO DECODE THE QUESTION	Each question in the independent free-choice task shows you *what* you should discuss and *how* you should organize your response. You must decode the topic carefully to determine the intended way of organizing your response. You must include a topic statement and support.
HOW TO DEVELOP SUPPORTING IDEAS	Support your topic statement with the kinds of support that the question asks for (such as *reasons, details,* or *examples*), and try to *personalize* your response as much as possible. The more support you have, the better your response will be.

SPEAKING EXERCISE 1: For each of the following questions, prepare a plan that shows the type of information you will include in your response.

1. What are the characteristics of a good neighbor? Use reasons and details to support your response.

TOPIC STATEMENT: The two most important characteristics are friendliness and helpfulness

SUPPORT: why these characteristics are important
(reasons):
- friendliness because I want to live in a place where people are friendly
- helpfulness because it is important for neighbors to help in times of need

2. What is your favorite holiday? Use reasons and details to support your response.

3. Which person has helped you the most to get where you are today, and how has he or she helped you? Use examples to support your response.

4. If you suddenly got $10 million, what would you spend it on? Use details to support your response.

5. What does your dream house look like? Use details to support your response.

6. What is your favorite food? Use reasons and details to support your response.

7. What are the characteristics of a good parent? Use reasons and details to support your response.

8. If you could live anywhere, where would you live? Use reasons to support your response.

9. What person who is alive today would you most like to meet? Use reasons and details to support your response.

10. Why are your preparing to take the TOEFL test? Use reasons to support your response.

Speaking Skill 2: MAKE THE FREE-CHOICE RESPONSE

After you have planned your response, you need to make your response. As you make your response, you should think about the following three things: (1) you should start with a topic statement, (2) you should support the topic statement, and (3) you should use transitions to show how the ideas are related.

Look at the plan for a response to the independent speaking task on where you would like to be in ten years and a sample response based on these notes.

TOPIC STATEMENT: I would like to own my own business

SUPPORT: how I will work toward owning my business
(details):
- will get master's in business (entrepreneurship)
- will work in company while planning my business
- will start my own business when I am ready

In ten years, I would like to own an import business of my own. Next year, I will be starting a master's program in business with a specialization in entrepreneurship. I will be getting this degree because I hope to start my own business and make it successful some day. After I finish my master's degree three years from now, I will most likely take a position in another company for a few years to make some money and to spend some time planning my own business. Within ten years, I hope to own my own company and be on the way to making it a success.

You should notice that this response includes a topic statement followed by several supporting details. The transitions *in ten years, next year, three years from now,* and *within ten years* are used to show how the ideas are related.

The following chart outlines the key information you should remember about making the response.

MAKING THE RESPONSE	
TOPIC	Start your response with a topic statement that states the main point of the response.
SUPPORT	Include details to support the topic statement.
TRANSITIONS	Use transitions to show how the ideas in the response are related.

SPEAKING EXERCISE 2: Create responses for the independent speaking tasks that you have been working on in Speaking Skills 1–2.

SPEAKING REVIEW EXERCISE (Skills 1–2): Read each question. On a piece of paper, take notes on the main points of each response. Then respond to each question.

1. If you could have any job in the world, what would it be? Use details to support your response.

2. At what age should a person be allowed to drive? Use reasons to support your response.

3. What is the best excuse to give your teacher when you have not done the homework? Use reasons to support your response.

4. What is your favorite day of the year? Use reasons to support your response.

5. What change would you like your government to make? Use reasons to support your response.

Speaking Skill 3: PLAN THE PAIRED-CHOICE RESPONSE

The first and most important step in the independent paired-choice task in the Speaking section of the *iBT* TOEFL test is to decode the question to determine what the intended outline is. Independent paired-choice questions generally give clear clues about how your answer should be constructed. It is important to follow the clues that are given in the topic when you are planning your answer. You will probably not be given too much credit for a response that does not cover the question in the way that is intended. Study the following question.

> **Question**
>
> Do you like to try new kinds of food or eat the same kind of food all the time? Use details and examples to support your response.

As you read this topic, you should quickly determine that you should state clearly whether you like to try new kinds of food or eat the same kind of food and support that statement with details and examples. You will have a little bit of time before you speak to plan your ideas. Study the following plan for the response to the question.

```
TOPIC STATEMENT:    I think I am the kind of person who tries new
                    food, but I am not

       SUPPORT:     I think I am adventurous, but not about food
       (details):   • I like to meet new people, go to new places,
                      try new things
                    • I don't like to try new food
       (example):   • time last week when I went to new
                      restaurant but didn't try new food
```

In this plan, there is a topic statement about the kind of person I am and supporting details and an example about what I really like.

The following chart outlines the key information that you should remember about planning the response.

PLANNING THE RESPONSE	
HOW TO DECODE THE QUESTION	Each question in the independent paired-choice task shows you *what* you should discuss and *how* you should organize your response. You must decode the topic carefully to determine the intended way of organizing your response. You must include a topic statement and support.
HOW TO DEVELOP SUPPORTING IDEAS	Support your topic statement with the kinds of support that the question asks for (such as *reasons, details,* or *examples*), and try to *personalize* your response as much as possible. The more support you have, the better your response will be.

SPEAKING EXERCISE 3: For each of the following questions, prepare a plan that shows the type of information you will include in your response.

1. Do you prefer to be in a large or a small class? Use reasons to support your response.

```
TOPIC STATEMENT:   I think it is better to be in a large class

      SUPPORT:     why I think large classes are better
      (reasons):   • hear ideas from many rather than from few
                   • one student can't dominate larger class
```

2. Would you prefer to go out to dinner or stay home and cook a meal? Use reasons to support your response.

3. Do you think it is better to marry before or after the age of 30? Use reasons to support your response.

4. Do you prefer to take essay exams or multiple-choice exams? Use reasons to support your response.

5. Would you prefer to take a trip by plane or by train? Use reasons to support your response.

6. Would you like to live in a big city or a small town? Use reasons to support your response.

7. Do you think it is better to study alone or study with friends? Use reasons to support your response.

8. Do you prefer to play sports or watch sports? Use reasons to support your response.

9. Would you prefer to go to the opera or to a football game? Use reasons and details to support your response.

10. Would you prefer to take the TOEFL test or a math test? Use reasons and details to support your response.

Speaking Skill 4: MAKE THE PAIRED-CHOICE RESPONSE

After you have planned your response, you need to make your response. As you make your response, you should think about the following three things: (1) you should start with a topic statement, (2) you should support the topic statement, and (3) you should use transitions to show how the ideas are related.

Look at the plan for a response to the independent speaking task on whether you like to try new foods or not and a sample response based on these notes.

TOPIC STATEMENT:	I think I am the kind of person who tries new food, but I am not
SUPPORT: (details):	I think I am adventurous, but not about food • I like to meet new people, go to new places, try new things • I don't like to try new food
(example):	• time last week when I went to new restaurant but didn't try new food

I like to think that I'm the kind of person who is willing to try new kinds of food, but when I get right down to it, it seems that I'm not that adventurous when it comes to trying new kinds of food. I think of myself as an adventurous person; I like to meet new people, go to new places, and try new things. However, whenever I'm given the choice of trying new food or sticking with the regular food I'm familiar with, I seem to avoid new kinds of food. Last week, for instance, my friends wanted to try a new restaurant, and they ordered new things while I ordered the same old hamburger and fries.

You should notice that this response includes a topic statement followed by several supporting details. The transitions *however* and *for instance* are used to show how the ideas are related.

The following chart outlines the key information you should remember about making the response.

MAKING THE RESPONSE	
TOPIC	Start your response with a topic statement that states the main point of the response.
SUPPORT	Include the details to support the topic statement.
TRANSITIONS	Use transitions to show how the ideas in the response are related.

SPEAKING EXERCISE 4: Create responses for the independent speaking tasks that you have been working on in Speaking Skills 3–4.

SPEAKING REVIEW EXERCISE (Skills 3–4): Read each question. On a piece of paper, take notes on the main points of each response. Then respond to each question.

1. If your teacher makes a mistake, is it better to correct the teacher or ignore the mistake? Use reasons to support your response.

2. Is it better to take chances in life or play it safe?

3. Is it better to have a career that pays a lot of money but keeps you away from your family or a career that does not pay so much but allows you time with your family? Use reasons to support your response.

4. Do you make decisions quickly or take your time making them? Use details and examples to support your response.

5. Do you think children should always obey their parents, or are there times when it is not necessary for children to obey?

INTEGRATED TASKS (Reading and Listening) _____

There are two integrated tasks that integrate speaking with reading and listening. These two integrated speaking tasks are on a campus topic and on an academic topic.

Speaking Skill 5: NOTE THE MAIN POINTS AS YOU READ

In the first reading, listening, and speaking integrated task in the Speaking section of the *iBT* TOEFL test, you will be asked to read a passage from a campus setting as part of the task. In this part of the integrated task, it is important for you to be able to read a campus passage of 100–120 words and take notes on the main points of the reading passage in a short period of time. Look at the following example of a reading passage that is part of the integrated speaking task.

Reading Passage

A notice from the office of the university president

The university president would like to make sure that it is perfectly clear to all university professors, administrators, students, and any other members of the university community that university policy requires that no pets be allowed on campus. The only exception to this rule, absolutely the only exception, is animals such as seeing-eye dogs that are trained for use in assisting persons with disabilities. Any other pets, no matter how large or small, are unequivocally not allowed. Anyone who fails to follow this policy, be they faculty, administrators, students, or others, will face immediate action by the university.

As you read the passage, you should take notes on the topic and main points of the reading passage. Look at these notes on the topic and main points of the reading passage.

TOPIC OF READING PASSAGE: notice from university president on policy against pets on campus

main points about notice:
- reminds university community about policy against pets on campus (except animals for persons with disabilities)
- tells campus community that action will be taken against anyone with pets on campus

---

These notes show that the topic of the reading passage is a notice from the university president on a policy against pets on campus; the main points about the notice are that it reminds the university community about the existing policy against pets on campus except for animals used by people with disabilities and that it tells the university community that action will be taken against anyone with pets on campus.

The following chart outlines the key information you should remember about dealing with the reading passage in the reading, listening, and speaking integrated speaking task.

NOTING THE MAIN POINTS IN THE READING PASSAGE	
TOPIC	Make sure that you understand (and take notes on) the *topic* of the reading passage.
MAIN POINTS	Then focus on (and take notes on) the *main points* that are used to support the topic of the reading passage.

SPEAKING EXERCISE 5: Read each of the following passages, and note the *topic* and the *main points* that are used to support the topic.

1. Read the passage. Take notes on the main points of the reading passage.

A notice from campus administration

This campus has a serious problem with bicycles: too many students are parking their bicycles in unauthorized places. Beginning on Monday, November 1, any bicycles left in unauthorized places will be ticketed. Please note that there is authorized parking for bicycles along the east and west sides of campus. Parking of bicycles is allowed only in places where signs are posted indicating that bicycle parking is allowed. In places where no signs are posted, bicycle parking is not allowed.

2. Read the passage. Take notes on the main points of the reading passage.

A message from the university president

It is with a sense of both joy and regret that the university announces the retirement of Dr. Margaret Connor, who has been something of an institution at this university for almost half a century. Dr. Connor will be retiring at the end of the spring semester next year, at which time she will have completed 50 years of service to the university. Dr. Connor came to this university as a graduate student, and then, after completing her doctorate in psychology, she became a professor in the Psychology Department. She has been praised for her commitment to her students over the decades and has published articles and books too numerous to mention. Though she will certainly be missed by the university community, we all wish her well in her retirement.

3. Read the passage. Take notes on the main points of the reading passage.

A part of a class syllabus

Just a word of warning to all of you. I have listed the assignments and the dates they are due here for you, so please pay attention to them. I do not accept late assignments, ever. On the date that an assignment is due, it is your responsibility to get it in on time. No excuses will be accepted, not even serious illness or injury. My strong advice to you is that you get your assignments done early so that you will be able to turn them in on time even if something serious comes up. Your grade on any assignment that is turned in late will be zero, so if you do not get an assignment done on time, do not bother to turn it in late.

Speaking Skill 6: NOTE THE MAIN POINTS AS YOU LISTEN

In the first reading, listening, and speaking integrated task in the Speaking section of the *iBT* TOEFL Test, you will also be asked to listen to a passage from a campus situation as part of the task. In this part of the integrated task, it is important for you to be able to listen to a campus passage of 1–2 minutes and takes notes on the main points of the listening passage as you listen. Look at the following example of a listening passage that is part of the integrated speaking task.

Listening Passage

(woman)   *You saw the notice from the university president?*

(man)   *I certainly did.*

(woman)   *From the tone of the notice, it sounded as if he was kind of upset, don't you think?*

(man)   *I do.*

(woman)   *I wonder why he created this new policy.*

(man)   *Well, it wasn't a new policy. . . . He was just reminding us of a policy that already existed. . . . But, you didn't hear why he put out this notice reminding us about the policy?*

(woman)   *No, I didn't. Did you?*

(man)   *Well, I heard something. This is what some of the other guys told me. They said that one of the professors in the Biology Department has a pet snake.*

(woman)   *A pet snake?*

(man)   *Yeah, a really big one. Anyway, the snake got out somehow, it escaped, and got into the president's office somehow.*

(woman)   *Oh, no!*

(man)   *Yeah, the president got quite a surprise when he sat down at his desk and felt this snake under his desk.*

(woman)   *Okay. Now I see why the president issued the notice.*

As you listen to the passage, you should take notes on the topic and main points of the listening passage. Look at these notes on the topic and main points of the listening passage.

TOPIC OF LISTENING PASSAGE: why the president issued the notice

reasons for issuing the notice:
- policy against pets on campus already existed
- professor in Biology Department had pet snake anyway
- snake escaped and got into president's office
- president wanted to remind campus of existing policy

These notes show that the topic of the listening passage is *why the president issued the notice*, and the details to explain why the notice was issued are that there was already a policy against pets on campus, that a professor in the Biology Department had a pet snake in spite of the policy, that the pet snake escaped and got into the president's office, and that the president wanted to remind the campus that there already was a policy against having pets on campus.

The following chart outlines the key information you should remember about dealing with the listening passage in the reading, listening, and speaking integrated speaking task.

NOTING THE MAIN POINTS IN THE LISTENING PASSAGE	
TOPIC	Make sure that you understand (and take notes on) the *topic* of the listening passage.
MAIN POINTS	Then focus on (and take notes on) the *main points* that are used to support the topic of the listening passage.

SPEAKING EXERCISE 6: Listen to each of the following passages, and note the *topic* and the *main points* that are used to support the topic.

1. Listen to the passage. On a piece of paper, take notes on the main points of the listening passage.

2. Listen to the passage. On a piece of paper, take notes on the main points of the listening passage.

3. Listen to the passage. On a piece of paper, take notes on the main points of the listening passage.

Speaking Skill 7: PLAN THE RESPONSE

After you have noted the main points of the reading passage and the main points of the listening passage in the campus integrated reading, listening, and speaking task, you need to read the question and plan your response.

The question will most likely be about how the main points of the reading passage and the main points of the listening passage are related. Look at the following example of a question in a reading, listening, and speaking integrated speaking task on the notice about the university policy on pets.

Question

How does the information in the students' conversation add to the information in the notice on the university's policy on pets?

You can see that, although the question does not specifically mention "main points" of the reading passage and listening passage, the question is in reality asking you to show how the main points of these two passages are related.

To prepare a plan for your response, you should look at the notes you have taken on the reading passage and the notes you have taken on the listening passage and focus on how the ideas in the two passages are related. Look at the following plan for a response to the integrated speaking task on the university's policy on pets.

Reading Passage = *a notice from the university president*

TOPIC OF READING PASSAGE: notice from university president on policy against pets on campus

main points about notice:
• reminds university community about policy against pets on campus (except animals for persons with disabilities)
• action will be taken against anyone with pets on campus

Listening Passage = *reasons for the notice*

TOPIC OF LISTENING PASSAGE: why the president issued the notice

reasons for issuing the notice:
• policy against pets on campus already existed
• professor in Biology Department had pet snake anyway
• snake escaped and got into president's office
• president wanted to remind campus of existing policy

From this plan, you can see the way that the ideas in the reading passage and the listening passage are related. The plan shows that the reading passage describes *a notice from the university president* and the listening passage provides *the reasons for the notice*.

The following chart outlines the key information you should remember about planning the response in a reading, listening, and speaking integrated speaking task.

PLANNING THE RESPONSE	
QUESTION	Study the question to determine what is being asked. Expect that the question is asking how the ideas in the reading passage and the listening passage are related.
RELATIONSHIP	Look at the notes you have taken on the reading passage and the listening passage, and focus on the main points or topics of each passage. Then describe how the ideas in each of the two passages are related.

SPEAKING EXERCISE 7: Look at the notes that you prepared for the reading passages in Speaking Exercise 5 and the listening passages in Speaking Exercise 6. Read the question for each task. Then prepare a plan for your response. Be sure to note the relationship between the reading passage and the listening passage in your plan.

1. How do the students seem to feel about the notice on bicycles from campus administration?

2. How does the students' conversation add to the information in the message about a certain university professor?

3. What is the students' reaction to the information in the syllabus that is presented in the reading passage?

Speaking Skill 8: MAKE THE RESPONSE

After you have planned your response, you need to make your response. As you make your response, you should think about the following three things: (1) you should start with a topic statement, (2) you should support the topic statement, and (3) you should use transitions to show how the ideas are related.

Look at the plan for a response on the integrated speaking task on the university's policy on pets and a sample response based on these notes.

Reading Passage = *a notice from the university president*

TOPIC OF READING PASSAGE: notice from university president on policy against pets on campus

main points about notice:
- reminds university community about policy against pets on campus (except animals for persons with disabilities)
- action will be taken against anyone with pets on campus

Listening Passage = *reasons for the notice*

TOPIC OF LISTENING PASSAGE: why the president issued the notice

reasons for issuing the notice:
- policy against pets on campus already existed
- professor in Biology Department had pet snake anyway
- snake escaped and got into president's office
- president wanted to remind campus of existing policy

In this set of materials, the reading passage describes a notice from the university president, and the listening passage provides a student discussion of the reasons for the notice.

The notice that is described in the reading passage reminds the university community about a policy against pets on campus, except for animals for persons with disabilities. The notice (also) tells the university community that action will be taken against anyone with pets on campus.

In the listening passage, the students discuss the reasons why this notice was issued. The students say that a policy against pets already existed on campus. (However), a professor in the Biology Department had a pet snake anyway, and the pet snake escaped and got into the president's office. The president most likely issued the notice to remind the campus of the existing policy.

You should notice that this response begins with a topic statement showing the relationship between the information in the reading passage and the listening passage. Two supporting paragraphs follow the topic statement, describing the main points of the reading passage and the listening passage. The transitions *also* and *however* are used to show how the ideas in the supporting paragraphs are related.

The following chart outlines the key information you should remember about making the response.

MAKING THE RESPONSE	
TOPIC	Start your response with a topic statement that shows how the ideas in the reading passage and the ideas in the listening passage are related.
SUPPORT	Include the key points of the reading passage and the listening passage in your response.
TRANSITIONS	Use transitions to show how the ideas are related.

SPEAKING EXERCISE 8: Create responses for the integrated reading, listening, and speaking tasks that you have been working on in Speaking Skills 5–8.

SPEAKING REVIEW EXERCISE (Skills 5–8):
Read the passage. On a piece of paper, take notes on the main points of the reading passage.

Part of the syllabus in a history class

The research paper is worth 40 percent of your grade. What you are to do is choose an event from history and research that event and then write a paper on the results of your research. However, I want you to do something a bit different from a typical research paper. I want you to write about the event from two perspectives, one positive and one negative. What you will find, in the study of history, is that a single event can be described in two very different ways. Thus, for your assignment, I want you to research a particular person or event from two perspectives, one positive and one negative.

Listen to the passage. On a piece of paper, take notes on the main points of the listening passage.

Now answer the following question:

How does the information in the listening passage add to the information in the reading passage?

Speaking Skill 9: NOTE THE MAIN POINTS AS YOU READ

In the second reading, listening, and speaking integrated task in the Speaking section of the *iBT* TOEFL test, you will be asked to read an academic passage as part of the task. In this part of the integrated task, it is important for you to be able to read an academic passage of 100–120 words and take notes on the main points of the reading passage in a short period of time. Look at the following example of a reading passage that is part of the integrated speaking task.

Reading Passage

Isaac Asimov

Isaac Asimov (1920–1992) was an amazing author who wrote an astounding amount of material on an even more astounding variety of subjects. His literary studies included line-by-line analyses of all of the plays of Shakespeare; his historical research included works on the history of Greece, the Roman Empire, England, and France; he also wrote well-researched tomes on physics, chemistry, and astronomy. What he is most likely best known for today, however, is science fiction: his *Foundation* series on a galactic empire inspired by Gibbon's *Decline and Fall of the Roman Empire* and the *I Robot* series about a future society where humans and robots coexist. In total, Asimov wrote more than 500 books on this wide variety of subjects.

As you read the passage, you should take notes on the topic and main points of the reading passage. Look at these notes on the topic and main points of the reading passage.

TOPIC OF READING PASSAGE: author Isaac Asimov

main points about Asimov:
- wrote a huge amount of material (more than 500 books)
- wrote on a wide variety of topics (literary analysis, history, physics, chemistry, astronomy, science fiction)

These notes show that the topic of the reading passage is the *author Isaac Asimov*; the main points about Asimov are that he *wrote a huge amount of material (more than 500 books)* and that he *wrote on a wide variety of topics* including *literary analysis, history, physics, chemistry, astronomy,* and *science fiction*.

The following chart outlines the key information you should remember about dealing with the reading passage in the integrated speaking task.

NOTING THE MAIN POINTS IN THE READING PASSAGE	
TOPIC	Make sure that you understand (and take notes on) the *topic* of the reading passage.
MAIN POINTS	Then focus on (and take notes on) the *main points* that are used to support the topic of the reading passage.

SPEAKING EXERCISE 9: Read each of the following passages, and note the *topic* and the *main points* that are used to support the topic.

1. Read the passage. Take notes on the main points of the reading passage.

The Dead Sea

The Middle Eastern body of water called *Bahr Lut* in Arabic is known as the Dead Sea in English. This body of water is said to be "dead" not because it is the dried-out remnant of a formerly living sea but instead because its high salinity makes it difficult for life-forms to survive in it. The Dead Sea is a landlocked body of water with the Jordan River as its source and no outlet. Its high salt content, which results from the rapid evaporation due to the area's extremely high temperatures, makes it the saltiest body of water on Earth.

2. Read the passage. Take notes on the main points of the reading passage.

Polling

Polling is, of course, a survey of certain people to find out how they feel about an issue or about a candidate for a government post in an election. Polling involves, simply, asking people how they feel about an issue or a person and then tallying the results. When it is not feasible to contact everyone involved to find out what each person thinks because there are, for example, too many people to contact each one individually, then a representative sample of people can be polled and the results of the representative sample can be attributed to the population as a whole.

3. Read the passage. Take notes on the main points of the reading passage.

The Polynesian Migration

One of the greatest migrations in history, one that perhaps is not traditionally given adequate credit, is the Polynesian migration throughout a 20,000-square-mile area of the Pacific Ocean. Around 4,000 years ago, the Polynesians began spreading out to cover the islands that are in a triangle from Hawaii in the north, to New Zealand in the South, and to Easter Island in the east. The Polynesians managed to cover this vast area of the Pacific Ocean using outrigger canoes, which are a type of vessel composed of two tree trunks joined together by a platform on which humans and animals rode across vast areas of the ocean.

Speaking Skill 10: NOTE THE MAIN POINTS AS YOU LISTEN

In the second reading, listening, and speaking integrated task in the Speaking section of the *iBT* TOEFL test, you will also be asked to listen to an academic passage as part of the task. In this part of the integrated task, it is important for you to be able to listen to an academic passage of 1–2 minutes and takes notes on the main points of the listening passage as you listen. Look at the following example of a listening passage that is part of the integrated speaking task.

Listening Passage	
(professor):	*Now I'm sure you're all wondering how Asimov managed to write so much. Well, the simple answer is that he did almost nothing except write because that's what he was driven to do.*
	Asimov's normal routine was to spend time, a lot of time, writing every day. He usually got up at 6 o'clock in the morning; he was at work writing by 7:30 in the morning, and he wrote until 10 o'clock in the evening. That's a lot of time to spend writing. This desire to spend so much time writing prompted Asimov himself to say, "Writing is my only interest. Even speaking is an interruption."

As you listen to the passage, you should take notes on the topic and main points of the listening passage. Look at these notes on the topic and main points of the listening passage.

TOPIC OF LISTENING PASSAGE: how Asimov wrote so much

main points about topic:
- Asimov wrote from 7:30 in the morning to 10 o'clock in the evening
- Asimov said, "Writing is my only interest"

These notes show that the topic of the listening passage is how Asimov managed to write so much; what Asimov did was to write *from 7:30 in the morning until 10 o'clock in the evening daily* and to say *"writing is my only interest."*

The following chart outlines the key information you should remember about dealing with the listening passage in the integrated speaking task.

NOTING THE MAIN POINTS IN THE LISTENING PASSAGE	
TOPIC	Make sure that you understand (and take notes on) the *topic* of the listening passage.
MAIN POINTS	Then focus on (and take notes on) the *main points* that are used to support the topic of the listening passage.

SPEAKING EXERCISE 10: Listen to each of the following passages, and note the *topic* and the *main points* that are used to support the topic.

1. Listen to the passage. On a piece of paper, take notes on the main points of the listening passage.

2. Listen to the passage. On a piece of paper, take notes on the main points of the listening passage.

3. Listen to the passage. On a piece of paper, take notes on the main points of the listening passage.

Speaking Skill 11: PLAN THE RESPONSE

After you have noted the main points of the reading passage and the main points of the listening passage in the academic integrated reading, listening, and speaking task, you need to read the question and plan your response.

The question will most likely be about how the main points of the reading passage and the main points of the listening passage are related. Look at the following example of a question in an integrated speaking task on the author Isaac Asimov.

Question

How does the information in the professor's lecture add to the information in the reading passage about Isaac Asimov?

You can see that, although the question does not specifically mention "main points" of the reading passage and listening passage, the question is in reality asking you to show how the main points of these two passages are related.

To prepare a plan for your response, you should look at the notes you have taken on the reading passage and the notes you have taken on the listening passage and focus on how the ideas in the two passages are related. Look at the plan for a response to the integrated speaking task on author Isaac Asimov.

Reading Passage = *an author who wrote an amazing amount*

TOPIC OF READING PASSAGE: author Isaac Asimov

main points about Asimov:
- wrote a huge amount of material (more than 500 books)
- wrote on a wide variety of topics (literary analysis, history, physics, chemistry, astronomy, science fiction)

Listening Passage = *how the author accomplished this*

TOPIC OF LISTENING PASSAGE: how Asimov wrote so much

main points about topic:
- Asimov wrote from 7:30 in the morning to 10 o'clock in the evening
- Asimov said, "Writing is my only interest"

From this plan, you can see the way that the ideas in the reading passage and the listening passage are related. The plan shows that the reading passage describes *an author who wrote an amazing amount* and the listening passage explains *how the author accomplished this.*

The following chart outlines the key information you should remember about planning the response in an integrated speaking task.

PLANNING THE RESPONSE	
QUESTION	Study the question to determine what is being asked. Expect that the question is asking how the ideas in the reading passage and the listening passage are related.
RELATIONSHIP	Look at the notes you have taken on the reading passage and the listening passage, and focus on the main points or topics of each passage. Then describe how the ideas in each of the two passages are related.

SPEAKING EXERCISE 11: Look at the notes that you prepared for the reading passages in Speaking Exercise 9 and the listening passages in Speaking Exercise 10. Read the question for each task. Then prepare a plan for your response. Be sure to note the relationship between the reading passage and the listening passage in your plan.

1. How does the information in the listening passage supplement the information in the reading passage?

2. How is the information in the listening passage related to the information in the reading passage?

3. What interesting point is provided in the listening passage to add to the information in the reading passage?

Speaking Skill 12: MAKE THE RESPONSE

After you have planned your response, you need to make your response. As you make your response, you should think about the following three things: (1) you should start with a topic statement, (2) you should support the topic statement, and (3) you should use transitions to show how the ideas are related.

Look at the plan for a response to the integrated speaking task on author Isaac Asimov and a sample response based on these notes.

Reading Passage = *an author who wrote an amazing amount*

TOPIC OF READING PASSAGE: author Isaac Asimov

main points about Asimov:
- wrote a huge amount of material (more than 500 books)
- wrote on a wide variety of topics (literary analysis, history, physics, chemistry, astronomy, science fiction)

Listening Passage = *how the author accomplished this*

TOPIC OF LISTENING PASSAGE: how Asimov wrote so much

main points about topic:
- Asimov wrote from 7:30 in the morning to 10 o'clock in the evening
- Asimov said, "Writing is my only interest"

In this set of materials, the reading passage discusses an author who wrote an amazing amount of material, and the listening passage explains how the author accomplished this.

The reading passage explains that Asimov wrote a huge amount of material, more than 500 books in total. (In addition), he wrote books on a wide variety of topic (such as) literary analysis, history, physics, chemistry, astronomy, and science fiction.

The listening passage explains how Asimov managed to accomplish all this work. Asimov wrote all day long, from 7:30 in the morning until 10 o'clock in the evening. (Moreover), he was interested only in writing, saying "writing is my only interest."

You should notice that this response begins with a topic statement showing the relationship between the information in the reading passage and the listening passage. Two supporting paragraphs describing the main points of the reading passage and the listening passage follow the topic statement. The transitions *in addition, such as,* and *moreover* are used to show how the ideas in the supporting paragraphs are related.

The following chart outlines the key information you should remember about making the response.

MAKING THE RESPONSE	
TOPIC	Start your response with a topic statement that shows how the ideas in the reading passage and the ideas in the listening passage are related.
SUPPORT	Include the key points of the reading passage and the listening passage in your response.
TRANSITIONS	Use transitions to show how the ideas are related.

SPEAKING EXERCISE 12: Create responses for the integrated reading, listening, and speaking tasks that you have been working on in Speaking Skills 9–12.

SPEAKING REVIEW EXERCISE (Skills 9–12):
Read the passage. On a piece of paper, take notes on the main points of the reading passage.

The Equity Theory

The equity theory of employee satisfaction in business focuses on comparisons between employees; the basis of this theory is that workers in an organization evaluate their treatment by the organization by comparing their treatment to the treatment of other workers in the organization. According to this theory, workers evaluate their *return for contribution*, what they contribute to the company and what they receive in return for it, and compare their return for contribution to what other employees contribute and receive in return. A worker who receives a return for contribution that is equal to or greater than the return for contribution of other employees will be content, while a worker whose return for contribution is less will not be content.

Listen to the passage. On a piece of paper, take notes on the main points of the listening passage.

Now answer the following question:

> How does the information in the listening passage add to the information in the reading passage?

INTEGRATED TASKS (Listening)

There are two integrated tasks that integrate speaking with listening. These two integrated speaking tasks are on a campus topic and on an academic topic.

Speaking Skill 13: NOTE THE MAIN POINTS AS YOU LISTEN

In one of the listening and speaking integrated tasks in the Speaking section of the *iBT* TOEFL test, you will be asked to listen to a passage from a campus setting as part of the task. In this part of the integrated task, it is important for you to be able to listen to a campus passage of 2–3 minutes and take notes on the main points of the listening passage as you listen. Look at the following example of a listening passage that is part of the integrated speaking task.

Listening Passage

(woman)   Hi, Brett.

(man)   Hi, Karen.

(woman)   You don't look too happy, Brett. Is anything the matter?

(man)   You can tell I'm upset just by looking at me?

(woman)   Yeah, it's pretty obvious. You want to tell me what's bothering you?

(man)   Well, it's that I'm having trouble in my economics class, and I just talked to the professor. She didn't seem too sympathetic.

(woman)   She didn't? What's the problem?

(man)   Well, it's that I'm on the baseball team.

(woman)   I know. I've seen you play. But what does that have to do with your economics class?

(man)   It's the away games. That's the problem. The away games are all on the weekend, but usually when we're traveling to another school for a weekend game, we leave on Friday. The team bus usually leaves about noon on Friday.

(woman)   And that has something to do with your economics class?

(man)   Yeah, my economics class meets on Mondays, Wednesdays, and Fridays, in the afternoon.

(woman)   I see. So you miss your economics class once in a while on Friday afternoons?

(man)   Not just once in a while. It's been every Friday for the last four weeks.

(woman)   And you talked to your economics professor about this?

(man)   Yes, I did. And I told her <u>why</u> I missed class on Fridays.

(woman)   But she wasn't very sympathetic you said.

(man)   She wasn't sympathetic at all.

(woman)   I think that's because you've missed so many classes. . . . Listen, have you thought about switching to a different section of the class? I think there's another section of the same class on Tuesdays and Thursdays.

(man)   I hadn't thought about that. Maybe that would be something to consider, since my professor's not at all happy that I miss class so much.

As you listen to the passage, you should take notes on the topic and main points of the listening passage. Look at these notes on the topic and main points of the listening passage.

> TOPIC OF LISTENING PASSAGE: problem man is having with economics class
>
> main points about problem:
> - man is missing economics class on Fridays because he is on baseball team
> - woman suggests changing to a different section of economics class that does not meet on Fridays

These notes show that the topic of the listening passage is a problem that the man is having in his economics class, and the main points about this topic are that the man is missing his economics class on Fridays because he is on the baseball team, and the woman suggests that he change to a different section of the economics class, one that does not meet on Fridays.

The following chart outlines the key information you should remember about dealing with the listening passage in the integrated speaking task.

NOTING THE MAIN POINTS IN THE LISTENING PASSAGE	
TOPIC	Make sure that you understand (and take notes on) the *topic* of the listening passage.
MAIN POINTS	Then focus on (and take notes on) the *main points* that are used to support the topic of the listening passage.

SPEAKING EXERCISE 13: Listen to each of the following passages, and note the *topic* and the *main points* that are used to support the topic.

1. Listen to the passage. On a piece of paper, take notes on the main points of the listening passage.

2. Listen to the passage. On a piece of paper, take notes on the main points of the listening passage.

3. Listen to the passage. On a piece of paper, take notes on the main points of the listening passage.

Speaking Skill 14: PLAN THE RESPONSE

After you have noted the main points of the listening passage in the campus integrated listening and speaking task, you need to read the question and plan your response.

The question will most likely be about the main points of the listening passage. Look at the following example of a question in an integrated speaking task on a problem the man is having in his economics class.

Question

How does the woman react to the man's problem?

You can see that, although the question does not specifically mention "main points" of the listening passage, the question is in reality asking you what the main points of the passage are.

To prepare a plan for your response, you should look at the notes you have taken on the listening passage and focus on the main points of the passage. Look at the plan for a response on the integrated speaking task on the problem the man is having in his economics class.

Listening Passage = *a woman's reaction to a man's problem*

TOPIC OF READING PASSAGE: *problem man is having with economics class*

main points about problem:
* *man is missing economics class on Fridays because he is on baseball team*
* *woman suggests changing to a different section of economics class that does not meet on Fridays*

From this plan, you can see the way that the listening passage is about *a woman's reaction to a man's problem*.

The following chart outlines the key information you should remember about planning the response in an integrated speaking task.

PLANNING THE RESPONSE	
QUESTION	Study the question to determine what is being asked. Expect that the question is asking about the main ideas of the listening passage.
FOCUS	Look at the notes you have taken on the listening passage, and focus on the main points of the passage. Then describe the main points of the listening passage.

SPEAKING EXERCISE 14: Look at the notes that you prepared for the listening passages in Speaking Exercise 13. Read the question for each task. Then prepare a plan for your response. Be sure to note the main points of the listening passage.

1. How does the woman seem to feel about the information she gets from the man?

2. How does the woman suggest that the man change his study habits?

3. How does the man respond to the woman's question about an independent study project?

Speaking Skill 15: MAKE THE RESPONSE

After you have planned your response, you need to make your response. As you make your response, you should think about the following three things: (1) you should start with a topic statement, (2) you should support the topic statement, and (3) you should use transitions to show how the ideas are related.

Look at the plan for a response to the independent speaking task on a problem the man is having in his economics class and a sample response based on these notes.

Listening Passage = *a woman's reaction to a man's problem*

TOPIC OF READING PASSAGE: problem man is having with economics class

main points about problem:
- man is missing economics class on Fridays because he is on baseball team
- woman suggests changing to a different section of economics class that does not meet on Fridays

---

    In this listening passage, two students discuss a problem the man has with his economics class. First, the man explains that he has the problem that he is missing his economics class on Fridays because he is on the baseball team and he travels to away games on Fridays. Then, after the woman understands this problem, she suggests that he change to a different section of economics class, one that does not meet on Fridays.

You should notice that this response includes a topic statement followed by several supporting details. The transitions *first* and *then* are used to show how the ideas are related.

The following chart outlines the key information you should remember about making the response.

MAKING THE RESPONSE	
TOPIC	Start your response with a topic statement that states the main point of the response.
SUPPORT	Include details to support the topic statement.
TRANSITIONS	Use transitions to show how the ideas in the response are related.

SPEAKING EXERCISE 15: Create responses for the independent speaking tasks that you have been working on in Speaking Skills 13–15.

SPEAKING REVIEW EXERCISE (Skills 13–15):

Listen to the passage. On a piece of paper, take notes on the main points of the listening passage.

Now answer the following question:

What does the woman suggest the man can do to deal with his problem?

Speaking Skill 16: NOTE THE MAIN POINTS AS YOU LISTEN

In the second listening and speaking integrated task in the Speaking section of the *iBT* TOEFL test, you will be asked to listen to an academic passage as part of the task. In this part of the integrated task, it is important for you to be able to listen to an academic passage of 2–3 minutes and take notes on the main points of the listening passage as you listen. Look at the following example of a listening passage that is part of the integrated speaking task.

Listening Passage

(professor)   *Today, I'm going to talk about certain types of political characters. One of these types of political characters is called a Hamlet, you know, after the character in the Shakespeare play.*

In Shakespeare's play, Hamlet was a tragic figure, one who spent a lot of time anguishing over what to do in a particularly terrible situation; Hamlet learned that his uncle had murdered Hamlet's father. Hamlet considered what to do in this situation and then he considered still more. He anguished over the decision, he vacillated back and forth, and he anguished some more over the decision.

In political terms, a Hamlet is someone who goes through this sort of decision-making process. A Hamlet is someone who, when faced with a decision, tends to overthink problems, to vacillate, to find it difficult to come to a decision.

As you listen to the passage, you should take notes on the topic and main points of the listening passage. Look at these notes on the topic and main points of the listening passage.

TOPIC OF LISTENING PASSAGE: a type of political character known as a Hamlet

details about a Hamlet:
- Hamlet in Shakespeare's play faced a difficult decision and had a hard time coming to a decision
- a political Hamlet is someone who has a hard time coming to a difficult decision

---

These notes show that the topic of the listening passage is *a type of political character known as a Hamlet,* and the details about a Hamlet are that the character named *Hamlet in Shakespeare's play faced a difficult decision and had a hard time coming to a decision,* and that a political Hamlet is someone who also has a hard time coming to a difficult decision.

The following chart outlines the key information you should remember about dealing with the listening passage in the integrated speaking task.

NOTING THE MAIN POINTS IN THE LISTENING PASSAGE	
TOPIC	Make sure that you understand (and take notes on) the *topic* of the listening passage.
MAIN POINTS	Then focus on (and take notes on) the *main points* that are used to support the topic of the listening passage.

SPEAKING EXERCISE 16: Listen to each of the following passages, and note the *topic* and the *main points* that are used to support the topic.

1. Listen to the passage. On a piece of paper, take notes on the main points of the listening passage.

2. Listen to the passage. On a piece of paper, take notes on the main points of the listening passage.

3. Listen to the passage. On a piece of paper, take notes on the main points of the listening passage.

Speaking Skill 17: PLAN THE RESPONSE

After you have noted the main points of the listening passage in the academic integrated listening and speaking task, you need to read the question and plan your response.

The question will most likely be about the main points of the listening passage. Look at the following example of a question in an integrated speaking task on a political character called a Hamlet.

Question

How is a certain type of political character described in the lecture?

You can see that, although the question does not specifically mention "main points" of the listening passage, the question is in reality asking you what the main points of the passage are.

To prepare a plan for your response, you should look at the notes you have taken on the listening passage and focus on the main points of the passage. Look at the plan for a response on the integrated speaking task on a certain type of political character.

Listening Passage = *a description of a political character*

TOPIC OF READING PASSAGE: a type of political character known as a Hamlet

details about a Hamlet:
- Hamlet in Shakespeare's play faced a difficult decision and had a hard time coming to a decision
- a political Hamlet is someone who has a hard time coming to a difficult decision

---

From this plan, you can see the way that the listening passage is about a *description of a political character.*

The following chart outlines the key information you should remember about planning the response in an integrated speaking task.

PLANNING THE RESPONSE	
QUESTION	Study the question to determine what is being asked. Expect that the question is asking about the main ideas of the listening passage.
FOCUS	Look at the notes you have taken on the listening passage, and focus on the main points of the passage. Then describe the main points of the listening passage.

SPEAKING EXERCISE 17: Look at the notes that you prepared for the listening passages in Speaking Exercise 16. Read the question for each task. Then prepare a plan for your response. Be sure to note the main points of the listening passage.

1. What can one learn from the listening passage about the Bank Holiday of 1933?

2. What can be learned from the listening passage about a definition of creativity?

3. According to the listening passage, how did the Amazon get its name?

Speaking Skill 18: MAKE THE RESPONSE

After you have planned your response, you need to make your response. As you make your response, you should think about the following three things: (1) you should start with a topic statement, (2) you should support the topic statement, and (3) you should use transitions to show how the ideas are related.

Look at the plan for a response to the independent speaking task on a certain political character and a sample response based on these notes.

Listening Passage = *a description of a political character*

TOPIC OF READING PASSAGE: *a type of political character known as a Hamlet*

details about a Hamlet:
- Hamlet in Shakespeare's play faced a difficult decision and had a hard time coming to a decision
- a political Hamlet is someone who has a hard time coming to a difficult decision

---

In this listening passage, the professor discusses a certain type of political character that is know as a Hamlet. Hamlet was a character in a play by Shakespeare, and in the play Hamlet faced a difficult decision and had a hard time coming to a decision. A political person who has a hard time coming to a difficult decision can therefore be called a Hamlet.

You should notice that this response includes a topic statement followed by several supporting details. The transition *therefore* is used to show how the ideas are related.

The following chart outlines the key information you should remember about making the response.

MAKING THE RESPONSE	
TOPIC	Start your response with a topic statement that states the main point of the response.
SUPPORT	Include details to support the topic statement.
TRANSITIONS	Use transitions to show how the ideas in the response are related.

SPEAKING EXERCISE 18: Create responses for the independent speaking tasks that you have been working on in Speaking Skills 16–18.

SPEAKING REVIEW EXERCISE (Skills 16–18):
Listen to the passage. On a piece of paper, take notes on the main points of the listening passage.

Now answer the following question:

What points does the professor make about SAD?

SPEAKING POST-TEST

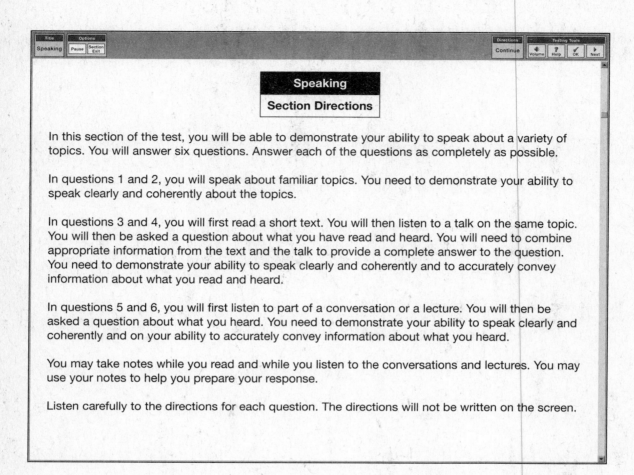

Speaking

Section Directions

In this section of the test, you will be able to demonstrate your ability to speak about a variety of topics. You will answer six questions. Answer each of the questions as completely as possible.

In questions 1 and 2, you will speak about familiar topics. You need to demonstrate your ability to speak clearly and coherently about the topics.

In questions 3 and 4, you will first read a short text. You will then listen to a talk on the same topic. You will then be asked a question about what you have read and heard. You will need to combine appropriate information from the text and the talk to provide a complete answer to the question. You need to demonstrate your ability to speak clearly and coherently and to accurately convey information about what you read and heard.

In questions 5 and 6, you will first listen to part of a conversation or a lecture. You will then be asked a question about what you heard. You need to demonstrate your ability to speak clearly and coherently and on your ability to accurately convey information about what you heard.

You may take notes while you read and while you listen to the conversations and lectures. You may use your notes to help you prepare your response.

Listen carefully to the directions for each question. The directions will not be written on the screen.

Questions 1–6

Question 1
Read the question. On a piece of paper, take notes on the main points of a response. Then respond to the question.

Which person who is living today do you admire most? Use reasons to support your response.

Question 2
Read the question. On a piece of paper, take notes on the main points of a response. Then respond to the question.

Is it better to learn about the news from newspapers or from television?

Question 3

Read the passage. On a piece of paper, take notes on the main points of the reading passage.

Notice from university food services

University Food Services is sorry to notify any students holding meal cards that the main cafeteria will be closed until November 1. It has been necessary to close the main cafeteria for the week of October 24 to November 1 in order to make much-needed repairs. During the period that the main cafeteria is closed, any students who have meal cards may use their meal cards at the three snack bars on campus. We recognize that this arrangement will be inconvenient both for students holding meal cards and for students who regularly purchase meals at the three snack bars. Please accept our sincere apologies for this inconvenience.

Listen to the passage. On a piece of paper, take notes on the main points of the listening passage.

Now answer the following question:

How does the information in the listening passage add to the information included in the reading passage?

Question 4

Read the passage. On a piece of paper, take notes on the main points of the reading passage.

Social Environments

It is important for an effective teacher to recognize that various types of social environments can be established in the classroom based upon the goals that are to be met. Three of the major types of social environments that an effective teacher can work to establish are a cooperative environment, a competitive environment, and an individualistic environment. In a cooperative social environment in the classroom, the students work together to complete tasks. In a competitive social environment, students try to come up with better answers more quickly or efficiently than other students. In an individualistic social environment, students work by themselves to come up with the best answers that they can working alone.

Listen to the passage. On a piece of paper, take notes on the main points of the listening passage.

Now answer the following question:

How does the information in the listening passage supplement the information in the reading passage?

Question 5

Listen to the passage. On a piece of paper, take notes on the main points of the listening passage.

Now answer the following question:

How does the man feel about the problem the woman has?

Question 6

Listen to the passage. On a piece of paper, take notes on the main points of the listening passage.

Now answer the following question:

What points does the professor make about the planet Mars?

After you have completed this test, fill in the chart on pages 546–551.

WRITING

WRITING DIAGNOSTIC PRE-TEST

Writing
Section Directions

This section measures your ability to use writing to communicate in an academic environment. There will be two writing tasks.

For the first writing task, you will read a passage and listen to a lecture and then answer a question based on what you have read and heard. For the second task, you will answer a question based on your own knowledge and experience.

Integrated Writing Directions

For the first task, you will read a passage about an academic topic. You will have **3 minutes** to read the passage. You may take notes on the passage while you read. The passage will then be removed and you will listen to a lecture about the same topic. While you listen, you may also take notes.

Then you will write a response to a question that asks you about the relationship between the lecture you heard and the reading passage. Try to answer the question as completely as possible using information from the reading passage and the lecture. The question does **not** ask you to express your personal opinion. You will be able to see the reading passage again when it is time for you to write. You may use your notes to help you answer the question. You will have **20 minutes** to write your response.

Typically, an effective response will be 150 to 225 words. You need to demonstrate your ability to write well and to provide complete and accurate content.

Remember you can look at the passage again when you write your response. Immediately after the reading time ends, the lecture begins.

Independent Writing Directions

For the second task, you will write an essay in response to a question that asks you to state, explain, and support your opinion on an issue. You will have **30 minutes** to plan, write, and revise your response.

Typically, an effective essay will contain a minimum of 300 words. You need to demonstrate your ability to write well. This includes the development of your ideas, the organization of your essay, and the quality and accuracy of the language you use to express your ideas.

Question 1

Read the passage. On a piece of paper, take notes on the main points of the reading passage.

Reading Time: 3 minutes

A truly amazing characteristic of human memory is that all people seem to experience a certain type of very specific amnesia, or the inability to remember events that have occurred in their lives. This particular kind of amnesia, which is apparently experienced quite universally, is the inability to remember events that took place in the first few years of life; even though the first few years of life are a time when learning is at its highest and tremendous amounts of information are learned, people seem to remember basically nothing from this period. When Freud first noted this interesting aspect of memory in 1905, he referred to it as **childhood amnesia**.

Since the time that Freud first noted this phenomenon, numerous studies have been conducted to learn about it, and the results of these studies are that people tend not to remember anything from the first three to five years of their lives. A possible difficulty in this type of study is that one cannot simply ask people if they remember events from the first five years of life because they may think that they remember things, but there is no way to check whether the remembered events actually occurred. Even when this difficulty is overcome in experiments, at least somewhat, by testing whether or not subjects can remember events that have been well documented from childhood, such as family celebrations or births of siblings, the results remain constant, that people tend not to remember anything from the first three to five years of life.

Listen to the passage. On a piece of paper, take notes on the main points of the listening passage.

Now answer the following question:

How does the information in the listening passage add to the ideas presented in the reading passage?

Preparation Time: 1 minute
Response Time: 20 minutes

Question 2

Read the question. On a piece of paper, take notes on the main points of a response. Then write your response.

What recent news story has affected you the most? In what ways has it affected you? Use reasons and examples to support your response.

Response Time: 30 minutes

After you have completed this test, fill in the chart on pages 552–553.

WRITING OVERVIEW

The last section on the *iBT* TOEFL test is the Writing section. This section consists of two tasks, one integrated task and one independent task. You write your responses to these two tasks on the computer.

- The **integrated** task consists of a 250–300 word reading passage and a 1–2 minute lecture on the same academic topic. The information in the reading passage and the information in the listening passage are related, but the listening passage does not simply repeat what is in the reading passage. You take notes on the information in each of the passages, and then you must write a 100–200 word response about how the information in the two passages is related.

- The **independent** task consists of an essay topic. You must write an essay on the topic that is given. The ideas in your essay come from your personal experience rather than from material that is given to you.

Because these tasks are different, there are different strategies for each task. The following strategies can help you on the integrated task in the Writing section.

STRATEGIES FOR THE INTEGRATED WRITING TASK

1. **Be familiar with the directions.** The directions on every test are the same, so it is not necessary to spend time reading the directions carefully when you take the test. You should be completely familiar with the directions before the day of the test.

2. **Dismiss the directions as soon as they come up.** You should already be familiar with the directions, so you can click on `Continue` as soon as it appears and use your time on the passages and questions.

3. **Do not worry if the material in the integrated task is on a topic that is not familiar to you.** All of the information that you need to write your response is included in the passage. You do not need any background knowledge to answer the questions.

4. **Read the reading passage carefully.** You will have only a limited amount of time to read the passage.

5. **Take careful notes as you read the passage.** You should focus on the main points and key supporting material. Do not try to write down everything you read. Do not write down too many unnecessary details.

6. **Listen carefully to the passage.** You will hear the passage one time only. You may not hear the passage again.

7. **Take careful notes as you listen to the spoken material.** You should focus on the main points and key supporting material. Do not try to write down everything you hear. Do not write down too many unnecessary details.

8. **Organize your response very clearly.** You should have an overall topic statement that shows the relationship between the reading passage and the listening passage. You should also have a paragraph about the reading passage and a paragraph about the listening passage.

---

9. **Use transitions to make your response cohesive.** Your essay is easier to read and understand if you show how the ideas in your response are related.

10. **Stick to vocabulary, sentence structures, and grammatical points that you know.** This is not the best time to try out new words, structures, or grammar points.

11. **Monitor the time carefully on the title bar of the computer screen.** The title bar indicates how much time you have to complete your response.

12. **Finish writing your response a few minutes early so that you have time to edit what you wrote.** You should spend the last three to five minutes checking your response for problems in sentence structure and grammatical errors.

The following strategies can help you on the independent task in the Writing section.

STRATEGIES FOR THE INDEPENDENT WRITING TASK

1. **Be familiar with the directions.** The directions on every test are the same, so it is not necessary to spend time reading the directions carefully when you take the test. You should be completely familiar with the directions before the day of the test.

2. **Dismiss the directions as soon as they come up.** You should already be familiar with the directions, so you can click on Continue as soon as it appears and use your time on the passages and questions.

3. **Read the question carefully, and answer the question exactly as it is asked.** Take some time at the beginning of the task to be sure that you understand the question and what the question is asking you to do.

4. **Organize your response very clearly.** You should think of having an introduction, body paragraphs that develop the introduction, and a conclusion to end your essay.

5. **Use transitions to make your essay cohesive.** Your essay is easier to read and understand if you show how the ideas in your essay are related.

6. **Whenever you make a general statement, be sure to support that statement.** You can use examples, reasons, facts, or personal information to support any general statement.

7. **Stick to vocabulary, sentence structures, and grammatical points that you know.** This is not the best time to try out new words, structures, or grammar points.

8. **Monitor the time carefully on the title bar of the computer screen.** The title bar indicates how much time you have to complete your essay.

9. **Finish writing your essay a few minutes early so that you have time to edit what you wrote.** You should spend the last three to five minutes checking your essay for problems in sentence structure and grammatical errors.

WRITING SKILLS

The following skills will help you to implement these strategies in the Writing section of the *iBT* TOEFL test.

INTEGRATED TASK

Writing Skill 1: NOTE THE MAIN POINTS AS YOU READ

In the integrated task in the Writing section of the *iBT* TOEFL test, you will be asked to read an academic passage as part of the task. In this part of the integrated task, it is important for you to be able to read an academic passage of 250–300 words and take notes on the main points of the reading passage in a short period of time. Look at the following example of a reading passage that is part of the integrated writing task.

Reading Passage

It is common knowledge that **forecasting** is an attempt by meteorologists to determine what weather will be like in the future. **Hindcasting** is the opposite of forecasting, an attempt to determine what weather was like in the past. Meteorologists wish that records of weather had been kept in full for at least a few millennia, but it has been only in the last century that detailed records of the weather have been kept. Thus, meteorologists need to hindcast the weather, and they do so by using all sorts of information from other fields as diverse as archeology, botany, geology, literature, and art. These pieces of information from other fields that are used as a basis for drawing conclusions about what the weather must have been like at some point in the past are called **proxies**.

As you read the passage, you should take notes on the topic and main points of the reading passage. Look at these notes on the topic and main points of the reading passage.

TOPIC OF READING PASSAGE: hindcasting (trying to determine what weather was like in the past)

main points about hindcasting:
- detailed weather records kept for less than a century
- proxies (information from various other fields) used to hindcast weather

---

These notes show that the topic of the reading passage is hindcasting, which means trying to determine what the weather was like in the past; the main points about hindcasting are that detailed weather records were kept for less than a century and that proxies, which are pieces of information from various other fields, are used to hindcast weather.

The following chart outlines the key information you should remember about dealing with the reading passage in the integrated writing task.

NOTING THE MAIN POINTS IN THE READING PASSAGE	
TOPIC	Make sure that you understand (and take notes on) the *topic* of the reading passage.
MAIN POINTS	Then focus on (and take notes on) the *main points* that are used to support the topic of the reading passage.

WRITING EXERCISE 1: Read each of the following passages, and note the *topic* and the *main points* that are used to support the topic.

1. Read the passage. Take notes on the main points of the reading passage.

   The Sahara is a massive desert, the world's largest, in fact. It is approximately equal in size to the United States and covers more than 9 million square kilometers. It is more than 5,500 kilometers from east to west and 2,000 kilometers from north to south.

   The Sahara has a very dry climate. The average annual rainfall is not even 10 centimeters, and many areas receive less than 2 centimeters per year. In the very driest places, it rains only about once a century.

   There is little surface water in the Sahara. The Nile River does run through the Sahara, and there are some oases there, but otherwise the surface is dry. Of the oases in the Sahara, about 90 are large enough to support tiny villages.

   > topic Sahara Desert.
   > main point Characteristics of the Sahara Desert
   > - large (9 million square km)
   > - dry climate (average annual rainfall is not even 10)
   > - no lakes / River

2. Read the passage. Take notes on the main points of the reading passage.

   It is very common in English for one word to have many different meanings. This condition, where one word has different meanings, is known as **polysemy**. (This term comes from *poly-* meaning "many" and *sem-* meaning "meaning.")

   Sound is one such polysemic word. As a noun, it refers to a noise (as in *a loud sound*) or a body of water (as in *Puget Sound*). As an adjective, it can refer to a state of health (as in *sound mind and body*). It can also be an intransitive verb (as in *sound angry*), a transitive verb (as in *sound the alarm*), or part of a verb phrase as an outburst (as in *sound off*) and an inquiry (as in *sound out*).

   You may think that the word *sound* is a truly wondrous polysemic word. After all, its definitions cover seven pages in one major dictionary and include 19 meanings as a noun, 12 meanings as an adjective, 12 meanings as a verb (some transitive and some intransitive), 4 meanings in verb phrases, and 2 meanings as an adverb.

Sahara, the world's largest

Sahara Desert

description

Polysem✓

Eny have many different meanings.

- One word there have mol diffent meanings
- Sound ver different

~~topic~~

~~Hinterstiny~~, what ~~weather was~~ like in the past

topic   Anthropologist [who is know ground breaking reser
on the effects of culture on gender roles

    - There are three different societies   in New Guinea
        1 Society that behavior
by men and women were remarkably similar

But what about the extraordinary word *set*? It looks like such a short, simple word, only three little letters in all. However, if you look it up in an unabridged dictionary, you will find at least 57 meanings for *set* when it is used as a noun and over 120 meanings when it is used as a verb.

[handwritten notes:]

Topic   Polysemy (one world differen meaning)

main points   Sound (14=N, 12=adj, 14=v, 4 phrases, 2 adv)

Set (57=N, 120=V)

3. Read the passage. Take notes on the main points of the reading passage.

Anthropologist Margaret Mead is known for her groundbreaking research on the effects of culture on gender roles. Her working hypothesis was that if gender behavior was the effect purely of biology, then what was considered masculine and feminine would be the same in all cultures. If gender behavior differed in different cultures, this would demonstrate that gender behavior resulted from culture rather than biology.

To test this hypothesis, Mead studied three different societies in New Guinea. The first society that she studied was the Arapesh. In this society, she observed that behavior by men and behavior by women were remarkably similar. She found that both men and women exhibited characteristics that are traditionally considered feminine: they were sensitive to each others' feelings and expressed emotions.

The second society that she studied in New Guinea were the Mundugumor, which was a society of headhunters and cannibals. The society was the opposite of the gentle and feminine Arapesh. In this second society, both men and woman exhibited characteristics that are traditionally considered male: they were harsh and aggressive.

In the third society that she studied, the Tchambuli, Mead found that males and females exhibited very different types of behavior. What was unusual was that the roles were the opposite of what we have come to expect. Mead found that in this society, the men were emotional and submissive to the women, and the women were dominant and aggressive.

Based on these findings, Margaret Mead came to the conclusion that culture, more than biology, determines gender behavior.

[handwritten notes:]

Margaret Mead   New Guinea research (Society)

main points   three Societies

(1) Arapesh m/F

(2) Mundugumor

(3) Tchambuli

Writing Skill 2: NOTE THE MAIN POINTS AS YOU LISTEN

In the integrated task in the Writing section of the *iBT* TOEFL test, you will also be asked to listen to an academic passage as part of the task. In this part of the integrated task, it is important for you to be able to listen to an academic passage of 1–2 minutes and take notes on the main points of the listening passage as you listen. Look at the following example of a listening passage that is part of the integrated writing task.

Listening Passage

(professor): *Now let me talk about how hindcasting was used in one particular situation. This situation has to do with the weather in seventeenth-century Holland. It appears, from proxies in paintings from the time by numerous artists, that the weather in Holland in the seventeenth century was much colder than it is today. Seventeenth-century paintings show really cold winter landscapes with huge snow drifts and ice skaters skating on frozen canals. Since it's unusual today for snow to drift as high as it is in the paintings and for the canals to freeze over so that skaters can skate across them as they are in the paintings, these paintings appear to serve as proxies that demonstrate that the weather when the paintings were created in the seventeenth century was much colder than it is today.*

As you listen to the passage, you should take notes on the topic and main points of the listening passage. Look at these notes on the topic and main points of the listening passage.

TOPIC OF LISTENING PASSAGE: paintings that are proxies showing weather in 17th-century Holland colder than today

details in 17th-century paintings showing colder weather:
- huge snow drifts higher than today's drifts
- skaters on canals that are not frozen today

These notes show that the topic of the listening passage is paintings that are proxies showing that the weather in seventeenth-century Holland was colder than it is today, and the details in seventeenth-century paintings that show that the weather was colder are huge snow drifts that are higher than today's snow drifts and skaters skating on canals that do not freeze today.

The following chart outlines the key information you should remember about dealing with the listening passage in the integrated writing task.

NOTING THE MAIN POINTS IN THE LISTENING PASSAGE	
TOPIC	Make sure that you understand (and take notes on) the *topic* of the listening passage.
MAIN POINTS	Then focus on (and take notes on) the *main points* that are used to support the topic of the listening passage.

WRITING EXERCISE 2: Listen to each of the following passages, and note the *topic* and the *main points* that are used to support the topic.

1. Listen to the passage. On a piece of paper, take notes on the main points of the listening passage.

2. Listen to the passage. On a piece of paper, take notes on the main points of the listening passage.

3. Listen to the passage. On a piece of paper, take notes on the main points of the listening passage.

Writing Skill 3: PLAN BEFORE YOU WRITE

After you have noted the main points of the reading passage and the main points of the listening passage in the integrated writing task, you need to read the question and plan your response.

The question will most likely be about how the main points of the reading passage and the main points of the listening passage are related. Look at the following example of a question in an integrated writing task on hindcasting and seventeenth-century weather in Holland.

Question

How does the information in the listening passage about the weather in seventeenth-century Holland shed light on the information on hindcasting in the reading passage?

You can see that, although the question does not specifically mention "main points" of the reading passage and listening passage, the question is in reality asking you to show how the main points of these two passage are related.

To prepare a plan for your response, you should look at the notes you have taken on the reading passage and the notes you have taken on the listening passage and focus on how the ideas in the two passages are related. Look at the plan for a response on the integrated writing task on hindcasting and seventeenth-century weather in Holland.

Reading Passage = *a technique used by meteorologists*

TOPIC OF READING PASSAGE: hindcasting (trying to determine what weather was like in the past)

main points about hindcasting:
- detailed weather records kept for less than a century
- proxies (information from various other fields) used to hindcast weather

Listening Passage = *an example of the technique*

TOPIC OF LISTENING PASSAGE: paintings that are proxies showing weather in 17th-century Holland colder than today

details in 17th-century paintings showing colder weather:
- huge snow drifts higher than today's drifts
- skaters on canals that are not frozen today

From this plan, you can see the way that the ideas in the reading passage and the listening passage are related. The plan shows that the reading passage describes *a technique used by meteorologists* and the listening passage provides *an example of the technique.*

The following chart outlines the key information you should remember about planning before you write in an integrated writing task.

PLANNING BEFORE YOU WRITE	
QUESTION	Study the question to determine what is being asked. Expect that the question is asking how the ideas in the reading passage and the listening passage are related.
RELATIONSHIP	Look at the notes you have taken on the reading passage and the listening passage, and focus on the main points or topics of each passage. Then describe how the ideas in each of the two passages are related.

WRITING EXERCISE 3: Look at the notes that you prepared for the reading passages in Writing Exercise 1 and the listening passages in Writing Exercise 2. Read the question for each task. Then prepare a plan for your response. Be sure to note the relationship between the reading passage and the listening passage in your plan.

1. How is the information in the listening passage related to the information in the reading passage?

2. What is the relationship between the words discussed in the listening passage and the words discussed in the reading passage?

3. How does the information in the listening passage cast doubt on what is discussed in the reading passage?

Writing Skill 4: WRITE A TOPIC STATEMENT

After you have planned your response, you should begin writing your response with an overall topic statement that directly indicates how the information in the reading passage and the information in the listening passage are related. To do this, you should study the information from your plan that shows the topics of the reading passage and the listening passage and the information about how the two passages are related. Look at this information from the integrated writing task on hindcasting and the weather in seventeenth-century Holland.

Reading Passage = *a technique used by meteorologists*

TOPIC OF READING PASSAGE: hindcasting (trying to determine what weather was like in the past)

Listening Passage = *an example of the technique*

TOPIC OF LISTENING PASSAGE: paintings that are proxies showing weather in 17th-century Holland colder than today

---

As you study this information, you should think about writing an overall topic statement that includes information about the topics of each of the passages and about how the two passages are related. Look at a possible topic statement for the integrated writing task on hindcasting and the weather in seventeenth-century Holland.

Topic Statement

> In this set of materials, the reading passage discusses a technique used by meteorologists, and the listening passage provides an example of this technique from seventeenth-century Holland.

You should notice that this topic statement does not include all the details about the topic. For example, it mentions a technique but does not say what the technique is, and it mentions an example from seventeenth-century Holland but does not say that the example refers to weather. The topic statement simply gives the overall idea, and the rest of the details will be included in the supporting paragraphs.

The following chart outlines the key information you should remember about writing a topic statement.

WRITING A TOPIC STATEMENT	
TOPIC STATEMENT	Start your response with a topic statement. This topic statement should show, in a general rather than a specific way, how the topic of the reading passage and the topic of the listening passage are related.

WRITING EXERCISE 4: Look at the plans that you prepared for the integrated writing tasks in Writing Exercise 3. Then write a topic statement for each task.

1. In this set of materials, the reading passage _____ _____ _____,

   and the listening passage _____ _____ _____.

2. In this set of materials, the reading passage _____ _____ _____,

   and the listening passage _____ _____ _____.

3. In this set of materials, the reading passage _____ _____ _____,

   and the listening passage _____ _____ _____.

Writing Skill 5: WRITE UNIFIED SUPPORTING PARAGRAPHS

A good way to begin writing effective supporting paragraphs in an integrated writing task is to study your notes carefully before you begin to write. Then, as you write, you should think about organizing and supporting each paragraph by introducing the main idea of each paragraph, supporting the main idea with adequate details, and connecting the ideas together in a unified paragraph (using cohesive techniques such as repeated key words, rephrased key ideas, pronouns and determiners for reference, and transition expressions).

> NOTE: For further work on cohesion, see APPENDIX A.

Look at the notes on the reading passage on hindcasting and the supporting paragraph that is based on the notes.

TOPIC OF READING PASSAGE: hindcasting (trying to determine what weather was like in the past)

main points about hindcasting:
- detailed weather records kept for less than a century
- proxies (information from various other fields) used to hindcast weather

---

The reading passage discusses the technique of (hindcasting), which is a method used by meteorologists to try to determine what the weather was like in the past. One point that is made about this (meteorological method) is that detailed weather records have not been kept for long. (As a result), meteorologists have had to find another way to determine what the weather was like in the past. (They) developed a method of hindcasting using proxies, which are pieces of information from other fields.

As you read the supporting paragraph on the reading passage, you should note that the first sentence of the paragraph is a topic sentence that indicates that the reading passage is about a certain method, and the rest of the sentences are details about the method. You should also note the techniques that have been used to make the paragraph cohesive. The word *hindcasting* is an example of a repeated key word, the phrase *meteorological method* is a rephrasing of the key idea *hindcasting*, the phrase *As a result* is a transition expression, and the word *They* is a pronoun that refers back to *meteorologists*.

Now look at the notes on the listening passage on seventeenth-century weather and the supporting paragraph that is based on the notes.

TOPIC OF LISTENING PASSAGE: paintings that are proxies showing weather in 17th-century Holland colder than today

details in 17th-century paintings showing colder weather:
- huge snow drifts higher than today's drifts
- skaters on canals that are not frozen today

The listening passage provides an example of a (situation) where hindcasting was used. (This) situation involves paintings that are proxies showing that the weather in 17th-century Holland was colder than it is today. There were many details in the 17th-century paintings that showed how (frigid) the weather was. (For instance), there were huge snow drifts that were higher than today's snow drifts, and there were skaters skating on canals that are not frozen today.

As you read the supporting paragraph on the reading passage, you should note that the first sentence of the paragraph is a topic sentence that indicates that the reading passage is about a certain method and that the rest of the sentences are details about the method. You should also note the techniques that have been used to make the paragraph cohesive. The word *situation* is an example of a repeated key word, the word *This* is a determiner that refers back to the previous *situation*, the word *frigid* is a rephrasing of the key idea *colder*, and the phrase *For instance* is a transition expression that shows that an example will follow.

The following chart outlines the key information that you should remember about writing unified supporting paragraphs.

WRITING UNIFIED SUPPORTING PARAGRAPHS	
ORGANIZATION	Each supporting paragraph should include a sentence with the main idea of the paragraph and several sentences with supporting ideas.
COHESION	To make a supporting paragraph cohesive, you should use a variety of techniques, such as repeated and rephrased key ideas, pronouns and determiners, and transition expressions.

WRITING EXERCISE 5: Read the paragraph. Then answer the questions that follow.

Paragraph

1   In this set of materials, the reading passage defines a certain legal concept, and the listening passage provides an example from the judicial system showing how this legal concept can come into play.

2   In the reading passage, the legal concept of reversible error is explained. This legal idea refers to an error that has been made in a legal proceeding and that affects the rights of the defendant in that procedure. If this kind of error has been made in a legal proceeding, it can be reversed should the defendant decide to appeal; thus, it is called a reversible error.

3   In the listening passage, an example of this concept is provided. This example is about a situation where a prosecuting attorney has made unfair remarks about the defendant and the judge has allowed his remarks to go unchallenged. In this situation, if the jury finds the person on trial guilty, perhaps because of the unfair remarks by the prosecutor, then this situation is one where there has been an error that can be reversed. In other words, it is a reversible error.

Repeated and rephrased key ideas

1. How many times does the key word *legal* appear in paragraph 2?
2. How many times does the key word *error* appear in paragraph 2?
3. How is the key word concept rephrased in paragraph 2?
4. How many times does the key word *remarks* appear in paragraph 3?
5. How many times does the key word *situation* appear in paragraph 3?
6. With what group of words is the key word defendant rephrased in paragraph 3?

7. What group of words does the pronoun it in paragraph 2 refer to?

8. What person does the determiner his in paragraph 3 refer to?

9. How many times is the determiner *this* used in the response to refer back to a previous idea?

10. How many times is the determiner *that* used in the response to refer back to a previous idea?

Transition expressions

11. Which transition expression in paragraph 2 shows that the result follows?

12. Which transition expression in paragraph 3 shows that a previous idea will be restated?

Now write unified supporting paragraphs for the integrated writing tasks that you worked on in Writing Exercises 1–4.

Writing Skill 6: REVIEW SENTENCE STRUCTURE

After you have written your response, it is important for you to review the sentence structure in your response. You should check the sentence structure of simple sentences, compound sentences, and complex sentences.

> NOTE: For a review of sentence structure, see APPENDIX B.

Look at the following sentences from a response about the development of a new theory.

Since a new <u>theory</u> <u>was developed</u> within the last decade.
            S   V

The <u>reading passage</u> <u>explains</u> a theory, the <u>listening passage</u>
            S   V   S
<u>discusses</u> the historical background of the theory.
    V

One <u>issue</u> that the lecturer points out <u>it</u> <u>is</u> that the main facts
      S   S   V
contradict the theory.

The sentence structure of each of these sentences is not correct. The first sentence is an incorrect simple sentence. In this sentence, the subordinate connector *Since* in front of the subject and verb *theory was developed* makes the sentence incomplete. The second sentence is an incorrect compound sentence. In this sentence, the main clauses *reading passage explains . . .* and *listening passage discusses . . .* are connected with a comma (,), and a comma cannot be used to connect two main clauses. The third sentence is an incorrect complex sentence. In this sentence, the main subject is *issue* and the verb is *is*; there is an extra subject *it*, which makes the sentence incorrect.

The following chart outlines the key information you should remember about reviewing sentence structure.

REVIEWING SENTENCE STRUCTURE	
SENTENCE STRUCTURE	Check for errors in sentence structure in your response. Be sure to check for errors in simple sentences, compound sentences, and complex sentences.

WRITING EXERCISE 6: Correct the errors in sentence structure in the following passages. (The number in parentheses at the end of each paragraph indicates the number of errors in the paragraph.)

1.

Paragraph

1   In this set of materials, the reading passage discusses one type of management style, the listening passage presents the opposite type of management style. Both of the management styles they were proposed by Douglas McGregor. *(2)*

2   The reading passage discusses the theory X management style, which an authoritarian management style. What a theory X manager believes it is that employees dislike work and will try to avoid it. Since this type of manager believes that employees do not like to work. He or she must force employees to work, a manager must force employees to work with threats and punishment. *(4)*

3   The listening passage discusses a very different management style, it discusses the theory Y management style, which is a participative style of management. A theory Y manager believes that employees to work for enjoyment. Employees do not need to be threatened, they work for the pleasure of working. The role that this type of manager needs to follow it is to set objectives and then to reward employees. As they meet these objectives. *(5)*

2.

Paragraph

1 In this set of materials, the reading passage describes the different types of waves that occur during earthquakes and the listening passage explains how much damage each of these types of waves causing. *(2)*

2 According to the reading passage, three different types of waves they occur during an earthquake: primary (or P) waves, secondary (or S) waves, and surface waves. Primary waves are the fastest-moving waves, secondary waves are not as fast as primary waves. Surface waves resemble the ripples in a pond after a stone has been thrown in it, they are very slow-moving waves. *(3)*

3 According to the listening passage, the types of waves that occur during an earthquake they do not cause equal amounts of damage to structures. What causes most damage to structures during earthquakes it is surface waves. The really slow-moving surface waves cause most of the differential movement of buildings during earthquakes, and is the differential movement of buildings that causes most of the damage. Because the primary and secondary waves vibrate much faster and with less movement than surface waves. They cause little damage to structures. *(4)*

Writing Skill 7: REVIEW GRAMMAR

After you have written your response, it is important for you to review the grammar in your response.

> NOTE: For a review of grammar, see APPENDIX C.

Look at the following sentence from a response on a scientific phenomenon.

> Though scientists are quite sure that this phenomenon *exist*, *it's* causes are not so clear.

In this sentence, the verb *exist* does not agree with the singular subject *phenomenon;* to correct this error, you can change *exist* to *exists*. The contracted subject and verb *it's* in front of the noun *causes* should be changed to a possessive adjective; to correct this error, you can change *it's* to *its*.

The following chart outlines the key information you should remember about reviewing grammar.

REVIEWING GRAMMAR	
GRAMMAR	Check for errors in grammar in your response. Be sure to check for errors with nouns and pronouns, verbs, adjectives and adverbs, articles, and agreement.

WRITING EXERCISE 7: Correct the errors in grammar in the following passages. (The number in parentheses at the end of each paragraph indicates the number of errors in the paragraph.)

1.
Paragraph

1   In this set of materials, the reading passage discusses attempt to deal with the problem of spelling in much words in American English; the listening passage explained why this attempt was not a successfully one. *(4)*

2   The reading passage explains that there is a problem in spelling a number of word in English where the spelling and pronunciation does not match; it then goes on to explain that philanthropist Andrew Carnegie made an efforts to resolve this. He gave an huge amount of dollars to establish a board calling the Simplified Spelling Board. As the name of a board indicates, its' purpose was to simplify the spellings of a words that are difficult to spell in English. Because of all of work that the board did, spellings like ax (instead of axe) and program (instead of programme) had become acceptable in American English. *(11)*

3   The listening passage explain why the work of the Simplified Spelling Board does not last. According to the listening passage, the main reason for the board's problems were that it went too far. They tried to establish spellings like yu (instead of you) and tuff (instead of tough). There was a real negative reaction to the attempt to change spelling too much, and eventually the board was dissolving. *(6)*

2.
Paragraph

1   In this set of materials, the reading passage describes type of learning, and the listening passage provided an extending example of this type of learning. *(3)*

2   The reading passage discusses aversive conditioning, which is define as learning involving an unpleasant stimulus. In this type of learning, an unpleasant stimulus is applying every times that a certain behavior occurs, in an attempt to stop the behavior. A learner can behaves in two different way in response to the knowledge that something unpleasant will soon occurs. Avoidance behavior is change in behavior before the stimulus was applied to avoid the unpleasant stimulus, while escape behavior is the opposite, a change in behavior after the application of the stimulus to cause them to stop. *(8)*

3   The listening passage provides long example of aversive conditioning. This extended example is about the alarm in much cars that buzzed if the driver's seat belt is not fastened. In this example, the method of aversive conditioning that is applied to drivers are that every time a driver tries to drive with the seat belt unfastened, the buzzer went off. The driver exhibits avoidance behavior if he or she has fasten the seat belt before driving to avoid hearing the buzzer. The driver exhibits escape behavior if he or she attach the seat belt after the alarm had started to buzz, to stop the buzzing. *(8)*

WRITING REVIEW EXERCISE (Skills 1–7): Read the passage. On a piece of paper, take notes on the main points of the reading passage.

Reading Time: 3 minutes

What is one of the oldest, if not actually the oldest, human bodies was discovered in 1991 by some rather surprised hikers who were traveling in the Alps of the Southern Tyrol close to the border between Austria and Italy. The hikers noticed what looked like a human body with dried-out skin. The body was originally taken to Innsbruck University in Austria; however, after some investigation, it was determined that the body had actually been discovered on the Italian, rather than the Austrian, side of the border, so it was sent to a museum in Italy for study. Numerous tests were conducted on the body to determine its age. Though it was believed that the body was rather old, there was considerable surprise among the researchers when various tests all arrived at the conclusion that the body was more than 5,000 years old.

The researchers who studied the body determined that it was a male who had darkish skin and was forty to fifty years old. He was rather short by today's standards, at around 5 feet 2 inches (1.58 meters) tall. He was wearing a tanned goatskin coat, a calfskin belt and leggings, shoes with bearskin soles and deerskin uppers, a bearskin cap, and a cape made of woven grass. He was carrying a dagger with a flint blade, a copper axe, a wooden bow, a fur backpack, and a deerskin quiver with arrows.

Listen to the passage. On a piece of paper, take notes on the main points of the listening passage.

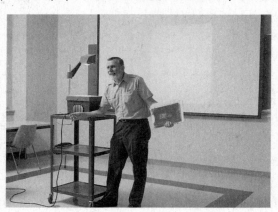

Now answer the following question:

How does the information in the listening passage add to the ideas presented in the reading passage?

Preparation Time: 1 minute
Response Time: 20 minutes

After you have completed this exercise, fill in the chart on page 552.

INDEGENDENT TASK

Writing Skill 8: PLAN BEFORE YOU WRITE

The first and most important step in the independent task in the Writing section of the *iBT* TOEFL test is to decode the essay topic to determine what the intended outline is. Writing topics generally give very clear clues about how your answer should be constructed. It is important to follow the clear clues that are given in the topic when you are planning your answer. You will probably not be given too much credit for a response that does not cover the topic in the way that is intended. Study the following essay topic.

Essay Topic

Some people prefer to work in groups on projects, while other people prefer to work alone. What are the advantages of each, and which do you prefer? Use details and examples to support your response.

As you read this topic, you should quickly determine that the overall organization of your response should be an introduction, supporting paragraphs about the advantages of working in groups and the advantages of working alone on projects (with examples showing the advantages), and a conclusion. You should take a few minutes before you begin to plan your ideas. Study the following plan for an essay on the given topic.

INTRODUCTION: advantages of working individually and in groups

SUPPORTING PARAGRAPH 1: advantages of working in groups
(advantages): • opportunity to learn from others
• less work for individual members
(example): • group project in history (four people, some know things others don't, one quarter of the work for each one)

SUPPORTING PARAGRAPH 2: advantages of working individually
(advantages): • previous success in working this way
• enjoyment of doing work when and how I want
(example): • individual project in history (working alone, doing work my way, getting good grade)

CONCLUSION: • better for me to work individually

In this example, there are two advantages of working in groups and two advantages of working individually, and examples are provided.

The following chart outlines the key information that you should remember about planning before you write.

PLANNING BEFORE YOU WRITE	
HOW TO DECODE THE ESSAY TOPIC	Each topic in the independent task shows you exactly *what* you should discuss and *how* you should organize your response. You must decode the topic carefully to determine the intended way of organizing your response, and you must include an introduction and a conclusion.
HOW TO DEVELOP SUPPORTING IDEAS	Support your essay with the kinds of support that the essay topic asks for (such as *reasons*, *details*, or *examples*), and try to *personalize* your essay as much as possible. The more support you have, the better your essay will be.

WRITING EXERCISE 8: For each of the following writing topics, prepare a plan that shows the type of information you will include in each paragraph of the essay.

1. People have various ways of relieving stress. What are some of the ways that you find most effective in relieving stress? Give reasons and examples to support your response.

INTRODUCTION: my ways of relieving stress

SUPPORTING PARAGRAPH 1: get away from the stress
    (examples): • read a book, see a movie, visit friends
    (reason): • necessary to leave stress to relieve it
    (personal story): • a time last month when I was able to finish a difficult assignment after leaving it for a while and going to see a movie

SUPPORTING PARAGRAPH 2: get moving
    (examples): • go for a walk, go dancing, go to the gym
    (reason): • helpful in providing an outlet for stress
    (personal story): • a time last year when I was finally able to deal with a problem with a friend after going on a long, long walk

CONCLUSION: • to relieve stress, get away from it and move
    • problems seem small and solutions seem clear

2. What famous place would you like to visit? Use details and reasons to support your response.

3. Do you agree or disagree with the following statement?

 Actions speak louder than words.

 Use specific reasons and examples to support your response.

4. Compare yourself today and yourself five years ago. In what ways are you the same or different? Use specific examples to support your response.

5. Some people prefer to play team sports, while others prefer to play individual sports. Discuss the advantages of each. Then indicate which you prefer and why.

6. What is the best age to marry? Give reasons and examples to support your response.

7. What are the characteristics of a good teacher? Use reasons and examples to support your response.

8. Do you agree or disagree with the following statement?

Haste makes waste.

Use specific reasons and examples to support your response.

9. It can be quite difficult to learn a new language. What do you think are the most difficult aspects of learning a new language? Give reasons and examples to support your response.

10. Do you agree or disagree with the following statement?

The TOEFL test is a wonderful test!

Use reasons and examples to support your response.

Writing Skill 9: WRITE THE INTRODUCTION

The purpose of the introduction is first to interest the reader in your topic and then to explain clearly to the reader what you are going to discuss and how you are going to organize the discussion. When finished with the introduction, the reader should be eager to continue reading your essay and should have an idea of what your topic is and how you are going to organize the discussion of your topic. You do not need to give the outcome of your discussion; you can save that for the conclusion. Study the following essay topic.

Essay Topic

Some people prefer to work in groups on projects, while other people prefer to work alone. What are the advantages of each, and which do you prefer? Use details and examples to support your response.

The following example shows one possible introduction to an essay on this topic.

INTRODUCTION

The educational system where I have been a student for the last 16 years is a system that places a high value on individual achievement and little value on group achievement. Having been a rather successful student in this educational system for the better part of my life, I am well aware of the advantages of working individually on projects. However, I can only imagine the advantages of working on projects in groups.

In the first part of the introduction, the writer provides background information that he or she has been a successful student in an educational system that is based on a lot of individual work, to interest the reader in the topic. By the end of the introduction, the reader also understands that the writer intends to discuss the advantages of individual work, based on personal experience, and then to discuss the advantages of working in groups from her or his imagination.

The following chart outlines the key information that you should remember about writing an introduction.

WRITING THE INTRODUCTION	
INTEREST	You should begin your introduction with information that will *interest* the reader in your topic.
TOPIC	You should state the *topic* directly in the middle of the introduction.
ORGANIZATION	You should end the introduction with a statement that shows the *organization* of the discussion of the topic.

WRITING EXERCISE 9: For each of the following writing topics, write introductions that include material to *interest* the reader in the topic, a statement of the specific *topic*, and a statement showing the *organization* of the discussion of the topic.

1.
> Some people prefer to work in one company for all their career. Others think it is better to move from company to company. Discuss the advantages of each position. Which do you think is better and why?

In my family we have experience both in staying with one company for a long time and in moving from one company to another. I find that one of these ways of working is better for me. However, each of these ways of working has its own advantages.

2.
> What famous place would you like to visit? Use details and reasons to support your response.

3.
> Do you agree or disagree with the following statement?
>   *Actions speak louder than words.*
> Use specific reasons and examples to support your response.

4.
> Compare yourself today and yourself five years ago. In what ways are you the same or different? Use specific examples to support your response.

5. Some people prefer to play team sports, while others prefer to play individual sports. Discuss the advantages of each. Then indicate which you prefer and why.

6. What is the best age to marry? Give reasons and examples to support your response.

7. What are the characteristics of a good teacher? Use reasons and examples to support your response.

8. Do you agree or disagree with the following statement?

Haste makes waste.

Use specific reasons and examples to support your response.

9. It can be quite difficult to learn a new language. What do you think are the most difficult aspects of learning a new language? Give reasons and examples to support your response.

10. Do you agree or disagree with the following statement?
The TOEFL test is a wonderful test!
Use reasons and examples to support your response.

Writing Skill 10: WRITE UNIFIED SUPPORTING PARAGRAPHS

A good way to begin writing effective supporting paragraphs in an independent writing task is to study your notes carefully before you begin to write. Then, as you write, you should think about introducing the main idea of each paragraph, supporting the main idea with adequate details, and connecting the ideas together in a unified paragraph (using cohesive techniques such as repeated key words, rephrased key ideas, pronouns and determiners for reference, and transition expressions).

> NOTE: For further work on cohesion, see APPENDIX A.

Look at the notes on the first supporting paragraph of the essay and the supporting paragraph that is based on the notes.

SUPPORTING PARAGRAPH 1: <u>advantages of working in groups</u>
(advantages):
- opportunity to learn from others
- less work for individual members

(example):
- group project in history (four people, some know things others don't, one quarter of the work for each one)

 The first point I would like to make is that there are strong advantages to working in groups. One (benefit) of this method of getting things done is that the members of the (group) can learn from each other. Something else that is good is that the work can be divided among the members of the group. If, (for example), four people have to work in a group to get a 20-page paper done for history class, the paper can get done quickly. The reason for (this) is that different members of the group know different things and each group member has to write only 5 pages.

As you read the first supporting paragraph in the essay on working in groups and working individually, you should note that the first sentence of the paragraph is a topic sentence that indicates that the first supporting paragraph is about advantages of working in groups, and the rest of the sentences are details about this topic. You should also note the techniques that have been used to make the paragraph cohesive. The word *benefit* is a rephrasing of the key idea *advantages,* the word *group* is an example of a repeated key word, the phrase *for example* is a transition expression, and the word *this* is a pronoun that refers back to the idea *the paper can get done quickly.*

Look at the notes on the second supporting paragraph of the essay and the supporting paragraph that is based on the notes.

SUPPORTING PARAGRAPH 2: <u>advantages of working individually</u>

(advantages):
- previous success in working this way
- enjoyment of doing work when and how I want

(example):
- individual project in history (me working alone, doing work my way, getting good grade)

Though there are strong advantages to working in groups, there are some even more compelling advantages for me to work by (myself). I have had a lot of success working (alone), and (this) is because I enjoy working by myself, working when I want, and getting things done the way that I want. (Thus), if I had to write that 20-page history paper, I would rather do it myself, even though I would have to write all 20 pages, because I could do it the way that I want.

As you read the second supporting paragraph in the essay on working in groups and working individually, you should note that the first sentence of the paragraph is a topic sentence that indicates that the second supporting paragraph is about advantages of working individually, and the rest of the sentences are details about this topic. You should also note the techniques that have been used to make the paragraph cohesive. The word *myself* is an example of a repeated key word, the word *alone* is a rephrasing of the key idea *by myself,* the word *this* is a pronoun that refers back to the idea *I have had a lot of success,* and the word *Thus* is a transition expression.

The following chart outlines the key information you should remember about writing unified supporting paragraphs.

WRITING UNIFIED SUPPORTING PARAGRAPHS	
ORGANIZATION	Each supporting paragraph should include a sentence with the main idea of the paragraph and several sentences with supporting ideas.
COHESION	To make a supporting paragraph cohesive, you should use a variety of techniques, such as repeated and rephrased key ideas, pronouns and determiners, and transition expressions.

WRITING EXERCISE 10: Read the paragraph. Then answer the questions that follow.

Paragraph 1

English is not an easy language to learn. Of all the possible problems that I have experienced when trying to learn this language, the most difficult problem that I have encountered is that English does not seem to be spoken by Americans in the same way that it was presented in my textbooks. For instance, the first time that I asked an American a question, I got a strange response. The man who answered my question said something that sounded like "Dunno." I was sure that I had never studied this expression in my textbooks, and I could not find anything like it in my textbooks, and I could not find anything like it in my dictionary. I was surprised to learn later from a friend that this mysterious-sounding answer was really nothing more than a shortened version of "I do not know." Not too long after that I had an even more interesting example of my most difficult problem in learning English. One evening, I was unable to do some chemistry homework problems, so the next morning I asked a classmate if she had been able to do them. I was amazed when she gave the rather bizarre answer that the assignment had been a "piece of cake." I was not quite sure what a piece of cake had to do with the chemistry assignment, so I responded that I was not quite sure that the assignment really was a piece of cake. I have learned by now that she meant that the assignment was quite easy. Overall, I'm sure it is clear from these two examples what I find so difficult about the English language.

Repeated and rephrased key ideas

1. How many times does the key word *difficult* appear in the passage?
2. How many times does the key word *problem(s)* appear in the passage?
3. How is the phrase strange response rephrased in the passage?
4. How is the expression Dunno rephrased in the passage?
5. How is the word surprised rephrased in the passage?

Pronouns and determiners

6. What noun does the pronoun it refer to?
7. What noun does the pronoun them refer to?
8. What noun does the pronoun she refer to?
9. How many times is the determiner *this* used to refer back to a previous idea?
10. How many times is the determiner *these* used to refer back to a previous idea?

Transition expressions

11. Which transition expression shows that the first example will follow?
12. Which transition expression shows that the second example will follow?
13. Which transition expression shows that the summary of the main point follows?

Now write unified supporting paragraphs for the independent writing tasks that you worked on in Writing Exercises 8–9.

Writing Skill 11: CONNECT THE SUPPORTING PARAGRAPHS

To make sure your essay is as clear as possible, you should show as clearly as you can how the ideas in the supporting paragraphs in your essay are related. This can be accomplished (1) with a transition expression such as *the first, the most important,* or *a final way,* or (2) with a transition sentence that includes the idea of the previous paragraph and the idea of the current paragraph. It is best to use a combination of these two types of transitions. The following example shows how transitions can be used to show the relationships between the supporting paragraphs in an essay.

Essay Outline

INTRODUCTION: *advantages of working in groups and individually*

SUPPORTING PARAGRAPH 1: *advantages of working in groups*

SUPPORTING PARAGRAPH 2: *advantages of working individually*

CONCLUSION: *better for me to work individually*

Transitions

(to introduce SP1): *The first point I would like to make is that there are strong advantages to working in groups.*

(to introduce SP2): *Though there are strong advantages to working in groups, there are some even more compelling advantages for me to work by myself.*

The first supporting paragraph is introduced with the transition expression *The first point* to show that this is the first of the points that you are going to discuss in your essay. The second supporting paragraph is introduced with a transition sentence that shows how this paragraph is related to the previous paragraph; it includes a reference to the first supporting paragraph *strong advantages to working in groups* and a reference to the second supporting paragraph *more compelling advantages for me to work by myself.*

The following chart outlines the key information that you should remember about connecting the supporting paragraphs in your essay.

CONNECTING THE SUPPORTING PARAGRAPHS	
TRANSITION EXPRESSIONS	You can use transition expressions such as *the first, the next, in addition, another, finally* to connect the supporting paragraphs.
TRANSITION SENTENCES	You can use a transition sentence that relates the topic of the previous paragraph to the topic of the current paragraph.

WRITING EXERCISE 11: For each outline of an essay, write sentences to introduce each of the supporting paragraphs. You should use a combination of transition expressions and transition sentences.

1. INTRO: *a decision about whether or not to own a car in a big city*
   SP1: • the advantages of owning a car in a big city
   SP2: • the disadvantages of owning a car in a big city

   SP1: <u>The advantages of having a car in a big city are numerous.</u>

   SP2: <u>There may be numerous advantages to owning a car in a big city; however, there</u>
         <u>are also distinct disadvantages.</u>

2. INTRO: *the types of reading that I enjoy*
   SP1: • science fiction
   SP2: • romances
   SP3: • sports magazines

   SP1: _____
   _____

   SP2: _____
   _____

   SP3: _____
   _____

3. INTRO: *a preference for traveling alone or traveling in groups*
   SP1: • benefits of traveling alone
   SP2: • benefits of traveling in groups

   SP1: _____
   _____

   SP2: _____
   _____

4. INTRO: *characteristics leading to success as a student*
   SP1: • self-motivation
   SP2: • desire to succeed
   SP3: • joy in learning

   SP1: _____
   _____

   SP2: _____
   _____

   SP3: _____

5. INTRO: *living for today versus living for tomorrow*
 SP1: • people who have a philosophy of living for today
 SP2: • people who have a philosophy of living for tomorrow

 SP1: _____

 _____

 SP2: _____

 _____

6. INTRO: *my reasons for going to the movies all the time*
 SP1: • to be entertained rather than taught
 SP2: • to feel good rather than depressed

 SP1: _____

 _____

 SP2: _____

 _____

7. INTRO: *advice to someone trying to learn a new language*
 SP1: • listen to videos, television programs, radio programs in the new language
 SP2: • talk with native speakers of the language every chance you get
 SP3: • read newspapers, magazines, books in the new language

 SP1: _____

 _____

 SP2: _____

 _____

 SP3: _____

 _____

8. INTRO: *steps the government should take to protect the earth's environment*
 SP1: • educate people about the causes and effects of environmental damage
 SP2: • create and enforce laws that penalize those who damage the environment
 SP3: • reward those who are environmentally conscious with tax incentives

 SP1: _____

 _____

 SP2: _____

 _____

 SP3: _____

 _____

Writing Skill 12: WRITE THE CONCLUSION

The purpose of the conclusion is to close your essay by summarizing the main points of your discussion. When finished with your conclusion, the reader should clearly understand your exact ideas on the topic and the reasons you feel the way that you do about the topic.

The ideas in your conclusion should be clearly related to the ideas that you began in the introduction. You should indicate what you intend to discuss in the essay in the introduction, and you should indicate the outcome or results of the discussion in the conclusion. Refer to the essay topic and sample introduction in Writing Skill 9.

Essay Topic

Some people prefer to work in groups on projects, while other people prefer to work alone. What are the advantages of each, and which do you prefer? Use details and examples to support your response.

The following example shows a possible conclusion to an essay on this topic.

CONCLUSION

I have worked individually throughout my education, and I have been successful working in this way because this style of work is a good match with my personality. I can imagine that, for some people, the cooperative benefits that come from working in groups might be a good thing. However, I prefer to continue with a style of work that has made me successful up to now. I hope that the success that I have had up to now by working in this way will continue to make me successful in the future.

Here the writer refers back to the personal information that was mentioned in the introduction, saying *I have worked individually throughout my education, and I have been successful working this way. . . .* The writer also briefly summarizes the advantages of each style of work by mentioning that working individually is *a good match with my personality* and that working in groups has *cooperative benefits.* Finally, the writer clearly states a preference for working individually because of the success that this style of work has brought *up to now.*

The following chart outlines the key information that you should remember about writing a conclusion.

WRITING THE CONCLUSION	
OVERALL IDEA	You should make sure that your *overall idea* is very clear.
MAIN POINTS	You should summarize the *main points* that you used to arrive at this overall idea.
INTEREST	You should refer back to the information that you used to *interest* the reader in the introduction.

WRITING EXERCISE 12: For each of the following writing topics, write conclusions that restate the main idea, summarize the main points, and refer back to the information that you used to interest the reader in the introduction.

1. Some people prefer to work in one company for all their career. Others think it is better to move from company to company. Discuss the advantages of each position. Which do you think is better and why?

From this, I think you can understand why I prefer to better my career by moving from company to company. I do understand that there are advantages in staying with one company for a long time; I certainly hear about these advantages from my family over and over. However, I have come to the conclusion that something different is better for me.

2. What famous place would you like to visit? Use details and reasons to support your response.

3. Do you agree or disagree with the following statement?
   Actions speak louder than words.
   Use specific reasons and examples to support your response.

4. Compare yourself today and yourself five years ago. In what ways are you the same or different? Use specific examples to support your response.

5. Some people prefer to play team sports, while others prefer to play individual sports. Discuss the advantages of each. Then indicate which you prefer and why.

6. What is the best age to marry? Give reasons and examples to support your response.

7. What are the characteristics of a good teacher? Use reasons and examples to support your response.

8. Do you agree or disagree with the following statement?

Haste makes waste.

Use specific reasons and examples to support your response.

9.

It can be quite difficult to learn a new language. What do you think are the most difficult aspects of learning a new language? Give reasons and examples to support your response.

10.

Do you agree or disagree with the following statement?
  The TOEFL test is a wonderful test!
Use reasons and examples to support your response.

Writing Skill 13: REVIEW SENTENCE STRUCTURE

After you have written your essay, it is important for you to review the sentence structure in your essay. You should check the sentence structure of simple sentences, compound sentences, and complex sentences.

> NOTE: For a review of sentence structure, see APPENDIX B.

Look at the following sentences from an essay about a test.

Because the <u>test</u> in history class <u>was</u> extremely difficult.
          S   V

<u>I</u> finally <u>passed</u> the test, otherwise <u>I</u> <u>would have had</u> to take it over.
S   V   S   V

The <u>grade</u> that I intended to get <u>it</u> <u>was</u> much higher.
     S   S V

The sentence structure of each of these sentences is not correct. The first sentence is an incorrect simple sentence. In this sentence, the subordinate connector *Because* in front of the subject and verb *test . . . was* makes the sentence incomplete. The second sentence is an incorrect compound sentence. In this sentence, the main clauses *I . . . passed . . .* and *I would have had . . .* are connected with a comma (,), and a comma cannot be used to connect two main clauses. The third sentence is an incorrect complex sentence. In this sentence, the main subject is *grade* and the verb is *was*; there is an extra subject *it*, which makes the sentence incorrect.

The following chart outlines the key information you should remember about reviewing sentence structure.

REVIEWING SENTENCE STRUCTURE	
SENTENCE STRUCTURE	Check for errors in sentence structure in your response. Be sure to check for errors in simple sentences, compound sentences, and complex sentences.

WRITING EXERCISE 13: Correct the errors in sentence structure in the following passages. (The number in parentheses at the end of each paragraph indicates the number of errors in the paragraph.)

Paragraph

1   I definitely believe that taking part in organized team sports is beneficial. However, is beneficial for much more than the obvious reasons. Everyone recognizes, of course, that participation in sports provides obvious physical benefits. It leading to improved physical fitness, it also provides a release from the stresses of life. I spent my youth taking part in a number of organized sports, including football, basketball, and volleyball, as a result of this experience I understand that the benefits of participation much greater than the physical benefits. *(5)*

2   One very valuable benefit that children get from taking part in sports it is that it teaches participants teamwork. What any player in a team sport needs to learn it is that individual team members must put the team ahead of individual achievement. Individuals on one team who are working for individual glory rather than the good of the team they often end up working against each other. A team made up of individuals unable to work together often not a very successful team, it is usually a complete failure. *(5)*

3   What also makes participation in team sports valuable it is that it teaches participants to work to achieve goals. Playing sports it involves setting goals and working toward them, examples of such goals are running faster, kicking harder, throwing straighter, or jumping higher. Athletes learn that can set goals and work toward them until the goals accomplished. Is through hard work that goals can be met. *(6)*

4   By taking part in sports, can learn the truly valuable skills of working together on teams and working to accomplish specific goals. These goals not just beneficial in sports, more importantly, the skills that are developed through sports they are the basis of success in many other aspects of life. Mastering these skills leading to success not only on the playing field but also in the wider arena of life. *(5)*

Writing Skill 14: REVIEW GRAMMAR

After you have written your essay, it is important for you to review the grammar in your response.

NOTE: For a review of grammar, see APPENDIX C.

Look at the following sentence from an essay on the effects of television.

Television certainly has changing society in very big way.

In this sentence, the past participle rather than the present participle *changing* should be used after the helping verb *has*; to correct this error, you can change *changing* to *changed*. The article *a* also needs to be added because the countable singular noun *way* requires an article; to correct this error, you can change *very* to *a very*.

The following chart outlines the key information you should remember about reviewing grammar.

REVIEWING GRAMMAR	
GRAMMAR	Check for errors in grammar in your response. Be sure to check for errors with nouns and pronouns, verbs, adjectives and adverbs, articles, and agreement.

WRITING EXERCISE 14: Correct the errors in grammar in the following passages. (The number in parentheses at the end of each paragraph indicates the number of errors in the paragraph.)

> Paragraph
>
> 1   In my first semester at the university, I was overwhelm by the differences between university studies and high school studies. In high school, I had easily be able to finish the number of work that was assigned, and if on certain occasion I did not complete an assignment, the teacher quickly tells me to make up the work. The situation in my university classes were not at all like the situation in high school. *(6)*
>
> 2   I was tremendously surprising at the volume of work assigned in the university. Unlike high school courses, which perhaps covered a chapter in two week, university courses regular covered two or three chapters in one week and two or three other chapters in the next week. I have been able to keep up with the workload in high school, but it was difficult for me to finish all the reading in mine university classes even though I tried real hard to finish all of them. *(7)*
>
> 3   The role that the teacher took in motivating students to get work done were also very different in my university. In high school, if an assignment was unfinishing on a date that it was due, my teacher would immediate let me know that I had made really a mistake and needed to finish an assignment right away. In my university classes, however, professors did not inform regularly students to make sure that we were get work done on schedule. It was really easy to put off studying in the beginning of each semesters and really have to work hard later in the semester to catch up on my assignments. *(9)*
>
> 4   During my first year in the university, I had to set firm goal to get things done by myself instead of relying on others to watch over me and make sure that I have done what I was supposed to do. With so much assignments, this was quite a task difficult, but I now regular try to do my best because I dislike being very far behind. It seems that I have turn into quite a motivating student. *(7)*

WRITING REVIEW EXERCISE (Skills 8–14)

Read the question. On a piece of paper, take notes on the main points of a response. Then write your response.

> Some people show their emotions, while other people work hard to keep their emotions from showing. What are the advantages of each type of behavior? Which do you try to do?
>
> Response Time: 20 minutes

After you have completed this exercise, fill in the chart on page 553.

WRITING POST-TEST

> ### Writing
> #### Section Directions
>
> This section measures your ability to use writing to communicate in an academic environment. There will be two writing tasks.
>
> For the first writing task, you will read a passage and listen to a lecture and then answer a question based on what you have read and heard. For the second task, you will answer a question based on your own knowledge and experience.
>
> **Integrated Writing Directions**
>
> For the first task, you will read a passage about an academic topic. You will have **3 minutes** to read the passage. You may take notes on the passage while you read. The passage will then be removed and you will listen to a lecture about the same topic. While you listen, you may also take notes.
>
> Then you will write a response to a question that asks you about the relationship between the lecture you heard and the reading passage. Try to answer the question as completely as possible using information from the reading passage and the lecture. The question does **not** ask you to express your personal opinion. You will be able to see the reading passage again when it is time for you to write. You may use your notes to help you answer the question. You will have **20 minutes** to write your response.
>
> Typically, an effective response will be 150 to 225 words. You need to demonstrate your ability to write well and to provide complete and accurate content.
>
> Remember you can look at the passage again when you write your response. Immediately after the reading time ends, the lecture begins.
>
> **Independent Writing Directions**
>
> For the second task, you will write an essay in response to a question that asks you to state, explain, and support your opinion on an issue. You will have **30 minutes** to plan, write, and revise your response.
>
> Typically, an effective essay will contain a minimum of 300 words. You need to demonstrate your ability to write well. This includes the development of your ideas, the organization of your essay, and the quality and accuracy of the language you use to express your ideas.

Questions 1–2

Question 1
Read the passage. On a piece of paper, take notes on the main points of the reading passage.

Reading Time: 3 minutes

According to the law of unintended consequences, actions of individuals, groups, or governments have effects, or "consequences" that are unexpected, or "unintended." These unexpected effects, or unintended consequences as they are called in academic literature, are effects that are not planned when an original action is taken, and the person or persons making the decision do not consider that these effects may result from the action taken.

Unintended consequences may turn out to be positive or negative. Unintended consequences that are positive may result, for example, from a decision by a city council to ban cars from Main Street in the city. If, as a result of this decision, there is an unexpected effect that many citizens improve their health because they need to park their cars and walk on a regular basis to get to the businesses that line Main Street, then this is a positive effect. There can, however, also be negative consequences of this decision by the city council to ban cars on Main Street. If, as a result of this decision, citizens decide that it is too much trouble to get to the businesses on Main Street because they cannot take their cars there, then they might decide to go to businesses elsewhere because it is easier to get there. A loss in the number of customers visiting the businesses along Main Street would be a definitely negative effect of the decision by the city council that was absolutely not intended by the city council when the decision was made.

Listen to the passage. On a piece of paper, take notes on the main points of the listening passage.

Now answer the following question:

How does the information in the listening passage add to the ideas presented in the reading passage?

Preparation Time: 1 minute
Response Time: 20 minutes

Question 2

Read the question. On a piece of paper, take notes on the main points of a response. Then write your response.

Do you agree or disagree with the following statement?

It is better to be safe than sorry.

Use reasons and examples to support your response.

Response Time: 30 minutes

After you have completed this test, fill in the chart on pages 552–553.

MINI-TEST 1

READING

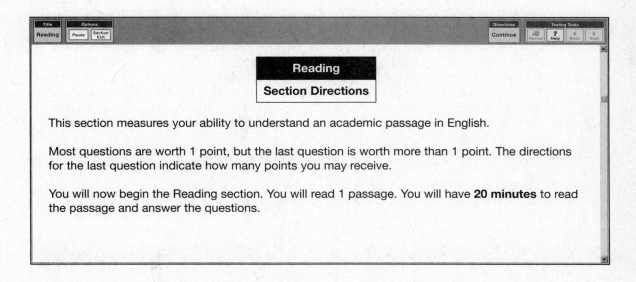

Reading

Section Directions

This section measures your ability to understand an academic passage in English.

Most questions are worth 1 point, but the last question is worth more than 1 point. The directions for the last question indicate how many points you may receive.

You will now begin the Reading section. You will read 1 passage. You will have **20 minutes** to read the passage and answer the questions.

Read the passage.

| 20 minutes |

Migration

1   A widely held theory today is that the ancestors of today's Native American peoples traveled to the Western Hemisphere from Asia between 25,000 and 30,000 years ago, which was around the same time that Japan was being settled by Stone Age inhabitants. There is dental evidence and blood-type evidence to support this theory. A dental pattern that is found among most ancient human fossils in the Americas is consistent with the dental pattern of ancient human fossils in northeastern Asia. In blood type, the fact that blood type B is almost nonexistent among Native American populations but exists in Asian populations leads to the conclusion that migrations to the Americas from Asia took place before the evolution of blood type B, which is believed to have occurred around 30,000 years ago. In addition to the dental and blood-type evidence, more general evolutionary evidence suggests that it took more than 20,000 years for the variety of physical traits common to Native American populations to evolve, and linguists broadly concur that the development of the approximately 500 distinct languages of the Native Americans would require approximately 25,000 years.

2   The proposed migration from Asia to the Americas took place during the Ice Age that characterized the Pleistocene epoch. During that period of time, there were huge glaciers holding enormous volumes of water, and, because of the huge glaciers, sea levels were as much as 100 meters lower than they are today. The reduced sea levels meant that Asia and North America were linked with a 750-mile-wide landmass, named Beringia after the Bering Straits that now cover it, and consisted of treeless grassland with warm summers and cold dry winters. Because of the geographical features of Beringia during the Pleistocene epoch, it was an environment well-suited to the large mammals of the time, such as mammoth, mastodon, bison, horse, and reindeer, as well as to the Stone Age hunters who depended on these animals for their existence. The Stone Age inhabitants of the area used these animals not only for food but also for shelter, clothing, and weapons; they were able to spread out and expand their hunting areas as their populations grew, and their populations most likely grew at a very high rate because of the huge amount of territory available for expansion.

3   In spite of the evidence, not all anthropologists are convinced that the migrations from Asia to the Americas took place as early as 25,000 to 30,000 years ago. There is general agreement that the migrations took place, but some believe that the migrations took place much later. No fossilized human bones have been found in what used to be Beringia; finding human bones dating from 25,000 to 30,000 years ago would be strong proof of the dates when the migrations took place. However, because what was once Beringia is submerged beneath ocean waters, it may be a formidable task to uncover fossil evidence of migration from Asia to the Americas through Beringia.

Refer to this version of the passage to answer the questions that follow.

Migration

1   A widely held theory today is that the ancestors of today's Native American peoples traveled to the Western Hemisphere from Asia between 25,000 and 30,000 years ago, which was around the same time that Japan was being settled by Stone Age inhabitants. There is dental evidence and blood-type evidence to support this theory. A dental pattern that is found among most ancient human fossils in the Americas is consistent with the dental pattern of ancient human fossils in northeastern Asia. In blood type, the fact that blood type B is almost nonexistent among Native American populations but exists in Asian populations leads to the conclusion that migrations to the Americas from Asia took place before the evolution of blood type B, which is believed to have occurred around 30,000 years ago. In addition to the dental and blood-type evidence, more general evolutionary evidence suggests that it took more than 20,000 years for the variety of physical traits common to Native American populations to evolve, and linguists broadly concur that the development of the approximately 500 distinct languages of the Native Americans would require approximately 25,000 years.

2   The proposed migration from Asia to the Americas took place during the Ice Age that characterized the Pleistocene epoch. During that period of time, there were huge glaciers holding enormous volumes of water, and, because of the huge glaciers, sea levels were as much as 100 meters lower than they are today. The reduced sea levels meant that Asia and North America were linked with a 750-mile-wide landmass, named Beringia after the Bering Straits that now cover it, and consisted of treeless grassland with warm summers and cold dry winters. Because of the geographical features of Beringia during the Pleistocene epoch, it was an environment well-suited to the large mammals of the time, such as mammoth, mastodon, bison, horse, and reindeer, as well as to the Stone Age hunters who depended on these animals for their existence. The Stone Age inhabitants of the area used these animals not only for food but also for shelter, clothing, and weapons; they were able to spread out and expand their hunting areas as their populations grew, and their populations most likely grew at a very high rate because of the huge amount of territory available for expansion.

3   **11A** In spite of the evidence, not all anthropologists are convinced that the migrations from Asia to the Americas took place as early as 25,000 to 30,000 years ago. **11B** There is general agreement that the migrations took place, but some believe that the migrations took place much later. **11C** No fossilized human bones have been found in what used to be Beringia; finding human bones dating from 25,000 to 30,000 years ago would be strong proof of the dates when the migrations took place. However, because what was once Beringia is submerged beneath ocean waters, it may be a formidable task to uncover fossil evidence of migration from Asia to the Americas through Beringia. **11D**

Questions

1. The word held in paragraph 1 could best be replaced by
   - Ⓐ accepted
   - Ⓑ possessed
   - Ⓒ contained
   - Ⓓ carried

2. The word support in paragraph 1 could best be replaced by
   - Ⓐ hold
   - Ⓑ finance
   - Ⓒ confirm
   - Ⓓ stiffen

3. Which of the following is NOT provided as evidence to support the hypothesis that the migration discussed in the passage occurred 25,000 to 30,000 years ago?
   - Ⓐ Dental patterns common to Asians and Native Americans
   - Ⓑ Variations in blood types between Asians and Native Americans
   - Ⓒ The number of Native American languages in existence today
   - Ⓓ The human bones found in Beringia

4. The phrase broadly concur in paragraph 1 is closest in meaning to
   - Ⓐ have the contrary idea
   - Ⓑ have extensive debates
   - Ⓒ openly question
   - Ⓓ are in general agreement

5. Which of the sentences below expresses the essential information in the highlighted sentence in paragraph 2? *Incorrect* choices change the meaning in important ways or leave out essential information.
   - Ⓐ Since the Ice Age, the amount of water in the oceans has decreased dramatically.
   - Ⓑ During the Ice Age, sea levels were low because of how much water was frozen.
   - Ⓒ Glaciers have grown tremendously since the last Ice Age.
   - Ⓓ During the Ice Age, huge glaciers displaced a lot of water, causing the oceans to rise.

6. It is stated in the passage that Beringia
   - Ⓐ was the source of the name Bering Straits
   - Ⓑ used to be covered with trees
   - Ⓒ is now submerged
   - Ⓓ was unable to support animal life

7. The phrase well-suited in paragraph 2 is closest in meaning to
   - Ⓐ equal to
   - Ⓑ appropriate for
   - Ⓒ flattering to
   - Ⓓ modified for

8. The word they in paragraph 2 refers to
   - Ⓐ Stone Age inhabitants
   - Ⓑ animals
   - Ⓒ weapons
   - Ⓓ their hunting areas

9. It is implied in the passage that the Stone Age inhabitants of Beringia were most likely
   - Ⓐ dependent on agriculture
   - Ⓑ poor hunters
   - Ⓒ involved in raising livestock
   - Ⓓ mobile

10. The author begins paragraph 3 with the expression In spite of to show that the fact that some anthropologists were not convinced by the evidence was
    - Ⓐ unexpected
    - Ⓑ a natural conclusion
    - Ⓒ unsurprising
    - Ⓓ logical

11. Look at the four squares [■] that indicate where the following sentence can be added to paragraph 3.

    Some, in fact, hypothesize that the migrations took place around 15,000 B.C.

    Click on a square [■] to add the sentence to the passage.

12. The word formidable in paragraph 3 is closest in meaning to
    - Ⓐ superior
    - Ⓑ maddening
    - Ⓒ powerful
    - Ⓓ difficult

13.

Directions: An introductory sentence or a brief summary of the passage is provided below. Complete the summary by selecting the FOUR answer choices that express the most important ideas in the passage. Some sentences do not belong in the summary because they express ideas that are not presented in the passage or are minor ideas in the passage. *This question is worth 3 points.*

The passage discusses a theory of migration from the Eastern Hemisphere to the Western Hemisphere 25,000 to 30,000 years ago.

-
-
-
-

Answer Choices (choose 4 to complete the chart):

(1) There are geographical reasons to support this theory.

(2) A number of fossils from the Pleistocene epoch have been found in Beringia.

(3) There are physiological reasons to support this theory.

(4) A study of blood types indicates that blood type B is rare among Native Americans.

(5) There are linguistic reasons to support this theory.

(6) Because there is no physiological evidence, not all experts agree with the theory.

Turn to the chart on page 544, and circle the numbers of the questions that you missed.

LISTENING

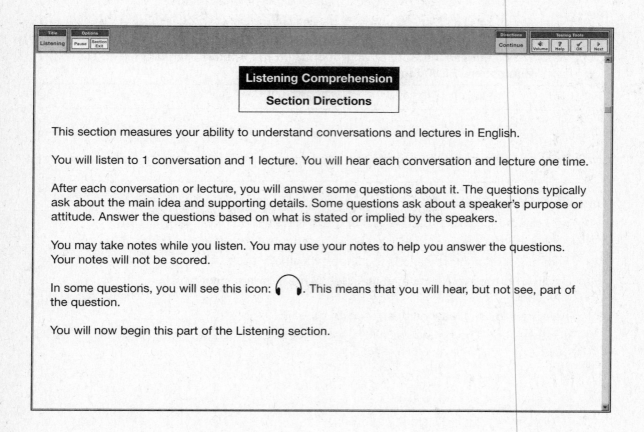

Listening Comprehension

Section Directions

This section measures your ability to understand conversations and lectures in English.

You will listen to 1 conversation and 1 lecture. You will hear each conversation and lecture one time.

After each conversation or lecture, you will answer some questions about it. The questions typically ask about the main idea and supporting details. Some questions ask about a speaker's purpose or attitude. Answer the questions based on what is stated or implied by the speakers.

You may take notes while you listen. You may use your notes to help you answer the questions. Your notes will not be scored.

In some questions, you will see this icon: 🎧. This means that you will hear, but not see, part of the question.

You will now begin this part of the Listening section.

Questions 1–5

Listen to a conversation between a student and a lab assistant.

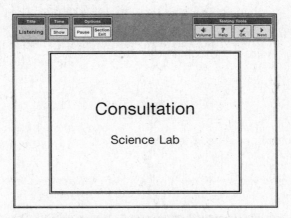

1. Why does the student go to see the lab assistant?

 Ⓐ To discuss two issues related to the science lab

 Ⓑ To discuss why he did not do a good job on his first lab assignment

 Ⓒ To find out what he must do to complete his lab report

 Ⓓ To talk about the members of his science lab group

2. Listen again to part of the passage. Then answer the question.

 Why does the lab assistant answer the student's question with this question:

 Ⓐ She has not understood what the student has asked.

 Ⓑ She is not sure who is in the student's group.

 Ⓒ She would like to know if the student has really done any work with his group.

 Ⓓ She has made an assumption about the group from the student's questions.

3. What does the lab assistant suggest that the group should try?

 Ⓐ Completing the lab session without talking

 Ⓑ Spending more time talking during the lab session

 Ⓒ Meeting before the lab session to have a discussion

 Ⓓ Working individually in the science lab

4. Listen again to part of the passage. Then answer the question.

 How does the student seem to feel about his group?

 Ⓐ He thinks his group does work quite deliberately.

 Ⓑ He feels that the group is not able to get things done effectively.

 Ⓒ He is not sure when or where the group is meeting.

 Ⓓ He is afraid that his group does not have enough time to do a good job.

5. What does the lab assistant say about the lab report?

 Ⓐ It must be completed by the group.

 Ⓑ Each member may decide how to prepare the report.

 Ⓒ Each individual must write a part of the report.

 Ⓓ The report must be prepared in a very specific way.

Questions 6–11

Listen to a lecture in an American literature class.

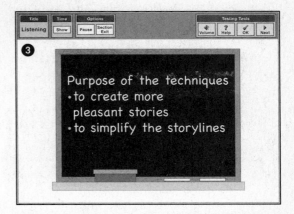

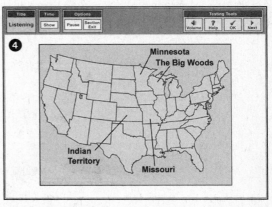

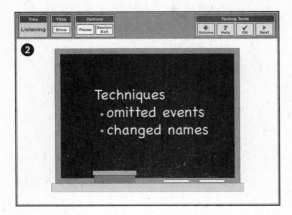

6. Listen again to part of the passage. Then answer the question. 🎧

Why does the professor begin the lecture in this way?

Ⓐ To show how the coming lecture is related to a previous lecture

Ⓑ To outline the various topics that will be covered in the course

Ⓒ To indicate that the topic will be covered in a future lecture

Ⓓ To impress the students with the importance of the coming topic

7. How is the information in the lecture presented?

Ⓐ Two different genres are contrasted.

Ⓑ Examples of a certain genre are described.

Ⓒ Various characteristics of a genre are classified.

Ⓓ Events in the life of a person are outlined chronologically.

8. How is the *Little House* series classified?

Ⓐ As historical fact

Ⓑ As autobiography

Ⓒ As historical fiction

Ⓓ As biography

9. What two statements are true about Laura Wilder's *Little House* series?

Click on 2 answers.

Ⓐ Laura made up many of the events.

Ⓑ Laura wrote the books during her childhood.

Ⓒ Every event recorded in the books happened.

Ⓓ Not every event in Laura's life was recorded.

10. What event did Laura omit from her books?

Ⓐ A move to the Indian Territory

Ⓑ A problem she had with Nellie Olsen

Ⓒ Her father's storytelling sessions

Ⓓ The birth and death of her brother

11. What conclusion can be drawn from the lecture?

Ⓐ That historical fiction is not always historically accurate

Ⓑ That historical fiction is always autobiographical

Ⓒ That historical fiction must be true to reality

Ⓓ That authors of historical fiction alter facts only unintentionally

Turn to the chart on page 545, and circle the numbers of the questions that you missed.

SPEAKING

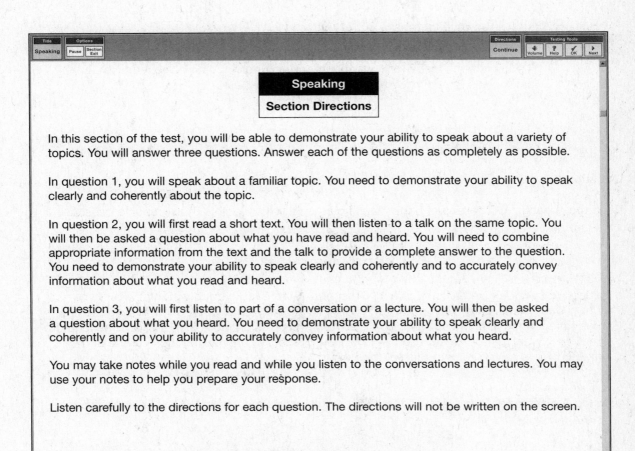

In this section of the test, you will be able to demonstrate your ability to speak about a variety of topics. You will answer three questions. Answer each of the questions as completely as possible.

In question 1, you will speak about a familiar topic. You need to demonstrate your ability to speak clearly and coherently about the topic.

In question 2, you will first read a short text. You will then listen to a talk on the same topic. You will then be asked a question about what you have read and heard. You will need to combine appropriate information from the text and the talk to provide a complete answer to the question. You need to demonstrate your ability to speak clearly and coherently and to accurately convey information about what you read and heard.

In question 3, you will first listen to part of a conversation or a lecture. You will then be asked a question about what you heard. You need to demonstrate your ability to speak clearly and coherently and on your ability to accurately convey information about what you heard.

You may take notes while you read and while you listen to the conversations and lectures. You may use your notes to help you prepare your response.

Listen carefully to the directions for each question. The directions will not be written on the screen.

Questions 1–3

Question 1

Read the question. On a piece of paper, take notes on the main points of a response. Then respond to the question.

> If you were the leader of your country, what would you do? Use reasons
> and details to support your response.

> Preparation Time: 15 seconds
> Response Time: 45 seconds

Question 2

Read the passage. On a piece of paper, take notes on the main points of the reading passage.

> Reading Time: 45 seconds

Part of the syllabus in a history class

One of the requirements for this class is that you watch a number of films on historical topics. You will be given a list of twenty films, and you are required to watch at least twelve of the twenty films. After you watch each film, you are to write a report summarizing the key information in the film. (If you want, you may turn in reports on more than twelve films for extra credit.) All twenty films are on reserve in the library, and you may watch them in one of the viewing rooms on the second floor of the library.

Listen to the passage. On a piece of paper, take notes on the main points of the listening passage.

Now answer the following question:

> How do the students seem to feel about the history class assignment?

> Preparation Time: 30 seconds
> Response Time: 60 seconds

Question 3

Listen to the passage. On a piece of paper, take notes on the main points of the listening passage.

Now answer the following question:

How are glaciers formed?

> Preparation Time: 20 seconds
> Response Time: 60 seconds

After you have completed this test, fill in the chart on pages 546–551.

WRITING

Writing
Section Directions

This section measures your ability to use writing to communicate in an academic environment. There will be one writing task.

For this writing task, you will read a passage and listen to a lecture and then answer a question based on what you have read and heard.

Integrated Writing Directions

For this task, you will read a passage about an academic topic. You will have **3 minutes** to read the passage. You may take notes on the passage while you read. The passage will then be removed and you will listen to a lecture about the same topic. While you listen, you may also take notes.

Then you will write a response to a question that asks you about the relationship between the lecture you heard and the reading passage. Try to answer the question as completely as possible using information from the reading passage and the lecture. The question does **not** ask you to express your personal opinion. You will be able to see the reading passage again when it is time for you to write. You may use your notes to help you answer the question. You will have **20 minutes** to write your response.

Typically, an effective response will be 150 to 225 words. You need to demonstrate your ability to write well and to provide complete and accurate content.

Now you will see the reading passage. Remember you can look at the passage again when you write your response. Immediately after the reading time ends, the lecture begins.

Read the passage. On a piece of paper, take notes on the main points of the reading passage.

Reading Time: 3 minutes

Garlic, a member of the lily family with its distinctive odor and taste, has been used throughout recorded history because it was considered to have beneficial properties. The earliest known record of its use is in Sanskrit records from 3,000 B.C.

It was used as a medicine in Ancient Egypt, where it was used to cure 22 different ailments. It was also fed to the slaves who were building the pyramids because the Egyptians believed that, in addition to keeping the slaves healthy so that they could continue to work, garlic would make the slaves stronger so that they could work harder.

The ancient Greeks and Romans found even more uses for garlic than the Egyptians had. In addition to using garlic to cure illnesses, as the Egyptians had, the Greeks and Romans believed that garlic had magical powers, that it could ward off evil spells and curses. Garlic was also fed to soldiers because it was believed to make men more courageous.

Quite a few seafaring cultures have also used garlic because they believed that it was beneficial in helping sailors to endure long voyages. Homer used it on his odysseys, the Vikings always carried garlic on their long voyages in the northern seas, and Marco Polo left records showing that garlic was carried on his voyages to the Orient.

Finally, even as late as early in the twentieth century, it was believed that garlic could fight infections. Because of this belief, garlic juice was applied to soldiers' wounds in World War I to keep infection at bay and to prevent gangrene.

Listen to the passage. On a piece of paper, take notes on the main points of the listening passage.

Now answer the following question:

How does the information in the listening passage support the information presented in the reading passage?

Preparation Time: 1 minute
Response Time: 20 minutes

After you have completed this test, fill in the chart on pages 546–551.

MINI-TEST 2

READING

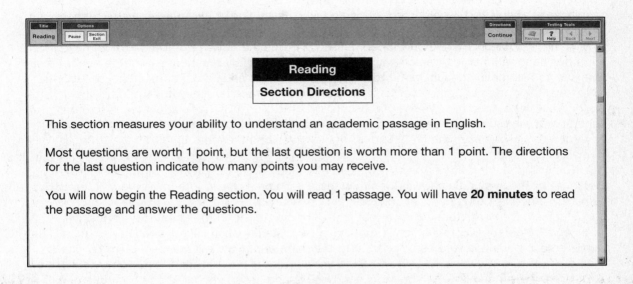

Reading

Section Directions

This section measures your ability to understand an academic passage in English.

Most questions are worth 1 point, but the last question is worth more than 1 point. The directions for the last question indicate how many points you may receive.

You will now begin the Reading section. You will read 1 passage. You will have **20 minutes** to read the passage and answer the questions.

Read the passage.

| 20 minutes |

Birth Order

1   A considerable body of research has demonstrated a correlation between birth order and aspects such as temperament and behavior, and some psychologists believe that birth order significantly affects the development of personality. Psychologist Alfred Adler was a pioneer in the study of the relationship between birth order and personality. A key point in his research and in the hypothesis that he developed based on it was that it was not the actual numerical birth position that affected personality; instead, it was the similar responses in large numbers of families to children in specific birth order positions that had an effect. For example, first-borns, who have their parents to themselves initially and do not have to deal with siblings in the first part of their lives, tend to have their first socialization experiences with adults and therefore tend to find the process of peer socialization more difficult. In contrast, later-born children have to deal with siblings from the first moment of their lives and therefore tend to have stronger socialization skills.

2   Numerous studies since Adler's have been conducted on the effect of birth order and personality. These studies have tended to classify birth order types into four different categories: first-born, second-born and/or middle, last, and only child.

3   Studies have consistently shown that first-born children tend to exhibit similar positive and negative personality traits. First-borns have consistently been linked with academic achievement in various studies; in one study, the number of National Merit scholarship winners who are first-borns was found to be equal to the number of second- and third-borns combined. First-borns have been found to be more responsible and assertive than those born in other birth-order positions and tend to rise to positions of leadership more often than others; more first-borns have served in the U.S. Congress and as U.S. presidents than have those born in other birth-order positions. However, studies have shown that first-borns tend to be more subject to stress and were considered problem children more often than later-borns.

4   Second-born and/or middle children demonstrate markedly different tendencies from first-borns. They tend to feel inferior to the older child or children because it is difficult for them to comprehend that their lower level of achievement is a function of age rather than ability, and they often try to succeed in areas other than those in which their older sibling or siblings excel. They tend to be more trusting, accepting, and focused on others than the more self-centered first-borns, and they tend to have a comparatively higher level of success in team sports than do first-borns or only children, who more often excel in individual sports.

5   The last-born child is the one who tends to be the eternal baby of the family and thus often exhibits a strong sense of security. Last-borns collectively achieve the highest degree of social success and demonstrate the highest levels of self-esteem of all the birth-order positions. They often exhibit less competitiveness than older brothers and sisters and are more likely to take part in less competitive group games or in social organizations such as sororities and fraternities.

6   Only children tend to exhibit some of the main characteristics of first-borns and some of the characteristics of last-borns. Only children tend to exhibit the strong sense of security and self-esteem exhibited by last-borns while, like first-borns, they are more achievement oriented and more likely than middle- or last-borns to achieve academic success. However, only children tend to have the most problems establishing close relationships and exhibit a lower need for affiliation than other children.

Refer to this version of the passage to answer the questions that follow.

Paragraph

Birth Order

1   A considerable body of research has demonstrated a correlation between birth order and aspects such as temperament and behavior, and some psychologists believe that birth order significantly affects the development of personality. Psychologist Alfred Adler was a pioneer in the study of the relationship between birth order and personality. A key point in his research and in the hypothesis that he developed based on it was that it was not the actual numerical birth position that affected personality; instead, it was the similar responses in large numbers of families to children in specific birth order positions that had an effect. For example, first-borns, who have their parents to themselves initially and do not have to deal with siblings in the first part of their lives, tend to have their first socialization experiences with adults and therefore tend to find the process of peer socialization more difficult. In contrast, later-born children have to deal with siblings from the first moment of their lives and therefore tend to have stronger socialization skills.

2   Numerous studies since Adler's have been conducted on the effect of birth order and personality. These studies have tended to classify birth order types into four different categories: first-born, second-born and/or middle, last, and only child.

3   Studies have consistently shown that first-born children tend to exhibit similar positive and negative personality traits. First-borns have consistently been linked with academic achievement in various studies; in one study, the number of National Merit scholarship winners who are first-borns was found to be equal to the number of second- and third-borns combined. First-borns have been found to be more responsible and assertive than those born in other birth-order positions and tend to rise to positions of leadership more often than others; more first-borns have served in the U.S. Congress and as U.S. presidents than have those born in other birth-order positions. However, studies have shown that first-borns tend to be more subject to stress and were considered problem children more often than later-borns.

4   **9A** Second-born and/or middle children demonstrate markedly different tendencies from first-borns. **9B** They tend to feel inferior to the older child or children because it is difficult for them to comprehend that their lower level of achievement is a function of age rather than ability, and they often try to succeed in areas other than those in which their older sibling or siblings excel. **9C** They tend to be more trusting, accepting, and focused on others than the more self-centered first-borns, and they tend to have a comparatively higher level of success in team sports than do first-borns or only children, who more often excel in individual sports. **9D**

5   The last-born child is the one who tends to be the eternal baby of the family and thus often exhibits a strong sense of security. Last-borns collectively achieve the highest degree of social success and demonstrate the highest levels of self-esteem of all the birth-order positions. They often exhibit less competitiveness than older brothers and sisters and are more likely to take part in less competitive group games or in social organizations such as sororities and fraternities.

6   Only children tend to exhibit some of the main characteristics of first-borns and some of the characteristics of last-borns. Only children tend to exhibit the strong sense of security and self-esteem exhibited by last-borns while, like first-borns, they are more achievement oriented and more likely than middle- or last-borns to achieve academic success. However, only children tend to have the most problems establishing close relationships and exhibit a lower need for affiliation than other children.

Questions

1. The word body in paragraph 1 could best be replaced by
   Ⓐ corpse
   Ⓑ amount
   Ⓒ organization
   Ⓓ skeleton

2. The word key in paragraph 1 could best be replaced by
   Ⓐ locked
   Ⓑ secret
   Ⓒ studied
   Ⓓ significant

3. The word it in paragraph 1 refers to
   Ⓐ personality
   Ⓑ component
   Ⓒ research
   Ⓓ hypothesis

4. What is stated in paragraph 1 about Adler?
   Ⓐ He was one of the first to study the effect of birth order on personality.
   Ⓑ He believed that it was the actual birth order that affected personality.
   Ⓒ He had found that the responses by family members had little to do with personality.
   Ⓓ He was the only one to study birth order.

5. The author includes the idea that These studies have tended to classify birth order types into four different categories in paragraph 2 in order to
   Ⓐ announce what ideas will be presented in the following paragraphs
   Ⓑ show how other studies differed from Adler's
   Ⓒ explain how Adler classified his work
   Ⓓ describe the various ways that different studies have categorized birth order groups

6. The word traits in paragraph 3 is closest in meaning to
   Ⓐ stresses
   Ⓑ marks
   Ⓒ characteristics
   Ⓓ fears

7. Which of the sentences below expresses the essential information in the highlighted sentence in paragraph 3? *Incorrect* choices change the meaning in important ways or leave out essential information.
   Ⓐ In spite of certain characteristics that first-borns possess, many of them become leaders.
   Ⓑ An interesting fact that is difficult to explain is that many first-borns have served in high government positions.
   Ⓒ Because first-borns tend to be very assertive, they are uncomfortable serving in government positions.
   Ⓓ Several examples support the idea that first-borns have characteristics that make them leaders.

8. The word accepting in paragraph 4 is closest in meaning to
   Ⓐ tolerant
   Ⓑ affectionate
   Ⓒ admissible
   Ⓓ respectable

9. Look at the four squares [■] that indicate where the following sentence can be added to paragraph 4.

   Thus, second-borns tend to be better at soccer, football, volleyball, and baseball than at tennis, diving, gymnastics, or archery.

   Click on a square [■] to add the sentence to the passage.

10. Which of the following is NOT true, according to the passage?
    Ⓐ First-borns tend to do well in individual sports.
    Ⓑ Middle children tend to have a preference for team sports.
    Ⓒ Last-borns tend to prefer games with fierce competition.
    Ⓓ Only children tend to prefer individual over team sports.

11. The phrase more achievement oriented in paragraph 6 is closest in meaning to

    Ⓐ more directly involved

    Ⓑ more focused on accomplishments

    Ⓒ more skilled as leaders

    Ⓓ more aware of surroundings

12. Which of the following would be most likely to have a successful career but few close friendships?

    Ⓐ A second-born

    Ⓑ A middle child

    Ⓒ A last-born

    Ⓓ An only child

13.

Directions:	Two of the answer choices below are used to describe each of the birth order groups. Complete the chart by matching appropriate answer choices to the birth order groups they are used to describe. ***This question is worth 3 points.***

first-borns	• •
second-borns and middle children	• •
last-borns	• •
only children	• •

Answer Choices (choose 8 to complete the chart):

  (1) Tendency to feel secure and to achieve social success

  (2) Tendency to concentrate on others rather than self

  (3) Tendency to feel secure and to do well in school

  (4) Tendency to do well in school and as leaders

  (5) Tendency to do poorly academically while excelling at individual sports

  (6) Tendency not to be highly competitive

  (7) Tendency to have problems maintaining relationships

  (8) Tendency to withdraw from others because of feelings of inferiority

  (9) Tendency to feel stressed

 (10) Tendency to feel inferior to siblings

Turn to the chart on page 544, and circle the numbers of the questions that you missed.

LISTENING

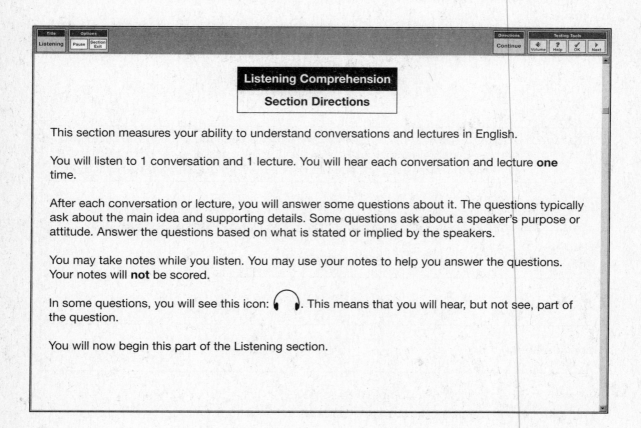

Questions 1–5

Listen to a conversation between a student and a professor.

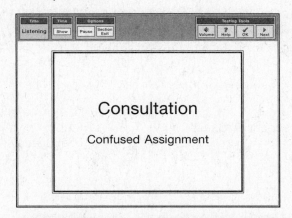

1. What is the student confused about?

   Click on 2 answers.

   Ⓐ Which professor gave the assignment
   Ⓑ When the assignment was given
   Ⓒ What she is supposed to read
   Ⓓ When the assignment is due

2. Listen again to part of the passage. Then answer the question.

   How does the professor seem to feel?
   Ⓐ Frustrated
   Ⓑ Enthusiastic
   Ⓒ Bored
   Ⓓ Calm

3. Is each of these part of the assignment?

For each answer, click in the YES or NO column.		
	YES	NO
Looking at various reports		
Reading journal articles from the library		
Determining the main ideas of articles		
Writing a journal article		
Comparing the main ideas of various reports		

4. Listen again to the end of the conversation. Then answer the question.

   Why does the professor end the conversation this way?
   Ⓐ To show that he enjoys going over information with students
   Ⓑ To indicate that he believes the student finally understands the assignment
   Ⓒ To show that he thinks the student may still be confused
   Ⓓ To indicate that he wants to end the conversation

5. What conclusion can be drawn about the student?
   Ⓐ She had not really needed to see the professor.
   Ⓑ She did not really need to write the report.
   Ⓒ She had already begun part of the assignment.
   Ⓓ She had understood almost nothing about the assignment.

Questions 6–11

Listen to a discussion in an archeology class.

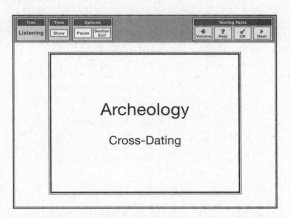

Archeology

Cross-Dating

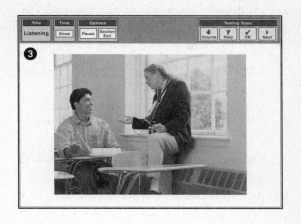

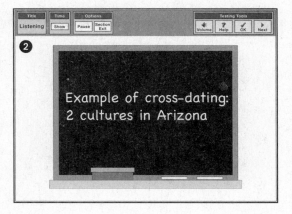

Example of cross-dating:
2 cultures in Arizona

6. What is the main topic of this discussion?
  Ⓐ A way of comparing two different archeological sites
  Ⓑ A method of determining the age of an ancient civilization
  Ⓒ Counting tree rings to date cultures
  Ⓓ The dates of various cultures in Arizona

7. How is the information in the discussion presented?
  Ⓐ Various cultures are contrasted.
  Ⓑ A series of cultures are presented in chronological order.
  Ⓒ The reasons why a certain technique works are listed.
  Ⓓ A concept is explained through an extended example.

8. What do archeologists compare when using cross-dating?
  Ⓐ Two cultures, each with unknown dates
  Ⓑ Two methods of dating cultures
  Ⓒ One culture with known and one culture with unknown dates
  Ⓓ The known dates of two cultures

9. What is NOT true about tree-ring dating, according to the discussion?
  Ⓐ It is a scientific method of dating.
  Ⓑ It can be used to date all types of areas.
  Ⓒ It was used effectively to date the northern culture.
  Ⓓ It was not used to date the southern culture.

10. Is each of these true about the areas discussed in the lecture?

For each statement, click in the YES or NO column.

	YES	NO
The dates of the northern culture were determined from tree-ring dating.		
Pieces of southern pottery were found in the northern area.		
The dates of the southern culture were determined from cross-dating.		
Pieces of northern pottery were found in the southern area.		

11. How does the student seem to feel about the material?
  Ⓐ Quite confident throughout the discussion
  Ⓑ Quite confident at first but confused later
  Ⓒ Quite confused throughout the discussion
  Ⓓ Quite confused at first but more confident later

Turn to the chart on page 545, and circle the numbers of the questions that you missed.

SPEAKING

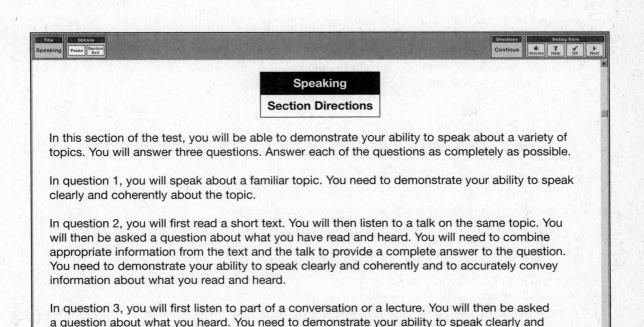

In this section of the test, you will be able to demonstrate your ability to speak about a variety of topics. You will answer three questions. Answer each of the questions as completely as possible.

In question 1, you will speak about a familiar topic. You need to demonstrate your ability to speak clearly and coherently about the topic.

In question 2, you will first read a short text. You will then listen to a talk on the same topic. You will then be asked a question about what you have read and heard. You will need to combine appropriate information from the text and the talk to provide a complete answer to the question. You need to demonstrate your ability to speak clearly and coherently and to accurately convey information about what you read and heard.

In question 3, you will first listen to part of a conversation or a lecture. You will then be asked a question about what you heard. You need to demonstrate your ability to speak clearly and coherently and on your ability to accurately convey information about what you heard.

You may take notes while you read and while you listen to the conversations and lectures. You may use your notes to help you prepare your response.

Listen carefully to the directions for each question. The directions will not be written on the screen.

Questions 1–3

Question 1

Read the question. On a piece of paper, take notes on the main points of a response. Then respond to the question.

> Do you think it is better to get up early in the morning or sleep in until later? Use reasons and details to support your response.

> Preparation Time: 15 seconds
> Response Time: 45 seconds

Question 2

Read the passage. On a piece of paper, take notes on the main points of the reading passage.

> Reading Time: 45 seconds

Leadership Roles

Have you ever considered the various roles that a group leader might take on? There can be many different kinds of leadership roles in groups; two of the many possible kinds of leadership roles are *instrumental* leadership and *expressive* leadership. Instrumental leadership is group leadership that emphasizes the completion of tasks by the group. Instrumental leadership is focused on getting the task done. Expressive leadership is different from instrumental leadership. Expressive leadership is leadership that is concerned with the well-being of the group; expressive leadership is leadership that is concerned with ensuring that all members of the group are comfortable working together.

Listen to the passage. On a piece of paper, take notes on the main points of the listening passage.

Now answer the following question:

> How does the information in the listening passage add to what is explained in the reading passage?

> Preparation Time: 30 seconds
> Response Time: 60 seconds

Question 3

Listen to the passage. On a piece of paper, take notes on the main points of the listening passage.

Now answer the following question:

How do the students seem to feel about what will be discussed at the student council meeting?

> Preparation Time: 20 seconds
> Response Time: 60 seconds

After you have completed this test, fill in the chart on pages 546–551.

WRITING

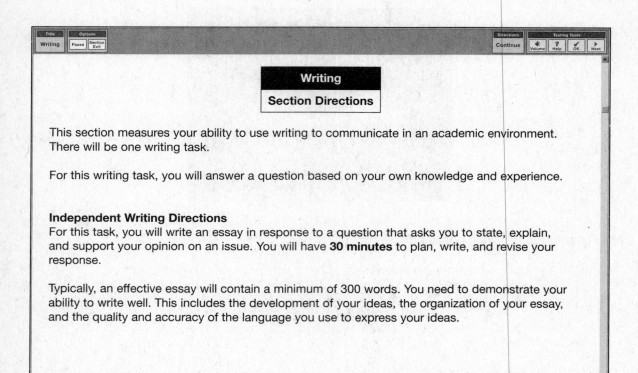

Read the question. On a piece of paper, take notes on the main points of a response. Then write your response.

What historical event in your country has had a major effect on your country? Give reasons and examples to support your response.

Response Time: 30 minutes

After you have completed this test, fill in the chart on pages 552–553.

MINI-TEST 3

READING

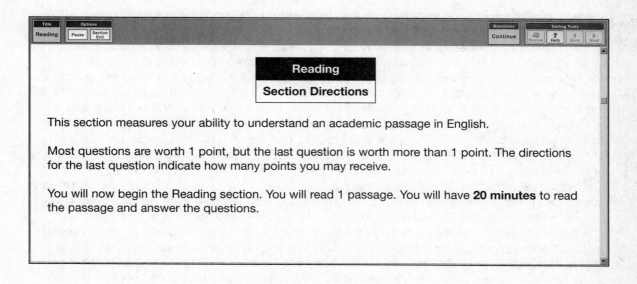

Title
Reading

Options
Pause | Section Exit

Directions
Continue

Testing Tools
Review | Help | Back | Next

Reading

Section Directions

This section measures your ability to understand an academic passage in English.

Most questions are worth 1 point, but the last question is worth more than 1 point. The directions for the last question indicate how many points you may receive.

You will now begin the Reading section. You will read 1 passage. You will have **20 minutes** to read the passage and answer the questions.

Read the passage.

20 minutes

Paragraph

Ketchup

1   The sauce that is today called ketchup (or catsup) in Western cultures is a tomato-based sauce that is quite distinct from the Eastern ancestors of this product. A sauce called *ke-tiap* was in use in China at least as early as the seventeenth century, but the Chinese version of the sauce was made of pickled fish, shellfish, and spices. The popularity of this Chinese sauce spread to Singapore and Malaysia, where it was called *kechap*. The Indonesian sauce *ketjab* derives its name from the same source as the Malaysian sauce but is made from very different ingredients. The Indonesian *ketjab* is made by cooking black soy beans, fermenting them, placing them in a salt brine for at least a week, cooking the resulting solution further, and sweetening it heavily; this process results in a dark, thick, and sweet variation of soy sauce.

2   Early in the eighteenth century, sailors from the British navy came across this exotic sauce on voyages to Malaysia and Singapore and brought samples of it back to England on return voyages. English chefs tried to recreate the sauce but were unable to do so exactly because key ingredients were unknown or unavailable in England; chefs ended up substituting ingredients such as mushrooms and walnuts in an attempt to recreate the special taste of the original Asian sauce. Variations of this sauce became quite the rage in eighteenth-century England, appearing in a number of recipe books and featured as an exotic addition to menus from the period.

3   The English version did not contain tomatoes, and it was not until the end of the eighteenth century that tomatoes became a main ingredient, in the ketchup of the newly created United States. It is quite notable that tomatoes were added to the sauce in that tomatoes had previously been considered quite dangerous to health. The tomato had been cultivated by the Aztecs, who had called it *tomatl*; however, early botanists had recognized that the tomato was a member of the *Solanacaea* family, which does include a number of poisonous plants. The leaves of the tomato plant are poisonous, though of course the fruit is not.

4   Thomas Jefferson, who cultivated the tomato in his gardens at Monticello and served dishes containing tomatoes at lavish feasts, often receives credit for changing the reputation of the tomato. Soon after Jefferson had introduced the tomato to American society, recipes combining the newly fashionable tomato with the equally fashionable and exotic sauce known as *ketchap* began to appear. By the middle of the nineteenth century, both the tomato and tomato ketchup were staples of the American kitchen.

5   Tomato ketchup, popular though it was, was quite time-consuming to prepare. In 1876, the first mass-produced tomato ketchup, a product of German-American Henry Heinz, went on sale and achieved immediate success. From tomato ketchup, Heinz branched out into a number of other products, including various sauces, pickles, and relishes. By 1890, his company had expanded to include sixty-five different products but was in need of a marketing slogan. Heinz settled on the slogan "57 Varieties" because he liked the way that the digits 5 and 7 looked in print, in spite of the fact that this slogan understated the number of products that he had at the time.

Refer to this version of the passage to answer the questions that follow.

Ketchup

1   The sauce that is today called ketchup (or catsup) in Western cultures is a tomato-based sauce that is quite distinct from the Eastern ancestors of this product. A sauce called *ke-tiap* was in use in China at least as early as the seventeenth century, but the Chinese version of the sauce was made of pickled fish, shellfish, and spices. The popularity of this Chinese sauce spread to Singapore and Malaysia, where it was called *kechap.* The Indonesian sauce *ketjab* derives its name from the same source as the Malaysian sauce but is made from very different ingredients. The Indonesian *ketjab* is made by cooking black soy beans, fermenting them, placing them in a salt brine for at least a week, cooking the resulting solution further, and sweetening it heavily; this process results in a dark, thick, and sweet variation of soy sauce.

2   Early in the eighteenth century, sailors from the British navy came across this exotic sauce on voyages to Malaysia and Singapore and brought samples of it back to England on return voyages. English chefs tried to recreate the sauce but were unable to do so exactly because key ingredients were unknown or unavailable in England; chefs ended up substituting ingredients such as mushrooms and walnuts in an attempt to recreate the special taste of the original Asian sauce. Variations of this sauce became quite the rage in eighteenth-century England, appearing in a number of recipe books and featured as an exotic addition to menus from the period.

3   The English version did not contain tomatoes, and it was not until the end of the eighteenth century that tomatoes became a main ingredient, in the ketchup of the newly created United States. It is quite notable that tomatoes were added to the sauce in that tomatoes had previously been considered quite dangerous to health. The tomato had been cultivated by the Aztecs, who had called it *tomatl*; however, early botanists had recognized that the tomato was a member of the *Solanacaea* family, which does include a number of poisonous plants. The leaves of the tomato plant are poisonous, though of course the fruit is not.

4   **10A** Thomas Jefferson, who cultivated the tomato in his gardens at Monticello and served dishes containing tomatoes at lavish feasts, often receives credit for changing the reputation of the tomato. **10B** Soon after Jefferson had introduced the tomato to American society, recipes combining the newly fashionable tomato with the equally fashionable and exotic sauce known as *ketchap* began to appear. **10C** By the middle of the nineteenth century, both the tomato and tomato ketchup were staples of the American kitchen. **10D**

5   Tomato ketchup, popular though it was, was quite time-consuming to prepare. In 1876, the first mass-produced tomato ketchup, a product of German-American Henry Heinz, went on sale and achieved immediate success. From tomato ketchup, Heinz branched out into a number of other products, including various sauces, pickles, and relishes. By 1890, his company had expanded to include sixty-five different products but was in need of a marketing slogan. Heinz settled on the slogan "57 Varieties" because he liked the way that the digits 5 and 7 looked in print, in spite of the fact that this slogan understated the number of products that he had at the time.

Questions

1. The word ancestors in paragraph 1 is closest in meaning to
   Ⓐ predecessors
   Ⓑ descendents
   Ⓒ creators
   Ⓓ ingredients

2. It is NOT stated in paragraph 1 that
   Ⓐ the Chinese sauce was in existence in the seventeenth century
   Ⓑ the Malaysian sauce was similar to the Chinese sauce
   Ⓒ the Chinese sauce was made from seafood and spices
   Ⓓ the Indonesian sauce was similar to the Chinese sauce

3. The word it in paragraph 1 refers to
   Ⓐ a salt brine
   Ⓑ a week
   Ⓒ the resulting solution
   Ⓓ this process

4. The expression came across in paragraph 2 could best be replaced by
   Ⓐ traversed
   Ⓑ discovered
   Ⓒ transported
   Ⓓ described

5. It can be inferred from paragraph 2 that mushrooms and walnuts were
   Ⓐ difficult to find in England
   Ⓑ not part of the original Asian recipe
   Ⓒ not native to England
   Ⓓ transported to England from Asia

6. The word rage in paragraph 2 could best be replaced by
   Ⓐ anger
   Ⓑ distinction
   Ⓒ misunderstanding
   Ⓓ fashion

7. The author mentions The English version at the beginning of paragraph 3 in order to
   Ⓐ indicate what will be discussed in the coming paragraph
   Ⓑ explain why tomatoes were considered dangerous
   Ⓒ make a reference to the topic of the previous paragraph
   Ⓓ provide an example of a sauce using tomatoes

8. According to paragraph 3, the tomato plant
   Ⓐ was considered poisonous by the Aztecs
   Ⓑ is related to some poisonous plants
   Ⓒ has edible leaves
   Ⓓ has fruit that is sometimes quite poisonous

9. The word staples in paragraph 4 could best be replaced by
   Ⓐ standard elements
   Ⓑ strong attachments
   Ⓒ necessary utensils
   Ⓓ rare alternatives

10. Look at the four squares [■] that indicate where the following sentence can be added to paragraph 4.

    It turned from very bad to exceedingly good.

    Click on a square [■] to add the sentence to the passage.

11. The expression branched out in paragraph 5 is closest in meaning to
    Ⓐ contracted
    Ⓑ stemmed
    Ⓒ converted
    Ⓓ expanded

12. Which of the sentences below expresses the essential information in the highlighted sentence in paragraph 5? *Incorrect* choices change the meaning in important ways or leave out essential information.

Ⓐ Heinz selected a certain slogan even though it was inaccurate because he liked the look of it.

Ⓑ Heinz was eventually able to settle a dispute about which slogan would be the best for his company.

Ⓒ Heinz was unable to print out the actual number of varieties, so he printed out a different number.

Ⓓ Heinz's company actually had far fewer products than the slogan indicated that it did.

13.

Directions: An introductory sentence or a brief summary of the passage is provided below. Complete the summary by selecting the FOUR answer choices that express the most important ideas in the passage. Some sentences do not belong in the summary because they express ideas that are not presented in the passage or are minor ideas in the passage. ***This question is worth 3 points.***
This passage discusses the history of a sauce known as ketchup.
•
•
•
•

Answer Choices (choose 4 to complete the chart):

(1) An English variation of the sauce, without tomatoes, became popular after sailors returned home with samples.

(2) A plant called the *tomatl* is known to have been cultivated by the Aztecs.

(3) A businessman achieved success with the introduction of a mass-produced tomato-based sauce.

(4) The sauce was first developed in Asia, without tomatoes.

(5) The sauce known as *ketjab* was a variation of the Chinese sauce that contained tomatoes.

(6) The American version added the exotic and newly fashionable tomato as a main ingredient.

Turn to the chart on page 544, and circle the numbers of the questions that you missed.

LISTENING

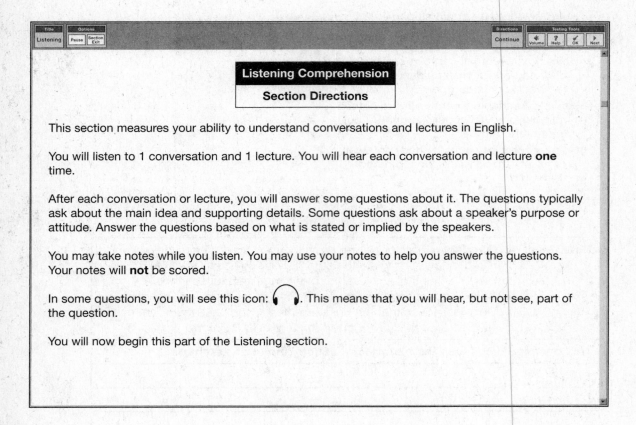

Questions 1–5

Listen to a conversation between a student and an advisor.

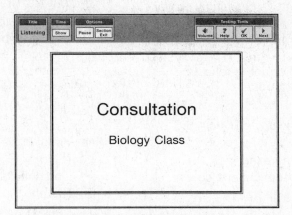

1. What problem does the student have?
   (A) Deciding whether or not to study biology
   (B) Deciding between two seemingly similar courses
   (C) Deciding whether to take a 100- or 200-level course
   (D) Deciding whether or not to take an introductory-level course

2. What differentiates Biology 101 from the other course?
   (A) Biology 101 has more lectures.
   (B) Biology 101 is a more general course.
   (C) Biology 101 has a laboratory component.
   (D) Biology 101 has fewer units.

3. Listen again to part of the passage. Then answer the question. 🎧

   What does the advisor mean when she says this: 🎧
   (A) "You really should have said it differently."
   (B) "It's not how I would say it, but it's close in meaning."
   (C) "You have your opinion, and I have mine."
   (D) "It would have been better to have said something else."

4. What decision does the advisor seem to think that the student should make fairly soon?
   (A) Whether his major will be within the sciences or not
   (B) How he should fulfill the general education requirements
   (C) Whether or not to study biology
   (D) Exactly what his major is

5. What can be concluded from the conversation?
   (A) That the student has made a decision on a major
   (B) That the student really does not like science
   (C) That the student has completed his general education requirements
   (D) That the student has decided which course to take

Questions 6–11

Listen to a lecture in a gemology class.

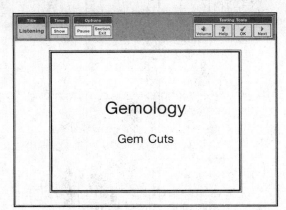

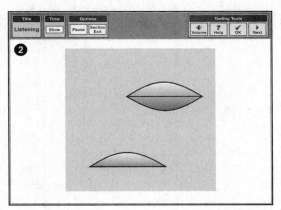

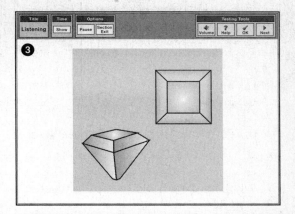

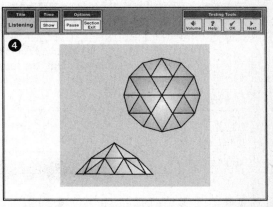

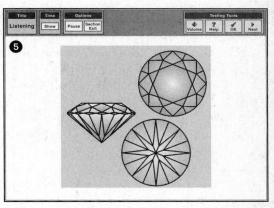

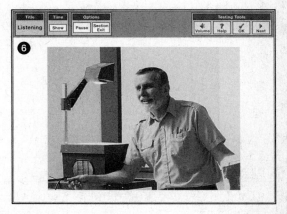

6. How does the professor present the different styles of gems?

   Ⓐ From the least common to the most common

   Ⓑ From the simplest to the most complex

   Ⓒ From the oldest to the most recently developed

   Ⓓ From the least expensive to the most expensive

7. What are the characteristics of these gemstone cuts?

For each gemstone cut, click in the correct column.			
	Unfaceted	**Faceted only on the top**	**Faceted on the top and bottom**
Cabochon			
Table cut			
Rose cut			
Brilliant cut			

8. What does the professor say about faceting?

Click on 2 answers.

   Ⓐ It was not done earlier than the fifteenth century.

   Ⓑ It may have been done earlier than the fifteenth century.

   Ⓒ It was done in the fifteenth century.

   Ⓓ It was not done until after the fifteenth century.

9. Which style of gem is no longer used much because it does not reflect light well?

   Ⓐ The rose cut

   Ⓑ The cabochon

   Ⓒ The table cut

   Ⓓ The brilliant cut

10. What overall conclusion can be drawn from the lecture?

   Ⓐ That the cutting of gemstones developed earlier than the polishing of gemstones

   Ⓑ That the cutting of gemstones developed at the same time as the polishing of gemstones

   Ⓒ That the polishing of gemstones developed earlier than the cutting of gemstones

   Ⓓ That the polishing of gemstones developed as a result of the cutting of gemstones

11. What is the assignment for the next class?

   Ⓐ To cut some gems

   Ⓑ To identify the style of some gems

   Ⓒ To polish some gems

   Ⓓ To read about some gems

Turn to the chart on page 545, and circle the numbers of the questions that you missed.

SPEAKING

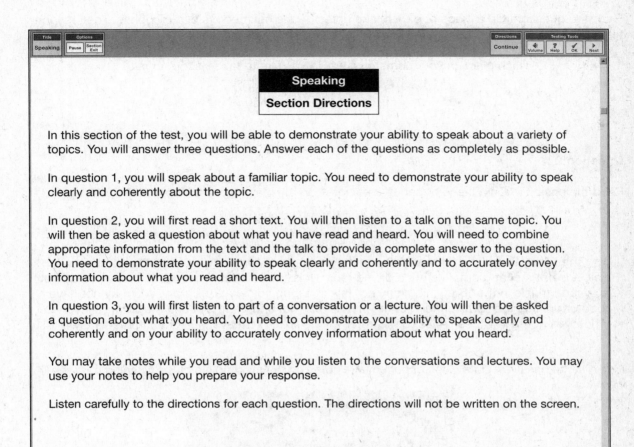

Questions 1–3

Question 1

Read the question. On a piece of paper, take notes on the main points of a response. Then respond to the question.

Which place in your hometown would you like to take visitors to see?

> Preparation Time: 15 seconds
> Response Time: 45 seconds

Question 2

Read the passage. On a piece of paper, take notes on the main points of the reading passage.

> Reading Time: 45 seconds

Notice posted around the library

The library is a place for reading, working on research, or studying only. It is not a concert hall. It is not a chat room. It is not a dining room. It is not a motel. This means that you may not play loud music in the library, you may not talk in a loud voice in the library, you may not have food or drink in the library, and you may not stretch out and go to sleep in the library. Anyone who does not follow these rules to the letter will be asked to leave the library immediately.

Listen to the passage. On a piece of paper, take notes on the main points of the listening passage.

Now answer the following question:

How do the students react to the notice posted in the library?

> Preparation Time: 30 seconds
> Response Time: 60 seconds

Question 3

Listen to the passage. On a piece of paper, take notes on the main points of the listening passage.

Now answer the following question:

Why does the professor use the example of split infinitives?

> Preparation Time: 20 seconds
> Response Time: 60 seconds

After you have completed this test, fill in the chart on pages 546–551.

WRITING

Writing
Section Directions

This section measures your ability to use writing to communicate in an academic environment. There will be one writing task.

For this writing task, you will read a passage and listen to a lecture and then answer a question based on what you have read and heard.

Integrated Writing Directions

For this task, you will read a passage about an academic topic. You will have **3 minutes** to read the passage. You may take notes on the passage while you read. The passage will then be removed and you will listen to a lecture about the same topic. While you listen, you may also take notes.

Then you will write a response to a question that asks you about the relationship between the lecture you heard and the reading passage. Try to answer the question as completely as possible using information from the reading passage and the lecture. The question does **not** ask you to express your personal opinion. You will be able to see the reading passage again when it is time for you to write. You may use your notes to help you answer the question. You will have **20 minutes** to write your response.

Typically, an effective response will be 150 to 225 words. You need to demonstrate your ability to write well and to provide complete and accurate content.

Now you will see the reading passage. Remember you can look at the passage again when you write your response. Immediately after the reading time ends, the lecture begins.

Read the passage. On a piece of paper, take notes on the main points of the reading passage.

Reading Time: 3 minutes

Many species of Asian bamboo have rather unique flowering and seeding cycles. What makes these cycles unique is that all the members of a species tend to flower and then seed at the same time; something else that is unique is that these simultaneous seeding cycles generally occur at rather lengthy intervals of perhaps fifteen to sixty years or more. This means that a particular species of Asian bamboo may not flower and seed for many, many decades and then, when this species does flower and seed, all of its members tend to flower at the same time and then simultaneously set tremendous quantities of seeds before they die so that the seeds can grow into new plants.

One particular species of Chinese bamboo is a rather extreme example of the unique flowering and seeding cycles of Asian bamboo. This species tends to flower and seed less than once a century, and, when it does flower and seed, it does so throughout the world. This special Chinese species is known to have flowered and seeded in the early 1700s and in the mid 1800s and then once again in the late 1960s. Its twentieth century flowering was quite well documented and showed how amazing the species' flowering and seeding cycle is. Astoundingly, when this species of bamboo flowered and seeded in the late 1960s, it flowered and seeded in widely divergent areas; the flowering and seeding of this species of bamboo was noted in many parts of the world, including northern and southern Asia, North America, South America, and Europe.

Listen to the passage. On a piece of paper, take notes on the main points of the listening passage.

Now answer the following question:

How is the information in the listening passage about the giant panda related to the ideas in the reading passage on Asian bamboo?

Preparation Time: 1 minute
Response Time: 20 minutes

After you have completed this test, fill in the chart on pages 552–553.

MINI-TEST 4

READING

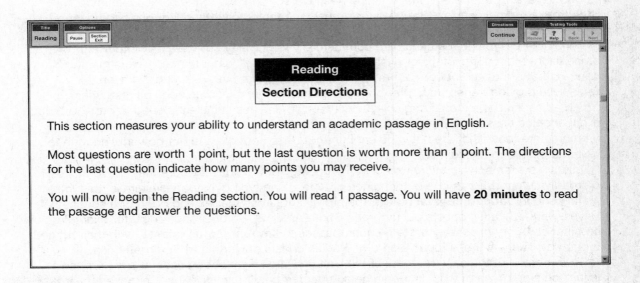

Title
Reading

Options
Pause | Section Exit

Directions
Continue

Testing Tools
Review | ? Help | Back | Next

Reading
Section Directions

This section measures your ability to understand an academic passage in English.

Most questions are worth 1 point, but the last question is worth more than 1 point. The directions for the last question indicate how many points you may receive.

You will now begin the Reading section. You will read 1 passage. You will have **20 minutes** to read the passage and answer the questions.

Read the passage.

> 20 minutes

Estuaries

1   Fresh water from land enters the ocean through rivers, streams, and groundwater flowing through valleys. These valleys that channel fresh water from land to the salty ocean, which range from extremely narrow stream-cut channels to remarkably broad lagoons behind long barrier islands, are called **estuaries**.

2   A number of types of estuaries are commercially vital. Many commercially important estuaries are the mouths of major rivers. The powerful flow of water in major rivers maintains channels that are deep enough for navigation by ocean-bound vessels, and the rivers themselves provide transportation of goods to points farther inland. In addition, estuaries formed as a result of tectonic or glacial activity are sometimes sufficiently deep to provide ports for oceangoing vessels. The types of estuaries that are not viable as ports-of-call for ocean commerce are those that are not wide enough, not deep enough, and not powerful enough to prevent the buildup of sediment.

3   Estuary systems, which vary to reflect the geology of the coasts where they are found, can be broadly categorized as one of two different types. One type of estuary system is the type that is found in **flooded coastal plains**, the broad land areas that extend out to the continental shelves, on the Atlantic coasts of North and South America, Europe, and Africa, for example. The other category of estuary system encompasses the **mountainous coasts**, with their rugged topography, such as those found along the Pacific coasts of North and South America.

4   Today, much of the eastern coast of the United States is a flooded coastal plain. During the last ice age, much of what is today the submerged continental shelf was exposed as an extended part of the continent. Intricate river systems composed of main rivers and their tributaries cut valleys across the plains to the edge of the shelf, where they released the fresh water that they carried into the ocean. Then, as the ice melted at the end of the ice age, rising waters extended inland over the lower areas, creating today's broad drowned river valleys. On today's flooded coastal plains, the water is comparatively shallow and huge amounts of sand and sediment are deposited. These conditions foster the growth of extensive long and narrow offshore deposits, many of which are exposed above the water as sandspits or barrier islands. These deposits are constantly being reshaped, sometimes extremely slowly and sometimes quite rapidly, by the forces of water and wind. It is common along flooded coastal plains for drowned river valleys to empty into lagoons that have been created behind the sandspits and barrier islands rather than emptying directly into the ocean. These lagoons support vigorous biological activity inasmuch as they are shallow, which causes them to heat up quickly, and they are fed by a constant inflow of nutrient-rich sediments.

5   Unlike the flooded coastal plains, the mountainous coasts have a more rugged and irregular topography with deeper coastal waters. There is less sand and sediment, and external systems of barrier islands are not as pervasive as they are on flooded coastal plains because the mountainous topography blocks the flow of sediments to the coast and because the deeper ocean water inhibits the growth of barrier islands, and without the protection of barrier beaches, mountainous coasts are more exposed to direct attack by the erosive forces of waves. Different geological processes contribute to the rugged topography along mountain coasts. The tectonic activity that creates the mountains along a mountainous coast can cause large blocks of the Earth's crust to fall below sea level; San Francisco Bay in California and the Strait of Juan de Fuca in Washington state in the north formed in this way. In the northern latitudes, coastal fjords were created as glaciers cut impressive u-shaped valleys through mountains and now carry fresh water from the land to the ocean.

Refer to this version of the passage to answer the questions that follow.

Paragraph

Estuaries

1   Fresh water from land enters the ocean through rivers, streams, and groundwater flowing through valleys. These valleys that channel fresh water from land to the salty ocean, which range from extremely narrow stream-cut channels to remarkably broad lagoons behind long barrier islands, are called **estuaries**.

2   A number of types of estuaries are commercially vital. Many commercially important estuaries are the mouths of major rivers. The powerful flow of water in major rivers maintains channels that are deep enough for navigation by ocean-bound vessels, and the rivers themselves provide transportation of goods to points farther inland. In addition, estuaries formed as a result of tectonic or glacial activity are sometimes sufficiently deep to provide ports for oceangoing vessels. The types of estuaries that are not viable as ports-of-call for ocean commerce are those that are not wide enough, not deep enough, and not powerful enough to prevent the buildup of sediment.

3   Estuary systems, which vary to reflect the geology of the coasts where they are found, can be broadly categorized as one of two different types. One type of estuary system is the type that is found in **flooded coastal plains**, the broad land areas that extend out to the continental shelves, on the Atlantic coasts of North and South America, Europe, and Africa, for example. The other category of estuary system encompasses the **mountainous coasts**, with their rugged topography, such as those found along the Pacific coasts of North and South America.

4   Today, much of the eastern coast of the United States is a flooded coastal plain. During the last ice age, much of what is today the submerged continental shelf was exposed as an extended part of the continent. Intricate river systems composed of main rivers and their tributaries cut valleys across the plains to the edge of the shelf, where they released the fresh water that they carried into the ocean. Then, as the ice melted at the end of the ice age, rising waters extended inland over the lower areas, creating today's broad drowned river valleys. On today's flooded coastal plains, the water is comparatively shallow and huge amounts of sand and sediment are deposited. **7A** These conditions foster the growth of extensive long and narrow offshore deposits, many of which are exposed above the water as sandspits or barrier islands. **7B** These deposits are constantly being reshaped, sometimes extremely slowly and sometimes quite rapidly, by the forces of water and wind. **7C** It is common along flooded coastal plains for drowned river valleys to empty into lagoons that have been created behind the sandspits and barrier islands rather than emptying directly into the ocean. **7D** These lagoons support vigorous biological activity inasmuch as they are shallow, which causes them to heat up quickly, and they are fed by a constant inflow of nutrient-rich sediments.

5   Unlike the flooded coastal plains, the mountainous coasts have a more rugged and irregular topography with deeper coastal waters. There is less sand and sediment, and external systems of barrier islands are not as pervasive as they are on flooded coastal plains because the mountainous topography blocks the flow of sediments to the coast and because the deeper ocean water inhibits the growth of barrier islands, and without the protection of barrier beaches, mountainous coasts are more exposed to direct attack by the erosive forces of waves. Different geological processes contribute to the rugged topography along mountain coasts. The tectonic activity that creates the mountains along a mountainous coast can cause large blocks of the Earth's crust to fall below sea level; San Francisco Bay in California and the Strait of Juan de Fuca in Washington state in the north formed in this way. In the northern latitudes, coastal fjords were created as glaciers cut impressive u-shaped valleys through mountains and now carry fresh water from the land to the ocean.

Questions

1. The phrase commercially vital in paragraph 2 is closest in meaning to
   - Ⓐ understandably lucky
   - Ⓑ by-products of business
   - Ⓒ the essence of professionality
   - Ⓓ important to trade

2. The word viable in paragraph 2 is closest in meaning to
   - Ⓐ workable
   - Ⓑ valuable
   - Ⓒ identifiable
   - Ⓓ verifiable

3. The passage indicates that all of the following are estuaries with commercial potential as ports of call EXCEPT
   - Ⓐ estuaries at the mouths of powerful rivers
   - Ⓑ estuaries formed from tectonic activity
   - Ⓒ estuaries formed by glaciers
   - Ⓓ estuaries on flooded coastal plains

4. The word Intricate in paragraph 4 is closest in meaning to
   - Ⓐ delicate
   - Ⓑ attractive
   - Ⓒ complex
   - Ⓓ individual

5. According to the passage, drowned river valleys
   - Ⓐ are covered with ice
   - Ⓑ are covered with shallow water
   - Ⓒ are covered with deep water
   - Ⓓ are land areas with rivers cutting through

6. The word foster in paragraph 4 is closest in meaning to
   - Ⓐ encourage
   - Ⓑ deter
   - Ⓒ adopt
   - Ⓓ relate

7. Look at the four squares [■] that indicate where the following sentence can be added to paragraph 4.

   Some changes to the deposits can take place gradually over decades, while other changes can be quite radical changes in a period of only a few hours as the result of major storm activity.

   Click on a square [■] to add the sentence to the passage.

8. Which of the sentences below expresses the essential information in the highlighted sentence in paragraph 4? *Incorrect* choices change the meaning in important ways or leave out essential information.
   - Ⓐ Biological activity contributes to the formation of lagoons by heating them up and providing a source of food.
   - Ⓑ Lagoons become more and more shallow as they heat up and flow into the ocean.
   - Ⓒ A lot of life exists in lagoons for two reasons: the low water level and the steady source of new residue.
   - Ⓓ The flow of sediments into lagoons causes biological activity, which in turn causes the lagoons to heat up.

9. The author begins paragraph 5 with the phrase Unlike the flooded coastal plains in order to
   - Ⓐ indicate that a thorough discussion of flooded coastal plains follows
   - Ⓑ show that flooded coastal plains and mountainous coasts have some similarities in spite of their differences
   - Ⓒ clarify the ideas of flooded coastal plains that were previously presented
   - Ⓓ indicate that the discussion is moving from one type of estuary system to the other

10. The phrase not as pervasive as in paragraph 5 is closest in meaning to
    - Ⓐ as simple as
    - Ⓑ less common than
    - Ⓒ more covered than
    - Ⓓ not as limited as

11. The phrase this way in paragraph 5 refers to

Ⓐ geological processes contributing to rugged topography

Ⓑ the sea level rising along the mountainous coast

Ⓒ large blocks of crust sinking as a result of tectonic activity

Ⓓ glaciers cutting valleys through mountains

12. It is implied in the passage that fjords

Ⓐ are a type of mountainous estuary system

Ⓑ are found throughout the world

Ⓒ were formed in the same way as the San Francisco Bay

Ⓓ have as much sediment as flooded coastal plains

13.

Directions: Four of the answer choices below are used to describe each of the different types of estuary systems. Complete the table by matching appropriate answer choices to the estuary systems they are used to describe. *This question is worth 3 points.*	
estuary systems on flooded coastal plains	• • • •
estuary systems on mountainous coasts	• • • •

Answer Choices (choose 8 to complete the chart):

(1) Lead into deeper bodies of water

(2) Have huge amounts of deposits

(3) Are never commercially viable

(4) Were created by tectonic or glacial activity

(5) Are covered with shallow water

(6) Are not protected by barrier beaches

(7) Are the primary way that fresh water is channeled to the ocean

(8) Were created on part of a submerged continent

(9) Are protected by barrier beaches

(10) Have smaller amounts of deposits

Turn to the chart on page 544, and circle the numbers of the questions that you missed.

LISTENING

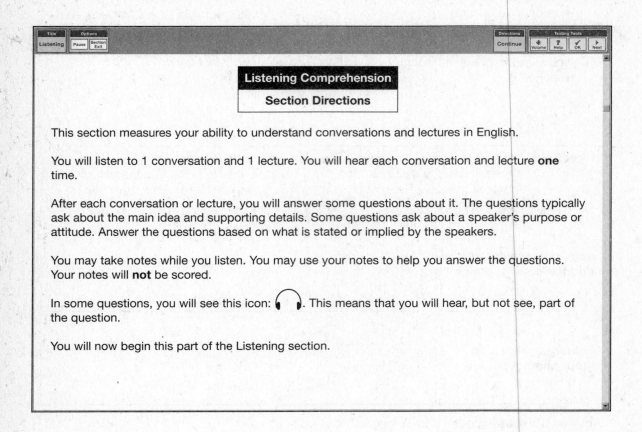

Questions 1–5

Listen to a conversation between a student and a professor.

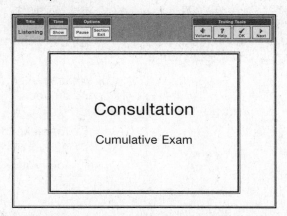

1. Why does the student go to see the professor?
   - Ⓐ To retake an exam she failed
   - Ⓑ To explain to the professor why the grade was so low
   - Ⓒ To make up an exam that she missed
   - Ⓓ To look for a solution to the problem of a bad grade

2. Listen again to part of the passage. Then answer the question.

   Why does the professor say this:

   - Ⓐ To revert to an earlier topic
   - Ⓑ To reinforce what he just said
   - Ⓒ To clarify what the student's question was
   - Ⓓ To ask the student a question

3. What are the professor's grades based on?

Click on 2 answers.

   - Ⓐ A unit exam
   - Ⓑ Unit exams
   - Ⓒ A cumulative exam
   - Ⓓ Several cumulative exams

4. What is a cumulative exam?
   - Ⓐ An exam on the final unit in the course
   - Ⓑ An exam that covers all the units in the course
   - Ⓒ The first exam given in the course
   - Ⓓ The exam with the highest grade

5. What solution does the professor offer to the student?
   - Ⓐ To accept a bad grade in the course
   - Ⓑ To retake the exam
   - Ⓒ To submit extra credit assignments
   - Ⓓ To prepare well for future exams

Questions 6–11

Listen to a lecture in a geography class.

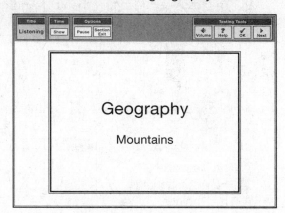

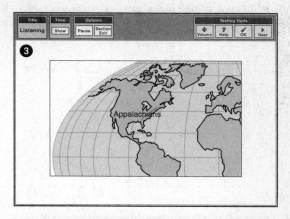

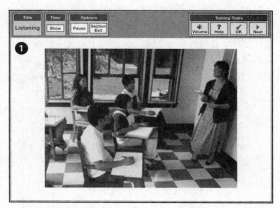

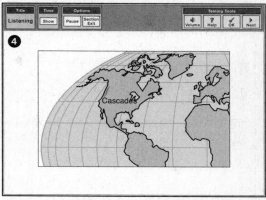

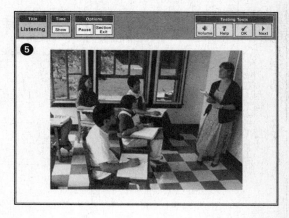

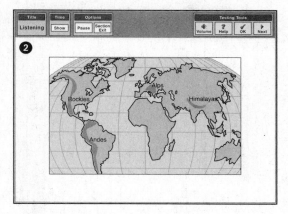

6. What is the topic of this lecture?
   A Examples of ways that volcanic mountains develop
   B The history of mountains in the last 100 million years
   C Examples of stages in the evolution of mountain-building
   D Methods of proving which mountains are really the oldest

7. What is true about the ages of various mountain ranges?

   Click on 2 answers.

   A The Appalachians are older than the Rockies.
   B The Cascades are younger than the Rockies.
   C The Himalayas are younger than the Andes.
   D The Alps are younger than the Cascades.

8. How were these mountain ranges formed?

   For each mountain range, click in the correct column.

	Created by volcanic action	Created by crashing tectonic plates
The Alps		
The Andes		
The Appalachians		
The Cascades		
The Himalayas		

9. What is true about the length of the mountain ranges?
   A The Rockies are longer than the Andes.
   B The Himalayas are 7,000 miles long.
   C The Andes are more than 4,000 miles long.
   D The Alps are 7,000 miles long.

10. Which mountain ranges are part of the Ring of Fire?

    Click on 2 answers.

    A The Cascades
    B The Appalachians
    C The Rockies
    D The Andes

11. Why does the professor discuss the Appalachians and Cascades?
    A They are examples of the world's tallest mountains.
    B They are among the world's oldest and youngest mountains.
    C They are the world's oldest mountains.
    D They were formed in different ways from other mountains.

Turn to the chart on page 545, and circle the numbers of the questions that you missed.

SPEAKING

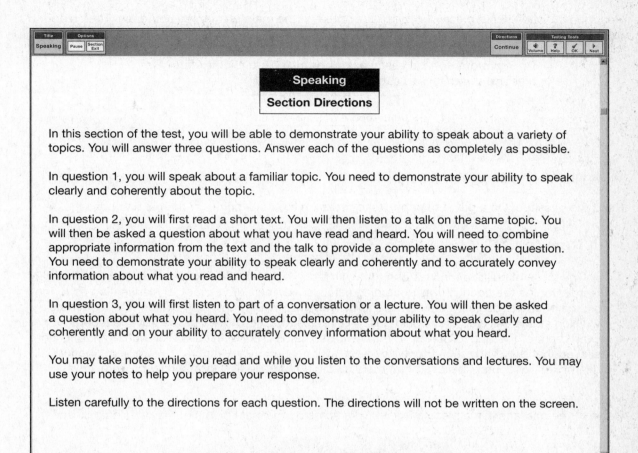

Speaking

Section Directions

In this section of the test, you will be able to demonstrate your ability to speak about a variety of topics. You will answer three questions. Answer each of the questions as completely as possible.

In question 1, you will speak about a familiar topic. You need to demonstrate your ability to speak clearly and coherently about the topic.

In question 2, you will first read a short text. You will then listen to a talk on the same topic. You will then be asked a question about what you have read and heard. You will need to combine appropriate information from the text and the talk to provide a complete answer to the question. You need to demonstrate your ability to speak clearly and coherently and to accurately convey information about what you read and heard.

In question 3, you will first listen to part of a conversation or a lecture. You will then be asked a question about what you heard. You need to demonstrate your ability to speak clearly and coherently and on your ability to accurately convey information about what you heard.

You may take notes while you read and while you listen to the conversations and lectures. You may use your notes to help you prepare your response.

Listen carefully to the directions for each question. The directions will not be written on the screen.

Question 1

Read the question. On a piece of paper, take notes on the main points of a response. Then respond to the question.

> Do you prefer to take essay exams or multiple-choice exams? Use reasons and details to support your response.

> | Preparation Time: 15 seconds |
> | Response Time: 45 seconds |

Question 2

Read the passage. On a piece of paper, take notes on the main points of the reading passage.

> | Reading Time: 45 seconds |

Nullification

The issue of nullification was one that was faced by the United States early in the history of the country. As the country was becoming established, there was a lack of clarification as to the balance of power between the states and the federal government. Nullification was a doctrine by which states believed they could nullify, or refuse to accept, laws passed by the federal government of the United States. In other words, states that believed in their right to nullification believed that they had the authority to reject laws passed by the federal government; the federal government, of course, believed that the states did not have the right to reject federal laws.

Listen to the passage. On a piece of paper, take notes on the main points of the listening passage.

Now answer the following question:

> How does the information in the listening passage supplement what is explained in the reading passage?

> | Preparation Time: 30 seconds |
> | Response Time: 60 seconds |

Question 3

Listen to the passage. On a piece of paper, take notes on the main points of the listening passage.

Now answer the following question:

What is happening with the students' assignments for their psychology class?

Preparation Time: 20 seconds
Response Time: 60 seconds

After you have completed this test, fill in the chart on pages 546–551.

WRITING

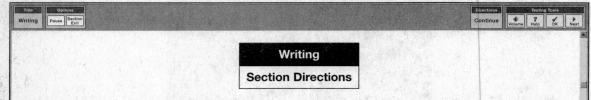

Title | Options
Writing | Pause | Section Exit

Directions
Continue

Testing Tools
Volume | Help | OK | Next

Writing
Section Directions

This section measures your ability to use writing to communicate in an academic environment. There will be one writing task.

For this writing task, you will answer a question based on your own knowledge and experience.

Independent Writing Directions

For this task, you will write an essay in response to a question that asks you to state, explain, and support your opinion on an issue. You will have **30 minutes** to plan, write, and revise your response.

Typically, an effective essay will contain a minimum of 300 words. You need to demonstrate your ability to write well. This includes the development of your ideas, the organization of your essay, and the quality and accuracy of the language you use to express your ideas.

Read the question. On a piece of paper, take notes on the main points of a response. Then write your response.

Some people prefer to take a position in a company and work for the company. Other people think it is better to go into business for themselves. Which do you think is better? Give reasons and examples to support your response.

Response Time: 30 minutes

After you have completed this test, fill in the chart on pages 552–553.

MINI-TEST 5

READING

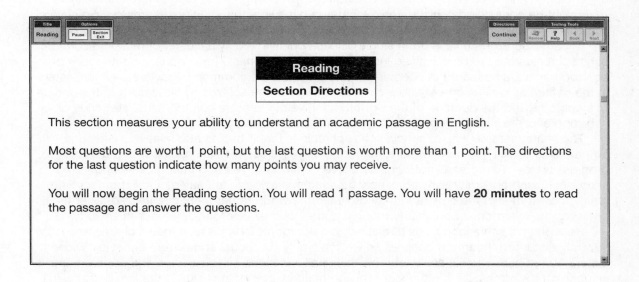

Reading
Section Directions

This section measures your ability to understand an academic passage in English.

Most questions are worth 1 point, but the last question is worth more than 1 point. The directions for the last question indicate how many points you may receive.

You will now begin the Reading section. You will read 1 passage. You will have **20 minutes** to read the passage and answer the questions.

Read the passage.

20 minutes

Paragraph

Schizophrenia

1   Schizophrenia is in reality a cluster of psychological disorders in which a variety of behaviors are exhibited and which are classified in various ways. Though there are numerous behaviors that might be considered schizophrenic, common behaviors that manifest themselves in severe schizophrenic disturbances are thought disorders, delusions, and emotional disorders.

2   Because schizophrenia is not a single disease but is in reality a cluster of related disorders, schizophrenics tend to be classified into various subcategories. The various subcategories of schizophrenia are based on the degree to which the various common behaviors are manifested in the patient as well as other factors such as the age of the schizophrenic patient at the onset of symptoms and the duration of the symptoms. Five of the more common subcategories of schizophrenia are simple, hebephrenic, paranoid, catatonic, and acute.

3   The main characteristic of simple schizophrenia is that it begins at a relatively early age and manifests itself in a slow withdrawal from family and social relationships with a gradual progression toward more severe symptoms over a period of years. Someone suffering from simple schizophrenia may early on simply be apathetic toward life, may maintain contact with reality a great deal of the time, and may be out in the world rather than hospitalized. Over time, however, the symptoms, particularly thought and emotional disorders, increase in severity.

4   Hebephrenic schizophrenia is a relatively severe form of the disease that is characterized by severely disturbed thought processes as well as highly emotional and bizarre behavior. Those suffering from hebephrenic schizophrenia have hallucinations and delusions and appear quite incoherent; their behavior is often extreme and quite inappropriate to the situation, perhaps full of unwarranted laughter, or tears, or obscenities that seem unrelated to the moment. This type of schizophrenia represents a rather severe and ongoing disintegration of personality that makes this type of schizophrenic unable to play a role in society.

5   Paranoid schizophrenia is a different type of schizophrenia in which the outward behavior of the schizophrenic often seems quite appropriate; this type of schizophrenic is often able to get along in society for long periods of time. However, a paranoid schizophrenic suffers from extreme delusions of persecution, often accompanied by delusions of grandeur. While this type of schizophrenic has strange delusions and unusual thought processes, his or her outward behavior is not as incoherent or unusual as a hebephrenic's behavior. A paranoid schizophrenic can appear alert and intelligent much of the time but can also turn suddenly hostile and violent in response to imagined threats.

6   Another type of schizophrenia is the catatonic variety, which is characterized by alternating periods of extreme excitement and stupor. There are abrupt changes in behavior, from frenzied periods of excitement to stuporous periods of withdrawn behavior. During periods of excitement, the catatonic schizophrenic may exhibit excessive and sometimes violent behavior; during the periods of stupor, the catatonic schizophrenic may remain mute and unresponsive to the environment.

7   A final type of schizophrenia is acute schizophrenia, which is characterized by a sudden onset of schizophrenic symptoms such as confusion, excitement, emotionality, depression, and irrational fear. The acute schizophrenic, unlike the simple schizophrenic, shows a sudden onset of the disease rather than a slow progression from one stage of it to the other. Additionally, the acute schizophrenic exhibits various types of schizophrenic behaviors during different episodes, sometimes exhibiting the characteristics of hebephrenic, catatonic, or even paranoid schizophrenia. In this type of schizophrenia, the patient's personality seems to have completely disintegrated.

Refer to this version of the passage to answer the questions that follow.

Paragraph

Schizophrenia

1   Schizophrenia is in reality a cluster of psychological disorders in which a variety of behaviors are exhibited and which are classified in various ways. Though there are numerous behaviors that might be considered schizophrenic, common behaviors that manifest themselves in severe schizophrenic disturbances are thought disorders, delusions, and emotional disorders.

2   Because schizophrenia is not a single disease but is in reality a cluster of related disorders, schizophrenics tend to be classified into various subcategories. The various subcategories of schizophrenia are based on the degree to which the various common behaviors are manifested in the patient as well as other factors such as the age of the schizophrenic patient at the onset of symptoms and the duration of the symptoms. Five of the more common subcategories of schizophrenia are simple, hebephrenic, paranoid, catatonic, and acute.

3   **5A** The main characteristic of simple schizophrenia is that it begins at a relatively early age and manifests itself in a slow withdrawal from family and social relationships with a gradual progression toward more severe symptoms over a period of years. **5B** Someone suffering from simple schizophrenia may early on simply be apathetic toward life, may maintain contact with reality a great deal of the time, and may be out in the world rather than hospitalized. **5C** Over time, however, the symptoms, particularly thought and emotional disorders, increase in severity. **5D**

4   Hebephrenic schizophrenia is a relatively severe form of the disease that is characterized by severely disturbed thought processes as well as highly emotional and bizarre behavior. Those suffering from hebephrenic schizophrenia have hallucinations and delusions and appear quite incoherent; their behavior is often extreme and quite inappropriate to the situation, perhaps full of unwarranted laughter, or tears, or obscenities that seem unrelated to the moment. This type of schizophrenia represents a rather severe and ongoing disintegration of personality that makes this type of schizophrenic unable to play a role in society.

5   Paranoid schizophrenia is a different type of schizophrenia in which the outward behavior of the schizophrenic often seems quite appropriate; this type of schizophrenic is often able to get along in society for long periods of time. However, a paranoid schizophrenic suffers from extreme delusions of persecution, often accompanied by delusions of grandeur. While this type of schizophrenic has strange delusions and unusual thought processes, his or her outward behavior is not as incoherent or unusual as a hebephrenic's behavior. A paranoid schizophrenic can appear alert and intelligent much of the time but can also turn suddenly hostile and violent in response to imagined threats.

6   Another type of schizophrenia is the catatonic variety, which is characterized by alternating periods of extreme excitement and stupor. There are abrupt changes in behavior, from frenzied periods of excitement to stuporous periods of withdrawn behavior. During periods of excitement, the catatonic schizophrenic may exhibit excessive and sometimes violent behavior; during the periods of stupor, the catatonic schizophrenic may remain mute and unresponsive to the environment.

7   A final type of schizophrenia is acute schizophrenia, which is characterized by a sudden onset of schizophrenic symptoms such as confusion, excitement, emotionality, depression, and irrational fear. The acute schizophrenic, unlike the simple schizophrenic, shows a sudden onset of the disease rather than a slow progression from one stage of it to the other. Additionally, the acute schizophrenic exhibits various types of schizophrenic behaviors during different episodes, sometimes exhibiting the characteristics of hebephrenic, catatonic, or even paranoid schizophrenia. In this type of schizophrenia, the patient's personality seems to have completely disintegrated.

Questions

1. The passage states that schizophrenia
   - (A) is a single psychological disorder
   - (B) always involves delusions
   - (C) is a group of various psychological disorders
   - (D) always develops early in life

2. The phrase manifested in in paragraph 2 is closest in meaning to
   - (A) internalized within
   - (B) demonstrated by
   - (C) created in
   - (D) maintained by

3. Which of the sentences below expresses the essential information in the highlighted sentence in paragraph 3? *Incorrect* choices change the meaning in important ways or leave out essential information.
   - (A) Simple schizophrenia generally starts at an early age and slowly worsens.
   - (B) All types of schizophrenics withdraw from their families as their disease progresses.
   - (C) Those suffering from simple schizophrenia tend to move more and more slowly over the years.
   - (D) It is common for simple schizophrenia to start at an early age and remain less severe than other types of schizophrenia.

4. The word apathetic in paragraph 3 is closest in meaning to
   - (A) sentimental
   - (B) logical
   - (C) realistic
   - (D) emotionless

5. Look at the four squares [■] that indicate where the following sentence can be added to paragraph 3.

   At this point, hospitalization will most likely be deemed necessary.

   Click on a square [■] to add the sentence to the passage.

6. The word unwarranted in paragraph 4 is closest in meaning to
   - (A) inappropriate
   - (B) uncontrolled
   - (C) insensitive
   - (D) underestimated

7. The phrase get along in paragraph 5 could best be replaced by
   - (A) mobilize
   - (B) negotiate
   - (C) manage
   - (D) travel

8. The author uses the word While in paragraph 5 in order to show that paranoid schizophrenics
   - (A) think in a way that is materially different from the way that they act
   - (B) have strange delusions at the same time that they have unusual thought patterns
   - (C) can think clearly in spite of their strange behavior
   - (D) exhibit strange behaviors as they think unusual thoughts

9. It is implied in paragraph 5 that a paranoid schizophrenic would be most likely to
   - (A) break into unexplained laughter
   - (B) believe that he is a great leader
   - (C) withdraw into a stuporous state
   - (D) improve over time

10. The word mute in paragraph 6 is closest in meaning to
    - (A) asleep
    - (B) quiet
    - (C) deaf
    - (D) frightened

11. The word it in paragraph 7 refers to
    - (A) the disease
    - (B) a slow progression
    - (C) one stage
    - (D) the other

12. It is NOT indicated in the passage that which of the following suffers from delusions?

Ⓐ A hebephrenic schizophrenic
Ⓑ A paranoid schizophrenic
Ⓒ A catatonic schizophrenic
Ⓓ An acute schizophrenic

13.

Directions: One of the answer choices below is used to describe each of the types of schizophrenia. Complete the table by matching appropriate answer choices to the types of schizophrenia they are used to describe. *This question is worth 3 points.*

simple schizophrenia	•
hebephrenic schizophrenia	•
paranoid schizophrenia	•
catatonic schizophrenia	•
acute schizophrenia	•

Answer Choices (choose 5 to complete the chart):

(1) Sometimes involves behavior that is quite normal, and even exceptional, and at other times involves delusions that cause negative behavior

(2) Appears suddenly and includes a variety of behaviors from various other types of schizophrenia

(3) Starts at a young age and progresses slowly, moving from withdrawal from society to serious emotional problems

(4) Involves violent behavior during phases of extreme stupor

(5) Involves irrational and irregular behavior on an ongoing basis that makes it impossible to take part in regular social interactions

(6) Is a less serious form of the disease that develops later in life and involves complete disintegration of personality

(7) Involves drastic changes from extremely quiet and withdrawn behavior to wild and uncontrolled behavior

Turn to the chart on page 544, and circle the numbers of the questions that you missed.

LISTENING

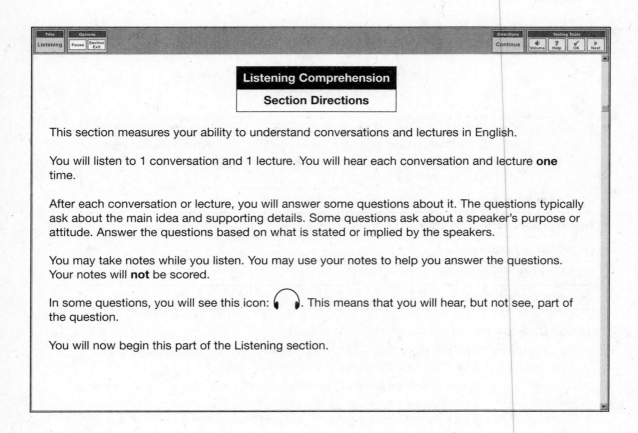

Questions 1–5

Listen to a conversation between a student and a worker in a university office.

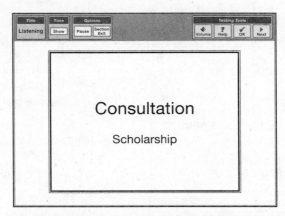

Consultation

Scholarship

1. Why does the student go to see this office worker?

    Ⓐ To ask for a letter of reference
    Ⓑ To turn in an application for a scholarship
    Ⓒ To ask for an application for university admission
    Ⓓ To find out how to apply for a particular program

2. Does the office worker emphasize each of these?

For each item, click in the YES or NO column.		
	YES	NO
The date the completed application is due		
The need to answer all questions		
The length of the essays		
The information to be included in the reference letters		

3. Why does the student ask about the question on high school ranking?

    Ⓐ It is an example of a question he finds difficult to answer.
    Ⓑ It seems like a question that would take too much time to answer.
    Ⓒ He thinks that his high school ranking might be too low.
    Ⓓ He thinks the question should be answered by someone else.

4. What does the advisor say about the essays?

    Ⓐ The student needs to answer the two essay questions on page four.
    Ⓑ The student needs to answer two of the four essay questions on page seven.
    Ⓒ The student needs to answer all four essay questions on page seven.
    Ⓓ The student needs to answer the four essay questions on page two.

5. What does the advisor say about the letters of reference?

Click on 2 answers.

    Ⓐ The student needs two of them.
    Ⓑ The student needs three of them.
    Ⓒ Two must be written by professors.
    Ⓓ Only one can be written by a professor.

Questions 6–11

Listen to a discussion by a group of students in an oceanography class.

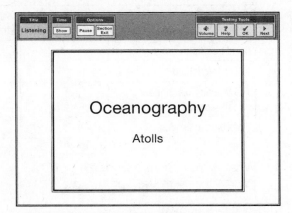

6. What is this discussion mainly about?

   Ⓐ How oceanic volcanoes occur

   Ⓑ The formation of certain coralline
      structures

   Ⓒ Where atolls most likely occur

   Ⓓ The formation of lagoons

7. What is an atoll made of?

   Ⓐ A combination of coral and algae

   Ⓑ A combination of algae and volcanic ash

   Ⓒ Only of algae

   Ⓓ Only of coral

8. Where do atolls tend to grow?

Click on 2 answers.

   Ⓐ In tropical areas

   Ⓑ In arctic areas

   Ⓒ In warm water

   Ⓓ In cool water

9. Listen again to part of the discussion. Then answer the question.

Why does the instructor say this: 🎧

   Ⓐ The student's response was incorrect.

   Ⓑ She would like a more thorough
      response from the student.

   Ⓒ The diagram they are looking at is not
      clear enough.

   Ⓓ She does not understand the student's
      response.

10. In what order do these occur?

For each statement, click in the correct column.	1st step	2nd step	3rd step	4th step
Coral begins to grow.				
A volcanic island forms.				
The volcano disappears underwater.				
The volcano erodes.				

11. What is true about a lagoon?

Click on 2 answers.

   Ⓐ It is a body of water.

   Ⓑ It encircles an atoll.

   Ⓒ It is made of coral.

   Ⓓ It is surrounded by an atoll.

Turn to the chart on page 545, and circle the numbers of the questions that you missed.

SPEAKING

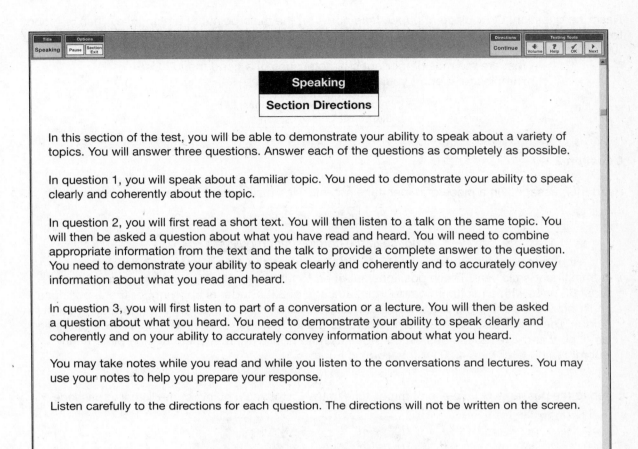

Speaking

Section Directions

In this section of the test, you will be able to demonstrate your ability to speak about a variety of topics. You will answer three questions. Answer each of the questions as completely as possible.

In question 1, you will speak about a familiar topic. You need to demonstrate your ability to speak clearly and coherently about the topic.

In question 2, you will first read a short text. You will then listen to a talk on the same topic. You will then be asked a question about what you have read and heard. You will need to combine appropriate information from the text and the talk to provide a complete answer to the question. You need to demonstrate your ability to speak clearly and coherently and to accurately convey information about what you read and heard.

In question 3, you will first listen to part of a conversation or a lecture. You will then be asked a question about what you heard. You need to demonstrate your ability to speak clearly and coherently and on your ability to accurately convey information about what you heard.

You may take notes while you read and while you listen to the conversations and lectures. You may use your notes to help you prepare your response.

Listen carefully to the directions for each question. The directions will not be written on the screen.

Questions 1–3

Question 1

Read the question. On a piece of paper, take notes on the main points of a response. Then respond to the question.

> What are the most important characteristics of a good friend? Use examples to support your response.
>
> | Preparation Time: 15 seconds |
> | Response Time: 45 seconds |

Question 2

Read the passage. On a piece of paper, take notes on the main points of the reading passage.

| Reading Time: 45 seconds |

A notice in the administration building

Eight positions for student assistants are available in the Administration Building for the coming academic year. These positions are open to full-time students who have completed at least 60 units with a minimum grade-point average of 3.0. Students applying for these positions must be available to work either from 9:00 AM to noon or from 1:00 to 4:00 PM Monday through Friday. They must also have basic computer and telephone skills. Applications may be obtained as of now at the reception desk in the Administration Building; they must be completed and submitted no later than 4:00 PM this coming Friday.

Listen to the passage. On a piece of paper, take notes on the main points of the listening passage.

Now answer the following question:

> How do the students respond to the notice about the positions in the Administration Building?
>
> | Preparation Time: 30 seconds |
> | Response Time: 60 seconds |

Question 3

Listen to the passage. On a piece of paper, take notes on the main points of the listening passage.

Now answer the following question:

How is the concept of zero-sum games related to the study of economic systems?

Preparation Time: 20 seconds
Response Time: 60 seconds

After you have completed this test, fill in the chart on pages 546–551.

WRITING

Writing
Section Directions

This section measures your ability to use writing to communicate in an academic environment. There will be one writing task.

For this writing task, you will read a passage and listen to a lecture and then answer a question based on what you have read and heard.

Integrated Writing Directions

For this task, you will read a passage about an academic topic. You will have **3 minutes** to read the passage. You may take notes on the passage while you read. The passage will then be removed and you will listen to a lecture about the same topic. While you listen, you may also take notes.

Then you will write a response to a question that asks you about the relationship between the lecture you heard and the reading passage. Try to answer the question as completely as possible using information from the reading passage and the lecture. The question does **not** ask you to express your personal opinion. You will be able to see the reading passage again when it is time for you to write. You may use your notes to help you answer the question. You will have **20 minutes** to write your response.

Typically, an effective response will be 150 to 225 words. You need to demonstrate your ability to write well and to provide complete and accurate content.

Now you will see the reading passage. Remember you can look at the passage again when you write your response. Immediately after the reading time ends, the lecture begins.

Read the passage. On a piece of paper, take notes on the main points of the reading passage.

Reading Time: 3 minutes

Joseph Heller's *Catch-22* (1961) is one of the most acclaimed novels of the twentieth century. It is a black comedy about life in the military during World War II. It features bombardier John Yossarian, who is trying to survive the military's inexhaustible supply of bureaucracy and who is frantically trying to do anything to avoid killing and being killed. Heller was able to use his own experiences in the Air Force during World War II to create this character and the novel.

Even though *Catch-22* eventually became known as a great novel, it was not originally considered one. When it was first published in 1961, the reviews were tepid and the sales were lackluster. It was not well received at this point at least in part because it presented such a cowardly protagonist at a time when World War II veterans were being lauded for their selfless courage.

Within a few years of the release of the book, as an unpopular war in Southeast Asia was heating up, Heller's *Catch-22* found a new audience eager to enjoy the exploits of Heller's war-averse protagonist. It was within the framework of this era that *Catch-22* was newly discovered, newly examined, and newly credited as one of the century's best novels.

Listen to the passage. On a piece of paper, take notes on the main points of the listening passage.

Now answer the following question:

How does the information in the listening passage add to the ideas presented in the reading passage?

Preparation Time: 1 minute
Response Time: 20 minutes

After you have completed this test, fill in the chart on pages 552–553.

MINI-TEST 6

READING

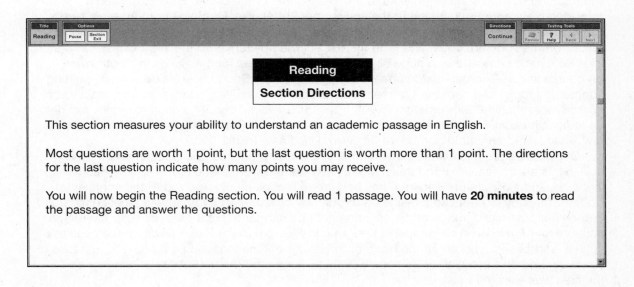

Reading

Section Directions

This section measures your ability to understand an academic passage in English.

Most questions are worth 1 point, but the last question is worth more than 1 point. The directions for the last question indicate how many points you may receive.

You will now begin the Reading section. You will read 1 passage. You will have **20 minutes** to read the passage and answer the questions.

Read the passage.

20 minutes

Exxon Valdez

1   In the late 1980s, a disaster involving the *Exxon Valdez,* an oil tanker tasked with transporting oil from southern Alaska to the West Coast of the United States, caused a considerable amount of damage to the environment of Alaska. Crude oil from Alaska's North Slope fields near Prudhoe Bay on the north coast of Alaska is carried by pipeline to the port of Valdez on the southern coast and from there is shipped by tanker to the West Coast. On March 24, 1989, the *Exxon Valdez,* a huge oil tanker more than three football fields in length, went off course in a 16-kilometer-wide channel in Prince William Sound near Valdez, Alaska, hitting submerged rocks and causing a tremendous oil spill. The resulting oil slick spread rapidly and coated more than 1,600 kilometers (1,000 miles) of coastline. Though actual numbers can never be known, it is believed that at least a half million birds, thousands of seals and otters, quite a few whales, and an untold number of fish were killed as a result.

2   Decades before this disaster, environmentalists had predicted just such an enormous oil spill in this area because of the treacherous nature of the waters due to the submerged reefs, icebergs, and violent storms there. They had urged that oil be transported to the continental United States by land-based pipeline rather than by oil tanker or by undersea pipeline to reduce the potential damage to the environment posed by the threat of an oil spill. Alyeska, a consortium of the seven oil companies working in Alaska's North Slope fields, argued against such a land-based pipeline on the basis of the length of time that such a pipeline would take to construct and on the belief, or perhaps wishful thinking, that the probability of a tanker spill in the area was extremely low.

3   Government agencies charged with protecting the environment were assured by Alyeska and Exxon that such a pipeline was unnecessary because appropriate protective measures had been taken, that within five hours of any accident there would be enough equipment and trained workers to clean up any spill before it managed to cause much damage. However, when the *Exxon Valdez* spill actually occurred, Exxon and Alyeska were unprepared, in terms of both equipment and personnel, to deal with the spill. Though it was a massive spill, appropriate personnel and equipment available in a timely fashion could have reduced the damage considerably. Exxon ended up spending billions of dollars on the clean-up itself and, in addition, spent further billions in fines and damages to the state of Alaska, the federal government, commercial fishermen, property owners, and others harmed by the disaster. The total cost to Exxon was more than $8 billion.

4   A step that could possibly have prevented this accident even though the tanker did run into submerged rocks would have been a double hull on the tanker. Today, almost all merchant ships have double hulls, but only a small percentage of oil tankers do. Legislation passed since the spill requires all new tankers to be built with double hulls, but many older tankers have received dispensations to avoid the $25 million cost per tanker to convert a single hulled tanker to one with a double hull. However, compared with the $8.5 billion cost of the *Exxon Valdez* catastrophe, it is a comparatively paltry sum.

Refer to this version of the passage to answer the questions that follow.

Paragraph

Exxon Valdez

1   In the late 1980s, a disaster involving the *Exxon Valdez,* an oil tanker tasked with transporting oil from southern Alaska to the West Coast of the United States, caused a considerable amount of damage to the environment of Alaska. Crude oil from Alaska's North Slope fields near Prudhoe Bay on the north coast of Alaska is carried by pipeline to the port of Valdez on the southern coast and from there is shipped by tanker to the West Coast. On March 24, 1989, the *Exxon Valdez,* a huge oil tanker more than three football fields in length, went off course in a 16-kilometer-wide channel in Prince William Sound near Valdez, Alaska, hitting submerged rocks and causing a tremendous oil spill. The resulting oil slick spread rapidly and coated more than 1,600 kilometers (1,000 miles) of coastline. Though actual numbers can never be known, it is believed that at least a half million birds, thousands of seals and otters, quite a few whales, and an untold number of fish were killed as a result.

2   **8A** Decades before this disaster, environmentalists had predicted just such an enormous oil spill in this area because of the treacherous nature of the waters due to the submerged reefs, icebergs, and violent storms there. **8B** They had urged that oil be transported to the continental United States by land-based pipeline rather than by oil tanker or by undersea pipeline to reduce the potential damage to the environment posed by the threat of an oil spill. **8C** Alyeska, a consortium of the seven oil companies working in Alaska's North Slope fields, argued against such a land-based pipeline on the basis of the length of time that such a pipeline would take to construct and on the belief, or perhaps wishful thinking, that the probability of a tanker spill in the area was extremely low. **8D**

3   Government agencies charged with protecting the environment were assured by Alyeska and Exxon that such a pipeline was unnecessary because appropriate protective measures had been taken, that within five hours of any accident there would be enough equipment and trained workers to clean up any spill before it managed to cause much damage. However, when the *Exxon Valdez* spill actually occurred, Exxon and Alyeska were unprepared, in terms of both equipment and personnel, to deal with the spill. Though it was a massive spill, appropriate personnel and equipment available in a timely fashion could have reduced the damage considerably. Exxon ended up spending billions of dollars on the clean-up itself and, in addition, spent further billions in fines and damages to the state of Alaska, the federal government, commercial fishermen, property owners, and others harmed by the disaster. The total cost to Exxon was more than $8 billion.

4   A step that could possibly have prevented this accident even though the tanker did run into submerged rocks would have been a double hull on the tanker. Today, almost all merchant ships have double hulls, but only a small percentage of oil tankers do. Legislation passed since the spill requires all new tankers to be built with double hulls, but many older tankers have received dispensations to avoid the $25 million cost per tanker to convert a single hulled tanker to one with a double hull. However, compared with the $8.5 billion cost of the *Exxon Valdez* catastrophe, it is a comparatively paltry sum.

Questions

1. What is stated in paragraph 1 about the oil industry in Alaska?
    - Ⓐ The oil fields are in the southern part of Alaska.
    - Ⓑ Oil is carried from the oil fields to Valdez by tanker.
    - Ⓒ Oil arrives in Valdez by pipeline and departs by ship.
    - Ⓓ Oil is transported from Valdez to the U.S. mainland through a pipeline.

2. The word coated in paragraph 1 could best be replaced by
    - Ⓐ covered
    - Ⓑ warmed
    - Ⓒ filled
    - Ⓓ blackened

3. An untold number in paragraph 1 is most likely a number
    - Ⓐ that has not been discussed
    - Ⓑ that is so high that it cannot be counted
    - Ⓒ that is of little importance to anyone
    - Ⓓ that has been hidden away from the public

4. The word They in paragraph 2 refers to
    - Ⓐ decades
    - Ⓑ environmentalists
    - Ⓒ waters
    - Ⓓ reefs

5. Which point is NOT made by the environmentalists mentioned in paragraph 2?
    - Ⓐ That a huge oil spill in the waters off Alaska was possible
    - Ⓑ That the waters off the coast of Alaska were dangerous for ships
    - Ⓒ That oil tankers should not be used to transport oil from Alaska
    - Ⓓ That an undersea pipeline was preferable to a land-based pipeline

6. In paragraph 2, a consortium is most likely
    - Ⓐ a board
    - Ⓑ a leader
    - Ⓒ an association
    - Ⓓ a contract

7. The author uses the expression wishful thinking in paragraph 2 in order to
    - Ⓐ emphasize the idea that the belief was misguided
    - Ⓑ emphasize the desire that the pipeline would be built
    - Ⓒ emphasize the hope that an oil spill could be cleaned up quickly
    - Ⓓ emphasize the wish that a lot of oil would be discovered

8. Look at the four squares [■] that indicate where the following sentence can be added to paragraph 2.

    Unfortunately, the line of reasoning proved incorrect, with disastrous results.

    Click on a square [■] to add the sentence to the passage.

9. What can be inferred from paragraph 3 about the preparations for a potential oil spill?
    - Ⓐ Government agencies assured the oil companies that the environment was protected.
    - Ⓑ The oil companies had equipment and staff ready to deal with a spill within five hours of a spill.
    - Ⓒ Neither Exxon nor Alyeska had prepared adequately for a tanker accident.
    - Ⓓ Exxon had spent billions of dollars preparing for a potential oil spill.

10. The word fashion in paragraph 3 could best be replaced by
    - Ⓐ style
    - Ⓑ direction
    - Ⓒ hour
    - Ⓓ manner

11. Which of the sentences below expresses the essential information in the highlighted sentence in paragraph 4? *Incorrect* choices change the meaning in important ways or leave out essential information.

Ⓐ In spite of the legislation requiring double hulls on all ships, many ship owners have paid millions of dollars to avoid installing double hulls.

Ⓑ Although new tankers are legally required to have double hulls, not all older tankers have been required to do so.

Ⓒ Laws have been passed requiring all tankers, both old and new, to have double hulls.

Ⓓ It is very expensive to build double-hulled tankers, so most new tankers do not have double hulls.

12. The word paltry in paragraph 4 is closest in meaning to

Ⓐ insignificant
Ⓑ unbelievable
Ⓒ inaccurate
Ⓓ enormous

13.

Directions: An introductory sentence or a brief summary of the passage is provided below. Complete the summary by selecting the THREE answer choices that express the most important ideas in the passage. Some sentences do not belong in the summary because they express ideas that are not presented in the passage or are minor ideas in the passage. *This question is worth 3 points.*

The passage discusses the tragedy of the *Exxon Valdez* and factors that could have prevented or lessened the damage.

-
-
-

Answer Choices (choose 3 to complete the chart):

(1) Higher fines and damage payments for Exxon

(2) Appropriate preparations by oil companies for tanker spills

(3) A land-based oil pipeline from southern Alaska to the West Coast

(4) Additional dispensations for single-hulled tankers

(5) The use of double-hulled ships to transport oil

(6) A land-based oil pipeline from the North Slope fields to Valdez

Turn to the chart on page 544, and circle the numbers of the questions that you missed.

LISTENING

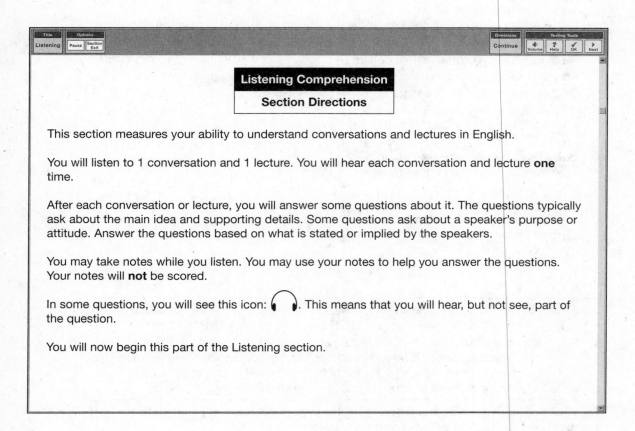

Questions 1–5

Listen to a conversation between a student and her advisor.

1. Why is the student in the advisor's office?
   - (A) To review the courses she has taken
   - (B) To learn about some general education requirements
   - (C) To discuss her schedule for the coming semester
   - (D) To talk about a problem in her chemistry course

2. Listen again to part of the passage. Then answer the question.

   Why does the advisor start the conversation this way?
   - (A) To indicate that the student is late for an appointment
   - (B) To explain what he has just been doing
   - (C) To apologize for starting the meeting late
   - (D) To clarify what time of day it is

3. How does the student seem to feel about chemistry?
   - (A) It is quite challenging.
   - (B) It is too easy.
   - (C) It is quite fun.
   - (D) It is not much work.

4. What does the student want to do?
   - (A) Skip the second part of chemistry permanently
   - (B) Change her major to athletics
   - (C) Enroll in an additional chemistry class immediately
   - (D) Take a break from chemistry for a while

5. How does the advisor seem to feel about the student's decision?
   - (A) It is unacceptable.
   - (B) It seems reasonable.
   - (C) It needs to be reconsidered.
   - (D) It is just what he would recommend.

Questions 6–11

Listen to a lecture in a zoology class.

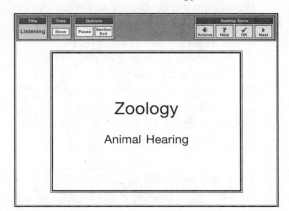

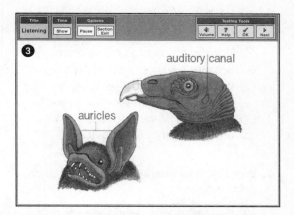

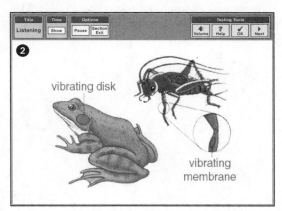

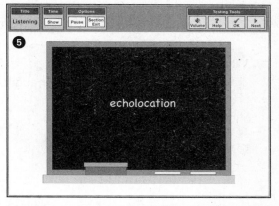

6. How is the information in the lecture organized?

   Ⓐ Various types of auricles are outlined.

   Ⓑ Smaller to larger animals are described.

   Ⓒ Various types of hearing organs are evaluated for their effectiveness.

   Ⓓ Examples of various hearing mechanisms are provided.

7. What type of hearing organ does each animal have?

For each animal, click in the correct column.			
	Disks behind eyes	**Membranes on legs**	**Auditory canals**
Cricket			
Frog			
Bird			

8. What do the disks on frogs do?

   Ⓐ They vibrate when struck by sound waves.

   Ⓑ They lead to the inner ear.

   Ⓒ They reflect sound waves off objects.

   Ⓓ They allow heat to escape the body.

9. What is true about mammals?

   Ⓐ They have membranes on their auditory canals.

   Ⓑ They use echolocation.

   Ⓒ They generally have auricles.

   Ⓓ They hear better than birds.

10. Listen again to part of the passage. Then answer the question.

Why does the professor say this?

   Ⓐ To indicate that the lecture is coming to an end

   Ⓑ To announce that a slightly different topic will follow

   Ⓒ To summarize previously stated information

   Ⓓ To reinforce a particularly important point

11. What is true about echolocation?

Click on 2 answers.

   Ⓐ It involves making sounds and then waiting to hear echoes.

   Ⓑ It can be used to detect objects in the way.

   Ⓒ It cannot be used to determine how distant objects are.

   Ⓓ It is only used by land animals.

Turn to the chart on page 545, and circle the numbers of the questions that you missed.

SPEAKING

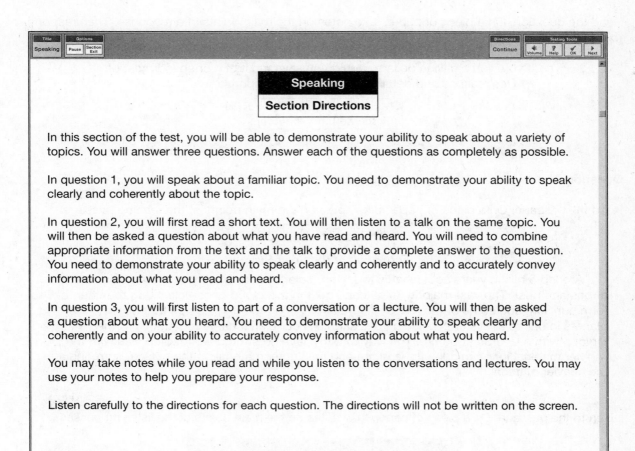

Speaking

Section Directions

In this section of the test, you will be able to demonstrate your ability to speak about a variety of topics. You will answer three questions. Answer each of the questions as completely as possible.

In question 1, you will speak about a familiar topic. You need to demonstrate your ability to speak clearly and coherently about the topic.

In question 2, you will first read a short text. You will then listen to a talk on the same topic. You will then be asked a question about what you have read and heard. You will need to combine appropriate information from the text and the talk to provide a complete answer to the question. You need to demonstrate your ability to speak clearly and coherently and to accurately convey information about what you read and heard.

In question 3, you will first listen to part of a conversation or a lecture. You will then be asked a question about what you heard. You need to demonstrate your ability to speak clearly and coherently and on your ability to accurately convey information about what you heard.

You may take notes while you read and while you listen to the conversations and lectures. You may use your notes to help you prepare your response.

Listen carefully to the directions for each question. The directions will not be written on the screen.

Questions 1–3

Question 1

Read the question. On a piece of paper, take notes on the main points of a response. Then respond to the question.

> If you won a million dollars, would you save most of it or spend most of it? Use reasons and details to support your response.

| Preparation Time: 15 seconds |
| Response Time: 45 seconds |

Question 2

Read the passage. On a piece of paper, take notes on the main points of the reading passage.

| Reading Time: 45 seconds |

Formation of the Solar System

Around 5 billion years ago, what is today our solar system was most likely a spinning cloud of gas and dust. The vast majority of gas and dust in this cloud began clumping together to form our Sun, and some of the rest of the material began forming clumps that became the planets in our solar system, including our Earth. As our planet came together, it formed into a globe with a layered structure. The way that this layered structure ended up was with the heavier material in the middle of the globe and the lighter material on the outside surrounding the heavier material.

Listen to the passage. On a piece of paper, take notes on the main points of the listening passage.

Now answer the following question:

> How does the information in the listening passage add to what is explained in the reading passage?

| Preparation Time: 30 seconds |
| Response Time: 60 seconds |

Question 3

Listen to the passage. On a piece of paper, take notes on the main points of the listening passage.

Now answer the following question:

How are the students dealing with the situation surrounding the guest speaker?

Preparation Time: 20 seconds
Response Time: 60 seconds

After you have completed this test, fill in the chart on pages 546–551.

WRITING

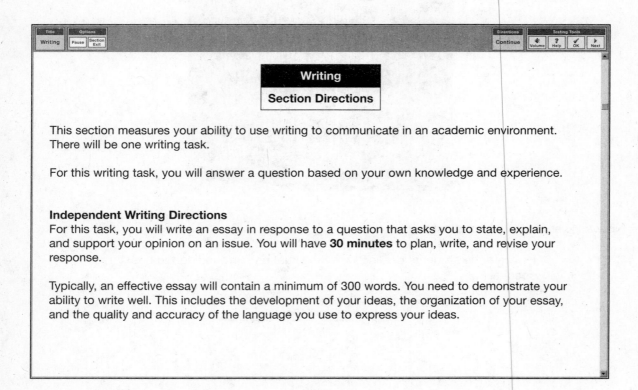

This section measures your ability to use writing to communicate in an academic environment. There will be one writing task.

For this writing task, you will answer a question based on your own knowledge and experience.

Independent Writing Directions
For this task, you will write an essay in response to a question that asks you to state, explain, and support your opinion on an issue. You will have **30 minutes** to plan, write, and revise your response.

Typically, an effective essay will contain a minimum of 300 words. You need to demonstrate your ability to write well. This includes the development of your ideas, the organization of your essay, and the quality and accuracy of the language you use to express your ideas.

Read the question. On a piece of paper, take notes on the main points of a response. Then write your response.

Traveling to a different country can be both exciting and frustrating at the same time. What are the most important pieces of advice that you would give visitors coming to your country? Give reasons and details to support your response.

Response Time: 30 minutes

After you have completed this test, fill in the chart on pages 552–553.

MINI-TEST 7

READING

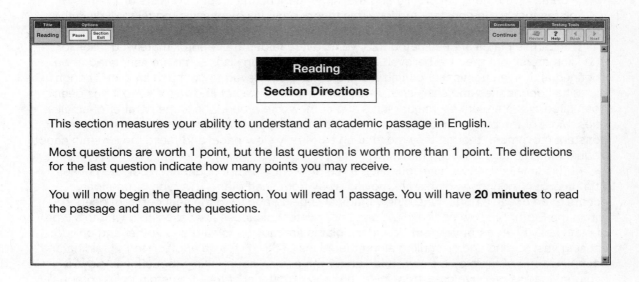

Reading
Section Directions

This section measures your ability to understand an academic passage in English.

Most questions are worth 1 point, but the last question is worth more than 1 point. The directions for the last question indicate how many points you may receive.

You will now begin the Reading section. You will read 1 passage. You will have **20 minutes** to read the passage and answer the questions.

Read the passage.

20 minutes

Plate Tectonics

Paragraph

1   According to the theory of plate tectonics, the upper portion of the Earth's lithosphere, which contains the heavier oceanic and the lighter continental crusts, consists of a series of rigid plates that are in constant motion. This theory provides a cohesive model to explain the integrated actions of continental drift, seafloor spreading, and mountain formation.

2   The Earth's plates are estimated to have an average depth of approximately 60 miles (or 100 kilometers), but they are believed to vary considerably in size. Some are estimated to be continental or even hemispheric in size, while other are believed to be much smaller. Though the actual boundaries and sizes and shapes of the plates are not known for sure, it has been postulated that there are six major plates and somewhere around the same number of smaller ones. Most of the plates consist of both *sial* (continental) and *sima* (oceanic) crust. They are in constant movement, though they move at an extremely slow pace, and these movements cause frequent interactions between plates.

3   At this time, scientists have identified three different types of boundaries between plates. At a **divergent** boundary, plates are moving away from each other. This type of boundary occurs at an oceanic ridge, where new material is being added to the seafloor from deeper within the Earth. Shallow earthquakes and underwater volcanoes are associated with this type of plate activity. At a **convergent** boundary, plates are moving toward each other and collide, causing vast folding and crumpling along the edges of the plates. In addition to the folding and crumpling, one of the plates slowly folds under the other. Though this subduction is slow, it can nonetheless be quite catastrophic as the crustal material of the submerging plate gradually melts into the fiery hot depths below. The area where subduction occurs is usually an area where the crust is relatively unstable and is characterized by numerous deep earthquakes and a significant amount of volcanic activity. The boundaries between convergent plates are generally found around the edges of ocean basins and are sometimes associated with deep ocean trenches. A third type of boundary is a **transcurrent** boundary, which involves two plates sliding past each other laterally, without the folding and crumpling that occurs at a convergent boundary. This third type of boundary is thought to be far less common than the other two types of boundaries.

4   The concept of plate tectonics provides an understanding of the massive rearrangement of the Earth's crust that has apparently taken place. It is now generally accepted that the single supercontinent known as Pangaea indeed existed, that Pangaea subsequently broke apart into two giant pieces, Gondwanaland in the south and Laurasia in the north, and that the continents attached to the various crustal plates separated and drifted in various directions. As the plates drifted, they may have diverged, which was associated with the spread of the seafloor, or they may have converged, which resulted in collision, subduction, and mountain building.

5   The majority of the Earth's major mountain ranges are found in zones where plates converge. The Himalayas, which are the world's highest mountains, along with the central Asian mountains of varying heights associated with them, were formed by the crumpling and folding of two massive plates that collided at a convergent boundary. The landmass that is today known as India was originally part of Gondwanaland, the giant supercontinent in the Southern Hemisphere, but it broke off from Gondwanaland approximately 200 million years ago and drifted north to collide with part of Laurasia, the giant supercontinent in the Northern Hemisphere, to create the world's tallest mountains.

Refer to this version of the passage to answer the questions that follow.

Paragraph

Plate Tectonics

1   According to the theory of plate tectonics, the upper portion of the Earth's lithosphere, which contains the heavier oceanic and the lighter continental crusts, consists of a series of rigid plates that are in constant motion. This theory provides a cohesive model to explain the integrated actions of continental drift, seafloor spreading, and mountain formation.

2   The Earth's plates are estimated to have an average depth of approximately 60 miles (or 100 kilometers), but they are believed to vary considerably in size. Some are estimated to be continental or even hemispheric in size, while other are believed to be much smaller. Though the actual boundaries and sizes and shapes of the plates are not known for sure, it has been postulated that there are six major plates and somewhere around the same number of smaller ones. Most of the plates consist of both *sial* (continental) and *sima* (oceanic) crust. They are in constant movement, though they move at an extremely slow pace, and these movements cause frequent interactions between plates.

3   At this time, scientists have identified three different types of boundaries between plates. At a **divergent** boundary, plates are moving away from each other. This type of boundary occurs at an oceanic ridge, where new material is being added to the seafloor from deeper within the Earth. Shallow earthquakes and underwater volcanoes are associated with this type of plate activity. At a **convergent** boundary, plates are moving toward each other and collide, causing vast folding and crumpling along the edges of the plates. In addition to the folding and crumpling, one of the plates slowly folds under the other. Though this subduction is slow, it can nonetheless be quite catastrophic as the crustal material of the submerging plate gradually melts into the fiery hot depths below. The area where subduction occurs is usually an area where the crust is relatively unstable and is characterized by numerous deep earthquakes and a significant amount of volcanic activity. The boundaries between convergent plates are generally found around the edges of ocean basins and are sometimes associated with deep ocean trenches. A third type of boundary is a **transcurrent** boundary, which involves two plates sliding past each other laterally, without the folding and crumpling that occurs at a convergent boundary. This third type of boundary is thought to be far less common than the other two types of boundaries.

4   The concept of plate tectonics provides an understanding of the massive rearrangement of the Earth's crust that has apparently taken place. It is now generally accepted that the single supercontinent known as Pangaea indeed existed, that Pangaea subsequently broke apart into two giant pieces, Gondwanaland in the south and Laurasia in the north, and that the continents attached to the various crustal plates separated and drifted in various directions. As the plates drifted, they may have diverged, which was associated with the spread of the seafloor, or they may have converged, which resulted in collision, subduction, and mountain building.

5   **12A** The majority of the Earth's major mountain ranges are found in zones where plates converge. **12B** The Himalayas, which are the world's highest mountains, along with the central Asian mountains of varying heights associated with them, were formed by the crumpling and folding of two massive plates that collided at a convergent boundary. **12C** The landmass that is today known as India was originally part of Gondwanaland, the giant supercontinent in the Southern Hemisphere, but it broke off from Gondwanaland approximately 200 million years ago and drifted north to collide with part of Laurasia, the giant supercontinent in the Northern Hemisphere, to create the world's tallest mountains. **12D**

Questions

1. The word cohesive in paragraph 1 is closest in meaning to
   (A) unified
   (B) contemporary
   (C) tenacious
   (D) lengthy

2. It can be inferred from paragraph 2 that
   (A) none of the plates has a depth of more than 100 kilometers
   (B) each of the plates has approximately the same dimensions
   (C) some plates are relatively stationary
   (D) there are most likely around 6 minor plates

3. The word postulated in paragraph 2 is closest in meaning to
   (A) postponed
   (B) hypothesized
   (C) proven
   (D) forgotten

4. The author uses the expression At this time at the beginning of paragraph 3 in order to indicate that
   (A) more types of boundaries might be found in the future
   (B) interactions are currently occurring between plates
   (C) all possible types of boundaries have already been located
   (D) the major plates are all currently moving away from each other

5. The word subduction in paragraph 3 is closest in meaning to
   (A) strong attack
   (B) lateral movement
   (C) sudden melting
   (D) downward force

6. According to the passage, subduction
   (A) occurs rapidly
   (B) has little effect
   (C) causes one of the plates to sink and melt
   (D) generally takes place in stable areas

7. The phrase associated with in paragraph 3 is closest in meaning to
   (A) related to
   (B) working with
   (C) hidden from
   (D) found inside

8. It is NOT stated in paragraph 4 that it is generally accepted that
   (A) there used to be a giant continent
   (B) the giant continent broke into parts
   (C) Gondwanaland moved to the south and Laurasia moved to the north
   (D) the continents moved in various directions

9. The word drifted in paragraph 4 is closest in meaning to
   (A) broke down
   (B) moved slowly
   (C) were formed
   (D) lifted up

10. The word them in paragraph 5 refers to
    (A) zones
    (B) the Himalayas
    (C) central Asian mountains
    (D) two massive plates

11. Which of the sentences below expresses the essential information in the highlighted sentence in paragraph 5? *Incorrect* choices change the meaning in important ways or leave out essential information.
    (A) India was formed when a landmass from the Southern Hemisphere broke off and collided with a landmass in the Northern Hemisphere.
    (B) Gondwanaland drifted north 200 million years ago to merge with Laurasia.
    (C) India was formed 200 million years ago when two giant supercontinents drifted north and collided.
    (D) The world's tallest mountains used to be in India, but they broke off from India and drifted to the north.

12. Look at the four squares [■] that indicate where the following sentence can be added to paragraph 5.

Mountain building is clearly explained through the concept of plate tectonics.

Click on a square [■] to add the sentence to the passage.

13.

Directions: Two of the answer choices below are used to describe each of the types of boundaries. Complete the table by matching appropriate answer choices to the boundaries they are used to describe. ***This question is worth 3 points.***		
divergent boundary	• •	
convergent boundary	• •	
transcurrent boundary	• •	

Answer Choices (choose 6 to complete the chart):

(1) Occurs when two plates remain stationary in relation to each other

(2) Occurs when plates moving toward each other do not collide

(3) Occurs when plates move away from each other

(4) Occurs when plates moving toward each other collide

(5) Can result in the creation of mountains

(6) Causes the continents to shift

(7) Is the least common type of boundary

(8) Can result in the spreading of the seafloor

Turn to the chart on page 544, and circle the numbers of the questions that you missed.

LISTENING

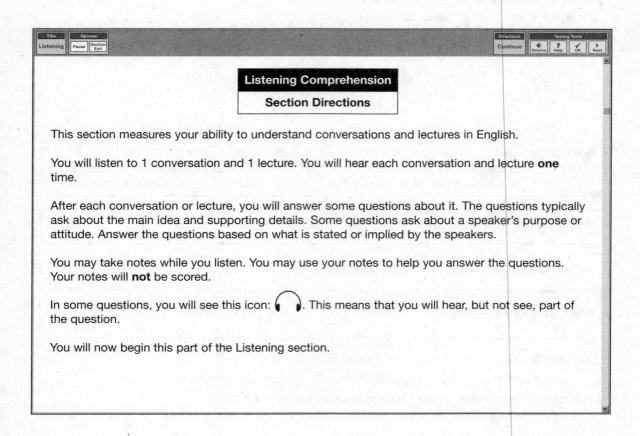

Listening Comprehension
Section Directions

This section measures your ability to understand conversations and lectures in English.

You will listen to 1 conversation and 1 lecture. You will hear each conversation and lecture **one** time.

After each conversation or lecture, you will answer some questions about it. The questions typically ask about the main idea and supporting details. Some questions ask about a speaker's purpose or attitude. Answer the questions based on what is stated or implied by the speakers.

You may take notes while you listen. You may use your notes to help you answer the questions. Your notes will **not** be scored.

In some questions, you will see this icon: 🎧. This means that you will hear, but not see, part of the question.

You will now begin this part of the Listening section.

Questions 1–5

Listen to a conversation between a student and a professor.

1. Why does the student go to talk with the professor?

   Ⓐ To find out who else is working on his group presentation

   Ⓑ To discuss how to resolve a problem his group is having

   Ⓒ To set up a meeting with his group and the professor

   Ⓓ To discuss the issues his group has developed for their presentation

2. Listen again to part of the passage. Then answer the question.

   What does the professor mean when she says this:

   Ⓐ "Your question is too hard for me to answer."

   Ⓑ "Can you please specify what your presentation is about?"

   Ⓒ "Your question is a really good one."

   Ⓓ "I can't answer until I understand better what your question is."

3. What does the professor think the students have done wrong?

   Ⓐ They are concentrating on dividing up topics too early.

   Ⓑ They have come up with too many issues.

   Ⓒ They need to determine more than one issue.

   Ⓓ They have determined the issues but not the solutions.

4. What should the students do first?

   Ⓐ Find the main issue the company is facing

   Ⓑ Determine how to organize their presentation

   Ⓒ Determine the main issues and how to solve them

   Ⓓ Determine which part of the presentation each student should work on

5. Listen again to part of the passage. Then answer the question.

   Why does the professor say this?

   Ⓐ To outline how the students should organize the presentation

   Ⓑ To apologize for not knowing how the students should organize the presentation

   Ⓒ To clarify that the students should discuss two issues

   Ⓓ To suggest that there are many possible ways to organize the presentation

Questions 6–11

Listen to a lecture in a music class.

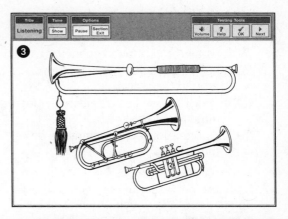

6. What can be concluded about the development of the trumpet?

  Ⓐ It was invented fairly recently.
  Ⓑ It has been used in various forms around the world.
  Ⓒ Its primary use has traditionally been as a musical instrument.
  Ⓓ Its current form is the same as earlier forms.

7. Does the professor make each of these points about the development of the trumpet?

For each statement, click in the YES or NO column.		
	YES	NO
The culture where the earliest trumpet developed is known.		
Today's trumpet is much like the earliest trumpet.		
The trumpet has been used in many different ways.		
Many different types of music have been written for the trumpet.		

8. Which was NOT mentioned as a material from which trumpets have been made?

  Ⓐ Tusks
  Ⓑ Cane
  Ⓒ Stone
  Ⓓ Silver

9. When did different parts of the trumpet develop?

  Click on 2 answers.

  Ⓐ The trumpet's tubing was initially straight and later the tubing became looped.
  Ⓑ Valves were added to the trumpet before a bell was added.
  Ⓒ The tubing on the trumpet was looped before a bell was added.
  Ⓓ A bell was added to an early trumpet that was a long straight tube.

10. Listen again to part of the passage. Then answer the question. 🎧

  Why does the professor say this?
  Ⓐ To indicate to the students where he is in his overall outline of points
  Ⓑ To make sure that the students are paying attention
  Ⓒ To correct an error he just made
  Ⓓ To summarize all the points in the passage

11. How did the professor categorize each of these uses of a trumpet?

For each use, click in the correct column.			
	Ceremony	Battle	Communication
Playing from a mountaintop			
Beginning a charge			
Announcing an arrival			

Turn to the chart on page 545, and circle the numbers of the questions that you missed.

SPEAKING

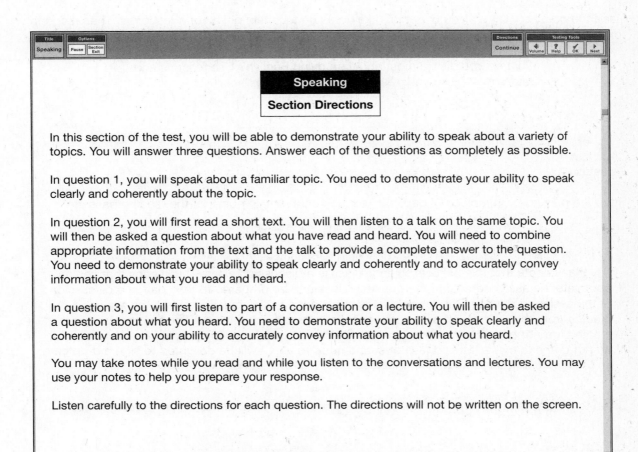

Question 1

Read the question. On a piece of paper, take notes on the main points of a response. Then respond to the question.

> What do you dislike most about studying English? Use reasons and details to support your response.
>
> | Preparation Time: 15 seconds |
> | --- |
> | Response Time: 45 seconds |

Question 2

Read the passage. On a piece of paper, take notes on the main points of the reading passage.

> | Reading Time: 45 seconds |
> | --- |

Part of a syllabus in a political science class

Please note that this political science class is a discussion class. This means that you must complete the assigned reading before each class and be prepared to take part in a discussion of the assigned reading. The reading list is attached, and you must complete the assigned reading from the reading list before you come to class. If you have not finished the assigned reading, do not bother to come to class. If you do not plan on taking part in class discussions, do not come to class. If this does not sound good to you, I will be delighted to sign a drop card so that you can transfer to a different class.

Listen to the passage. On a piece of paper, take notes on the main points of the listening passage.

Now answer the following question:

> How do the students seem to feel about the professor's policy on class discussions?
>
> | Preparation Time: 30 seconds |
> | --- |
> | Response Time: 60 seconds |

Question 3

Listen to the passage. On a piece of paper, take notes on the main points of the listening passage.

Now answer the following question:

> What points does the professor make about a certain kind of response from the public?

| Preparation Time: 20 seconds |
| Response Time: 60 seconds |

After you have completed this test, fill in the chart on pages 546–551.

WRITING

Writing
Section Directions

This section measures your ability to use writing to communicate in an academic environment. There will be one writing task.

For this writing task, you will read a passage and listen to a lecture and then answer a question based on what you have read and heard.

Integrated Writing Directions

For this task, you will read a passage about an academic topic. You will have **3 minutes** to read the passage. You may take notes on the passage while you read. The passage will then be removed and you will listen to a lecture about the same topic. While you listen, you may also take notes.

Then you will write a response to a question that asks you about the relationship between the lecture you heard and the reading passage. Try to answer the question as completely as possible using information from the reading passage and the lecture. The question does **not** ask you to express your personal opinion. You will be able to see the reading passage again when it is time for you to write. You may use your notes to help you answer the question. You will have **20 minutes** to write your response.

Typically, an effective response will be 150 to 225 words. You need to demonstrate your ability to write well and to provide complete and accurate content.

Now you will see the reading passage. Remember you can look at the passage again when you write your response. Immediately after the reading time ends, the lecture begins.

Read the passage. On a piece of paper, take notes on the main points of the reading passage.

Reading Time: 3 minutes

Hemophilia is a condition in which the blood either clots slowly or fails to clot at all. Most people who get a little cut on a finger can put a bandage on the cut, and the cut on the finger will heal because the blood will clot. A blood clot forms from the polymerization of protein fibers that circulate in the blood. A number of protein factors take part in the process, and it is necessary for all of the protein factors to function correctly for blood to clot. Hemophilia exists when any of the factors is either missing or not functioning.

The most common kinds of hemophilia are hemophilia A (or classic hemophilia) and hemophilia B (or Christmas hemophilia), which was named after the first person known to have contracted it. Hemophilia A occurs when clotting factor 8 is not functioning properly; 85 percent of those who suffer from hemophilia have hemophilia type A. Hemophilia B occurs when factor 9 is not functioning properly; almost all of the rest of those who suffer from hemophilia have hemophilia B.

Hemophilia is generally passed from mother to son, though sometimes it seems to develop spontaneously in some women. Women carry the recessive gene but do not generally develop the disease. A mother who carries the defective gene may or may not pass it on to her children. If a mother passes the defective gene to a daughter, the daughter will carry the gene but will most likely not develop the disease. If a mother passes the defective gene to a son, then the son will most likely develop the disease.

Listen to the passage. On a piece of paper, take notes on the main points of the listening passage.

Now answer the following question:

How is the information in the listening passage related to the information presented in the reading passage?

Preparation Time: 1 minute
Response Time: 20 minutes

After you have completed this test, fill in the chart on pages 552–553.

MINI-TEST 8

READING

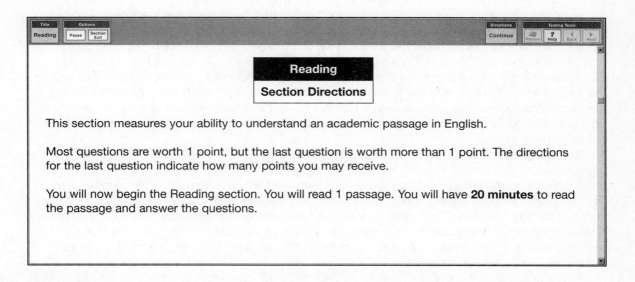

Reading

Section Directions

This section measures your ability to understand an academic passage in English.

Most questions are worth 1 point, but the last question is worth more than 1 point. The directions for the last question indicate how many points you may receive.

You will now begin the Reading section. You will read 1 passage. You will have **20 minutes** to read the passage and answer the questions.

Read the passage.

| 20 minutes |

Paragraph

Limners

1 The earliest known American painters, who were active in the latter part of the seventeenth century and the early part of the eighteenth century, were described in documents, journals, and letters of the time as limners. Most of the paintings created by limners were portraits, and they were unsigned because the finished pieces did not belong to the limners who created them but were instead the possessions of the subjects in the portraits. The portraits today are named after the subjects portrayed in them, and a particular artist is known only as the creator of a particular portrait; thus a particular portrait is named *Mrs. Elizabeth Freake and Baby Mary* after the people in the portrait, and the limner who created the portrait is known only as the Freake Limner. Art historians who specialize in art from this era have been able to identify clusters of portraits painted by each of a number of limners but, in many cases, do not know the name of the actual limner.

2 As can be seen from the fact that portraits created by limners went unsigned, limners were regarded more as artisans or skilled tradesmen than as artists. They earned their living as many artisans and tradesmen did at the time, as itinerant workers moving from town to town offering their services to either those who could pay or, more likely, to those who had goods or services to offer in return. They were able to paint portraits for those desiring to have a tangible representation of a family member for posterity; they also took on a variety of other types of painting jobs to stay employed, such as painting the walls of buildings, painting signs for businesses, and painting furniture.

3 Some of the early portraitists most likely received their education in art or trained as artisans in Europe prior to their arrival in America and then trained others in America in their craft; because they were working in undeveloped or minimally developed colonial areas, their lives were quite difficult. They had little access to information about the world of art and little access to art supplies, so they needed to mix their own paints and make their own brushes and stretched canvasses. They also needed to be prepared to take on whatever painting jobs were needed to survive.

4 There seem to be two broad categories of painting styles used by the portraitists, the style of the New England limners and the style of the New York limners. The style of the New England limners was a decorative style with flat characters, characters that seemed to lack mass and volume. This is not because the New England limners had no knowledge of painting techniques but was instead because the New England limners were using the style of Tudor painting that became popular during the reign of Queen Elizabeth I, a style that included characters with a flat woodenness yet with the numerous highly decorative touches and frills popular in the English court.

5 The New York limners had a rather different style from the New England limners, and this was because New York had a different background from the rest of New England. Much of New England had been colonized by the English, and thus the basis for the style of the New England limners was the Tudor style that had been popularized during the reign of the Tudor queen Elizabeth I. However, the Dutch had settled the colony of New Amsterdam, and though New Amsterdam became an English colony in 1664 and was renamed New York, the Dutch character and influence was strongly in place during the era of the limners. The New York limners, as a result, were influenced by the Dutch artists of the time rather than the Tudor artists. Dutch art, unlike the more flowery Tudor art, was considerably more sober and prosaic. In addition, the New York limners lacked the flat portrayals of characters of the New England limners and instead made use of light and shade to create more lifelike portraits.

Refer to this version of the passage to answer the questions that follow.

Limners

1   The earliest known American painters, who were active in the latter part of the seventeenth century and the early part of the eighteenth century, were described in documents, journals, and letters of the time as limners. Most of the paintings created by limners were portraits, and they were unsigned because the finished pieces did not belong to the limners who created them but were instead the possessions of the subjects in the portraits. The portraits today are named after the subjects portrayed in them, and a particular artist is known only as the creator of a particular portrait; thus a particular portrait is named *Mrs. Elizabeth Freake and Baby Mary* after the people in the portrait, and the limner who created the portrait is known only as the Freake Limner. Art historians who specialize in art from this era have been able to identify clusters of portraits painted by each of a number of limners but, in many cases, do not know the name of the actual limner.

2   As can be seen from the fact that portraits created by limners went unsigned, limners were regarded more as artisans or skilled tradesmen than as artists. They earned their living as many artisans and tradesmen did at the time, as itinerant workers moving from town to town offering their services to either those who could pay or, more likely, to those who had goods or services to offer in return. They were able to paint portraits for those desiring to have a tangible representation of a family member for posterity; they also took on a variety of other types of painting jobs to stay employed, such as painting the walls of buildings, painting signs for businesses, and painting furniture.

3   **9A** Some of the early portraitists most likely received their education in art or trained as artisans in Europe prior to their arrival in America and then trained others in America in their craft; because they were working in undeveloped or minimally developed colonial areas, their lives were quite difficult. **9B** They had little access to information about the world of art and little access to art supplies, so they needed to mix their own paints and make their own brushes and stretched canvasses. **9C** They also needed to be prepared to take on whatever painting jobs were needed to survive. **9D**

4   There seem to be two broad categories of painting styles used by the portraitists, the style of the New England limners and the style of the New York limners. The style of the New England limners was a decorative style with flat characters, characters that seemed to lack mass and volume. This is not because the New England limners had no knowledge of painting techniques but was instead because the New England limners were using the style of Tudor painting that became popular during the reign of Queen Elizabeth I, a style that included characters with a flat woodenness yet with the numerous highly decorative touches and frills popular in the English court.

5   The New York limners had a rather different style from the New England limners, and this was because New York had a different background from the rest of New England. Much of New England had been colonized by the English, and thus the basis for the style of the New England limners was the Tudor style that had been popularized during the reign of the Tudor queen Elizabeth I. However, the Dutch had settled the colony of New Amsterdam, and though New Amsterdam became an English colony in 1664 and was renamed New York, the Dutch character and influence was strongly in place during the era of the limners. The New York limners, as a result, were influenced by the Dutch artists of the time rather than the Tudor artists. Dutch art, unlike the more flowery Tudor art, was considerably more sober and prosaic. In addition, the New York limners lacked the flat portrayals of characters of the New England limners and instead made use of light and shade to create more lifelike portraits.

Questions

1. The word pieces in paragraph 1 could best be replaced by
   - (A) parts
   - (B) works
   - (C) ideas
   - (D) fragments

2. The word them in paragraph 1 refers to
   - (A) limners
   - (B) portraits
   - (C) possessions
   - (D) subjects

3. Which of the sentences below expresses the essential information in the highlighted sentence in paragraph 1? *Incorrect* choices change the meaning in important ways or leave out essential information.
   - (A) Art historians have been able to identify characteristics in paintings indicating that the paintings were created by limners.
   - (B) Artists from the era of limners painted clusters of portraits without knowing whom they were painting.
   - (C) People studying art have been able to identify clusters of artists who had painted portraits of the same subjects.
   - (D) Certain groups of portraits are known to have been painted by the same limner, though the limner's name is often not known.

4. The word itinerant in paragraph 2 is closest in meaning to
   - (A) successful
   - (B) uneducated
   - (C) wandering
   - (D) professional

5. It is NOT mentioned in paragraph 2 that a limner might
   - (A) work as a carpenter
   - (B) receive pay for a painting
   - (C) offer his services in return for other services
   - (D) paint a house

6. The word posterity in paragraph 2 is closest in meaning to
   - (A) prominent display
   - (B) future generations
   - (C) social acceptance
   - (D) delayed gratification

7. It can be inferred from paragraph 3 that limners
   - (A) would not possibly have had any formal training
   - (B) were quite knowledgeable about the world of art
   - (C) were held in high esteem by the population
   - (D) were not all formally trained artists

8. The phrase take on in paragraph 3 could best be replaced by
   - (A) accept
   - (B) attack
   - (C) admit
   - (D) allow

9. Look at the four squares [■] that indicate where the following sentence can be added to paragraph 3.

   Few limners were formally trained artists.

   Click on a square [■] to add the sentence to the passage.

10. Why does the author state that the Dutch had settled the colony of New Amsterdam in a passage about limners?
    - (A) To provide background information about the New England limners
    - (B) To indicate why the Tudor style of painting was possible
    - (C) To give a reason for the highly flowery Dutch paintings
    - (D) To explain why the style of the New York limners differed from that of the New England limners

11. It is stated in the passage that New Amsterdam

    Ⓐ was settled by the English

    Ⓑ was a Dutch colony after 1664

    Ⓒ moved from English control to Dutch control

    Ⓓ later became New York

12. The word prosaic in paragraph 5 is closest in meaning to

    Ⓐ realistic

    Ⓑ poetic

    Ⓒ lively

    Ⓓ strict

13.

Directions: Two of the answer choices below are used to describe each of the groups of limners. Complete the table by matching appropriate answer choices to the groups of limners they are used to describe. ***This question is worth 3 points.***	
only the New York limners	• •
only the New England limners	• •
both the New York and New England limners	• •

Answer Choices (choose 6 to complete the chart):

(1) Used a Tudor style of painting

(2) Painted for Queen Elizabeth I

(3) Were influenced by the Dutch style of painting

(4) Did not sign portraits

(5) Had flat characters and lots of ornamentation

(6) Had flat characters with little ornamentation

(7) Earned a living by traveling from town to town

(8) Had more lifelike characters and less ornamentation

Turn to the chart on page 544, and circle the numbers of the questions that you missed.

LISTENING

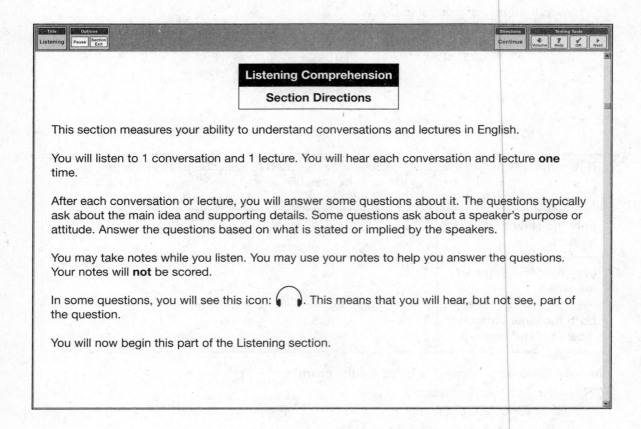

Questions 1–5

Listen to a conversation between a student and an advisor.

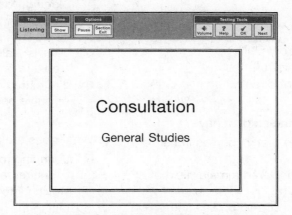

1. Listen again to part of the passage. Then answer the question. 🎧

   What does the advisor mean when he says this: 🎧

   Ⓐ "It's no big deal."
   Ⓑ "I need to put it down."
   Ⓒ "I'm telling you the truth."
   Ⓓ "I'm going to say it directly."

2. What problem does the student have?

   Ⓐ She has taken too many courses in her major.
   Ⓑ She has not yet declared a major field of study.
   Ⓒ She has not taken some courses she needs for her major.
   Ⓓ She does not know what the required courses for her major are.

3. What is stated about the courses the student has taken?

   Click on 2 answers.

   Ⓐ She has taken only courses in her major.
   Ⓑ She has taken only required courses.
   Ⓒ She has taken only courses she finds interesting.
   Ⓓ She has taken a wide variety of courses.

4. Which sentence best describes what the advisor seems to think?

   Ⓐ "I'm really not sure what you've been doing; why don't you tell me?"
   Ⓑ "You seem to have a bit of a problem; let's look for a solution."
   Ⓒ "This is really terrible; you'll never be able to graduate."
   Ⓓ "I'm extremely impressed with what you've been doing; keep doing it!"

5. What does the advisor suggest?

   Ⓐ Changing to a major with broader requirements
   Ⓑ Moving into different classes now
   Ⓒ Taking the required courses for her major as soon as possible
   Ⓓ Changing the way that she chooses courses

Questions 6–11

Listen to a discussion by some students taking a chemistry class.

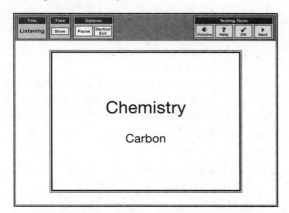

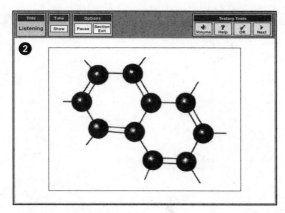

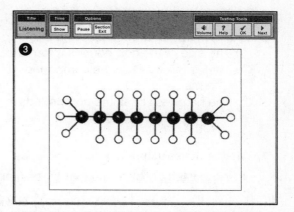

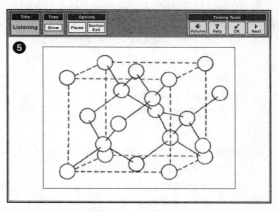

6. What is unusual about carbon?

    Ⓐ The number of compounds it forms

    Ⓑ The size of the compounds it forms

    Ⓒ The simplicity of all the compounds it forms

    Ⓓ The hardness of all the compounds it forms

7. What is the structure of each substance?

For each item, click in the correct column.

	Soap	Graphite	Diamond	Octane
Has rings of 6 carbon atoms each				
Has a chain of 8 carbon atoms				
Has a chain of 15–17 atoms				
Has a complex pattern of carbon atoms				

8. Which two molecules do NOT contain only carbon atoms?

Click on 2 answers.

    Ⓐ A graphite molecule

    Ⓑ An octane molecule

    Ⓒ A soap molecule

    Ⓓ A diamond molecule

9. What is NOT true about the uses of molecules containing carbon?

    Ⓐ One carbon compound can be used to make soap.

    Ⓑ Graphite can be used in pencils.

    Ⓒ Octane is the only type of gasoline molecule.

    Ⓓ Diamond can be used to cut other substances.

10. Listen again to part of the passage. Then answer the question.

Why does the man say this:

    Ⓐ To demonstrate to the woman that what he said was wrong

    Ⓑ To explain to the others in the group that he needs to leave

    Ⓒ To let the others know that he had a good reason for what he said

    Ⓓ To indicate that he had previously said something incorrect

11. What overall conclusion can be drawn from the discussion?

    Ⓐ Carbon atoms can be part of many extremely different molecules.

    Ⓑ Carbon can form molecules only with other carbon atoms.

    Ⓒ Carbon must have other substances with it to form molecules.

    Ⓓ Carbon atoms attach easily to all other kinds of atoms.

Turn to the chart on page 545, and circle the numbers of the questions that you missed.

SPEAKING

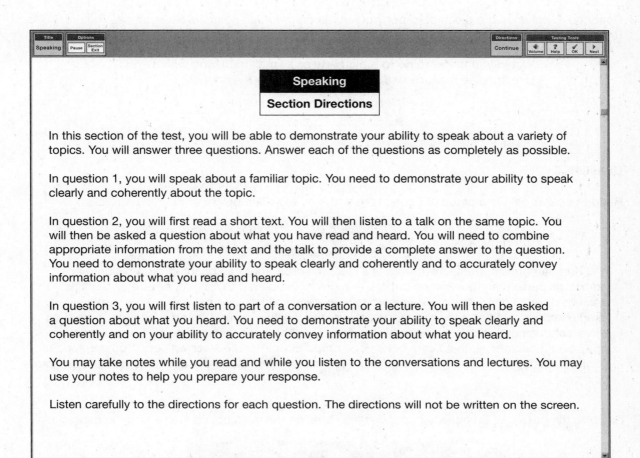

Speaking

Section Directions

In this section of the test, you will be able to demonstrate your ability to speak about a variety of topics. You will answer three questions. Answer each of the questions as completely as possible.

In question 1, you will speak about a familiar topic. You need to demonstrate your ability to speak clearly and coherently about the topic.

In question 2, you will first read a short text. You will then listen to a talk on the same topic. You will then be asked a question about what you have read and heard. You will need to combine appropriate information from the text and the talk to provide a complete answer to the question. You need to demonstrate your ability to speak clearly and coherently and to accurately convey information about what you read and heard.

In question 3, you will first listen to part of a conversation or a lecture. You will then be asked a question about what you heard. You need to demonstrate your ability to speak clearly and coherently and on your ability to accurately convey information about what you heard.

You may take notes while you read and while you listen to the conversations and lectures. You may use your notes to help you prepare your response.

Listen carefully to the directions for each question. The directions will not be written on the screen.

Questions 1–3

Question 1

Read the question. On a piece of paper, take notes on the main points of a response. Then respond to the question.

Would you prefer to go to a big party or a small gathering with friends?
Use specific reasons and details to support your response.

| Preparation Time: 15 seconds |
| Response Time: 45 seconds |

Question 2

Read the passage. On a piece of paper, take notes on the main points of the reading passage.

| Reading Time: 45 seconds |

Somnambulism

   Somnambulism, or sleepwalking, is a sleep disorder that can occur in both children and adults. Its causes are not known but are thought to be related to fatigue, severe exhaustion, anxiety, or reaction to drugs. While someone is sleepwalking, he or she may take part in simple actions such as sitting up or getting up and walking around before returning to bed; more complex activities such as getting dressed, washing dishes, moving furniture, and even operating machines such as cars have been noted among some sleepwalkers. Some episodes of sleepwalking are very brief, lasting only seconds or minutes; longer episodes can last an hour or more.

Listen to the passage. On a piece of paper, take notes on the main points of the listening passage.

Now answer the following question:

How does the information in the listening passage add to what is explained in the reading passage?

| Preparation Time: 30 seconds |
| Response Time: 60 seconds |

Question 3

Listen to the passage. On a piece of paper, take notes on the main points of the listening passage.

Now answer the following question:

What possible solutions does the woman offer to the man's problem?

Preparation Time: 20 seconds
Response Time: 60 seconds

After you have completed this test, fill in the chart on pages 546–551.

WRITING

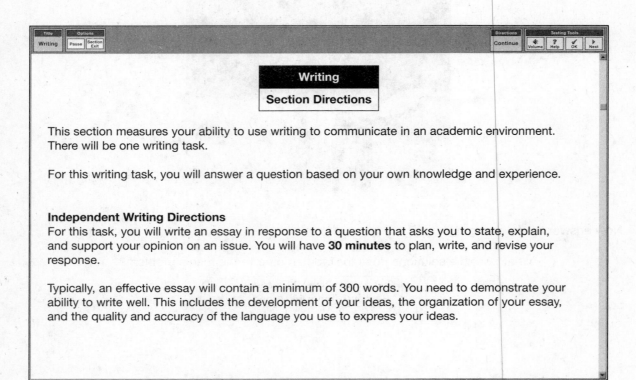

Read the question. On a piece of paper, take notes on the main points of a response. Then write your response.

Do you agree or disagree with the following statement?

I think there is too much violence in movies.

Give specific reasons and examples to support your response.

Response Time: 30 minutes

After you have completed this test, fill in the chart on pages 546–551.

COMPLETE TEST 1

READING 1

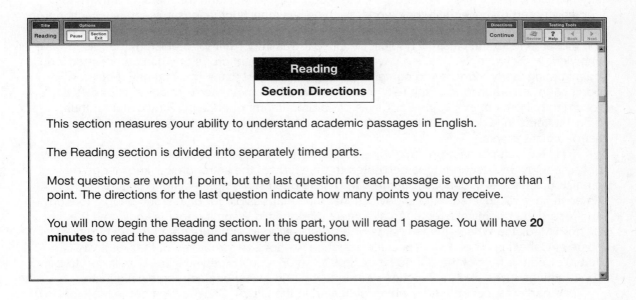

This section measures your ability to understand academic passages in English.

The Reading section is divided into separately timed parts.

Most questions are worth 1 point, but the last question for each passage is worth more than 1 point. The directions for the last question indicate how many points you may receive.

You will now begin the Reading section. In this part, you will read 1 pasage. You will have **20 minutes** to read the passage and answer the questions.

Read the passage.

20 minutes

Paragraph

Prehistoric Astronomers

1   Prehistoric peoples most certainly took note of the recurring patterns of movements in the sky of such celestial bodies as the Sun, the Moon, the planets, and the stars, and they most certainly noted that events in their world, such as seasonal fluctuations in weather, which in turn had an effect on the lives of the plants and animals in their world, were often correlated with the movements of the celestial bodies. Because it was important for prehistoric people to have knowledge, for example, of when it was the best time to plant crops or when game herds would be migrating, early farmers and hunters took a great interest in the movements of celestial bodies. An understanding of the relationship between the movements of celestial bodies and recurring patterns of events on Earth was of paramount importance in many cultures; thus, many cultures in widely separated areas of the world developed methods for monitoring astronomical events.

2   The field of archeoastronomy, which combines knowledge and expertise from the fields of archeology and astronomy, is dedicated to the study of the astronomical knowledge of prehistoric cultures. Archeoastronomers who have been studying prehistoric cultures in North America have discovered various devices that made it possible for prehistoric people to study and record astronomical events. An alignment of stones in Wyoming that is known as the Bighorn Medicine Wheel, the remnants of a circular-shaped structure created with wooden posts at Cahoki in Illinois, and specially designed windows in structures of the Southwest that allowed the rays of the Sun to hit designated marks on inside walls are all believed to be constructions that serve the function of monitoring and measuring astronomical events.

3   One particular construction, which is located in the Chaco Canyon area of the state of New Mexico, has been the subject of considerable attention and discussion among archeologists and astronomers. This construction, which is at least 700 years old, consists of large slabs of rock located on top of the flat surface of a high butte that seem to form an observatory of sorts. What makes it appear to experts to be an observatory is that the slabs of rock are positioned so that shafts of sunlight fall between them and hit spiral markings carved into the side of a cliff. As the Sun changes positions with the progression of the seasons, the shafts of light fall in different places on the markings in the cliff wall. Using this system, it must have been possible for early inhabitants of the area to predict upcoming seasonal changes and the events based on them.

4   One question that has been the focus of considerable discussion is whether the stones were actually placed in their current location by early inhabitants of the region or whether the forces of nature created the arrangement. While some scientists argue that the stones could not have fallen in the current arrangement by mere happenstance and must have been purposefully positioned, others find it harder to believe that the huge stones could have been moved and easier to believe that the marks on the cliff wall were placed to reflect the positions where the slabs had fallen naturally. Whether or not the slabs were positioned by the local population, the structure correlating the positions of the slabs and the markings on the cliff wall represents a remarkably sophisticated method of following astronomical events.

Refer to this version of the passage to answer the questions that follow.

Paragraph

Prehistoric Astronomers

1   Prehistoric peoples most certainly took note of the recurring patterns of movements in the sky of such celestial bodies as the Sun, the Moon, the planets, and the stars, and they most certainly noted that events in their world, such as seasonal fluctuations in weather, which in turn had an effect on the lives of the plants and animals in their world, were often correlated with the movements of the celestial bodies. Because it was important for prehistoric people to have knowledge, for example, of when it was the best time to plant crops or when game herds would be migrating, early farmers and hunters took a great interest in the movements of celestial bodies. An understanding of the relationship between the movements of celestial bodies and recurring patterns of events on Earth was of paramount importance in many cultures; thus, many cultures in widely separated areas of the world developed methods for monitoring astronomical events.

2   **7A** The field of archeoastronomy, which combines knowledge and expertise from the fields of archeology and astronomy, is dedicated to the study of the astronomical knowledge of prehistoric cultures. **7B** Archeoastronomers who have been studying prehistoric cultures in North America have discovered various devices that made it possible for prehistoric people to study and record astronomical events. **7C** An alignment of stones in Wyoming that is known as the Bighorn Medicine Wheel, the remnants of a circular-shaped structure created with wooden posts at Cahoki in Illinois, and specially designed windows in structures of the Southwest that allowed the rays of the Sun to hit designated marks on inside walls are all believed to be constructions that serve the function of monitoring and measuring astronomical events. **7D**

3   One particular construction, which is located in the Chaco Canyon area of the state of New Mexico, has been the subject of considerable attention and discussion among archeologists and astronomers. This construction, which is at least 700 years old, consists of large slabs of rock located on top of the flat surface of a high butte that seem to form an observatory of sorts. What makes it appear to experts to be an observatory is that the slabs of rock are positioned so that shafts of sunlight fall between them and hit spiral markings carved into the side of a cliff. As the Sun changes positions with the progression of the seasons, the shafts of light fall in different places on the markings in the cliff wall. Using this system, it must have been possible for early inhabitants of the area to predict upcoming seasonal changes and the events based on them.

4   One question that has been the focus of considerable discussion is whether the stones were actually placed in their current location by early inhabitants of the region or whether the forces of nature created the arrangement. While some scientists argue that the stones could not have fallen in the current arrangement by mere happenstance and must have been purposefully positioned, others find it harder to believe that the huge stones could have been moved and easier to believe that the marks on the cliff wall were placed to reflect the positions where the slabs had fallen naturally. Whether or not the slabs were positioned by the local population, the structure correlating the positions of the slabs and the markings on the cliff wall represents a remarkably sophisticated method of following astronomical events.

Questions

1. The word correlated in paragraph 1 could best be replaced by

   (A) in disagreement
   (B) in coordination
   (C) in touch
   (D) in spirit

2. It is NOT mentioned in paragraph 1 that prehistoric peoples were interested in

   (A) the movements of the stars
   (B) changes in the weather
   (C) migration patterns of certain animals
   (D) the evolution of various plants

3. The word paramount in paragraph 1 could best be replaced by

   (A) tall
   (B) dependable
   (C) supreme
   (D) computed

4. Which of the following would an archeoastronomer be most likely to study?

   (A) Plans to send a spacecraft to Mars
   (B) Potential remnants of an early civilization's lunar calendar
   (C) Tools used by a prehistoric tribe to prepare food
   (D) Geographic formations on the Moon

5. The author mentions An alignment of stones in Wyoming, a circular-shaped structure . . . at Cahoki, and specially designed windows in structures of the Southwest in paragraph 2 in order to

   (A) provide proof that archeoastronomers have been studying prehistoric cultures
   (B) provide support for the idea that North American cultures built creative structures
   (C) provide evidence that certain astronomical events have not changed over time
   (D) provide examples of ways that prehistoric peoples monitored occurrences in the sky

6. The word serve in paragraph 2 could best be replaced by

   (A) fulfill
   (B) provide
   (C) assist
   (D) demonstrate

7. Look at the four squares [■] that indicate where the following sentence can be added to paragraph 2.

   This apparent understanding of certain aspects of astronomy by certain prehistoric cultures is of great academic interest today.

   Click on a square [■] to add the sentence to the passage.

8. What is stated in paragraph 3 about the construction in Chaco Canyon?

   (A) It was created from a single piece of stone.
   (B) It prevents sunlight from entering the area.
   (C) It was built before the fourteenth century.
   (D) It is located in a canyon.

9. The phrase of sorts in paragraph 3 is closest in meaning to

   (A) of opportunity
   (B) of some kind
   (C) of the past
   (D) of fate

10. The word them in paragraph 3 refers to

    (A) experts
    (B) slabs
    (C) shafts
    (D) markings

11. Which of the sentences below expresses the essential information in the highlighted sentence in paragraph 4? *Incorrect* choices change the meaning in important ways or leave out essential information.

(A) One issue is whether the stones were positioned by nature or by people.

(B) Early inhabitants often discussed where the stones should be placed.

(C) The current location of the stones was chosen because it provides the most natural setting.

(D) There is much discussion about how often early inhabitants moved the stones.

12. The word happenstance in paragraph 4 is closest in meaning to

(A) standing

(B) event

(C) order

(D) chance

13.

Directions: An introductory sentence or a brief summary of the passage is provided below. Complete the summary by selecting the THREE answer choices that express the most important ideas in the passage. Some sentences do not belong in the summary because they express ideas that are not presented in the passage or are minor ideas in the passage. *This question is worth 2 points.*
This passage discusses the study of astronomy as it refers to prehistoric cultures in North America.
•
•
•

Answer Choices (choose 3 to complete the chart):

(1) The structure at Chaco Canyon was most likely used for something other than astronomy.

(2) Prehistoric cultures in North America were not as advanced in their study of astronomy as were cultures in other parts of the world.

(3) One structure used by a certain prehistoric culture to monitor astronomical events was either discovered or created by the culture.

(4) Prehistoric cultures in North America created devices to monitor astronomical events.

(5) The Bighorn Medicine Wheel was constructed with stones.

(6) Prehistoric cultures in North America most likely understood the relationship between astronomy and their daily lives.

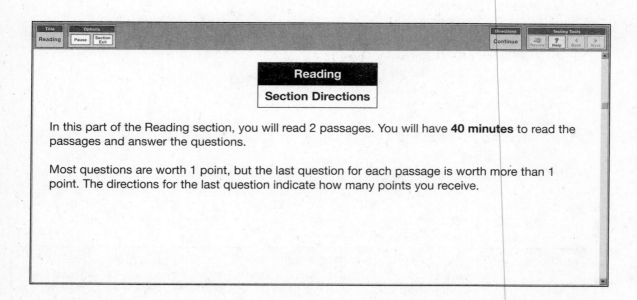

Reading

Section Directions

In this part of the Reading section, you will read 2 passages. You will have **40 minutes** to read the passages and answer the questions.

Most questions are worth 1 point, but the last question for each passage is worth more than 1 point. The directions for the last question indicate how many points you receive.

READING 2

Read the passage.

> 40 minutes

Paragraph

Truman and the Railroads

1   The period following World War II was filled with a succession of crises as the United States dealt with the difficulty of postwar reconversion to a peacetime economy. A threatened railroad strike in 1946 was one of many crises that led to a reconsideration of the interrelationships among government, management, and labor.

2   Organized labor, which had fared well during the war years of 1939–1945, faced severe problems because of the swift demobilization of 13 million service personnel following the war and the destabilizing results of industrial reconversions from wartime to peacetime uses. During late 1945 and early 1946, a record wave of labor disputes and strikes hit the United States, and even more strikes and disputes were expected. At the height of the problems, more than 500 strikes were under way, some of them in industries that were highly critical to the overall U.S. economy, including coal, steel, cars, and oil. When a national strike was threatened by the railroads in the spring of 1946, the government moved into action, believing that the U.S. economy was threatened were it to take place.

3   President Harry S. Truman had dealt rather patiently with the labor problems until the spring of 1946. Throughout his political career, Truman had been a friend of organized labor and had been strongly supported by labor in his elections, and when the railroad strike was first threatened, he called for a 60-day mediation period while the issues, particularly the main issue of a wage hike for railroad workers, were negotiated between management and labor. By April, 18 of the 20 unions related to the railroads had arrived at an agreement; however, the remaining unions which together controlled 280,000 workers and were essential to the operation of the railroads, were dissatisfied and set a date for a strike.

4   The day before the strike deadline, Truman's patience wore thin, and he signed an executive order authorizing government seizure of the railroads. Under threat of having the government take over the operation of the railroads, the two unions in question agreed to a five-day delay in the strike. Truman even suggested an 18.5-cent per hour pay raise for railroad workers. However, as the strike deadline approached, negotiations remained at a stalemate. The strike began as scheduled and had an immediate impact; of the country's 200,000 trains, only a few hundred remained in operation. Infuriated, Truman took to the radio waves and delivered a burning speech to the public; two days later, he delivered a speech to Congress blasting the striking workers and urging Congress to take unprecedented steps to break the strike, including urging approval to draft striking workers into military service. As Truman was delivering the speech, he was handed a note stating that the strike had been settled.

5   Even though the strike was resolved, deep issues had been raised over what role the government should play in disputes between management and labor. Truman's proposal to use the federal government to break a strike by drafting strikers into the armed forces brought this issue to the fore. Although management was pleased with the toughness that Truman had shown and many citizens were pleased that disruption of the economy had been avoided, concern was expressed about the constitutionality of having Congress take such a step. The Labor Management Relations Act (also known as the Taft-Hartley Act), which was enacted in the year following the strike, was an attempt to clarify some of the interrelationships among government, management, and labor.

Refer to this version of the passage to answer the questions that follow.

Paragraph

Truman and the Railroads

1   The period following World War II was filled with a succession of crises as the United States dealt with the difficulty of postwar reconversion to a peacetime economy. A threatened railroad strike in 1946 was one of many crises that led to a reconsideration of the interrelationships among government, management, and labor.

2   Organized labor, which had fared well during the war years of 1939–1945, faced severe problems because of the swift demobilization of 13 million service personnel following the war and the destabilizing results of industrial reconversions from wartime to peacetime uses. During late 1945 and early 1946, a record wave of labor disputes and strikes hit the United States, and even more strikes and disputes were expected. At the height of the problems, more than 500 strikes were under way, some of them in industries that were highly critical to the overall U.S. economy, including coal, steel, cars, and oil. When a national strike was threatened by the railroads in the spring of 1946, the government moved into action, believing that the U.S. economy was threatened were it to take place.

3   President Harry S. Truman had dealt rather patiently with the labor problems until the spring of 1946. Throughout his political career, Truman had been a friend of organized labor and had been strongly supported by labor in his elections, and when the railroad strike was first threatened, he called for a 60-day mediation period while the issues, particularly the main issue of a wage hike for railroad workers, were negotiated between management and labor. By April, 18 of the 20 unions related to the railroads had arrived at an agreement; however, the remaining unions which together controlled 280,000 workers and were essential to the operation of the railroads, were dissatisfied and set a date for a strike.

4   The day before the strike deadline, Truman's patience wore thin, and he signed an executive order authorizing government seizure of the railroads. **22A** Under threat of having the government take over the operation of the railroads, the two unions in question agreed to a five-day delay in the strike. **22B** Truman even suggested an 18.5-cent per hour pay raise for railroad workers. **22C** However, as the strike deadline approached, negotiations remained at a stalemate. **22D** The strike began as scheduled and had an immediate impact; of the country's 200,000 trains, only a few hundred remained in operation. Infuriated, Truman took to the radio waves and delivered a burning speech to the public; two days later, he delivered a speech to Congress blasting the striking workers and urging Congress to take unprecedented steps to break the strike, including urging approval to draft striking workers into military service. As Truman was delivering the speech, he was handed a note stating that the strike had been settled.

5   Even though the strike was resolved, deep issues had been raised over what role the government should play in disputes between management and labor. Truman's proposal to use the federal government to break a strike by drafting strikers into the armed forces brought this issue to the fore. Although management was pleased with the toughness that Truman had shown and many citizens were pleased that disruption of the economy had been avoided, concern was expressed about the constitutionality of having Congress take such a step. The Labor Management Relations Act (also known as the Taft-Hartley Act), which was enacted in the year following the strike, was an attempt to clarify some of the interrelationships among government, management, and labor.

Questions

14. The phrase fared well in paragraph 2 is closest in meaning to
    - Ⓐ recovered from illness
    - Ⓑ won battles
    - Ⓒ made good wages
    - Ⓓ experienced good fortune

15. According to paragraph 2, in late 1945 and early 1946
    - Ⓐ there were labor problems because too many workers were in the military
    - Ⓑ there were labor problems because too many people were leaving the military
    - Ⓒ there were 500 strikes in the railroad industry
    - Ⓓ there were 500 strikes in critical industries

16. The word it in paragraph 2 refers to
    - Ⓐ a national strike
    - Ⓑ the government
    - Ⓒ action
    - Ⓓ the U.S. economy

17. The phrase called for in paragraph 3 is closest in meaning to
    - Ⓐ criticized
    - Ⓑ cheered
    - Ⓒ proposed
    - Ⓓ postponed

18. According to paragraph 3, it is NOT true that the railroad workers
    - Ⓐ were all in favor of the strike
    - Ⓑ were interested in higher pay
    - Ⓒ from two unions set a strike date
    - Ⓓ turned down Truman's offer of a pay raise

19. Why does the author mention 280,000 workers in paragraph 3?
    - Ⓐ To indicate how many workers were opposed to the strike
    - Ⓑ To demonstrate that the railroads were not really a critical industry
    - Ⓒ To support management's claim that a wage increase was not possible
    - Ⓓ To illustrate how serious the strike threat was

20. The phrase wore thin in paragraph 4 is closest in meaning to
    - Ⓐ was extended
    - Ⓑ decreased
    - Ⓒ lightened
    - Ⓓ lost weight

21. The phrase remained at a stalemate in paragraph 4 is closest in meaning to
    - Ⓐ stayed on target
    - Ⓑ proceeded on a friendly basis
    - Ⓒ suddenly started up again
    - Ⓓ were at a standstill

22. Look at the four squares [■] that indicate where the following sentence can be added to paragraph 4.

    This was an offer that was considerably more generous than previous offers.

    Click on a square [■] to add the sentence to the passage.

23. The word steps in paragraph 4 could best be replaced by
    - Ⓐ paces
    - Ⓑ measures
    - Ⓒ stairs
    - Ⓓ suggestions

24. It can be inferred from paragraph 4 that
    - Ⓐ Truman actually drafted striking workers into the military
    - Ⓑ Congress passed a law allowing the drafting of striking workers
    - Ⓒ it was the threat of drafting strikers that ended the strike
    - Ⓓ Truman was actually opposed to drafting workers into the military

25. Which of the sentences below expresses the essential information in the highlighted sentence in paragraph 5? *Incorrect* choices change the meaning in important ways or leave out essential information.

    Ⓐ Though some were pleased that Truman had kept the economy going, there was concern about how he had done it.

    Ⓑ During the strike, the economy was disrupted, and Congress was forced to take steps to fix it.

    Ⓒ Because of the effects of the strike on the citizens of the country, it was necessary for Congress to make changes to the Constitution.

    Ⓓ Management took tough actions during the strike; as a result, Congress expressed concern about the steps that management had taken.

26.

Directions: An introductory sentence or a brief summary of the passage is provided below. Complete the summary by selecting the FOUR answer choices that express the most important ideas in the passage. Some sentences do not belong in the summary because they express ideas that are not presented in the passage or are minor ideas in the passage. ***This question is worth 3 points.***
This passage discusses Truman and organized labor.
•
•
•
•

Answer Choices (choose 4 to complete the chart):

(1) In response to a threatened strike by railroad workers, Truman took strong actions.

(2) A law was passed after the railroad strike in an attempt to clarify the relationship between labor and government.

(3) The railroad workers went on strike in order to obtain shorter working days.

(4) Truman's actions with the railroad workers raised issues about the relationship between labor and government.

(5) During the railroad strike, only a small percentage of the country's trains were operating.

(6) Truman initially dealt calmly with the many labor problems immediately following the war.

READING 3

Read the passage.

Paragraph

Mathematical Bases

1   The system of numeration that is now most widely used is a base-10 system with the following characteristics: each number from 1 to 10 as well as the powers of 10 (such as one hundred or one thousand) has a distinctive name, and the names of the other numbers tend to be combinations of the names of the numbers from 1 to 10 and the powers of 10. In most Indo-European, Semitic, and Mongolian languages, the numerical systems have a decimal base and conform at least approximately to this theoretical model. The almost universal adoption of the base-10 numerical system was undoubtedly influenced by the fact that humans have ten fingers, since people most likely first learned to count on their fingers. Though the base-10 numerical systems are convenient for reasons of anatomy, they are not as mathematically practical as would be systems based on perhaps 11 or 12. Some mathematicians have suggested that a base-11 system would be preferable to a base-10 system because 11 is a prime number (and is thus divisible only by 1 and 11), while 10 is not a prime number (because it is divisible by 1, 2, 5, and 10); others have suggested that a base-12 system would be preferable to a base-10 system because 12 is divisible by more whole numbers (1, 2, 3, 4, 6, 12) than is 10.

2   Base-10 numerical systems were not the only systems based on anatomical parts: there were also systems based on 5 and 20. While it is difficult to find a number system that is a purely base-5, or quinary, system, it is possible to find number systems that have traces of groupings by fives, and these systems are most likely what remains of older systems that developed from counting the fingers on one hand. In a quinary system, there would be distinct units for numbers 1 through 5, but the words for numbers 6 through 9 are compounds of five-and-one, five-and-two, five-and-three, and so on. Remnants of quinary systems can be found today only in historical records of ancient languages, such as the language of the early Sumerians.

3   Examples of base-20, or vigesimal, systems, which most likely developed from counting by making use of all the digits, are more common than are those of base-5 systems. A number of early cultures, including the Mayans, the Aztecs, and the Celts, developed numerical systems that involved counting by 20s. The Mayan calendar had 20 months of 20 days each, and the Mayans counted years in terms of 20-year periods rather than decades; study of the Aztec numbers for 1 through 20 shows that the names of the first five numbers are related to the fingers of one hand, the names of the next five numbers are related to the fingers of the other hand, the names of the numbers 11 through 16 are related to the toes on one foot, and the names of numbers 16 through 20 are related to the toes on the other foot. In Celtic languages, counting is also done by 20s, and a number of other European languages maintain remnants of this characteristic. In French and Latin, the words for 20 are clearly remnants of a vigesimal system in that they are distinct words not derived from words for *two-tens,* which would occur in a purely base-10 system, and the way of expressing the number 80 is by counting by 20s and saying *four-twenties.* In English, the way of counting by 20s was to use the word *score;* this method of counting was commonly used by Shakespeare and was still in use at the time of Abraham Lincoln, who opened his famous address at Gettysburg by saying: "Four score and seven years ago. . . ."

4   Some cultures had systems based upon 60, a system with a major drawback in that it requires 60 distinct words for numbers 1 through 60. In Sumerian, Babylonian, Greek, and Arab cultures, for example, the sexagesimal system was a scholarly numerical system. Sexagesimal systems were obviously not developed based on body parts, and numerous theories have been raised to explain how such systems came about, but it is not know conclusively which of these theories is correct. One hypothesis is that 60 was chosen as the base because it is the lowest number with a great many divisors (1, 2, 3, 4, 5, 6, 10, 12, 15, 20, 30, 60). Another

theory provides a more natural explanation for the use of 60 as a base: the approximate number of days in a year is 360, which supposedly led to the use of 360 degrees in a circle and was reduced to the more manageable 60, which is one-sixth of 360. A third theory suggests that the use of 60 as a base must have come about as a result of interchange between two different civilizations, one using a decimal (base 10) system and the other using a base-6 system. A weakness of this theory is that there is no historical foundation to support the existence of a base-6 system.

Refer to this version of the passage to answer the questions that follow.

Paragraph

Mathematical Bases

1   The system of numeration that is now most widely used is a base-10 system with the following characteristics: each number from 1 to 10 as well as the powers of 10 (such as one hundred or one thousand) has a distinctive name, and the names of the other numbers tend to be combinations of the names of the numbers from 1 to 10 and the powers of 10. In most Indo-European, Semitic, and Mongolian languages, the numerical systems have a decimal base and conform at least approximately to this theoretical model. The almost universal adoption of the base-10 numerical system was undoubtedly influenced by the fact that humans have ten fingers, since people most likely first learned to count on their fingers. Though the base-10 numerical systems are convenient for reasons of anatomy, they are not as mathematically practical as would be systems based on perhaps 11 or 12. Some mathematicians have suggested that a base-11 system would be preferable to a base-10 system because 11 is a prime number (and is thus divisible only by 1 and 11), while 10 is not a prime number (because it is divisible by 1, 2, 5, and 10); others have suggested that a base-12 system would be preferable to a base-10 system because 12 is divisible by more whole numbers (1, 2, 3, 4, 6, 12) than is 10.

2   Base-10 numerical systems were not the only systems based on anatomical parts: there were also systems based on 5 and 20. While it is difficult to find a number system that is a purely base-5, or quinary, system, it is possible to find number systems that have traces of groupings by fives, and these systems are most likely what remains of older systems that developed from counting the fingers on one hand. In a quinary system, there would be distinct units for numbers 1 through 5, but the words for numbers 6 through 9 are compounds of five-and-one, five-and-two, five-and-three, and so on. Remnants of quinary systems can be found today only in historical records of ancient languages, such as the language of the early Sumerians.

3   Examples of base-20, or vigesimal, systems, which most likely developed from counting by making use of all the digits, are more common than are those of base-5 systems. A number of early cultures, including the Mayans, the Aztecs, and the Celts, developed numerical systems that involved counting by 20s. The Mayan calendar had 20 months of 20 days each, and the Mayans counted years in terms of 20-year periods rather than decades; study of the Aztec numbers for 1 through 20 shows that the names of the first five numbers are related to the fingers of one hand, the names of the next five numbers are related to the fingers of the other hand, the names of the numbers 11 through 16 are related to the toes on one foot, and the names of numbers 16 through 20 are related to the toes on the other foot. In Celtic languages, counting is also done by 20s, and a number of other European languages maintain remnants of this characteristic. In French and Latin, the words for 20 are clearly remnants of a vigesimal system in that they are distinct words not derived from words for *two-tens,* which would occur in a purely base-10 system, and the way of expressing the number 80 is by counting by 20s and saying *four-twenties.* In English, the way of counting by 20s was to use the word *score*; this method of counting was commonly used by Shakespeare and was still in use at the time of Abraham Lincoln, who opened his famous address at Gettysburg by saying: "Four score and seven years ago. . . ."

4   Some cultures had systems based upon 60, a system with a major drawback in that it requires 60 distinct words for numbers 1 through 60. **36A** In Sumerian, Babylonian, Greek, and Arab cultures, for example, the sexagesimal system was a scholarly numerical system. **36B** Sexagesimal systems were obviously not developed based on body parts, and numerous theories have been raised to explain how such systems came about, but it is not know conclusively which of these theories is correct. **36C** One hypothesis is that 60 was chosen as the base because it is the lowest number with a great many divisors (1, 2, 3, 4, 5, 6, 10, 12, 15, 20, 30, 60). **36D** Another theory provides a more natural explanation for the use of 60 as a base: the approximate number of days in a year is 360, which supposedly led to the use of 360 degrees in a circle and was reduced to the more manageable 60, which is one-sixth of 360. A third theory suggests that the use of 60 as a base must have come about as a result of interchange between two different civilizations, one using a decimal (base 10) system and the other using a base-6 system. A weakness of this theory is that there is no historical foundation to support the existence of a base-6 system.

Questions

27. The phrase of anatomy in paragraph 1 is closest in meaning to

  Ⓐ related to mathematical precision
  Ⓑ related to the history of the language
  Ⓒ related to the structure of the body
  Ⓓ related to ease of counting

28. Which of the sentences below expresses the essential information in the highlighted sentence in paragraph 1? *Incorrect* choices change the meaning in important ways or leave out essential information.

  Ⓐ It has been suggested that either base 11 or base 12 would be preferable to base 10, for opposite reasons.
  Ⓑ The number 10 has fewer divisors than the number 11 but more divisors than the number 12.
  Ⓒ All mathematicians agree that a numerical system based on a number with the most divisors would be the best system.
  Ⓓ Mathematicians have suggested that either base 11 or base 12 would be better than base 10 because both 11 and 12 are prime numbers.

29. The author begins paragraph 2 by mentioning Base-10 numerical systems in order to

  Ⓐ introduce a new topic in paragraph 2
  Ⓑ indicate that base-10 systems are based on anatomy, while other systems are not
  Ⓒ emphasize that base-10 systems were less common than other systems
  Ⓓ relate the topic of paragraph 1 to the topic of paragraph 2

30. The word traces in paragraph 2 could best be replaced by

  Ⓐ remnants
  Ⓑ tracks
  Ⓒ results
  Ⓓ processes

31. The word digits in paragraph 3 could best be replaced by

  Ⓐ hands
  Ⓑ numbers
  Ⓒ fingers and toes
  Ⓓ measurements

32. The phrase this characteristic in paragraph 3 refers to

  Ⓐ using Celtic words
  Ⓑ counting by 20s
  Ⓒ relating the names of numbers to the toes
  Ⓓ counting on the toes of one foot

33. The passage indicates that all of the following languages show characteristics of a vigesimal system EXCEPT

Ⓐ Latin
Ⓑ Celtic
Ⓒ English
Ⓓ Greek

34. It can be determined from paragraph 3 that four score and seven is equal to

Ⓐ 47
Ⓑ 87
Ⓒ 327
Ⓓ 749

35. The word drawback in paragraph 4 is closest in meaning to

Ⓐ disadvantage
Ⓑ attraction
Ⓒ reversal
Ⓓ interest

36. Look at the four squares [■] that indicate where the following sentence can be added to paragraph 4.

It was one that was used mainly for scientific study and analysis.

Click on a square [■] to add the sentence to the passage.

37. The word interchange in paragraph 4 is closest in meaning to

Ⓐ barter
Ⓑ absorption
Ⓒ finance
Ⓓ contact

38. The number 25 would most likely be

Ⓐ a distinct number from 1 through 24 in a quinary system
Ⓑ a variation of *five-fives* in a decimal system
Ⓒ a variation of *twenty-plus-five* in a vigesimal system
Ⓓ a variation of *two-tens-plus-five* in a sexagesimal system

39.

Directions: Two of the answer choices below are used to describe each of the numerical systems. Complete the table by matching appropriate answer choices to the numerical systems they are used to describe. ***This question is worth 4 points.***	
quinary system	• •
decimal system	• •
vigesimal system	• •
sexagesimal system	• •

Answer Choices (choose 8 to complete the chart):

(1) Most likely based on the fingers of one hand

(2) The most commonly used system

(3) Most likely based on the fingers and toes

(4) Most likely not based on the fingers and toes

(5) Most likely based on the toes on both feet

(6) Remnants found in some of today's languages

(7) Came about as a result of the merging of two different numerical systems

(8) Remnants found only in ancient languages

(9) Not know to have been used by the masses in any culture

(10) Most likely based on the fingers on both hands

Turn to the chart on page 544, and circle the numbers of the questions that you missed.

LISTENING

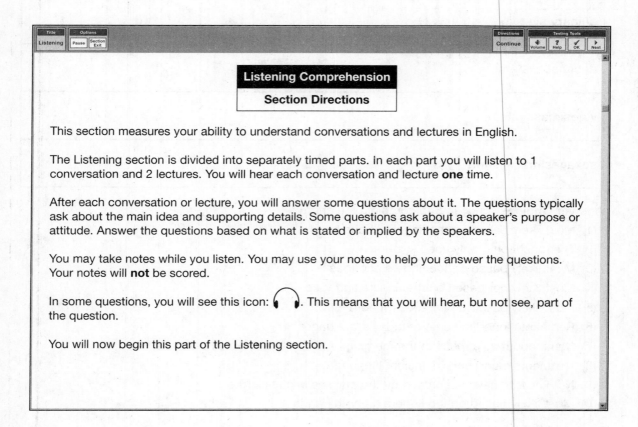

Within the screen:

Listening Comprehension

Section Directions

This section measures your ability to understand conversations and lectures in English.

The Listening section is divided into separately timed parts. In each part you will listen to 1 conversation and 2 lectures. You will hear each conversation and lecture **one** time.

After each conversation or lecture, you will answer some questions about it. The questions typically ask about the main idea and supporting details. Some questions ask about a speaker's purpose or attitude. Answer the questions based on what is stated or implied by the speakers.

You may take notes while you listen. You may use your notes to help you answer the questions. Your notes will **not** be scored.

In some questions, you will see this icon: 🎧. This means that you will hear, but not see, part of the question.

You will now begin this part of the Listening section.

Questions 1–5

Listen to a conversation between a student and a university office worker.

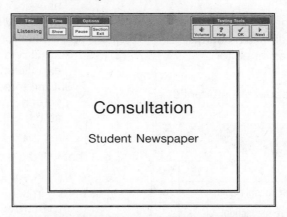

1. Why does the student go to this university office?

   Ⓐ To find out about writing for the school paper
   Ⓑ To get a copy of the student paper
   Ⓒ To sign up for a journalism course
   Ⓓ To apply for a job as an editor

2. Is each of these true about the student's experience?

For each statement, click in the YES or NO column.		
	YES	NO
She has worked on the high school paper.		
She has worked on the university school paper.		
She has taken a high school journalism course.		
She has taken a university journalism course.		
She has been an editor on the high school paper.		
She has been an editor on the university paper.		

3. Listen again to part of the passage. Then answer the question.

   Why does the office worker say this:

   Ⓐ To try to convince the student to change her mind
   Ⓑ To verify that what the student just said was accurate
   Ⓒ To encourage the student
   Ⓓ To correct something he just said

4. What must a student do to become a staff writer on the university paper?

   Ⓐ Submit three articles about any single aspect of the student's life
   Ⓑ Submit any articles he or she has written for other papers
   Ⓒ Submit one article about his or her experience as a writer
   Ⓓ Submit three articles he or she has written about different aspects of student life

5. What will the student most likely do next?

   Ⓐ Turn in some of her high school articles
   Ⓑ Turn in some university articles tomorrow
   Ⓒ Forget about joining the paper
   Ⓓ Take some time to write the articles carefully

Questions 6–11

Listen to a discussion from a geography class.

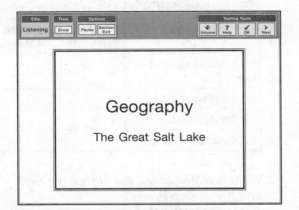

Geography

The Great Salt Lake

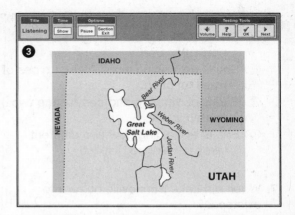

1

2

IDAHO

WYOMING

Great Salt Lake

N

Lake Bonneville

NEVADA

UTAH

3

IDAHO

NEVADA

Bear River

Great Salt Lake

Weber River

Jordan River

WYOMING

UTAH

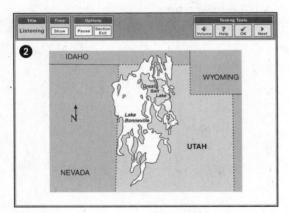

4

6. What is the instructor trying to accomplish?

    Ⓐ She is outlining the history of a particular area.

    Ⓑ She is describing how different types of lakes function.

    Ⓒ She is comparing and contrasting two related lakes.

    Ⓓ She is explaining how two different lakes developed distinctly.

7. When did Lake Bonneville come into existence?

    Ⓐ 10,000 years ago

    Ⓑ 100,000 years ago

    Ⓒ 1,000,000 years ago

    Ⓓ 10,000,000 years ago

8. Listen again to part of the passage. Then answer the question. 🎧

    What does the instructor mean when she says this: 🎧

    Ⓐ "Take more time to answer if you want."

    Ⓑ "I think your answer is not correct."

    Ⓒ "You didn't say anything; please say something."

    Ⓓ "I think you're not very sure of yourself."

9. What is stated in the lecture about each lake?

For each statement, click in the correct column.		
	Lake Bonneville	Great Salt Lake
It is a 20,000-square-mile lake.		
It is a freshwater lake.		
It is the older lake.		
It is the lake with no outlet.		

10. What is stated about the Weber, the Bear, and the Jordan Rivers?

Click on 2 answers.

    Ⓐ They feed into the Great Salt Lake.

    Ⓑ They carry deposits out of the Great Salt Lake.

    Ⓒ They are saltier than the Great Salt Lake.

    Ⓓ They bring a million tons of deposits into the Great Salt Lake each year.

11. How much salt has built up in the Great Salt Lake?

    Ⓐ 6 tons

    Ⓑ 600 tons

    Ⓒ 6 million tons

    Ⓓ 6 billion tons

Questions 12–17

Listen to a group of students who are taking a business class.

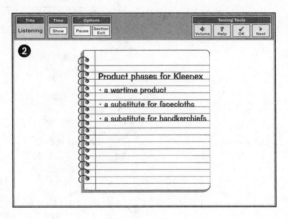

12. Why are the students meeting?

    Ⓐ They are reviewing class lecture notes.

    Ⓑ They are preparing for a presentation.

    Ⓒ They are working on a paper.

    Ⓓ They are preparing for an exam.

13. Listen again to part of the discussion. Then answer the question.

Why does the man say this:

    Ⓐ He thinks the marketing of the products is not as important as the history.

    Ⓑ He is afraid the other students do not know what course they are taking.

    Ⓒ He is concerned that the presentation does not have the correct focus.

    Ⓓ He would like to remind the others that they are taking two different courses.

14. With what product was each of these periods of time associated?

For each period of time, click in the correct column.			
	Facecloths	**Bandages**	**Handkerchiefs**
Before 1920			
In the 1920s			
In the 1930s			

15. What was the situation at Kimberly-Clark at the end of World War I?

Click on 2 answers.

    Ⓐ It had a surplus of its product.

    Ⓑ It needed to develop a new product.

    Ⓒ It no longer needed to market its product.

    Ⓓ It needed to begin marketing its product.

16. How did Kimberly-Clark learn that its product had a use as a handkerchief?

    Ⓐ From customer letters

    Ⓑ From research scientists

    Ⓒ From marketing experts

    Ⓓ From famous actresses

17. With what product was each of these marketing strategies associated?

For each marketing strategy, click in the correct column.			
	Facecloths	**Bandages**	**Handkerchiefs**
Consumer testing			
No marketing			
Famous actresses			

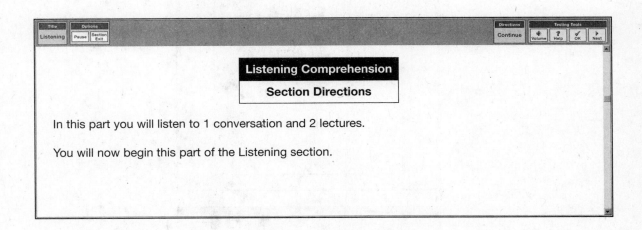

Listening Comprehension

Section Directions

In this part you will listen to 1 conversation and 2 lectures.

You will now begin this part of the Listening section.

Questions 18–22

Listen to a conversation between a student and a professor.

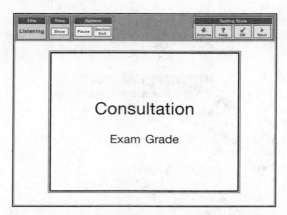

18. Why does the student go to see the professor?

    Ⓐ To talk about how to prepare for a coming exam

    Ⓑ To figure out why she did not do well on an exam

    Ⓒ To discuss the answer to an exam question

    Ⓓ To find out how the professor wants her to evaluate information

19. How had the student most likely prepared for the exam?

    Ⓐ She had most likely not studied at all.

    Ⓑ She had most likely studied only a little.

    Ⓒ She had most likely spent a lot of time memorizing information.

    Ⓓ She had most likely prepared the way that the professor wanted.

20. What problem did the student have with the question regarding the process?

    Ⓐ She did not know what the process was.

    Ⓑ She did not know what the steps in the process were.

    Ⓒ She did not list all of the steps in the process.

    Ⓓ She failed to evaluate the steps in the process.

21. What problem did the student have with the question regarding the theories?

    Ⓐ She did not know what the theories were.

    Ⓑ She wrote about only one of the theories.

    Ⓒ She stated incorrect information about the theories.

    Ⓓ She did not clearly compare and contrast the theories.

22. Which exam question would this professor most likely use?

    Ⓐ What are the key points of a certain policy?

    Ⓑ Who supports a certain policy?

    Ⓒ What are the strengths and weaknesses of a certain policy?

    Ⓓ When was a certain policy developed?

Questions 23–28

Listen to a lecture in an American history class.

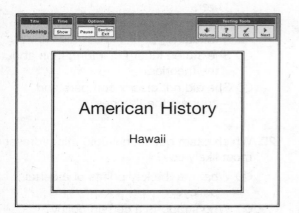

American History

Hawaii

23. What does the lecturer mainly discuss?

Ⓐ The role of Captain Cook in the history of Hawaii

Ⓑ How the Hawaiian monarchy came to be

Ⓒ Events leading up to the end of the Hawaiian monarchy

Ⓓ The queen who built up the Hawaiian monarchy

24. Why does the lecturer most likely mention King Kamehameha and Captain Cook?

Ⓐ They played important roles in the history of Hawaii leading up to Liliuokalani.

Ⓑ They succeeded in convincing Liliuokalani to change what she was doing.

Ⓒ They were both instrumental in causing the monarchy of Hawaii to fall.

Ⓓ They were in Hawaii at the time that the monarchy was established there.

25. What does the professor say about James Cook?

Ⓐ He was the Earl of Sandwich.

Ⓑ He fought to unite the islands under one king.

Ⓒ He served as one of the kings of Hawaii.

Ⓓ He named the islands after a British earl.

26. What did Liliuokalani believe, according to the professor?

Ⓐ That the monarchy should end

Ⓑ That the monarch's power should be limited

Ⓒ That someone else should be the monarch

Ⓓ That the monarch should have complete power

27. Which of the following did NOT happen to Liliuokalani?

Ⓐ She became queen in 1891.

Ⓑ She ruled Hawaii until the end of her life.

Ⓒ She received a pension from the government.

Ⓓ She was removed from power.

28. When did each person live?

For each person, click in the correct column.			
	End of the 18th century	**Beginning of the 19th century**	**End of the 19th century**
Kamehameha			
James Cook			
Liliuokalani			

Questions 29–34

Listen to a lecture in a science class.

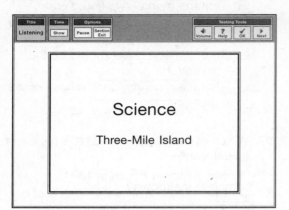

29. What is the main topic of the lecture?
- (A) The causes of an accident
- (B) The history of a nuclear power plant
- (C) An accident and its effects
- (D) The construction of the reactors at Three-Mile Island

30. How many pressurized water reactors are there at Three-Mile Island?
- (A) One
- (B) Two
- (C) Three
- (D) Four

31. What does the lecturer say about the PWRs during the accident?
- (A) There were no problems with the PWRs.
- (B) There was a problem with only one of the PWRs.
- (C) There were problems with one PWR after another.
- (D) There were problems with more than one PWR.

32. Did each of these happen during the accident discussed in the lecture?

For each statement, click in the YES or NO column.		
	YES	NO
A cooling valve was stuck closed.		
Instruments were misread.		
The emergency cooling was turned on.		
A partial meltdown occurred.		

33. What is stated in the lecture about a complete meltdown?
- (A) One occurred at Three-Mile Island.
- (B) One occurs if uranium begins to melt.
- (C) It requires the emergency water cooling system to be turned on.
- (D) It involves the complete meltdown of the uranium in the fuel core.

34. How does the lecturer seem to feel about the accident at Three-Mile Island?
- (A) It was not at all serious.
- (B) Its seriousness was extremely exaggerated.
- (C) It was not as serious as it could have been.
- (D) It was quite catastrophic.

Turn to the chart on page 545, and circle the numbers of the questions that you missed.

SPEAKING

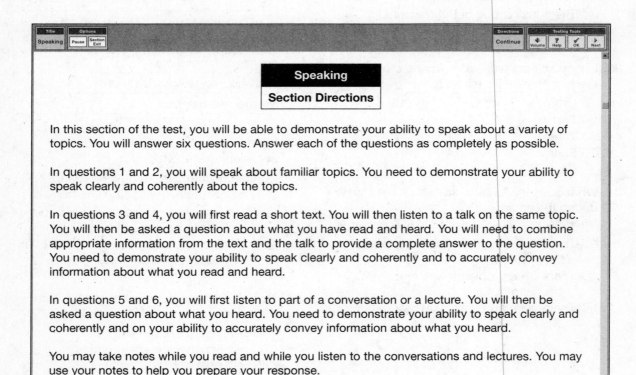

> ### Speaking
> #### Section Directions
>
> In this section of the test, you will be able to demonstrate your ability to speak about a variety of topics. You will answer six questions. Answer each of the questions as completely as possible.
>
> In questions 1 and 2, you will speak about familiar topics. You need to demonstrate your ability to speak clearly and coherently about the topics.
>
> In questions 3 and 4, you will first read a short text. You will then listen to a talk on the same topic. You will then be asked a question about what you have read and heard. You will need to combine appropriate information from the text and the talk to provide a complete answer to the question. You need to demonstrate your ability to speak clearly and coherently and to accurately convey information about what you read and heard.
>
> In questions 5 and 6, you will first listen to part of a conversation or a lecture. You will then be asked a question about what you heard. You need to demonstrate your ability to speak clearly and coherently and on your ability to accurately convey information about what you heard.
>
> You may take notes while you read and while you listen to the conversations and lectures. You may use your notes to help you prepare your response.
>
> Listen carefully to the directions for each question. The directions will not be written on the screen.

Question 1

Read the question. On a piece of paper, take notes on the main points of a response. Then respond to the question.

> What would be your dream job? Use reasons and details to support your reponse.
>
> | Preparation Time: 15 seconds |
> | --- |
> | Response Time: 45 seconds |

Question 2

Read the question. On a piece of paper, take notes on the main points of a response. Then respond to the question.

> Would you prefer to write a paper by yourself or with a group? Use reasons and details to support your response.
>
> | Preparation Time: 15 seconds |
> | --- |
> | Response Time: 45 seconds |

Question 3

Read the passage. On a piece of paper, take notes on the main points of the reading passage.

Reading Time: 45 seconds

Announcement from the music department

The Spring Show is an annual program of vocal and instrumental music to celebrate the spring season. Tickets for this fantastic event will go on sale for students at 9:00 A.M. on Monday, March 1 at the music auditorium ticket office. Any tickets that are still available will go on sale to the public on Monday, March 8. Get your tickets early for this fabulous annual event because they always sell out soon after they go on sale to the public. Get your tickets early so that you will not have to miss out on this fabulous event.

Listen to the passage. On a piece of paper, take notes on the main points of the listening passage.

Now answer the following question:

How do the students react to the notice about the Spring Show?

Preparation Time: 30 seconds
Response Time: 60 seconds

Question 4

Read the passage. On a piece of paper, take notes on the main points of the reading passage.

Reading Time: 45 seconds

Great Ape Communication

Quite a few scientific studies have been conducted on communication by the great apes, a group of primates composed of gorillas, chimpanzees, and orangutans. What has been concluded in these studies is that the great apes communicate in a variety of ways that include, but are not limited to, facial expressions, gestures with their appendages, and a variety of calls. The large primates use this wide variety of methods of communication to express a broad range of ideas to other members of their group, such as anger, fear, approaching danger, dominance over the group, or acceptance of members into the group.

Listen to the passage. On a piece of paper, take notes on the main points of the listening passage.

Now answer the following question:

How does the information in the listening passage add to what is explained in the reading passage?

Preparation Time: 30 seconds
Response Time: 60 seconds

Question 5

Listen to the passage. On a piece of paper, take notes on the main points of the listening passage.

Now answer the following question:

How is the woman dealing with the problem she is facing?

Preparation Time: 20 seconds
Response Time: 60 seconds

Question 6

Listen to the passage. On a piece of paper, take notes on the main points of the listening passage.

Now answer the following question:

How does the professor describe mercantilism?

Preparation Time: 20 seconds
Response Time: 60 seconds

After you have completed this test, fill in the chart on pages 546–551.

WRITING

Writing
Section Directions

This section measures your ability to use writing to communicate in an academic environment. There will be two writing tasks.

For the first writing task, you will read a passage and listen to a lecture and then answer a question based on what you have read and heard. For the second task, you will answer a question based on your own knowledge and experience.

Integrated Writing Directions

For the first task, you will read a passage about an academic topic. You will have **3 minutes** to read the passage. You may take notes on the passage while you read. The passage will then be removed and you will listen to a lecture about the same topic. While you listen, you may also take notes.

Then you will write a response to a question that asks you about the relationship between the lecture you heard and the reading passage. Try to answer the question as completely as possible using information from the reading passage and the lecture. The question does **not** ask you to express your personal opinion. You will be able to see the reading passage again when it is time for you to write. You may use your notes to help you answer the question. You will have **20 minutes** to write your response.

Typically, an effective response will be 150 to 225 words. You need to demonstrate your ability to write well and to provide complete and accurate content.

Remember you can look at the passage again when you write your response. Immediately after the reading time ends, the lecture begins.

Independent Writing Directions

For the second task, you will write an essay in response to a question that asks you to state, explain, and support your opinion on an issue. You will have **30 minutes** to plan, write, and revise your response.

Typically, an effective essay will contain a minimum of 300 words. You need to demonstrate your ability to write well. This includes the development of your ideas, the organization of your essay, and the quality and accuracy of the language you use to express your ideas.

Question 1

Read the passage. On a piece of paper, take notes on the main points of the reading passage.

> Reading Time: 3 minutes

Originally named after the Roman goddess of love, the planet Venus also used to be known as the morning star and the evening star because it shines so brightly that it is visible on Earth even when the Sun is only partially visible in the morning and the evening.

Why does Venus shine so brightly? One reason is certainly because Venus is so close to Earth; it is, in fact, the closest planet to Earth. However, its proximity to Earth is not the only reason that Venus appears to shine so brightly. Another reason that Venus shines so brightly is that it is covered in thick white clouds that reflect sunlight off of them.

For quite some time, all that we have been able to see of Venus is the thick clouds that surround it, and little else was known of the planet itself. Dozens of space probes were sent to Venus in the last part of the twentieth century, and most of them were destroyed before they were able to send back information about Venus's surface. One probe, however, did manage to transmit some messages before it, too, failed.

From this one partially successful probe, numerous amazing facts about Venus have been learned. The thick clouds that cover Venus, for example, are made of sulfuric acid rather than oxygen, and these thick clouds never part to let any sunshine in at all. Most amazingly, the temperature on Venus is extremely hot, somewhere around 900 degrees Fahrenheit.

Listen to the passage. On a piece of paper, take notes on the main points of the listening passage.

Now answer the following question:

How does the information in the listening passage expand on the information presented in the reading passage?

> Preparation Time: 1 minute
> Response Time: 20 minutes

Question 2

Read the question. On a piece of paper, take notes on the main points of a response. Then write your response.

> Many families have important traditions that family members share. What is one of your family's important traditions? Use specific reasons and details to support your response.

> Response Time: 30 minutes

After you have completed this test, fill in the chart on pages 552–553.

COMPLETE TEST 2

READING 1

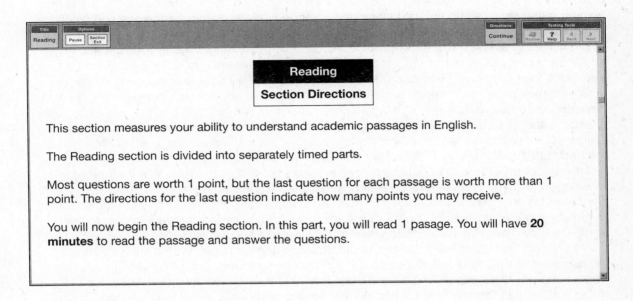

Reading
Section Directions

This section measures your ability to understand academic passages in English.

The Reading section is divided into separately timed parts.

Most questions are worth 1 point, but the last question for each passage is worth more than 1 point. The directions for the last question indicate how many points you may receive.

You will now begin the Reading section. In this part, you will read 1 pasage. You will have **20 minutes** to read the passage and answer the questions.

Read the passage.

20 minutes

Paragraph

Navigational Devices

1   From the earliest of times, sailors have found ways to navigate their ships on the seas and oceans of the world. The earliest sailors navigated by simply following the coastline. Aside from being a rather slow method of navigating, this method was also rather dangerous and limited. It was dangerous in that waters close to the shoreline could be shallow enough to strand a ship or the waters could be full of rocky protrusions capable of sending ships to their graves. When seafarers began sailing out of sight of land more than 4,000 years ago, they used the stars to determine their direction. They calculated the distance traveled from their speed and sailing time, and they drew rough charts and maps to find their way and to exchange information about navigational routes with others. It had also been known as early as 300 B.C. that a sundial casts a longer shadow as it is moved farther north of the equator, and this information was used by sailors from that time to get an idea of how far north of the equator a ship was. All of these methods provided only very rudimentary means of navigating.

2   It was not until more than 3,000 years after sailors set out on the seas that the compass was developed. The premise of a compass is that the magnetized needle of a compass, when it is balanced on a central pivot or left to float on liquid, will always turn to point in the direction of magnetic north. Navigators on Chinese ships were the first ones who were known to use compasses to determine the direction their ships were heading, as early as 1100.

3   Numerous inventions were created to determine a ship's latitude. With the invention of the astrolabe in the fourteenth century, sailors were able to measure the Sun's height with better accuracy than with a sundial, and they were able to use the information provided by the astrolabe to determine how far north of the equator they were. An astrolabe was a metal circle with a sighting rule that rotated in the circle; the rule could be aligned with the Sun, and measurements on the ring indicated the Sun's height. Other devices followed that were better able to determine the Sun's height and thus provide an idea of the ship's latitude. The backstaff, invented in 1595, and the sextant, invented in 1757, were devices that each improved a navigator's ability to determine latitude. The backstaff was a device that required the navigator to face away from the Sun and make a calculation of the shadow in relation to the horizon. The sextant was a measuring device that required the navigator to look into an eyepiece and calculate the Sun's position relative to the horizon and then check printed tables to convert this information into latitude.

4   The missing piece in the navigational puzzle was the ability to calculate longitude, or how far east or west a ship had traveled. The need for a device to calculate longitude was so important to navigators that the English Parliament offered a reward of 20,000 pounds (an extraordinarily large sum at the time, perhaps $10 million in today's currency) to anyone who could invent a method for calculating longitude. In 1759, English clockmaker John Harrison built a chronometer that was accurate enough for navigation. The premise of the device was that the Sun rises two seconds later each day for each kilometer traveled in a westerly direction, so the accurately measured change in time was an accurate way to calculate longitude. Harrison was easily able to convince Parliament that the reward was warranted.

Refer to this version of the passage to answer the questions that follow.

Paragraph

Navigational Devices

1   From the earliest of times, sailors have found ways to navigate their ships on the seas and oceans of the world. The earliest sailors navigated by simply following the coastline. Aside from being a rather slow method of navigating, this method was also rather dangerous and limited. It was dangerous in that waters close to the shoreline could be shallow enough to strand a ship or the waters could be full of rocky protrusions capable of sending ships to their graves. When seafarers began sailing out of sight of land more than 4,000 years ago, they used the stars to determine their direction. They calculated the distance traveled from their speed and sailing time, and they drew rough charts and maps to find their way and to exchange information about navigational routes with others. It had also been known as early as 300 B.C. that a sundial casts a longer shadow as it is moved farther north of the equator, and this information was used by sailors from that time to get an idea of how far north of the equator a ship was. All of these methods provided only very rudimentary means of navigating.

2   It was not until more than 3,000 years after sailors set out on the seas that the compass was developed. The premise of a compass is that the magnetized needle of a compass, when it is balanced on a central pivot or left to float on liquid, will always turn to point in the direction of magnetic north. Navigators on Chinese ships were the first ones who were known to use compasses to determine the direction their ships were heading, as early as 1100.

3   Numerous inventions were created to determine a ship's latitude. With the invention of the astrolabe in the fourteenth century, sailors were able to measure the Sun's height with better accuracy than with a sundial, and they were able to use the information provided by the astrolabe to determine how far north of the equator they were. An astrolabe was a metal circle with a sighting rule that rotated in the circle; the rule could be aligned with the Sun, and measurements on the ring indicated the Sun's height. Other devices followed that were better able to determine the Sun's height and thus provide an idea of the ship's latitude. The backstaff, invented in 1595, and the sextant, invented in 1757, were devices that each improved a navigator's ability to determine latitude. The backstaff was a device that required the navigator to face away from the Sun and make a calculation of the shadow in relation to the horizon. The sextant was a measuring device that required the navigator to look into an eyepiece and calculate the Sun's position relative to the horizon and then check printed tables to convert this information into latitude.

4   The missing piece in the navigational puzzle was the ability to calculate longitude, or how far east or west a ship had traveled. **10A** The need for a device to calculate longitude was so important to navigators that the English Parliament offered a reward of 20,000 pounds (an extraordinarily large sum at the time, perhaps $10 million in today's currency) to anyone who could invent a method for calculating longitude. **10B** In 1759, English clockmaker John Harrison built a chronometer that was accurate enough for navigation. **10C** The premise of the device was that the Sun rises two seconds later each day for each kilometer traveled in a westerly direction, so the accurately measured change in time was an accurate way to calculate longitude. **10D** Harrison was easily able to convince Parliament that the reward was warranted.

Questions

1. The expression to their graves in paragraph 1 could best be replaced by

   (A) to shipyards
   (B) to the seafloor
   (C) to be repaired
   (D) to their destination

2. According to the passage, sailors 4,000 years ago

   (A) were able to calculate their speed
   (B) were dependent on stars to tell time
   (C) never ventured away from the coastline
   (D) used the compass to navigate

3. The word rudimentary in paragraph 1 is closest in meaning to

   (A) reliable
   (B) direct
   (C) established
   (D) elementary

4. The word it in paragraph 2 refers to

   (A) premise
   (B) compass
   (C) needle
   (D) pivot

5. It is NOT stated in the passage that the astrolabe

   (A) was used to determine distance from the equator
   (B) was similar in shape to a sundial
   (C) had moving parts
   (D) was a circular-shaped device

6. The word rule as used in paragraph 3 is most likely

   (A) a regulation followed by sailors on a ship
   (B) a device used to make measurements
   (C) a law enacted by a government
   (D) a customary way of acting

7. The word convert in paragraph 3 is closest in meaning to

   (A) change
   (B) develop
   (C) twist
   (D) reassign

8. The author refers to The missing piece of the navigational puzzle in paragraph 4 in order to

   (A) show that navigation was considered an amusing game
   (B) highlight that the ability to determine longitude was the final problem to be solved
   (C) indicate that missing ships were difficult to find
   (D) determine that it was difficult to calculate latitude

9. A chronometer in paragraph 4 most likely measures

   (A) speed
   (B) distance
   (C) time
   (D) height

10. Look at the four squares [■] that indicate where the following sentence can be added to paragraph 4.

    Though many tried, it took a number of years after the offer was made for someone to succeed.

    Click on a square [■] to add the sentence to the passage.

11. Which of the sentences below expresses the essential information in the highlighted sentence in paragraph 4? *Incorrect* choices change the meaning in important ways or leave out essential information.

    (A) A chronometer could be used to measure longitude by combining knowledge about the rising Sun and accurate measurement of time.
    (B) A chronometer could be used to determine when the Sun was going to rise.
    (C) A chronometer could be used only to calculate longitude if one was traveling in a westerly direction.
    (D) A chronometer was an inaccurate measure of time because of the movement of the ship.

12. It is implied in the passage that

Ⓐ Harrison's device was not very accurate

Ⓑ Harrison spent considerable time traveling

Ⓒ Harrison received 20,000 pounds from Parliament

Ⓓ Harrison's device was better than any other device in determining latitude

13.

Directions: Various navigational devices were used to resolve different navigational issues. Complete the table by matching appropriate navigational devices to the navigational problems they were used to resolve. ***This question is worth 3 points.***	
direction	• • •
latitude	• • • •
longitude	•

Answer Choices (choose 8 to complete the chart):

(1) Astrolabe

(2) Stars

(3) Sextant

(4) Navigational puzzle

(5) Chronometer

(6) Sundial

(7) Coastline

(8) Reward

(9) Backstaff

(10) Compass

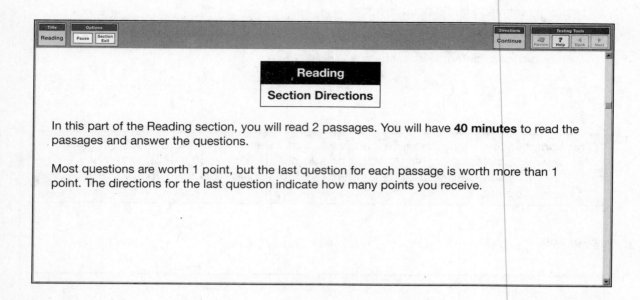

Title
Reading

Options
Pause | Section Exit

Directions
Continue

Testing Tools
Review | ? Help | ◄ Back | ► Next

Reading
Section Directions

In this part of the Reading section, you will read 2 passages. You will have **40 minutes** to read the passages and answer the questions.

Most questions are worth 1 point, but the last question for each passage is worth more than 1 point. The directions for the last question indicate how many points you receive.

READING 2

Read the passage.

40 minutes

The Neanderthals

Paragraph

1   Relatively recent archaeological finds have brought about a considerable change in perception about the Neanderthals. Neanderthals had previously been characterized more as primitive grunting beasts than as intelligent and compassionate human ancestors. However, evidence suggests that they may have exhibited more learned skills and social compassion than had previously been thought.

2   The Neanderthals lived during a period that extended from at least 40,000 to 100,000 years ago in a variety of environments ranging from relatively warm and dry to extremely cold areas. The Neanderthals differed from modern man in that they had a stronger and heavier skeleton and facial structure with a more projecting brow, a broader nose, and larger teeth. Casts made of Neanderthal brains by archeologists show little difference in size from those of modern man.

3   It has been known for some time that Neanderthals were rather skilled stone artisans. They are best known for their production of stone tools, which included a large number of scrapers and pointed implements. The techniques that the Neanderthals used to prepare these tools demonstrated a clear and important technological advance over their predecessors. Edges of their stone tools have been studied under microscopes for evidence of how the tools may have been used. Many of the tools seem to have been used for working with wood, both for hacking at large branches and for doing more detailed work on smaller pieces; other tools were clearly used to prepare food, both meat and vegetables; still others, which resemble many of today's suede and leather tools, were used to work with animal skins.

4   A clearer picture of Neanderthals has come about recently as archeologists have determined that, in addition to the known ability to develop and employ tools in a rather skilled way, Neanderthals also exhibited evidence of beliefs and social rituals, aspects of life that were newly introduced by Neanderthals and that provide evidence of humanlike thoughts and feelings. Neanderthal cemeteries have been discovered in places like La Ferrassie in France and Shanidar in Iraq; Neanderthal remains in these cemeteries have provided proof of social organization and ritual in the Neanderthals. One skeleton of a Neanderthal was found with a crushed skull; the blow on the top of the head, perhaps from a falling boulder, had quite obviously been the cause of death. What was interesting was that study of the skeleton showed that while he had been alive this man had been seriously handicapped with a defect that had limited use of the upper right side of his body, that he suffered from arthritis, and that he was blind in one eye. The fact that he had survived well into old age was a strong indication that others had been helping to care for him and to provide him with food rather than allowing him to die because he was no longer fit. Other skeletal remains of Neanderthals show clear examples of burial rituals. Another skeleton of a grown male was found surrounded by pollen from eight different flowers, including ancestors of today's hyacinth, bachelor's button, and hollyhock; experts are convinced that the flowers could not have been growing in the cave where they were found and that they had been arranged around the body in a burial ritual. In a different Neanderthal cemetery, a young child was found buried with a deposit of ibex horns laid out with the body. These discoveries about Neanderthals help to create a picture of Neanderthals as beings with the feelings and emotions that go along with developed social customs and rituals.

Refer to this passage to answer the questions that follow.

Paragraph

The Neanderthals

1   Relatively recent archaeological finds have brought about a considerable change in perception about the Neanderthals. Neanderthals had previously been characterized more as primitive grunting beasts than as intelligent and compassionate human ancestors. However, evidence suggests that they may have exhibited more learned skills and social compassion than had previously been thought.

2   **16A** The Neanderthals lived during a period that extended from at least 40,000 to 100,000 years ago in a variety of environments ranging from relatively warm and dry to extremely cold areas. **16B** The Neanderthals differed from modern man in that they had a stronger and heavier skeleton and facial structure with a more projecting brow, a broader nose, and larger teeth. **16C** Casts made of Neanderthal brains by archeologists show little difference in size from those of modern man. **16D**

3   It has been known for some time that Neanderthals were rather skilled stone artisans. They are best known for their production of stone tools, which included a large number of scrapers and pointed implements. The techniques that the Neanderthals used to prepare these tools demonstrated a clear and important technological advance over their predecessors. Edges of their stone tools have been studied under microscopes for evidence of how the tools may have been used. Many of the tools seem to have been used for working with wood, both for hacking at large branches and for doing more detailed work on smaller pieces; other tools were clearly used to prepare food, both meat and vegetables; still others, which resemble many of today's suede and leather tools, were used to work with animal skins.

4   A clearer picture of Neanderthals has come about recently as archeologists have determined that, in addition to the known ability to develop and employ tools in a rather skilled way, Neanderthals also exhibited evidence of beliefs and social rituals, aspects of life that were newly introduced by Neanderthals and that provide evidence of humanlike thoughts and feelings. Neanderthal cemeteries have been discovered in places like La Ferrassie in France and Shanidar in Iraq; Neanderthal remains in these cemeteries have provided proof of social organization and ritual in the Neanderthals. One skeleton of a Neanderthal was found with a crushed skull; the blow on the top of the head, perhaps from a falling boulder, had quite obviously been the cause of death. What was interesting was that study of the skeleton showed that while he had been alive this man had been seriously handicapped with a defect that had limited use of the upper right side of his body, that he suffered from arthritis, and that he was blind in one eye. The fact that he had survived well into old age was a strong indication that others had been helping to care for him and to provide him with food rather than allowing him to die because he was no longer fit. Other skeletal remains of Neanderthals show clear examples of burial rituals. Another skeleton of a grown male was found surrounded by pollen from eight different flowers, including ancestors of today's hyacinth, bachelor's button, and hollyhock; experts are convinced that the flowers could not have been growing in the cave where they were found and that they had been arranged around the body in a burial ritual. In a different Neanderthal cemetery, a young child was found buried with a deposit of ibex horns laid out with the body. These discoveries about Neanderthals help to create a picture of Neanderthals as beings with the feelings and emotions that go along with developed social customs and rituals.

Questions

14. The phrase brought about in paragraph 1 is closest in meaning to
    - Ⓐ carried
    - Ⓑ raised
    - Ⓒ led
    - Ⓓ caused

15. The word those in paragraph 2 refers to
    - Ⓐ teeth
    - Ⓑ casts
    - Ⓒ brains
    - Ⓓ archeologists

16. Look at the four squares [■] that indicate where the following sentence can be added to paragraph 2.

    Neanderthals have been found in areas as diverse as desertlike regions of the Middle East and glacial areas of northern Europe.

    Click on a square [■] to add the sentence to the passage.

17. The word predecessors in paragraph 3 is closest in meaning to
    - Ⓐ ancestors
    - Ⓑ precedents
    - Ⓒ survivors
    - Ⓓ successors

18. It is NOT stated in the passage that Neanderthal tools were used to
    - Ⓐ chop wood
    - Ⓑ make woven clothing
    - Ⓒ prepare things to eat
    - Ⓓ prepare animal skins for use

19. The word picture in paragraph 4 could best be replaced by
    - Ⓐ fantasy
    - Ⓑ photograph
    - Ⓒ conception
    - Ⓓ sight

20. The author refers to cemeteries in paragraph 4 in order to
    - Ⓐ indicate that Neanderthals buried their dead as their predecessors had
    - Ⓑ make a point about the use of Neanderthal tools in the construction of cemeteries
    - Ⓒ demonstrate that Neanderthals were unsuccessful in their attempt to initiate social rituals
    - Ⓓ provide an example of a Neanderthal social ritual

21. The word proof in paragraph 4 is closest in meaning to
    - Ⓐ evidence
    - Ⓑ motivation
    - Ⓒ details
    - Ⓓ logic

22. Which of the following is stated in the passage about Neanderthal burial sites?
    - Ⓐ They have all been found in only one place.
    - Ⓑ They all seem to demonstrate the existence of Neanderthal social structure.
    - Ⓒ They have all held the remains of old people.
    - Ⓓ They have all been surrounded by flowers.

23. The word fit in paragraph 4 could best be replaced by
    - Ⓐ healthy
    - Ⓑ appropriate
    - Ⓒ necessary
    - Ⓓ old

24. Which of the sentences below expresses the essential information in the highlighted sentence in paragraph 4? *Incorrect* choices change the meaning in important ways or leave out essential information.

Ⓐ The large number of flowers found in a particular cave proves that the skeleton was a Neanderthal.

Ⓑ The fact that the flowers could not have grown there indicates that the burial site must have been moved.

Ⓒ Because only pollen and not actual flowers was found, experts believe that there had originally been more than eight types of flowers.

Ⓓ Because of the pollen around one grave, experts believe that the body was buried during a ceremony.

25. An ibex in paragraph 4 is most likely a type of

Ⓐ clothing

Ⓑ weapon

Ⓒ animal

Ⓓ gemstone

26.

Directions: An introductory sentence or a brief summary of the passage is provided below. Complete the summary by selecting the THREE answer choices that express the most important ideas in the passage. Some sentences do not belong in the summary because they express ideas that are not presented in the passage or are minor ideas in the passage. *This question is worth 2 points.*

The passage discusses our understanding of the Neanderthals.

-
-
-

Answer Choices (choose 3 to complete the chart):

(1) The discovery of what are apparently Neanderthal rituals shows that they possessed a degree of social structure.

(2) The language skills of the Neanderthals are not known.

(3) It has been discovered that the brains of Neanderthals were much smaller than those of humans.

(4) It was previously believed that Neanderthals were lacking in intelligence and social structure.

(5) Remnants of Neanderthal cultures have been found in what is today Iraq.

(6) The use of stone tools by the Neanderthals is an indication of the skills that they possessed.

READING 3

Read the passage.

Paragraph

The Silent Era

1   The first 35 years of motion picture history are called the silent era, even though films were accompanied by the music of pianists or organists or small orchestras of house musicians, because there was no practical means for recording and playing back recorded dialogue or music in synchronization with the reel of film. Films of this era progressed from very rudimentary to much more elaborate in the years 1894 to 1928 that bookend the era of silent films. The films of this era can quite logically be divided into three phases: the primitive era (1894–1907), the transitional era (1908–1917), and the mature era (1918–1928).

2   The primitive era began when the Kinetograph and the Kinetoscope, inventions created in Thomas Edison's New Jersey laboratory in 1892 to film and to view short sequences resepctively, were used to create and present 30-second vignettes of novelty acts in U.S. and European cities in 1894. An alternative to Edison's equipment, the Cinématographe, was developed by Auguste and Louis Lumière; the Cinématographe was a camera that was lighter than Edison's and could be easily converted into a projector, and it was this machine that turned the motion picture into a worldwide phenomenon. The Lumières held the first public screening of their motion pictures in Paris in 1895. For the next few years, the films created were rather short and primitive: each film consisted of a single shot from a lone stationary viewpoint.

3   The period from 1908 to 1917 was known as the transitional era. In this era, motion pictures changed from a primitive form of recreation to a well-respected part of popular culture. Actors developed in their ability to convey ideas without words, and creative intertitles provided commentary and narrative between sections of frames. Filming techniques were developed, with the introduction of such stylistic devices as alternating close-ups and long shots. Films became much longer, and the repertoire of film topics expanded considerably from the earlier scenes of real life to include film adaptations of popular and classic literature and plays. During this period, newspapers also began carrying reviews of films so that audiences would know which films were worth seeing. By 1917, a major shift in the film industry had occurred. France had been the world's leading exporter of films prior to World War I, but the war had decimated the film industry in France. By 1917, the United States had assumed leadership in the motion-picture industry, and the sleepy town of Hollywood, California, which had been used as a winter shooting site for filmmakers from the East Coast as early as 1907, had become the seat of the filmmaking industry. By 1920, Hollywood boasted a clique of movie stars with worldwide fame, and, as the decade progressed, fan magazines and gossip columns devoted to publicizing both the public and private lives of the stars flourished. The 1920s were also a time of great expansion of the Hollywood studios, as Metro-Goldwyn-Mayer (MGM) was created from a merger to form the largest studio in Hollywood, as Universal, Paramount, and Fox became firmly established as studios, and as the small company Warner Brothers, which was to grow immensely in later decades, introduced a series of films featuring the canine star Rin Tin Tin.

4   However, by the end of the 1920s, the era of silent films ended rather abruptly. Edison and other inventors had introduced technology for creating motion pictures with sound at various times throughout the early decades of the twentieth century, but those early devices could not ensure good enough sound quality and amplification to induce studios to try any of them out. Finally, Warner Brothers took a chance with the 1927 film, *The Jazz Singer,* which starred popular recording artist Al Jolson and featured both singing and talking. When *The Jazz Singer* became a tremendous hit, Warner Brothers and Fox immediately converted to producing motion pictures with sound; the other large studios, believing that talking pictures might be only a passing fad, continued making silent pictures for one more year. When it became clear that talking pictures were the future of film rather than a passing fad, the remaining studios converted to the exclusive production of talking films a year later; by 1929, all of the films produced in Hollywood studios were talking pictures, and the era of silent films was over.

Refer to this version of the passage to answer the questions that follow.

Paragraph

The Silent Era

1   The first 35 years of motion picture history are called the silent era, even though films were accompanied by the music of pianists or organists or small orchestras of house musicians, because there was no practical means for recording and playing back recorded dialogue or music in synchronization with the reel of film. Films of this era progressed from very rudimentary to much more elaborate in the years 1894 to 1928 that bookend the era of silent films. The films of this era can quite logically be divided into three phases: the primitive era (1894–1907), the transitional era (1908–1917), and the mature era (1918–1928).

2   The primitive era began when the Kinetograph and the Kinetoscope, inventions created in Thomas Edison's New Jersey laboratory in 1892 to film and to view short sequences resepctively, were used to create and present 30-second vignettes of novelty acts in U.S. and European cities in 1894. **31A** An alternative to Edison's equipment, the Cinématographe, was developed by Auguste and Louis Lumière; the Cinématographe was a camera that was lighter than Edison's and could be easily converted into a projector, and it was this machine that turned the motion picture into a worldwide phenomenon. **31B** The Lumières held the first public screening of their motion pictures in Paris in 1895. **31C** For the next few years, the films created were rather short and primitive: each film consisted of a single shot from a lone stationary viewpoint. **31D**

3   The period from 1908 to 1917 was known as the transitional era. In this era, motion pictures changed from a primitive form of recreation to a well-respected part of popular culture. Actors developed in their ability to convey ideas without words, and creative intertitles provided commentary and narrative between sections of frames. Filming techniques were developed, with the introduction of such stylistic devices as alternating close-ups and long shots. Films became much longer, and the repertoire of film topics expanded considerably from the earlier scenes of real life to include film adaptations of popular and classic literature and plays. During this period, newspapers also began carrying reviews of films so that audiences would know which films were worth seeing. By 1917, a major shift in the film industry had occurred. France had been the world's leading exporter of films prior to World War I, but the war had decimated the film industry in France. By 1917, the United States had assumed leadership in the motion-picture industry, and the sleepy town of Hollywood, California, which had been used as a winter shooting site for filmmakers from the East Coast as early as 1907, had become the seat of the filmmaking industry. By 1920, Hollywood boasted a clique of movie stars with worldwide fame, and, as the decade progressed, fan magazines and gossip columns devoted to publicizing both the public and private lives of the stars flourished. The 1920s were also a time of great expansion of the Hollywood studios, as Metro-Goldwyn-Mayer (MGM) was created from a merger to form the largest studio in Hollywood, as Universal, Paramount, and Fox became firmly established as studios, and as the small company Warner Brothers, which was to grow immensely in later decades, introduced a series of films featuring the canine star Rin Tin Tin.

4   However, by the end of the 1920s, the era of silent films ended rather abruptly. Edison and other inventors had introduced technology for creating motion pictures with sound at various times throughout the early decades of the twentieth century, but those early devices could not ensure good enough sound quality and amplification to induce studios to try any of them out. Finally, Warner Brothers took a chance with the 1927 film, *The Jazz Singer,* which starred popular recording artist Al Jolson and featured both singing and talking. When *The Jazz Singer* became a tremendous hit, Warner Brothers and Fox immediately converted to producing motion pictures with sound; the other large studios, believing that talking pictures might be only a passing fad, continued making silent pictures for one more year. When it became clear that talking pictures were the future of film rather than a passing fad, the remaining studios converted to the exclusive production of talking films a year later; by 1929, all of the films produced in Hollywood studios were talking pictures, and the era of silent films was over.

Questions

27. The phrase in synchronization with in paragraph 1 is closest in meaning to
    Ⓐ in time with
    Ⓑ in agreement with
    Ⓒ as many times as
    Ⓓ on top of

28. The author includes the last sentence in paragraph 1 in order to
    Ⓐ describe events leading up to the events in the following paragraphs
    Ⓑ provide examples showing that there were many different types of silent films
    Ⓒ announce the organization of the passage
    Ⓓ present a concluding idea to summarize paragraph 1

29. It is implied in paragraph 2 that
    Ⓐ the Kinetoscope was invented some time before the Kinetograph
    Ⓑ the Kinetoscope was used to view films created with the Kinetograph
    Ⓒ the Cinématographe could create films but could not be used to view them
    Ⓓ the Cinématographe was used to view films created with the Kinetograph

30. The word turned in paragraph 2 could best be replaced by
    Ⓐ rotated
    Ⓑ accepted
    Ⓒ changed
    Ⓓ alternated

31. Look at the four squares [■] that indicate where the following sentence can be added to paragraph 2.

    They depicted short everyday scenes of people taking part in outdoor activities, laborers working at a construction site, and travellers scurrying through a train station.

    Click on a square [■] to add the sentence to the passage.

32. The word convey in paragraph 3 is closest in meaning to
    Ⓐ communicate
    Ⓑ understand
    Ⓒ transport
    Ⓓ contradict

33. It is NOT true according to paragraph 3 that Hollywood
    Ⓐ was the leading producer of films before World War I
    Ⓑ was used as a winter site for films early in the twentieth century
    Ⓒ was a small town prior to the success of the film industry
    Ⓓ took over the role of leader in the film industry from France

34. The word seat in paragraph 3 could best be replaced by
    Ⓐ chair
    Ⓑ basis
    Ⓒ center
    Ⓓ success

35. The word them in paragraph 4 refers to
    Ⓐ early decades
    Ⓑ early devices
    Ⓒ sound quality and amplification
    Ⓓ studios

36. The phrase took a chance in paragraph 4 is closest in meaning to
    Ⓐ behaved randomly
    Ⓑ lost an opportunity
    Ⓒ took a risk
    Ⓓ had good fortune

37. According to paragraph 4, *The Jazz Singer*
    Ⓐ was produced by Fox Studios
    Ⓑ was the last great silent film
    Ⓒ featured a famous Hollywood movie star
    Ⓓ was extremely successful

38. Which of the sentences below expresses the essential information in the highlighted sentence in paragraph 4? *Incorrect* choices change the meaning in important ways or leave out essential information.

Ⓐ After studios were sure that pictures with sound were going to be successful, they converted to talking pictures relatively quickly.

Ⓑ The future of film was presented in a series of talking films that were produced in Hollywood for release in 1929.

Ⓒ The era of silent films ended when the exclusive production for making talking pictures was granted to Hollywood studios.

Ⓓ It was clear to studios that talking pictures were only a fad, so they decided not to produce them until sometime in the future.

39.

Directions: Three of the answer choices below are used to describe each of the eras in the history of silent films. Complete the table by matching appropriate answer choices to the eras they are used to describe. ***This question is worth 4 points.***	
primitive era	• • •
transitional era	• • •
mature era	• • •

Answer Choices (choose 9 to complete the chart):

(1) The era of the introduction of adaptations of novels and plays

(2) The era of Hollywood stars

(3) The era of *The Jazz Singer*

(4) The era of single-shot films

(5) The era of the introduction of close-ups and long shots

(6) The era of films showing unusual acts

(7) The era of fan magazines

(8) The era of the introduction of film review

(9) The era of short films

(10) The era of Hollywood studios

Turn to the chart on page 544, and circle the numbers of the questions that you missed.

LISTENING

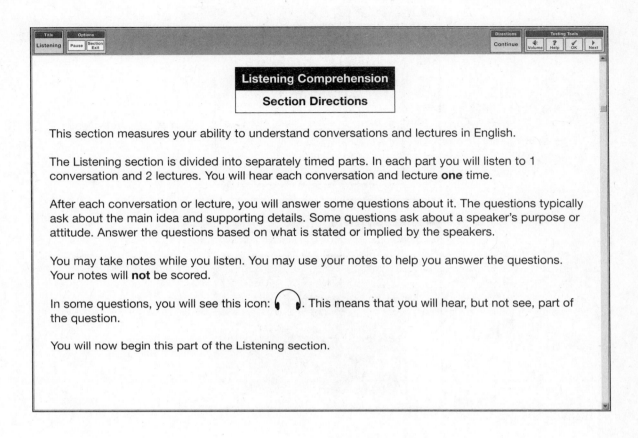

Questions 1–5

Listen to a conversation between a student and a university office worker.

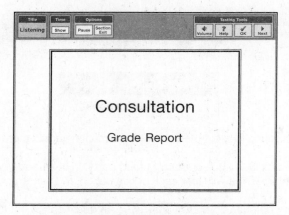

1. Why does the student go to see the office worker?
   - (A) To determine why his grades were so low
   - (B) To find out why he did not receive a grade report
   - (C) To ask where he could find the student with the same name
   - (D) To replace an incorrect document with a correct one

2. What incorrect assumption did the clerk make?
   - (A) That the student had already talked with the professor
   - (B) That grades had not yet been sent out
   - (C) That the student's problem should be dealt with by the professors
   - (D) That the student knew the other person with the same name

3. What is stated about the grade report the student received?

   Click on 2 answers.

   - (A) It had the correct name.
   - (B) It had an incorrect name.
   - (C) It listed the correct classes.
   - (D) It listed incorrect classes.

4. What did the confusion turn out to be?
   - (A) Two students had similar names.
   - (B) Two students lived at the same address.
   - (C) Two students took the same classes.
   - (D) Two students took courses from the same professors.

5. What did the office worker promise to do?

   Click on 2 answers.

   - (A) Verify information with the student's professors
   - (B) Contact the student with the same name
   - (C) Prepare another grade report for him to pick up
   - (D) Send out a new grade report

Questions 6–11

Listen to a lecture in a government class.

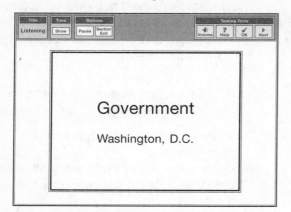

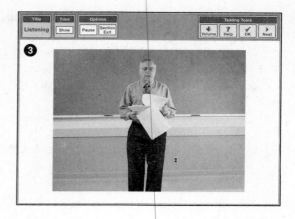

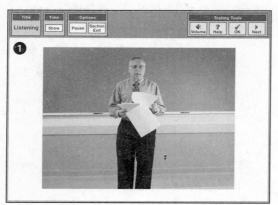

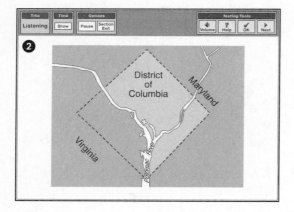

6. What does the professor mainly discuss in the lecture?
   - Ⓐ How Washington, D.C. got its name
   - Ⓑ Where Washington, D.C. is located
   - Ⓒ How Washington, D.C. is governed
   - Ⓓ How Washington, D.C. differs from other U.S. cities

7. Which name has NOT been used for the city discussed in the lecture?
   - Ⓐ Columbia
   - Ⓑ Washington City
   - Ⓒ District of Columbia
   - Ⓓ Washington, D.C.

8. Listen again to part of the lecture. Then answer the question.

   Why does the professor say this:

   - Ⓐ Because he thinks the students are not familiar with the topic of the lecture
   - Ⓑ Because he expects that everyone has been to Washington, D.C.
   - Ⓒ Because he wants to introduce the topic of the lecture to the students
   - Ⓓ Because he is trying to slow down the pace of the lecture

9. What two points make Washington, D.C. different from other U.S. cities?
   ### Click on 2 answers.
   - Ⓐ It was named, in part, after Columbus.
   - Ⓑ It is not part of any state.
   - Ⓒ It is on the Potomac River.
   - Ⓓ It became self-governing only recently.

10. Are these statements true about Washington, D.C. and the state of Virginia?

	YES	NO
For each statement, click once in the YES or NO column.		
Part of the original state of Virginia was used to create Washington, D.C.		
Washington, D.C. used to be part of the state of Virginia.		
Part of Washington, D.C. was returned to the state of Virginia.		
Today, Washington D.C. is part of the state of Virginia.		

11. What is stated in the lecture about the government of Washington, D.C.?
    ### Click on 2 answers.
    - Ⓐ In the beginning, it did not elect its own government.
    - Ⓑ In the beginning, it did elect its own government.
    - Ⓒ Today, it does not elect its own government.
    - Ⓓ Today, it does elect its own government.

Questions 12–17

Listen to a lecture in a linguistics class.

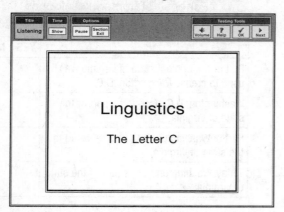

Linguistics

The Letter C

①

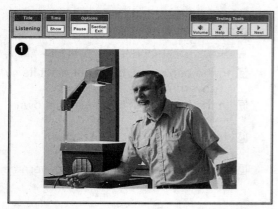

②

Early
Semitic   Phoenician   Early
Greek

③

Early
Latin
Letter   Classical
Latin C   Classical
Latin G

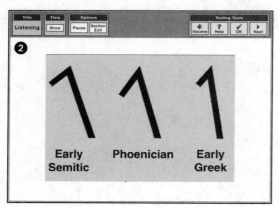

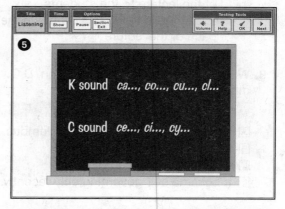

④

⑤

K sound   ca..., co..., cu..., cl...

C sound   ce..., ci..., cy...

⑥

12. What is the main idea of the lecture?

   Ⓐ That the letter *c* has always had the same pronunciation

   Ⓑ That the shape of the letter *c* has changed over time

   Ⓒ That precursors of the letter *c* existed in early cultures

   Ⓓ That various historical influences caused the letter *c* to have two different pronunciations

13. What is true about the shape of the third letter of the alphabet?

   Ⓐ It has always been rounded.

   Ⓑ Initially it was angular, but later it became rounded.

   Ⓒ It has always been angular.

   Ⓓ Initially it was rounded, but later it became angular.

14. Is each of these true about sounds in early languages?

For each statement, click in the YES or NO column.	YES	NO
In early Greek, the third letter of the alphabet was pronounced like a *g*.		
The *c* in early Latin was pronounced only with a *k* sound.		
In classical Latin, the letter *c* had a *k* sound.		
In classical Latin, a *c* with a line through it had a hard *g* sound.		

15. Which of the following are true, according to the lecture?

   Click on 2 answers.

   Ⓐ In 1066, the Normans defeated the Saxons.

   Ⓑ In 1066, the Saxons defeated the Normans.

   Ⓒ Because of the French influence, the letter *c* took on an *s* sound.

   Ⓓ Because of the French influence, the letter *c* took on a *g* sound.

16. Which of the following English words most likely begin with an *s* sound?

   Click on 2 answers.

   Ⓐ Coxswain

   Ⓑ Cytoplasm

   Ⓒ Curmudgeon

   Ⓓ Cephalization

17. Listen again to part of the passage. Then answer the question. 🎧

   What does the professor mean?

   Ⓐ "It's important to have a good time."

   Ⓑ "It's important to break things down into parts."

   Ⓒ "It's important to put everything away."

   Ⓓ "It's important to understand how the details fit together."

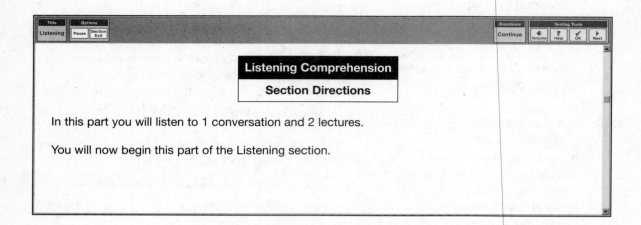

Listening Comprehension

Section Directions

In this part you will listen to 1 conversation and 2 lectures.

You will now begin this part of the Listening section.

Questions 18–22

Listen to a conversation between a student and a professor.

Consultation

The Space Shuttle

18. Why does the student want to talk to the professor?

   Ⓐ To discuss something he read

   Ⓑ To clear up some confusion from a previous lecture

   Ⓒ To get some help with a homework assignment

   Ⓓ To have a conversation about an interesting topic

19. Listen again to part of the passage. Then answer the question.

What does the professor mean when she says this:

   Ⓐ "I'll create a quiz."

   Ⓑ "I'll try to figure out what you mean."

   Ⓒ "You'll answer some questions."

   Ⓓ "I'll add the parts you don't know."

20. Which sources of power did the student have in his notes?

   Click on 2 answers.

   Ⓐ The main engine

   Ⓑ The smaller engines

   Ⓒ The boosters

   Ⓓ The batteries

21. What is the role of each of these sources of power?

For each answer, click in the correct column.			
	The main engine	**The boosters**	**The smaller engines**
To lift the shuttle off of the ground and then return to Earth			
To lift the shuttle off of the ground and then help it get close to orbital velocity			
To push the shuttle into orbit			

22. What is the purpose of the parachute?

   Ⓐ To break the fall of the boosters

   Ⓑ To help the shuttle return to Earth

   Ⓒ To slow down the main engine

   Ⓓ To steady the smaller engines

Questions 23–28

Listen to a lecture in a geology class.

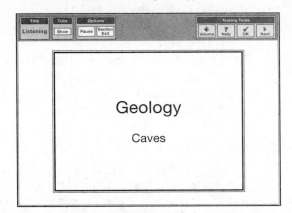

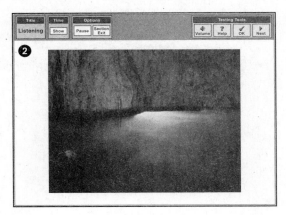

23. What main point does the professor make about various types of caves?

Ⓐ They are named after the area in which they are found.

Ⓑ They are named after the process by which they were formed.

Ⓒ They are named after the people who discovered them.

Ⓓ They are named after the features in their interiors.

24. Listen again to part of the passage. Then answer the question. 🎧

How does the professor seem to feel about answering the student's question?

Ⓐ It is impossible to answer the question.

Ⓑ Answering the question is not necessary.

Ⓒ It is quite all right to answer the question.

Ⓓ Answering the question can be postponed.

25. What type of cave is each of these?

For each cave, click in the correct column.			
	Sea cave	**Lava cave**	**Solution cave**
Blue Grotto			
Carlsbad Caverns			
Lava Beds National Monument			

26. What is stated in the lecture about where the caves are found?

Click on 2 answers.

Ⓐ Lava Beds National Monument is found in Hawaii.

Ⓑ Carlsbad Caverns is found in California.

Ⓒ The Blue Grotto is found in Capri.

Ⓓ Lava Beds National Monument is found in California.

27. How is each type of cave formed?

For each type of cave, click in the correct column.			
	Created by erosion	**Created during volcanic eruptions**	**Created by weak acids dissolving rock**
Lava caves			
Solution caves			
Sea caves			

28. What is NOT a usual way for a solution cave to develop an entrance?

Ⓐ An earthquake lifts the cave opening to surface levels.

Ⓑ Erosion exposes a cave opening.

Ⓒ An area collapses, exposing an entrance to the cave.

Ⓓ Pounding surf wears away an entrance to the cave.

Questions 29–34

Listen to a discussion in a biology class.

Biology

The Compound Eye

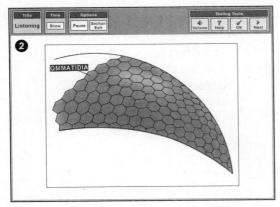

29. How is the information in the passage organized?

Ⓐ The causes of a certain phenomenon are explained.

Ⓑ Various types of compound eyes are contrasted.

Ⓒ A topic is explained through an extended example.

Ⓓ The steps of a process are outlined.

30. What is stated in the lecture about ommatidia?

Click on 2 answers.

Ⓐ There are thousands of ommatidia on a compound eye.

Ⓑ The ommatidia each have thousands of sides.

Ⓒ The ommatidia cover the surface of a compound eye.

Ⓓ The ommatidia all point in the same direction.

31. What is NOT stated in the lecture about the butterfly?

Ⓐ It has a compound eye.

Ⓑ It is nearsighted.

Ⓒ It can discern movement well.

Ⓓ It has a six-sided eye.

32. Are these statements true about the compound eye?

For each statement, click in the YES or NO column.

	YES	NO
A compound eye can easily detect tiny movements.		
A compound eye can focus extremely well.		
A compound eye can see compound pictures.		
A compound eye can see a single detailed image.		

33. Listen again to part of the passage. Then answer the question.

Why does the professor say this:

Ⓐ She is presenting a concrete example of a difficult idea.

Ⓑ She is contrasting the actions of two insects.

Ⓒ She is injecting a bit of humor into the lecture.

Ⓓ She is suggesting something for the students to try.

34. What is the most likely title for Chapter 3 of the text for this class?

Ⓐ The Brain and Light

Ⓑ Eye Structures

Ⓒ Detection of Light and Motion

Ⓓ Butterflies

Turn to the chart on page 545, and circle the numbers of the questions that you missed.

SPEAKING

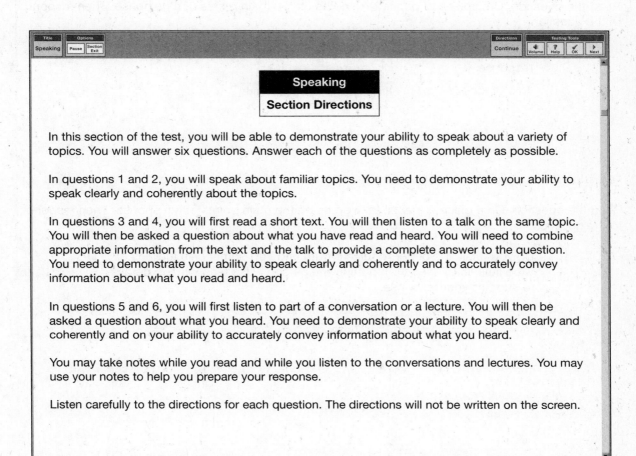

Question 1

Read the question. On a piece of paper, take notes on the main points of a response. Then respond to the question.

What is your favorite movie? Use reasons and details to support your response.

| Preparation Time: 15 seconds |
| Response Time: 45 seconds |

Question 2

Read the question. On a piece of paper, take notes on the main points of a response. Then respond to the question.

Do you think it is better to tell the truth and hurt someone's feelings or tell a little lie to keep from hurting the person? Use reasons and details to support your response.

| Preparation Time: 15 seconds |
| Response Time: 45 seconds |

Question 3

Read the passage. On a piece of paper, take notes on the main points of the reading passage.

Reading Time: 45 seconds

A notice for students in the business department

A limited number of internships in local businesses are available for the coming semester. An internship is an unpaid position that requires 10 hours of work per week for 12 weeks. Students who are selected for the internship program must sign up for Business 500 and submit reports on their internship to the internship advisor; three graduate units will be awarded for successful completion of Business 500. To apply for an internship, pick up an application from the Business Department office, fill it out, and submit it along with references from three professors in the Business Department by May 1.

Listen to the passage. On a piece of paper, take notes on the main points of the listening passage.

Now answer the following question:

How do the students seem to feel about the internships offered by the Business Department?

Preparation Time: 30 seconds
Response Time: 60 seconds

Question 4

Read the passage. On a piece of paper, take notes on the main points of the reading passage.

Reading Time: 45 seconds

Supersonic Speed

The terms *subsonic* and *supersonic* are used to describe the speed of various aircraft in relation to the speed of sound. Subsonic aircraft fly at speeds that are slower than the speed of sound, and supersonic aircraft fly at speeds that are faster than the speed of sound. Austrian physicist Ernst Mach (1838–1916) was a pioneer in the study of objects moving faster than the speed of sound and the shock waves that they produce; as a result, the term *Mach* is used to describe the speed of supersonic aircraft. An aircraft flying at Mach 1 is flying at the speed of sound, and an aircraft flying at twice the speed of sound is flying at Mach 2.

Listen to the passage. On a piece of paper, take notes on the main points of the listening passage.

Now answer the following question:

How does the information in the listening passage add to what is explained in the reading passage?

Preparation Time: 30 seconds
Response Time: 60 seconds

Question 5

Listen to the passage. On a piece of paper, take notes on the main points of the listening passage.

Now answer the following question:

How are the students dealing with the project they are working on?

Preparation Time: 20 seconds
Response Time: 60 seconds

Question 6

Listen to the passage. On a piece of paper, take notes on the main points of the listening passage.

Now answer the following question:

How does the professor describe multiple personality disorder?

Preparation Time: 20 seconds
Response Time: 60 seconds

After you have completed this test, fill in the chart on pages 546–551.

WRITING

This section measures your ability to use writing to communicate in an academic environment. There will be two writing tasks.

For the first writing task, you will read a passage and listen to a lecture and then answer a question based on what you have read and heard. For the second task, you will answer a question based on your own knowledge and experience.

Integrated Writing Directions
For the first task, you will read a passage about an academic topic. You will have **3 minutes** to read the passage. You may take notes on the passage while you read. The passage will then be removed and you will listen to a lecture about the same topic. While you listen, you may also take notes.

Then you will write a response to a question that asks you about the relationship between the lecture you heard and the reading passage. Try to answer the question as completely as possible using information from the reading passage and the lecture. The question does **not** ask you to express your personal opinion. You will be able to see the reading passage again when it is time for you to write. You may use your notes to help you answer the question. You will have **20 minutes** to write your response.

Typically, an effective response will be 150 to 225 words. You need to demonstrate your ability to write well and to provide complete and accurate content.

Remember you can look at the passage again when you write your response. Immediately after the reading time ends, the lecture begins.

Independent Writing Directions
For the second task, you will write an essay in response to a question that asks you to state, explain, and support your opinion on an issue. You will have **30 minutes** to plan, write, and revise your response.

Typically, an effective essay will contain a minimum of 300 words. You need to demonstrate your ability to write well. This includes the development of your ideas, the organization of your essay, and the quality and accuracy of the language you use to express your ideas.

Question 1

Read the passage. On a piece of paper, take notes on the main points of the reading passage.

Reading Time: 3 minutes

The library at Alexandria was said to have been a marvel, the greatest collection of scholarship in the ancient world. It was founded by Ptolemy I, the general that Alexander the Great installed as ruler of the city named after himself. It was Ptolemy's son, Ptolemy II Philadelphus, who had the vision of expanding the library to make it the largest collection imaginable.

Under Ptolemy II and those who followed, the library was expanded tremendously. Ptolemy II's vision was to create a library with every Greek work ever written as well as with as many works from other parts of the Western world as could be gathered together. The number of *volumen,* or scrolls, in the library has been estimated at anywhere between 300,000 and 700,000.

A huge number of people were employed in preparing scrolls for the library, inasmuch as each scroll to enter the library had to be copied by hand. Manuscripts were bought or borrowed or taken from all over the Western world to be copied and placed in the library (although it was rather common to copy an original manuscript and then return the copy to the owner and keep the original for the library). Ptolemy II often asked for manuscripts from foreign powers in return for traded goods, and manuscripts were often demanded from citizens to pay debts to the government. In addition, any time that manuscripts were found on trading ships in the port at Alexandria, the manuscripts were taken and copied and added to the library. It was in these ways that so many manuscripts were collected in the library at Alexandria.

Listen to the passage. On a piece of paper, take notes on the main points of the listening passage.

Now answer the following question:

What further information does the listening passage provide to add to the information presented in the reading passage?

Preparation Time: 1 minute
Response Time: 20 minutes

Question 2

Read the question. On a piece of paper, take notes on the main points of a response. Then write your response.

What are the characteristics of a good leader? Give reasons and examples to support your response.

Response Time: 30 minutes

After you have completed this test, fill in the chart on pages 552–553.

APPENDIX A
COHESION _____

It is important when you are producing material on the *iBT* TOEFL test that you use a variety of methods of creating **cohesion**[1]. You should be sure that you know how to use repeated and rephrased key ideas, pronouns and determiners, and transition expressions to create cohesion.

Appendix A1: USE REPEATED AND REPHRASED KEY IDEAS

One way to make your written and spoken English more cohesive is to use repeated and rephrased key ideas. Look at the following example of repeated and rephrased key ideas used for cohesion.

Example

I think that the most important characteristic in a friend is honesty. If someone is a friend, then he or she must be *honest*. I can trust someone only if he or she is truthful. If a friend of mine does not tell me the *truth,* then he or she can no longer be considered a friend.

In this example, the key idea *honesty* is repeated as *honest* and rephrased as *truthful* and *truth* to make the passage cohesive.

The following chart outlines the key information that you should remember about using repeated key ideas to make your written and spoken English more cohesive.

USING REPEATED AND REPHRASED KEY IDEAS FOR COHESION

1. It is important to make your written and spoken English as cohesive as possible.
2. One way to make your written and spoken English more cohesive is to use repeated key ideas.
3. Another way to make your written and spoken English more cohesive is to use rephrased key ideas.
4. Repeated and rephrased key ideas are not the only way to make your written and spoken English cohesive. You should use a variety of ways to make your English cohesive.

---

[1] **Cohesion** is a characteristic of language in which ideas flow or attach together smoothly.

APPENDIX EXERCISE A1: Fill in the blank in each pair of sentences with one of the words from the box above the pair of sentences to make the sentences cohesive. You should use each answer one time only.

chance	competitor	energy	outcome	pleases	shocked	speaks

1. I am happy you have the opportunity to go there. It _____ me that you have been given such a _____.

2. She is quite a dynamic speaker. She always _____ with a great amount of _____.

3. The results of the competition were entirely unexpected. The _____ was _____ by the _____.

acts	brief	determined	positive	problems	remarks	resolved

4. The lawyer made a short statement. His _____ were quite _____.

5. The problems are not insurmountable. The _____ can be _____.

6. If you look at his actions in a negative way, you might say that he is stubborn. Conversely, if you look at the way he _____ in a _____ way, you might say that he is _____.

answers	complex	eventually	explanation	finish	indicated	succinct

7. She said that she would get it done sometime. She _____ that she would _____ it _____.

8. I do not want you to ramble on and on in your responses. Your _____ should be _____.

9. You have explained this in an overly simplistic way. You really need a more _____ _____.

animated	appreciates	concept	discussions	episode	involved	novel	reasons

10. Your idea is quite innovative. It is a _____ _____.

11. This professor seems to welcome lively debate. He _____ _____ _____.

12. Can you explain why you took part in this incident? Can you give me your _____ for being _____ in this _____?

Appendix A2: USE PRONOUNS AND DETERMINERS

Another way to make your written and spoken English more cohesive is to use **pronouns**[2] and **determiners**[3] to refer back to previous ideas. Some pronouns and determiners that can be used for cohesion are listed in the following table.

PRONOUNS					DETERMINERS	
SUBJECT	OBJECT	POSSESSIVE	REFLEXIVE	DEMONSTRATIVE	POSSESSIVE	DEMONSTRATIVE
I	me	mine	myself	this	my	this
you	you	yours	yourself	that	your	that
he	him	his	himself	these	his	these
she	her	hers	herself	those	her	those
it	it		itself		its	
we	us	ours	ourselves		our	
you	you	yours	yourselves		your	
they	them	theirs	themselves		their	

Look at the following example showing pronouns and determiners used for cohesion.

> **Example**
>
> A certain student worked very hard on a project. *He* did all of the work on *it* by *himself*, and *his* professor was very pleased with *this* work.

In this example, the pronoun *He* refers to the noun *student,* the pronoun *it* refers to the noun *project,* the pronoun *himself* refers to the noun *students,* the determiner *his* refers to the noun *student,* and the determiner *this* refers to the noun *work.* These pronouns and determiners help to make the passage cohesive.

The following chart outlines the key information that you should remember about using pronouns and determiners to make your written and spoken English more cohesive.

> **USING PRONOUNS AND DETERMINERS FOR COHESION**
>
> 1. It is important to make your written and spoken English as cohesive as possible.
> 2. One way to make your written and spoken English more cohesive is to use pronouns to refer back to previous ideas.
> 3. Another way to make your written and spoken English more cohesive is to use determiners to refer back to previous ideas.
> 4. Pronouns and determiners are not the only way to make your written and spoken English cohesive. You should use a variety of ways to make your English cohesive.

---

[2] **Pronouns** are words that take the place of nouns.
[3] **Determiners** are words that accompany nouns to identify the nouns.

APPENDIX EXERCISE A2: Fill in each blank in a passage with one of the pronouns or determiners from the box above the passage to make the passage cohesive. You should use each answer one time only.

her	herself	she	them	this	this

1. A researcher has been conducting a study on the causes of a certain disease. She has been conducting _____ study by _____. Up to now, _____ has determined several possible causes of the disease and has decided to focus on the most promising of _____. Though _____ research has not yet yielded a conclusive result, the researcher hopes _____ will happen soon.

it	mine	our	our	ourselves	ourselves	this	we	your

2. You and I have _____ work cut out for _____. You have to finish _____ part of the project, and I have to finish _____. Then when we have each finished _____ own parts of the project, _____ can get together to finish _____. We have to take it upon _____ to get _____ project done.

their	them	themselves	themselves	these	they	they

3. Some students have a huge assignment to complete by Friday. However, _____ students have procrastinated for quite some time, and now _____ are in a bit of a fix, so _____ only hope of finishing the assignment on time is for _____ to stay up all night for the next two nights to get it done. The students have gotten _____ into this situation, and now _____ will have to work very hard to get _____ out of it.

he	he	he	him	himself	his	his	it	this

4. A particular student is regretting that he signed up for a particular course. Unfortunately, _____ signed up for _____ course because _____ thought that _____ could be quite interesting. It did not take long for _____ to figure out that _____ reasoning had been rather faulty. He told _____ that _____ needed to be more careful in _____ decision-making in the future.

Appendix A3: USE TRANSITION EXPRESSIONS

A third way to make your written and spoken English more cohesive is to use transition expressions to show how ideas are related. Some transition expressions that can be used for cohesion are listed in the following table.

TRANSITION EXPRESSIONS			
EXPRESSION	MEANING	EXPRESSION	MEANING
therefore	result follows	*in addition*	more information follows
as a result	result follows	*moreover*	more information follows
thus	result follows	*furthermore*	more information follows
consequently	result follows		
		in contrast	opposite information follows
for example	example follows	*on the other hand*	opposite information follows
for instance	example follows	*nevertheless*	unexpected information follows
		nonetheless	unexpected information follows
in conclusion	conclusion follows	*however*	opposite or unexpected information follows
in summary	conclusion follows		
in fact	emphasis follows	*fortunately*	something lucky follows
indeed	emphasis follows	*surprisingly*	something unexpected follows
		interestingly	something unexpected follows

Look at the following example showing transition expressions used for cohesion.

Example

A group of students really wanted a certain program to be added to the university curriculum. The students presented their request to the university; *in addition,* they got hundreds of signatures on a petition. *Nonetheless,* their request was denied.

In this example, the transitions *in addition* and *Nonetheless* are used to make the passage cohesive.

The following chart outlines the key information that you should remember about using transition expressions to make your written and spoken English more cohesive.

USING TRANSITION EXPRESSIONS FOR COHESION

1. It is important to make your written and spoken English as cohesive as possible.
2. One way to make your written and spoken English more cohesive is to use transitions expressions to show how ideas are related.
3. Transition expressions are not the only way to make your written and spoken English cohesive. You should use a variety of ways to make your English cohesive.

APPENDIX EXERCISE A3: Fill in each blank with one of the transition expressions from the box above each passage to make the passage cohesive. You should use each answer one time only.

For instance	Fortunately	Furthermore	However	In fact

1. I certainly thought he would do a good job. _____, he failed miserably.

2. There are many ways to make a good impression on your boss. _____, one way is to come to work on time.

3. You should always show up for work on time. _____, you should never leave work early.

4. I can argue that you need to spend more time on this job. _____, you should spend several hours on it.

5. He tried recently to get that job. _____, that job is now his.

in contrast	in summary	moreover	nonetheless	therefore

6. Freshmen are taking the introductory course; juniors, _____, are taking the advanced course.

7. Freshmen have already studied biology; _____, they must still take the introductory biology course.

8. A certain course is required for freshmen; all freshmen, _____, must take the course.

9. Freshmen must take three lecture courses; _____, they must take one laboratory course.

10. Juniors must take three lecture courses and three laboratory courses; _____, they will be very busy.

as a result	for example	in conclusion	on the other hand	surprisingly

11. One student studied really hard for the exam; _____, she failed the exam.

12. A few students did quite well on the exam; the rest, _____, did quite poorly.

13. There were a few high grades on the exam. One student, _____, had 99% correct.

14. Some students did not prepare for the exam; _____, they did not do so well.

15. The students who studied hard did well on the exam, and those who did not study hard did poorly; _____, one can say that the exam grades depended on preparation.

| consequently | in addition | indeed | interestingly | nevertheless |

16. Tickets are required for the concert; _____, anyone who wants to go to the concert must purchase a ticket.

17. A sonata will be performed at the concert; _____, a concerto will be performed.

18. One students does not like classical music; _____, her friends have talked her into going.

19. There will be a guest performer at the concert; _____, the guest performer is someone quite famous.

20. The audience truly appreciated the performance; _____, the audience thought the performance was wonderful.

APPENDIX REVIEW EXERCISE (A1–A3): Put parentheses around the cohesive devices in the following passages. Label each as (A) a repeated or rephrased key idea, (B) a pronoun or determiner, and (C) a transition expression.

1. The young man gave an explanation for his unusual behavior. (It) was that (he) had been afraid. (His) (fear) had caused him to (act) this way.

2. The board has indicated that it is now in accord on the key point of the bill. However, agreement on this main point was not easy for the board to reach.

3. The professor discussed several important concepts in the lecture. The focus of her lecture was the development of these concepts.

4. One member of the group was opposed to the plan. He objected vociferously. Nonetheless, the plan was implemented immediately.

5. Assignments must be turned in on time. Absolutely no late assignments will be accepted. In fact, any assignment that is not submitted on time will receive a grade of zero.

6. An account of the incident appeared in the newspaper. Unfortunately, many of the details in this account were not accurate. The newspaper needs to print a retraction to correct these inaccuracies.

7. You must decide whether to write a thesis or to take a comprehensive exam, and you must make this decision yourself. Choosing between a thesis and a comprehensive exam is a major decision.

8. Even in the beginning, all the members of the group worked very hard on the project. Indeed, from the outset, a huge amount of effort was invested in the project. Not surprisingly, their effort was not wasted; they were rewarded with a high grade on the project.

9. The professor gave an assignment in class today. However, the students are confused about what the assignment actually is. The professor spoke for quite some time about the assignment, but he said a number of contradictory things. These contradictory things are what caused the students to be confused.

10. A number of major corporations are sending representatives to campus this week to interview students who are seeking jobs in these corporations. Any students wishing to have interviews should sign up in the campus placement office. The corporate representatives will be on campus for only a short time, and the number of interviews is limited. Thus, it is important to sign up for interviews immediately.

APPENDIX B
SENTENCE STRUCTURE_____

It is important when you are producing material on the *iBT* TOEFL test that you use a variety of correct sentence structures. You should be sure that you know how to use simple sentences, compound sentences, and complex sentences.

Appendix B1: USE CORRECT SIMPLE SENTENCES

A simple sentence is a sentence that has only one **clause**.[4] Two types of sentence structure errors are common in sentences with only one clause: (1) the clause can be missing a subject or a verb, and (2) the clause can be introduced by a subordinate adjective clause connector.

The first type of incorrect simple sentence is a sentence that is missing a subject or a verb. (Note that an asterisk is used to indicate that a sentence contains an error.)

Generally, is important to fill out the form completely.*
    VERB

The ideas for the construction of the project.*
    SUBJECT

The first sentence is incorrect because it has the verb *is* but is missing a subject. The second sentence is incorrect because it has a subject *ideas* but is missing a verb.

Another type of incorrect simple sentence is one that includes a subordinate adverb clause connector in front of the subject and the verb. The following chart lists common subordinate adverb clause connectors.

SUBORDINATE ADVERB CLAUSE CONNECTORS							
TIME		CAUSE	CONDITION	CONTRAST	MANNER	PLACE
after as as long as as soon as before by the time	once since until when whenever while	as because inasmuch as now that since	if in case provided providing unless whether	although even though though while whereas	as in that	where wherever

Look at the following examples of incomplete sentences.

Because the manager of the company instructed me to do it.*
        SUBJECT   VERB

Even though the contest was run in an unfair manner.*
        SUBJECT   VERB

The first sentence is incorrect because the subordinate adverb clause connector *Because* is in front of the subject *manager* and the verb *instructed*. The second sentence is incorrect because

---

[4] A **clause** is a group of words that has both a subject and a verb.

the subordinate adverb clause connector *Even though* is in front of the subject *contest* and the verb *was run*.

The following chart outlines the key information that you should remember about using correct simple sentences.

USING CORRECT SIMPLE SENTENCES
1. A simple sentence is a sentence with one clause.
2. A simple sentence must have both a subject and a verb.
3. A simple sentence may not be introduced by a subordinate adverb clause connector.

APPENDIX EXERCISE B1: Underline the subjects once and the verbs twice. Put parentheses around the subordinate clause connectors. Then indicate if the sentences are correct (C) or incorrect (I).

_____ 1. The obvious reasons for the selection of the candidate.

_____ 2. When everyone in the room decided to leave.

_____ 3. I found the ideas rather unsettling.

_____ 4. Often discusses the advantages of the situation.

_____ 5. A preference for movies with lots of action.

_____ 6. Fortunately, the piece of paper with the crucial information was found.

_____ 7. As soon as the article appears in the newspaper.

_____ 8. Definitely is not proper to make that suggestion.

_____ 9. His agreement with me about the important issues.

_____ 10. It happened that way.

_____ 11. As no one else in the world would have made the same decision.

_____ 12. Without any hesitation made a decision not to return.

_____ 13. An agreement as to the amount to be paid has been reached.

_____ 14. A poem written on a piece of faded parchment.

_____ 15. Now that you have told me about your childhood.

_____ 16. We forgot.

_____ 17. To take the medicine at the right time to be the most effective.

_____ 18. If you think about the problem just a little more.

_____ 19. Unfortunately, the manager already made the decision.

_____ 20. Even though you gave me a gift for my birthday.

Appendix B2: USE CORRECT COMPOUND SENTENCES

A compound sentence is a sentence that has more than one **main clause**.[5] The main clauses in a compound sentence can be connected correctly with a coordinate conjunction (*and, but, or, so, yet*) and a comma (,) or with a semi-colon (;). Look at the following examples.

> Jack studies hard. He gets high grades.
>
> Jack studies hard, so he gets high grades.
>
> Jack studies hard; he gets high grades.

In the first example, the two main clauses *Jack studies hard* and *He gets high grades* are not combined into a compound sentence. In the second example, the two main clauses are combined into a compound sentence with the coordinate conjunction so and a comma. In the third example, the same two main clauses are combined into a compound sentence with a semi-colon.

It is possible to use adverb transitions in compound sentences. (See Appendix A3 for a list of transition expressions.) It is important to note that adverb transitions are not conjunctions, so either a semi-colon or a coordinate conjunction with a comma is needed.

Look at the following examples of sentences with adverb transitions.

> Jack studies hard. As a result, he gets high grades.
>
> Jack studies hard, and, as a result, he gets high grades.
>
> Jack studies hard; as a result, he gets high grades.

In the first example, the two main clauses *Jack studies hard* and *he gets high grades* are not combined into a compound sentence even though the adverb transition *As a result* is used. In the second example, the two main clauses are combined into a compound sentence with the coordinate conjunction and and a comma; the adverb transition *as a result* is included after the coordinate conjunction. In the third example, the same two main clauses are combined into a compound sentence with a semi-colon, and the adverb transition is set off from the second main clause with a comma.

The following chart outlines the key information that you should remember about using correct compound sentences.

USING CORRECT COMPOUND SENTENCES

1. A compound sentence is a sentence with more than one main clause.
2. The main clauses in a compound sentence may be joined with either a semi-colon (;) or a coordinate conjunction (and, but, or, so, yet) and a comma (,).
3. An adverb transition can be used in a compound sentence, but either a semi-colon or a coordinate conjunction and a comma is still needed.

---

[5] **A main clause** is an independent clause that has both a subject and a verb and is not introduced by a subordinate clause connector.

APPENDIX EXERCISE B2: Underline the subjects once and the verbs twice in the main clauses. Put parentheses around the punctuation, transitions, and connectors that join the main clauses. Then indicate if the sentences are correct (C) or incorrect (I).

_____ 1. The matter was really important(,) I could to decide too quickly.

_____ 2. The children broke the rules, but their parents did not find out.

_____ 3. She expected to graduate in the spring, however she did not graduate until fall.

_____ 4. My family moved a lot during my youth; as a result, I always had to make new friends.

_____ 5. I made a firm promise to my friend and I vowed to keep it.

_____ 6. Sam did not sign in before work, so he signed in afterwards.

_____ 7. The students waited in a long line to register. Finally, they got to the front of the line.

_____ 8. His parents advised him to think about it some more he did not take their advice.

_____ 9. My first job in the company was as a part-time worker, later I was given a full-time job.

_____ 10. Tom really wanted to be successful, yet he did not know how to accomplish this.

_____ 11. We must return the books to the library today, otherwise we will have to pay a fine.

_____ 12. She always tries not to get too angry. However, she sometimes loses her temper.

_____ 13. Therefore she has gotten a job, she can pay all of her bills.

_____ 14. She had the surgery recommended by her doctor; as a result, she is doing better now.

_____ 15. They left the money in a savings account, it began to collect some interest.

_____ 16. I wanted to get a high-paying job last summer; unfortunately, this was impossible.

_____ 17. I will have to study harder, or I will not be able to get a scholarship.

_____ 18. An accident happened at the corner, afterwards, the police came and wrote a report.

_____ 19. The plan has a number of advantages it also has a number of disadvantages.

_____ 20. The directions must be followed exactly; otherwise, the outcome will be very bad.

Appendix B3: USE CORRECT COMPLEX SENTENCES

A complex sentence is a sentence with one main clause and at least one **subordinate clause**.[6] Noun, adjective, and adverb clauses are all types of subordinate clauses. Each of the following sentences is a complex sentence because it contains a subordinate clause.

> I cannot believe (what he did).
>
> NOUN CLAUSE

> The runner (who finishes first) wins the trophy.
>
> ADJECTIVE CLAUSE

> I will return to the job (when I am able).
>
> ADVERB CLAUSE

The first complex sentence contains the subordinate noun clause *what he did*. The second complex sentence contains the subordinate adjective clause *who finishes first*. The final complex sentence contains the subordinate adverb clause *when I am able*.

A variety of errors with complex structures can occur in student writing, but two errors that occur with great frequency are (1) repeated subjects after adjective clauses, and (2) repeated subjects after noun clauses as subjects. To understand these two problems, you must recognize adjective and noun clauses. The following chart lists connectors that introduce adjective and noun clauses.

SUBORDINATE ADJECTIVE AND NOUN CLAUSE CONNECTORS			
ADJECTIVE CLAUSE CONNECTORS	NOUN CLAUSE CONNECTORS		
who whom which that	who whoever what whatever	when where why how	whether if that

Look at the following examples of errors with adjective and noun clauses.

> A good <u>friend</u> (who lives down the street) <u>she</u>* <u><u>did</u></u> me a favor.
>
> SUBJECT   SUBJECT VERB

> (<u>What my advisor told me yesterday</u>) <u>it</u>* <u><u>was</u></u> very helpful.
>
> NOUN CLAUSE SUBJECT   SUBJECT VERB

The first sentence is incorrect because it contains an extra subject. The correct subject *friend* comes before the adjective clause *who lives down the street*, and an extra subject *she* comes after the adjective clause. To correct this sentence, you should omit the extra subject *she*. The second sentence is also incorrect because it contains an extra subject. *What my advisor told me yesterday* is a noun clause subject, and this noun clause subject is followed by the extra subject *it*. To correct this sentence, you should omit the extra subject *it*.

---

[6] A **subordinate clause** is a dependent clause that has both a subject and a verb and is introduced by a subordinate clause connector.

The following chart outlines the key information that you should remember about using correct complex sentences.

USING CORRECT COMPLEX SENTENCES

1. A complex sentence is a sentence with one main clause and one or more subordinate clauses.
2. Noun clauses, adjective clauses, and adverb clauses are subordinate clauses.
3. When a subject comes before an adjective clause, you should not add an extra subject after the adjective clause.
4. When a noun clause is used as a subject, you should not add an extra subject after the noun clause.

APPENDIX EXERCISE B3: Underline the subjects once and the verbs twice in the main clauses. Put parentheses around the subordinate noun and adjective clauses. Then indicate if the sentences are correct (C) or incorrect (I).

_____ 1. The reason (that) he took the money it was to pay the bills.

_____ 2. Why the man did something so terrible will never be known.

_____ 3. The ticket that I need to get onto the plane was not included in the packet.

_____ 4. What the lifeguard did it was quite heroic.

_____ 5. The day when I found out the news it was a good day.

_____ 6. The teacher whose advice I remember to this day was my sixth grade teacher.

_____ 7. Where we went on vacation it was such a gorgeous place.

_____ 8. That he really said those words it could not be refuted.

_____ 9. The man who helped me the most in my life he was my high school coach.

_____ 10. How the paper got finished on time remains unclear to me.

_____ 11. What caused the accident on the freeway it is still unknown.

_____ 12. The plans that we made for our trip were not carefully thought out.

_____ 13. The process by which the decisions were made it was very slow.

_____ 14. Whatever she gets is what she deserves.

_____ 15. The employee who has the information that you need is out of the office.

_____ 16. What he wrote in the letter it could not be taken back.

_____ 17. The officer who stopped me on the highway he gave me a ticket for speeding.

_____ 18. How he could believe something that is so incredible is beyond me.

_____ 19. The reason that I applied to the public school was that the tuition was lower.

_____ 20. Why they said what they said to the man who tried to help them it was not clear.

APPENDIX REVIEW EXERCISE (B1–B3): Correct the errors in the following passages.

1. I have two very personal reasons for coming to this conclusion. One of the reasons is related to my family relationships, the other is related to my finances.

2. A decision has been reached but the decision has not yet been announced. We must wait until 4 o'clock, that is when the decision will be announced.

3. What just happened this morning it was a complete shock to me. My math professor announced in class this morning that the exam that was scheduled for next Friday it would be given this morning. Unfortunately, I was not prepared for the exam this morning because did not expect the exam to be given then.

4. The department has announced that only two scholarships will be awarded and that more than a hundred applications for the scholarship they have already been received. Nonetheless, I am still going to submit my application.

5. My family never really wanted to make so many moves, it had to do so. Because it was necessary for my father's career, so we moved almost every year.

6. I expect your papers to be very clearly organized; thus, you are required to turn in an outline before you complete your papers. Your outline should be turned in within two weeks; the final paper is not due for two months.

7. The university is considering implementing an increase in tuition for the coming year. The students believe that tuition should not be raised, however, the students will most likely not get what they want.

8. The details of the report are confidential, they will not be made public. If want to find out about the report, what you must do it is to file a petition to get hold of the report.

9. My dream house is one that would be in the mountains. It would be surrounded by trees and it would have a view of a gorgeous lake. Moreover, the only noises that could be heard they would be the sounds of birds singing.

10. You must develop your ideas thoroughly. If you make a statement, you should be sure to support that statement. You may use many kinds of ideas to support a statement. For example, you may use details, or reasons, or examples.

APPENDIX C

ERROR CORRECTION _____

It is important when you are producing material on the *iBT* TOEFL test that your English should be grammatically correct. You should be sure that you know how to use subject/verb agreement, parallel structure, comparatives and superlatives, verb forms, verb uses, passives, nouns, pronouns, adjectives and adverbs, and articles correctly.

SUBJECT/VERB AGREEMENT

Subject/verb agreement is simple: if a sentence is singular, then the verb that accompanies it must be singular, and if a subject is plural, then the verb that accompanies it must be plural.

> The <u>student</u> <u>takes</u> many exams.
>
> The <u>students</u> <u>take</u> many exams.

In the first example, the singular subject *student* requires the singular verb *takes*. In the second example, the plural subject *students* requires the plural verb *take*.

Although this might seem quite simple, there are some situations with subject/verb agreement that can be confusing. You should be careful of subject/verb agreement (1) after prepositional phrases, and (2) after expressions of quantity.

Appendix C1: MAKE VERBS AGREE AFTER PREPOSITIONAL PHRASES

Sometimes prepositional phrases can come between the subject and the verb. If the object of the preposition is singular and the subject is plural, or if the object of the preposition is plural and the subject is singular, there can be confusion in making the subject and verb agree. (Note that an asterisk indicates that there is an error.)

> The <u>key</u> (to the doors) <u>are</u>* in the drawer.
>
> The <u>keys</u> (to the door) <u>is</u>* in the drawer.

In the first example, you might think that *doors* is the subject because it comes directly in front of the verb *are*. However, *doors* is not the subject because it is the object of the preposition *to*. The subject is *key*, so the verb should be *is*. In the second example, you might think that *door* is the subject because it comes directly in front of the verb *is*. You should recognize in this example that *door* is not the subject because it is the object of the preposition *to*. Because the subject is *keys*, the verb should be *are*.

The following chart outlines the key information that you should understand about subject/verb agreement with prepositional phrases.

SUBJECT/VERB AGREEMENT WITH PREPOSITIONAL PHRASES
S   *(prepositional phrase)*   V
When a prepositional phrase comes between the subject and the verb, be sure that the verb agrees with the subject.

APPENDIX EXERCISE C1: Each of the following sentences has one or more prepositional phrases between the subject and the verb. Put parentheses around the prepositional phrases between the subject and verb. Underline the subjects once and the verbs twice. Then indicate if the sentences are correct (C) or incorrect (I).

_____ 1. The forest <u>rangers</u> (in the eastern section) (of the park) <u><u>have spotted</u></u> a bear.

_____ 2. The <u>flowers</u> (on the plum tree) (in the garden) <u><u>has started</u></u> to bloom.

   (flowers . . . have started)

_____ 3. The cost of the books for all of his classes are quite high.

_____ 4. The reports prepared by the staff for the manager contain many graphs and charts.

_____ 5. The light from the candles on the end tables provide a soft glow to the room.

_____ 6. The ideas suggested at the meeting of the council was well received by most attendees.

_____ 7. The gemstones in the necklace worn by the actress were beautifully matched.

_____ 8. The speech on a variety of topics of great importance to the citizens are being broadcast this evening.

_____ 9. The new tires for the front of the car are being installed at this moment.

_____ 10. The exams scheduled for the last week of the semester is going to be comprehensive exams.

Appendix C2: MAKE VERBS AGREE AFTER EXPRESSIONS OF QUANTITY

A particular agreement problem occurs when the subject is an expression of quantity, such as _all_, _most_, or _some_, followed by the preposition _of_. In this situation, the subject (_all_, _most_, or _some_) can be singular or plural, depending on what follows the preposition _of_.

   <u>All</u> (of the book) <u><u>was</u></u> interesting.

   <u>All</u> (of the books) <u><u>were</u></u> interesting.

   <u>All</u> (of the information) <u><u>was</u></u> interesting.

In the first example, the subject _All_ refers to the singular noun _book_. In the second example, the subject _All_ refers to the plural noun _books_, so the correct verb is the plural verb _were_. In the third example, the subject _All_ refers to the uncountable noun _information_, so the correct verb is therefore the singular verb _was_.

The following chart outlines the key information that you should understand about subject/verb agreement after expressions of quantity.

SUBJECT/VERB AGREEMENT AFTER EXPRESSIONS OF QUANTITY
all most some   of the (OBJECT)   V half part
When an expression of quantity is the subject, the verb agrees with the object.

APPENDIX EXERCISE C2: Each of the following sentences has a quantity expression as the subject. Underline the subjects once and the verbs twice. Put parentheses around the objects that the verbs agree with. Then indicate if the sentences are correct (C) or incorrect (I).

_C_   1. All of his past (experience) has contributed to his present success.

_I_   2. Most of the (dishes) served at the banquet was quite spicy.
       (Most of the dishes served at the banquet were quite spicy.)

_____   3. Some of the details of the plan requires clarification.

_____   4. Half of the material needs to be completed this week.

_____   5. All of the homes on this block of town was flooded during the storm.

_____   6. Most of the children in the class has improved their reading scores tremendously.

_____   7. Some of the money from the inheritance has to be used to pay taxes.

_____   8. I bought a carton of eggs yesterday, but half of the eggs in the carton was broken.

_____   9. For her health to improve, all of the medicine has to be taken on schedule.

_____ 10. At the conference, most of the time allocated for speeches was actually devoted to discussion.

PARALLEL STRUCTURE

In good English, an attempt should be made to make the language as even and balanced as possible. This balance is called "parallel structure." You can achieve parallel structure by making the forms as similar as possible. The following is an example of a sentence that is not parallel.

> I like to sing and dancing.*

The problem in this sentence is not the expression *to sing,* and the problem is not the word *dancing.* The expression *to sing* is correct by itself, and the word *dancing* is correct by itself. Both of the following sentences are correct.

I like to sing.

I like dancing.

The problem in the incorrect example is that *to sing* and *dancing* are joined together in one sentence with *and*. They are different forms where it is possible to have similar forms; the example is therefore not parallel. It can be corrected in two different ways.

I like to sing and to dance.

I like singing and dancing.

Two issues in parallel structure that you should be familiar with are (1) the use of parallel structure with coordinate conjunctions, and (2) the use of parallel structure with paired conjunctions.

Appendix C3: USE PARALLEL STRUCTURE WITH COORDINATE CONJUNCTIONS

The job of coordinate conjunctions (*and, but, or*) is to join together equal expressions. In other words, what is on one side of these words must be parallel to what is on the other side. These conjunctions can join nouns, or verbs, or adjectives, or phrases, or subordinate clauses; they just must join together two of the same thing. Look at the following examples.

She is not a teacher *but* a lawyer.

You can stay home *or* go to the movies with us.

My boss is sincere, friendly, *and* nice.

The papers are on my desk *or* in the drawer.

I am here because I have to be *and* because I want to be.

In the first example, the coordinate conjunction *but* joins two nouns, *teacher* and *lawyer*. In the second example, the coordinate conjunction *or* joins two verbs, *stay* and *go*. In the third example, the coordinate conjunction *and* joins three adjectives, *sincere, friendly,* and *nice*. In the fourth example, the coordinate conjunction *or* joins two prepositional phrases, *on my desk* and *in the drawer*. In the last example, the coordinate conjunction *and* joins two clauses, *because I have to be* and *because I want to be*.

The following chart describes the use of parallel structures with coordinate conjunctions.

PARALLEL STRUCTURE WITH COORDINATE CONJUNCTIONS			
(same structure)		and but or	(same structure)
(same structure),	(same structure),	and but or	(same structure)

APPENDIX EXERCISE C3: Each of the following sentences contains words or groups of words that should be parallel. Put parentheses around the word that indicates that the sentence should have parallel parts. Underline the parts that should be parallel. Then indicate if the sentences are correct (C) or incorrect (I).

  I   1. The movie was really scary (but) was still quite pleasure.
(was still quite pleasurable)

  C   2. He said that he was sorry (and) that he would make amends.

_____ 3. The leader spoke of the need for idealism, integrity, and dedicate.

_____ 4. The ball player was not very tall yet was quite athlete.

_____ 5. To contact me, you may call on the phone, write a letter, or send a fax.

_____ 6. The course is offered in the spring semester but not in the fall semester.

_____ 7. For his job, he travels back and forth between Los Angeles and New York to pick up packages and delivers them.

_____ 8. He can work on the report in the library or studies at home.

_____ 9. The news report described the pain, anger, resentment, frustration, and disbelief in the aftermath of the accident.

_____ 10. She gave a well-rehearsed yet natural-sounding speech.

Appendix C4: USE PARALLEL STRUCTURE WITH PAIRED CONJUNCTIONS

The paired conjunctions *both . . . and, either . . . or, neither . . . nor,* and *not only . . . but also* require parallel structures. Look at the following examples.

> I know *both* <u>where you went</u> *and* <u>what you did</u>.
>
> *Either* <u>Mark</u> or <u>Sue</u> has the book.
>
> The tickets are *neither* <u>in my pocket</u> *nor* <u>in my purse</u>.
>
> He *not only* <u>works hard</u> *but also* <u>plays hard</u>.

In the first example, the paired conjunction *both . . . and* is followed by parallel clauses, *where you went* and *what you did*. In the second example, the paired conjunction *Either . . . or* is followed by parallel nouns, *Mark* and *Sue*. In the third example, the paired conjunction *neither . . . nor* is followed by parallel phrases, *in my pocket* and *in my purse*. In the last example, the paired conjunction *not only . . . but also* is followed by parallel verb phrases, *works hard* and *plays hard*.

The following chart describes the use of parallel structure with paired conjunctions.

PARALLEL STRUCTURE WITH PAIRED CONJUNCTIONS			
both either neither not only	(same structure)	and or nor but also	(same structure)

APPENDIX EXERCISE C4: Each of the following sentences contains words or groups of words that should be parallel. Put parentheses around the word or words that indicate that the sentence should have parallel parts. Underline the parts that should be parallel. Then indicate if the sentences are correct (C) or incorrect (I).

__I__   1. He (not only) plays football (but also) baseball.
            (plays baseball)

__C__   2. The children were (either) praised (or) scolded for their behavior.

_____   3. There is food to eat both in the refrigerator and the freezer.

_____   4. It has been decided to do neither what you prefer or what I prefer.

_____   5. She not only misplaced her textbook but also couldn't find her notebook.

_____   6. Either you can work on this committee or join a different one.

_____   7. She was both challenged by and frustrated with her job.

_____   8. Neither the manager nor any members of the staff are staying late today.

_____   9. You can either register for three courses or for four courses.

_____ 10. Both the children as well as the baby-sitter fell asleep.

COMPARATIVES AND SUPERLATIVES

A comparative (formed with *-er* or *more*) shows how two items relate to each other, while a superlative (formed with *-est* or *most*) shows how one item relates to a group.

> My history class is much *harder* than my science class.
> My history class is much *more interesting* than my science class.
>
> My history class is *the hardest* of all my classes.
> My history class is *the most interesting* of all my classes.

In the first two examples, the comparatives *harder* and *more interesting* show how the history class relates to the science class. In the last two examples, the superlatives *the hardest* and *the most interesting* show how the history class relates to all of the classes.

Comparatives and superlatives are important in academic language. It is important for you to know how to do the following: (1) form the comparative and superlative correctly, and (2) use the comparative and superlative correctly.

Appendix C5: FORM COMPARATIVES AND SUPERLATIVES CORRECTLY

The comparative is formed with either *-er* or *more* and *than*. In the comparative, *-er* is used with shorter (one-syllable and some two-syllable) adjectives such as *tall*, and *more* is used with longer (some two-syllable and all three-or-more-syllable) adjectives such as *beautiful*.

> Rich is *taller than* Ron.
> Sally is *more beautiful than* Sharon.

The superlative is formed with *the*, either *-est* or *most*, and sometimes *in*, *of*, or a *that-clause*. In the superlative, *-est* is used with shorter adjectives such as *tall*, and *most* is used with longer adjectives such as *beautiful*.

> Rich is *the tallest* man *in* the room.
> Sally is *the most beautiful* of all the women in the room.
> The spider by the window is *the largest* one *that* I have ever seen.
> *The fastest* runner wins the race. (no *in*, *of*, or *that*)

The following chart outlines the possible forms of comparatives and superlatives.

FORMS OF COMPARATIVES AND SUPERLATIVES			
COMPARATIVE	short adjective + *-er* *more* + long adjective	*than*	
SUPERLATIVE	*the*	short adjective + *-est* *most* + long adjective	maybe *in, of, that*
Shorter adjectives are all one-syllable adjectives and some two-syllable adjectives. Longer adjectives are some two-syllable adjectives and all adjectives with three or more syllables.			

APPENDIX EXERCISE C5: Each of the following sentences contains a comparative or superlative. Put parentheses around the comparative or superlative. Then indicate if the sentences are correct (C) or incorrect (I).

__I__ 1. This morning I heard (the unsualest) story in the news.
(the most unusual)

__C__ 2. This bicycle is (more expensive than) mine.

_____ 3. Today she became the angriest that I have ever seen her.

_____ 4. This classroom is the hotter than the one next door.

_____ 5. The weather today is much more cloudier today than it was yesterday.

_____ 6. This room houses the most ancient pieces of sculpture in the museum.

_____ 7. The seats on this airline are wider than those on the airline that I took last week.

_____ 8. The building where he works is the most tallest in town.

_____ 9. This restaurant has most efficient service of all the restaurants I have visited.

_____ 10. This type of coffee is stronger and more flavorful than my regular coffee.

Appendix C6: USE COMPARATIVES AND SUPERLATIVES CORRECTLY

The comparative and superlative have different uses, and it is important to understand these differences. The comparative is used to describe two unequal things.

> The math class is larger than the philosophy class.
>
> Jean is more intelligent than Joan.

In the first example, the *math class* is being compared with the *philosophy class*, and they are not equal. In the second example, *Jean* is being compared with *Joan*, and they are not equal.

The superlative is used when there are more than two items to compare and one of them is outstanding in some way.

> The math class is the largest in the school.
>
> Jean is the most intelligent in the class.

In the first example, the *math class* is compared with all of the other classes *in the school*, and the math class is larger than each of the other classes. In the second example, *Jean* is compared with all of the other students *in the class*, and Jean is more intelligent than each of the other students.

The following chart outlines the uses of comparatives and superlatives.

USES OF COMPARATIVES AND SUPERLATIVES	
COMPARATIVES	Are used to show the relationship between two things, and these two things are not equal.
SUPERLATIVES	Are used to show how one item is outstanding in a group of three or more.

APPENDIX EXERCISE C6: Each of the following sentences contains a comparative or superlative. Put parentheses around the comparative or superlative. Then indicate if the sentences are correct (C) or incorrect (I).

__C__ 1. We have (the friendliest) pets of all.

__I__ 2. This set of problems is (the most difficult of) the last set was.
(*more difficult than*)

_____ 3. The grey cat has a nicest disposition than the black cat.

_____ 4. You missed the best party of the year last night.

_____ 5. Her car is the most fuel-efficient of most other cars.

_____ 6. The weather this year is the drier that it has been in a decade.

_____ 7. My boss is not the most understanding of bosses.

_____ 8. This is earlier that I have ever arrived at work.

_____ 9. The scores on the second exam were the highest of those on the first exam.

_____ 10. Cathy is more reticent than the other students in the class to volunteer answers.

APPENDIX REVIEW EXERCISE (C1–C6): Indicate if the following sentences are correct (C) or incorrect (I).

_____ 1. The new movie is not only deeply moving but also very well paced.

_____ 2. Some of the rooms were scheduled to be painted this week.

_____ 3. Please drop these letters off at the most near post office.

_____ 4. The man wrote and signed the check, presented it to the cashier, and leaving with cash.

_____ 5. The noises coming from outside the house was frightening the family inside.

_____ 6. Today she has scheduled the more important interview of her career.

_____ 7. Your excuses are neither credible nor acceptable.

_____ 8. Half of your answers on the exam were less than adequate.

_____ 9. Hal is trying to behave in a more honorabler way than he has in the past.

_____ 10. After dinner, we can take a walk, play a game, or go bowling.

_____ 11. The stairs leading to the top floor of the building is blocked now.

_____ 12. This is a more ridiculous plan than you have ever made.

_____ 13. The politician claimed that he had neither asked for nor accepted any illegal donations.

_____ 14. I believe that most of the reasons presented in the report was convincing.

_____ 15. The trip by train is longer but less expensive than the trip by plane.

VERB FORMS

You should be familiar with the following verb forms: the base form, the third-person singular form, the past form, the past participle, and the present participle.

BASE FORM	THIRD-PERSON SINGULAR	PAST FORM	PAST PARTICIPLE	PRESENT PARTICIPLE
walk	walks	walked	walked	walking
hear	hears	heard	heard	hearing
take	takes	took	taken	taking
begin	begins	began	begun	beginning
come	comes	came	come	coming
think	thinks	thought	thought	thinking

You should be particularly aware of the following three problematic situations with verb forms because they are the most common and the easiest to correct: (1) using the correct form after _have_, (2) using the correct form after _be_, and (3) using the correct form after modals.

Appendix C7: AFTER *HAVE,* USE THE PAST PARTICIPLE

The verb *have* in any of its forms (*have, has, had, having*) can be followed by another verb. Whenever you use the verb *have* in any of its forms, you should be sure that a verb that follows it is in the past participle form.

They *had walk** to school.	(should be *had walked*)
We *have see** the show.	(should be *have seen*)
He *has took** the test.	(should be *has taken*)
*Having ate**, he went to school.	(should be *Having eaten*)
She *should have did** the work.	(should be *should have done*)

In addition, you should be sure that, if you have a subject and a past participle, you also have a form of the verb *have.*

My friend *sung** in the choir.	(should be *sang* or *has sung*)
He *become** angry at his friend.	(should be *became* or *has become*)
The boat *sunk** in the ocean.	(should be *sank* or *has sunk*)

The following chart outlines the use of verb forms after *have.*

VERB FORMS AFTER *HAVE*
have + past participle

APPENDIX EXERCISE C7: Each of the following sentences contains a verb formed with *have.* Underline the verbs twice, and study the forms following *have.* Then indicate if the sentences are correct (C) or incorrect (I).

_____ 1. Her sisters <u><u>have came</u></u> to help plan the party.
       (have come)

_____ 2. I <u>thought</u> that I <u>had told</u> you everything.

_____ 3. The girl has wore the same dress to school each day this week.

_____ 4. High winds have blown the plane off course.

_____ 5. The computer cartridge has running out of ink.

_____ 6. Lightning had struck and had knocked the tree down.

_____ 7. Perhaps you have drew the wrong conclusion.

_____ 8. The professor has taught this course many times before.

_____ 9. The surprised student had not knew that there was an exam that day.

_____ 10. All the family members have always gotten together to celebrate Thanksgiving.

Appendix C8: AFTER *BE,* USE THE PRESENT PARTICIPLE OR THE PAST PARTICIPLE

The verb *be* in any of its forms (*am, is, are, was, were, be, been, being*) can be followed by another verb. This verb should be in the present participle or past participle form.

We *are do** our homework.	(should be *are doing*)
The homework *was do** early.	(should be *was done*)
Tom *is take** the book.	(should be *is taking*)

The following chart outlines the use of verb forms after *be.*

VERB FORMS AFTER *BE*
be + (1) present participle (2) past participle

APPENDIX EXERCISE C8: Each of the following sentences contains a verb formed with *be.* Underline the verbs twice, and study the forms following *be.* Then indicate if the sentences are correct (C) or incorrect (I).

__I__ 1. The new president <u>will be inaugurate</u> next week.
(will be inaugurated)

__C__ 2. The plans that <u>were presented</u> last week <u>are unchanged.</u>

_____ 3. The photograph was took without her permission.

_____ 4. She has been promoted because of her excellent work.

_____ 5. We are always arguing about what is happens in politics.

_____ 6. He should not have been smoke in the office, but he was.

_____ 7. The telephone was ringing constantly throughout the day.

_____ 8. All of the plants were froze because of the cold weather.

_____ 9. Everyone is wondering when the train will be departing.

_____ 10. The planes were take off and land right on schedule.

Appendix C9: AFTER *WILL, WOULD,* OR OTHER MODALS, USE THE BASE FORM OF THE VERB

Modals such as *will, would, shall, should, can, could, may, might,* and *must* are helping verbs that will be followed by a base form of the verb. Whenever you see a modal, you should be sure that the verb that follows it is its base form.

The boat *will leaving** at 3:00.	(should be *will leave*)
The doctor *may arrives** soon.	(should be *may arrive*)
The students *must taken** the exam.	(should be *must take*)

The following chart outlines the use of verb forms after modals.

VERB FORMS AFTER MODALS
modal + base form of the verb

APPENDIX EXERCISE C9: Each of the following sentences contains a verb formed with a modal. Underline the verbs twice, and study the forms following the modals. Then indicate if the sentences are correct (C) or incorrect (I).

__C__ 1. The professor <u>cannot return</u> the papers until tomorrow.

__I__ 2. The tour guide <u>may preferring</u> to leave within an hour.
(*may prefer*)

_____ 3. The next step in the process will depends on the results of the medical tests.

_____ 4. He asked if you might be coming to the party.

_____ 5. The team members must to try a lot harder in the second half of the game.

_____ 6. My friend told me that he could taken care of the problem.

_____ 7. When do you think the company might announce its decision?

_____ 8. The teaching assistant must not gave the students any more time for the test.

_____ 9. Many of the cars on the lot will going on sale this weekend.

_____ 10. He was angry because his car would not start this morning.

VERB USES

Many different problems in using verb tenses are possible in English. Three of them occur frequently, so you need to pay careful attention to them: (1) knowing when to use the past with the present, (2) using *had* and *have* tenses correctly, and (3) using the correct tense with time expressions.

Appendix C10: KNOW WHEN TO USE THE PAST WITH THE PRESENT

One common verb tense problem is the switch from the past tense to the present tense for no particular reason. Often, when a sentence has both a past tense and a present tense, the sentence is incorrect.

> He *took* the money when he *wants** it.

This sentence says that *he took the money* (in the past) *when he wants it* (in the present). This sentence does not make sense because it is impossible to do something in the past as a result of wanting it in the present. This sentence can be corrected in several ways, depending on the desired meaning.

> He *took* the money when he *wanted* it.
> He *takes* the money when he *wants* it.

The first example means that *he took the money* (in the past) *when he wanted it* (in the past). This meaning is logical, and the sentence is correct. The second example means that *he takes the money* (habitually) *when he wants it* (habitually). This meaning is also logical, and the second example is also correct.

It is necessary to point out, however, that it is possible for a logical sentence in English to have both a present tense and a past tense.

> I *know* that he *took* the money yesterday.

The meaning of this sentence is logical: *I know* (right now, in the present) that he *took the money* (yesterday, in the past). You can see from this example that it is possible for an English sentence to have both a present tense and a past tense. When you see a sentence with both a present tense and a past tense, you must think about whether the meaning is logical or not.

The following chart outlines the use of the past tense and the present tense.

USING THE PAST WITH THE PRESENT

1. If you see a sentence with one verb in the past and one verb in the present, the sentence is probably incorrect.
2. However, it is possible for a logical sentence to have both the past and the present together.
3. If you see the past and the present together, you must check the meaning to determine whether or not the sentence is logical.

APPENDIX EXERCISE C10: Each of the following sentences has at least one verb in the past and one verb in the present. Underline the verbs twice, and decide if the meanings are logical. Then indicate if the sentences are correct (C) or incorrect (I).

__I__ 1. The audience members <u>need</u> to take their seats because the play <u>was</u> about to start. *(is)*

__C__ 2. Today's newspaper <u>has</u> a story that <u>describes</u> what <u>happened</u> during the tragedy.

_____ 3. When he told her the truth, she is pleased with what she heard.

_____ 4. The teacher is well aware that the students did not understand the assignment.

_____ 5. I had problems in my last math course, but this one is going much better.

_____ 6. Every morning Rob leaves the house at the same time and took the bus to work.

_____ 7. As the plane was landing, the passengers remain in their seats with their seat belts fastened.

_____ 8. The police are certain that the suspect committed the crime.

_____ 9. On the way home from work, they filled the car up with gas and then heads to the supermarket.

_____ 10. People understand what happened, but they are unclear about why it occurred this way.

Appendix C11: USE *HAVE* AND *HAD* CORRECTLY

Two tenses that are often confused are the present perfect (*have* + past participle) and the past perfect (*had* + past participle). These two tenses have completely different uses, and you should understand how to differentiate them.

The present perfect (*have* + past participle) can refer to the period of time *from the past until the present*.

> Sue *has lived* in Los Angeles for ten years.

This sentence means that Sue has lived in Los Angeles for the ten years up to the present. According to this sentence, Sue is still living in Los Angeles.

Because the present perfect can refer to a period of time from the past until the present, it is not correct in a sentence that indicates past only.

> *At the start of the nineteenth century,* Thomas Jefferson *has become**
> president of the United States.

In this example, the phrase *at the start of the nineteenth century* indicates that the action of the verb was in the past only, but the verb indicates the period of time from the past until the present. Since this is not logical, the sentence is not correct. The verb *has become* should be changed to *became*.

The past perfect (*had* + past participle) refers to a period of time that *started in the past and ended in the past, before something else happened in the past*.

> Sue *had lived* in Los Angeles for ten years when she *moved* to San Diego.

This sentence means that Sue lived in Los Angeles for ten years in the past, before she moved to San Diego. She no longer lives in Los Angeles.

Because the past perfect begins in the past and ends in the past, it is generally not correct in the same sentence with the present tense.

> Tom *had finished* the exam when the teacher *collects** the papers.

This sentence indicates that *Tom finished the exam* (in the past), and that action ended in the past at the same time that *the teacher collects the papers* (in the present). This sentence is not logical, so the sentence is not correct.

The following chart outlines the uses of the present perfect and the past perfect.

USING (*HAVE* + PAST PARTICIPLE) AND (*HAD* + PAST PARTICIPLE)			
TENSE	FORM	MEANING	USE
present perfect	*have* + past participle	past up to now	not with a past tense**
past perfect	*had* + past participle	before past	not with a present tense
**Except when the time expression *since* is part of the sentence (see C12).			

APPENDIX EXERCISE C11: Each of the following sentences contains *had* or *have*. Underline the verbs twice and decide if the meanings are logical. Then indicate if the sentences are correct (C) or incorrect (I).

_____ 1. She is very pleased that her son has graduated with honors.

_____ 2. After the bell had rung, the students leave class quickly.
  (left)

_____ 3. I have visited that museum each time that I traveled to the city.

_____ 4. The lawyer suddenly found out that he had made a big mistake.

_____ 5. Admissions are based on what you have done throughout your high school years.

_____ 6. When all the papers had been collected, the teacher dismisses the class.

_____ 7. The garden was not growing well because there had not been much rain for months.

_____ 8. She knows that you have always tried to be helpful.

_____ 9. I can tell you what I know about what has transpired during the investigation.

_____ 10. We will be able to discuss the situation thoroughly after you have submitted your report.

Appendix C12: USE THE CORRECT TENSE WITH TIME EXPRESSIONS

When a time expression is used in a sentence, it commonly indicates what tense is needed in the sentence.

> We moved to New York *in 1998*.
>
> We had left there *by 2002*.
>
> We have lived in San Francisco *since 2004*.

In the first example, the time expression *in 1998* indicates that the verb should be in the simple past (*moved*). In the second example, the time expression *by 2002* indicates that the verb should be in the past perfect (*had left*). In the third example, the time expression *since 2004* indicates that the verb should be in the present perfect (*have lived*).

Some additional time expressions that clearly indicate the correct tense are *ago, last,* and *lately*.

> She got a job *two years ago*.
>
> She started working *last week*.
>
> She has worked very hard *lately*.

In the first example, the time expression *two years ago* indicates that the verb should be in the simple past (*got*). In the second example, the time expression *last week* indicates that the verb should be in the simple past (*started*). In the third example, the time expression *lately* indicates that the verb should be in the present perfect (*has worked*).

The following chart lists time expressions that indicate the correct verb tense.

USING CORRECT TENSES WITH TIME EXPRESSIONS		
PAST PERFECT	SIMPLE PAST	PRESENT PERFECT
by (1920)	(one century) ago last (century) in (1920)	since (1920) lately

APPENDIX EXERCISE C12: Each of the following sentences contains a time expression. Put parentheses around the time expressions, and underline the verbs twice. Then indicate if the sentences are correct (C) or incorrect (I).

__I__ 1. (By 1995), Steve <u>has decided</u> to pursue a different career.
(had decided)

__C__ 2. This university <u>was established</u> (in 1900), at the turn of the century.

_____ 3. Since I last saw you, I got a job at the United Nations.

_____ 4. Mike has applied to law school a few months ago.

_____ 5. The organization elected new officers just last month.

_____ 6. We experienced problem after problem lately.

_____ 7. By the end of the meeting, all of the participants had reached an agreement.

_____ 8. Sara has finally graduated from the university in June.

_____ 9. I am living in the same neighborhood since I was a child.

_____ 10. I was glad that you called me because I tried to call you just a few minutes ago and got a busy signal.

PASSIVE VERBS

In a passive sentence, the subject and object are reversed from where they are found in an active sentence. A passive verb consists of a form of the verb *be* and a past participle, and *by* is used in front of the object in a passive verb.

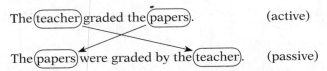

The (teacher) graded the (papers).   (active)

The (papers) were graded by the (teacher).   (passive)

The first example is an active statement, and the second example is a passive statement. The subject from the active statement (*teacher*) has become the object following *by* in the passive example; the object from the active example (*papers*) has become the subject in the passive example. The verb in the passive example consists of a form of *be* (*were*) and a past participle (*graded*).

It should be noted that, in a passive sentence, *by + object* does not need to be included to have a complete sentence.

> The papers were graded by the teacher.
>
> The papers were graded.

Each of these examples is a correct sentence. The first example is a passive statement that includes *by the teacher*. The second example is a passive statement that does not include *by*.

You should pay attention to the passive in your English. You should pay attention to (1) the form of the passive, and (2) the use of the passive.

Appendix C13: USE THE CORRECT FORM OF THE PASSIVE

One possible problem with the passive is an incorrect form of the passive. A correctly formed passive will always have a form of *be* and a past participle. The following are examples of common errors in the form of the passive.

> The portrait *was painting** by a famous artist.
>
> The project *will finished** by the group.

In the first example, the passive is formed incorrectly because the past participle *painted* should be used rather than the present participle *painting*. In the second example, the verb *be* has not been included, and some form of *be* is necessary for a passive verb. The verb in the second example should be *will be finished*.

The following chart outlines the way to form the passive correctly.

THE FORM OF THE PASSIVE
be + past participle

APPENDIX EXERCISE C13: Each of the following sentences has a passive meaning. Underline twice the verbs that should be passive. Then indicate if the sentences are correct (C) or incorrect (I).

__I__ 1. The trees and hedges <u>will be trim</u> this week.
  (will be trimmed)

__C__ 2. That kind of decision <u>is made</u> by the board of directors.

_____ 3. The bank robbed yesterday by a masked gunman.

_____ 4. The plans for the building complex were describing by the architect.

_____ 5. The oil has been changed, and the tires have been filled with air.

_____ 6. Some tickets to the concert have given away by the concert promoters.

_____ 7. As soon as the food was cooked, it was brought to the table.

_____ 8. The money for the purchase was accepted the clerk.

_____ 9. Students will not be allowed to register if their fees have not been pay.

_____ 10. The election is being held, and the results will be posted by the election committee.

Appendix C14: RECOGNIZE ACTIVE AND PASSIVE MEANINGS

When there is no object (with or without *by*) after a verb, you must look at the meaning of the sentence to determine if the verb should be active or passive. Look at the following examples.

> We <u>mailed</u> the *package* at the post office.
>
> The letter <u>was mailed</u> *by us* today before noon.
>
> The letter <u>was mailed</u> today before noon.
>
> The letter <u>mailed</u>* today before noon.

The first three examples are all correct. The first example has the active verb *mailed* used with the object *package*; the second example has the passive verb *was mailed* used with *by us*; the third example has the passive verb *was mailed* used without an object. The last example is not correct. The verb *mailed* looks like a correct active verb, but a passive verb is needed. There is no *by* and an object to tell you that a passive verb is needed; instead, you must understand from the meaning that it is incorrect. You should ask yourself *if the letter mails itself* (the letter *does* the action) or if *someone mails the letter* (the letter *receives* the action of being mailed). Since a letter does not mail itself, the passive is required in this sentence. The verb in the last example should be changed from the active *mailed* to the passive *was mailed*.

The following chart outlines the difference in meaning between active and passive verbs.

ACTIVE AND PASSIVE MEANINGS	
ACTIVE	The subject does the action of the verb.
PASSIVE	The subject receives the action of the verb.

APPENDIX EXERCISE C14: Each of the following sentences contains at least one active verb; however, some of the verbs should be passive. Underline the verbs twice. Then indicate if the sentences are correct (C) or incorrect (I).

__I__ 1. The game <u>won</u> in overtime.
(was won)

__C__ 2. The engine <u>started</u> on the very first try.

_____ 3. The photos placed in frames on the mantle.

_____ 4. The top students selected to receive scholarships.

_____ 5. The store opened right on schedule.

_____ 6. The outcome expected because of the lack of effort.

_____ 7. The comedian's jokes amused the audience.

_____ 8. The policy changes announced late yesterday afternoon.

_____ 9. The chair knocked over, and the child fell off.

_____ 10. The surgical procedure lasted for more than six hours.

APPENDIX REVIEW EXERCISE (C7–C14): Indicate if the following sentences are correct (C) or incorrect (I).

_____ 1. The director may has to cut a few of the more violent scenes from the movie.

_____ 2. He feels the way that he does today because of what happened in the past.

_____ 3. The vegetables washed and chopped up for salad.

_____ 4. The children have drank all of the milk from the refrigerator.

_____ 5. The family did not take any long vacations lately.

_____ 6. It is expects that many of the employees will be transferred to new positions.

_____ 7. The company was found more than a hundred years ago.

_____ 8. The report clearly proved that no one had been treated unfairly.

_____ 9. I would like to know when you will be able to give me the money.

_____ 10. The home owner knew that he has paid his insurance premiums on time.

_____ 11. I am worrying about the decisions that I am try to make.

_____ 12. By the end of the final talk, the lecturer has managed to convey his main points.

_____ 13. I am satisfied that you did everything possible to resolve the problem.

_____ 14. I had sought advice from my counselor before I registered for classes.

_____ 15. The story appeared in the newspaper soon after the politician interviewed.

NOUNS

A noun is the part of speech that is used to refer to a person, place, thing (or idea). Two issues related to nouns are (1) whether they are singular or plural, and (2) whether they are countable or uncountable.

Appendix C15: USE THE CORRECT SINGULAR OR PLURAL NOUN

A common problem with nouns is whether to use a singular or a plural noun.

> On the table there were many _dish*_.
>
> The lab assistant finished every _tests*_.

In the first example, _many_ indicates that the plural _dishes_ is needed. In the second example, _every_ indicates that the singular _test_ is needed.

You should watch very carefully for key words such as *each, every, one, single,* and *a* that indicate that a noun should be singular. You should also watch carefully for such key words as *many, several, both, various,* and *two* (or any other number except *one*) that indicate that a noun should be plural.

The following chart lists the key words that indicate to you whether a noun should be singular or plural.

KEY WORDS FOR SINGULAR AND PLURAL NOUNS					
FOR SINGULAR NOUNS	*each*	*every*	*single*	*one*	*a*
FOR PLURAL NOUNS	*both*	*two*	*many*	*several*	*various*

APPENDIX EXERCISE C15: Each of the following sentences contains at least one key word to tell you if a noun should be singular or plural. Put parentheses around the key words. Underline the nouns they describe. Then indicate if the sentences are correct (C) or incorrect (I).

__I__ 1. (Each) <u>exhibits</u> in the zoo is open today.
(exhibit)

__C__ 2. (Both) <u>children</u> have (various) <u>assignments</u> to complete tonight.

_____ 3. Would you like a single scoop of ice cream or two scoops?

_____ 4. She must take several pills every days.

_____ 5. Final exam week is an exhausting time for many students.

_____ 6. Various plans for a new community centers have been offered.

_____ 7. Every times that I go there, I run into several acquaintances.

_____ 8. A single serving at this restaurant consists of more food than one people can consume.

_____ 9. One incident last week caused many misunderstandings.

_____ 10. There are several candidates for the position, and each ones of them is extremely qualified.

Appendix C16: DISTINGUISH COUNTABLE AND UNCOUNTABLE NOUNS

In English, nouns are classified as either countable or uncountable. It is necessary to distinguish countable and uncountable nouns in order to use the correct modifiers with them.

As the name implies, countable nouns are nouns that can be counted. Countable nouns can come in quantities of one, or two, or a hundred, and so forth. The noun *book* is countable because you can have one book or several books.

Uncountable nouns, on the other hand, are nouns that cannot be counted because they come in some indeterminate quantity or mass. A noun such as *happiness* cannot be counted; you cannot have one happiness or two happinesses.

It is important for you to recognize the difference between countable and uncountable nouns when you come across such key words as *much* and *many*.

> He has seen *much** foreign *films*.
>
> He did not have *many** fun at the movies.

In the first example, much is incorrect because *films* is countable. This example should say *many foreign films*. In the second example, *many* is incorrect because *fun* is uncountable. This example should say *much fun*.

The following chart lists the key word that indicate to you whether a noun should be countable or uncountable.

KEY WORDS FOR COUNTABLE AND UNCOUNTABLE NOUNS				
FOR COUNTABLE NOUNS	*many*	*number*	*few*	*fewer*
FOR UNCOUNTABLE NOUNS	*much*	*amount*	*little*	*less*

APPENDIX EXERCISE C16: Each of the following sentences contains at least one key word to tell you if a noun should be countable or uncountable. Put parentheses around the key words. Underline the nouns they describe. Then indicate if the sentences are correct (C) or incorrect (I).

__C__ 1. (Many) <u>applicants</u> came to see about the job.

__I__ 2. Today, there is an unusually large (amount) of <u>people</u> in the room. *(number)*

_____ 3. Few suggestions and little help were offered.

_____ 4. We need to have more opportunities and less restrictions.

_____ 5. The official gave us much sincere assurances that we would receive assistance.

_____ 6. A large number of the facts in the report are being disputed.

_____ 7. I have less concern than she does about the much unpaid bills.

_____ 8. There are fewer men than women serving on the committee.

_____ 9. Of the many potential problems, only a little have been resolved.

_____ 10. A huge amount of paper was used to prepare the report.

PRONOUNS

Pronouns are words such as *he, us,* or *them* that take the place of nouns. The following pronoun problems are quite common: (1) distinguishing subject and object pronouns, (2) distinguishing possessive pronouns and possessive determiners, and (3) checking pronoun reference for agreement.

Appendix C17: DISTINGUISH SUBJECT AND OBJECT PRONOUNS

Subject and object pronouns can easily be confused, so you need to think carefully about these pronouns.

PRONOUNS	
SUBJECT	OBJECT
I	me
you	you
he	him
she	her
it	it
we	us
they	them

A subject pronoun is used as the subject of a verb. An object pronoun can be used as the object of a preposition. Compare the following two examples.

> Sally gave the book to John.
> She gave it to him.

In the second sentence, the subject pronoun *she* is replacing the noun *Sally*. The object of the verb *it* is replacing the noun *book,* and the object of the preposition *him* is replacing the noun *John*.

The following are examples of the types of subject or object pronoun errors you might see.

> *Him and me** are going to the movies.
> The secret is between *you and I**.

In the first example, the object pronouns *Him and me* are incorrect because these pronouns serve as the subject of the verb *are*. The object pronouns *Him and me* should be changed to *He and I*. In the second example, the subject pronouns *you and I* are incorrect because these pronouns serve as the object of the preposition *between*. The subject pronouns *you and I* should be changed to *you and me*.

APPENDIX EXERCISE C17: Each of the following sentences contains at least one subject or object pronoun. Put parentheses around the pronouns. Then indicate if the sentences are correct (C) or incorrect (I).

__I__ 1. (Him) and (me) are going to be taking the early bus today.
 (*He and I*)

__C__ 2. (We) will talk to (them), and (they) will listen to (us).

_____ 3. Just between you and I, I think that they made the best decision.

_____ 4. He and she have agreed to assist us with the project that we are trying to complete.

_____ 5. You and I have to try harder to do more for he and her.

_____ 6. It is difficult for we students to complete so many projects.

_____ 7. She said that I did not give it to her, but I am sure that she is wrong.

_____ 8. They sent you and I an invitation, so I think that we should attend the party.

_____ 9. It is not about us; instead, it is all about him and her.

_____ 10. They could not have done any more to help you and I.

Appendix C18: DISTINGUISH POSSESSIVE DETERMINERS AND PRONOUNS

Possessive determiners (or adjectives) and pronouns both show who or what "owns" a noun. However, possessive determiners and possessive pronouns do not have the same function, and these two kinds of possessives can easily be confused. A possessive determiner (or adjective) describes a noun: it must be accompanied by a noun. A possessive pronoun takes the place of a noun. It cannot be accompanied by a noun.

> They lent me _their book_.
>
> They lent me _theirs_.

In the first example, the possessive determiner _their_ is accompanied by the noun _book_. In the second example, the possessive pronoun _theirs_ is not accompanied by a noun.

The following are examples of errors that are possible with possessive determiners and pronouns.

> Each morning they read _theirs*_ newspapers.
>
> Could you lend me _your*_?

In the first example, the possessive pronoun _theirs_ is incorrect because it is accompanied by the noun _newspapers_, and a possessive pronoun cannot be accompanied by a noun. The possessive determiner _their_ is needed in the first example. In the second example, the possessive determiner _your_ is incorrect because it is not accompanied by a noun, and a possessive determiner must be accompanied by a noun. The possessive pronoun _yours_ is needed.

The following chart outlines the possessives and their uses.

POSSESSIVES	
DETERMINERS	PRONOUNS
my	mine
your	yours
his	his
her	hers
its	—
our	ours
their	theirs
must be accompanied by a noun	may not be accompanied by a noun

APPENDIX EXERCISE C18: Each of the following sentences contains at least one possessive pronoun or adjective. Put parentheses around the possessives. Then indicate if the sentences are correct (C) or incorrect (I).

__I__ 1. We must do (our) part to encourage (ours) teammates.
(our teammates)

__C__ 2. I will pick up (your) children when I go to pick up (mine).

_____ 3. I am worried about both his response and hers.

_____ 4. She lost her notes, so she asked to borrow my.

_____ 5. Your explanation is, in my opinion, a bit weak.

_____ 6. Why don't you show them where theirs offices are?

_____ 7. It was my mistake and not your.

_____ 8. He thinks that his argument is more convincing than hers.

_____ 9. If these are not ours keys, then they must be theirs.

_____ 10. Do you think that your answer is better than hers or that her answer is better than yours?

Appendix C19: CHECK PRONOUN REFERENCE FOR AGREEMENT

After you have checked that the subject and object pronouns and the possessives are used correctly, you should also check each of these pronouns and possessives for agreement. The following are examples of errors of this type.

The *boys* will cause trouble if you let *him**.

Everyone must give *their** name.

In the first example, the singular pronoun *him* is incorrect because it refers back to the plural noun *boys*. This pronoun should be replaced with the plural pronoun *them*. In the second example, the plural possessive adjective *their* is incorrect because it refers back to the singular *everyone*. This adjective should be replaced with the singular *his or her*.

The following chart outlines what you should remember about checking pronoun reference.

PRONOUN AGREEMENT
1. Be sure that every pronoun and possessive agrees with the noun it refers to.
2. You generally check back in the sentence for agreement.

APPENDIX EXERCISE C19: Each of the following sentences contains at least one pronoun or possessive. Put parentheses around the pronouns and possessives. Underline any nouns they refer to. Then indicate if the sentences are correct (C) or incorrect (I).

_I_   1. <u>Papers</u> are due today at 5:00; be sure to turn (it) in on time.
     (them)

_C_   2. The <u>party</u> is for (my) <u>neighbors</u>, and (they) know all about (it).

_____ 3. Everyone must submit an application if you want to be considered for the scholarship.

_____ 4. The concert is tonight, and we will be going with our friends to hear them.

_____ 5. The sunshine today is lovely; I enjoy feeling it on my face.

_____ 6. The man has a problem, and he will have to resolve it all by herself.

_____ 7. My friend has a book on that subject, and she said that I could borrow her.

_____ 8. Your brothers have the money, and they know that you want it for yourself.

_____ 9. Each person has their own individual set of fingerprints.

_____ 10. Your classmates will have to finish the project by yourselves.

APPENDIX REVIEW EXERCISE (C15–C19): Indicate if the following sentences are correct (C) or incorrect (I).

_____ 1. She has tried much times to raise a little extra money.

_____ 2. We saw them getting into their car.

_____ 3. Of the two assignments, only one is complete; the other one has many errors in it.

_____ 4. Him and her never even asked us to lend them the money.

_____ 5. She told him about her decision, and he expressed his dissatisfaction with it.

_____ 6. Few issues have raised so many problems.

_____ 7. I have numerous questions about the situation, and I hope you can answer it.

_____ 8. You and I should not open this package because it was not given to you and I.

_____ 9. Many students have tried for perfect grades, but little of them have succeeded.

_____ 10. Our friends are coming to visit us after they visit their parents.

_____ 11. It will take a miracle to meet the various need of each person in the room.

_____ 12. They saw you and me, but we did not see them even though they called out to us.

_____ 13. You have done your part, but they have not done their.

_____ 14. This diet food has less fat and less calories.

_____ 15. We have our reasons, and they have theirs.

ADJECTIVES AND ADVERBS

An adjective is a modifier that is used to describe a noun or pronoun, while an adverb is a modifier that is used to describe a verb, an adjective, or another adverb.

> He is a *nice* man, and he is *generous*.
>
> He is *really* generous, and he *almost always* has a smile on his face.

In the first example, the adjective *nice* is describing the noun *man*, and the adjective *generous* is describing the pronoun *he*. In the second example, the adverb *really* is describing the adjective *generous*, the adverb *almost* is describing the adverb *always*, and the adverb *always* is describing the verb *has*.

Three issues with adjectives and adverbs that it is important to master are the following: (1) the basic uses of adjectives and adverbs, (2) the correct positioning of adjectives and adverbs, and (3) the use of *-ed* and *-ing* verbal adjectives.

Appendix C20: USE BASIC ADJECTIVES AND ADVERBS CORRECTLY

Adjectives and adverbs have very different uses. Adjectives describe nouns and pronouns, and adverbs describe verbs, adjectives, and other adverbs. The following are examples of incorrectly used adjectives and adverbs.

> They were seated at a *largely** table.
>
> The child talked *quick** to her mother.
>
> We read an *extreme** long story.

In the first example, the adverb *largely* is incorrect because the adjective *large* is needed to describe the noun *table*. In the second example, the adjective *quick* is incorrect because the adverb *quickly* is needed to describe the verb *talked*. In the last example, the adjective *extreme* is incorrect because the adverb *extremely* is needed to describe the adjective *long*.

The following chart outlines the important information that you should remember about the basic uses of adjectives and adverbs.

BASIC USES OF ADJECTIVES AND ADVERBS	
ADJECTIVES	Describe nouns or pronouns.
ADVERBS	Describe verbs, adjectives, or other adverbs.

APPENDIX EXERCISE C20: Each of the following sentences has at least one adjective or adverb. Put parentheses around the adjectives and adverbs, and indicate which words they describe. Then indicate if the sentences are correct (C) or incorrect (I).

_____ 1. The race was held under (extreme) (humid) conditions.

    extreme describes humid

    humid describes conditions

    (extremely)

_____ 2. The hungry baby wailed quite plaintively.

hungry describes baby

quite describes plaintively

plaintively describes wailed

_____ 3. We saw a real exciting movie with an unexpected ending.

_____

_____

_____ 4. The striking workers marched slowly and deliberately outside of the locked front gates of the company.

_____

_____

_____

_____ 5. The manager studied the complex issue thoroughly before making the difficultly decision.

_____

_____

_____

_____ 6. The parking lot had recently been resurfaced with thick black asphalt.

_____

_____

_____

_____ 7. We proceeded extremely cautious in order to arrive at a totally acceptable outcome.

_____

_____

_____

_____ 8. The couple decided rather suddenly to alter the plans for their vacation considerable.

_____

_____

_____

_____ 9. The large white building at the end of the circular driveway houses the main office.

_____

_____

_____

_____ 10. Whose brilliantly idea was it to take this supposed shortcut when none of us actually knew where it led?

_____

_____

_____

Appendix C21: POSITION ADJECTIVES AND ADVERBS CORRECTLY

It is important to pay attention to the position of both adjectives and adverbs. In English, a one-word adjective comes before the noun. Look at this example of an incorrectly positioned adjective.

> The information *important** is on the first page.

In this example, the adjective *important* should come before the noun *information* because *important* describes *information*.

Adverbs can be used in many different positions in English, but there is at least one position where an adverb cannot be used. If a verb has an object, then an adverb describing the verb cannot be used between the verb and its object. Look at these examples.

> The man drove *quickly*.
>
> The man drove *quickly** the car.

In the first example, the adverb *quickly* describes the verb *drove*. It is positioned correctly after the verb *drove* because *drove* does not have an object. In the second example, the adverb *quickly* is incorrectly positioned. The adverb *quickly* describes the verb *drove*, but the adverb cannot come directly after the verb because the verb has an object (*car*). To correct the last example, you would have to say *the man drove the car quickly*.

The following chart outlines the key information you should remember about the position of adjectives and adverbs.

THE POSITION OF ADJECTIVES AND ADVERBS	
ADJECTIVES	A one-word adjective comes before the noun it describes.
ADVERBS	An adverb can appear in many positions. One place that an adverb cannot be used is between the verb it describes and the object of the verb.

APPENDIX EXERCISE C21: Each of the following sentences has at least one adjective or adverb. Put parentheses around the adjectives and adverbs, and indicate which words they describe. Then indicate if the sentences are correct (C) or incorrect (I).

___I___ 1. Can you return (immediately) the necklace?

    immediately describes return

    (return the necklace immediately)

    _____

___C___ 2. He is a (serious) man who (always) works (diligently).

    serious describes man

    always describes works

    diligently describes works

_____ 3. The worried mother gently scolded the little girl.

    _____

    _____

    _____

_____ 4. He uses often his checks to pay for purchases.

    _____

    _____

    _____

_____ 5. The lifeguard attentive jumped quickly into the pool.

    _____

    _____

    _____

_____ 6. In the paper, you need to explain the reasons for your hypothesis more clearly.

    _____

    _____

    _____

_____ 7. The accountant studied carefully the figures before preparing the monthly report.

    _____

    _____

    _____

_____ 8. The lawyer skillfully questioned the hostile witness.

    _____

    _____

    _____

_____ 9. I cannot remember always the number of the account.

_____

_____

_____

_____ 10. The temperature dropped suddenly, and the people local bundled up to face the

chilly weather.

_____

_____

_____

Appendix C22: USE -*ED* AND -*ING* ADJECTIVES CORRECTLY

Verb forms ending in -*ed* and -*ing* can be used as adjectives. For example, the verbal adjectives *cleaned* and *cleaning* come from the verb *to clean*.

> The woman *cleans* the car.
>
> The *cleaning* woman worked on the car.
>
> The woman put the *cleaned* car back in the garage.

In the first example, *cleans* is the verb of the sentence. In the second example, *cleaning* is a verbal adjective describing *woman*. In the third example *cleaned* is a verbal adjective describing *car*.

Look at the following examples of incorrectly used -*ing* and -*ed* adjectives.

> The *cleaning** car...
>
> The *cleaned** woman...

The difference between an -*ed* adjective and an -*ing* adjective is similar to the difference between the active and the passive (see C13–C14). An -*ing* adjective (like the active) means that the noun it describes is doing the action. The example above about the *cleaning car* is not correct because a car cannot do the action of cleaning: you cannot say that a car cleans itself. An -*ed* adjective (like the passive) means that the noun it describes is receiving the action from the verb. The example above about the *cleaning woman* is not correct because in this example a woman cannot receive the action of the verb *clean*; this sentence does not mean that *someone cleaned the woman*. To correct the examples above, you should say *the cleaned car* and *the cleaning woman*.

The following chart outlines the key information that you should remember about -*ed* and -*ing* adjectives.

-*ED* AND -*ING* ADJECTIVES			
TYPE	MEANING	USE	EXAMPLE
-*ing*	active	It does the action of the verb.	the happily *playing* children
-*ed*	passive	It receives the action of the verb.	the frequently *played* CD

APPENDIX EXERCISE C22: Each of the following sentences contains either an *-ed* or an *-ing* verbal adjective. Put parentheses around the verbal adjectives, and indicate which words they describe. Then indicate if the sentences are correct (C) or incorrect (I).

_C_   1. The line is long, but at least it is a (fast-moving) line.

fast-moving describes line

_I_   2. The (satisfying) customers thanked the salesperson for the good service.

satisfying describes customers
(satisfied)

_____   3. The people felt shocked as they heard the disturbed news.

_____   4. The delighted girl thanked her friend for the unexpected gift.

_____   5. It was such a depressed situation that no one smiled.

_____   6. The snow-capped mountains ringed the charmed village.

_____   7. An annoying guest made a number of rude comments to the frustrated host.

_____   8. The correcting papers are being returned to the waiting students.

_____ 9. An unidentified attacker tried to rob the strolling couple.

_____

_____

_____

_____ 10. The most requesting room in the hotel is the one with the unobstructing view of

the lake.

_____

_____

_____

ARTICLES

Articles are very difficult to learn because there are many rules, many exceptions, and many special cases. It is possible, however, to learn a few rules that will help you to use articles correctly much of the time.

Nouns in English can be either countable or uncountable. If a noun is countable, it must be either singular or plural. In addition to these general types of nouns, there are two types of articles: definite (specific) and indefinite (general).

ARTICLES	COUNTABLE SINGULAR NOUNS	COUNTABLE PLURAL NOUNS	UNCOUNTABLE NOUNS
INDEFINITE (General)	*a* pen *an* apple	___ pens ___ apples	___ ink ___ juice
DEFINITE (Specific)	*the* pen *the* apple	*the* pens *the* apples	*the* ink *the* juice

Appendix C23: USE ARTICLES WITH SINGULAR NOUNS

You can see from the chart that if a noun is either countable plural or uncountable, it is possible to have either the definite article *the* or no article (indefinite). With <u>all</u> countable singular nouns, however, you must have an article unless you already have another determiner such as *my* or *each*.

> I have *money*. (uncountable — no article needed)
>
> I have *books*. (countable plural — no article needed)
>
> I have *a book*. (countable singular — article needed)

The following chart outlines the key information that you should remember about articles with singular nouns.

ARTICLES WITH SINGULAR NOUNS
A singular noun must have an article (*a, an, the*) or some other determiner such as *my* or *each*. (A plural noun or uncountable noun may or may not have an article.)

APPENDIX EXERCISE C23: The following sentences contain different types of nouns. Underline the countable singular nouns. Put parentheses around any articles in front of the countable singular nouns. Then indicate if the sentences are correct (C) or incorrect (I).

__I__ 1. Man wearing stylish hat is standing at door.
   (*A man . . . a . . . hat . . . the door*)

__C__ 2. I am working on (a) difficult task, and I need help with it.

_____ 3. Sam is taking classes in geography, math, and science as well as holding part-time job.

_____ 4. I need advice about problems that I have been having with my neighbors.

_____ 5. She has funny feeling about surprising event that she just witnessed.

_____ 6. We would like to buy a van that has enough space for a family of six.

_____ 7. In the science course, the students must read textbook, take exams, give presentation, and participate in discussions.

_____ 8. The family likes pets; they have turtles, parakeets, snake, cats, and large dog.

_____ 9. She has a strong opinion about a situation involving acquaintances of ours.

_____ 10. Plants need water and air to grow.

Appendix C24: DISTINGUISH *A* AND *AN*

The basic difference between *a* and *an* is that *a* is used in front of consonant, and *an* is used in front of vowels (a, e, i, o, u).

a **b**ook	*an* **o**range
a **m**an	*an* **i**llness
a **p**age	*an* **a**utomobile

In reality, the rule is that *a* is used in front of a word that begins with a consonant *sound* and that *an* is used in front of a word that begins with a vowel *sound*. Pronounce the following examples.

a university	*a* hand	*a* one-way street	*a* euphemism	*a* xerox machine
an unhappy man	*an* hour	*an* omen	*an* event	*an* x-ray machine

These examples show that certain beginning letters can have either a consonant or a vowel sound. A word that begins with *u* can begin with the consonant sound *y* as in *university* or with a vowel sound as in *unhappy*. A word that begins with *h* can begin with a consonant *h* sound as in *hand* or with a vowel sound as in *hour*. A word that begins with *o* can begin with a consonant *w* sound as in *one* or with a vowel sound as in *omen*. A word that begins with *e* can begin with either a consonant *y* sound as in *euphemism* or with a vowel sound as in *event*. A word that begins with *x* can begin with either a consonant *z* sound as in *xerox* or with a vowel sound as in *x-ray*.

The following chart outlines the key information about the use of *a* and *an*.

A AND *AN*	
A	*A* is used in front of a singular noun that begins with a consonant sound.
AN	*An* is used in front of a singular noun that begins with a vowel sound.
Be careful with words beginning with *u, o, e, x,* or *h.* These words may begin with either a vowel or a consonant sound.	

APPENDIX EXERCISE C24: Each of the following sentences contains at least one *a* or *an*. Put parentheses around each *a* or *an*. Underline the beginning of the word that directly follows. Pronounce the word. Then indicate if the sentences are correct (C) or incorrect (I).

_C_ 1. You have (an) <u>op</u>portunity to attend (a) <u>one</u>-time event.

_I_ 2. He made (a) <u>mi</u>stake, but it was (a) <u>hon</u>est mistake.
    (an honest mistake)

_____ 3. They are staying in a hotel with a jacuzzi, a sauna, and a heated pool.

_____ 4. It is a honor to be a guest at such a important celebration.

_____ 5. The family is planning a once-in-a-lifetime trip to a faraway country.

_____ 6. Is this a usual occurrence or a unusual occurrence?

_____ 7. The party decorations included a colorful banner, a hand-painted sign, and a helium balloon.

_____ 8. She had an euphoric feeling after she unexpectedly won an huge sum of money.

_____ 9. A person who is unable to write may use a X rather than a signature when signing a document.

_____ 10. The class read a traditional story about a unicorn that saved a helpless child.

Appendix C25: MAKE ARTICLES AGREE WITH NOUNS

The definite article (*the*) is used for both singular and plural nouns, so agreement is not a problem with the definite article. However, because the use of the indefinite article is different for singular and plural nouns, you must be careful of agreement between the indefinite article and the noun. One very common agreement error is to use the singular definite article (*a* or *an*) with a plural noun.

> He saw *a* new movies*.
>
> They traveled to *a** nearby *mountains*.
>
> Do you have *another* books*?

In these examples, you should not have *a* or *an* because the nouns are plural. The following sentences are possible corrections of the sentences above.

He saw a new movie.	(singular)
He saw new movies.	(plural)
They traveled to a nearby mountain.	(singular)
They traveled to nearby mountains.	(plural)
Do you have another book?	(singular)
Do you have other books?	(plural)

The following chart outlines the key point for you to remember about the agreement of articles with nouns.

AGREEMENT OF ARTICLES WITH NOUNS
You should never use *a* or *an* with a plural noun.

APPENDIX EXERCISE C25: Each of the following sentences contains *a* or *an*. Put parentheses around each *a* or *an*. Underline the noun that it describes. Then indicate if the sentences are correct (C) or incorrect (I).

__I__ 1. The team needs (a) new uniforms before the start of the season.
(a new uniform OR *new uniforms)*

__C__ 2. I need to buy pens, pencils, (a) notebook, and (a) textbook.

_____ 3. They are buying a new house with a swimming pool, with a roomy balconies, and with a wonderful views from the balconies.

_____ 4. The visiting professor shared an interesting new theories.

_____ 5. The office has a computer, a phone, a table and chairs, and office supplies.

_____ 6. The mother told her children a bedtime stories, gave them gentle kisses, and then tucked them into bed.

_____ 7. She went shopping and bought a new dress, a new shoes, a new purse, and a new earrings.

_____ 8. I have a good reason for answering questions this way.

_____ 9. The hostess served her guests tea and a vanilla biscuits.

_____ 10. The executive needs a secretary to prepare reports and take phone messages.

Appendix C26: DISTINGUISH SPECIFIC AND GENERAL IDEAS

With countable singular nouns, it is possible to use either the definite or the indefinite article, but the definite and indefinite articles will have different meanings. The definite article is used to refer to one specific noun.

> Tom will bring *the* book tomorrow.
> (There is one specific book that Tom will bring tomorrow.)
>
> He will arrive on *the* first Tuesday in July.
> (There is only one first Tuesday in July.)
>
> He sailed on *the* Pacific Ocean.
> (There is only one Pacific Ocean.)

The definite article is used when the noun could be one of several different nouns.

> Tom will bring *a* book tomorrow.
> (Tom will bring any one book tomorrow.)
>
> He will arrive on *a* Tuesday in July.
> (He will arrive on one of the four or five Tuesdays in July.)
>
> He sailed on *an* ocean.
> (He sailed on any one of the world's oceans.)

The following chart outlines the key information that you should understand about specific and general ideas.

SPECIFIC AND GENERAL IDEAS		
A or *AN*	general idea	Use when there are many, and you do not know which one it is. Use when there are many, and you do not care which one.
THE	specific idea	Use when it is the only one. Use when there are many, and you know which one it is.

APPENDIX EXERCISE C26: Each of the following sentences contains one or more articles. Put parentheses around each article. Underline the noun it describes. Then indicate if the sentences are correct (C) or incorrect (I).

__I__ 1. We took (a) balloon ride over (an) African continent.
(the African continent)

__C__ 2. Last evening, my friends and I went to see (a) movie that had (a) very unusual ending.

_____ 3. Today there is a big dark cloud in a sky.

_____ 4. The spacecraft that was recently launched is heading toward a planet Mars.

_____ 5. The teacher stood in a middle of the classroom and talked to the students.

_____ 6. Can you think of an idea for a topic for an interesting research paper?

_____ 7. I would like to stay in a same hotel that we stayed in a last time that we visited here.

_____ 8. A hat that you are wearing now is really quite a cute hat.

_____ 9. We won a prize for a best essay in the school's essay contest.

_____ 10. After the man standing over there was punched in a nose, he suffered a bloody nose.

APPENDIX REVIEW EXERCISE (C20–C26): Indicate if the following sentences are correct (C) or incorrect (I).

_____ 1. She offered an apology for a unbelievably rude comment.

_____ 2. The recipe calls for sugar, eggs, butter, flour, and vanilla.

_____ 3. The forgetful man misplaces often his keys.

_____ 4. An engine of the car that I am driving is making a funny noises.

_____ 5. The customer became increasingly impatient as she stood in an unmoving line.

_____ 6. A friend of mine works as an orderly in a hospital.

_____ 7. His job provides a good salary and a substantial benefits.

_____ 8. The student triumphantly finished the final part of the project and then turned the completed paper in.

_____ 9. She is taking an undergraduate course at nearby university.

_____ 10. The really angry father explained explicitly why his son's behavior was unacceptable.

_____ 11. It is delight to be a part of such a wonderful organization.

_____ 12. The unmaking beds and the unwashing dishes need some attention.

_____ 13. A dinner guest seated at the table should have a plate, a glass, a napkin, and eating utensils.

_____ 14. The teacher collected swiftly the exams from the anxious students.

_____ 15. At the school assembly this morning, a school principal gave speech to the students.

SCORES AND CHARTS

SCORING INFORMATION

Scoring 1: UNDERSTAND OVERALL SCORES

The highest possible score on the *iBT* TOEFL test is 120. Each of the four sections (Reading, Listening, Speaking, and Writing) receives a scaled score from 0 to 30. The scaled scores from the four sections are added together to determine the overall score.

Scoring 2: DETERMINE READING AND LISTENING PRE- AND POST-TEST SCALED SCORES

To determine a scaled score in a Reading or Listening Pre- or Post-Test section, you must first determine the number of points you received in the section. In Listening, you simply need to count the number of questions you answered correctly (out of 12) because the number of points is the number of questions you answered correctly. In Reading, you must determine the number of points you receive on the last two questions before you can determine the total number of points. The last two questions are chart questions that are worth more than one point, and you may received partial credit for a partially correct answer. (For example, perhaps a question is worth three points and has 6 correct answers. If you correctly answer all 6, then you get 3 points. If you correctly answer 4 or 5, then you get 2 points. If you correctly answer 2 or 3, then you get 1 point. If you correctly answer 0 or 1, then you get 0 points.) After you have determined the number of points you have earned on the last two questions, add this number to the number correct on questions 1 through 18 to determine your total points out of 25. When you know the total points you received in a Reading or Listening Pre- or Post-Test section, you can refer to the following chart to determine your scaled score out of 30 for this section.

TOTAL POINTS	READING SCALED SCORE	LISTENING SCALED SCORE	TOTAL POINTS	READING SCALED SCORE	LISTENING SCALED SCORE
25	30	—	12	14	30
24	29	—	11	13	27
23	28	—	10	12	24
22	26	—	9	11	21
21	25	—	8	10	18
20	24	—	7	8	15
19	23	—	6	7	13
18	21	—	5	6	11
17	20	—	4	5	9
16	19	—	3	4	6
15	21	—	2	2	4
14	17	—	1	1	2
13	16	—	0	0	0

Scoring 3: DETERMINE READING AND LISTENING MINI-TEST SCALED SCORES

To determine a scaled score in a Reading or Listening Mini-Test section, you must first determine the number of points you received in the section. In Listening, you simply need to count the number of questions you answered correctly (out of 11) because the number of points is the number of questions you answered correctly. In Reading, you must determine the number of points you receive on the last question before you can determine the total number of points. The last question is a chart question that is worth more than one point, and you may receive partial credit for a partially correct answer. (For example, perhaps a question is worth three points and has 6 correct answers. If you correctly answer all 6, then you get 3 points. If you correctly answer 4 or 5, then you get 2 points. If you correctly answer 2 or 3, then you get 1 point. If you correctly answer 0 or 1, then you get 0 points.) After you have determined the number of points you have earned on the last question, add this number to the number correct on questions 1 through 12 to determine your total points out of 15. When you know the total points you received in a Reading or Listening Mini-Test section, you can refer to the following chart to determine your scaled score out of 30 for this section.

TOTAL POINTS	READING SCALED SCORE	LISTENING SCALED SCORE	TOTAL POINTS	READING SCALED SCORE	LISTENING SCALED SCORE
15	30	—	7	8	15
14	28	—	6	7	13
13	25	—	5	5	9
12	22	—	4	4	6
11	19	30	3	2	4
10	16	26	2	1	2
9	14	23	1	1	1
8	11	19	0	0	0

Scoring 4: DETERMINE READING AND LISTENING COMPLETE TEST SCORES

To determine a scaled score in a Reading or Listening Complete Test section, you must first determine the number of points you received in the section. In Listening, you simply need to count the number of questions you answered correctly (out of 34) because the number of points is the number of questions you answered correctly. In Reading, you must determine the number of points you received on the last question of each reading (numbers 13, 26, and 39) before you can determine the total number of points. The last question of each reading is a chart question that is worth more than one point, and you may receive partial credit for a partially correct answer. (For example, perhaps a question is worth three points and has 6 correct answers. If you correctly answer all 6, then you get 3 points. If you correctly answer 4 or 5, then you get 2 points. If you correctly answer 2 or 3, then you get 1 point. If you correctly answer 0 or 1, then you get 0 points.) After you have determined the number of points you have earned on the chart questions, add this number to the number correct on the rest of questions 1 through 39 to determine your total points out of 45. When you know the total points you received in a Reading or Listening Mini-Test section, you can refer to the following chart to determine your scaled score out of 30 for this section.

TOTAL POINTS	READING SCALED SCORE	LISTENING SCALED SCORE	TOTAL POINTS	READING SCALED SCORE	LISTENING SCALED SCORE
45	30	—	22	9	15
44	29	—	21	8	15
43	29	—	20	8	14
42	28	—	19	7	13
41	27	—	18	7	11
40	26	—	17	6	9
39	25	—	16	6	8
38	24	—	15	5	8
37	23	—	14	5	7
36	22	—	13	4	6
35	21	—	12	4	5
34	20	30	11	3	4
33	19	29	10	3	4
32	18	27	9	2	3
31	17	26	8	2	3
30	16	25	7	1	2
29	16	24	6	1	2
28	15	23	5	0	1
27	14	22	4	0	0
26	13	21	3	0	0
25	12	19	2	0	0
24	11	17	1	0	0
23	10	16	0	0	0

Scoring 5: UNDERSTAND WRITING SCORING CRITERIA

In the Writing section, you will receive a score of 0 through 5; this score of 0 through 5 will then be converted to a scaled score out of 30. The criteria for Writing scores of 0 through 5 are listed below.

5	ANSWER TO QUESTION	The student answers the question thoroughly.
	COMPREHENSIBILITY	The student can be understood completely.
	ORGANIZATION	The student's response is maturely organized and developed.
	FLOW OF IDEAS	The student's ideas flow cohesively.
	GRAMMAR	The student uses advanced grammatical structures with a high degree of accuracy.
	VOCABULARY	The student uses advanced vocabulary with a high degree of accuracy.
4	ANSWER TO QUESTION	The student answers the question adequately but not thoroughly.
	COMPREHENSIBILITY	The student can generally be understood.
	ORGANIZATION	The student's response is adequately organized and developed.
	FLOW OF IDEAS	The student's ideas generally flow cohesively.
	GRAMMAR	The student uses either accurate easier grammatical structures or more advanced grammatical structures with a few errors.
	VOCABULARY	The student uses either accurate easier vocabulary or more advanced vocabulary with some errors.
3	ANSWER TO QUESTION	The student gives a basically accurate response to the question.
	COMPREHENSIBILITY	The student's basic ideas can be understood.
	ORGANIZATION	The student's response is organized basically and is not thoroughly developed.
	FLOW OF IDEAS	The student's ideas flow cohesively sometimes and at other times do not.
	GRAMMAR	The student has a number of errors in grammar or uses only very basic grammar fairly accurately.
	VOCABULARY	The student has a number of errors in vocabulary or uses only very basic vocabulary fairly accurately.

2	ANSWER TO QUESTION	The student discusses information from the task but does not answer the question directly.
	COMPREHENSIBILITY	The student's ideas are not always intelligible.
	ORGANIZATION	The student's response is not clearly organized and is incomplete or contains some inaccurate points.
	FLOW OF IDEAS	The student's ideas often do not flow cohesively.
	GRAMMAR	The student has numerous errors in grammar that interfere with meaning.
	VOCABULARY	The student has numerous errors in vocabulary that interfere with meaning.
1	ANSWER TO QUESTION	The student's response is only slightly related to the topic.
	COMPREHENSIBILITY	The student's ideas are occasionally intelligible.
	ORGANIZATION	The student's response is not clearly organized and is only minimally on the topic.
	FLOW OF IDEAS	The student's ideas do not flow smoothly.
	GRAMMAR	The student produces very little grammatically correct language.
	VOCABULARY	The student uses very little vocabulary correctly.
0	The student either writes nothing or fails to answer the question.	

Scoring 6: UNDERSTAND SPEAKING SCORING CRITERIA

In the Speaking section, you will receive a score of 0 through 4; this score of 0 through 4 will then be converted to a scaled score out of 30. The criteria for Speaking scores of 0 through 4 are listed below.

4	ANSWER TO QUESTION	The student answers the question thoroughly.
	COMPREHENSIBILITY	The student can be understood completely.
	ORGANIZATION	The student's response is well organized and developed.
	FLUENCY	The student's speech is generally fluent.
	PRONUNCIATION	The student has generally good pronunciation.
	GRAMMAR	The student uses advanced grammatical structures with a high degree of accuracy.
	VOCABULARY	The student uses advanced vocabulary with a high degree of accuracy.
3	ANSWER TO QUESTION	The student answers the questions adequately but not thoroughly.
	COMPREHENSIBILITY	The student can generally be understood.
	ORGANIZATION	The student's response is organized basically and is not thoroughly developed.
	FLUENCY	The student's speech is generally fluent, with minor problems.
	PRONUNCIATION	The student has generally good pronunciation, with minor problems.
	GRAMMAR	The student uses either accurate easier grammatical structures or more advanced grammatical structures with some errors.
	VOCABULARY	The student uses either accurate easier vocabulary or more advanced vocabulary with some errors.

2	ANSWER TO QUESTION	The student discusses information from the task but does not answer the question directly.
	COMPREHENSIBILITY	The student is not always intelligible.
	ORGANIZATION	The student's response is not clearly organized and is incomplete or contains some inaccurate points.
	FLUENCY	The student's speech is not very fluent and has a number of problems.
	PRONUNCIATION	The student's pronunciation is not very clear, with a number of problems.
	GRAMMAR	The student has a number of errors in grammar or uses only very basic grammar fairly accurately.
	VOCABULARY	The student has a number of errors in vocabulary or uses only very basic vocabulary fairly accurately.
1	ANSWER TO QUESTION	The student's response is only slightly related to the topic.
	COMPREHENSIBILITY	The student is only occasionally intelligible.
	ORGANIZATION	The student's response is not clearly organized and is only minimally on the topic.
	FLUENCY	The student has problems with fluency that make the response difficult to understand.
	PRONUNCIATION	The student has problems with pronunciation that make the response difficult to understand.
	GRAMMAR	The student has numerous errors in grammar that interfere with meaning.
	VOCABULARY	The student has numerous errors in vocabulary that interfere with meaning.
0	The student either says nothing or fails to answer the question.	

Scoring 7: ESTIMATE SPEAKING AND WRITING PRE- AND POST- TEST AND COMPLETE TEST SCORES

One way to estimate Writing and Speaking Pre- and Post-Test and Complete Test scaled scores is to use the Self-Assessment Checklists on pages 546–553. (Estimated Speaking and Writing Complete Test scores on the CD-ROM are also based on the Self-Assessment Checklists.) After you have completed a Speaking or Writing Complete Test section, you should evaluate your responses by putting checkmarks next to what you did well on in your responses on the Self-Assessment Checklist. Then count the number of checks you made out of 14 in Writing or out of 36 in Speaking. After you have counted the number of checks, you can refer to the following chart to determine your scaled score out of 30 for this section.

CHECKS	WRITING SCALED SCORE	SPEAKING SCALED SCORE	CHECKS	WRITING SCALED SCORE	SPEAKING SCALED SCORE
36	—	30	17	—	11
35	—	29	16	—	10
34	—	28	15	—	9
33	—	27	14	30	8
32	—	26	13	28	7
31	—	25	12	25	6
30	—	24	11	23	5
29	—	23	10	21	5
28	—	22	9	19	4
27	—	21	8	17	4
26	—	20	7	14	3
25	—	19	6	12	3
24	—	18	5	10	2
23	—	17	4	8	2
22	—	16	3	5	1
21	—	15	2	3	1
20	—	14	1	1	0
19	—	13	0	0	0
18	—	12			

Scoring 8: ESTIMATE SPEAKING AND WRITING MINI-TEST SCORES

One way to estimate Speaking and Writing Mini-Test scaled scores is to use the Self-Assessment Checklists on pages 546–553. (Estimated Speaking and Writing Mini-Test scores on the CD-ROM are also based on the Self-Assessment Checklists.) After you have completed a Speaking or Writing Mini-Test section, you should evaluate your responses by putting checkmarks next to what you did well on in your responses on the Self-Assessment Checklist. Then count the number of checks you made out of 7 in Writing or out of 18 in Speaking. After you have counted the number of checks, you can refer to the following chart to determine your scaled score out of 30 for this section.

CHECKS	WRITING SCALED SCORE	SPEAKING SCALED SCORE	CHECKS	WRITING SCALED SCORE	SPEAKING SCALED SCORE
18	—	30	8	—	10
17	—	28	7	30	8
16	—	26	6	25	6
15	—	24	5	21	5
14	—	22	4	17	4
13	—	20	3	12	3
12	—	18	2	8	2
11	—	16	1	3	1
10	—	14	0	0	0
9	—	12			

READING SKILLS CHART

Circle the number of each of the questions that you *answered incorrectly* or *were unsure of*. Then you will see which skills you need to review.

	PRE-TEST	POST-TEST	MINI-TESTS								COMPLETE TESTS					
			1	2	3	4	5	6	7	8	1–1	1–2	1–3	2–1	2–2	2–3
SKILL 1	3 9 16 17	2 8 11 15	1 2 4 7 12	1 2 6 8 11	1 4 6 9 11	1 2 4 6 10	2 4 6 7 10	2 3 6 10 12	1 3 6 7 9	1 4 6 8 12	1 3 6 9 12	1 4 7 8 10	1 4 5 9 11	1 3 6 7 9	1 4 6 8 10	1 4 6 8 10
SKILL 2	11 14	6 17	8	3	3	11	11	4	10	2	10	3	6	4	2	9
SKILL 3	4 13	7 12	5	7	12	8	3	11	11	3	11	12	2	11	11	12
SKILL 4	8 18	5 16	11	9	10	7	5	8	12	9	7	9	10	10	3	5
SKILL 5	5 15	10 14	6	4	8	5	1	1	5	11	8	2	8	2	9	11
SKILL 6	1 10	3 18	3	10	2	3	12	5	8	5	2	5	7	5	5	7
SKILL 7	6 7	4 9	9	12	5	12	9	9	2	7	4	11	12	12	12	3
SKILL 8	2 12	1 13	10	5	7	9	8	7	4	10	5	6	3	8	7	2
SKILL 9	20	19	13		13		13				13	13			13	
SKILL 10	19	20		13		13	13		13	13			13	13		13

LISTENING SKILLS CHART

Circle the number of each of the questions that you *answered incorrectly* or *were unsure of.* Then you will see which skills you need to review.

	PRE-TEST	POST-TEST	MINI-TESTS 1	2	3	4	5	6	7	8	COMPLETE TESTS 1–10	11–22	23–34	1–10	11–22	23–34
SKILL 1	1 7	1 7	1	6	1	1 6	1 6	1	1	2	1 6	11 17	23 29	1 6	11 17	23
SKILL 2	2 8	4 9	3 5 8 9 10	1 9	2 4 8 9 11	3 4 7 9 10	4 5 7 8 11	4 8 9 11	3 4 8 9	3 5 6 8 9	4 8 9	12 15 16 19 20 21	26 27 30 31 33	2 3 4 5 8 10	12 14 16 20 22	24 26 30 31
SKILL 3	3 9	2 8	2 6	4 8		2 11	3 9	2 10	5 10	10	3	18	24	7	13	33
SKILL 4	4 11	5 10	4	2 11	3		3 5	2		1 4		13	34		18	28
SKILL 5	5 10	3 11	7	3 7 10	6 7	8	2 10	6 7	7 11	7	2	14 22	25 28 32	9	15 19 21	25 29 32
SKILL 6	6 12	6 12	11	5	5 10	5			6	11	5 7 10					27 34

SPEAKING SELF-ASSESSMENT CHECKLISTS _____

After you complete each speaking task, put check marks in the appropriate boxes in the following checklists.

Integrated Task, Free Choice: Skills 1–2	PRE-TEST, Question 1	REVIEW EXERCISE (Skills 1–2)	POST-TEST, Question 1	MINI-TEST 1, Question 1	MINI-TEST 3, Question 1	MINI-TEST 5, Question 1	MINI-TEST 7, Question 1	COMPLETE TEST 1, Question 1	COMPLETE TEST 2, Question 1
SKILL 1 I read the **question** carefully.									
SKILL 1 I used careful **planning** to outline my response.									
SKILL 2 I began with the overall **topic statement**.									
SKILL 2 I used strong **supporting ideas**.									
SKILL 2 I used **transitions** to connect the supporting ideas.									

SPEAKING SELF-ASSESSMENT CHECKLISTS _____

Integrated Task, Paired Choice: Skills 3–4	PRE-TEST, Question 2	REVIEW EXERCISE (Skills 3–4)	POST-TEST, Question 2	MINI-TEST 2, Question 1	MINI-TEST 4, Question 1	MINI-TEST 6, Question 1	MINI-TEST 8, Question 1	COMPLETE TEST 1, Question 2	COMPLETE TEST 2, Question 2
SKILL 3 I read the **question** carefully.									
SKILL 3 I used careful **planning** to outline my response.									
SKILL 4 I began with the overall **topic statement**.									
SKILL 4 I used strong **supporting ideas**.									
SKILL 4 I used **transitions** to connect the supporting ideas.									

SPEAKING SELF-ASSESSMENT CHECKLISTS

Independent Tasks, Reading and Listening: Skills 5–8

	PRE-TEST, Question 3	REVIEW EXERCISE (5–8)	POST-TEST, Question 3	MINI-TEST 1, Question 2	MINI-TEST 3, Question 2	MINI-TEST 5, Question 2	MINI-TEST 7, Question 2	COMPLETE TEST 1, Question 3	COMPLETE TEST 2, Question 3
SKILL 5 I noted the **main points** of the **reading passage**.									
SKILL 6 I noted the **main points** of the **listening passage**.									
SKILL 7 I read the **question** carefully.									
SKILL 7 I used careful **planning** to outline my response.									
SKILL 8 I began with an overall **topic statement**.									
SKILL 8 I used strong **supporting ideas**.									
SKILL 8 I used **transitions** to connect the supporting ideas.									

SPEAKING SELF-ASSESSMENT CHECKLISTS

Independent Tasks, Reading and Listening: Skills 9–12	PRE-TEST, Question 4	REVIEW EXERCISE (9–12)	POST-TEST, Question 4	MINI-TEST 2, Question 2	MINI-TEST 4, Question 2	MINI-TEST 6, Question 2	MINI-TEST 8, Question 2	COMPLETE TEST 1, Question 4	COMPLETE TEST 2, Question 4
SKILL 9 I noted the **main points** of the **reading passage**.									
SKILL 10 I noted the **main points** of the **listening passage**.									
SKILL 11 I read the **question** carefully.									
SKILL 11 I used careful **planning** to outline my response.									
SKILL 12 I began with an overall **topic statement**.									
SKILL 12 I used strong **supporting ideas**.									
SKILL 12 I used **transitions** to connect the supporting ideas.									

SPEAKING SELF-ASSESSMENT CHECKLISTS

Independent Tasks, Listening: Skills 13–15								
	PRE-TEST, Question 5	REVIEW EXERCISE (13–15)	POST-TEST, Question 5	MINI-TEST 1, Question 3	MINI-TEST 3, Question 3	MINI-TEST 5, Question 3	MINI-TEST 7, Question 3	COMPLETE TEST 1, Question 5	COMPLETE TEST 2, Question 5
SKILL 13 I noted the **main points** of the **listening passage**.									
SKILL 14 I read the **question** carefully.									
SKILL 14 I used careful **planning** to outline my response.									
SKILL 15 I began with an overall **topic statement**.									
SKILL 15 I used strong **supporting** ideas.									
SKILL 15 I used **transitions** to connect the supporting ideas.									

SPEAKING SELF-ASSESSMENT CHECKLISTS

Independent Tasks, Listening: Skills 16–18									
	PRE-TEST, Question 6	REVIEW EXERCISE (16–18)	POST-TEST, Question 6	MINI-TEST 2, Question 3	MINI-TEST 4, Question 3	MINI-TEST 6, Question 3	MINI-TEST 8, Question 3	COMPLETE TEST 1, Question 6	COMPLETE TEST 2, Question 6
SKILL 16 I noted the **main points** of the **listening passage**.									
SKILL 17 I read the **question** carefully.									
SKILL 17 I used careful **planning** to outline my response.									
SKILL 18 I began with an overall **topic statement**.									
SKILL 18 I used strong **supporting** ideas.									
SKILL 18 I used **transitions** to connect the supporting ideas.									

WRITING SELF-ASSESSMENT CHECKLISTS _____

After you complete each writing task, put check marks in the appropriate boxes in the following checklists.

		PRE-TEST, Question 1	REVIEW EXERCISE (1–7)	POST-TEST, Question 1	MINI-TEST 1	MINI-TEST 3	MINI-TEST 5	MINI-TEST 7	COMPLETE TEST 1, Question 1	COMPLETE TEST 2, Question 1
Integrated Tasks: Skills 1–7										
SKILL 1	I noted the **main points of the reading** passage.									
SKILL 2	I noted the **main points of the listening** passage.									
SKILL 3	I used careful **planning** to outline my response.									
SKILL 4	I began with the overall **topic statement**.									
SKILL 5	I wrote unified **supporting paragraphs**.									
SKILL 6	I checked the **sentence structure** in my response.									
SKILL 7	I checked the **grammar** in my response.									

WRITING SELF-ASSESSMENT CHECKLISTS _____

	Independent Tasks: Skills 8–14								
	PRE-TEST, Question 2	REVIEW EXERCISE (8–14)	POST-TEST, Question 2	MINI-TEST 2	MINI-TEST 4	MINI-TEST 6	MINI-TEST 8	COMPLETE TEST 1, Question 2	COMPLETE TEST 2, Question 2
SKILL 8 I used careful **planning** to outline my response.									
SKILL 9 I included the topic and organization in the **introduction**.									
SKILL 10 I wrote unified **supporting paragraphs**.									
SKILL 11 I used **transitions** to connect the supporting paragraphs.									
SKILL 12 I summarized the main points in the **conclusion**.									
SKILL 13 I checked the **sentence structure** in my response.									
SKILL 14 I checked the **grammar** in my response.									

PROGRESS CHART

Each time that you take a Pre-Test, a Post-Test, a Mini-Test, or a Complete Test, you should record the results in the chart that follows. In this way, you will be able to keep track of the progress you are making.

	READING	LISTENING	SPEAKING	WRITING
Pre-Test				
Post-Test				
Mini-Test 1				
Mini-Test 2				
Mini-Test 3				
Mini-Test 4				
Mini-Test 5				
Mini-Test 6				
Mini-Test 7				
Mini-Test 8				
Complete Test 1				
Complete Test 2				

RECORDING SCRIPT

LISTENING DIAGNOSTIC PRE-TEST

Questions 1 through 6. Listen to a discussion between a student and an advisor.

(advisor) Hi, Brad, thanks for coming in.

(student) No problem. What did you want to see me about?

(advisor) Well, I saw your mid-semester grade report, and there was something of a problem on it.

(student) You mean my history class?

(advisor) Yes, exactly. . . . You do understand that there's a problem in your history class, don't you? What is the problem? You're doing fairly well in your other classes, but in history you're, frankly, not doing very well at all. Your grades in your other classes show that you're capable of doing good work. What's the problem in history?

(student) Well, history's so early in the morning.

(advisor) It's at nine o'clock; that's not so early.

(student) It seems early to me.

(advisor) So, set your alarm clock . . . This brings up a question, by the way . . . you do get up and go to history class, don't you?

(student) Usually.

(advisor) Usually? Since it's a class you're not doing well in, you should be there all the time.

(student) I'll try.

(advisor) And take a seat in the front of the class near the professor so you can get involved in the class.

(student) But it's such a big class. You have to get there early to get a seat in the front.

(advisor) *(smiles)* Well, maybe you should try getting there early. . . .

(student) I'll try. . . .

(advisor) And get there early for every class. . . .

(student) I'll try that, too.

(advisor) Now, is that your only problem in the class, that you miss class sometimes and get there late other times?

(student) No, not exactly.

(advisor) What else is a problem?

(student) Well, I didn't, uh, I . . . I didn't do too well on the exam.

(advisor) And what was your problem, do you think?

(student) I studied for the exam, I really did. . . . But there were a lot of questions on the exam that weren't in the class textbook, in the chapters that were covered on the exam. At least half the questions on the exam weren't from the book.

(advisor) Do you understand why?

(student) I think there must've been a lot of questions from the lectures, stuff that wasn't covered in the text.

(advisor) Are you sure?

(student) No, but I think so.

(advisor) Well, maybe you should check with the professor and find out if that's the case.

(student) OK.

(advisor) And if it is, maybe you should concentrate on taking good notes during the lectures.

(student) OK.

(advisor) And of course you should be in class all the time to take good notes.

(student) That's for sure.

(advisor) OK, so check back with me in a couple of weeks, and let me know how you're handling this.

(student) I'll do that.

1. WHY DOES THE ADVISOR WANT TO TALK WITH THE STUDENT?
2. WHAT PROBLEMS DOES THE STUDENT HAVE?
3. LISTEN AGAIN TO PART OF THE PASSAGE. THEN ANSWER THE QUESTION.

   (advisor) This brings up a question, by the way, you do get up and go to history class, don't you?

   (student) Usually.

   (advisor) Usually?

   WHAT DOES THE ADVISOR MEAN WHEN SHE SAYS THIS:

   (advisor) Usually?

4. HOW DOES THE ADVISOR SEEM TO FEEL ABOUT THE STUDENT'S RESPONSES?
5. DOES THE ADVISOR RECOMMEND EACH OF THESE?
6. WHAT CAN BE CONCLUDED FROM THE CONVERSATION?

Questions 7 through 12. Listen as an instructor leads a discussion of some material from a psychology class.

(instructor) Today, we're going to review the characteristics of sleep, in both humans and other types of living beings. We talked about this some in the last class, and you should have done the reading, so this should all be clear to you. First of all, what are the main characteristics of sleep? Let's talk about this diagram. ❶ What happens to the human body when a person is sleeping? Uh . . . can you start this off for us, Pam?

(Pam) Well, during sleep, the, um, muscles relax, both breathing and heart rate slow down, and . . . brain waves change.

(instructor) Exactly. Now, let's look at these drawings of brain wave patterns. ❷ Ron, can you explain how brain waves change?

(Ron) I think so. The brain of a person who's awake and relaxed gives off about 10 small waves per second, like in the drawing on the left. But it's different in deep sleep.

(instructor) What's different about deep sleep?

(Ron)	Well, I think that in deep sleep, the, uh, brain waves become much slower and larger, like in the drawing on the right.
(instructor)	Well . . . you don't sound quite sure of your answers, Ron, but you've got them exactly right. Brain waves are the slowest and largest during the first few hours of a period of sleep. This is called the period of slow-wave sleep. Are brain waves always large and slow during sleep? Nancy?
(Nancy)	No, um, there are periods of small and fast waves at intervals during a period of sleep. These short and fast waves are similar to the brain waves of a person who's awake.
(instructor)	And what happens to the eyes during these periods of fast brain activity?
(Pam)	The sleeper's eyes move rapidly. This is called "rapid-eye-movement sleep" or REM sleep.
(instructor)	Yes, Pam, exactly. And what other name does the period of REM, or rapid-eye-movement, sleep have?
(Pam)	REM sleep is called "dreaming sleep" because this is when dreaming occurs.
(instructor)	OK, let's stop for a moment and make sure it's all clear so far. . . . We've seen that when a person sleeps, there're different types of brain-wave activity. There're periods of large, slow brain waves during deep sleep, and there're periods of small, fast brain waves during REM, or dreaming, sleep. Now, we're going to compare human sleep patterns with the sleep patterns of certain animals. What can you tell me about the sleep patterns of mammals, Ron?
(Ron)	Mammals seem to experience true sleep, with changes in brain-wave patterns. They have periods of dreaming sleep and periods of slow-wave sleep.
(instructor)	And what about reptiles and fish? Nancy?
(Nancy)	Reptiles also experience sleep with changes in brain-wave patterns, but they don't seem to have periods of dreaming sleep. Fish have periods when they become less aware of their surroundings, but, um, there's no scientific evidence of changes in brain waves.
(instructor)	❸ Excellent. Now, Pam, let's see if you can summarize the information for us. Which types of animals seem to experience changes in brain waves while they're sleeping?
(Pam)	Humans, of course, and also mammals, birds, and reptiles. Fish don't seem to experience changes in brain waves.
(instructor)	And what about periods of dreaming?
(Pam)	Again, humans, of course, experience periods of dreaming, and most mammals seem to experience the same type of dreaming, with periods of dreaming sleep and periods of slow-wave sleep.

	Birds may experience short periods of dreaming, but reptiles and fish don't.
(instructor)	That's very good. That's all for today.

7. WHAT DOES THE INSTRUCTOR MAINLY WANT TO GET ACROSS IN THE DISCUSSION?
8. WHAT HAPPENS DURING HUMAN SLEEP?
9. WHAT DOES THE INSTRUCTOR MEAN WHEN HE SAYS THIS:

(instructor)	OK, let's stop for a moment and make sure it's all clear so far.

10. HOW LONG ARE THE PERIODS OF DREAMING FOR EACH OF THESE GROUPS OF ANIMALS?
11. HOW DOES THE PROFESSOR SEEM TO FEEL ABOUT THE STUDENTS' RESPONSES?
12. WHAT CONCLUSION CAN BE DRAWN FROM THE DISCUSSION?

EXAMPLE (Listening Skill 1)

Listen as a student talks to his advisor.

(student)	I see that a comprehensive exam is required for my major, and I'm not exactly sure what a comprehensive exam is.
(advisor)	A comprehensive exam is an exam that you take in the final quarter of your studies. Its purpose is to determine your overall competency.
(student)	How is this comprehensive exam different from a final exam?
(advisor)	A final exam covers all the material taught in a specific course; a comprehensive exam, on the other hand, covers all of the materials taught in the entire program.
(student)	And it's true that the comprehensive exam is required for my major? It's not an option?
(advisor)	(laughs) No, it's not an option. A comprehensive exam isn't required for all majors at this university, but it is required for your major. Sorry, it's not optional.

1. WHY DOES THE STUDENT GO TO SEE THE ADVISOR?
2. WHAT IS THE TOPIC OF THIS CONVERSATION?

LISTENING EXERCISE 1

PASSAGE ONE

Questions 1 and 2. Listen to a conversation between a student and a professor.

(student)	Professor, I have a question about taking the engineering course that you'll be teaching. I already took this course once, but I didn't do very well in it, and I'd like to take it over again.
(professor)	Why do you want to try it again? Do you think you can do better this time?
(student)	Well, I understood about half of the material last time, and if I concentrate on the rest of the material, I think I can do much better next time.
(professor)	It's . . . uh . . . possible to repeat a course to try for a higher grade, as long as the appropriate form is filled out.

(student) I've got the form right here, and I've already filled out most of it. All I need is your signature at the bottom.

(professor) That's fine. You really do seem prepared. Give me the form, and I'll sign it.

1. WHY DOES THE STUDENT GO TO SEE THE PROFESSOR?
2. WHAT DOES THE STUDENT WANT TO DO?

PASSAGE TWO

Questions 3 and 4. Listen as a student visits a university office.

(student) I have a problem, and I hope you can help.

(worker) What's your problem?

(student) I haven't received my grade report from last quarter, and my friends have already received their grade reports.

(worker) Grade reports from last quarter were mailed out two weeks ago. You haven't received yours yet?

(student) No, I haven't.

(worker) Did you move in the last quarter? Has your address changed? Um, . . . maybe the grade report went to the wrong address.

(student) No, I'm still in the same place. I haven't moved. The address should be accurate.

(worker) And did you take all of your final exams? If you missed an exam, then your grade report would be held up.

(student) No, I took all my exams. . . .

(worker) Then, uh, you should've received your grade report by now. Give me a moment, please, and I'll look your grade report up in the computer system and see if I can figure out what the problem is.

(student) Thanks very much for your help.

3. WHY DOES THE STUDENT GO TO THE OFFICE?
4. WHAT IS THE TOPIC OF THE CONVERSATION?

PASSAGE THREE

Questions 5 and 6. Listen to some students having a discussion.

(woman 1) OK. Let's see where we are on this project for geography class. Our presentation's in two days, and I hope we're almost ready.

(man) I hope so, too. We were each going to look up information about a different lake—with an emphasis on how each lake was formed—and we'll each present information on that lake to the, to the class. My job was to look up information on Lake Superior, and I've done that.

(woman 2) I've done my research on the Caspian Sea.

(woman 1) And I'm ready with information about Lake Baikal.

(woman 2) Great. I'll go first. I'll be discussing the Caspian Sea, which is the largest inland body of water in the world. The Caspian Sea is a saltwater lake between Europe and Asia. It is believed that this lake was originally connected to the world's oceans, which would account for its saltwater content. As the earth's plates moved, this arm of the ocean was cut off.

(man) Well, here's what I found on Lake Superior. Lake Superior is, of course, one of the Great Lakes in North America, and it's the largest freshwater lake in the world. Along with the other Great Lakes, it was formed by glaciers. Glaciers covered the northern part of North America until 10,000 years ago and were responsible for carving out the Great Lakes, including Lake Superior.

(woman 1) OK, now for Lake Baikal, which is the lake I'll be discussing. Lake Baikal's in Russia, and it was formed when the earth's crust broke apart at a fault. Because Lake Baikal formed over a split in the earth's crust, it's a very deep lake, the deepest lake in the world. Lake Baikal's so deep that, even though its surface area is much smaller than the surface area of Lake Superior, it could hold the water of all the Great Lakes combined.

(man) Well, it looks like we've all found information about each of these lakes, and, in particular, how they were formed. Now we need to talk about how we can present the information to the rest of the class.

5. WHAT ARE THE STUDENTS DISCUSSING?
6. WHY ARE THE STUDENTS DISCUSSING THIS MATERIAL?

PASSAGE FOUR

Questions 7 and 8. Listen as a professor leads a class discussion.

(professor) Today, instead of lecturing, I'm going to start out by taking questions. You all know that the exam's tomorrow, so today I'd like to spend time talking about whatever's unclear to you. Yes, Anne, what's your question?

(Anne) I've got a question about the theories of Redfield and Espy. I understand that they were meteorologists, American meteorologists in the nineteenth century, and that they had different theories about how storms behave, but I'm . . . um, not quite sure I really understand the two theories. Could you explain them again?

(professor) OK. It's true that William Redfield and James Espy were two nineteenth-century meteorologists and they had different theories on the behavior of storms. Espy argued that centripetal force was at work in storms. Anne, do you understand what direction the winds would be moving if centripetal force were involved?

(Anne) I think so. Centripetal force would cause winds to move inward from all directions toward the center of the storm. But that's not what really happens during a storm, is it? Winds don't move inward toward the center of the storm.

(professor) That's right, Anne. Espy's theory was that centripetal force pushed the winds of a storm inward toward the center from all directions, but this theory hasn't proven very accurate. . . . Now, the other meteorologist was Redfield. Did Redfield agree or disagree with Espy?

(Anne) I know that Redfield disagreed with Espy, but I'm not quite sure how.

(professor) Can someone else explain what Redfield believed? What about you, Chris?

(Chris) Sure. Redfield argued that the winds in a storm rotated around the center of the storm, so the winds would be moving in a circular path. And he believed that the winds moved in a counterclockwise direction, which means that they move in the opposite direction from the direction that a clock moves.

(professor) Yes, that's correct. Is that clear to you, Anne?

(Anne) So, Espy believed that centripetal force caused winds to move inward toward the center of a storm, and, um, Redfield believed that the winds in a storm moved in a counterclockwise direction.

(professor) Exactly. Now, for the most important question . . . We've already said that Espy's theory on how the winds in a storm behave wasn't very accurate. What about Redfield's theory? Was his theory accurate or inaccurate? Anne?

(Anne) I think Redfield's description was quite close to what actually happens in a storm.

(professor) That's right. Now, . . . who has another question?

7. WHAT IS THE TOPIC OF THIS DISCUSSION?
8. WHY IS THIS TOPIC BEING DISCUSSED?

EXAMPLE (Listening Skill 2)

Listen to a part of a lecture in an astronomy class.

(professor) Halley's comet, which passes by our planet every 76 years, last came by our planet in 1986. . . .

This comet was named after astronomer Edmund Halley who correctly predicted its return in 1758, 16 years after his death. . . .

1. WHAT IS STATED IN THE LECTURE ABOUT HALLEY'S COMET?
2. WHAT DOES THE LECTURER SAY ABOUT EDMUND HALLEY?

LISTENING EXERCISE 2

PASSAGE ONE

Questions 1 through 6. Listen as a student talks to an office worker on campus.

(student) Hi, I need to get a parking sticker.

(worker) Well, you've come to the right place. Let me ask you a few questions. First, are you a student?

(student) Yes, I am.

(worker) And have you ever purchased a student parking sticker before?

(student) No, I haven't. This is the first time I've gotten a parking sticker.

(worker) OK, and do you have your student I.D. with you?

(student) I do.

(worker) And how are you going to pay for the sticker, with cash, check, credit card, or debit card?

(student) By check.

(worker) That's fine. All right . . . all you need to do is fill out this form and write your check, give me the form and the check, and then show me your student I.D.

(student) Do I have to bring my car over here so you can put the sticker on it?

(worker) No, that's not necessary. I'll give you the sticker, and you can put it on your car. Just be sure to put it in the right place.

(student) Where do I need to put it?

(worker) On the front window of the car, on the right-hand side . . . no, wait a minute, not on the right-hand side . . . it should be on the left-hand side.

(student) Front window, left side. OK, I've got it.

(worker) Now, do you know about the various parking areas on campus?

(student) Well, I've noticed that the parking areas on campus are marked with different colors, but I'm not sure what these different colors mean.

(worker) It's really very easy. The parking areas are marked with two different colors. The blue parking areas are for faculty and staff, and the yellow parking areas are for students.

(student) And I'm a student, so that means I can park in the yellow parking areas and not the blue ones.

(worker) That's exactly right. Now, let me get that sticker for you.

1. WHAT IS THE STUDENT'S SITUATION?
2. HOW IS THE STUDENT GOING TO PAY?
3. WHAT DOES THE STUDENT NOT NEED TO DO?
4. WHERE DOES THE STICKER GO?
5. WHAT IS STATED ABOUT PARKING ON CAMPUS?
6. WHO PARKS IN WHICH AREAS?

PASSAGE TWO

Questions 7 through 11. Listen to a discussion by some students who are taking a drama class.

(Bill) We need to get going on our class project for drama class. We have to present a scene from *Our Town*, in costume and with props. Our performance is only in three weeks, and that's not very much time for all we have to do.

(Tina) Let's see. We've already decided on a scene from *Our Town*.

(Chuck) And we know who's going to play each part. Bill, you're going to be the Stage Manager—that's a big part in this play. Tina, you're going to play Emily, and I'm going to play George. We're going to do a scene from the part of the play that takes place before George and Emily's wedding. I've already started learning my lines. What about you two?

(Bill) I've already started working on my lines.

(Tina) And I'm familiar with mine, too. I think we're ready to read through the scene together.

(Chuck) Why don't we discuss what we're going to do about costumes and props first, and then we can run through the scene together.

(Tina) That sounds like a good idea to me.

(Bill) I think so, too.

7. WHEN IS THE STUDENTS' PERFORMANCE?
8. WHICH OF THESE IS NOT A CHARACTER IN THE SCENE?
9. HOW FAMILIAR ARE THE STUDENTS WITH THEIR LINES?
10. WHAT IS STATED ABOUT THE SCENE?
11. WHAT ARE THE STUDENTS GOING TO DISCUSS NEXT?

PASSAGE THREE
Questions 12 through 17. Listen to a lecture in an education class.

(professor) All of you are enrolled in this introductory education course because you want to become teachers. I'd like to introduce this course with a little information about the life of a teacher a century ago. I hope you'll understand this information about early teachers, and I think you'll appreciate how much the life of a teacher has changed over the past century.

Early in the twentieth century, the life of a teacher was quite different from what it is now. There were very strict rules that governed every aspect of the teacher's life. The rules weren't just about how a teacher could conduct herself in the classroom and on the school grounds. There were also numerous rules that governed just about everything a teacher did.

Here are some of the rules. Teachers had to follow, um, strict rules about their appearance; they were sometimes told not to wear colorful clothing, not to dye their hair or wear it loose, and not to wear their skirts above the ankle. Teachers' whereabouts during after-school hours were also strictly regulated; there were rules forbidding teachers to go to bars and to ice-cream parlors; there were rules requiring teachers to be home after 8:00 in the evening, and there were some rules forbidding them to leave town without permission. Just about any action a teacher wanted to take could be regulated. Teachers could be forbidden to smoke or to drink; they were also sometimes forbidden to spend time with

men or to marry if they wanted to remain teachers.

12. WHO IS LISTENING TO THE LECTURE?
13. THE RULES DISCUSSED IN THE LECTURE RELATE TO WHAT PERIOD OF TIME?
14. WHAT IS STATED IN THE LECTURE ABOUT THE RULES FOR TEACHERS?
15. WHAT RULES ABOUT CLOTHING ARE DISCUSSED IN THE LECTURE?
16. WHAT WERE TEACHERS REQUIRED TO DO IN THE EVENING?
17. WHERE WERE TEACHERS FORBIDDEN TO GO?

PASSAGE FOUR
Questions 18 through 23. Listen to a discussion by some students taking a geology class.

(woman 1) OK. So, the next type of mineral we need to talk about is iron pyrite.

(man) Iron pyrite? Isn't that what's also called fool's gold?

(woman 1) Yes, it is.

(woman 2) Why is iron pyrite called fool's gold?

(man) It's called fool's gold because it can look sort of like gold, and sometimes people who found iron pyrite thought they'd found gold.

(woman 1) So iron pyrite kind of looks like gold? What exactly does it look like?

(man) It can be shiny golden in color, but its crystals have a different shape from, from golden crystals. Iron pyrite crystals are cubical in shape. Crystals of gold aren't.

(woman 2) How does iron pyrite get its shiny golden color if it's not gold?

(woman 1) I know the answer to that. . . . Iron pyrite gets its shiny golden color from the mix of elements in it, the elements it contains.

(man) Iron pyrite's made from a mix of elements?

(woman 1) Yes, iron pyrite's a compound of iron and sulfur, so it's very different from gold because it's made of this compound.

(woman 2) And it's also quite different from gold in how it reacts to heat. Iron pyrite has a very strong reaction to heat.

(man) Why? What happens when iron pyrite's heated?

(woman 2) When iron pyrite's heated, it smokes and develops a strong, uh, an awful odor.

(man) And gold doesn't have that kind of reaction to heat?

(woman 1) No, it doesn't.

(woman 2) Do you know where the name pyrite came from?

(man) I think I know that. It came from the Greek word for fire, didn't it?

(woman 1) Yes, it did. If you strike iron pyrite with metal, then it produces sparks. Some ancient cultures used to use iron pyrite to start fires. They couldn't have used gold that way.

(man) So iron pyrite did have some use, even if it really wasn't gold.

18. IN WHAT WAY IS IRON PYRITE SIMILAR TO GOLD?
19. WHY IS IRON PYRITE CALLED FOOL'S GOLD?
20. WHAT IS IRON PYRITE COMPOSED OF?
21. HOW DOES IRON PYRITE REACT TO HEAT?
22. WHERE DID THE WORD *PYRITE* COME FROM?
23. HOW DID SOME ANCIENT CULTURES USE IRON PYRITE?

LISTENING REVIEW EXERCISE (Skills 1 and 2)

Questions 1 through 7. Listen to a conversation between a student and a professor.

(student) ❶ Thanks for seeing me, Dr. Barton.

(professor) No problem. It's my office hour. . . . What did you want to talk about?

(student) I wanted to discuss the topic I've chosen for the paper I'm supposed to be writing for your anthropology course. The topic I'm thinking about is a bit unusual.

(professor) Oh you know, it has to be related to some aspect of anthropology that we're studying . . . What topic did you have in mind?

(student) I wanted to write about a test used by the Roman military to test soldiers' eyesight.

(professor) Hmm . . . an eyesight test used by the Roman military? Are you sure this is related to our anthropology class? . . . Well, tell me about it. . . . What is this eyesight test that the Roman military used?

(student) Well, it was a test that the Romans used to determine if their soldiers would fight as foot soldiers on the front lines or as archers behind the front lines. Roman soldiers were required to undergo certain tests to determine their ability to perform as soldiers. One of these tests was simply to count the stars in the constellation, the Big Dipper. This test determined the acuity of their vision. See. Look at this picture of the Big Dipper. ❷ You can see the seven stars in the Big Dipper. The star at the bend of the handle of the Big Dipper is called Mizar, and Mizar is a binary star. If you look closely, there's a second star called Alcor next to Mizar. If a Roman soldier's eyesight was good enough to see Alcor, he could fight as an archer. If he couldn't see Alcor, he had to fight on the front lines as a foot soldier.

(professor) So this eye test was based on the ability of the soldier to see Alcor next to Mizar.

(student) Yes, exactly.

(professor) Well, that's a very interesting test, but I'm not sure that it's related to the material in our anthropology class. Well, let's put it this way . . . how would you relate this to the material in the anthropology course?

(student) I'd relate it to the idea of "survival of the fittest."

(professor) Um . . . Interesting . . . and how would you relate it to this concept? Survival of the fittest has to do with the idea that those who're strongest or have some other physical or mental advantage will be more likely to survive.

(student) Well, this test for eyesight was used not only by the Romans but also other groups of people for hundreds of years. The interesting point is that over time more people have been able to pass the test, and the fact that more people have been able to pass this test over time has been attributed to survival of the fittest. It was certainly true for Roman soldiers that those who passed the test had a better chance of surviving for longer.

(professor) And why is that? Why did Roman soldiers who passed the test stand a better chance of surviving longer?

(student) Well, soldiers with better eyesight weren't on the front lines. Those with worse eyesight were sent to the front lines and, more often than not, were killed on the front lines. Archers stood a better chance of survival and were around to father children, who would also tend to have better eyesight than those who failed the test. This is what supports the concept of survival of the fittest.

(professor) ❸ Hmm. That's an interesting idea. As long as you concentrate on the idea of survival of the fittest in your paper and use this example of an eye test to support the concept, I think you would have a solid paper.

(student) That's what I'll do then. Thanks, Dr. Barton.

1. WHY DOES THE STUDENT GO TO SEE THE PROFESSOR?
2. WHAT IS THE TOPIC OF THE PAPER HE WANTS TO WRITE?
3. WHY WERE ROMAN SOLDIERS ASKED TO COUNT THE STARS IN THE BIG DIPPER?
4. WHICH OF THE FOLLOWING IS NOT TRUE?
5. WHAT TWO STATEMENTS DESCRIBE POSSIBLE OUTCOMES FROM THE ROMAN EYESIGHT TEST?
6. HOW DOES THE TERM "SURVIVAL OF THE FITTEST" RELATE TO THE TEST THAT THE STUDENT DESCRIBES?
7. WHAT DOES THE PROFESSOR FINALLY DECIDE?

EXAMPLE (Listening Skill 3)

Listen as a student asks her professor about an assignment.

(student) Professor Roberts, I have a question for you about the assignment.

(professor) OK, if it's a short question.

(student) It is. The assignment on the syllabus lists pages 101 through 120 in the text, and the last page of the assigned reading is a list of questions. I was wondering if we were supposed to read through the questions and just think about the answers or actually write out the answers to the questions.

(professor) Well, you don't need to write out neat and formal answers to the questions, but you should be really familiar with the answers because we'll be talking about the questions during class and I expect you to have answers ready.

(student) You mean, we don't need to turn in written answers to the questions?

(professor) That's right, but you might want to jot down notes about your answers so that you can refer to them during our discussion.

1. LISTEN AGAIN TO PART OF THE PASSAGE. THEN ANSWER THE QUESTION.
(student) Professor Roberts, I have a question for you about the assignment.
(professor) OK, if it's a short question.
WHAT DOES THE PROFESSOR MEAN WHEN HE SAYS THIS:
(professor) OK, if it's a short question.

2. LISTEN AGAIN TO PART OF THE PASSAGE. THEN ANSWER THE QUESTION.
(professor) Well, you don't need to write out neat and formal answers to the questions, but you should be really familiar with the answers because we'll be talking about the questions during class, and I expect you to have answers ready.
(student) You mean, we don't need to turn in written answers to the questions?
WHY DOES THE STUDENT SAY THIS:
(student) You mean, we don't need to turn in written answers to the questions?

LISTENING EXERCISE 3

PASSAGE ONE
Questions 1 through 4. Listen as a student talks to a librarian.

(student) Excuse me. Can you help me, please?
(librarian) That's why I'm here. What do you need?
(student) I need to find a specific magazine, and I'm not sure where to look.
(librarian) How old is the magazine you need to find? Is it a recent magazine—less than a year old—or is it an older magazine?
(student) You need to know how old the magazine is to find it?
(librarian) That's why I asked. The more recent magazines—those that are less than a year old—are in the Magazine Reading Room, on the second floor. But after a year, magazines are bound together and put in hard covers, and the bound magazines are on the third floor.
(student) Well, the magazine I want to find is more than a year old, so that means that I need to go to the second floor, oh, excuse me . . . what am I saying? . . . The third floor.
(librarian) That's right. The third floor.
(student) Thanks for your help. I really appreciate it.

(librarian) You're quite welcome. Feel free to come by any time.

1. LISTEN AGAIN TO PART OF THE CONVERSATION. THEN ANSWER THE QUESTION.
(student) Excuse me. Can you help me, please?
(librarian) That's why I'm here. What do you need?
WHY DOES THE LIBRARIAN SAY THIS:
(librarian) That's why I'm here.

2. LISTEN AGAIN TO PART OF THE CONVERSATION. THEN ANSWER THE QUESTION.
(student) You need to know how old the magazine is to find it?
(librarian) That's why I asked.
WHAT DOES THE LIBRARIAN MEAN WHEN HE SAYS THIS:
(librarian) That's why I asked.

3. LISTEN AGAIN TO PART OF THE CONVERSATION. THEN ANSWER THE QUESTION.
(student) Well, the magazine I want to find is more than a year old, so that means that I need to go to the second floor, oh, excuse me . . . what am I saying? . . . The third floor.
WHY DOES THE STUDENT SAY THIS:
(student) Oh, excuse me . . . what am I saying?

4. LISTEN AGAIN TO PART OF THE CONVERSATION. THEN ANSWER THE QUESTION.
(student) Thanks for your help. I really appreciate it.
(librarian) You're quite welcome. Feel free to come by any time.
WHAT DOES THE LIBRARIAN MEAN WHEN HE SAYS THIS:
(librarian) Feel free to come by any time.

PASSAGE TWO
Questions 5 through 9. Listen to two students having a conversation.

(woman) Hey, Sam, I have a question for you.
(man) (laughs) All you have to do is ask.
(woman) I think it's a pretty easy question. All I need to know is how I can get a copy of my transcript. I need one for a scholarship I'm applying for.
(man) Oh, I think I can handle that one. You need to go to the registrar's office to get a copy of your transcript.
(woman) That's all there is to it? I just go to the registrar's office and ask for a copy of my transcript, and I'll get it?
(man) Well, it's not quite that easy. You need to go to the registrar's office and fill out a form, a transcript request form. Then you turn in the form with a ten-dollar fee.
(woman) That doesn't sound like it'll take too long.
(man) I hope you don't need the transcript too soon.
(woman) I need it within a week.
(man) Well, you may get lucky . . . but don't count on it.
(woman) I really need it within a week, or else I won't be able to turn the application in on time, and that means I won't get a scholarship.

(man) Well, if I were you, I'd get over to the registrar's office immediately. And it wouldn't hurt to explain that you need the transcript right away. But I wouldn't count on it. I don't think transcripts are processed that quickly.

(woman) I'll get over there right now and see what happens.

5. LISTEN AGAIN TO PART OF THE CONVERSATION. THEN ANSWER THE QUESTION.
(woman) Hey, Sam, I have a question for you.
(man) (laughs) All you have to do is ask.
WHY DOES THE MAN SAY THIS:
(man) (laughs) All you have to do is ask.

6. LISTEN AGAIN TO PART OF THE CONVERSATION. THEN ANSWER THE QUESTION.
(woman) I think it's a pretty easy question. All I need to know is how I can get a copy of my transcript. I need one for a scholarship I'm applying for.
(man) Oh, I think I can handle that one.
WHAT DOES THE MAN MEAN WHEN HE SAYS THIS:
(man) Oh, I think I can handle that one.

7. LISTEN AGAIN TO PART OF THE CONVERSATION. THEN ANSWER THE QUESTION.
(man) You need to go to the registrar's office to get a copy of your transcript.
(woman) That's all there is to it? I just go to the registrar's office and ask for a copy of my transcript, and I'll get it?
WHAT DOES THE WOMAN MEAN WHEN SHE SAYS THIS:
(woman) That's all there is to it?

8. LISTEN AGAIN TO PART OF THE CONVERSATION. THEN ANSWER THE QUESTION.
(man) Well, you may get lucky . . . but don't count on it.
(woman) I really need it within a week, or else I won't be able to turn the application in on time, and that means I won't get a scholarship.
WHY DOES THE MAN SAY THIS:
(man) Well, you may get lucky . . . but don't count on it.

9. LISTEN AGAIN TO PART OF THE CONVERSATION. THEN ANSWER THE QUESTION.
(woman) I really need it within a week, or else I won't be able to turn the application in on time, and that means I won't get a scholarship.
(man) Well, if I were you, I'd get over to the registrar's office immediately.
WHAT DOES THE MAN IMPLY WHEN HE SAYS THIS:
(man) Well, if I were you, I'd get over to the registrar's office immediately.

PASSAGE THREE
Questions 10 through 13. Listen to a group of students discussing information from a zoology class.

(man 1) The next animal we need to discuss is the opossum. The opossum is another kind of marsupial.

(woman) A marsupial? Oh no, I think we're supposed to know what that is.
(man 2) We are. A marsupial's an animal that carries its young in a pouch.
(woman) Oh, that's right. It's like a kangaroo.
(man 2) Exactly.
(woman) And young opossums stay in their mother's pouch for what, a few days?
(man 1) No, not exactly. It's about two months. Then, when the babies are about two months old, they come out of their mother's pouch, but they don't go very far. For the next few months, they go everywhere with their mother.
(man 2) They just ride along on their mother's back.
(woman) So young opossums spend the first two months in their mother's pouch and the next two months hanging on her back?
(man 1) You've got it. Now, aren't opossums animals that play dead?
(man 2) Oh, I don't think it's opossums that play dead. . . . Oh, wait a minute. . . . Maybe it is. We do talk about playing 'possum if we're talking about pretending that we're asleep or dead.
(man 2) Exactly.
(woman) So when an opossum's frightened by an attacker, it doesn't run away?
(man 2) No, it doesn't. It just rolls over on its back, kind of curls up, and pretends it's dead.
(woman) I guess it's just hoping the attacker will think it's dead and will go away and leave it alone.

10. LISTEN AGAIN TO PART OF THE DISCUSSION. THEN ANSWER THE QUESTION.
(man 1) The next animal we need to discuss is the opossum. The opossum is another kind of marsupial.
(woman) A marsupial? Oh no, I think we're supposed to know what that is.
WHAT DOES THE WOMAN MEAN WHEN SHE SAYS THIS:
(woman) Oh no, I think we're supposed to know what that is.

11. LISTEN AGAIN TO PART OF THE DISCUSSION. THEN ANSWER THE QUESTION.
(woman) And young opossums stay in their mother's pouch for what, a few days?
(man 1) No, not exactly. It's about two months.
WHY DOES THE MAN SAY THIS:
(man 1) No, not exactly.

12. LISTEN AGAIN TO PART OF THE DISCUSSION. THEN ANSWER THE QUESTION.
(woman) So young opossums spend the first two months in their mother's pouch and the next two months hanging on her back?
(man 1) You've got it.
WHAT DOES THE MAN MEAN WHEN HE SAYS THIS:
(man 1) You've got it.

13. LISTEN AGAIN TO PART OF THE DISCUSSION. THEN ANSWER THE QUESTION.
(man 2) Oh, I don't think it's opossums that play dead. . . . Oh, wait a minute. Maybe it is.

WHY DOES THE MAN SAY THIS:
(man 2) Oh, wait a minute. Maybe it is.

PASSAGE FOUR
Questions 14 through 19. Listen to a discussion in an astronomy class.

(professor) Today we'll be discussing the planet Venus, which is the second planet in our solar system. I'm sure you all know which planet is the third planet in our solar system. Yes, Beth?

(Beth) Is Earth the third planet?

(professor) You don't sound too sure of your answer, Beth . . . but, yes, that's true. Venus is the second planet in our solar system, and Earth is the third. Venus is almost the same size as our Earth, which is the fifth largest planet in, ah, the solar system.

The planet Venus is easily visible in the sky from Earth, although not always as a complete sphere. It goes through some phases, just like the Moon. Sometimes it's fully visible, like a full moon, sometimes it's half visible, and sometimes it's only a small crescent. When do you think Venus is the brightest, when it's fully visible or when it's a crescent? Mark?

(Mark) Well, it makes sense that it would be the brightest when it's fully visible.

(professor) Well, things aren't always as they seem. Try again.

(Mark) You mean, Venus is actually brighter when it's only a small crescent than when it's fully visible?

(professor) That's exactly what I mean. . . . Now, does anyone know if Venus is a hot or cold planet? . . . What would you expect since Venus is closer to the Sun than our planet is?

(Beth) Since it's so close to the Sun, I think it would be very hot.

(professor) And it is. The temperature there can reach almost to 500 degrees centigrade. What is this in Fahrenheit? . . . Anyone? . . . Come on, we've talked about this before.

(Mark) I think that's around 900 degrees Fahrenheit.

(professor) Yes, it is. Now, we've said that the temperature on Venus is quite hot, and the temperature there is hot because Venus is so close to the Sun. But that's not the only reason that Venus is so hot. It's also hot for another reason. Does anyone know? Could it be the atmosphere? What is its atmosphere made of? Beth?

(Beth) Its atmosphere's almost entirely carbon dioxide.

(professor) Yes, that's right, Beth, and this type of atmosphere holds in the heat from the Sun extremely well. . . . Now, let's talk about the clouds that cover Venus. As you know, Venus is visible to us on Earth, but it's not actually the planet that we see; it's the clouds. The surface of Venus can't be seen, even with a telescope, because of the clouds that surround the planet. What can you tell me about the clouds that cover Venus?

(Mark) Uh . . . the clouds around Venus?

(professor) Yes, I'm asking about the clouds around Venus. I want to know about the clouds around Venus.

(Mark) Do you want to know what they're made of? They're made of carbon dioxide. No . . . wait a minute. The atmosphere's made of carbon dioxide. . . . The clouds're made of sulfuric acid.

(professor) That's right. The clouds on Venus are actually made of sulfuric acid. These clouds help to contribute to the brightness of Venus in our sky. When Venus appears to shine so brightly, it's because the light of the Sun is reflecting off Venus's clouds of sulfuric acid.

14. LISTEN AGAIN TO PART OF THE DISCUSSION. THEN ANSWER THE QUESTION.
(professor) I'm sure you all know which planet is the third planet in our solar system. Yes, Beth?
(Beth) Is Earth the third planet?
(professor) You don't sound too sure of your answer, Beth.
WHY DOES THE PROFESSOR SAY THIS:
(professor) You don't sound too sure of your answer, Beth.

15. LISTEN AGAIN TO PART OF THE DISCUSSION. THEN ANSWER THE QUESTION.
(professor) When do you think Venus is the brightest, when it's fully visible or when it's a crescent? Mark?
(Mark) Well, it makes sense that it would be the brightest when it's fully visible.
(professor) Well, things aren't always as they seem. Try again.
WHAT DOES THE PROFESSOR MEAN WHEN SHE SAYS THIS:
(professor) Well, things aren't always as they seem. Try again.

16. LISTEN AGAIN TO PART OF THE DISCUSSION. THEN ANSWER THE QUESTION.
(professor) The temperature there can reach almost to 500 degrees centigrade. What is this in Fahrenheit? . . . Anyone? . . . Come on, we've talked about this before.
WHAT DOES THE PROFESSOR MEAN WHEN SHE SAYS THIS:
(professor) Come on, we've talked about this before.

17. LISTEN AGAIN TO PART OF THE DISCUSSION. THEN ANSWER THE QUESTION.
(professor) But that's not the only reason that Venus is so hot. It's also hot for another reason. Does anyone know? Could it be the atmosphere?
WHY DOES THE PROFESSOR SAY THIS:
(professor) Could it be the atmosphere?

18. LISTEN AGAIN TO PART OF THE DISCUSSION. THEN ANSWER THE QUESTION.

(professor) What can you tell me about the clouds that cover Venus?

(Mark) Uh . . . the clouds around Venus?

(professor) Yes, I'm asking about the clouds around Venus. I want to know about the clouds around Venus.

WHY DOES THE PROFESSOR SAY THIS:

(professor) Yes, I'm asking about the clouds around Venus. I want to know about the clouds around Venus.

19. LISTEN AGAIN TO PART OF THE DISCUSSION. THEN ANSWER THE QUESTION.

(Mark) Do you want to know what they're made of? They're made of carbon dioxide. No . . . wait a minute. . . . The atmosphere's made of carbon dioxide. . . . The clouds're made of sulfuric acid.

WHAT DOES THE STUDENT MEAN WHEN HE SAYS THIS:

(Mark) No . . . wait a minute.

EXAMPLE (Listening Skill 4)

Listen to a conversation between two students.

(woman) Do you enjoy playing chess?

(man) Yes, I really do.

(woman) Well, you might think about joining the chess club. I belong to it, and I think you might really enjoy it, too.

(man) What does the chess club do?

(woman) The members get together once a week for friendly competitions. Then each semester, the three best players from the club compete in a tournament with players from other schools.

(man) The meetings once a week sound like a lot of fun, but . . . uh . . . my chess playing just . . . uh . . . might not be quite up to the level of tournament play.

(woman) Well, why don't you come with me this Wednesday and try out one of the weekly meetings? You can come to the meetings for a while and then see if you're ready to compete in a tournament in a few months.

1. LISTEN AGAIN TO PART OF THE CONVERSATION. THEN ANSWER THE QUESTION.

(woman) Do you enjoy playing chess?

(man) Yes, I really do.

(woman) Well, you might think about joining the chess club. I belong to it, and I think you might really enjoy it, too.

HOW DOES THE WOMAN SEEM TO FEEL ABOUT THE CHESS CLUB?

2. LISTEN AGAIN TO PART OF THE CONVERSATION. THEN ANSWER THE QUESTION.

(man) The meetings once a week sound like a lot of fun, but . . . uh . . . my chess playing just . . . uh . . . might not be quite up to the level of tournament play.

WHICH SENTENCE BEST EXPRESSES HOW THE MAN FEELS?

LISTENING EXERCISE 4

PASSAGE ONE

Questions 1 and 2. Listen as an advisor discusses a student's course load with the student.

(advisor) I'd like to talk with you about the number of courses you'll be taking next semester.

(student) I took five courses last semester, I'm taking five courses this semester, and I'm planning on taking five courses again next semester. I always like to take the maximum number of courses because I don't mind working hard and because I want to finish my undergraduate degree as quickly as possible and get into graduate school.

(advisor) I understand that you're trying to finish your undergraduate program quickly in order to go to graduate school. However, the problem is that your grades are passable but not very high, and you'll need higher grades to get into a good graduate school.

(student) I definitely want to go to a good graduate school. Do you think it's better for me to take a lighter course load next semester in order to try to get higher grades in those courses?

(advisor) Well, . . . because you're taking the maximum number of courses, I don't think you have enough time to put sufficient time and effort into each of your courses.

1. LISTEN AGAIN TO PART OF THE DISCUSSION. THEN ANSWER THE QUESTION.

(advisor) I'd like to talk with you about the number of courses you'll be taking next semester.

(student) I took five courses last semester, I'm taking five courses this semester, and I'm planning on taking five courses again next semester. I always like to take the maximum number of courses because I don't mind working hard and because I want to finish my undergraduate degree as quickly as possible and get into graduate school.

HOW DOES THE STUDENT SEEM TO FEEL ABOUT TAKING THE MAXIMUM NUMBER OF COURSES?

2. LISTEN AGAIN TO PART OF THE DISCUSSION. THEN ANSWER THE QUESTION.

(student) Do you think it's better for me to take a lighter course load next semester in order to try to get higher grades in those courses?

(advisor) Well, . . . because you're taking the maximum number of courses, I don't think you have enough time to put sufficient time and effort into each of your courses.

WHICH SENTENCE BEST EXPRESSES WHAT THE ADVISOR MIGHT SAY TO THE STUDENT?

PASSAGE TWO

Questions 3 and 4. Listen to a conversation between two students.

(woman) This is an interesting assignment we have for psychology class.

(man) Interesting? It's going to be a lot of work.

(woman) What's so hard about it? We just have to make up a survey questionnaire related to theories from the class.

(man) Making up a survey questionnaire isn't so hard. But we have to find 50 people to fill out the questionnaire and then write up a report analyzing the data.

(woman) It'll be easy to find 50 people to fill out the questionnaire. We can do that in one afternoon at the student center. That actually sounds like fun to me.

(man) That's good. I don't mind preparing the questionnaire and analyzing the data, but getting 50 people to answer the questionnaire does not seem like fun to me.

3. LISTEN AGAIN TO PART OF THE CONVERSATION. THEN ANSWER THE QUESTION.

(woman) This is an interesting assignment we have for psychology class.

(man) Interesting? . . . It's going to be a lot of work . . . Making up a survey questionnaire isn't so hard. But we have to find 50 people to fill out the questionnaire and then write up a report analyzing the data.

HOW DOES THE MAN SEEM TO FEEL ABOUT THE ASSIGNMENT?

4. LISTEN AGAIN TO PART OF THE CONVERSATION. THEN ANSWER THE QUESTION.

(woman) This is an interesting assignment we have for psychology class.

(man) Interesting? It's going to be a lot of work.

(woman) What's so hard about it? We just have to make up a survey questionnaire related to theories from the class.

WHICH SENTENCE BEST EXPRESSES HOW THE WOMAN FEELS ABOUT THE ASSIGNMENT?

PASSAGE THREE
Questions 5 and 6. Listen to a lecture in a course on Native American studies.

(professor) Our topic for today is Iroquois villages, and I'm going to have a rather unusual assignment for you based on this topic, so you need to listen carefully to the information. First of all, I'll be describing an Iroquois village, and then, for your assignment, I want you to draw a village.

(student) Excuse me, Dr. Thomas. You want us to draw an Iroquois village?

(professor) Yes, that's exactly what I want you to do. I think this will help you to understand the efficient simplicity of the design of an Iroquois village.

Now, let me describe an Iroquois village and what makes it so special. An Iroquois village consisted of a number of longhouses. Iroquois longhouses were long, single-story houses with U-shaped roofs, and they were very elegant in their simplicity. Iroquois villages were also well defended. Around an Iroquois village, there was usually a stockade, which is a defensive wall or barrier made of wooden posts. The stockade around an Iroquois village was typically hexagonal in shape, which means that it was six-sided. It had vertical wood posts around the outside of the stockade, and these posts had sharpened ends pointing upward for further protection.

Now, for the assignment . . . your assignment is to create a pencil drawing of an Iroquois village. You can use the information I just provided, and you can find more information in Chapter 22 of the text.

(student) But, Dr. Thomas, what if I can't draw? I'm not very good at drawing.

(professor) Well, just try your best. I want you to make a good effort.

(student) Are you expecting just a simple drawing, or does the drawing need to be complicated?

(professor) I'd like you to do the best you can do.

(student) Well, for me, my best might not be what you're expecting.

5. LISTEN AGAIN TO PART OF THE LECTURE. THEN ANSWER THE QUESTION.

(professor) Now, let me describe an Iroquois village and what makes it so special. An Iroquois village consisted of a number of longhouses. Iroquois longhouses were long, single-story houses with U-shaped roofs, and they were very elegant in their simplicity. Iroquois villages were also well defended. Around an Iroquois village, there was usually a stockade, which is a defensive wall or barrier made of wooden posts.

HOW DOES THE PROFESSOR SEEM TO FEEL ABOUT THE DESIGN OF THE IROQUOIS VILLAGE?

6. LISTEN AGAIN TO PART OF THE LECTURE. THEN ANSWER THE QUESTION.

(student) But, Dr. Thomas, what if I can't draw? I'm not very good at drawing.

(professor) Well, just try your best. I want you to make a good effort.

(student) Are you expecting just a simple drawing, or does the drawing need to be complicated?

(professor) I'd like you to do the best you can do.

(student) Well, for me, my best might not be what you're expecting.

WHICH SENTENCE BEST EXPRESSES HOW THE STUDENT SEEMS TO FEEL ABOUT THE ASSIGNMENT?

PASSAGE FOUR
Questions 7 and 8. Listen to a discussion by two students taking a meteorology class.

(man) OK, I think we understand how snow and rain are formed. Now we need to discuss the formation of hail, and this part isn't very clear to me. What exactly is hail? And how does it differ from snow and rain?

(woman) Well, it's not really too hard to understand. Hail is really just frozen drops of rain.

(man) That's all it is? When I was reading about it, it seemed rather hard to understand. How is hail formed?

(woman) Hailstones develop in cumulonimbus clouds that've grown very tall.

(man) Cumulonimbus clouds?

(woman) That's right. Cumulonimbus clouds are very tall clouds. They can actually be as tall as six miles. Because they're so tall, they're much warmer at the bottom than at the top.

(man) That's really tall.

(woman) And sometimes air currents blow drops of water in a cloud up higher into the cloud.

(man) Where it's colder, so the drops freeze into ice. Do the drops fall to the earth then?

(woman) Usually not just after the trip up. Usually the drops aren't yet heavy enough to fall to the Earth.

(man) So the drops rise and fall a number of times within the cloud, and each time a drop rises and falls, it adds another layer of ice?

(woman) Yes, you've got it.

(man) Really? This isn't as difficult as I thought. I can understand it.

(woman) Yes, you can. A hailstone actually has a number of layers of ice on it, one layer for each time that it's pushed up and freezes again. After it builds up enough layers, it gets too heavy.

(man) And that's when it falls to Earth.

(woman) Exactly.

7. LISTEN AGAIN TO PART OF THE DISCUSSION. THEN ANSWER THE QUESTION.

(man) Now, we need to discuss the formation of hail, and this part isn't very clear to me. What exactly is hail? And how does it differ from snow and rain?

(woman) Well, it's not really too hard to understand. Hail is really just frozen drops of rain.

(man) That's all it is? When I was reading about it, it seemed rather hard to understand.

HOW DOES THE MAN SEEM TO FEEL ABOUT THE TOPIC IN THE BEGINNING OF THE CONVERSATION?

8. LISTEN AGAIN TO PART OF THE DISCUSSION. THEN ANSWER THE QUESTION.

(man) So the drops rise and fall a number of times within the cloud, and each time a drop rises and falls, it adds another layer of ice?

(woman) Yes, you've got it.

(man) Really? This isn't as difficult as I thought. I can understand it.

WHICH SENTENCE BEST EXPRESSES HOW THE MAN FEELS AT THE END OF THE CONVERSATION?

LISTENING EXERCISE (Skills 3 and 4)

Questions 1 through 6. Listen to a discussion in an American history class.

(professor) ❶ Today we're going to talk about a coin from early in the history of the United States. It was the first coin issued by the U.S. government, and it was issued soon after the government was established. Do you know when this was? . . . Any idea? . . . Come on, you must have some idea when this was. Yes, Sam?

(Sam) Was it in the late 1700s?

(professor) That's right, Sam. This coin was issued in 1789. It was known by two names; it was known as both the Fugio coin and the Franklin coin. First of all, can you tell me why it was called the Fugio coin? Laura?

(Laura) It was called the Fugio coin because it had the word *fugio* on the front of the coin. Fugio is a Latin word that means "I fly."

(professor) That's right, Laura. And this coin was also called the Franklin coin. Why was it called the Franklin coin? It was because Benjamin Franklin was on it, wasn't it?

(Doug) No, it was called the Franklin coin because Franklin was given credit for the wording on the coin.

(professor) That's right. ❷ Now, this is the coin we're talking about. Let's look at the front of the coin. Can you describe the front for me? Sam?

(Sam) The front of the coin has a sundial in the middle with a sun shining down on the sundial.

(professor) Yes, both a sun and a sundial are there. And what else?

(Sam) Well, . . . uh . . . there's a date along one side and . . . um, . . . there seems to be some wording at the bottom.

(professor) Sam needs some help. Who can help Sam answer the question? Yes, Doug?

(Doug) The wording along the bottom is "mind your business." This coin's called the Franklin coin because Benjamin Franklin was given credit for the wording.

(professor) ❸ Now let's talk about the other side of the coin. Let me describe the front of the coin for you. Oh, . . . excuse me, . . . did I say front? I meant back. On the back of the coin, there's a large circle made up of 13 linked circles, and in the middle of the circle are the words "We are one." Do you understand what these words mean?

(Laura) I think so, particularly with the words "We are one." This design on the back of the coin symbolizes the 13 original colonies linked into one country.

(professor) That's a very appropriate idea for the first coin issued by the United States after the country won its independence.

❹ Now, that's all for today. However, I'd like to suggest that some of you might want to be somewhat more prepared for the next class. And just to check on whether or not you're prepared, there just might be a quiz.

1. LISTEN AGAIN TO PART OF THE DISCUSSION. THEN ANSWER THE QUESTION.
   (professor) Today we're going to talk about a coin from early in the history of the United States. It was the first coin issued by the U.S. government, and it was issued soon after the government was established. Do you know when this was? . . . Any idea? . . . Come on, you must have some idea when this was.
   HOW DOES THE PROFESSOR SEEM TO FEEL WHEN SHE SAYS THIS:
   (professor) Do you know when this was? . . . Any idea? . . . Come on, you must have some idea when this was.

2. LISTEN AGAIN TO PART OF THE DISCUSSION. THEN ANSWER THE QUESTION.
   (professor) And this coin was also called the Franklin coin. Why was it called the Franklin coin? It was because Benjamin Franklin was on it, wasn't it?
   WHY DOES THE PROFESSOR SAY THIS:
   (professor) It was because Benjamin Franklin was on it, wasn't it?

3. LISTEN AGAIN TO PART OF THE DISCUSSION. THEN ANSWER THE QUESTION.
   (Sam) Well, . . . uh . . . there's a date along one side and . . . um, . . . there seems to be some wording at the bottom.
   (professor) Sam needs some help. Who can help Sam answer the question?
   WHY DOES THE PROFESSOR SAY THIS:
   (professor) Sam needs some help. Who can help Sam answer the question?

4. LISTEN AGAIN TO PART OF THE DISCUSSION. THEN ANSWER THE QUESTION.
   (professor) Let me describe the front of the coin for you because we don't have a photograph of it. Oh, . . . excuse me, . . . did I say front? I meant back.
   WHY DOES THE PROFESSOR SAY THIS:
   (professor) Oh, . . . excuse me, . . . did I say front? I meant back.

5. LISTEN AGAIN TO PART OF THE DISCUSSION. THEN ANSWER THE QUESTION.
   (professor) On the back of the coin, there's a large circle made up of 13 linked circles, and in the middle of the circle are the words "We are one." Do you understand what these words mean?
   (Laura) I think so, particularly with the words "We are one." This design on the back of the coin symbolizes the thirteen original colonies linked into one country.
   (professor) That's a very appropriate idea for the first coin issued by the United States after the country won its independence.
   HOW DOES THE PROFESSOR SEEM TO FEEL WHEN SHE SAYS THIS:
   (professor) That's a very appropriate idea for the first coin issued by the United States after the country won its independence.

6. LISTEN AGAIN TO PART OF THE DISCUSSION. THEN ANSWER THE QUESTION.
   (professor) However, I'd like to suggest that some of you might want to be somewhat more prepared for the next class. And just to check on whether or not you're prepared, there just might be a quiz.
   WHAT MIGHT THE PROFESSOR SAY?

LISTENING REVIEW EXERCISE (Skills 1 through 4)

Questions 1 through 8. Listen to a lecture in a zoology class.

(professor) ❶ OK, calm down, please. . . . It's time to get started . . . You can continue your chitchat after class. Our topic for today is hibernation.

When it begins getting cold in the north as winter approaches, uh, different types of animals deal with the approach of the cold weather in different ways. Some animals move south to warmer weather, some animals increase their activity to stay warm, and other animals hibernate during the cold weather. So today, we'll be discussing this third category of animals, the animals that hibernate. Now, these are the animals like groundhogs and bears that go into a state of unconsciousness or semiconsciousness during the cold winter months.

❷ The first animal we'll look at is the groundhog. The groundhog's one of the best-known hibernators. It goes into its burrow 4 or 5 feet underground sometime in the fall, and, uh, it doesn't come out until spring. A groundhog stays in its underground burrow for the entire winter, without coming out. Now, because the groundhog hibernates so completely, it's the groundhog that has achieved prominence in our folklore as the animal that's responsible for determining whether or not winter's over and it's safe to come out of hibernation.

You see, according to folklore, the groundhog will come out of the burrow where it's hibernating on Groundhog Day in February. If winter's over, the groundhog will remain out of its burrow, but if winter's going to last for a while longer, the groundhog will scurry back into its burrow . . . Yes, Amanda, do you have a question?

(Amanda) Yes, I do. Does the groundhog have a good record, you know, about predicting whether winter's over?

(professor) (laughs) Uh, no, not really. It's just a folktale, and the groundhog isn't . . . um . . . batting much more than fifty-fifty. Now, back to the discussion of hibernation, with a little more emphasis on its scientific nature.

❸ We've discussed the groundhog, which hibernates throughout the cold weather. Other animals that hibernate in a similar fashion are bats and squirrels. Now, we'll look at the bear, which hibernates in a different manner.

❹ You see, bears don't hibernate as completely as groundhogs, bats, or squirrels. In the southern half of the United States, bears don't hibernate at all because the weather doesn't get cold enough for them to hibernate. In the northern half of the United States, bears may not stay in hibernation for the entire winter. They may come out of their hibernation during the winter and wander about before returning to hibernation . . . Yes, Tom, what's your question?

(Tom) Well, professor, I'm not . . . uh . . . exactly sure what . . . um . . . hibernation is. I mean, . . . how is hibernation different from sleep?

(professor) ❺ Ah, . . . that's a good question, Tom, one that I'm a little late in clarifying. Hibernation is different from sleep, and these differences between sleep and hibernation are seen in body temperature and heart rate. You see, the main characteristics of hibernation, which are very different from sleep, are that body temperature and heart rate decrease significantly. When an animal comes out of hibernation, the heart rate and body temperature increase to the levels normal during waking hours. During the period when a large animal, uh . . . such as a bear, is coming out of hibernation, the animal's entire body does not warm at once. The area around the heart warms up first. As the heart warms up, it begins beating at its normal rate, and it's then able to pump blood around the rest of the body and heat up the rest of the body.

❻ These are the main points that we need to cover about hibernation. Now, we'll take a short break before moving on to the next subject.

1. LISTEN AGAIN TO PART OF THE LECTURE. THEN ANSWER THE QUESTION.
   (professor) OK, calm down, please. . . . It's time to get started . . . You can continue your chitchat after class.
   WHAT DOES THE PROFESSOR MEAN WHEN HE SAYS THIS:
   (professor) You can continue your chitchat after class.
2. WHAT IS THE TOPIC OF THE TALK?
3. WHAT IS NOT MENTIONED BY THE PROFESSOR AS A WAY THAT VARIOUS TYPES OF ANIMALS PREPARE FOR THE COLD WEATHER?
4. LISTEN AGAIN TO PART OF THE LECTURE. THEN ANSWER THE QUESTION.

(Amanda) Yes, I do. Does the groundhog have a good record, you know, about predicting whether winter's over?

(professor) (laughs) Uh, no . . . not really. It's just a folktale, and the groundhog isn't . . . um . . . batting much more than fifty-fifty. Now, back to the discussion of hibernation, with a little more emphasis on its scientific nature.

HOW DOES THE PROFESSOR SEEM TO FEEL ABOUT THE ABILITY OF THE GROUNDHOG TO PREDICT THE END OF WINTER WHEN HE SAYS THIS:
(professor) It's just a folktale, and the groundhog isn't . . . um . . . batting much more than fifty-fifty. Now, back to the discussion of hibernation, with a little more emphasis on its scientific nature.

5. WHICH IS NOT A GOOD HIBERNATOR?
6. LISTEN AGAIN TO PART OF THE LECTURE. THEN ANSWER THE QUESTION.
   (Tom) Well, professor, I'm not . . . uh . . . exactly sure what . . . um . . . hibernation is. I mean, . . . how is hibernation different from sleep?
   (professor) Ah, . . . that's a good question, Tom, one that I'm a little late in clarifying.
   WHY DOES THE PROFESSOR SAY THIS:
   (professor) Ah, . . . that's a good question, Tom, one that I'm a little late in clarifying.
7. WHAT HAPPENS TO BODY TEMPERATURE AND HEART RATE DURING HIBERNATION?
8. WHAT PART OF THE BEAR MOST LIKELY WARMS UP FIRST FROM HIBERNATION?

EXAMPLE (Listening Skill 5)

Listen to a part of a lecture in a geography class.

(professor) Today, I'll be talking about the major rivers of the world. The four longest are the Nile, the Amazon, the Mississippi, and the Yangtze.

The Nile River in Africa is the longest, at 4,145 miles in length. It flows north from the equator to empty into the Mediterranean and irrigates more than a million acres of land.

The Amazon River in South America is slightly shorter than the Nile at just over 4,000 miles in length. Though it is the world's second longest river, it carries more water than any other river.

Asia also has a massive river system. The Yangtze River in China is Asia's longest at 3,436 miles. Because the mountains at its source are at such a high altitude, the Yangtze flows more rapidly than other major rivers for most of its length.

The Mississippi River is the best-known river system in North America, and it's the United States' chief inland waterway. However, it's not the longest river in North America; the Missouri River, at

2,340 miles in length, is slightly longer than the Mississippi.

1. HOW IS THE INFORMATION IN THE LECTURE ORGANIZED?
2. IS EACH OF THESE RIVERS DISCUSSED IN THE LECTURE?
3. WHAT IS THE LENGTH OF EACH OF THESE RIVERS?

LISTENING EXERCISE 5

PASSAGE ONE

Questions 1 through 3. Listen to a lecture in a biology class.

(professor) Today I'll be talking about the concept of tropism as it relates to plants. Tropism, for those of you who don't know, refers to a bending of a plant or a part of a plant in response to an outside stimulus.

There are three important kinds of tropism. They are phototropism, geotropism, and hydrotropism. In each of these kinds of tropism, a plant, or a part of a plant, bends in response to a different kind of outside stimulus.

First, we'll discuss phototropism. The outside stimulus in phototropism is light. When a plant is affected by phototropism, it grows in the direction of a light source such as the Sun.

The second kind of tropism is geotropism. In geotropism, the outside stimulus is gravity. In a plant affected by geotropism, the affected part of the plant grows directly downward because of the pull of gravity. When a plant's affected by geotropism, it's often the root structure that's affected.

OK. The final kind of tropism I'll discuss today is hydrotropism. When hydrotropism affects a plant, this means that the plant is drawn toward water. A plant under the effect of hydrotropism will grow in the direction of its water source.

1. HOW IS THE INFORMATION IN THE PASSAGE ORGANIZED?
2. IS EACH OF THESE KINDS OF TROPISM DESCRIBED IN THE PASSAGE?
3. WHAT IS EACH OF THESE TYPES OF TROPISM?

PASSAGE TWO

Questions 4 through 6. Listen to a lecture in an archeology class.

(professor) Today, we're going to be talking about fossils. A basic definition of fossils is that they are the remains of plants and animals that have turned to stone, and today we're going to be talking about how animals become fossils.

The process begins when a living being dies. After an animal dies, its soft tissues break down. When the soft tissues have decomposed, only the hard parts of the body, such as the bones and teeth, remain.

Over a long period of time, um, the hard tissue becomes buried under layers of sediment. As more layers of sediment cover the hard tissue, it becomes buried more and more deeply.

When the bones are buried deep in the earth, they come into contact with groundwater, and a change begins to occur. Minerals from the groundwater seep into the bones and, over long periods of time, the minerals eventually replace the bones. This is the actual step when fossilization occurs, when minerals from the groundwater have replaced the actual hard tissue from the original body.

The buried fossilized remains, which are buried deep within the earth, may then make their way back to the surface. As the earth moves, the remains are pushed around . . . if they get closer to the surface, where they can be seen, or get near enough to the surface, where they can be dug out.

4. HOW IS THE INFORMATION IN THE PASSAGE ORGANIZED?
5. THE PROFESSOR EXPLAINS THE STEPS IN THE PROCESS OF ANIMAL FOSSIL FORMATION. PUT THESE STEPS IN ORDER.
6. INDICATE WHETHER EACH OF THESE STEPS OCCURS AS AN ANIMAL BECOMES A FOSSIL.

PASSAGE THREE

Questions 7 through 9. Listen to a discussion by a group of students taking a law class.

(man 1) We need to know about Clarence Darrow and some of his more famous cases.

(woman) OK, uh, I know that Clarence Darrow was a famous lawyer. What were some of his most famous cases?

(man 2) He was famous for the Eugene Debs case, and the Loeb-Leopold case, and the Scopes trial.

(woman) He was also famous for his part in resolving a coal strike.

(man 1) OK, let's go over each of these cases and make sure we understand them. The first one was the Eugene Debs case in 1895. Darrow defended Debs, who was the president of the railroad workers union, after the railroad workers went on strike.

(man 2) Wasn't the strike by the railroad workers called the Pullman Strike?

(man 1) Yes, it was; it was named after the Pullman, which was a type of railroad car.

(woman) Uh, the next situation was the Pennsylvania coal strike in 1902. Clarence Darrow was asked by the president of the United States to arbitrate the coal strike.

(man 1)	So this wasn't actually a trial; it was an arbitration.
(woman)	That's true. Now, there are two other trials we need to know about: the Loeb-Leopold trial and the Scopes trial.
(man 2)	The Loeb-Leopold trial was in 1924. This was a very famous murder trial.
(woman)	And Clarence Darrow was the defense attorney in this trial?
(man 2)	Exactly.
(woman)	Now, the last case we need to be familiar with is the Scopes trial, but I don't know much about that.
(man 1)	The Scopes trial in 1925—also known as the Scopes monkey trial—was about evolution, about whether humanity evolved from monkeys.
(woman)	And who was Scopes?
(man 1)	Scopes was a high school biology teacher who was charged with breaking the law because he taught evolution in school.
(woman)	And Clarence Darrow was the defense attorney in this trial?
(man 1)	Yes, he was.
(man 2)	I think we've covered the information we need to know about Darrow. We know about three of the trials in which he served as defense attorney.
(woman)	And we also know about the strike he helped to arbitrate.

7. HOW DO THE STUDENTS ORGANIZE THEIR DISCUSSION?
8. DO THE STUDENTS DISCUSS EACH OF THESE CASES IN WHICH DARROW PARTICIPATED?
9. THE STUDENTS DISCUSS A NUMBER OF CASES IN WHICH CLARENCE DARROW WAS INVOLVED. WHAT WAS EACH OF THESE CASES ABOUT?

PASSAGE FOUR
Questions 10 through 14. Listen to a discussion in a physiology class.

(instructor)	Now, we're going to review the information on various types of fractures, or broken bones. Yesterday, we talked about three types of fractures. Do you remember what they were? Clair?
(Clair)	They were simple, compound, and, ah, greenstick fractures.
(instructor)	Yes, exactly. Now, can you tell me how a simple fracture and a compound fracture differ? Are they different because of the number of fractures? Dave?
(Dave)	No, the difference between a simple and a compound fracture refers to how much damage there is to the tissue around the broken bone rather than the number of breaks in the bone. In a simple fracture, the bone is broken, but there's little damage to the tissue around the, um, around the bone. In a compound fracture, the bone is broken and there's a lot of damage to the tissue around the broken bone.
(instructor)	So, how much tissue damage is there in a compound fracture? Gail?

(Gail)	A lot. In a compound fracture, the broken bone actually comes through the skin.
(instructor)	So, when we talk about the difference between a simple and a compound fracture, this doesn't refer to the number of breaks in a bone; instead, it refers to the amount of tissue damage. How do we refer to the number of breaks in a bone? Clair?
(Clair)	To talk about the number of breaks in a bone, we talk about a, a single, a double, or a multiple break. A single fracture means one break, a double fracture means two breaks, and the, uh, a multiple fracture means more than two breaks.
(instructor)	OK, I hope this distinction's clear, that we talk about single, double, and multiple fractures to refer to the number of fractures and simple and compound fractures to refer to how much tissue damage there is around the break. Now, we have just one more type of fracture to discuss, and that's the greenstick fracture. Dave can you tell me who generally suffers from greenstick fractures?
(Dave)	Greenstick fractures are usually found in children.
(instructor)	That's true. And what is a greenstick fracture? Gail?
(Gail)	A greenstick fracture means that the bone bends and maybe it breaks part of the way, but it doesn't break all the way through. The name "greenstick" refers to a young green plant that might bend instead of breaking.
(instructor)	So, is a greenstick fracture a very serious fracture? Clair?
(Clair)	No, a greenstick fracture's usually the least serious type of fracture because the bone isn't broken all the way through. The compound fracture, where the broken bone comes through the skin, is the most serious type of fracture.

10. HOW IS THE INFORMATION IN THE DISCUSSION ORGANIZED?
11. WHAT DOES EACH TYPE OF FRACTURE DESCRIBE?
12. HOW CAN EACH TYPE OF FRACTURE BE DESCRIBED?
13. HOW MANY BREAKS DOES EACH TYPE OF FRACTURE HAVE?
14. HOW SERIOUS IS EACH TYPE OF FRACTURE?

EXAMPLE (Listening Skill 6)

Listen as two students discuss campus parking.

(man)	Can you tell me about parking on campus? I've just gotten a car, and I'm going to be parking on campus. I'm so glad I don't have to be riding my bicycle to class anymore.

(woman) Parking is kind of difficult on campus because there just aren't enough spaces for all the people who want to park. You do know that if you're going to park on campus, you'll need a parking sticker?

(man) A parking sticker? What kind of parking sticker?

(woman) Well, if you're only going to park on campus once in a while, you can get a daily sticker each day that you park. But if you're going to be parking on campus often, then you should really get a permanent sticker.

(man) I have classes almost every day of the week, so I know what I've got to do.

1. WHAT WILL THE MAN MOST LIKELY DO?

LISTENING EXERCISE 6

PASSAGE ONE

Questions 1 and 2. Listen as a student asks her advisor about a placement test.

(student) I'm scheduled to take a placement test in math on Saturday. Is this something I really need to do?

(advisor) It's to your advantage to take the placement test, but you don't have to.

(student) What's the advantage of taking the placement test?

(advisor) If you take the math placement test and do well on it, you don't have to take the beginning math class. You'll be able to start with an intermediate or even an advanced math class if you get a high score on the placement test.

(student) And if I don't take the math placement test, then I have to start with the beginning math class?

(advisor) That's right.

(student) Well, then, . . . I think I can save myself an entire semester-long course if I do as well as I think I can.

1. WHAT IS IMPLIED ABOUT THE MATH PLACEMENT TEST?
2. WHAT IS THE STUDENT MOST LIKELY GOING TO DO?

PASSAGE TWO

Questions 3 and 4. Listen as a student meets with his professor to discuss a term paper he is writing.

(professor) Thanks for stopping by.

(student) No problem. Why did you want to see me?

(professor) I need to go over the outline for your term paper.

(student) The outline for my term paper? . . . Is there a problem?

(professor) Well, you have a good topic and lots of interesting ideas here, but the outline itself could still be better.

(student) Well, what can I do to improve the outline?

(professor) I have two suggestions to improve the outline. First of all, you need to organize the ideas a little more clearly.

(student) So, you think I have enough ideas, but they need to be better organized?

(professor) Exactly. And for my second suggestion, you don't . . . uh . . . have much of a conclusion. You should really think about . . . uh . . . strengthening your conclusion.

(student) OK, I'll work on the overall organization and the conclusion. Then what?

(professor) Well, after you've improved these two areas, I'd like you to resubmit the outline, and we can discuss it some more.

(student) And when would you like the revised outline?

(professor) Well, don't take too long working on it. You really need to get the outline squared away so you can work on writing the paper. Let's say within a week? You should get it to me no later than next week.

3. HOW WAS THIS MEETING MOST LIKELY INITIATED?
4. WHAT IS THE PROFESSOR'S OVERALL ASSESSMENT OF THE OUTLINE?

PASSAGE THREE

Questions 5 and 6. Listen to a lecture in a botany class.

(professor) Today, I'll be talking about the information in Chapter 22 from the text, the chapter on conifers. You should've read the chapter already and turned in the answers to the ten questions at the end of the chapter.

Do you know what conifers are? Well, conifers are the type of trees, such as pines, that have cones instead of colorful flowers. About a third of the world's trees are conifers, and the vast majority of conifers are found in the great conifer forests of North America and Siberia.

Conifers are hardy trees that have been able to survive well, and as a result, both the oldest and the biggest trees in the world belong to the conifer family. The oldest known living tree is a four-thousand-year-old bristlecone pine, which is located in California. The giant redwoods, which are also found in California, are the largest trees; they can be several hundred feet tall and weigh as much as 2,000 tons. An interesting note about the giant redwoods is that, even though the trees are so large, they have relatively small cones.

What is true of most, but not all, conifers is that they are evergreens with needle-like leaves. The needle-like shape of conifer leaves evolved as a reaction to drought. When compared with a flat leaf, a needle presents a much smaller surface area, which decreases the amount of water lost through the leaves. Because most conifers are evergreens, they lose and replace their needles throughout the year, rather than shedding all their leaves in one season, as deciduous trees do.

That's all for today. For next class, you should read the next chapter and do the same with it that you did with the chapter for today. See you next class.

5. WHAT DOES THE PROFESSOR IMPLY ABOUT CONIFERS IN THE LECTURE?
6. WHAT ARE THE STUDENTS MOST LIKELY SUPPOSED TO DO FOR THE NEXT CLASS?

PASSAGE FOUR

Questions 7 through 9. Listen as a professor talks to a group of students in an economics class.

(professor) Today, I'm going to go over the presentations you'll be giving and what I'm looking for in them. I'm sure you'll want to give really good presentations; the presentations are, by the way, 50 percent of your grade in the course. . . . Did that get your attention? . . . That's right. For each of you, your presentation is fully half of your grade in the course.

Um, first, let me talk about the topic. This is a course about economic theory, so for your presentation I want you to choose one of the economic theories from the course and apply it to some present-day situation. This means that you need to include both the theory and the present-day situation and make it clear how, uh, how the theory is applicable to the present-day situation. And . . . you'll need to include enough facts about the present-day situation to demonstrate that it provides a good example of the theory you selected.

Now, let me make it clear what I expect regarding the timing of your presentations. I'm going to be very strict about the timing. You have exactly five minutes to present, not a second more. And in this five minutes you have to present both the theory and the present-day example to show how they're related. You'll be stopped at the end of five minutes whether you're finished or not, and . . . you can believe me . . . if you haven't finished all the main points of your presentation within five minutes, your grade will suffer. Then, after you make your presentation, the other students'll have five minutes to question you on your presentation. The question-and-answer period following the presentation will also last for five minutes, and all of the students in the audience are expected to be involved in questioning the presenter.

(student) Professor, what if we don't know enough about the situation to ask questions about it?

(professor) It's the responsibility of the presenter to provide enough information about

the situation. If you're unable to ask questions, then the presenter hasn't done a very good job. The presentation needs to provide enough details about the present-day situation.

7. WHAT TOPIC WOULD BE MOST ACCEPTABLE TO THE PROFESSOR?
8. WHICH WOULD MOST LIKELY GET A GOOD GRADE?
9. WHICH OF THE FOLLOWING WOULD THE PROFESSOR MOST LIKELY SAY?

LISTENING EXERCISE (Skills 5 and 6)

Questions 1 through 7. Listen to a discussion about a history course.

(woman 1) ❶ We certainly have a lot of study questions to review for our history exam.

(man) Yes, we do, but we're almost finished. We only have two more questions to go.

(woman 2) Only two more questions? That's great. Let's get going on them, and we'll be finished preparing for this exam. . . . Now, what's the next question on the study list?

(woman 1) The next question on the study list asks about famous historical places on the Outer Banks.

(woman 2) The Outer Banks? Where're the Outer Banks?

(man) ❷ Look at the map in the book. The Outer Banks are a series of islands stretching along the coast of North Carolina.

(woman 1) Now, the question asks about famous historical places on the Outer Banks. Can you come up with any?

(man) Um, let's see. There's the Lost Colony on Roanoke.

(woman 1) Can you see Roanoke Island on the map? That was where the Lost Colony was located.

(woman 2) Wait a minute. The Lost Colony? What was the Lost Colony?

(man) The Lost Colony was the group of settlers from England that landed on Roanoke Island in 1587. When a supply ship returned there three years later, the colonists had disappeared. To this day, no one knows what happened to them.

(woman 1) OK, I think Roanoke Island is one good answer to a question about famous historical places on the Outer Banks. Now, what about Ocracoke Island? Isn't Ocracoke Island famous for something?

(woman 2) All I know about Ocracoke Island is that it's where Blackbeard had his hideout.

(man) Blackbeard, the pirate?

(woman 2) Yes. Blackbeard had his hideout on Ocracoke Island, early in the eighteenth century. He used to move up and down the coast from his hideout on Ocracoke and attack ships and steal their goods.

(woman 1) OK, so we've got historical places on Roanoke Island and Ocracoke Island for answers to the question. Can you come up with any other historical places on the Outer Banks?

(man) What about the Wright Brothers? Didn't they make their flights on the Outer Banks?

(woman 2) Yes, it was at Kill Devil Hills, outside of Kitty Hawk, that the Wright Brothers made their flights.

(man) On December 7, 1903, they managed to get a power-driven plane in the air, for just a short time. But the plane was flying.

(woman 2) Their first flight was only 12 seconds long. They tried four flights on the same day, and by the end of the day, they got the plane to stay up for 59 seconds, almost a full minute.

(woman 1) ❸ OK. I think we have enough information to answer that question. We've got historical places on Roanoke Island, Ocracoke Island, and Kitty Hawk.

(man) I agree. Why don't we leave the question on the Outer Banks and move on?

(woman 2) Good idea. Only one more to go. We're almost there.

1. WHAT DOES THE DISCUSSION FOCUS ON?
2. HOW ARE THE LOCATIONS PRESENTED?
3. WHEN DID THESE PEOPLE LIVE?
4. WITH WHAT PEOPLE ARE THESE LOCATIONS ASSOCIATED?
5. DO THE STUDENTS DISCUSS THESE PLACES?
6. WHAT CAN BE INFERRED FROM THE PASSAGE ABOUT THE EVENTS SELECTED BY THE STUDENTS?
7. WHAT WILL THE STUDENTS MOST LIKELY DO NEXT?

LISTENING REVIEW EXERCISE (Skills 1 through 6)

Questions 1 through 6. Listen to a lecture in a botany class.

(professor) ❶ Today, we're going to talk about phyllotaxy. Phyllotaxy is a scientific term that refers to the arrangement of leaves on the stem of a plant. On most plants, leaves are arranged in a definite pattern. It's very unusual for a plant to have randomly placed leaves. One of the main reasons why the leaves on a plant stem are arranged in an orderly way is to ensure that each leaf is exposed to the maximum amount of light with a minimum amount of interference from other leaves.

❷ The first type of leaf arrangement is the alternate arrangement. You can see this type of leaf arrangement in the diagram. In this type of leaf arrangement, there's only one leaf at each node, and a node, by the way, is the spot where the leaf's attached to the stem.

❸ The next type of leaf arrangement is the opposite arrangement, which you can see in the diagram. In this type of leaf arrangement, there're two leaves at each node, and these two leaves are opposite each other on the stem. This type of leaf arrangement isn't as common as the alternate arrangement, with one leaf at each node.

❹ Where was I? Oh, OK. The last type of leaf arrangement that we're going to look at is called the whorled leaf arrangement. This type of leaf arrangement is the least common of all. It isn't as common as either the opposite or the alternate arrangement. In this type of arrangement, in the whorled arrangement, three or more leaves are attached to the stalk of the plant at the same node. In the diagram, you can see three leaves at the same node, but it's also possible for there to be more than three leaves at the same node, and the leaf arrangement would still be considered a whorled arrangement.

❺ Now, . . . I hope you've been paying careful attention to this information about phyllotaxy, . . . because I . . . um . . . have an assignment for you that's a bit different from the homework assignments you've had so far. Your assignment is to visit the university's botanical garden. Were you aware that this university has quite an extensive botanical garden? In the botanical garden, there're examples of many different kinds of plants, and each plant is labeled with the name of the plant as well as other information about the plant. For your assignment, you are to find three examples of each of these different types of leaf structures, write down the names of the plants that have these leaf structures, and then turn in your lists on Friday. It'll be quite easy for you to find examples of the alternate leaf structure because, as I said before, this is the most common type of leaf structure. It'll be a bit more difficult to find examples of the opposite structure, but by far the most difficult leaf arrangement for you to find will be the whorled structure because this leaf arrangement's so rare. You'll have to spend some time finding examples of the whorled leaf arrangement in our botanical garden. See you on Friday with your lists . . . eh . . . uh . . . Hold on for a minute! Just a word of warning. . . . You'd better not put off the assignment until Thursday evening, as I'm sure many of you are used to doing. The botanical gardens close at sunset each day, so if you try to put this assignment off until Thursday evening, you won't be able to get it done.

1. WHY IS THE PROFESSOR DISCUSSING LEAF ARRANGEMENTS WITH THE STUDENTS?

2. WHAT POINTS DOES THE PROFESSOR WANT TO MAKE ABOUT LEAF ARRANGEMENTS ON PLANTS?
3. WITH WHAT TYPE OF LEAF ARRANGEMENTS ARE THESE NODE PATTERNS ASSOCIATED?
4. HOW COMMON ARE THESE TYPES OF LEAF ARRANGEMENTS?
5. WHAT DOES THE PROFESSOR SAY ABOUT THE BOTANICAL GARDEN?
6. LISTEN AGAIN TO PART OF THE LECTURE. THEN ANSWER THE QUESTION.

> (professor) See you on Friday with your lists. . . . Eh . . . uh . . . Hold on for a minute! Just a word of warning. . . . You'd better not put off the assignment until Thursday evening, as I'm sure many of you are used to doing.

WHAT DOES THE PROFESSOR MEAN WHEN HE SAYS THIS:

> (professor) Hold on for a minute!

LISTENING POST-TEST

Questions 1 through 6. Listen to a conversation between a student and a professor.

> (student) Hello, Dr. Trent.
> (professor) Hi, Sandy. Come on in. Is there something you wanted to talk about with me?
> (student) Yes, it's about the project in music class.
> (professor) I though I explained it pretty well in class, . . . but, what's your question?
> (student) Um, . . . I'm just not sure what you want me to do for the project.
> (professor) I think I explained it clearly in class. . . . You were in class, weren't you?
> (student) Yes, I certainly was.
> (professor) Well, then, why don't you tell me what you heard about the project.
> (student) OK. I know you said that we should choose a composer. . . .
> (professor) Yes, that's right.
> (student) Well, does it have to be a composer that we've talked about in class, or can it be a different composer?
> (professor) I think the project's a bit easier if you choose one of the composers from class, but you really can choose any composer for the project.
> (student) OK.
> (professor) So do you have a composer in mind?
> (student) Yes, I do. . . .
> (professor) And is it one of the composers from class?
> (student) No, it's not. . . .
> (professor) That's OK . . . now what are you supposed to do for the rest of the project, after you've chosen a composer?
> (student) The next step is to research the composer. I haven't started the research yet, but that doesn't sound too bad to me.
> (professor) And what're you supposed to learn about the composer?

> (student) I know we were supposed to learn about the composer's style . . . his style of writing music.
> (professor) Yes, exactly.
> (student) But are we also supposed to learn about him—I mean about his life?
> (professor) Some background about his life would be helpful, but really, the focus is on the composer's style of writing. Is that clear?
> (student) Yes, it is.
> (professor) And now for the final part of the project. What are you supposed to do for the final part of the project?
> (student) That's the hard part, if I understood you correctly in class.
> (professor) Well, it's the most interesting and challenging part, I think. . . .
> (student) We're supposed to write a short piece of music in the style of this composer.
> (professor) Yes, that's right.
> (student) That's a lot harder than doing some research. When you do research you just have to find things, but in this part of the project I have to create something on my own. I'm not sure I can do that.
> (professor) I'm sure you can. Keep in mind that it's just a very short piece, but it does have to be in the style of the composer you've chosen.
> (student) That's what I thought you said in class . . . but it sounds so hard.
> (professor) It's a challenge, maybe, but I'm sure you'll enjoy it once you get into it.

1. WHY IS THE STUDENT TALKING WITH THE PROFESSOR?
2. LISTEN AGAIN TO PART OF THE PASSAGE. THEN ANSWER THE QUESTION.

> (student) Um, . . . I'm just not sure what you want me to do for the project.
> (professor) I think I explained it clearly in class. . . . You were in class, weren't you?
> (student) Yes, I certainly was.
> (professor) Well, then, why don't you tell me what you heard about the project.

WHY DOES THE PROFESSOR SAY THIS:

> (professor) Well, then, why don't you tell me what you heard about the project.

3. IS EACH OF THESE PART OF THE ASSIGNMENT?
4. WHAT DOES THE STUDENT SAY ABOUT A COMPOSER FOR HER PROJECT?
5. HOW DOES THE STUDENT SEEM TO FEEL ABOUT THE ASSIGNMENT?
6. WHAT CONCLUSION CAN BE DRAWN ABOUT THE ASSIGNMENT?

Questions 7 through 12. Listen as an instructor leads a discussion of some material from a geography class.

> (instructor) ❶ Today we're going to be reviewing some information about the Great Lakes, and we're going to see that traditional beliefs about the Great Lakes do not reflect scientific reality. ❷ First of all, can you identify the Great Lakes on this map? Hannah?

(Hannah)	Lake Superior is the largest and northernmost of the five Great Lakes. The two smaller lakes to the southeast of the other lakes are Lake Erie and Lake Ontario. The two lakes in the middle are Lake Michigan and Lake Huron.
(instructor)	All right. Now I'm going to ask a question that sounds like an easy question but really isn't. This deceptively easy question is, which of the Great Lakes is the largest? Jack?
(Jack)	It seems like an easy question because, on the map, you can clearly see that Lake Superior is the largest, and any almanac of world information lists Lake Superior as the world's largest freshwater lake. But I know Lake Superior really isn't the answer you want.
(instructor)	And do you know why Lake Superior isn't the answer I was looking for to the question about which Great Lake is the largest?
(Jack)	Yes, I think so. I believe I read that scientists who have studied the interactions of the lakes have found that Lake Michigan and Lake Huron actually interact as one lake.
(instructor)	That's exactly right. . . . So, in reality, which of the Great Lakes is the largest?
(Jack)	In reality, Lakes Michigan and Huron together are one lake. You could say that Lake Michigan-Huron is the largest of the Great Lakes and the world's largest freshwater lake.
(instructor)	OK. ❸ Now, let's go over the arguments for considering Lake Huron and Lake Michigan one lake rather than two. Pat?
(Pat)	Well, first of all, Lake Huron and Lake Michigan are at the same elevation, and they are connected by the Mackinac Strait, which is also at the same elevation. If they were two distinct lakes, they might be divided by a stream or a river. However, the Mackinac Strait is not a stream or a river. Instead, it is a body of water that is 3 to 5 miles wide, wider than most lakes.
(instructor)	That's right. So what does this mean?
(Pat)	Mackinac Strait is not a river that separates two lakes; instead, it could be argued that there is one giant lake, Michigan-Huron, and this one giant lake narrows at the spot known as Mackinac Strait.
(instructor)	Not bad at all, Pat. I couldn't have done better. Now let's see if some of the rest of you can match that. What about you, Hannah? What about the flow of water between Lake Michigan and Lake Huron?
(Hannah)	The flow of water between the two lakes can reverse. Whenever there's an imbalance in the water levels in the two lakes, the water levels can equalize rapidly, in either direction.

(instructor)	Very good, Hannah. And what does this mean?
(Hannah)	It means that if the water level becomes higher in Lake Huron, water will flow from Lake Huron into Lake Michigan, and if the water level becomes higher in Lake Michigan, water will flow from Lake Michigan into Lake Huron.
(instructor)	So the flow of water between the two lakes can move in either direction, from Lake Huron into Lake Michigan or from Lake Michigan into Lake Huron, and the water levels in Huron and Michigan will always equalize. What conclusion can be drawn from this information? Pat?
(Pat)	This means that the two lakes, Michigan and Huron, are, in reality, acting like one lake instead of two.
(instructor)	Exactly. You seem to have a good understanding of this material. I'll see you at the next session.

7. WHAT IS THE INSTRUCTOR'S MAIN POINT?
8. WHY DOES THE INSTRUCTOR SAY THIS:

(instructor)	Now I'm going to ask a question that sounds like an easy question but really isn't.

9. WHICH OF THE GREAT LAKES HAS TRADITIONALLY BEEN CONSIDERED THE LARGEST?
10. LISTEN AGAIN TO PART OF THE PASSAGE. THEN ANSWER THE QUESTION.

(instructor)	Not bad at all, Pat. I couldn't have done better. Now let's see if some of the rest of you can match that. What about you, Hannah? What about the flow of water between Lake Michigan and Lake Huron?

HOW DOES THE PROFESSOR SEEM TO FEEL ABOUT THE STUDENT'S RESPONSE?

11. WHAT IS TRUE ABOUT LAKES MICHIGAN AND HURON?
12. WHAT CAN BE INFERRED FROM THE DISCUSSION?

SPEAKING DIAGNOSTIC PRE-TEST

Question 3

Listen to the passage. On a piece of paper, take notes on the main points of the listening passage.

(woman)	You're going to take some classes in the Humanities Department next semester, aren't you, Paul?
(man)	I'm taking two of them.
(woman)	I think you're going to sign up for the same two I'm taking.
(man)	Yeah, we both have the same two classes to take.
(woman)	Have you gotten a signature yet?
(man)	A signature? Whose signature do I have to get?
(woman)	You have to get your advisor's signature so that you can register for the two humanities courses you want to take.

(man)	Since when? I've never had to get a signature from my advisor to register for classes.
(woman)	There's a new policy. I saw a notice on the door of the Humanities Department office.
(man)	I haven't seen the notice. I'll have to go check it out . . . but it says that every student has to get an advisor's signature to register for any class?
(woman)	To register for any class in the Humanities Department, any class except the introductory classes.
(man)	I guess I'll have to go see my advisor.
(woman)	Me, too.
(man)	But first I'm going to go over to the Humanities Department and look at the notice. Listen, thanks for telling me about this.

HOW DOES THE STUDENTS' CONVERSATION ADD TO THE INFORMATION INCLUDED IN THE NOTICE?

Question 4

Listen to the passage. On a piece of paper, take notes on the main points of the listening passage.

(professor)	I'd like to make a couple of points, now, about nonverbal communication. The first point is that nonverbal communication does <u>not</u> require intent. One can communicate nonverbally without intending to do so. Think about a student who's feeling bored listening to a professor drone on and on; this student might not want to make his or her boredom clear to the professor, might not want to offend the professor, but perhaps the student's boredom is clear to anyone who looks at him or her.
	Now, there's another point I'd like to make about nonverbal communication. This second point is that nonverbal communication doesn't take place automatically simply because one person has tried to communicate nonverbally. There has to be <u>communication</u>. If one person makes a certain gesture or expression, for example, but no one understands it, then no communication has taken place. There is communication <u>only</u> if the gesture or expression is understood.

HOW DOES THE PROFESSOR SUPPLEMENT THE INFORMATION INCLUDED IN THE READING?

Question 5

Listen to the passage. On a piece of paper, take notes on the main points of the listening passage.

(woman)	Hey, Mark, you're studying French, aren't you?
(man)	No, I'm studying Spanish.
(woman)	Spanish? Oh, I thought you were studying French, like me. I was going to ask you about some of the French courses.

(man)	I don't know about French courses; I only know about Spanish courses, but I think the courses in the two departments are the same. What's your question? Maybe I can help.
(woman)	My question's about the intermediate courses.
(man)	I'm taking intermediate Spanish.
(woman)	I'm enrolled in the intermediate French course, but it doesn't seem right for me.
(man)	Why not? It's too easy?
(woman)	(laughs) I wish. No, it's too hard.
(man)	Did you study French in high school?
(woman)	Yes, for three years. I had three years of French in high school.
(man)	I had three years of Spanish in high school, and now I'm in the intermediate Spanish class, and it seems to be the right level for me.
(woman)	I guess that answers my question. I must be in the class I'm supposed to be in. I had three years of French in high school, but intermediate French just seems too hard for me. I just can't believe that I might need to go back to beginning French when I studied three years of French in high school.
(man)	What's the problem in your intermediate French class? Are you sure it's too hard for you?
(woman)	The problem is that I don't understand anything in class, anything at all.
(man)	Do the other students seem to understand better than you?
(woman)	I don't know. I haven't really noticed.
(man)	Maybe you should talk with the other students and see if they're having trouble understanding, too. That would help you know if you're in the right place . . . And maybe you should talk with the professor, too, and find out if he thinks . . .
(woman)	<u>She</u> thinks. . . .
(man)	OK, find out if <u>she</u> thinks you're in the right class.
(woman)	So you think I should talk to the other students and to the professor?
(man)	I do.
(woman)	But not in French. That's too hard for me.

WHAT DOES THE MAN SUGGEST THE WOMAN SHOULD DO TO DEAL WITH THE PROBLEM SHE IS HAVING?

Question 6

Listen to the passage. On a piece of paper, take notes on the main points of the listening passage.

(professor)	Today, I'll be talking about whales, specifically about how whales use echolocation. Do you know what echolocation is? Well, in broad terms, it's a technique used by whales to determine what's going on in their surroundings. The term is *echolocation*; this term is composed of two ideas, *echo* and *location*. Basically, echolocation refers to the

technique of using <u>echoes</u> to determine the <u>location</u> of whatever is in the surrounding area.

I have a few points to make about echolocation. The first point is that it seems that only toothed whales can use echolocation. I'm sure you understand that some whales have teeth and others don't. It's only the toothed whales that seem to have this capability.

Next, I'd like to talk about what happens during echolocation. A whale uses echolocation by sending out a series of clicks. The clicks then bounce off objects in the water and are reflected back to the whale. So echolocation is actually a series of clicks sent out by a whale that bounce off objects and are then reflected back to the whale.

Now, what is it exactly that a whale can learn from these clicks that bounce off an object? Quite a bit, actually. A whale can learn the size and shape of objects that are out there. But that's not all. From the reflected clicks a whale can learn more than the size and shape of an object. It can also understand how far away the object is and if the object is moving, the whale can understand how fast the object is moving and what direction it's moving.

WHAT POINTS DOES THE PROFESSOR MAKE ABOUT ECHOLOCATION?

SPEAKING EXERCISE 6

1. Listen to the passage. On a piece of paper, take notes on the main points of the listening passage.

(man) Beth, you ride a bicycle to school, don't you?

(woman) Yes, I do.

(man) And I do, too. You saw the notice about bicycle parking?

(woman) What notice about bicycle parking?

(man) You didn't see it, then?

(woman) No, I didn't. What did it say?

(man) It said that we can't park our bicycles on campus near our classrooms.

(woman) What do you mean?

(man) The notice says that bicycles can be parked only along the east and west sides of campus, in the official bicycle parking locations.

(woman) And we can't leave our bicycles anywhere else on campus?

(man) No, we can't.

(woman) Well, what's going to happen if I leave my bicycle on campus, next to the building where I have class?

(man) If you leave your bicycle anywhere on campus except the authorized lots on the east and west sides of campus, you'll get a ticket.

(woman) Oh, no. That doesn't sound fair. I don't like that at all.

(man) You can say that again!

2. Listen to the passage. On a piece of paper, take notes on the main points of the listening passage.

(man) Cathy, did you hear that Dr. Connor's retiring?

(woman) I certainly did. I can't believe it. It seems like she's been here forever.

(man) It's too bad she's leaving. I was hoping to take one of her classes.

(woman) Me, too. You know, my father took several classes from Dr. Connor.

(man) He did? You mean, he was a student here?

(woman) Yeah, he graduated from here 30 years ago.

(man) And he took classes from Dr. Connor when he was here?

(woman) That's right. He's told me how much he enjoyed her classes, so I really want to take at least one before she retires.

(man) Well, she'll only be here for one more semester before she retires, so that'll be your only chance to take one, and my only chance, too.

(woman) Then we really have to make sure to sign up for at least one of her classes for the spring semester, don't we?

(man) We sure do.

3. Listen to the passage. On a piece of paper, take notes on the main points of the listening passage.

(man) Hey, Alice. Did you read the syllabus from Professor Thompson's class?

(woman) I looked it over.

(man) Well, did you see the part about the assignments?

(woman) You mean the part describing the assignments, what we have to do for each assignment?

(man) No, I mean the part about the due dates for the assignments.

(woman) Oh, you mean the part about late assignments, about how the professor doesn't like late assignments?

(man) Yeah, that part. It seems kind of strict, doesn't it? You don't think he actually means it, do you, that he won't accept any late assignments even if we're sick?

(woman) Actually, I'm quite sure he does mean it, absolutely.

(man) Why are you so sure of that?

(woman) Because that's how he's always been, from what I know. I heard about a student who was in his class, and this student was in an accident on his bicycle, one that wasn't his fault, and he was in the hospital. He'd even broken his arm and couldn't write, and Professor Thompson wouldn't even accept any late papers from him.

(man) Not even from a guy who was in the hospital with a broken arm and couldn't write because of the broken arm?

(woman) Not even from him.

(man)	Well, then, I guess Professor Thompson's pretty serious about the policy on late papers.
(woman)	He certainly is.

SPEAKING EXERCISE (Skills 5 through 8)

Listen to the passage. On a piece of paper, take notes on the main points of the listening passage.

(woman)	Do you understand the assignment for the research project in our history class?
(man)	I think so.
(woman)	Well, I'm not quite sure what the assignment is. What do you think we're supposed to do?
(man)	Well, we're supposed to choose one event or person and research that event or person and then write about it from positive and negative perspectives.
(woman)	That's what I thought the syllabus said, but it seems strange. Why do you think the professor wants us to do this?
(man)	I don't know for sure, but I can think of two reasons why he might.
(woman)	What are they?
(man)	Number one, I think he wants to get across to us that research involves a number of sources, not just one.
(woman)	Yeah, it seems easier to look at just one source, but I understand that we need to look in several sources. That makes sense. Now, what's your second reason?
(man)	Number two, I think the professor wants to get across that a single event can be viewed in different ways. Think of someone like Columbus. In some accounts he's viewed as a hero, while in other accounts he's viewed as a villain.
(woman)	OK, that makes sense. Now all I need is a good topic. It sounds like maybe you already have yours.

HOW DOES THE INFORMATION IN THE LISTENING PASSAGE ADD TO THE INFORMATION IN THE READING PASSAGE?

SPEAKING EXERCISE 10

1. Listen to the passage. On a piece of paper, take notes on the main points of the listening passage.

(professor) An interesting point that I'd like to add about the body of water called the Dead Sea is that it's not actually a sea but is instead a lake, a rather large lake, but a lake, not a sea. A sea refers to either a division of the ocean or to a large body of water that's partially, but not entirely, enclosed by land, one that opens into an ocean; a lake is a body of water that's entirely enclosed. The North Sea, for example, is a sea because it's a section of the northeastern part of the Atlantic Ocean, and the Mediterranean is a sea because it opens into the Atlantic.

Because the Dead Sea is landlocked with no outlet, it's a lake rather than a sea.

2. Listen to the passage. On a piece of paper, take notes on the main points of the listening passage.

(professor) Now I'd like to discuss one particular type of polling, a negative and unfair type of polling known as push polling. Push polling involves trying to plant negative information under the guise of conducting an opinion poll. By this, I mean that a pollster tells someone that he simply wants to ask the person's opinion and then, instead of merely finding out that person's opinion, tries to surreptitiously implant negative information in the person's mind. A pollster who uses the technique of push polling may call a potential voter who supports candidate X not to find out which candidate the voter supports but to implant negative information about candidate X in the voter's mind. The pollster might ask leading questions such as "Would you support candidate X if you knew that he spent time in prison?" or "Would you support candidate X if you knew he had a problem with alcohol?" The questions asked by a pollster who is push polling are designed more to implant negative information than to find out how the voter actually feels.

3. Listen to the passage. On a piece of paper, take notes on the main points of the listening passage.

(professor) I'd like to talk about something that the Polynesians may have done in their travels. It seems quite possible that the Polynesians actually made it all the way to South America in their travels, and this seems quite astounding when you consider that they were traveling on outrigger canoes made of only two tree trunks and a platform. There are a number of indications that the Polynesians may have traveled all the way to South America. One important piece of information that leads historians to believe that the Polynesians made it to South America is that there were plants from South America in Hawaii when Europeans first arrived in Hawaii. How did these plants from South America get to Hawaii before the Europeans arrived there? Quite possibly it was the Polynesians who carried the plants from South America to the Hawaiian Islands in their outrigger canoes.

SPEAKING EXERCISE (Skills 9 through 12)

Listen to the passage. On a piece of paper, take notes on the main points of the listening passage.

(professor) Let's look at a couple of situations to see the equity theory in action. We'll talk about this theory in terms of a mythical employee, employee X.

In the first situation, a coworker of employee X has the same job title as employee X, does the same amount of work, makes the same amount of money, and has a similar office. In this situation, employee X will feel satisfied with his job because he and his coworker receive equal returns for their contributions.

The second situation is different. In the second situation, a coworker of employee X has the same job title but does less work, makes more money, and has a bigger office than employee X. In this situation, employee X will not feel satisfied because he receives a lower return for his contribution than the coworker.

HOW DOES THE INFORMATION IN THE LISTENING PASSAGE ADD TO THE INFORMATION IN THE READING PASSAGE?

SPEAKING EXERCISE 13

1. Listen to the passage. On a piece of paper, take notes on the main points of the listening passage.

(man) Hey there, how are you doing?

(woman) Oh, just fine, thanks. Listen, can I ask you a question?

(man) Sure. About what?

(woman) About the course Cultural History of the United States.

(man) Oh, yeah, that's a great class. I took it last year.

(woman) And you really enjoyed it?

(man) I did. I took it with Dr. Abbott. I really enjoyed his course.

(woman) I'm glad. Listen, I saw that two different professors are teaching the course next quarter, and I was wondering if you could recommend one of them. It sounds like you enjoyed Dr. Abbott's course and would recommend him.

(man) I did enjoy Dr. Abbott's class, but . . . well . . . it's not for everyone.

(woman) What do you mean, that it's not for everyone?

(man) Oh, I really enjoyed it, but not everyone did.

(woman) Why not?

(man) In Dr. Abbott's course, we didn't need to memorize a lot of details.

(woman) That sounds good.

(man) And there was a lot of interesting discussion.

(woman) That sounds good, too. Why were some of the students unhappy with the course?

(man) It was the exams. The exams were all essay exams. Some people didn't like that.

(woman) Yeah, I probably wouldn't like that either. . . . By the way, do you know anything about the other professor who teaches the same course, Dr. Becker? Do you know anything about Dr. Becker's course? Is it just like Dr. Abbott's course?

(man) I've heard it's really different. Dr. Becker's a lot more concerned about details; she really concentrates on the details.

(woman) Do you know what her exams are like? Are they essay exams, like Dr. Abbott's?

(man) I've heard that her exams are all multiple choice; there aren't any essays.

(woman) That part of it sounds good to me, but memorizing a lot of details doesn't. The lively discussion in Dr. Abbott's course also sounds good, but the essay exams don't. I've got to think about this some more before I make a decision, but thanks for your help.

2. Listen to the passage. On a piece of paper, take notes on the main points of the listening passage.

(woman) Hey, Alan, are you going to the game tonight?

(man) Oh, I can't, Anne, I have an exam on Friday, and I need to study for it.

(woman) It's too bad you're going to miss the game. It's going to be a great one. . . . You should've studied earlier so that you could go to the game, you know.

(man) I wish I had, but I didn't, and now I've got to spend tonight and tomorrow reviewing my notes.

(woman) It takes that much time for you to review your notes?

(man) I know it shouldn't take that much time, but it does.

(woman) Why does it, do you think?

(man) Well, when I'm in class, I think I take really good notes, I mean, I think I understand what the professor's talking about and I write down lots of stuff . . . it all makes sense at the time. But then it's usually a few weeks until there's an exam, and when I go back to my notes from a few weeks earlier, the notes don't make any sense. That's why it takes so much time for me to review my notes. The notes from a few weeks ago, the ones that I thought were so good, just don't make sense after a few weeks, so it takes a lot of time to sort them out. You see what my problem is?

(woman) I think I understand what your problem is, and, even better, I think I know what you could do to solve the problem.

(man) You do? What?

(woman) I think the most important thing I do, right after I take notes during a lecture, is to go over the notes and reorganize them.

(man) Really? You do that?

(woman) I do. I think that one of the most important things my high school advisor told me about university studies, and about lecture notes in particular, was to "never let them get cold." What she meant was that you shouldn't just take notes during class and forget about the notes for a while until the last minute before an exam. Instead, you should review the notes within a day or so, review them and organize them, if necessary.

(man) Is that what you do?

(woman) Yes, and it saves me so much time because it's much easier to prepare for exams this way.

(man) I guess it can't hurt me to give it a try with the lectures that are coming up, but right now I need to go prepare for the exam on Friday.

(woman) So you can't go to the game?

(man) I really do wish I could, but I can't.

3. Listen to the passage. On a piece of paper, take notes on the main points of the listening passage.

(woman) Hi, Mike, do you have a moment? I'd like to talk with you about something.

(man) Sure, Nicky. I have a few minutes before I have to head over to my next class. What's your question?

(woman) It's about independent study, about an independent study project with Dr. Lee. You did an independent study project last year, and you did your project with Dr. Lee, didn't you?

(man) I sure did. You have a question about that?

(woman) I do. I'd like to know what it's like. I mean, how to do a good job of it.

(man) Uh . . . maybe I'm not the best person to talk about this because I . . . uh . . . didn't do a very good job on my project, I don't think.

(woman) (laughs) Well, then, maybe you can talk with me about what <u>not</u> to do, how <u>not</u> to do a project.

(man) Now that's my area of expertise. I can tell you about what you shouldn't do . . . OK, well first of all, and most important, you need to work on your project regularly. You'll only have meetings with Dr. Lee once a month. What I did was, uh, to not do any work on my project for about three and a half weeks each month, and then I'd spend a couple of days just before meeting with Dr. Lee working on nothing but my project.

(woman) That certainly doesn't sound like the best way to do a project like this. I need to work on the project throughout each month before I meet with Dr. Lee instead of putting all the work off until the last few days of each month. That makes sense . . . OK, what else can you tell me to help me with the project? Or what else can you tell me <u>not</u> to do?

(man) Let's see . . . OK, something else you should keep in mind, and I had trouble with this, too, when I was working on my project, is that it's an <u>independent</u> study project.

(woman) So it means that you work on the project independently?

(man) It also means that <u>you</u> determine the direction your research will take; Dr. Lee doesn't do that.

(woman) What do you mean exactly?

(man) Well, I kept expecting Dr. Lee to tell me what I should do next, but he expected me to figure out what I should do and then discuss it with him.

(woman) Oh, I see now. I need to take charge of figuring out the direction the project should take and not expect Dr. Lee to do that.

(man) Exactly. Think about these things if you decide to work on an independent study project with Dr. Lee. Then you should be able to do a much better job than I did.

SPEAKING EXERCISE (Skills 13 through 15)

Listen to the passage. On a piece of paper, take notes on the main points of the listening passage.

(woman) Are you enjoying Professor Taylor's class?

(man) Not exactly.

(woman) Why not? Why don't you like it?

(man) Well, I get bored in class. It's a two-hour class twice a week, and usually within 15 minutes of the start of the class, I'm nodding off, and it's really hard for me to keep my head up and try to keep my eyes open for the next two hours. One of these days I'm going to fall asleep outright and start snoring out loud right in the middle of class.

(woman) Well, maybe you need to get involved in the class. If you're involved in the class, you can't possibly fall asleep.

(man) But how do I do that?

(woman) Um, let me think about it. . . . Let's see, how many students are in your class?

(man) It's a big class, there are about 60 students in a large classroom.

(woman) Where do you sit?

(man) I sit in the back because I always start falling asleep.

(woman) Well, sit in the front of the classroom, sit right up in the front. It's too easy to let your mind wander when you're in the back of the classroom, and you need to be involved in the class. So you should sit right up at the front of the classroom, close to the professor.

(man) OK, I can try sitting in the front and hope that I don't fall asleep right under the professor's nose. Now, do you have anything else to suggest?

(woman) Well, does the professor just lecture, or does he talk with the students, ask the students questions or answer questions from the students?

(man) He lectures mostly, but sometimes he asks questions, and he'll always answer questions if the students ask.

(woman) Do you ever answer any questions the professor asks?

(man) No, I can't because I'm usually sitting in the back of the room.

(woman) Well, then sit in the front and answer questions the professor asks. . . . Now, have you ever asked the professor a question in class?

(man) No.

(woman) Not ever?

(man) No, not ever.

(woman) Well, ask questions. Sit in the front of the classroom and ask questions. No wonder you're not involved in the class. You can take steps to get yourself involved in the class, and then you just might begin to enjoy it a whole lot.

WHAT DOES THE WOMAN SUGGEST THE MAN CAN DO TO DEAL WITH HIS PROBLEM?

SPEAKING EXERCISE 16

1. Listen to the passage. On a piece of paper, take notes on the main points of the listening passage.

   (professor) Today we're going to be talking about the Bank Holiday of 1933. A holiday. A bank holiday. Sounds like a nice thing, doesn't it? But it really wasn't. It occurred when the U.S. banking system was in serious trouble in 1933, but somehow this situation became known as a holiday rather than as a disaster.

   Let's talk about what led up to the Bank Holiday of 1933. In the 1920s, banking in the United States hadn't been very stable, and it wasn't unusual for banks to fail. Then, after the stock market crashed in 1929, the problem with banks became much worse. By 1933, more than half the states had closed banks.

   The solution to this problem was when President Roosevelt called a bank holiday. This bank holiday meant that all banks were closed for a period of days while the federal government worked to reorganize the banking system. One of the bills passed by the government at the time was federal deposit insurance, which means that any money deposited in U.S. banks would be insured by the federal government.

   Since the time of the bank holiday, the situation has improved considerably. The number of banks that fail has decreased sharply, and the number of people to lose money by depositing it in a federally insured account has remained at zero.

2. Listen to the passage. On a piece of paper, take notes on the main points of the listening passage.

   (professor) Today we're going to talk about creativity. Think about it for a moment. What is creativity? How would you define creativity? It's kind of difficult, isn't it?

   Let's look at what the experts have to say about this. Rather than actually defining creativity, experts try to list what characteristics are part of creativity. Many researchers have studied creativity and have come up with lists of characteristics that their research has shown to be part of creativity. Unfortunately, as I'm sure you understand, various researchers are not in complete agreement as to what actually constitutes creativity.

   There are, however, two characteristics that are widely accepted in research as being constituent parts of creativity. These two components of creativity are originality and appropriateness. Let's think about these two components of creativity, originality and appropriateness, in terms of a problem you need to solve, a problem that requires a creative solution. Can you see how originality and appropriateness would be part of a creative solution?

   First, let's think about originality. If you need a creative solution to a problem, the solution you need isn't the normal, everyday solution that everyone comes up with. It must be an original solution, something new, something different.

   Now let's think about appropriateness, when you're looking for a solution to a problem, it has to be an appropriate solution, doesn't it? If you suggest a solution to a problem but the solution isn't appropriate, say it can't be used because it will offend people or it won't solve the problem because it doesn't fit the problem, this isn't a good solution.

   Thus, we've seen that for an idea to be creative, it has to, minimally, be original and appropriate. There may be other component parts to creativity, but originality and appropriateness are certainly part of it.

3. Listen to the passage. On a piece of paper, take notes on the main points of the listening passage.

   (professor) Have you ever wondered why the huge river in South America is called the Amazon? Well, two sources seem to have contributed to this name. One of these two sources for the modern name of the river is the original native name for the river, and the other source is a chronicle written when Europeans first explored the river in the sixteenth century.

   The native inhabitants living near the giant river certainly must've contributed in part to the modern name of this river. The name given by the native inhabitants to this large river was something like the modern name. The native inhabitants called the river *Amazunu*, which in their language meant "big wave." I'm sure you can hear the similarity between the native name *Amazunu* and today's modern name Amazon.

   However, today's modern name didn't come entirely from the native name for the river; there was another important source for the name Amazon, and this source comes from a sixteenth-century chronicle of the European exploration of the river. In early Greek literature, there were descriptions of a society of brave female warriors called Amazons. When the Europeans were exploring the river in the sixteenth century, a chronicle of the trip was kept. This chronicle of the exploration of the river in the sixteenth century contains descriptions of courageous female warriors much like the female warriors described in ancient Greek literature. The chronicler made reference to the Amazon-like warriors on the river called Amazunu by the natives, which both helped to contribute to the river's modern name Amazon.

SPEAKING EXERCISE (Skills 16 through 18)

Listen to the passage. On a piece of paper, take notes on the main points of the listening passage.

(professor) Something that affects some residents of Alaska and other societies in the far north of the globe during the winter months is a disorder call SAD. SAD is actually an acronym S-A-D, and it stands for seasonal affective disorder. S for seasonal, A for affective, and D for disorder.

In the summertime, Alaska is blessed with a tremendous amount of sunshine, 20 hours of sunshine a day in Anchorage and 22 hours of sunshine a day in Fairbanks. In the winter, however, the opposite occurs, and there are long, long hours of darkness and only an occasional few hours of sunshine if the sky during the hours when sunshine is possible isn't cloudy or stormy.

During these long periods of darkness interrupted by little or no sunlight, residents can be afflicted by SAD, or seasonal affective disorder, a serious kind of clinical depression. Estimates of the percentage affected by SAD range from 10 to 20 percent of the population.

There's actually a physiological cause of this disorder, one that's related to the lack of regular sunlight. When the human body receives less sunlight, it produces less serotonin and more melatonin than usual. Seratonin is a hormone that causes humans to feel cheerful and positive, and less seratonin is produced when there's inadequate sunlight. Melatonin is a hormone that causes humans to feel drowsy and fall asleep, and more melatonin is produced when there's inadequate sunlight. It's this combination of reduced seratonin and increased melatonin that's the cause of seasonal affective disorder in areas where sunlight is reduced considerably for several months at a time.

WHAT POINTS DOES THE PROFESSOR MAKE ABOUT SAD?

SPEAKING POST-TEST

Question 3

Listen to the passage. On a piece of paper, take notes on the main points of the listening passage.

(man) Hey, Sue, are you heading over to the snack bar?

(woman) Yes, I am. So you heard that the main cafeteria's closed?

(man) I didn't <u>hear</u> about it. I read the notice.

(woman) There's a notice about the main cafeteria being closed?

(man) Yeah, there is. It's posted on the door of the main cafeteria. I went over to the cafeteria for lunch, and I read the notice, so now I'm going to one of the snack bars.

(woman) Sorry you had to walk all the way over there for nothing. I heard about the cafeteria being closed from one of the students in my class, so I didn't have to walk all the way over there for nothing.

(man) Listen, do you know why the cafeteria's closed? I can't believe it's closed during the semester.

(woman) I heard there was a fire. Some people were in there cooking this morning, and a fire got started.

(man) That would explain why the cafeteria's closed.

HOW DOES THE INFORMATION IN THE LISTENING PASSAGE ADD TO THE INFORMATION IN THE READING PASSAGE?

Question 4

Listen to the passage. On a piece of paper, take notes on the main points of the listening passage.

(professor) As a teacher, it's important for you to recognize that you can take steps to establish the appropriate kind of social environment to meet the goals of each activity. It's not enough to recognize that certain types of social environments can exist in the classroom; it's also necessary to understand that you can take steps to ensure that the social environment is appropriate for a particular activity. To establish a cooperative environment, your role is to get across to the students that a particular task is to be completed in pairs or in groups and that only those responses that have been agreed upon by the entire group will be accepted. To establish a competitive environment, your role is to get across to the students that they must work alone and that their responses will be evaluated in comparison with responses from other students. To establish an individualistic environment, your role is to get across to the students that they are to work alone and that they are to do the best job they can and that they'll be evaluated based upon a predetermined scale rather than on how well they do in comparison with other students.

HOW DOES THE INFORMATION IN THE LISTENING PASSAGE SUPPLEMENT THE INFORMATION IN THE READING PASSAGE?

Question 5

Listen to the passage. On a piece of paper, take notes on the main points of the listening passage.

(man) Hey, Beth. I saw you running across campus this morning. What was the hurry?

(woman) Oh, hi, Todd. I do that every morning I'm on campus. This morning was nothing unusual.

(man) You go running across the campus every morning just for fun?

(woman) Oh, I'm not running for fun. I have to do that. It's the only way I can get to class on time.

(man) You have two classes in a row that are on opposite sides of the campus?

(woman) Oh, it's much worse than that. I have four classes in a row, and I seem to have managed to choose four classes with one in each of the four corners of campus. So every day I end up running from the first class to the second, and from the second class to the third, and from the third class to the last one.

(man) Why on earth did you schedule your classes that way?

(woman) It sounded like a good idea when I scheduled my classes. I thought it was a good idea to bunch my classes together. I have classes at 8 o'clock in the morning, at 9 o'clock, 10 o'clock, and at 11 o'clock Monday through Thursday. It means that I'm finished with all of my classes by noon.

(man) But it's not working out for you, is it?

(woman) No, it's not. I can't get from one class to the next without running because the classes are so far apart. And even though I move pretty quickly from class to class, I'm still usually late to each class. Here I thought I was making such a great schedule for myself when I selected these classes. I mean, it does sound nice to have all of my classes in the morning four days a week, doesn't it?

(man) That part of it sounds good. It would be nice to have afternoons and evenings free . . . but the part where the classes are so far apart and you have to run from class to class and you're still late all of the time, that part doesn't sound so good.

(woman) It's not, I can assure you.

(man) Maybe next semester you need to consider where your classes meet and not just when they meet.

(woman) That absolutely makes sense to me.

HOW DOES THE MAN FEEL ABOUT THE PROBLEM THE WOMAN HAS?

Question 6

Listen to the passage. On a piece of paper, take notes on the main points of the listening passage.

(professor) Today we're going to talk about the planet Mars and, in particular, how people got the notion that Mars was inhabited by intelligent beings. We know today that there are no English-speaking humanlike beings with intelligence superior to ours populating the planet, but for quite some time people believed that there were. Where did this idea come from? Do you know?

As often happens, we'll see that the idea that there might be humanlike inhabitants on Mars at least in part was based on an error, a linguistic error of sorts. This linguistic error has to do with the word *canali* in Italian.

In 1877 an Italian astronomer was looking through a telescope at Mars, and he saw what looked like thin, straight lines on its surface. He called these faint lines *canali*. In Italian the word *canali* can refer to either something natural or something man-made. In English, however, a canal is something man-made, and a channel is something natural; a canal is man-made, as in the Erie Canal, while a channel is a natural depression, as in the English Channel. When the Italian astronomer called the lines on Mars *canali*, he most likely meant natural geographic features. However, when the word *canali* was translated into English, it was translated as *canal*. From this, it was understood that astronomers were saying that there were features that had been constructed on Mars. If the features had been constructed, then the obvious conclusion would be that there were living beings on Mars who constructed the canals. Unfortunately, that wasn't what the astronomer meant; the astronomer was describing natural features on Mars rather than constructed ones.

WHAT POINTS DOES THE PROFESSOR MAKE ABOUT THE PLANET MARS?

WRITING DIAGNOSTIC PRE-TEST

Question 1

Listen to the passage. On a piece of paper, take notes on the main points of the listening passage.

(professor) Now, I'd like to talk about the cause of childhood amnesia. Though its cause is not known for certain and various explanations have been hypothesized, one explanation is more generally accepted than others.

The generally accepted explanation for childhood amnesia has to do with a huge difference in the way that young children and adults encode their experiences. Young children simply encode their experiences randomly as they happen, while adults retain their memories in an organized way. Because a young child encodes events randomly, without forming associations between events or categorizing events in an organized way, the memories of the encoded events of young children don't last.

There are most likely numerous causes of the shift from early childhood random encoding to adult encoding in organized patterns. A major factor in this shift is the maturing of the hippocampus. . . . Do you know what the hippocampus is? H-I-P-P-O-C-A-M-P-U-S? It's a part of the brain; it's the part of the brain that helps organize and consolidate memories, and this part of the brain is not mature for at least the first two to three years of life. As a result, events that take place in the first two or three years can't be organized and consolidated and therefore most likely won't be remembered later in life.

HOW DOES THE INFORMATION IN THE LISTENING PASSAGE ADD TO THE IDEAS PRESENTED IN THE READING PASSAGE?

WRITING EXERCISE 2

1. Listen to the passage. On a piece of paper, take notes on the main points of the listening passage.

   (professor) Something that many people find quite surprising about the Sahara is that it actually used to be quite green. It once used to be a lush green jungle-like area.

   When an ice age, the Pleistocene Ice Age, ended about 10,000 years ago, the area that today is the massive Sahara Desert actually had a rather wet climate. The area was a lush green land of forests and grasslands with rivers and lakes throughout. There were large animals such as giraffes and elephants, and there were even hippopotamuses, which need water year round to live, in the area. The area was also populated by prehistoric peoples who lived at first by hunting and fishing and later by farming and raising animals.

   Around 6,000 years ago, the climate there began to dry out, and the region began turning into a desert. Within 2,000 years, by 4,000 years ago, a dramatic shift had taken place, and the Sahara had become the huge desert that it is today.

2. Listen to the passage. On a piece of paper, take notes on the main points of the listening passage.

   (professor) We've seen that polysemic words are words that have numerous meanings. Well, there is a really special group of polysemic words, and this special group consists of words that have not just different meanings but opposite meanings. Think about this, that there can be one word in English that has not just different meanings but meanings that are, in some sense, opposite.

   Think about the words bolt and fast. If you bolt something, perhaps you bolt your door, then this means that it's locked <u>fast</u>, or fastened and cannot move or open. However, if someone decides to bolt, then he or she is running away, and running away very fast. So the word *bolt* can mean "locked and not moving" or conversely can mean "moving very quickly." The same can be said of the word *fast*. This word can also mean "locked and not moving" or "moving very quickly."

   Another interesting word of this type is the word *sanction*. Just think about what this word means. If you sanction something, it means that you permit it. However, if you put a sanction on something, then it means the opposite. In this case it means that you don't permit it.

   OK, keep in mind that these words that you just learned about, *bolt* and *fast* and *sanction*, are polysemic words because each can have different meanings. But they are special kinds of polysemic words because their meanings aren't simply different; their meanings are opposite in some sense.

3. Listen to the passage. On a piece of paper, take notes on the main points of the listening passage.

   (professor) Now I'd like to talk about what some critics have to say about Margaret Mead's research. There is one very general criticism that comes out in critical reviews of Mead's work.

   This general criticism of Mead's work is that what she saw in the three societies that she studied was just too pat, too neat, that it all fit too neatly into specific categories. She found these three societies that exhibited remarkably different gender roles, three societies that neatly fit into categories that she was looking to fill. It's not very normal for any society to have behavior that's so extreme, where one can say that all the people in the society act in the same extreme way. It's not very common, in anthropological research, in the study of human societies, that people fit very neatly into a limited number of categories because humans are far more complex than that.

Stated another way, this general criticism of Mead is that perhaps she was looking for societies that exhibit certain extreme behaviors as a whole, and when she found these three particular societies, she paid more attention to the behaviors that fit in with the theory she was trying to prove and perhaps did not pay enough attention to the behaviors that didn't fit into her theory.

WRITING REVIEW EXERCISE (Skills 1 through 7)

Listen to the passage. On a piece of paper, take notes on the main points of the listening passage.

(professor) What is really important about this discovery is that the Iceman was found with all of his clothing and tools intact. He is the first prehistoric man ever to have been found this way; other prehistoric bodies have been found, but these bodies had generally been prepared for death. The Iceman was most likely going about his day in a normal way, wearing his regular clothes and carrying the tools he used in his daily life. The Iceman, thus, can give us a very good idea about what the Iceman's daily life was like.

It was originally believed that the Iceman was out traveling in the mountains when he became unable to continue, perhaps overcome by the elements around him or by exhaustion. However, there is more recent evidence of a fatal knife wound in the Iceman's back and several other wounds on his body that leads researchers to believe that the Iceman was in close combat when he died. Whatever the cause of death, the body was preserved in ice for thousands of years until the ice around it thawed and it became visible to the hikers who found it.

HOW DOES THE INFORMATION IN THE LISTENING PASSAGE ADD TO THE IDEAS PRESENTED IN THE READING PASSAGE?

WRITING POST-TEST

Question 1

Listen to the passage. On a piece of paper, take notes on the main points of the listening passage.

(professor) Do you understand the concept of unintended consequences? That sometimes, when a decision is made, there are consequences of that decision that are unexpected? This, of course, can take place in any field, in any field where decisions are made, but we're going to look at this concept in terms of government decision-making.

Let's take, for example, a situation where a local government needed to increase revenue, so it decided to raise taxes. Makes sense, doesn't it, that the government should have raised taxes if it wanted to increase revenues?

Well, let's look at what happened in this situation. This government wanted to raise revenue, so it increased taxes, and, for a short while, tax revenue was higher. But then, guess what happened! The citizens of the area who were paying higher taxes had less money to spend, because they were paying higher taxes, you see. Well, because the citizens had less money to spend, they bought fewer goods. And what happened to companies when they were selling fewer goods? Well, they paid less in taxes, for one thing, and they had to lay off employees, for another. And these employees who lost their jobs paid no taxes because they weren't working, you see. So, look at the overall situation in this area after a few years. The local government had raised taxes to increase revenue; however, when the government raised taxes, revenue actually went down rather than up. That's an unexpected consequence.

HOW DOES THE INFORMATION IN THE LISTENING PASSAGE ADD TO THE IDEAS PRESENTED IN THE READING PASSAGE?

MINI-TEST 1

LISTENING

Questions 1 through 5. Listen to a conversation between a student and a lab assistant.

(student) Hi, I have a few questions about how we need to handle our work in the science laboratory.

(lab assistant) I gave very specific instructions at the first lab meeting.

(student) And we have to complete the lab work exactly that way?

(lab assistant) That's what I'd like, yes.

(student) Do we need to work in the lab in a group?

(lab assistant) Yes.

(student) And work with the exact group members we were assigned?

(lab assistant) Is there a problem with your group?

(student) Well, during the first lab session, we had a difficult time agreeing on how to proceed with the experiment.

(lab assistant) Of course you did! That's to be expected. There are four people in your group, so you most likely had four different ideas on how to proceed. Part of the task is for the four of you to work together as a group, to discuss as a group how the experiment should proceed and arrive at a consensus before you begin.

(student) During the first experiment, we spent almost the entire three hours in the lab discussing what to do next.

(lab assistant) Perhaps your group should meet before the next lab session to figure out how you're going to proceed with the experiment when you get to the lab.

(student) OK, I'll see if I can get my group to try that, but it'll probably take my group several hours even to decide when to meet, much less actually figure out what we're going to do during the lab session.

(lab assistant) (laughs) OK, please try that and see if you and your group can work it out. Now, was that the only question you had, or do you have another?

(student) Uh, I actually do have another question. It's about the, um, lab report. Is the lab report supposed to be a group assignment or an individual assignment?

(lab assistant) The lab report is to be an individual assignment. Each person involved in the experiment should write up a separate lab report about the experiment.

(student) So, the experiment has to be conducted by the group, and a report about the experiment has to be written up individually by each participant?

(lab assistant) That's exactly right.

(student) And does the report need to follow the format you described to us?

(lab assistant) It absolutely does. I'm extremely strict about the format; I want the format of the report to be exactly as I described.

(student) OK. I get the point.

1. WHY DOES THE STUDENT GO TO SEE THE LAB ASSISTANT?
2. LISTEN AGAIN TO PART OF THE PASSAGE. THEN ANSWER THE QUESTION.

(student) Do we need to work in the lab in a group?

(lab assistant) Yes.

(student) And work with the exact group members we were assigned?

(lab assistant) Is there a problem with your group?
WHY DOES THE LAB ASSISTANT ANSWER THE STUDENT'S QUESTION WITH THIS QUESTION:

(lab assistant) Is there a problem with your group?

3. WHAT DOES THE LAB ASSISTANT SUGGEST THAT THE GROUP SHOULD TRY?
4. LISTEN AGAIN TO PART OF THE PASSAGE. THEN ANSWER THE QUESTION.

(student) OK, I'll see if I can get my group to try that, but it'll probably take my group several hours even to decide when to meet, much less actually figure out what we're going to do during the lab session.

HOW DOES THE STUDENT SEEM TO FEEL ABOUT HIS GROUP?
5. WHAT DOES THE LAB ASSISTANT SAY ABOUT THE LAB REPORT?

Questions 6 through 11. Listen to a lecture in an American literature class.

(professor) ❶ Continuing our discussion of different genres of American literature, today we'll be discussing historical fiction. Historical fiction is a kind of fiction that tries to portray a certain time period or historical event while adding to or altering the facts to create a storyline. Often the historical event is told through the eyes of a fictional character, and sometimes the historical facts are altered to improve the storyline. One of the finest examples of historical American fiction is the *Little House* series of books written by Laura Ingalls Wilder.

How many of you are familiar with this series of books? I'm sure you're all familiar with the television series that was based on it. The *Little House* books began as a record of the stories Pa told Laura when she was little. When her first book, *Little House in the Big Woods*, was a success, Laura Wilder was asked to write a series of stories, not the history, of her childhood.

❷ The point I want you to understand clearly is that every incident in Laura Wilder's books is true, but Laura purposefully did not tell the whole truth. She wanted to write books that she felt were appropriate for children. What she did was to leave out events and to alter names that were unpleasant. An example of an event that Laura omitted because it was unpleasant was the life of the fourth Ingalls child. The fourth child was a boy, a boy named Charles Fredrick Ingalls, who died before his first birthday; the life of this child was omitted from her books. Another example shows how Laura changed the names of people portrayed in a bad light. Nellie Olsen was a character in the book rather than a real person. This character was based on a composite of two girls in Plum Creek, Nellie Owens and Ginny Masters, two girls who caused Mary and Laura a lot of trouble. Laura didn't want to use the real names of these bothersome girls in her books.

❸ From these examples, we can see that one of the ways that Laura made her stories more appropriate for children was to make her stories a little more pleasant than her life had actually been. Another technique she used to make her stories more appropriate for children was to simplify the storylines. Now we'll see another example of how

Laura simplified storylines by omitting events that actually happened because she wanted to make the story easier to follow. ❹ Laura altered the description of the moves that her family actually made, for the sake of simplicity. In real life, the Ingalls family moved from the Big Woods to Missouri, then to the Indian Territory, back to the Big Woods, and finally to Minnesota. In the *Little House* books, Laura recorded the Ingalls moving from the Big Woods to Indian Territory and then to Minnesota. There are many other such details and events that Laura felt were not appropriate for children. These changes are what move her work from the genre of autobiography to the genre of historical fiction.

❺ In summary, although the *Little House* books record true historical events as they happened, the series is considered historical fiction rather than autobiography because Laura Wilder omitted events and altered names to improve the storyline and make her books appropriate for her readers.

6. LISTEN AGAIN TO PART OF THE PASSAGE. THEN ANSWER THE QUESTION.
    (professor) Continuing our discussion of different genres of American literature, today we'll be discussing historical fiction.
    WHY DOES THE PROFESSOR BEGIN THE LECTURE IN THIS WAY?
7. HOW IS THE INFORMATION IN THE LECTURE PRESENTED?
8. HOW IS THE *LITTLE HOUSE* SERIES CLASSIFIED?
9. WHAT TWO STATEMENTS ARE TRUE ABOUT LAURA WILDER'S *LITTLE HOUSE* SERIES?
10. WHAT EVENT DID LAURA OMIT FROM HER BOOKS?
11. WHAT CONCLUSION CAN BE DRAWN FROM THE LECTURE?

SPEAKING

Question 2

Listen to the passage. On a piece of paper, take notes on the main points of the listening passage.

(woman) Isn't that a great assignment for history class?
(man) Which assignment?
(woman) The assignment where we have to watch a lot of films.
(man) I don't know. It seems like it's going to take a lot of time.
(woman) But we'll be spending time watching films.
(man) Watching films and writing reports. We have to write a report for each film we watch, you know.
(woman) I know we do, but we just have to write a report summarizing the key points of each film. We don't have to research anything, and we don't have to analyze anything.

We can just summarize the main points of each film, and that really shouldn't take too much time at all.
(man) You've got a point there, . . . and I guess watching films is a better assignment than most assignments the professor could give. . . . I guess I'll have to get to work on watching those 12 films.
(woman) Only 12? I'm going to try and watch all 20.
(man) But we only have to watch 12 of them, right?
(woman) Yes, but we can watch more than 12 for extra credit, and I think watching films is a great way to earn some extra credit.

HOW DO THE STUDENTS SEEM TO FEEL ABOUT THE HISTORY CLASS ASSIGNMENT?

Question 3

Listen to the passage. On a piece of paper, take notes on the main points of the listening passage.

(professor) Today, I'll be talking about glaciers and, in particular, how glaciers are formed. First of all, do you know what a glacier is? Well, a glacier is a mass of ice, but there's more to it than that. A glacier is a mass of ice that's <u>moving</u>.

Glaciers form where snow accumulates, where more snow falls than melts, so it piles up. If all the snow melts every year in a particular place, a glacier can't form there. And there needs to be considerable accumulation. If there's only a small amount of accumulation, then a glacier can't form because there needs to be considerable weight for a glacier to form, so there must be enough accumulation of sufficient weight for a glacier to form.

When enough snow has accumulated, there's pressure on the snow underneath, enough pressure to transform the loose snowflakes into ice crystals. The weight of the accumulated snow causes the snowflakes to compress into ice crystals. And with more and more pressure, the smaller ice crystals pack together to create even larger crystals.

The final step in the formation of a glacier is for the packed ice to begin to move. When the amount of crystallized ice becomes large enough, the packed ice begins to move and a glacier is born.

HOW ARE GLACIERS FORMED?

WRITING

Listen to the passage. On a piece of paper, take notes on the main points of the listening passage.

(professor) You may read all of this information about garlic, about how it was used in the past, and think that this was all just a lot of superstition, like breaking a mirror brings seven years of bad luck or

throwing salt over your shoulder protects you from bad luck. But this is different. It's not all just superstition, though some of it is. There's actually a lot of scientific evidence that garlic does have certain medicinal benefits.

First of all, garlic does kill bacteria. In 1858, Louis Pasteur conducted some research that showed that garlic does actually kill bacteria. When garlic was used during World War I to prevent infection, there was good reason. There is actually research to back up garlic's ability to kill bacteria. It's raw, or uncooked, garlic that has this property. Raw garlic has been shown to kill 23 different kinds of bacteria.

Then, when garlic is heated, it's been shown to have different medicinal properties. When it's heated, garlic forms a compound that thins the blood. The blood-thinning property can help prevent arteries from clogging and reduce blood pressure, which may have some impact on preventing heart attacks and strokes.

HOW DOES THE INFORMATION IN THE LISTENING PASSAGE SUPPORT THE INFORMATION PRESENTED IN THE READING PASSAGE?

MINI-TEST 2

LISTENING

Questions 1 through 5. Listen to a conversation between a student and a professor.

(student)	Hi, Dr. Lane. Uh, do you have a moment? Can I ask you a question?
(professor)	Sure. Come on in. . . . Now . . . what's your question?
(student)	Well, it's about the assignment . . .
(professor)	The assignment? Which assignment?
(student)	The assignment you gave yesterday in class?
(professor)	The . . . uh . . . assignment I gave in class yesterday?
(student)	Yeah. . . .
(professor)	But I didn't give an assignment in class yesterday . . . did I? I don't remember giving an assignment yesterday in class.
(student)	You know, the assignment about the reports we're supposed to read. . . .
(professor)	Oh! . . . I think you mean the assignment about the journals you're supposed to read . . . and the report you're supposed to write.
(student)	Yeah, that assignment.
(professor)	I'm sorry. I was a bit unsure what you were asking about because I discussed that assignment with the class last week and not yesterday.
(student)	Oh, I thought it was yesterday, but maybe it was last week. Anyway, that's the assignment I need to know about.

(professor)	What do you need to know about the assignment?
(student)	Well, I think the assignment was about reading some reports. . . .
(professor)	No, . . . did you understand what I just said . . . and did you understand anything about the assignment? You're supposed to read journals.
(student)	Oh, that's right, that's what you said before . . . we're supposed to read journals, . . . but what journals are we supposed to read?
(professor)	I _did_ go over that is class . . . last week . . . but, . . . anyway . . . I put some journal articles on reserve in the library . . . there are three journals on reserve.
(student)	So, I'm supposed to go to the library and read those two journal articles. . . .
(professor)	Three journal articles.
(student)	OK, I'm supposed to read three journal articles.
(professor)	Yes, that's right.
(student)	And that's all I need to do? Just read those three journal articles on reserve?
(professor)	No, not quite. That's only the first part of the assignment. After you read the three journal articles, you're supposed to write a report. . . .
(student)	Oh, I see, that's where the report comes in. We're not supposed to read a report; we're supposed to write a report.
(professor)	That's right.
(student)	And I should write about the three journal articles in my report?
(professor)	Yes, you should discuss the main points of each article in your report, and then compare the ideas in the three articles.
(student)	OK, I get it now.
(professor)	Are you sure? (_dryly_) Maybe I should go over it again.

1. WHAT IS THE STUDENT CONFUSED ABOUT?
2. LISTEN AGAIN TO PART OF THE PASSAGE. THEN ANSWER THE QUESTION.

(student)	Well, I think the assignment was about reading some reports. . . .
(professor)	No, . . . did you understand what I just said . . . and did you understand anything about the assignment?

HOW DOES THE PROFESSOR SEEM TO FEEL?

3. IS EACH OF THESE PART OF THE ASSIGNMENT?
4. LISTEN AGAIN TO THE END OF THE CONVERSATION. THEN ANSWER THE QUESTION.

(student)	OK, I get it now.
(professor)	Are you sure? Maybe I should go over it again.

WHY DOES THE PROFESSOR END THE CONVERSATION THIS WAY?

5. WHAT CONCLUSION CAN BE DRAWN ABOUT THE STUDENT?

Questions 6 through 11. Listen to a discussion in an archeology class.

(professor) ❶ I hope all of you read the assigned material. Do any of you have any questions about it?

(student) I do. I'm really having difficulty understanding some of the material.

(professor) Which material?

(student) The material in the tenth chapter in the text, on cross-dating. Can you explain it a bit more?

(professor) Sure. No problem. What do you need me to explain?

(student) First of all, exactly what is cross-dating?

(professor) That's a pretty broad question . . . OK, cross-dating is . . . uh . . . a method of dating one archeological area by extending relative dates from another area.

(student) And just what exactly does that mean? I still don't understand.

(professor) It means that archeologists may be certain of the dates when one particular culture existed, from scientific data in that area, but they may not have scientific information to be sure of the dates of another culture in the area. They can draw a conclusion about the dates that the second culture existed by comparing it with the first culture.

(student) You mean that archeologists compare two cultures in one area and determine the dates of one culture from the other?

(professor) Exactly. ❷ Let me give you an example. Archeologists found two areas of ancient cultural development, one in what is today northern Arizona and the other in what is today southern Arizona. They were able to date the cultural development in the northern area scientifically, but they were unable to date the cultural development in the southern area in the same way.

(student) So let me guess. Because they were able to date the northern area but not the southern area using scientific methods, they used cross-dating to infer the dates of the southern culture.

(professor) Exactly.

(student) And what type of scientific method did the archeologists use to date the culture in the northern area?

(professor) They used tree-ring remnants to determine the dates of the northern culture.

(student) Well, why couldn't they use the same method to determine the dates of the southern culture?

(professor) They couldn't date the cultural development in the southern area in the same way because there were no trees in that area, so they had to use the technique of cross-dating to determine the dates of the southern area.

(student) But, can you tell me, how exactly did the archeologists do that?

(professor) They used pottery. The culture in the northern area, which had been scientifically dated at 700 to 900 A.D. using tree-ring dating, had a distinctive type of pottery. Pieces of this distinctive northern pottery were found in the southern area.

(student) How did the pottery from the northern culture get to the southern culture?

(professor) Apparently, the pottery from the northern culture came to the southern culture through trade.

(student) And if the two cultures were involved in trade, then they must've existed at the same time.

(professor) Exactly. Because these pieces of northern pottery were found in the southern culture, archeologists were able to infer that the culture of the southern area was active in the same era as the northern culture.

(student) So the southern culture must have existed sometime around the period of 700 to 900 A.D., just as the northern culture did.

(professor) ❸ You've got it. Now do you understand how cross-dating works?

(student) Thanks. I actually think I do!

(professor) OK, then. . . . Now, are there any other questions?

6. WHAT IS THE MAIN TOPIC OF THIS DISCUSSION?
7. HOW IS THE INFORMATION IN THE DISCUSSION PRESENTED?
8. WHAT DO ARCHEOLOGISTS COMPARE WHEN USING CROSS-DATING?
9. WHAT IS NOT TRUE ABOUT TREE-RING DATING, ACCORDING TO THE DISCUSSION?
10. IS EACH OF THESE TRUE ABOUT THE AREAS DISCUSSED IN THE LECTURE?
11. HOW DOES THE STUDENT SEEM TO FEEL ABOUT THE MATERIAL?

SPEAKING

Question 2

Listen to the passage. On a piece of paper, take notes on the main points of the listening passage.

(professor) In a certain company, work was completed in work groups. Each employee was assigned to a work group, and each employee was evaluated, not on individual work, but on the quality of the work of his or her group. Two of the work groups in the company had very different leaders.

In the first group, the leader started off each group meeting with an activity designed to help the group members get to know each other. The leader then had the group members each make a positive comment about how the work on the group project was going. The leader ended each meeting by asking group members to send him an e-mail describing how they felt that the meeting had gone.

Work in the second group was very different. The group leader in the second group prepared a detailed list of what each group member was to get done in the following week. In each weekly meeting, the group leader grilled each group member about what he or she had and had not managed to accomplish since the last meeting and made it clear that the work on the list needed to be completed on time.

HOW DOES THE INFORMATION IN THE LISTENING PASSAGE ADD TO THE INFORMATION IN THE READING PASSAGE?

Question 3

Listen to the passage. On a piece of paper, take notes on the main points of the listening passage.

(woman)	Are you going to the meeting tonight, Jeff?
(man)	Which meeting?
(woman)	The student council meeting.
(man)	Oh, the open meeting, the one where any students can attend?
(woman)	Yeah, that meeting.
(man)	I don't think I'm going.
(woman)	Why not? Didn't you want to take part in the discussion about the exam schedule?
(man)	I'm happy with the exam schedule as it is. I like having a six-day final exam schedule.
(woman)	But that's why you need to go to the meeting.
(man)	What do you mean?
(woman)	Well, the student council's holding an open meeting to discuss changing the final exam schedule, and a lot of students want to change the schedule. I think a lot of students who want to change the exam schedule will be at the open meeting this evening.
(man)	You mean, if I want the final exam schedule to stay just like it is, then I need to go to the meeting to support the idea of keeping the schedule just like it is?
(woman)	That's right. That's why I'm going.
(man)	You mean, you don't want the schedule to change?
(woman)	No way. You know how they're considering changing the schedule?
(man)	They want to shorten it a little bit, don't they?
(woman)	They want to shorten it <u>a lot</u>. They want to cut it in half.
(man)	You mean, they want to reduce the final exam schedule from six days to three days?
(woman)	That's right.
(man)	But I have five final exams. If my five exams are spread out over six days, then I'll be OK, but if I have five exams in three days, I'm going to have a really hard time.
(woman)	Me, too. I have five final exams, too.
(man)	But why would anyone want to reduce the exam schedule from six to three days?

(woman)	So that summer vacation will start three says earlier.
(man)	But it would make the final exam schedule really horrible.
(woman)	That's why we need to go to that meeting tonight, to try and keep the exam schedule just like it is.
(man)	OK, you've convinced me. I'll be there.
(woman)	So will I.

HOW DO THE STUDENTS SEEM TO FEEL ABOUT WHAT WILL BE DISCUSSED AT THE STUDENT COUNCIL MEETING?

MINI-TEST 3

LISTENING

Questions 1 through 5. Listen to a conversation between a student and an advisor.

(advisor)	Yes, Sean, what can I do for you? Do you have a question?
(student)	Yes, I do.
(advisor)	Then come on in and take a seat. . . . OK, what's your question?
(student)	I'm working on planning my schedule for next quarter, and I'm trying to decide which biology class to take. There seem to be two that are quite similar.
(advisor)	Which two courses are you considering?
(student)	One is Introduction to Biological Science and the other is Biology 101. I thought that a 101-numbered course was a beginning course, so Biology 101 should be an introductory-level course, but then Introduction to Biological Science also seems to be an introductory-level course.
(advisor)	Well, uh, there's a difference between the courses. Introduction to Biological Science is an overview of biology in a more general way, and Biology 101 is a more detailed and scientific view of the material.
(student)	I'm sorry, but I don't quite understand the difference. . . .
(advisor)	Well, uh, a clear example of the difference is the fact that there's work in the lab as part of Biology 101, but there's no lab work in Introduction to Biological Science. Introduction to Biological Science is a lecture class, while Biology 101 includes both lecture and lab.
(student)	You mean that in Introduction to Biological Science, the students read about science, and in Biology 101, the students actually take part in science experiments in the lab.
(advisor)	Mmhm. You could put it that way.
(student)	It seems like Biology 101 is a lot more work than Introduction to Biological Science, with the lab work and all.
(advisor)	It certainly is. That's why Biology 101 is a four-unit course, and Introduction to Biological Science is only a three-unit course. . . . Um, listen, there's another really important difference between these two courses, and it has to do with what your major is. What is your major, by the way?

(student) I'm not actually sure, yet. . . . Is that . . . um . . . a problem?

(advisor) You're a freshman, aren't you? You're in your first year?

(student) Yes, I am.

(advisor) OK, so you actually don't need to declare your major until the end of your second year. But, you would be better off making certain decisions a bit earlier than that, and, uh, right now you're making one of them. One really important difference between Biology 101 and Introduction to Biological Science has to do with majors. Biology 101 is required for students who're majoring in science, while Introduction to Biological Science satisfies a general education requirement in science for students who're majoring in subjects outside of science. . . . I know you haven't decided on your major, but have you at least decided whether you'll be majoring in some area within the sciences or an area outside of science?

(student) No, I haven't even gotten that far in deciding on a major. I may want to major in science, or maybe not.

(advisor) OK, well, what I can suggest to you is that you really should start narrowing down your choices for a major area of studies. Perhaps if you're considering a major in science, you should take Biology 101 as a way of helping you to decide whether or not you enjoy studying science.

(student) If I take Biology 101 and then decide not to major in science, will I still need to take Introduction to Biological Science after Biology 101 to satisfy the general education requirement in science?

(advisor) No, absolutely not! If you take Biology 101, that'll also satisfy the general education requirement for non-science majors.

(student) OK, that makes sense. It'll be a good way to help me either to decide that I want to major in science or to find out that I really don't like science.

1. WHAT PROBLEM DOES THE STUDENT HAVE?
2. WHAT DIFFERENTIATES BIOLOGY 101 FROM THE OTHER COURSE?
3. LISTEN AGAIN TO PART OF THE PASSAGE. THEN ANSWER THE QUESTION.

(advisor) Introduction to Biological Science is a lecture class, while Biology 101 includes both lecture and lab.

(student) You mean that in Introduction to Biological Science, the students read about science, and in Biology 101, the students actually take part in science experiments in the lab.

(advisor) Mmhm. You could put it that way. . . .
WHAT DOES THE ADVISOR MEAN WHEN SHE SAYS THIS:

(advisor) Mmhm. You could put it that way. . . .

4. WHAT DECISION DOES THE ADVISOR SEEM TO THINK THAT THE STUDENT SHOULD MAKE FAIRLY SOON?

5. WHAT CAN BE CONCLUDED FROM THE CONVERSATION?

Questions 6 through 11. Listen to a lecture in a gemology class.

(professor) ❶ Today, I'll be talking about different styles of gem-cutting, particularly about how these different styles developed historically. The various styles of gems that I'll be talking about are the cabochon, the table cut, the rose cut, and the brilliant cut.

❷ The first style of gem-cutting, which you can see in this drawing, is the cabochon. The cabochon is a rounded shape, without facets. The cabochon style is quite old. It was the earliest style used to finish gems. The cabochons in these drawings are shown from the side. A cabochon could be a simple cabochon, with a rounded top and a flat bottom, or it could be a double cabochon, which is rounded on both the top and the bottom. It was discovered early on that powders of harder materials such as diamonds could be used to polish gemstones, and many ancient cultures used this method to finish gems.

The cabochon cut was not a faceted cut. A facet, for those of you who don't know, is a flat surface cut into a gem. It's not clear when faceting of stones first developed. Stones were faceted as early as the fifteenth century in Europe, and they may have been faceted earlier than that in other cultures.

❸ Now, we'll look at one of the earliest styles of faceted gems, the table cut. You can see a table-cut stone, from the top and from the side, in these drawings. An interesting thing to note is that early stones faceted in this way were probably not actually cut but were polished to this shape, using powders of harder stones such as diamonds. It does look like it was cut, but this stone was polished to this shape. Some stones, including diamonds, occur naturally in eight-sided double pyramids. To create a table cut from an eight-sided double pyramid, it's necessary only to polish a flat surface on the top of one side of the naturally occurring eight-sided shapes.

❹ The next stage in the development of gem-cutting is the rose cut. In a rose cut, a stone is actually cut rather than polished. This was one of the earliest methods of faceting the entire surface of a diamond, or other gem. . . . It's a very pretty cut, isn't it? . . . As you can tell from its name, it's supposed to look like a rose in bloom. The rose cut involved cutting up to 32 triangular facets on the top of a diamond and a flat surface on the bottom. You can see a rose cut in the drawing from the top and from the bottom. . . . Oh, excuse me, that's a top view and a side view. There's no bottom view of the rose cut. . . . Now, you should note that this type of cut was beneficial because it maintained much of the original stone. However, it doesn't reflect light in a way that maximizes the stone's shine and brilliance. Because it doesn't reflect light as well as other cuts, the rose cut's no longer used much today.

❺ The last type of cut we'll look at is the brilliant cut. The brilliant cut came into use after the other styles. You can see a brilliant cut from the top and from the side and from the bottom. The brilliant cut's faceted on the sides and top and also on the bottom. A stone with a brilliant cut in the correct proportion reflects the maximum amount of light out through the top of the stone and creates a stone that, as its name indicates, shines the most brilliantly. This style of stone is used quite often today because it's so reflective.

❻ We've seen four different styles of gems today, in the order that they developed historically. Two of them, the cabochon and the table cut, are polished rather than cut to create the style, while the other two are actually cut. Before next class, please look over the photos of gems at the end of the chapter and identify the style of each stone.

6. HOW DOES THE PROFESSOR PRESENT THE DIFFERENT STYLES OF GEMS?
7. WHAT ARE THE CHARACTERISTICS OF THESE GEMSTONE CUTS?
8. WHAT DOES THE PROFESSOR SAY ABOUT FACETING?
9. WHICH STYLE OF GEM IS NO LONGER USED MUCH BECAUSE IT DOES NOT REFLECT LIGHT WELL?
10. WHAT OVERALL CONCLUSION CAN BE DRAWN FROM THE LECTURE?
11. WHAT IS THE ASSIGNMENT FOR THE NEXT CLASS?

SPEAKING

Question 2

Listen to the passage. On a piece of paper, take notes on the main points of the listening passage.

(man) Boy, that notice is terrible!
(woman) You really think so? I kind of like it. I mean, I really like it.
(man) But it means we can't do anything in the library.
(woman) Not exactly. We can study, we can do homework, we can work on research, and we can do all of these things in peace and quiet.
(man) But so many of the students, myself included, like to talk to friends, maybe

have a little snack, take a little nap if we get tired, play a little music to relax.
(woman) I know. That's why students like me can't get any work done in the library.
(man) I like to get some work done in the library, but I can't work all the time.
(woman) Well, I'm glad this notice was posted, and now I only hope that it's enforced.
(man) If it is, I may have to go somewhere else to work.
(woman) (laughs) It's not the work that's the problem. It's the noise and the mess. I'm really glad something's finally getting done about this.

HOW DO THE STUDENTS REACT TO THE NOTICE POSTED IN THE LIBRARY?

Question 3

Listen to the passage. On a piece of paper, take notes on the main points of the listening passage.

(professor) I'd like to talk today about some of the formal grammar rules in English, rules about what's considered formally correct and incorrect. I'd like to talk in particular about rules that were formed in the seventeenth and eighteenth centuries during the period of neoclassicism.

During the seventeenth and eighteenth centuries in Europe, there was a widely held view that the culture of ancient Greece and Rome was superior to the culture of the day. This period in the seventeenth and eighteenth century is known as the neoclassic period.

During the neoclassic period, academics held the view that the Latin language of the classic age of the Roman Empire was the purest language possible; as a result, there was an attempt to Latinize the English of the time to make it resemble what was considered the most perfect language, Latin.

An example of a formal grammar rule that developed in English during the neoclassic revival is the rule against split infinitives. The infinitive is the form of the verb that includes the word *to* and the base form of the verb, such as *to go* or *to walk* or *to make*. There is a formal rule today in English against splitting the infinitive, against saying something like *to never go* or *to always work* or *to usually finish*, though many native speakers of English do break this formal rule fairly often.

This formal rule against split infinitives did not exist before the neoclassic period. Instead, it came about as seventeenth and eighteenth century academics during the neoclassic period noted that it's impossible to split infinitives in Latin; it's impossible to split infinitives in Latin because a Latin verb is one word rather than the two words that make up an English infinitive. However, because infinitives were never split in Latin, the rule against splitting infinitives was created. English speakers still, however, regularly split their infinitives; the attempt by seventeenth and eighteenth century academics to impose a rule against split infinitives in order to make English more like Latin did not succeed entirely.

WHY DOES THE PROFESSOR USE THE EXAMPLE OF SPLIT INFINITIVES?

WRITING

Listen to the passage. On a piece of paper, take notes on the main points of the listening passage.

(professor) A particular problem that attracted a lot of attention in the second half of the twentieth century is how the survival of the giant panda is related to the unusual flowering and seeding cycle of Asian bamboo. The giant panda still lives in the wild in only a few mountain ranges in the southwestern part of China because its survival has been threatened both by hunters and by the destruction of the habitat it needs to survive.

What has been noted in the last few decades is that the panda's survival is also threatened by the flowering and seeding cycles of the bamboo where the pandas live. Here's what the problem is. Bamboo is the main source of food for the giant panda. However, when there's a massive flowering and seeding of the bamboo, the bamboo that has just seeded dies, and there's a lag of quite a few years before the new young seedlings grow enough to provide food for the giant panda. When the bamboo where the giant panda's living dies, the giant panda needs to move to new areas to find food. The search for food has led the giant panda into areas that are more settled and more full of danger for the giant panda.

HOW IS THE INFORMATION IN THE LISTENING PASSAGE ABOUT THE GIANT PANDA RELATED TO THE IDEAS IN THE READING PASSAGE ON ASIAN BAMBOO?

MINI-TEST 4

LISTENING

Questions 1 through 5. Listen to a conversation between a student and a professor.

(student) Hello, Professor Norton. May I speak with you now? . . . I mean, is now a good time to talk with you?

(professor) Uh . . . I have . . . let me see . . . just a few minutes before I have to head over to Anderson Hall for a class, so if it's a short question, I can handle it.

(student) My question is about . . . about . . . my grade on the last exam. . . . My grade . . . it was . . . well, it wasn't very high. In fact, . . . it was pretty bad . . . a 62. And, well . . . I was wondering if there's anything I can do about it, some extra credit, . . . or retaking the exam, . . . something?

(professor) A 62? That's quite low.

(student) I know.

(professor) That may even have been the lowest in the class.

(student) Oh . . .

(professor) What happened? . . . I mean, why was the grade so low?

(student) I don't know. . . .

(professor) Did you attend class regularly?

(student) All the time. . . .

(professor) And were you paying attention and taking good notes . . . things like that?

(student) I guess I didn't take very good notes, and then, well, . . . uh . . . I didn't study as much as I should've.

(professor) Clearly . . . now, . . . uh . . . as to your original question about retaking the exam . . .

(student) Or maybe an extra credit assignment, something like that. . . .

(professor) I don't do things like that. . . . The grades in my courses are based solely on the exams.

(student) Oh . . .

(professor) But there is something you can do about that grade. . . .

(student) There is? What is it?

(professor) Well, you know, I explained about my grading system on the first day of the course. Did you understand it then?

(student) I think so, but, . . . well . . . maybe you could explain it again, so I can see how it can help me out of this predicament.

(professor) Well, there are three unit exams in the course, you just had one of them, the one you did so poorly on.

(student) Yes . . .

(professor) And then there's a final exam, a cumulative final exam.

(student) Cumulative?

(professor) That means it covers all the material in the course.

(student) Including the material on the exam we just took?

(professor) Yes, including the material on the exam you just took. . . .

(student) And how will the cumulative exam help me?

(professor) Because the final exam is cumulative, it counts for half of your final grade. The three unit exams together count as the other half. That means, if you do well on the remaining two unit exams and then do really well on the cumulative final, then your grade won't suffer too much.

(student)   It also means that the material I didn't understand too well on the last exam is also going to be tested again on the final.

(professor)   It certainly does mean that.

(student)   So I need to work some more on the unit we just finished in addition to working hard on the next two units. . . .

(professor)   That's exactly what it means. Oh, look what time it is! I need to get going now!

(student)   Well, thanks for your help, I guess.

1. WHY DOES THE STUDENT GO TO SEE THE PROFESSOR?

2. LISTEN AGAIN TO PART OF THE PASSAGE. THEN ANSWER THE QUESTION.

(professor)   And were you paying attention and taking good notes . . . things like that?

(student)   I guess I didn't take very good notes, and then, well, . . . uh . . . I didn't study as much as I should've.

(professor)   Clearly . . . now, . . . uh . . . as to your original question about retaking the exam . . .

WHY DOES THE PROFESSOR SAY THIS?

(professor)   now, . . . uh . . . as to your original question about retaking the exam . . .

3. WHAT ARE THE PROFESSOR'S GRADES BASED ON?

4. WHAT IS A CUMULATIVE EXAM?

5. WHAT SOLUTION DOES THE PROFESSOR OFFER TO THE STUDENT?

Questions 6 through 11. Listen to a discussion in a geography class.

(professor)   ❶ Today, we'll be discussing the formation of various mountain ranges around the world. What are some of the major mountain ranges?

(student)   The Rockies and the Himalayas . . .

(professor)   Mmhm. What about in Europe?

(student)   The Alps . . .

(professor)   And in South America?

(student)   Uh . . . I know it . . . uh . . . it's the Andes.

(professor)   That's right. You got it. The major mountain chains are the Himalayas, the Rockies, the Alps, and the Andes, and we'll be discussing them today. We'll also be discussing two smaller North American chains, the Appalachians and the Cascades, which do not rank among the world's tallest. The development of these two ranges, when compared with the development of the Himalayas, Rockies, Andes, and Alps, provides a clear overall picture of the . . . um . . . evolutionary process of the development of mountain ranges.

❷ Look at the world map showing the mountain ranges of the world. The tall mountain ranges of today's world were all formed within the last hundred million years. The Rocky Mountains began forming about a hundred million years ago and today comprise a 3,300-mile range. The Andes began forming about 65 million years ago, through volcanic activity. The Andes are actually part of the volcanically active Ring of Fire that encircles the Pacific Ocean. This range is more than 1,000 miles longer than the Rockies. The Alps and Himalayas are actually part of the same 7,000-mile mountain system. They began forming about 80 million years ago from the crashing action of major tectonic plates.

❸ Now, if you were asked to name the world's major mountain ranges, you might not think of the Appalachians. As you can see from the map, the Appalachians are a range of north-south mountains running in the eastern part of North America. These mountains are actually far older than the major mountain ranges of today, the Himalayas, the Andes, the Alps, and the Rockies, and in all probability the Appalachians used to be just as big and majestic. The Appalachians began forming more than 400 million years ago and were completely formed 200 million years ago; that's more than 100 million years before the Rockies began forming. The Appalachians were formed during major collisions of the North American plate with other, um, others of the world's great plates. At their height, the Appalachians were a grand and impressive mountain range, perhaps rivaling the Himalayas of today. Over millions of years, however, these mountains've been eroded by the forces of nature and no longer have the impressive height they used to.

❹ Now, before we wrap up for today, I'd like to add a final note about the Cascade Mountains. You can see from the map that the Cascades are in the western part of North America. These mountains completed their rise from the sea scarcely a million years ago and are among the youngest of the world's mountains ranges. They're volcanic mountains that're also part of the volcanically active Ring of Fire encircling the Pacific Ocean.

❺ Well, that's all for today. I hope that this lecture has helped you to understand the evolution of the mountains of the Earth. You'll find additional details on this topic in the assigned reading in the textbook.

6. WHAT IS THE TOPIC OF THIS LECTURE?

7. WHAT IS TRUE ABOUT THE AGES OF VARIOUS MOUNTAIN RANGES?

8. HOW WERE THESE MOUNTAIN RANGES FORMED?

9. WHAT IS TRUE ABOUT THE LENGTH OF THE MOUNTAIN RANGES?

10. WHICH MOUNTAIN RANGES ARE PART OF THE RING OF FIRE?

11. WHY DOES THE PROFESSOR DISCUSS THE
APPALACHIANS AND CASCADES?

SPEAKING

Question 2

Listen to the passage. On a piece of paper, take notes on
the main points of the listening passage.

(professor) The issue of nullification caused a serious
controversy in one particular situation in
the first part of the nineteenth century.
In 1828, the U.S. Congress passed a bill
that authorized new tariffs on some
imported manufactured goods. This
meant that taxes would have to be paid
to the federal government when certain
manufactured goods were imported, and
since many goods were not manufactured
in the United States at the time, if people
wanted to have these goods, then the
goods had to be imported.

The issue of nullification arose in this
situation when one of the southern states
in the United States held a convention
to discuss the tariffs on some imported
products; the convention voted to nullify
the law that required that tariffs be paid
on those imported goods. In other words,
the state voted not to follow a law passed
by the federal government.

The president of the United States,
Andrew Jackson, sent federal troops into
the state to impose the federal law on
tariffs there. A compromise was reached
when the government passed a new law
that lowered the tariff, and the southern
state agreed to pay this lower tariff.

HOW DOES THE INFORMATION IN THE
LISTENING PASSAGE SUPPLEMENT WHAT IS
EXPLAINED IN THE READING PASSAGE?

Question 3

Listen to the passage. On a piece of paper, take notes on
the main points of the listening passage.

(woman) Hey, Steve, can I ask you something?
(man) Sure, Chris, what do you want to know?
(woman) It's about the paper in our psychology class.
(man) The one for next week?
(woman) No, the first one we did. The one we got
back in class today.
(man) Oh, that one. What do you want to know
about it?
(woman) You seem to have done a good job
on it. I mean, the professor certainly
complimented you on it when she returned
it to you.
(man) Oh, you heard what the professor said?
That was kind of embarrassing.
(woman) You shouldn't be embarrassed. The
professor said you did a nice job on the
paper. . . . Listen, I was wondering if you
could help me a little, I mean, give me an

idea about what you did that the professor
liked.
(man) I'm sure the professor liked your paper, too.
(woman) Uh . . . no she didn't like it. The only
comment she wrote on my paper was
"Needs work." I don't think she liked it very
much.
(man) Well, I didn't do anything special. I mean, I
just read the question she asked and wrote
a very simple and direct answer to the
question.
(woman) You don't think she wanted something
creative? I worked really hard to come up
with a creative answer. I sort of told a story
that indirectly implied my answer to the
question.
(man) You did? Really? Well, it sounds like the
professor didn't appreciate the effort you
put into your paper to make such a creative
response.
(woman) So you just wrote a simple answer?
(man) A really simple, direct answer.
(woman) And the professor certainly seemed to like
that.
(man) I guess so.
(woman) Then I'll have to try that on the next paper.
And here I was working so hard to try to
think of a creative way to write the next
paper.
(man) I guess you don't need to do that.
(woman) Not if I want to write a paper the professor
likes . . . and I do.

WHAT IS HAPPENING WITH THE STUDENTS'
ASSIGNMENTS FOR THEIR PSYCHOLOGY
CLASS?

MINI-TEST 5

LISTENING

Questions 1 through 5. Listen to a conversation between
a student and a worker in a university office.

(office worker) Yes, how can I help you?
(student) I'm not sure if I'm in the right
place . . . I'm looking for an
application for the Academic
Scholarship program. Is that
something I can pick up here?
(office worker) Yes, you're in the right place.
Applications for the Academic
Scholarship program are right here.
Let me get one for you. . . . Here you
are.
(student) Thanks very much. . . . By the way,
is there anything I need to know to
complete the application, or is the
application self-explanatory?
(office worker) It's fairly self-explanatory, but let me
go over a few things with you, just
to be sure. . . . OK, the first really
important thing is the date. The
application's due by March 1, by the
end of the business day on March 1.
(student) That's really soon . . .

(office worker)	It is, and the date is absolute. No applications will be accepted after the first.
(student)	I'll have to hurry to get it done.
(office worker)	You will.
(student)	Anything else?
(office worker)	Uh, yes . . . make sure you fill the application out completely. Every single question must be answered. If you omit any questions, your application won't be considered.
(student)	But some of these questions don't seem to pertain to me.
(office worker)	Like what, for example?
(student)	Well, look, question number 20 asks about my high school ranking.
(office worker)	Why doesn't that pertain to you?
(student)	Well, the high school I attended didn't give rankings. I didn't go to high school here in the United States, and my high school didn't give out rankings.
(office worker)	Well, for that question, just give the explanation you gave me. Just be sure not to omit any questions; if you think a question doesn't pertain to you, then write an explanation why.
(student)	OK, I can do that. . . . Anything else you can tell me?
(office worker)	Well, there're the essays. . . . You know you have to write two essays to accompany the application?
(student)	Oh, my. That's a lot of work. I assume the essay questions are included somewhere in the application?
(office worker)	Yes, on page seven of the application. . . . Do you see them . . . at the bottom of the page?
(student)	Yes, I see them . . . there are four questions there. . . . I thought you said I needed to write two essays . . . oh . . . I see. It says to choose two of the four essay questions to answer. . . . Now, is that all I need to do? That must be all. . . .
(office worker)	Well, not quite.
(student)	Oh, no! What else?
(office worker)	There are the letters of reference.
(student)	Letters of reference? Are these letters that I write?
(office worker)	(laughs) Oh, no . . . you don't write the letters of reference yourself. You need to get three people to write letters of reference for you.
(student)	Do the letters of reference need to be written by professors, or can they be written by other people?
(office worker)	Two of the three letters need to be written by professors . . . you're applying for an academic scholarship, after all.
(student)	So I need two letters of reference from professors and one from someone else?
(office worker)	Yes.

(student)	Can the third letter of reference be written by a friend, by a student?
(office worker)	No, the third letter can't be written by a student.
(student)	How about by my advisor? Would that be OK?
(office worker)	That would be great.
(student)	And do I need all of this by March 1st, even the letters of reference?
(office worker)	All of it, if you want to be considered for the Academic Scholarship program.

1. WHY DOES THE STUDENT GO TO SEE THIS OFFICE WORKER?
2. DOES THE OFFICE WORKER EMPHASIZE EACH OF THESE?
3. WHY DOES THE STUDENT ASK ABOUT THE QUESTION ON HIGH SCHOOL RANKING?
4. WHAT DOES THE ADVISOR SAY ABOUT THE ESSAYS?
5. WHAT DOES THE ADVISOR SAY ABOUT THE LETTERS OF REFERENCE?

Questions 6 through 11. Listen to a discussion by a group of students in an oceanography class.

(instructor)	❶ OK, in this course, we've discussed a number of the ocean's unusual features. Today, we're going to discuss atolls and how they're formed. First, can you tell me what an atoll is? Beth?
(Beth)	An atoll's a ring-shaped mass of coral and algae.
(instructor)	That's right. An atoll's made of coral and algae, and it's in the shape of a ring. . . . And where're atolls found? Jim?
(Jim)	Atolls're found in tropical and subtropical areas of the ocean.
(instructor)	It's true that atolls're found in tropical and subtropical areas. . . . Why is that, do you think?
(Jim)	It's where the water temperature's fairly warm. The coral and reef-building algae grow best in fairly warm water.
(instructor)	OK, now, let's look at how atolls're formed. We'll look at a series of three diagrams and discuss what's happening in each. ❷ This diagram shows the first step in the process. What does the diagram show? Linda?
(Linda)	Well, it . . . uh . . . looks like a volcano.
(instructor)	(dryly) It certainly does . . . but perhaps there's something more you could add.
(Linda)	Uh, it's a volcanic island . . . a newer volcanic island that has formed recently.
(instructor)	And what's growing around the volcanic island?
(Linda)	Ah . . . a coral reef's growing around this new volcanic island.
(instructor)	Yes, good. . . . ❸ OK, now let's look at the second diagram. Beth, can you describe what's happening in this diagram?
(Beth)	The second diagram shows that the volcanic island has started to erode—it's wearing down.

(instructor)	And what's been happening with the coral reef while the volcanic island has been eroding?
(Beth)	The coral reef has continued to grow.
(instructor)	❹ Excellent. Now let's look at the third diagram in the series. What's happening in this diagram? Jim?
(Jim)	Well, in this diagram, you can see that the volcanic island has, um, worn down so far that it's below the level of the ocean. The coral has built up even further, so the coral's above the water, and the remains of the volcano are under water.
(instructor)	Yes, and it's at this stage when the ring of coral's called an atoll. The volcano has sunk, and there's a pool of water inside the atoll. Now, what do we call the pool of water that remains inside an atoll? Linda?
(Linda)	The pool of water inside the atoll is called a lagoon.
(instructor)	That's correct. The body of water inside an atoll is called a lagoon.

❺ Well, you seem to understand quite clearly how atolls result when coral reefs around volcanic islands continue to grow as the volcanic island themselves diminish. That's all for today. I'll see you next class.

6. WHAT IS THIS DISCUSSION MAINLY ABOUT?
7. WHAT IS AN ATOLL MADE OF?
8. WHERE DO ATOLLS TEND TO GROW?
9. LISTEN AGAIN TO PART OF THE DISCUSSION. THEN ANSWER THE QUESTION.

(instructor)	Now, let's look at how atolls are formed. We'll look at a series of three diagrams and discuss what's happening in each. This diagram shows the first step in the process. What does the diagram show? Linda?
(Linda)	Well, it . . . uh . . . looks like a volcano.
(instructor)	It certainly does . . . but perhaps there's something more you could add.

WHY DOES THE INSTRUCTOR SAY THIS:

(instructor)	but perhaps there's something more you could add.

10. IN WHAT ORDER DO THESE OCCUR?
11. WHAT IS TRUE ABOUT A LAGOON?

SPEAKING

Question 2

Listen to the passage. On a piece of paper, take notes on the main points of the listening passage.

(woman)	Have you seen the notice about the positions in the Administration Building?
(man)	Yeah, I have, but I can't apply for them because of the requirements.
(woman)	Well, I'm going to apply for one of the positions.
(man)	But look at the requirements for the positions. The notice says that you need to have completed 60 units.
(woman)	I've finished 45. That should be enough.
(man)	And is your grade point average 3.0 or higher? The notice says that a 3 point average is required.
(woman)	My grade point average is 2.5. I'm sure that's close enough.
(man)	And what about your availability? The notice says you have to be free either in the mornings or in the afternoons, and I know you have at least one class in the morning and one in the afternoon.
(woman)	I'm sure that won't be a problem either. And the notice says that good computer and telephone skills are required, and I have both.
(man)	You may have good telephone skills, but you're always having to ask me for help with your computer. I think you're wasting your time thinking about these positions.
(woman)	I think this job sounds perfect for me. I've already submitted my application.

HOW DO THE STUDENTS RESPOND TO THE NOTICE ABOUT THE POSITIONS IN THE ADMINISTRATION BUILDING?

Question 3

Listen to the passage. On a piece of paper, take notes on the main points of the listening passage.

(professor)	In economics class today, I'll be talking about zero-sum games. Theoretically, zero-sum games are a part of gaming theory, but the concept of zero-sum games has applications in a variety of academic areas. We'll be talking today first about the theoretical concept of zero-sum games and later about its application, of course, in the field of economics.

Theoretically, a zero-sum game is a game where the total number of points is fixed. If two players, players A and B, are playing a zero-sum game with a total of 100 points possible, then A and B each play to win the highest number of the 100 points available. If A wins 60 points, then B wins the remaining 40 points; if A wins 25 points, then B wins the remaining 75 points.

A non-zero-sum game is the opposite, a game where the total number of points is not fixed. In one game, perhaps player A wins 20 points and player B wins 30 points for a total of 50 points; in another game A wins 80 points and B wins 70 points for a total of 150 points.

Now let's take this gaming theory, the zero-sum gaming theory, and apply it to economics. Let's think first about a zero-sum economic system. In a zero-sum economy, there's a fixed amount of resources. In this economy, A has some of the resources and B has the rest. If A wants more in a zero-sum economy, the only way to get more is to take from B because there's only a fixed amount and B has whatever A doesn't have.

In a non-zero-sum economic system, the total amount of resources is not fixed; more resources can be created. If A has a certain amount of resources, A can either take some resources from B or can simply create more resources because the total amount of resources isn't fixed.

Your assignment for tomorrow is to look at the different economic theories we've been discussing so far—they're listed on page 20 in the text if you don't remember what they are. Look at the different theories in terms of the gaming theory I've just talked about and decide whether you think each of these theories is based upon the belief that the economy is a zero-sum economy or a non-zero-sum economy.

HOW IS THE CONCEPT OF ZERO-SUM GAMES RELATED TO THE STUDY OF ECONOMIC SYSTEMS?

WRITING

Listen to the passage. On a piece of paper, take notes on the main points of the listening passage.

(professor) Let me talk a bit about the expression *catch-22*. Do you understand what a catch-22 is? This expression is so well known now that it has entered the American lexicon: well, a catch-22 is a situation that is unresolvable, one where there is no good choice, no best path to take.

In Heller's novel, the catch-22 is a very specific catch in a very specific situation. The situation in which the protagonist found himself was that he wanted to get out of combat by declaring himself insane. So you see that in this situation there was a very specific catch. In American culture now, though, this expression is used more generally. It refers to any situation where there's a catch, where there's no solution, where there's no way out.

One more bit of information about the expression *catch-22*, about the number 22 in the expression. This number doesn't have any real meaning; it just signifies one in a long line of catches. Heller really could have used any number; it didn't have to be 22. When Heller was first writing the book, he used the number 14; the book was originally titled *Catch-14*. Then, in the production process, the number was changed to 18, so the title was *Catch-18*. But then there was a problem with the number 18 because there was another book with 18 in the title, so Heller's title became *Catch-22*.

HOW DOES THE INFORMATION IN THE LISTENING PASSAGE ADD TO THE IDEAS PRESENTED IN THE READING PASSAGE?

MINI-TEST 6

LISTENING

Questions 1 through 5. Listen to a conversation between a student and her advisor.

(advisor) Hi. Sorry I'm running a bit late. Are you ready to talk now?

(student) Yes, I am.

(advisor) And do you have your schedule planner with you?

(student) Yes, I do.

(advisor) And have you looked over the schedule of classes and thought about what courses you'd like to take then?

(student) Uh, yes to that, too.

(advisor) OK, let's see what courses you have on your list . . . uh . . . I see. . . . Let's talk about what you have here. I see that you'd like to take the American literature class on nineteenth-century novels. . . . That looks just fine. . . . You've already taken the prerequisite English courses for this one, haven't you?

(student) Yes, I have. I've taken both the prerequisites for the nineteenth-century novels course.

(advisor) OK. And you'd like to sign up for both world geography and sociology? . . . That's good. They both satisfy general education requirements, so they're good classes to take.

(student) Yes, those're some of my last required courses.

(advisor) Hmm. And music. You've listed a music course.

(student) Yes. I'm in the school choir, so I take the choir course every semester.

(advisor) That sounds fine, too. . . . Now, what's the last course you've listed? Canoeing? . . . You want to take a canoeing course? . . . Wait a minute . . . what about chemistry? . . . You're taking Chemistry 101 this semester?

(student) Yes, I'm taking it, but . . .

(advisor) You do know that you need to take Chemistry 102, also? Chemistry 101 isn't enough; it's part of a two-semester series. Chemistry 101 and 102 go together.

(student) I know that, but I just don't want to take Chemistry 102 next semester.

(advisor) Why not?

(student) Chemistry 101 isn't exactly a lot of fun. I'm working really hard in that course, but I'm not doing very well.

(advisor) OK. So maybe you should get a tutor. You do need to take the second semester of chemistry.

(student) I know I need to take another semester of chemistry, but I'd like to take some time off from it before I try the second semester.

(advisor) By taking canoeing instead?

(student) Exactly. I thought it would be a good break from chemistry.

(advisor) It certainly is. . . . Well, as long as you know that you need to take the second semester of chemistry and if you take only one semester off from it, then I guess it'll be OK.

(student) Thank you.

1. WHY IS THE STUDENT IN THE ADVISOR'S OFFICE?
2. LISTEN AGAIN TO PART OF THE PASSAGE. THEN ANSWER THE QUESTION.
   (advisor) Sorry I'm running a bit late. Are you ready to talk now?
   WHY DOES THE ADVISOR START THE CONVERSATION THIS WAY?
3. HOW DOES THE STUDENT SEEM TO FEEL ABOUT CHEMISTRY?
4. WHAT DOES THE STUDENT WANT TO DO?
5. HOW DOES THE ADVISOR SEEM TO FEEL ABOUT THE STUDENT'S DECISION?

Questions 6 through 11. Listen to a lecture in a zoology class.

(professor) ❶ Today, we'll be talking about how different types of animals hear. Many animals have sense organs that allow them to process sound waves. However, the sense organs are structured and function in very different ways in different types of animals.

❷ First, we'll look at the hearing abilities of some examples of insects and amphibians. Let's look now at an example of an insect. A cricket's a type of insect, and it has thin membranes that vibrate when sound hits them. The thin "hearing" membranes on a cricket are found on the side of each front leg. On other insects, these vibrating membranes can be found on various other body parts.

Now, let's look at an example of an amphibian. . . . The frog's a good example of one. The frog has large disks that serve as eardrums. These disks are located farther back on the head, behind each eye. The disks, or eardrums, behind each eye vibrate when sound hits them. So you see that the frog has large disks on its head that serve as eardrums, unlike the cricket that I talked about earlier, which is able to hear by means of vibrating membranes on the side of each front leg.

❸ Now, let's look at the hearing of birds and bats. Birds have external auditory canals along the sides of the head. The auditory canal on a bird is merely an opening that leads to the middle and inner ear, and this auditory opening on a bird is usually covered with feathers. Birds lack auricles, which are external portions of the ear that protrude from the body.

Bats are not birds; they're mammals. And like most mammals, they have auricles. You can see the large auricles on the bat, the part of the ear that protrudes from the bat's head. Bats are dependent on their hearing to navigate in the dark; they have very effective auricles that move to enhance their ability to pick up sound waves as they enter the ear. So we've seen that birds and bats have different ways of hearing because bats are mammals so they have auricles. But birds are not mammals, so they don't have auricles. They have auditory canals instead.

❹ Now, let's look at some other types of mammals, the elephant and the rabbit. Mammals are the only animals that have auricles, and elephants and rabbits are mammals, so they have auricles. The auricles of the African elephant are the largest of any animal, and rabbits have auricles that are unusually large in proportion to their bodies. These large auricles allow heat to escape the body and assist these animals in cooling off in hot weather.

❺ Now let me switch gears and talk for a moment about echolocation. Some animals are dependent on their hearing to navigate in the dark. The process that they use is called echolocation. Animals that use echolocation produce sounds and then listen for echos as the sound waves they have produced are reflected off of objects around them. They use echolocation to determine when objects are in their path and how far away the objects are. Bats and whales are two animals that navigate using echolocation, and there are many more.

❻ Today we've discussed the types of hearing organs that various animals have. You should be familiar with animals that have external vibrating membranes, animals that have auditory canals, animals that have auricles, and animals that use echolocation. If you understand these various types of hearing organs, then you understand the important points of this lecture.

6. HOW IS THE INFORMATION IN THE LECTURE ORGANIZED?
7. WHAT TYPE OF HEARING ORGAN DOES EACH ANIMAL HAVE?
8. WHAT DO THE DISKS ON FROGS DO?
9. WHAT IS TRUE ABOUT MAMMALS?
10. LISTEN AGAIN TO PART OF THE PASSAGE. THEN ANSWER THE QUESTION.
    (professor) Now let me switch gears and talk for a moment about echolocation.
    WHY DOES THE PROFESSOR SAY THIS?
11. WHAT IS TRUE ABOUT ECHOLOCATION?

SPEAKING

Question 2

Listen to the passage. On a piece of paper, take notes on the main points of the listening passage.

(professor) It's not clear to scientists exactly how this layered structure came to be. The various theories about how the layered structure came about can be classified into two general categories. In one category of theories about how the layered structure came to be, the core formed first and then the lighter layers came later. In the second category of theories, all the material clumped together first and then later separated into layers. In other words, in the first category of theories the Earth started out only as the core, with the lighter layers coming later, and in the second category of theories the Earth started out with all of its material and later separated into layers.

HOW DOES THE INFORMATION IN THE LISTENING PASSAGE ADD TO WHAT IS EXPLAINED IN THE READING PASSAGE?

Question 3

Listen to the passage. On a piece of paper, take notes on the main points of the listening passage.

(woman) Hey, Lee, are you going to the outdoor theater tonight?

(man) What for? Is something going on there tonight?

(woman) A guest speaker you said you wanted to go listen to is going to be there.

(man) Which one? I didn't know about any guest speaker at the outdoor theater tonight.

(woman) You know, the guest speaker from the governor's office. You said you wanted to go hear him speak.

(man) But I thought that wasn't until next week. He's scheduled to speak next week. Not tonight.

(woman) No, really. He's going to be speaking at the outdoor theater tonight. I just saw a notice posted over by the theater, and it said he would be speaking tonight.

(man) Wow, I really thought it was next week. I have it written on my calendar that it's next week.

(woman) I actually thought it was scheduled for next week, too.

(man) You know, I really think the schedule must've been changed if we both thought it was next week and not tonight.

(woman) Yeah, the schedule must've been changed, but if it was, then no one did a very good job of letting people know. There's just a sign over at the theater, but most people won't see it until it's too late.

(man) I think we really should let our friends know.

(woman) That sounds like a good idea. Maybe they don't know the speaker's tonight, either.

HOW ARE THE STUDENTS DEALING WITH THE SITUATION SURROUNDING THE GUEST SPEAKER?

MINI-TEST 7

LISTENING

Questions 1 through 5. Listen to a conversation between a student and a professor.

(professor) Come in, Will. Did you want to discuss something with me?

(student) Thank you, yes, I have something I need to talk about with you. It's about our group presentation. I'm here on behalf of our group. We've been trying to plan our presentation, but . . . well . . . we're kind of stuck. So we decided that one of us should come here and talk about it with you, and I'm the one.

(professor) That's fine, but can you be a bit more specific? I'm not quite sure how to answer your question.

(student) Well, we're not sure how to get started, how to get organized. We've had a number of meetings, but we just sit around discussing how we should prepare the presentation, and we never get anywhere. Sometimes it seems like everyone in the group has a different idea about how to proceed.

(professor) OK, I see. . . . Tell me, what's the topic of your presentation? I mean, which company are you discussing?

(student) The Northwest Paper Company.

(professor) OK, so, with your group, first of all you should be outlining what issues the Northwest Paper Company is facing.

(student) But we've been trying to divide up tasks first, trying to figure out who's going to do what part of the presentation.

(professor) That most likely won't work. You need to concentrate on the issues first, as a group and not individually.

(student) OK, so we should concentrate on the issues first. . . . You did say "issues," didn't you? There can be more than one issue?

(professor) Certainly. The company may be facing more than one issue . . . maybe two or three issues. Just concentrate on the major issues.

(student) So, as a group, the first thing we need to do is to decide what the issues are, maybe two or three main issues.

(professor) That's right. Then, after the group has agreed on what the issues are, as a group, you need to decide on the best solution for each issue.

(student) OK, first we figure out the issues, and then we figure out the best solutions for the issues.

(professor) Yes. Together as a group, you should agree on the issues and the solutions. And then, only then, you should think about how you're going to organize your presentation.

(student) And how would you suggest that we organize our presentation?

(professor) Oh, there are many different ways to organize the presentation . . . let me give you a couple of examples. How many students are in your group? Four or five?

(student) Four. Our group has four members.

(professor) Well, let's say you decide that there are two major issues. Then, one person could introduce the presentation, give an overview, you know, and a second person could discuss one issue and its solution, and the third person could discuss the second issue and its solution, and the fourth person could summarize it all. Or maybe you decide that there're three issues and three of you present issues and solutions and one person introduces and summarizes the presentation. Or maybe two of you present issues and the other two of you discuss possible solutions.

(student) OK. I understand. . . .

(professor) What, exactly, do you understand?

(student) That we need to figure out what the issues and solutions are together as a group before we can decide how we're going to organize the presentation.

(professor) Exactly!

1. WHY DOES THE STUDENT GO TO TALK WITH THE PROFESSOR?
2. LISTEN AGAIN TO PART OF THE PASSAGE. THEN ANSWER THE QUESTION.

(student) We've been trying to plan our presentation, but . . . well . . . we're kind of stuck. So we decided that one of us should come here and talk about it with you, and I'm the one.

(professor) That's fine, but can you be a bit more specific? I'm not quite sure how to answer your question.

WHAT DOES THE PROFESSOR MEAN WHEN SHE SAYS THIS?

(professor) I'm not quite sure how to answer your question.

3. WHAT DOES THE PROFESSOR THINK THE STUDENTS HAVE DONE WRONG?
4. WHAT SHOULD THE STUDENTS DO FIRST?
5. LISTEN AGAIN TO PART OF THE PASSAGE. THEN ANSWER THE QUESTION.

(professor) Well, let's say you decide that there are two major issues. Then, one person could introduce the presentation, give an overview, you know, and a second person could discuss one issue and its solution, and the third person could discuss the second issue and its solution, and the fourth person could summarize it all. Or maybe you decide that there're three issues and three of you present issues and solutions and one person introduces and summarizes the presentation. Or maybe two of you present issues and the other two of you discuss possible solutions.

WHY DOES THE PROFESSOR SAY THIS?

Questions 6 through 11. Listen to a lecture in a music class.

(professor) ❶ The trumpet of today, with its long oblong loop of metal and three piston valves, is a brass instrument that has a commanding role in modern-day bands and orchestras. This modern musical instrument has a long and interesting history. As we take a look at the development of the trumpet, you should keep the following points about the trumpet in mind. ❷ First, the trumpet is a universal instrument that has been part of numerous cultures. Second, the trumpet has undergone numerous mutations in its development. Third, the trumpet has served a variety of purposes in its various mutations and in different cultures.

The first point that we want to understand about the trumpet is that many early cultures had their own distinct version of a trumpet, so it's difficult to say that the trumpet originated in one specific culture. Early cultures in Africa and Australia had trumpet-like hollow tubes, and by 1400 B.C. the Egyptians had developed wide-belled trumpets made from bronze and silver. Assyrian, Greek, Etruscan, Roman, Celtic, and Teutonic civilizations all had some form of the trumpet, and during the Crusades in the Middle Ages, the Europeans were introduced to the Arab trumpa.

Now for the second point. . . . The second point to understand about the trumpet is that it has undergone extensive changes in construction, both in the materials used and in its shape. ❸ In this drawing, you can see various types of trumpets that've been used throughout the ages. Some of the materials that've been used to construct trumpets are the cane plant, horns or tusks of animals, and metals such as bronze, silver, and brass. In shape, the trumpet began as a long, hollow, straight tube to which a wide-mouthed bell was later added to magnify the sound. Then, as the tubing got longer and longer, it was bent to make the instrument more convenient, first into an S-shape and then into the circling loop of today. To increase the number and accuracy of tones produced, keys and a slide similar to the slide on a trombone were added to the trumpet before the three piston valves of the modern trumpet became the norm.

❹ OK, so far we've discussed the first and second points I wanted to make. Now on to the third point. The third point to understand about the trumpet is that it has served a variety of purposes. The trumpet has only relatively recently been considered a musical instrument. For most of its long history, it's been used in other ways. First, the trumpet has been used for ceremonial purposes, perhaps to herald the arrival of an important personage or to provide what you could call resonant ornamentation during a celebration or rite. In addition, the trumpet has been used for communication over distances; ancient versions of the trumpet with a limited range of low powerful notes were used for communication from village to village and from mountaintop to mountaintop. Finally, the trumpet has been used by numerous cultures in battle, to announce the charge into battle and to exhort troops to fight more intensely during battle. It wasn't until the last few centuries, when changes and improvements to the trumpet made it more versatile, that it became established in its role as a musical instrument.

❺ Of course, there's a whole lot more we could say about the trumpet. However, for today, these points will suffice.

6. WHAT CAN BE CONCLUDED ABOUT THE DEVELOPMENT OF THE TRUMPET?
7. DOES THE PROFESSOR MAKE EACH OF THESE POINTS ABOUT THE DEVELOPMENT OF THE TRUMPET?
8. WHICH WAS NOT MENTIONED AS A MATERIAL FROM WHICH TRUMPETS HAVE BEEN MADE?
9. WHEN DID DIFFERENT PARTS OF THE TRUMPET DEVELOP?
10. LISTEN AGAIN TO PART OF THE PASSAGE. THEN ANSWER THE QUESTION.
    (professor) OK, so far we've discussed the first and second points I wanted to make. Now on to the third point.
    WHY DOES THE PROFESSOR SAY THIS?
11. HOW DID THE PROFESSOR CATEGORIZE EACH OF THESE USES OF A TRUMPET?

SPEAKING

Question 2

Listen to the passage. On a piece of paper, take notes on the main points of the listening passage.

(woman) Brian, did you see the part of the syllabus about discussion in class?
(man) I sure did!
(woman) Do you think the professor means it? I mean, it sounds so strict.
(man) I'm actually really sure she means it.
(woman) Really? Why are you so sure?
(man) Because I know someone who took a class from this professor last year. One of my friends did.
(woman) And what did your friend tell you about the class?

(man) He said the professor really makes the point that she wants everyone to read the material and come prepared to take part in the discussion. Each day, the professor starts the class by asking students questions about the reading. If any students can't answer the questions, she tells them to leave the classroom before the discussion starts.
(woman) I guess she is serious about this. I think I'll go to the library and work on the first reading assignment.
(man) From what I've heard, that would be a very sensible idea.

HOW DO THE STUDENTS SEEM TO FEEL ABOUT THE PROFESSOR'S POLICY ON CLASS DISCUSSIONS?

Question 3

Listen to the passage. On a piece of paper, take notes on the main points of the listening passage.

(professor) When governments want to construct facilities of some kind, particularly those with some sort of negative effect on their surroundings, they commonly encounter a problem that's now called, simply, NIMBY. That's N-I-M-B-Y, NIMBY. Can you guess what the letters N-I-M-B-Y stand for? Well, they stand for not-in-my-backyard. So, governments encounter the NIMBY response when they want to construct a facility that might have a negative impact on the community where it's built, a facility such as a prison, a landfill, a mental hospital, or a power plant in a community. The community wants these facilities somewhere; communities want facilities like prisons, landfills, mental hospitals, and power plants somewhere, but not in their communities, or NIMBY. When a government announces, for example, that planning for a new prison in a certain area is underway, a strong NIMBY reaction to the news can be expected. This NIMBYism might take the form of neighborhood meetings, demonstrations, picketing, letters to newspapers, letter-writing campaigns directed at decision-making officials, or confrontational meetings with these officials.

WHAT POINTS DOES THE PROFESSOR MAKE ABOUT A CERTAIN KIND OF RESPONSE FROM THE PUBLIC?

WRITING

Listen to the passage. On a piece of paper, take notes on the main points of the listening passage.

(professor) Probably the most famous case of hemophilia is often called Royal hemophilia. In this case, Queen Victoria of England, who lived from 1819–1901, was a carrier of the mutating factor 8 that leads to hemophilia type A. Queen Victoria may have inherited the mutated gene from one of her parents, though there is no sign of the mutated gene in the families of Victoria's parents up to that time that she was born. The mutated factor 8 may also have mutated spontaneously in Victoria, as seems to happen sometimes.

However Victoria came to be a carrier of the gene with the mutated factor, she unfortunately passed it on to some of her children. She had nine children, and three of them, her daughters Alice and Beatrice and her son Leopold, received the mutated gene from their mother. Victoria's daughters then intermarried with other royal houses of Europe and carried the disease with them. Through Queen Victoria's daughter Beatrice, the disease was carried into the royal family of Spain. Through Queen Victoria's daughter Alice, the disease was introduced into the royal families of Austria and Russia, though the disease no longer exists in the Russian family because Victoria's granddaughter Alexandra and her children were all killed during the Russian revolution.

HOW IS THE INFORMATION IN THE LISTENING PASSAGE RELATED TO THE INFORMATION PRESENTED IN THE READING PASSAGE?

MINI-TEST 8

LISTENING

Questions 1 through 5. Listen to a conversation between a student and an advisor.

(advisor) Thanks for coming in, Beth.

(student) You wanted to see me? Is there some sort of problem?

(advisor) Well, not exactly a problem, but there is something we need to discuss. I asked you to come here because I want to talk with you about your schedule. I mean about the courses you've already taken and the courses you've signed up to take next year.

(student) Is there something wrong?

(advisor) It's not exactly wrong, but it's something we need to deal with. Let me lay it out for you . . . here it is. . . . You've declared that your major is sociology?

(student) Yes, that's right.

(advisor) But you haven't been taking too many sociology courses.

(student) No, I guess I haven't.

(advisor) There are some required courses for a sociology major that you should've taken but you haven't. If you want to graduate on time with a degree in sociology, then you're behind . . . you haven't taken some courses that you should've taken by now.

(student) I guess I understand that, I mean, I know I haven't taken some courses I need for a sociology major, but let me tell you what I've done and why. When the new schedule of classes comes out each semester, I like to sign up for courses that seem interesting to me . . . so I take a whole bunch of really interesting classes, and I don't seem to sign up for the required classes, particularly the ones I need for a sociology major.

(advisor) Well, if you aren't really interested in the courses that're required for sociology, maybe you're not in the right major.

(student) I think I was coming to that conclusion . . . each time the class schedule comes out, the courses that're offered in sociology don't seem very interesting to me.

(advisor) Is there some other major that interests you? Have you thought about that?

(student) Well, you can see from the list of courses I've already taken that I'm not very interested in a single subject. I seem to enjoy courses in a bunch of different areas.

(advisor) Well, then, I have something to suggest to you. There's a major in General Studies at this university. To get a degree in General Studies, you need to take courses from four different departments, so you need to take a wide variety of courses.

(student) That sounds like it might be the best thing for me.

(advisor) Let me give you some information about the General Studies degree, and you can look it over and see what you think.

(student) I'll do that. . . .

(advisor) And then come back to see me after you've made a decision about it.

(student) I'll do that, too!

1. LISTEN AGAIN TO PART OF THE PASSAGE. THEN ANSWER THE QUESTION.
   (student) Is there something wrong?
   (advisor) It's not exactly wrong, but it's something we need to deal with. Let me lay it out for you.
   WHAT DOES THE ADVISOR MEAN WHEN HE SAYS THIS?
   (advisor) Let me lay it out for you.

2. WHAT PROBLEM DOES THE STUDENT HAVE?

3. WHAT IS STATED ABOUT THE COURSES THE STUDENT HAS TAKEN?

4. WHICH SENTENCE BEST DESCRIBES WHAT THE ADVISOR SEEMS TO THINK?

5. WHAT DOES THE ADVISOR SUGGEST?

Questions 6 through 11. Listen to a discussion by some students taking a chemistry class.

(woman 1) ❶ I hope you're ready to discuss the chapter on carbon in our chemistry text. We're going to be having a quiz on this chapter later today.

(man) I think the main point of the chapter is that carbon is unique because of how many compounds it can form. I believe the chapter said there are more than seven million compounds that contain carbon.

(woman 2) Yeah, that's right. More than seven million carbon compounds are now known, and there're only 100,000 compounds made from all the other elements. That's because the carbon atom attaches easily with other carbon atoms and with many other kinds of atoms.

(woman 1) I think that we need to become familiar with some of the better-known carbon compounds. The chapter discusses a few of them. Ah, I remember that it discusses graphite and gasoline, and some others.

(man) It discusses graphite and gasoline, as well as soap and diamonds.

(woman 2) You know, graphite and gasoline seem like they're made from carbon, but it really seems strange that soap and diamonds are also derived from carbon. . . . Let's look at graphite first. What does the chapter say about graphite?

(woman 1) Graphite is made only of carbon. ❷ Look at the diagram of a graphite molecule in the text. It has rings of six carbon atoms each, and two of the carbon atoms are part of each ring.

(man) Isn't graphite what's found in pencils?

(woman 1) Yes. Graphite is the primary component of the lead in pencils.

(woman 2) Um, the next carbon compound is gasoline.

(woman 2) ❸ Look at the gasoline molecule in the book. The carbon atoms in this molecule are in a chain rather than in rings, as they were in the graphite molecule.

(man) And, unlike the graphite molecule, which was made only of carbon, the gasoline molecule is a compound of carbon and hydrogen.

(woman 1) This gasoline molecule is a molecule of octane because it contains a chain of eight carbon atoms, and *octane* means eight. The chapter says that different types of gasoline molecules each contain a chain of, uh, between five and ten carbon atoms.

(man) ❹ Now on to the soap molecule. I really didn't know that soap contained carbon.

(woman 2) Yeah, it does seem strange to think that soap contains carbon, but it does. . . . Now, what about the soap molecule?

(woman 1) There doesn't seem to be a picture of a soap molecule in the text. Oh but the text does say that the soap molecule has a long chain of carbon atoms, a much longer chain than the gasoline atom.

(man) The text says that soap atoms can have anywhere between five and seven carbon atoms in a chain.

(woman 2) Um, are you sure it says five to seven? It's supposed to be a long chain of carbon atoms, and five to seven doesn't seem right.

(man) Oh, here it is. Excuse me. You really do seem to have a good grasp of the material. The book doesn't say five to seven, it says 15 to 17.

(woman 1) Let me get this straight. A soap molecule has 15 to 17 carbon atoms in a chain, not five to seven.

(woman 2) You got it!

(man) Sorry for the confusion. . . .

(woman 2) It's OK. All right, now that we understand this, that makes three of the types of carbon molecules we have to deal with, so there's only one more. The last example of a carbon molecule is diamond. ❺ Oh, here's the diagram of a diamond molecule.

(woman 1) This diamond molecule consists only of carbon, and the carbon atoms are arranged in a very complex pattern. Oh, that's what helps to make diamond harder than any other natural substance.

(man) ❻ OK. I think we've got all the necessary information on carbon and a few of the many compounds that're formed from it. In graphite, the carbon was in rings, while in octane and soap, it was in long chains. And in diamond, it was in a very complex pattern.

(woman 2) And graphite and diamond molecules are formed solely from carbon, while gasoline and soap are compounds of carbon atoms and other types of atoms.

(woman 1) I think we're ready for the quiz today. See you at our next study session, the day after tomorrow.

6. WHAT IS UNUSUAL ABOUT CARBON?
7. WHAT IS THE STRUCTURE OF EACH SUBSTANCE?
8. WHICH TWO MOLECULES DO NOT CONTAIN ONLY CARBON ATOMS?
9. WHAT IS NOT TRUE ABOUT THE USES OF MOLECULES CONTAINING CARBON?
10. LISTEN AGAIN TO PART OF THE PASSAGE. THEN ANSWER THE QUESTION.

(man) The text says that soap atoms can have anywhere between five and seven carbon atoms in a chain.

(woman 2) Um, are you sure it says five to seven? It's supposed to be a long chain of carbon atoms, and five to seven doesn't seem right.

(man) Oh, here it is. Excuse me. You really do seem to have a good grasp of the material. The book doesn't say five to seven, it says 15 to 17.

WHY DOES THE MAN SAY THIS?

(man) Excuse me.

11. WHAT OVERALL CONCLUSION CAN BE DRAWN FROM THE DISCUSSION?

SPEAKING

Question 2

Listen to the passage. On a piece of paper, take notes on the main points of the listening passage.

(professor) There are several common misconceptions about sonnambulism, or sleepwalking, and I'd like to talk about two of them now.

One common misconception about sleepwalking is that someone who is sleepwalking should not be awakened. Many people will say that it's dangerous to awaken someone who's sleepwalking, but this is not true. It's not really dangerous to awaken someone who's sleepwalking.

Another common misconception about sleepwalking is that someone who's sleepwalking can't get hurt. This is also not true. Someone who's sleepwalking can easily get hurt by running into something or by tripping and falling.

HOW DOES THE INFORMATION IN THE LISTENING PASSAGE ADD TO WHAT IS EXPLAINED IN THE READING PASSAGE?

Question 3

Listen to the passage. On a piece of paper, take notes on the main points of the listening passage.

(man)	Hey, Tina, you took Dr. Hall's sociology class last year, didn't you?
(woman)	Yes, I did.
(man)	And you liked it?
(woman)	Not at first, but later on I did.
(man)	Really? I've just started his class, and I don't like it at all. What made you change your mind about it?
(woman)	It wasn't that I changed my mind about it. It's that the class changed, and I liked it better later on. At first, I didn't understand very much of the class at all.
(man)	That's the problem I'm having now. How did the class change when you took it?
(woman)	Well, it wasn't that the class changed on its own. We students caused the class to change.
(man)	How did you do that?
(woman)	We started asking questions, asking a lot of questions. Do any of you ask any questions?
(man)	We can't. There's not any time to do that. Dr. Hall just charges on and on. He doesn't even seem to stop to take a breath.
(woman)	I know what you mean. If no one asks any questions, he just assumes that everyone understands everything. For the first few weeks of my class, no one asked any questions, and he just moved so fast.
(man)	And how did you change that?
(woman)	Well, after a couple of weeks, someone started asking questions, and Dr. Hall answered them. Pretty soon, we all figured out that we were supposed to ask questions, lots of questions, to keep him from going so fast.
(man)	But nobody asks any questions because he's going so fast.
(woman)	You just need to start asking questions. At first Dr. Hall will seem a bit surprised because nobody has asked any questions

so far, but he'll answer your question, and then ask another question.

| (man) | And another after that. |
| (woman) | Exactly. That's how you get him to slow down. |

WHAT POSSIBLE SOLUTIONS DOES THE WOMAN OFFER TO THE MAN'S PROBLEM?

COMPLETE TEST 1

LISTENING

Questions 1 through 5. Listen to a conversation between a student and a university office worker.

(student)	Hi, I'd like to talk with someone about joining the staff of the school paper.
(office worker)	You're talking to the right person. I can help you with that. Let me ask you a few questions. First, what year of school are you in?
(student)	I'm a freshman. I'm in my first year.
(office worker)	So you've never worked on the school paper before?
(student)	Not on this school paper. I worked on the school paper in high school. In fact, I was the editor of the school paper in my senior year.
(office worker)	Oh, that's very good. So you do have some experience.
(student)	Yes, lots!
(office worker)	But not on a university paper. . . .
(student)	No, on a high school paper.
(office worker)	And you haven't taken any journalism courses here at the university?
(student)	No, not yet. I did take journalism in high school, but I can't take journalism here until next year because I have so many required classes to take this year.
(office worker)	OK, let me tell you how we select staff writers for the university newspaper. . . . Oh, you <u>do</u> want to be a staff writer on the paper, don't you?
(student)	For now, yes, I want to be a staff writer. And maybe one day I'd like to have an editorial position.
(office worker)	Editorial positions are open only to juniors and seniors.
(student)	OK, so maybe my junior or senior year I'd like to have an editorial position. For now, I'd like to be a staff writer.
(office worker)	That sounds good. Now let me tell you how we select staff writers. Quite a few people would like to be staff writers on the school paper, and we don't have enough positions for everyone who'd like to be one.
(student)	Of course.
(office worker)	So we have students who'd like to be on the paper submit three articles.
(student)	Can they be articles I've already written, for the high school paper?

(office worker) No, they need to be articles about this university, from a student's perspective.
(student) OK, three articles about the university . . . .
(office worker) And they need to be from three different areas.
(student) What do you mean by three different areas?
(office worker) Three different aspects of student life, like academics, sports, theater, student government, dormitories, the cafeteria. You understand?
(student) Yes, I see. And when should I submit these articles?
(office worker) Whenever you want. After you've submitted your articles, they'll be evaluated by the editorial committee, and a decision will be made as to whether or not you will be awarded a position as a staff writer on the paper.
(student) It sounds like I should hand them in soon if I want to get to work on the paper.
(office worker) Yes, but don't submit them too quickly. Take a few weeks. You want to do your best work, after all, so take your time and work carefully.
(student) I'll do that!

1. WHY DOES THE STUDENT GO TO THIS UNIVERSITY OFFICE?
2. IS EACH OF THESE TRUE ABOUT THE STUDENT'S EXPERIENCE?
3. LISTEN AGAIN TO PART OF THE PASSAGE. THEN ANSWER THE QUESTION.
    (office worker) OK, let me tell you how we select staff writers for the university newspaper . . . Oh you do want to be a staff writer on the paper, don't you?
    (student) For now, yes, I want to be a staff writer.
    WHY DOES THE OFFICE WORKER SAY THIS:
    (office worker) You do want to be a staff writer on the paper, don't you?
4. WHAT MUST A STUDENT DO TO BECOME A STAFF WRITER ON THE UNIVERSITY PAPER?
5. WHAT WILL THE STUDENT MOST LIKELY DO NEXT?

Questions 6 through 11. Listen to a discussion from a geography class.

(instructor) ❶ Today, we're going to talk about two lakes, the Great Salt Lake and Lake Bonneville. Most people are quite familiar with the Great Salt Lake, but not everyone is quite as familiar with Lake Bonneville.

❷ First of all, let's look at a map that shows both the Great Salt Lake and Lake Bonneville. Now, uh, Gwen, what can you tell me about the Great Salt Lake and Lake Bonneville?
(woman) Um, Lake Bonneville was a lake during prehistoric times. The Great Salt Lake

is the largest surviving remnant of the prehistoric Lake Bonneville.
(instructor) Yes, and how old is Lake Bonneville?
(woman) Lake Bonneville came into existence a million years ago.
(instructor) And how big was it?
(woman) It was an enormous lake that covered about 20,000 square miles.
(instructor) Gwen has explained that the Great Salt Lake is a small remnant of Lake Bonneville and that Lake Bonneville was 20,000 square miles in size. Now, Nick, just how big is the Great Salt Lake?
(man 1) Uh, the present Great Salt Lake is much bigger than Lake Bonneville was.
(instructor) Are you sure? You want to try again?
(man 1) Oops! Did I get it backwards? What did I say? . . . I mean, what I meant was that the Great Salt Lake is much smaller than Lake Bonneville; Lake Bonneville was much larger than the Great Salt Lake is today.
(instructor) You got it this time. The Great Salt Lake is much smaller than Lake Bonneville, less than 10 percent of the size of Lake Bonneville, in fact. The Great Salt Lake covers about 1,700 square miles. This is a rather large lake today, and it's much bigger than the lake that preceded it. And there's another big difference between the two lakes, besides the size. It has to do with the water. Can you tell me how the water in the Great Salt Lake differs from the water in Lake Bonneville? Paul?
(man 2) Uh, a big difference between Lake Bonneville and the Great Salt Lake is that Lake Bonneville was a freshwater lake, while the Great Salt Lake, as you can tell from its name, is a saltwater lake.
(instructor) Exactly. ❸ Now let's look at the reasons why this lake has become a saltwater lake and in fact has water that is much saltier than ocean water. And what is it that makes the Great Salt Lake so salty, Gwen?
(woman) What makes the Great Salt Lake so salty is that it has no outlet. Three rivers feed into it, the Bear, the Weber, and the Jordan River. These rivers carry a million tons of minerals and salts into the Great Salt Lake each year.
(instructor) And what about these three rivers, the Bear River, the Weber River, and the Jordan River? Nick?
(man 1) Uh, these rivers all feed into the Great Salt Lake. They don't provide any outlet from the lake.
(instructor) And how does this make the lake so salty? Paul?
(man 2) Well, there's no way for these minerals and salts to exit from the lake because the lake has no outlet. The water that flows into the lake from these three rivers evaporates and leaves the salts.

(instructor) And how much salt is there in the lake today?

(man 2) Over the lifetime of the lake, 6 billion tons of salts have built up. This is why the Great Salt Lake has a much higher salt content than the oceans.

(instructor) ❹ Excellent. You seem to understand the important points about the Great Salt Lake and Lake Bonneville. Now let's move on to another topic.

6. WHAT IS THE INSTRUCTOR TRYING TO ACCOMPLISH?

7. WHEN DID LAKE BONNEVILLE COME INTO EXISTENCE?

8. LISTEN AGAIN TO PART OF THE PASSAGE. THEN ANSWER THE QUESTION.

(man 1) The present Great Salt Lake is much bigger than Lake Bonneville was.

(instructor) Are you sure? You want to try again? WHAT DOES THE INSTRUCTOR MEAN WHEN SHE SAYS THIS?

(instructor) Are you sure? You want to try again?

9. WHAT IS STATED IN THE LECTURE ABOUT EACH LAKE?

10. WHAT IS STATED ABOUT THE WEBER, THE BEAR, AND THE JORDAN RIVERS?

11. HOW MUCH SALT HAS BUILT UP IN THE GREAT SALT LAKE?

Questions 12 through 17. Listen to a group of students who are taking a business class.

(man 1) ❶ Our presentation for marketing class is in a few days. Let's see what information we've come up with.

(woman) OK. Our topic for the presentation is the marketing of Kleenex early in its history. We're supposed to show how the early marketing of Kleenex helped to turn it into such a successful product.

(man 2) ❷ There seem to be three clear phases in the early history of Kleenex: first, its use during World War I, second its use as a substitute for facecloths during the 1920s, and third, its use as a substitute for handkerchiefs during the 1930s. For the presentation, how about if I talk about the first phase, the use of Kleenex during World War I?

(man 1) And I'll talk about the second phase, its use as a substitute for facecloths.

(woman) And that leaves me with the third phase, the use of Kleenex as a substitute for handkerchiefs.

(man 2) Now, don't forget . . . we're talking about a marketing class, not a history class.

(man 1) Yes, that's important to remember. Now, why don't we review the key points for each of these phases, with an emphasis on the marketing of the product during each phase?

(woman) Sounds like a good idea to me.

(man 2) So, I'll go first. The first phase of the product was its use during World War I. Cotton was in short supply during the war,

so the Kimberley-Clark company developed Kleenex for use in bandages and gas masks. During this first phase, the company didn't need to worry about marketing the product. Because it was during a war, there was very high demand for the product.

(man 1) Now, for the second phase. After the war, after World War I, the company had a huge surplus of Kleenex, and it had to market the product. During the 1920s, Kimberly-Clark decided to market Kleenex as a high-end and glamorous substitute for facecloths. It used famous actresses in its marketing, and women who wanted to be glamorous like the celebrities used Kleenex in place of facecloths.

(woman) Now, on to the second phase . . . oh, sorry, that was the second phase. I'm going to be discussing the third phase. While Kimberly-Clark was marketing Kleenex only for use as a facecloth, a number of people began writing in to the company saying that there was another use for Kleenex besides its use as a facecloth: Kleenex was even more useful as a replacement for handkerchiefs. In 1930, the company's marketing department decided to conduct consumer testing to determine if the product should be presented as a facecloth or as a handkerchief. The results of the consumer testing showed that a large majority thought Kleenex was more useful as a handkerchief than as a facecloth.

12. WHY ARE THE STUDENTS MEETING?

13. LISTEN AGAIN TO PART OF THE DISCUSSION. THEN ANSWER THE QUESTION.

(man 2) There seem to be three clear phases in the early history of Kleenex: first, its use during World War I, second its use as a substitute for facecloths during the 1920s, and third, its use as a substitute for handkerchiefs during the 1930s. For the presentation, how about if I talk about the first phase, the use of Kleenex during World War I?

(man 1) And I'll talk about the second phase, its use as a substitute for facecloths.

(woman) And that leaves me with the third phase, the use of Kleenex as a substitute for handkerchiefs.

(man 2) Now, don't forget . . . we're talking about a marketing class, not a history class.

WHY DOES THE MAN SAY THIS?

(man 2) Now, don't forget . . . we're talking about a marketing class, not a history class.

14. WITH WHAT PRODUCT WAS EACH OF THESE PERIODS OF TIME ASSOCIATED?

15. WHAT WAS THE SITUATION AT KIMBERLY-CLARK AT THE END OF WORLD WAR I?

16. HOW DID KIMBERLY-CLARK LEARN THAT ITS PRODUCT HAD A USE AS A HANDKERCHIEF?

17. WITH WHAT PRODUCT WAS EACH OF THESE MARKETING STRATEGIES ASSOCIATED?

Questions 18 through 22. Listen to a conversation between a student and a professor.

(student)   Hello, professor. I need to talk with you, please. Do you have some time to talk with me now?

(professor)   Yes, certainly. What did you want to discuss?

(student)   Well . . . I'd like to talk about the . . . uh . . . last exam . . . my grade on the last exam.

(professor)   What about your grade on the last exam?

(student)   It was, um, very low . . . I was surprised at how low it was.

(professor)   If your grade was low, perhaps you should've studied harder . . . you know, prepared more for the exam.

(student)   No, it's not that, really. I really studied hard. I went over the material, and I learned everything!

(professor)   OK. Do you have your exam paper with you?

(student)   Yes, I do.

(professor)   Let me look at it. No, that's not a very high grade. . . . Here's the first question . . . let me see what you wrote . . . OK, let's talk about this . . . I see what the problem is. . . . Look at the first question. Do you see what it is?

(student)   Yes, it asks about four steps in a process. . . .

(professor)   Yes, but do you see this word: *evaluation*? The question asks you to evaluate the four steps in the process. You simply listed the steps. Do you understand what *evaluate* means?

(student)   It means "to show the strengths and weaknesses of something."

(professor)   That's right. So in this question, you weren't supposed to simply list the steps. You needed to evaluate them. . . .

(student)   Show the strengths and weaknesses of each one?

(professor)   Yes, exactly. You see, you did list each step accurately. . . .

(student)   Yes.

(professor)   So that shows you knew the steps in the process. . . .

(student)   Yes.

(professor)   But you didn't provide any evaluation at all, and that's what I was looking for, not just a list of the steps in the process. So you see that?

(student)   Yes, I do now.

(professor)   OK, then, let's see what happened in a different question. . . . OK, now look at the next question . . . What does it ask?

(student)   It asks about two theories.

(professor)   It does. It asks about two theories, but . . . very important . . . it asks you to compare and contrast these two theories. Now, look at your response. . . . What did you do in your response?

(student)   I wrote about the two theories. . . .

(professor)   You did. You provided a lot of information about the two theories, I mean a lot of information, and this information about the two theories seems quite accurate . . . but . . . and this is the key point . . . you didn't do what the question asked you to do. Do you see what the question asks you to do with these two theories?

(student)   To compare and contrast them?

(professor)   Exactly. So, instead of listing a lot of information about the first theory and then giving a lot of information about the second theory, you should've clearly stated the ways that these two theories are similar and different.

(student)   Ah, I should've compared and contrasted them.

(professor)   Exactly. I think the important thing for you to make sure you understand is precisely what I'm asking in a particular question. Now please understand that on exams I generally don't ask you to just restate information from the text or lectures. Instead, I usually ask you to respond to the material somehow. It's not merely a matter of memorizing a lot of material, something that you clearly do well. So, is that clear to you now?

(student)   I think so.

(professor)   I would read and think about the actual questions very carefully because, uh, the next exam will be the same type of exam.

(student)   I certainly will, and thanks for taking the time to help me.

(professor)   You're welcome.

18. WHY DOES THE STUDENT GO TO SEE THE PROFESSOR?
19. HOW HAD THE STUDENT MOST LIKELY PREPARED FOR THE EXAM?
20. WHAT PROBLEM DID THE STUDENT HAVE WITH THE QUESTION REGARDING THE PROCESS?
21. WHAT PROBLEM DID THE STUDENT HAVE WITH THE QUESTION REGARDING THE THEORIES?
22. WHICH EXAM QUESTION WOULD THIS PROFESSOR MOST LIKELY USE?

Questions 23 through 28. Listen to a lecture in an American history class.

(professor)   ❶ Today, we're going to talk about the last monarch to rule land that today makes up part of the United States. This last monarch was a queen, and she was named Queen Liliuokalani of Hawaii. To understand Queen Liliuokalani's situation, I'm going to give you some background about the history of Hawaii before I discuss Queen Liliuokalani. I'm going to be talking about two people today in addition to Queen Liliuokalani: These two people are Captain James Cook and King Kamehameha. The reason I'm going to talk about these two people is, of course, that they'll help you to understand Queen Liliuokalani and the situation in which she found herself.

❷ So, first of all, let's talk about Captain James Cook. You must be familiar with Captain Cook. Captain Cook arrived in the Hawaiian Islands in 1778 and gave the islands the name Sandwich Islands in honor of a British nobleman, the Earl of Sandwich. When Captain Cook arrived in the islands near the end of the eighteenth century, the islands were not a single unified society. Instead, various islands in the chain were under the control of different native kings.

❸ The next person we're going to look at is King Kamehameha. Kamehameha spent almost 30 years uniting the Hawaiian Islands under one ruler, and by 1810, only a few decades after Captain Cook's arrival, all of the islands were united under this one king, King Kamahameha. King Kamehameha was the first ruler to reign over all of the islands together. He ruled over all the islands together until he died in 1819. A number of other kings of the Hawaiian Islands followed Kamehameha during the nineteenth century.

❹ Now we'll discuss Queen Liliuokalani, the last monarch of Hawaii. Liliuokalani became queen after her brother, King Kalakaua, died in 1891. Liliuokalani was the first and only female monarch to rule the Hawaiian Islands, and she was the final monarch of Hawaii. Liliuokalani became queen during a period when a large percentage of the population believed that it was better to have a democratic government than a monarchy. Liliuokalani refused to consider ending the monarchy and also refused to consider limiting the power of the monarchy and initiating a democratic government. In 1893, two years after she became queen, she developed a constitution granting complete power to the monarch. At that point, she was removed from the monarchy. Over the next few years, there were a number of plots to try to reinstitute the monarchy. By 1898, Liliuokalani had renounced her claim to the royal throne of Hawaii. She received a pension from the government and returned to her royal estates, where she lived out her life for the next 20 years with the title of queen but without the authority as the last monarch of the Hawaiian Islands.

❺ I know that the Hawaiian names can be a bit difficult to remember, but I hope you got the important main points, that it was King Kamehameha who unified the Hawaiian Islands under one monarch and it was Queen Liliuokalani who was the final monarch of the Hawaiian Islands. That's all for today.

23. WHAT DOES THE LECTURER MAINLY DISCUSS?
24. WHY DOES THE LECTURER MOST LIKELY MENTION KING KAMEHAMEHA AND CAPTAIN COOK?
25. WHAT DOES THE PROFESSOR SAY ABOUT JAMES COOK?
26. WHAT DID LILIUOKALANI BELIEVE, ACCORDING TO THE PROFESSOR?
27. WHICH OF THE FOLLOWING DID NOT HAPPEN TO LILIUOKALANI?
28. WHEN DID EACH PERSON LIVE?

Questions 29 through 34. Listen to a lecture in a science class.

(professor) ❶ Today, I'll be talking about an accident at a nuclear power plant. The accident I'll be discussing is the one that occurred at Three-Mile Island in 1979. This was an accident that, uh, while it was very serious, was not as catastrophic as it could've been. By the end of the lecture, you should understand what factors contributed to the accident there.

❷ Now you can see Three-Mile Island in this photograph. The nuclear reactor at Three-Mile Island is in the middle of a river in the state of Pennsylvania. This nuclear reactor has two PWRs, which means that it has two pressurized water reactors. The problem that occurred in 1979 was in the Number Two pressurized water reactor.

Now we're going to discuss what happened in the Number Three reactor. . . . Oh, excuse me, did I really say that? There are only two reactors, and the problem was with the Number Two reactor at Three-Mile Island. The important thing to understand about this accident with the Number Two reactor was that there was a series of problems rather than a single problem.

The series of problems occurred in the water-cooling system. The initial problem was that a cooling system valve stuck open and cooling water ran out.

Now unfortunately, the problem didn't end when the cooling valve was stuck open because operators misinterpreted the instrument readings. They knew there was a problem. Let me repeat this because it's important. They did know there was a problem, but they were mistaken about what the problem was. They thought the cooling system had too much water rather than too little water. Because they thought there was too much water, they shut off the emergency cooling water. As a result, there was no water to cool the nuclear reactor.

Now there wasn't a complete nuclear meltdown when the emergency cooling water was turned off, but there was a partial nuclear meltdown. A nuclear meltdown would occur if the uranium in the fuel core melted completely. In this situation, heat built up in the fuel core until the uranium began to melt, but it didn't melt down completely.

❸ I hope you understood the series of events that led to the problem at Three-Mile Island, one that, while serious, could've been catastrophic. It all started with the stuck valve in the cooling system and was exacerbated by the misinterpreted readings and the improper shutdown of the emergency cooling system. Fortunately, the meltdown that did occur was only partial and not complete.

29. WHAT IS THE MAIN TOPIC OF THE LECTURE?
30. HOW MANY PRESSURIZED WATER REACTORS ARE THERE AT THREE-MILE ISLAND?
31. WHAT DOES THE LECTURER SAY ABOUT THE PWRS DURING THE ACCIDENT?
32. DID EACH OF THESE HAPPEN DURING THE ACCIDENT DISCUSSED IN THE LECTURE?
33. WHAT IS STATED IN THE LECTURE ABOUT A COMPLETE MELTDOWN?
34. HOW DOES THE LECTURER SEEM TO FEEL ABOUT THE ACCIDENT AT THREE-MILE ISLAND?

SPEAKING

Question 3

Listen to the passage. On a piece of paper, take notes on the main points of the listening passage.

(man)   Have you gotten your tickets yet?
(woman) What tickets?
(man)   The tickets for the Spring Show. . . . Didn't you see the notice?
(woman) I didn't see any notice, and I don't even know what the Spring Show is.
(man)   Oh, you must be new to the school this year.
(woman) I am. I just transferred here this year . . . but how did you know that?
(man)   Because anyone who's been here for a while knows what the Spring Show is. It's a really big event.
(woman) I understand that from what you're saying. But do I really need to get tickets now?
(man)   Absolutely, if you want to get tickets. Tickets went on sale last Monday, and any remaining tickets will go on sale to the public next Monday. After tickets go on sale to the public, they sell out almost immediately.
(woman) I don't know exactly what the Spring Show is, but it sounds like I should get tickets right away and find out what it is.
(man)   Trust me, you won't regret it.

HOW DO THE STUDENTS REACT TO THE NOTICE ABOUT THE SPRING SHOW?

Question 4

Listen to the passage. On a piece of paper, take notes on the main points of the listening passage.

(professor) I'm sure you understand from the text that the great apes are able to communicate in a variety of ways within their species. I'd like to talk now about what studies have shown to be some of the limitations of their communication, in particular in two ways that are referred to as a lack of displacement and a lack of productivity.

First, let me talk about a lack of displacement. In terms of communication, a lack of displacement means that the great apes communicate only about things that are physically present. They do not communicate about things that are not physically present. This inability to communicate about things that aren't within range of their senses is called a lack of displacement.

Now, let me talk about a lack of productivity. In terms of communication, a lack of productivity is an inability to manipulate communication, to combine gestures and sounds or use gestures and sounds in different ways to create new meanings. Because the great apes do not manipulate their sounds and gestures to create new meanings, they're said to have a lack of productivity in their communication.

HOW DOES THE INFORMATION IN THE LISTENING PASSAGE ADD TO WHAT IS EXPLAINED IN THE READING PASSAGE?

Question 5

Listen to the passage. On a piece of paper, take notes on the main points of the listening passage.

(man)   Hey, Tina, what's up? You don't look too happy.
(woman) Oh, I've been trying to choose my classes for next semester.
(man)   And that's a problem? You don't like choosing your classes for next semester? I actually enjoy doing that.
(woman) Sometimes I enjoy it, but not this time.
(man)   Why not?
(woman) Because I've put off taking some of my required classes, a science class in particular, and now I can't put it off any longer. I have to take a science class next semester.
(man)   You're dreading taking a science class? That doesn't sound too terrible to me.
(woman) It doesn't? Have you taken any science classes yet? Maybe you can recommend one to me.
(man)   I haven't taken any science classes yet, but I'm looking forward to taking some.
(woman) You are? Really? I don't like science.

(man)   But all you have to do is take one science class, and there're so many to choose from, I mean you can take astronomy, or oceanography, or health, or physiology, or geography, or environmental studies. There are so many interesting science classes to choose from.

(woman)   (unsure) I guess so. . . .

(man)   You know, you really might enjoy one of these science classes. I think you've made such a big deal about taking a science class that you're dreading it, but you might actually enjoy it if you think more positively about it.

(woman)   OK, I'll try to do that.

(man)   Listen, why don't you let me know what science class you decide to take, and then maybe I'll sign up for the same course, and we can take it together.

(woman)   Now, that sounds like a good idea. I'll do that.

HOW IS THE WOMAN DEALING WITH THE PROBLEM SHE IS FACING?

Question 6

Listen to the passage. On a piece of paper, take notes on the main points of the listening passage.

(professor)   Today, I'll be discussing the economic policy known as mercantilism. Mercantilism was the overriding economic policy of major trading nations for almost two centuries, from the last part of the sixteenth century through the beginning of the eighteenth century, or from the 1580s through the 1720s. Mercantilism. Do you understand this word? It sounds kind of like the word *merchant*, and it's related in meaning to the word *merchant*. Mercantilism was an economic policy of nations based on developing international business, a policy dedicated to encouraging business production and to encouraging trade between nations.

The goal of mercantilism wasn't simply for nations to encourage business or for nations to try to trade with other nations; and the goal of a mercantilist society wasn't merely to achieve a balance of trade, for each nation to try to balance its imports and exports. Instead, each mercantilist nation was dedicated to amassing national wealth, and to do this each nation wanted to export more than it imported. Any goods that were exported over and above the amount of goods that were imported would be paid for in gold. It was this amassing of gold in payment for exports in excess of imports that would allow a nation to build wealth.

HOW DOES THE PROFESSOR DESCRIBE MERCANTILISM?

WRITING

Question 1

Listen to the passage. On a piece of paper, take notes on the main points of the listening passage.

(professor)   It was really surprising to scientists when they found out that Venus was so hot because the clouds around Venus reflect almost all the light from the Sun back into space. The small amount of sunlight that's able to filter through the clouds doesn't seem like anywhere near enough light to make the temperature on Venus so high. Instead, because it's always so cloudy on the surface of Venus, the temperature should be rather cool.

You might think that the temperature on Venus is so hot because Venus is so close to the Sun, but this isn't really a good explanation for the heat on Venus. The temperature on Venus is even hotter than the temperature on Mercury, which is closer than Venus to the Sun, so the proximity of Venus to the Sun doesn't explain the high temperature on Venus.

Scientists are still not certain why the temperature on Venus is so high, but one possible explanation is Venus's carbon dioxide atmosphere. The very dense atmosphere on Venus is almost entirely carbon dioxide. This carbon dioxide may create a barrier that traps any heat that gets through beneath it and doesn't let it escape.

HOW DOES THE INFORMATION IN THE LISTENING PASSAGE EXPAND ON THE INFORMATION PRESENTED IN THE READING PASSAGE?

COMPLETE TEST 2

LISTENING

Questions 1 through 5. Listen to a conversation between a student and a university office worker.

(clerk)   Next in line, please . . . yes . . . how can I help you?

(student)   Um, I have a question . . . a question about my grade record.

(clerk)   Your grade record? For which quarter?

(student)   For last quarter.

(clerk)   Grade reports for last quarter were mailed out a week ago. You should've received yours by now.

(student)   I received a grade report for last quarter . . . I just received it in the mail. . . .

(clerk)   Then what's the problem?

(student)   I received a grade report in the mail, but the grades on it are wrong.

(clerk)   Oh, we don't handle that here. Here we only record the grades that the professors submit. If you have any questions about the grades you received, you should talk with your professors. That's not something we deal with here.

(student) No, that's not what I mean. The problem is not that I received grades in the courses I took and the grades were lower than I expected. The problem is different from that. The problem is that I received grades in courses I didn't take and didn't receive grades in courses I did take.

(clerk) And the grade report had your name on it?

(student) It did.

(clerk) You're saying that you received a grade report with your name on it but that the courses listed on the grade report were courses you didn't take? That's really odd.

(student) Look . . . here's my grade report. That's my name at the top . . . Anthony Taylor . . . and that's my address . . . 320 4th Avenue, apartment B. But those aren't the courses I took.

(clerk) That's your name and address on the grade report, but you didn't take the courses listed there?

(student) No, this grade report lists a biology course, and I didn't take biology, and it lists calculus, and I most certainly did not take calculus. It also lists courses in English and track that I didn't take.

(clerk) What courses did you take?

(student) I took courses in history, drama, philosophy, and composition. None of those are listed there.

(clerk) Well, this certainly isn't the correct grade report for you. . . . Wait a minute. . . . Let me look up something in my files on the computer. . . . OK . . . you said your name was Anthony Taylor?

(student) Yes.

(clerk) But what's your middle initial?

(student) B. I'm Anthony B. Taylor.

(clerk) And you took courses in history, drama, philosophy, and composition . . . OK . . . I think I know what the problem is. We have two students here named Anthony Taylor.

(student) Really? There's another Anthony Taylor?

(clerk) Yes, but you're Anthony B. Taylor, and the other is Anthony M. Taylor. The courses listed for Anthony M. Taylor are history, drama, philosophy, and composition. These are the courses you took, and I think these must be your grades.

(student) So you think the grades for the two Anthony Taylors are mixed up? . . . I got his grade report, and he got mine?

(clerk) Not exactly. I think his grades ended up on your grade report and your grades ended up on his.

(student) I see. So what happens now?

(clerk) Let me check with your professors and make sure I have the correct information in the right places. Then I'll send out a new corrected grade report to you.

(student) And when should I have it?

(clerk) You probably won't have it for two weeks because it may take that long to resolve the issue and then mail out new grade reports.

(student) That's fine as long as the problem gets solved.

(clerk) It certainly will get solved.

1. WHY DOES THE STUDENT GO TO SEE THE OFFICE WORKER?
2. WHAT INCORRECT ASSUMPTION DID THE CLERK MAKE?
3. WHAT IS STATED ABOUT THE GRADE REPORT THE STUDENT RECEIVED?
4. WHAT DID THE CONFUSION TURN OUT TO BE?
5. WHAT DID THE OFFICE WORKER PROMISE TO DO?

Questions 6 through 11. Listen to a lecture in a government class.

(professor) ❶ Today, we'll be talking about the city of Washington, D.C. First of all, let me give you a little background about its name. The original name of the city was Washington City; it was, of course, named after the first president of the United States, George Washington. In later years, the name was changed to the District of Columbia, and I'm sure you can all guess who "Columbia" was named after. Today it's most commonly called Washington, D.C., where D.C. is the abbreviated form of District of Columbia.

Now, before we go on, let me ask you a question. Can I see from a show of hands, how many of you have ever been to Washington, D.C.? . . . Ah, about half of you. Well, the half of you who've been there may have a bit to contribute to this discussion, based on your experience there.

There are two points that I'd like to make about Washington, D.C. First of all, this city is unusual in the United States because it's the only U.S. city that is not part of any state. Second of all, this city was the only U.S. city which, for quite some time, was not self-governing.

❷ Now, let's look at a map of Washington, D.C. as we discuss the first point. In the early years of the country, the founding fathers believed that the capital of the United States should not be part of any state. When a location was chosen for the capital city, two states, Maryland and Virginia, were asked to give up land for a capital city. You can see on the map that the District of Columbia was originally a square, with the Potomac River cutting through the square. The area to the northeast of the Potomac originally belonged to the state of Maryland, and the area to the southwest of the Potomac originally belonged to the state of Virginia. In the middle of the nineteenth century, the portion of the square that had previously belonged to Virginia, the portion to the southwest of the Potomac, was returned to the state of

Virginia. Today, the District of Columbia's no longer a square. Instead, the District of Columbia is the portion of the square to the northeast of the Potomac.

❸ The second unusual point that I'd like to make about Washington D.C. is that, for most of its history, it was not a self-governing city. When the city was established, it was decided that its government would be appointed by the president of the United States; the citizens of Washington, D.C, would not elect their own city government. In addition, the citizens of Washington, D.C. for quite some time had no representation in Congress, and they were ineligible to vote for the president of the United States. The citizens of Washington, D.C. were given the right to vote for their government only relatively recently. Citizens of Washington, D.C. were first eligible to vote for the president of the United States in the 1964 election, they didn't have a representative in Congress until 1970, and they didn't elect their own city officials until 1974.

Please read the chapter on Washington, D.C. in your textbook and answer the questions at the end of the chapter before next class. I'll see you then.

6. WHAT DOES THE PROFESSOR MAINLY DISCUSS IN THE LECTURE?
7. WHICH NAME HAS NOT BEEN USED FOR THE CITY DISCUSSED IN THE LECTURE?
8. LISTEN AGAIN TO PART OF THE LECTURE. THEN ANSWER THE QUESTION.
   (professor) Now, before we go on, let me ask you a question. Can I see from a show of hands, how many of you have ever been to Washington, D.C.? . . . Ah, about half of you. Well, the half of you who've been there may have a bit to contribute to this discussion, based on your experience there.

   WHY DOES THE PROFESSOR SAY THIS?
   (professor) Now, before we go on, let me ask you a question.

9. WHAT TWO POINTS MAKE WASHINGTON, D.C. DIFFERENT FROM OTHER U.S. CITIES?
10. ARE THESE STATEMENTS TRUE ABOUT WASHINGTON, D.C. AND THE STATE OF VIRGINIA?
11. WHAT IS STATED IN THE LECTURE ABOUT THE GOVERNMENT OF WASHINGTON, D.C?

Questions 12 through 17. Listen to a lecture in a linguistics class.

   (professor) ❶ Something I'm sure you all understand clearly is that the letter *c* in today's English has two very different pronunciations. It can be pronounced like a *k*, as in the words *car, can,* or *coal*. It can also be pronounced like an *s*, as in the words *cent, circle,* or *cease*. What is maybe not so clear is <u>why</u> the letter *c* has two different pronunciations. So let's look at the history and development of the letter *c* to understand how these two very different pronunciations for one letter came to be.

❷ Precursors of the letters *c* existed as the third letter of a number of early alphabets. Look at the letters from these early alphabets, from early Semitic, from Phoenician, and from early Greek. These letters were the predecessors of the letter *c*. They were each the third letter in their respective alphabets, and they were all formed with a shorter and a longer line meeting at a sharp angle. Now, in each of these languages, the letter was pronounced with a hard *g* sound, as in *go* or *get*. This letter did not have an *s* or *k* sound.

❸ As languages developed, this early *c* was used for both the *g* sound as in *go* and *get* and the *k* sound as in *kite* or *kid*. The angular letter seen here from early Latin had two sounds, a *k* sound and a *g* sound. By the classical Latin period, these two sounds were differentiated. The early Latin angular letter was rounded to create the letter *c* of today; this letter was pronounced with a *k* sound. A new letter was created by adding a line to the *c*. This new letter had a *g* sound. Thus, in classical Latin, the letter *c* was pronounced only with a *k* sound.

❹ OK, the final change was the addition of the *s* sound to the letter *c*. This happened because of the French influence on English. You see, there was a major influence of French on the English language with the victory of the Normans over the Saxons in Britain in 1066. Now, because of this French influence, the letter *c* took on the *s* sound in addition to the *k* sound that it already had.

❺ Uh, let's look at this chart of the pronunciation of the letter *c*. At this point in the English language, the letter *c* has a *k* sound when it precedes the vowels *a, o, u,* or a consonant such as *l*. The letter *c* generally has an *s* sound in front of the vowels *e, i,* and *y*.

❻ OK now, it's important to make sure that all the pieces of the puzzle are in the right place. There were four stages in the development of the pronunciation of the third letter of the alphabet. In the beginning, the third letter of the alphabet was pronounced with a *g* sound. Then, in early Latin, the third letter had two sounds, *g* and *k*. In later Latin, a new letter was created for the *g* sound, and the letter *c* had only a *k* sound. Finally, because of the French influence on English, the letter *c* also took on an *s* sound.

12. WHAT IS THE MAIN IDEA OF THE LECTURE?
13. WHAT IS TRUE ABOUT THE SHAPE OF THE THIRD LETTER OF THE ALPHABET?
14. IS EACH OF THESE TRUE ABOUT SOUNDS IN EARLY LANGUAGES?
15. WHICH OF THE FOLLOWING ARE TRUE, ACCORDING TO THE LECTURE?
16. WHICH OF THE FOLLOWING ENGLISH WORDS MOST LIKELY BEGIN WITH AN *S* SOUND?
17. LISTEN AGAIN TO PART OF THE PASSAGE. THEN ANSWER THE QUESTION.

> (professor) Now, it's important to make sure that all the pieces of the puzzle are in the right place.

WHAT DOES THE PROFESSOR MEAN?

Questions 18 through 22. Listen to a conversation between a student and a professor.

> (student) Hello.
>
> (professor) Hi, come on in . . . I'll be with you in a moment . . . OK, what can I do for you?
>
> (student) I have a question about . . . some of the material from your last lecture. . . .
>
> (professor) Ah, about which material?
>
> (student) Something from yesterday's lecture . . . I didn't understand it completely . . . the part where you were talking about the space shuttle. . . .
>
> (professor) Well, I was discussing the space shuttle during most of the lecture. What part didn't you understand? Oh, I hope it wasn't the whole lecture you didn't understand.
>
> (student) The part about how the space shuttle gets its power, about how it gets propelled into orbit.
>
> (professor) Yes, that was a key point of the lecture; you really need to understand that part. . . . Listen, why don't you tell me what you did understand about the propulsion system for the space shuttle, and I'll try to fill in the blanks.
>
> (student) OK. Do you mind if I look at my notes? That'll help. . . .
>
> (professor) No problem.
>
> (student) OK . . . you said that the shuttle has <u>three</u> sources of power. I heard you say that . . . but I didn't hear what the three sources of power <u>are</u>.
>
> (professor) Which ones did you hear?
>
> (student) Uh, I heard you talk about the main engine and the boosters.
>
> (professor) OK, two of the sources of power are, indeed, the main engine and the booster; you've got that right. And then there are the smaller engines; that's the power source you missed.
>
> (student) The smaller engines.
>
> (professor) Yes, that's right. Now, do you understand how these sources of power work to get the space shuttle into orbit?
>
> (student) Well, I heard you say that the main engine and the boosters work together to lift the shuttle off the ground.

> (professor) That's right. And then what happens to the boosters?
>
> (student) Ah, the boosters separate from the shuttle and fall back to Earth.
>
> (professor) That's almost right. The boosters do separate from the shuttle, and they do return to Earth, but they don't exactly fall, as in free fall.
>
> (student) How do they get back to Earth?
>
> (professor) They have parachutes attached to them; they parachute back to Earth.
>
> (student) OK, now I understand that. I did hear you talking about a parachute in class, but I wasn't sure how that fit in.
>
> (professor) OK, so you do understand that it's the main engines and the boosters that lift the shuttle off the ground and that the boosters separate from the shuttle and parachute back to Earth?
>
> (student) Yes.
>
> (professor) But, it's the next part that I'm not sure you understand. It's about the smaller engines.
>
> (student) You're right. That's the part of the process I didn't get.
>
> (professor) Well, after the boosters have dropped off, the main engines power the shuttle until it's almost at orbital velocity. But then, how does the shuttle actually get into orbit? It needs more power to get into orbit.
>
> (student) Oh, it must be the smaller engines that do that.
>
> (professor) Good guess! When the shuttle is almost at orbital velocity, the smaller engines kick in and push the shuttle into orbit. . . . Is this clear to you now?
>
> (student) It is. . . . This is all so much clearer now. Thanks so much for your help.
>
> (professor) You're quite welcome.

18. WHY DOES THE STUDENT WANT TO TALK TO THE PROFESSOR?
19. LISTEN AGAIN TO PART OF THE PASSAGE. THEN ANSWER THE QUESTION.

> (professor) Listen, why don't you tell me what you did understand about the propulsion system for the space shuttle, and I'll try to fill in the blanks?

WHAT DOES THE PROFESSOR MEAN WHEN SHE SAYS THIS?

> (professor) I'll try to fill in the blanks.

20. WHICH SOURCES OF POWER DID THE STUDENT HAVE IN HIS NOTES?
21. WHAT IS THE ROLE OF EACH OF THESE SOURCES OF POWER?
22. WHAT IS THE PURPOSE OF THE PARACHUTE?

Questions 23 through 28. Listen to a lecture in a geology class.

> (professor) ❶ Good morning, class. Today, we're going to look at the three basic cave structures: sea caves, lava caves, and solution caves. As you may've guessed by

the names, the cave structures're named for the process that formed them.

(student 1) Excuse me, Professor, but can you please repeat that? I didn't quite get it.

(professor) You bet. I don't want you to miss it because it's important. What I said was that we'll be talking about the three basic cave structures and that the names of the different types of caves are actually derived from the process that formed them. You'll see what I mean after I finish talking about different types of caves and how they're formed.

(student 1) OK, thanks.

(professor) ❷ No problem. Now, let's look at this picture of a sea cave. Sea caves are found along rocky shores. Sea caves are formed when pounding water washes away areas of rock, creating a cave. The cave in this picture is one of the most famous sea caves, the Blue Grotto on the Isle of Capri. Have any of you ever been there? . . . None of you? . . . Oh, that's too bad. It's gorgeous.

❸ OK, now let's look at a lava cave. Lava caves form during volcanic eruptions when the outer surface of flowing lava cools and the lava underneath remains hot. The hot lava below continues to flow and leaves a lava tunnel or lava cave underneath. This picture shows one of the approximately 300 lava caves in Lava Beds National Monument. . . . What does it look like to you? . . . Have you ever seen any place that looks like this? It certainly looks like volcanic areas of Hawaii, and you might expect to find this monument on the volcanic islands of Hawaii, but it's not there. It's actually in northern California.

❹ OK, now . . . let me go back to my main point for just a moment. Remember I said that cave structures are named for the process that formed them. Have you understood this in terms of the first two types of caves, the sea cave and the lava cave? Well, the same concept applies to the last type of cave structure I'm going to talk about now.

❺ Here's a solution cave, which is the most complicated type of cave structure. You can see that this kind of cave has the stalagmites and stalactites that most people picture when you talk about caves. Now what does this picture show? Does anyone recognize it? Yes?

(student 2) It looks like Carlsbad Caverns.

(professor) That's exactly right. This picture shows the Carlsbad Caverns in New Mexico, and this is one of the most famous American solution caves. A solution cave is formed in areas with a large amount of limestone, marble, or dolomite. Surface water works its way into tiny cracks in the rock. As the surface water trickles through soil, a mild acid is formed, and this mild acid is a <u>solution</u> that creates this type of cave. Over thousands of years, this acid solution dissolves the limestone or similar rock. And what do you think happens as a result? . . . Well, this causes passages and chambers to form underground. If the water table drops, or an earthquake lifts the cave up, the water drains out. Rainwater then continues the process by seeping through cracks into the rocks. At this point, the dripping or flowing water begins to form the marvelous structures found in solution caves, and entrances may develop. These caves usually have very few entrances. An earthquake can lift the cave to the surface, opening the cave. Sometimes land over a solution cave collapses to create a sinkhole entrance. A solution cave can also develop an entrance as soil erodes from a hillside or as a spring flows from the cave. Now what's very important to understand from all this is that this type of cave is a very complicated cave structure, and I think you see that. I think you also see that it's called a solution cave because it's an acid solution that forms it.

❻ OK, that's all for now. Next week we'll discuss speleothems, the beautiful structures that form from various crystal deposits in solution caves. The most famous of these are, of course, the stalagmites and stalactites. See you next week.

23. WHAT MAIN POINT DOES THE PROFESSOR MAKE ABOUT VARIOUS TYPES OF CAVES?

24. LISTEN AGAIN TO PART OF THE PASSAGE. THEN ANSWER THE QUESTION.

(student) Excuse me, Professor, but can you please repeat that? I didn't quite get it.

(professor) You bet. I don't want you to miss it because it's important.

HOW DOES THE PROFESSOR SEEM TO FEEL ABOUT ANSWERING THE STUDENT'S QUESTION?

25. WHAT TYPE OF CAVE IS EACH OF THESE CAVES?

26. WHAT IS STATED IN THE LECTURE ABOUT WHERE THE CAVES ARE FOUND?

27. HOW IS EACH TYPE OF CAVE FORMED?

28. WHAT IS NOT A USUAL WAY FOR A SOLUTION CAVE TO DEVELOP AN ENTRANCE?

Questions 29 through 34. Listen to a discussion in a biology class.

(professor) ❶ For class today, you should've reviewed the section on compound eyes in Chapter 3 of your text. Yesterday we discussed eye structures called light spots, structures that can only sense light but can't see images as we do. Today we'll look at one example of a compound eye by looking at the eye of a monarch butterfly.

❷ Let's look at the compound eye of the monarch butterfly in this drawing. The compound eye is a very interesting structure. Magnified, the eye looks a bit like a pincushion full of round-headed pins. The surface of the eye is curved and made up of thousands of ommatidia. Who can tell me what ommatidia are? Yes, Josh?

(man 1) Aren't they lenses of some sort . . . lenses on the surface of the compound eye?

(professor) Yes, that's right. The ommatidia are lenses, and they cover the surface of the compound eye. Now, how many lenses are there covering the surface of a compound eye? Joyce?

(woman) Are there six? I think I read that there were six.

(professor) Well, you may have read something about the number six, but six wasn't the number of ommatidia covering the surface of a compound eye. Who knows? Roger?

(man 2) There are thousands, uh, thousands of ommatidia covering the compound eye.

(professor) That's right, Roger, there are thousands of ommatidia covering the compound eye, not six. . . . Now, we said that the omatidia are lenses, but they're not flat lenses, they're lenses with a number of sides. How many sides are there on each lens? Joyce?

(woman) There're . . . um . . . two sides? Two sides on each omma . . . omma . . .

(professor) Ommatidium.

(woman) Ommatidium. There're two sides on its lens.

(professor) Uh, no, that's not right. There're more than two sides on each lens. Who knows? Who knows how many sides are on the lens of each ommatidium. Yes, Roger?

(man 2) Each ommatidium is covered by a six-sided lens.

(professor) Yes, that's true. Here's where the number six comes in. It's the number of sides on each ommatidium's lens, it's not the number of ommatidia on each lense. Hopefully now we understand this. There are thousands of ommatidia on the surface of a compound eye, each ommatidium has a curved surface with six-sided lenses, and the six-sided lenses allow each ommatidium to face a slightly different direction and sense a slightly different image. As light enters each lense, photoreceptors under the lenses send messages to the brain. The brain reconstructs the image of the butterfly's surroundings by combining the thousands of messages from each of the thousands of lenses into one image.

❸ Now, we're going to discuss what a compound eye sees, and I have two points that I'd like to make. The first point I'd like to make is that a compound eye can see movement well, but it does not focus well. Butterflies are very nearsighted, so their eyesight isn't very clear, yet they're remarkably able to detect movement.

Have any of you tried to catch a butterfly in flight? Possibly some of you have been frustrated while trying to swat a fly? Researchers have known for a long time that insects of all kinds can sense movement very well. The compound eye allows insects to detect the slightest movement much better than our eye can in spite of the fact that it doesn't focus well.

Now, can you summarize for me what this first point is? Josh?

(man 1) It's that a compound eye can detect movement unbelievably well, even though it doesn't focus well and therefore doesn't see extremely clearly.

(professor) Yes, that's right. Now for the second point about the compound eye. The second point I'd like to make is that it's now believed that a compound eye probably sees one image rather than a compound picture. At one time it was thought that a compound eye saw a compound picture. Some thought that monarchs and other insects could detect movement well because each ommatidium registered six complete images, so the monarch saw some 6,000 pictures of the same item. This would be a bit like standing in a store and looking at a wall of TVs all tuned to the same channel. Every movement on the screen produces thousands of like movements.

Now most researchers think something different is happening; they think that a compound eye sees one image that is blurred because of the huge number of lenses in the compound eye. Because the eye senses light from so many directions, the butterfly detects movement easily. The slightest movement alters the light sensed in hundreds or thousands of the ommatidia, allowing the butterfly to react quickly, even if it can't clearly see what it's reacting to.

OK, I would like someone to summarize the second key point about the compound eye. Joyce, can you do that for me, please?

(woman) The second point is that researchers used to believe that the compound eye could see only one image, but now researchers believe that the compound eye can see a compound image.

(professor) No, it's the other way around. Try again.

(woman) (laughs) OK, then, the second point is that researchers used to believe that the compound eye could only see a compound image, but they now believe a compound eye can see a single image.

(professor) Now you've got it. Listen, that's all for today. Tomorrow we'll continue our study of eye structures. Please review the section in Chapter 3 about the human eye. I've put several interesting articles about recent research on the compound eye on reserve in the library. These articles are considered required reading in addition to the information in your textbook. As I think some of you figured out the hard way the last time around, tests in this course do cover both the textbook and the additional articles I assign, so please be aware of this and please be prepared.

29. HOW IS THE INFORMATION IN THE PASSAGE ORGANIZED?

30. WHAT IS STATED IN THE LECTURE ABOUT OMMATIDIA?

31. WHAT IS NOT STATED IN THE LECTURE ABOUT THE BUTTERFLY?

32. ARE THESE STATEMENTS TRUE ABOUT THE COMPOUND EYE?

33. LISTEN AGAIN TO PART OF THE PASSAGE. THEN ANSWER THE QUESTION.

(professor) Have any of you tried to catch a butterfly in flight? Possibly some of you have been frustrated while trying to swat a fly? Researchers have known for a long time that insects of all kinds can sense movement very well. The compound eye allows insects to detect the slightest movement much better than our eye can in spite of the fact that it doesn't focus well.

WHY DOES THE PROFESSOR SAY THIS?

(professor) Have any of you tried to catch a butterfly in flight? Possibly some of you have been frustrated while trying to swat a fly?

34. WHAT IS THE MOST LIKELY TITLE FOR CHAPTER 3 OF THE TEXT FOR THIS CLASS?

SPEAKING

Question 3

Listen to the passage. On a piece of paper, take notes on the main points of the listening passage.

(man) Have you seen the notice about the internships?

(woman) I have. So?

(man) Are you going to apply for the internship program?

(woman) I don't think so.

(man) Why not? It sounds like a great program to me.

(woman) It does? But it's a lot of work, and there's no pay. If I get a job, I want it to be a job that pays something.

(man) But this isn't for pay. It's for units, for graduate units, and for the work experience.

(woman) Oh, we get units for an internship?

(man) Yeah. Three graduate units. I'd much rather work in a company for units and get some actual work experience than study a textbook and take exams on the text.

(woman) The work experience does sound good, I guess. I mean, it would be good to have some work experience already when I begin applying for jobs after I get my degree.

(man) See, it seems like I might have convinced you to apply for an internship.

(woman) I think you have. Getting three graduate units and some work experience sounds good.

HOW DO THE STUDENTS SEEM TO FEEL ABOUT THE INTERNSHIPS OFFERED BY THE BUSINESS DEPARTMENT?

Question 4

Listen to the passage. On a piece of paper, take notes on the main points of the listening passage.

(professor) As you should understand from the reading, supersonic jets are jets that fly faster than the speed of sound. Think about this for a moment, that a supersonic jet moves faster than sound moves. What this means is that a person on the ground won't hear a supersonic jet as it approaches because the supersonic jet's moving faster than the speed of sound; the jet will move toward a person faster than any sound it makes moves. When the sound does catch up, it is heard as a sonic boom, a loud booming noise that results from the shock wave produced when a supersonic jet flies by. So, if you hear a sonic boom, it means that a supersonic aircraft has just passed by.

HOW DOES THE INFORMATION IN THE LISTENING PASSAGE ADD TO WHAT IS EXPLAINED IN THE READING PASSAGE?

Question 5

Listen to the passage. On a piece of paper, take notes on the main points of the listening passage.

(man) When do you want to start working on our project?

(woman) Right away. We should start on it really soon.

(man) Do we really need to start on it right away?

(woman) It's really a good idea to do that. I know all about this project.

(man) You do? How do you know about it?

(woman) My roommate took the same class last quarter, and I heard all about it then.

(man) What did you hear about it?

(woman) I heard that the professor talks a little bit about the project each week.

(man) That seems about right. He didn't tell us very much about it this week. I mean, he didn't explain all the steps. He just talked about the beginning steps.

(woman) That's right. He'll talk about a few steps each week, if he does it the same way he did last quarter when my roommate took the class.

(man)	And you think that we should do the steps he talks about each week?
(woman)	Yes, I do. My roommate said that if we do a few steps each week, then the project really isn't a big deal, but if we put everything off and try to do it all at the end it'll be very difficult.
(man)	So you think we should do the first steps that the professor has already talked about?
(woman)	Yes, we should. We're supposed to find partners first.
(man)	And we've done that. We're going to work together, aren't we?
(woman)	Of course.
(man)	And then we're supposed to decide on a topic.
(woman)	And find ten sources on that topic.
(man)	And that's what we need to do this week?
(woman)	Yes, so let's meet at the library tomorrow and start on that.
(man)	Sounds good to me. . . . By the way, is this how your roommate did the project? She did everything step-by-step with her partner?
(woman)	No, not exactly. She and her partner put everything off to the end and then really suffered getting the project done. She told me we definitely should <u>not</u> do the project the same way she did.

HOW ARE THE STUDENTS DEALING WITH THE PROJECT THEY ARE WORKING ON?

Question 6

Listen to the passage. On a piece of paper, take notes on the main points of the listening passage.

(professor) Today, I'll be talking about the psychological disorder known as multiple personality disorder. As you can most likely tell from the name of the disorder, multiple personality disorder is a psychological condition in which one person has two or more distinct and well-developed personalities. These two or more personalities exist simultaneously within a single individual.

It's quite common for the distinct personalities in an individual who suffers from multiple personality disorder to have different names, genders, and ages. It's quite possible that one personality in an individual could be a young female named Mary and another personality could be an older male named Michael.

It's also quite common for the attitudes and behaviors of the different personalities in an individual suffering from multiple personality disorder to be radically different. One personality may be a shy and quiet person who doesn't have any friends and who likes to stay home alone watching television, while the other's an outgoing person who likes to spend time getting to know people at wild parties.

Finally, in cases of multiple personality disorder, it's also quite possible that the different personalities may have different talents, abilities, or knowledge. There have been documented cases of multiple personality disorder where one of the personalities has musical talent that other personalities don't, that one personality knows how to play a card game that other personalities don't, and that one personality knows how to speak a foreign language that other personalities don't.

HOW DOES THE PROFESSOR DESCRIBE MULTIPLE PERSONALITY DISORDER?

WRITING

Question 1

Listen to the passage. On a piece of paper, take notes on the main points of the listening passage.

(professor) The great library of Alexandria no longer exists, but it's not known for sure when the library was destroyed. There's actually considerable debate among historians about who destroyed the library and when.

One culprit who has traditionally been accused of destroying the library at Alexandria is Julius Caesar. It's true that Julius Caesar led an invasion of Alexandria in 48–47 B.C. and that, at that time, his forces set the fleet of ships sitting in the Alexandria harbor on fire. Some historians believe that this fire in the harbor that was set by Caesar's forces, spread into the city of Alexandria and burned the library down, but this belief is no longer widely held today. The main reason that the theory that Julius Caesar destroyed the library at Alexandria isn't widely believed is that there are numerous references to the library in works written long after Caesar's death.

The conclusion that seems to be most accepted today is that the library at Alexandria existed, at least in part, until the late fourth century, centuries after the death of Julius Caesar, so it could not have been completely destroyed by Caesar. At that time, at the end of the fourth century, there was a large movement to destroy pagan temples and libraries. It seems likely that whatever remained of the library of Alexandria was destroyed at this time.

WHAT FURTHER INFORMATION DOES THE LISTENING PASSAGE PROVIDE TO ADD TO THE INFORMATION PRESENTED IN THE READING PASSAGE?

ANSWER KEY

READING ANSWER KEY

READING DIAGNOSTIC PRE-TEST

1. A	5. D	9. D	13. B	17. C
2. C	6. A	10. B	14. C	18. D
3. A	7. D	11. A	15. C	
4. C	8. B	12. D	16. B	

19. | theories attributing aggression to instinct: | (2) (6) |
    | theories attributing aggression to learned behaviors: | (1) (4) |

20. | causes of aggression: | (2) (3) (5) (6) |

Note: These answers may be in any order.

READING EXERCISE 1

1. B	6. B	11. C	16. B	21. A
2. D	7. D	12. A	17. C	22. A
3. C	8. A	13. B	18. B	23. A
4. A	9. C	14. D	19. A	24. C
5. B	10. B	15. A	20. D	

READING EXERCISE 2

1. C	5. A	9. B	13. B	17. C
2. B	6. B	10. A	14. B	18. A
3. A	7. A	11. C	15. D	
4. A	8. C	12. A	16. B	

READING EXERCISE (Skills 1–2)

1. A	4. A	7. A	10. B	13. A
2. C	5. B	8. C	11. D	
3. B	6. D	9. D	12. A	

READING EXERCISE 3

1. A	4. B	7. A	10. D	13. B
2. D	5. C	8. C	11. D	14. C
3. A	6. D	9. B	12. A	

READING EXERCISE 4

1. A	3. B	5. D	7. D	9. C
2. C	4. D	6. D	8. D	

READING EXERCISE (Skills 3–4)

1. C	3. B	5. B	7. B	9. D
2. A	4. C	6. C	8. D	10. B

READING REVIEW EXERCISE (Skills 1–4)

1. A	4. B	7. B	10. A	13. D
2. C	5. D	8. A	11. B	
3. B	6. D	9. C	12. C	

READING EXERCISE 5

1. D	6. C	11. A	16. A	21. C
2. A	7. A	12. D	17. B	22. D
3. D	8. D	13. C	18. A	
4. C	9. B	14. B	19. C	
5. B	10. C	15. D	20. D	

READING EXERCISE 6

1. D	6. C	11. D	16. D	21. C
2. C	7. A	12. A	17. A	22. A
3. A	8. D	13. B	18. B	
4. D	9. C	14. D	19. D	
5. B	10. D	15. C	20. D	

READING EXERCISE (Skills 5–6)

1. C	4. B	7. B	10. A	13. B
2. C	5. B	8. C	11. D	
3. A	6. D	9. D	12. D	

READING REVIEW EXERCISE (Skills 1–6)

1. C	4. A	7. D	10. A	13. B
2. B	5. D	8. C	11. D	
3. D	6. B	9. B	12. A	

READING EXERCISE 7

1. B	5. A	9. A	13. D	17. B
2. A	6. A	10. C	14. C	18. B
3. D	7. D	11. D	15. B	19. D
4. C	8. C	12. B	16. A	

READING EXERCISE 8

1. D	5. B	9. C	13. D	17. D
2. A	6. A	10. B	14. A	18. B
3. C	7. D	11. A	15. B	19. D
4. C	8. D	12. D	16. A	

READING EXERCISE (Skills 7–8)

1. B	3. D	5. D	7. C	9. B
2. C	4. A	6. A	8. C	10. A

READING REVIEW EXERCISE (Skills 1–8)

1. B	4. C	7. A	10. A	13. C
2. A	5. C	8. B	11. D	
3. D	6. A	9. D	12. B	

READING EXERCISE 9

1. | the ways that plant life is able to develop on islands: | (2) (4) (6) |

2. | Ben and Jerry's unconventional company: | (2) (4) (5) |

3. | radical shifts in population that the bald eagle has undergone: | (1) (2) (4) (6) |

4. | characteristics shared by modernism in art: | (1) (2) (4) (6) |

READING EXERCISE 10

1. | amount of sand: | (5) (7) |
   | directions of winds: | (1) (3) |

2. | *buckaroo* and *vaquero*: | (2) (7) |
   | *buckaroo* and *vaccine*: | (5) (8) |
   | *vacca* and *vaccine*: | (1) (4) |

READING EXERCISE (Skills 9–10)

1.

| processes affecting the development of millions of species: | (1) (3) (6) |

2.

| speciation: | (2) (5) |
| extinction: | (1) (4) (7) |

READING REVIEW EXERCISE (Skills 1–10)

1. B	4. D	7. B	10. A
2. A	5. C	8. A	11. D
3. D	6. B	9. B	12. C

13.

| different models for analyzing the process of decision making: | (2) (3) (6) |

READING POST-TEST

1. C	5. B	9. A	13. C	17. C
2. B	6. B	10. C	14. C	18. D
3. D	7. D	11. B	15. A	
4. A	8. C	12. D	16. A	

19.

| schooling behavior in certain fish: | (2) (4) |

20.

| hypotheses related to purpose: | (1) (5) (7) |
| hypotheses related to manner: | (2) (6) |

LISTENING ANSWER KEY

LISTENING DIAGNOSTIC PRE-TEST

1. B	5. Y, N, N, Y, Y	9. A
2. C, D	6. A	10. C1, C3, C2
3. C	7. D	11. C
4. B	8. A, C	12. D

LISTENING EXERCISE 1

| 1. C | 3. B | 5. A | 7. A |
| 2. A | 4. D | 6. C | 8. D |

LISTENING EXERCISE 2

1. C	9. B	17. B, D
2. B	10. A, C	18. A
3. D	11. B, D	19. B
4. A, D	12. D	20. B, D
5. B	13. C	21. A, B
6. B, C	14. A, C	22. D
7. C	15. B, C	23. C
8. C	16. B	

LESSON REVIEW EXERCISE (Skills 1–2)

| 1. B | 3. C | 5. A, D | 7. C, D |
| 2. D | 4. A | 6. B | |

LISTENING EXERCISE 3

1. B	5. D	9. B	13. B	17. B
2. A	6. B	10. D	14. D	18. A
3. C	7. C	11. A	15. C	19. D
4. D	8. A	12. C	16. A	

LISTENING EXERCISE 4

| 1. B | 3. D | 5. B | 7. D |
| 2. C | 4. A | 6. D | 8. B |

LISTENING EXERCISE (Skills 3–4)

| 1. D | 3. B | 5. B |
| 2. A | 4. D | 6. A |

LISTENING REVIEW EXERCISE (Skills 1–4)

| 1. D | 3. A | 5. D | 7. B, D |
| 2. C | 4. D | 6. B | 8. C |

LISTENING EXERCISE 5

1. B	8. Y, N, Y, Y, N
2. Y, N, N, Y, N, Y	9. C2, C3, C1
3. C1, C3, C2	10. C
4. A	11. C1, C2, C1, C3, C2, C2, C3
5. C3, C1, C4, C2	12. C2, C3, C1
6. N, Y, N, Y, Y	13. C1, C2, C3
7. D	14. C2, C3, C1

LISTENING EXERCISE 6

| 1. D | 3. D | 5. B | 7. C | 9. A |
| 2. A | 4. B | 6. C | 8. D | |

LISTENING EXERCISE (Skills 5–6)

1. A	4. C3, C1, C2	7. C
2. D	5. N, Y, Y, N, N, Y	
3. C2, C3, C1	6. B	

LISTENING REVIEW EXERCISE (Skills 1–6)

| 1. A | 3. C2, C1, C3 | 5. A, D |
| 2. B, D | 4. C3, C1, C2 | 6. B |

LISTENING POST-TEST

1. B	5. C	9. B
2. A	6. D	10. C
3. N, Y, N, Y	7. A	11. Y, Y, N, N
4. A, C	8. D	12. A

SPEAKING ANSWER KEY

SPEAKING DIAGNOSTIC PRE-TEST

Sample Notes

Question 3

TOPIC OF READING PASSAGE: notice about registering for classes in Humanities Department

main points of notice:

- too many students registering for classes without fulfilling prerequisites
- now students need signatures from advisors to register for humanities classes (except intro classes)
- advisors must check that students have fulfilled prerequisites

TOPIC OF LISTENING PASSAGE: student conversation about notice

main points of conversation:

- woman has read the notice but man hasn't
- they each need to go see their advisors
- man wants to read notice first

Question 4

TOPIC OF READING PASSAGE: nonverbal communication

definition and examples of nonverbal communication:
- definition (any communication without words)
- examples (smiling, frowning, nodding, shaking head, shaking hands, waving hand)

TOPIC OF LISTENING PASSAGE: two points of clarification about nonverbal communication

points of clarification:
- there can be nonverbal communication without intent
- there cannot be nonverbal communication without communication

Question 5

TOPIC OF LISTENING PASSAGE: problem the woman is having with her college French class

what the woman's problem is:
- took 3 years of French in high school
- intermediate French is too difficult (she can't understand anything)

what the man suggests:
- find out if other students have the same problem
- talk with her professor

Question 6

LISTENING TOPICS: echolocation used by whales

points about echolocation used by whales:
- only toothed, not toothless, whales use echolocation
- whales send out clicks, clicks reflected from objects back to whales
- whales can learn size, shape, distance, speed, direction

SPEAKING EXERCISE 5
Sample Notes

1. TOPIC OF READING PASSAGE: notice on problem with bicycle parking on campus

   main points about problem:
   - too many students parking bicycles in unauthorized places
   - new policy ticketing bicycles parked in unauthorized places
   - authorized parking for bicycles along east and west sides of campus

2. TOPIC OF READING PASSAGE: message on retirement of professor

   main points about message:
   - retiring professor has served at university for 50 years
   - will retire at end of next spring semester
   - praised for commitment to students and for publications

3. TOPIC OF READING PASSAGE: part of a class syllabus on professor's policy against late assignments

   main points in part of class syllabus:
   - assignments and due dates listed

- no late assignment accepted, ever
- grade on late assignment always zero

SPEAKING EXERCISE 6
Sample Notes

1. TOPIC OF LISTENING PASSAGE: student conversation on unhappiness with notice on bicycle parking

   main points about conversation:
   - man has seen notice but woman hasn't
   - neither one is happy about notice
   - it seems unfair to both that they cannot park bicycles near classrooms

2. TOPIC OF LISTENING PASSAGE: student conversation about professor who is retiring

   main points about conversation:
   - both students sorry professor is retiring
   - woman's father took classes from professor 30 years ago
   - both students want to take class from professor spring semester

3. TOPIC OF LISTENING PASSAGE: student conversation about part of class syllabus on late assignments

   main points about conversation:
   - man initially does not believe what syllabus says about late assignments
   - woman tells story about injured student whose late papers were not accepted
   - man then believes what syllabus says about late papers

SPEAKING EXERCISE 7
Sample Notes

1. reading passage describes a *notice*; listening passage shows *students' unhappiness* about the notice

2. reading passage describes a *message about a professor*; listening passage shows *students' reaction* to the message

3. reading passage describes part of a *syllabus*; listening passage shows *students' reaction* to the part of the syllabus

SPEAKING EXERCISE 8
Sample Answers

1. In this set of materials, the reading passage is a notice, and the listening passage shows some students' unhappiness with the notice.

   The reading passage is a notice on a problem with bicycle parking on campus. The notice states that too many students are parking bicycles in unauthorized places, that there is a new policy ticketing bicycles parked in unauthorized places, and that the only authorized parking for their bicycles is along two sides of campus.

   The listening passage is a conversation between students who are unhappy with the notice on bicycle parking. In the conversation, the woman has already seen the notice, but the man hasn't. Neither one is happy about the notice because it seems unfair to both of them that they can't park their bicycles near their classrooms.

2. In this set of materials, the reading passage is a message about a professor, and the listening passage shows some students' reaction to the message.

The reading topic is a message on the retirement of a long-time professor. The message states that the professor who is retiring has served at the university for almost 50 years and will retire at the end of next spring semester. Throughout her career, the professor has been praised for her commitment to students and for her publications.

The listening topic is a student conversation about the professor who is retiring. In the conversation, both students are sorry the professor is retiring. The woman's father took classes from the same professor 30 years ago, and both students want to take class from the professor in the coming spring semester.

3. In this set of materials, the reading passage describes part of a syllabus, and the listening passage shows the students' reaction to that part of the syllabus.

The reading passage is part of a class syllabus on a professor's policy against late assignments. The reading passage lists assignments and due dates. It also states that no late assignments are accepted, ever, and that the grade on any late assignment is always zero.

The listening passage is a student conversation about the part of the class syllabus on late assignments. In the conversation, the man initially does not believe what the syllabus says about late assignments. Then the woman tells a story about an injured student whose late papers were not accepted, and the man then believes what the syllabus says about late papers.

SPEAKING REVIEW EXERCISE (Skills 5–8)
Sample Notes

TOPIC OF READING PASSAGE: part of history syllabus on research assignment

main points about research assignment:
• students must choose event or person from history
• students must research the event or person
• students must write about the event or person from positive and negative perspectives

TOPIC OF LISTENING PASSAGE: student conversation about research assignment

main points about conversation:
• man has better understanding of assignment than woman
• man gives reasons why he thinks the professor gave this assignment (students should look at various sources, students should understand that a person or event can be viewed in different ways)

Sample Answer

In this set of materials, the reading passage is part of a syllabus, and the listening passage is a student conversation about this part of the syllabus.

The reading passage is about a research assignment or part of the history syllabus. The main points about

the syllabus are that students must choose an event or person from history, they must research the event or person, and they must write about the event or person from positive and negative perspectives.

The listening passage is a student conversation about the research assignment. In the conversation, the man has a better understanding of the assignment than the woman. The man gives reasons why he thinks the professor gave this assignment; the reasons are that the students should look at various sources and that the students should understand that a person or event can be viewed in different ways.

SPEAKING EXERCISE 9
Sample Notes

1. TOPIC OF READING PASSAGE: the Dead Sea

main points about Dead Sea:
• "dead" because high salt level prevents life in it
• landlocked with no outlet
• in area with high temperature, which causes rapid evaporation

2. TOPIC OF READING PASSAGE: polling

main points about polling:
• involves asking people how they feel about an issue or candidate
• representative sample can be polled if the group to be polled is too large

3. TOPIC OF READING PASSAGE: Polynesian migration in the Pacific Ocean

details about Polynesian migration:
• started 4,000 years ago
• covered 20,000 square miles of Pacific Ocean (Hawaii to New Zealand to Easter Island)
• made use of outrigger canoes (2 tree trunks joined with a platform)

SPEAKING EXERCISE 10
Sample Notes

1. TOPIC OF LISTENING PASSAGE: additional point about Dead Sea

Dead Sea is not a sea:
• sea is body of water that is part of ocean or opens into ocean
• lake is body of water that is entirely enclosed
• Dead Sea has no outlet and is therefore lake

2. TOPIC OF LISTENING PASSAGE: push polling

characteristics of push polling:
• negative and unfair kind of polling
• involves asking leading questions to influence person being polled

3. TOPIC OF LISTENING PASSAGE: one special aspect of Polynesian migration

Polynesians may have made it to South America:
• surprising because they were traveling on outrigger canoes
• South American plants in Hawaii may be indication this happened

SPEAKING EXERCISE 11

1. reading passage describes *a body of water*; listening passage provides *additional information* about the body of water

2. reading passage describes *polling in general*; listening passage describes *one specific kind of polling*

3. reading passage describes *a migration by one culture*; listening passage describes *one special aspect of that migration*

SPEAKING EXERCISE 12
Sample Answers

1. In this set of materials, the reading passage describes a body of water, and the listening passage provides additional information about the body of water.

   The reading passage describes the body of water named the Dead Sea. This body of water is said to be "dead" because its high salt level prevents life in it. It's so salty because it's landlocked with no outlet and it's in an area with a high temperature, which causes rapid evaporation.

   The listening passage makes an additional point about the Dead Sea. This point is that the Dead Sea isn't really a sea. A sea is a body of water that's part of the ocean or opens into the ocean, while a lake is a body of water that's entirely enclosed. The Dead Sea has no outlet and is therefore a lake.

2. In this set of materials, the reading passage describes polling in general, and the listening passage describes one specific kind of polling.

   The reading passage describes polling, which is a process that involves asking people how they feel about an issue or candidate. A representative sample can be polled if the group to be polled is too large.

   The listening passage describes one particular kind of polling, which is called push polling. Push polling is a negative and unfair kind of polling that involves asking leading questions to influence the person being polled.

3. In this set of materials, the reading passage describes a migration by one culture, and the listening passage describes one special aspect of that migration.

   The reading passage describes the Polynesian migration across the Pacific Ocean. This migration started 4,000 years ago and covered 20,000 square miles of Pacific Ocean, from Hawaii to New Zealand to Easter Island. This migration was accomplished using outrigger canoes, which consisted of two tree trunks joined with a platform.

   The listening passage describes one special aspect of Polynesian migration. This special aspect is that the Polynesians may have made it to South America, which would be surprising because the Polynesians were traveling on outrigger canoes. One indication that this might have happened is that there are plants from South America in Hawaii.

SPEAKING REVIEW EXERCISE (Skills 9–12)
Sample Notes

TOPIC OF READING PASSAGE: equity theory of employee satisfaction

main points about equity theory:
• employee determines return for contribution and compares their return for contribution to other employees
• employee content if return for contribution is higher than or equal to return for contribution of other employees and unhappy if it is lower

TOPIC OF LISTENING PASSAGE: examples of equity theory

examples related to employee X:
• employee X satisfied when he and coworker have equal returns for contributions (similar job title, work, salary, office)
• employee X dissatisfied when he gets less return for contribution than coworker (same job title but more work, less money, smaller office)

Sample Answer

In this set of materials, the reading passage describes a theory, and the listening passage provides examples of this theory.

The reading passage describes the equity theory of employee satisfaction. According to this theory, the employee determines his or her return for contribution and compares it to the return for contribution of other employees. An employee will be content if his or her return for contribution is higher than or equal to the return for contribution of other employees and unhappy if it is lower.

The listening passage provides examples of the equity theory of employee satisfaction. In the first example, employee X is satisfied when he and his coworker have equal returns for their contributions such as similar job titles, similar work, similar salaries, and similar offices. In the second example, employee X is dissatisfied when he receives less return for contribution than his coworker, such as having the same job titles but having to do more work, making less money, and having a smaller office.

SPEAKING EXERCISE 13
Sample Notes

1. TOPIC OF LISTENING PASSAGE: woman wants to know about two different professors who teach the same course

   what the woman learns about the two professors:
   • Dr. Abbott has interesting discussions and gives essay exams
   • Dr. Becker concentrates on details and gives multiple-choice exams

   what the woman thinks about the two professors:
   • interesting discussions sound good but essay exams do not
   • concentration on details doesn't sound good but multiple-choice exams do

2. TOPIC OF LISTENING PASSAGE: man unable to go to big game because he needs to review notes for an exam

   what woman suggests to the man:
   • review and reorganize notes soon after taking them
   • not wait until just before exam to review notes

what man decides:
- can try this method with future notes
- needs to review old notes now and can't go to game

3. TOPIC OF LISTENING PASSAGE: woman's question about an independent study project

what the man says he did wrong:
- put off the project until a couple of days before each monthly meeting
- expected professor to tell him what to do

what the woman should do:
- work on project regularly throughout each month
- determine direction research should go and discuss ideas with professor

SPEAKING EXERCISE 14

1. woman learns about two professors and states what she thinks about them

2. woman offers suggestion to help man solve a problem, and he reacts to this

3. woman learns how man completed a project and learns from what he says

SPEAKING EXERCISE 15
Sample Answers

1. In this listening passage, the woman learns about two professors and states what she thinks about them.

   The woman wants to know about two different professors who teach the same course. She learns that Dr. Abbott has a lot of interesting discussions and gives essay exams and that Dr. Becker concentrates on details and gives multiple-choice exams.

   After the woman learns about the two professors, she comes to the conclusion that interesting discussions sound good but essay exams do not and that concentration on details doesn't sound good but multiple-choice exams do.

2. In this listening passage, the woman offers a suggestion to the man to help him solve a problem he is having, and the man reacts to her suggestion.

   The situation is that the man is unable to go to a big game because he needs to review his notes before an exam. The woman suggests that the man review and reorganize his notes soon after taking them and that he not wait until just before an exam to review his notes.

   After this discussion, the man decides that he can try this method with his notes in the future but that he needs to review his old notes now and he cannot go to the game.

3. In this listening passage, the woman learns how the man completed a project, and she learns what she should do from what he says.

   The woman asks the man about an independent study project he worked on with Dr. Lee. The man tells the woman that the two problems he had were that he put off working on the project until a couple of days before each monthly meeting and that he expected the professor to tell him what to do.

After she hears this, the woman comes to the conclusion that she should work on the project regularly throughout each month and that she should determine the direction her research should go and then discuss her ideas with the professor.

SPEAKING REVIEW EXERCISE (Skills 13–15)
Sample Notes

TOPIC OF LISTENING PASSAGE: man's boredom in class because of lack of involvement

how man shows he's bored:
- sits in the back
- almost falls asleep

how woman suggests that he can become more involved:
- should sit in the front
- should answer questions and ask the professor questions

Sample Answer

In this listening passage, the man describes a problem he's having in a certain class, and the woman offers suggestions to solve the problem.

The problem the man has is that he's bored in class. The man shows that he's bored by sitting in the back of the classroom and almost falling asleep.

The woman suggests that the man can take specific steps to become more involved in the class. He can try sitting in the front of the classroom. He can also answer questions the professor asks and ask the professor questions.

SPEAKING EXERCISE 16
Sample Notes

1. TOPIC OF LISTENING PASSAGE: Bank holiday of 1933

   main points about Bank Holiday of 1933:
   - was not a holiday (was a closing of unstable banks)
   - banks were closed while federal government reorganized the banking system
   - one part of reorganization was federal deposit insurance
   - since then bank failures have decreased considerably

2. TOPIC OF LISTENING PASSAGE: definition of creativity

   main points in definition of creativity:
   - originality (idea must not be normal, everyday idea)
   - appropriateness (idea must fit the situation)

3. TOPIC OF LISTENING PASSAGE: how the Amazon River got its name

   two sources contributed to its name:
   - native inhabitants gave river the name Amanuzu ("big wave")
   - chronicle by European explorers describes female warriors who resembled Amazons in Greek literature

SPEAKING EXERCISE 17

1. professor describes Bank Holiday of 1933
2. professor discusses definition of creativity
3. professor discusses how the Amazon river got its name

SPEAKING EXERCISE 18
Sample Answers

1. In this listening passage, a professor describes the Bank Holiday of 1933. The main point the professor makes about the Bank Holiday of 1933 is that it was not a holiday but was instead a closing of unstable banks. Banks were closed while the federal government reorganized the banking system. One part of the reorganization was federal deposit insurance, and since then, bank failures have decreased considerably.

2. In this listening passage, a professor discusses a definition of creativity. The point the professor makes about this definition is that it must include the ideas of originality and appropriateness. Originality means that a creative idea must not be a normal, everyday idea, and appropriateness means that a creative idea must fit the situation.

3. In this listening passage, a professor discusses how the Amazon River got its name. Two sources contributed to its name. The first source is the name given to the river by native inhabitants; this name was Amanuzu, which meant "big wave." The second source was a chronicle by European explorers. This chronicle described female warriors who resembled Amazons in Greek literature.

SPEAKING REVIEW EXERCISE (Skills 16–18)
Sample Notes

TOPIC OF LISTENING PASSAGE: seasonal affective disorder (SAD)

main points about SAD:
- affects people living in areas where sunlight is low in winter (such as Alaska)
- reduced sunlight causes reduced seratonin (hormone that causes cheerfulness) and increased melatonin (hormone that causes sleepiness)

Sample Answer

In this listening passage, the professor discusses seasonal affective disorder, or SAD. The professor makes the point that SAD affects people living in areas where sunlight is low in winter, such as Alaska. The reduced sunlight causes reduced seratonin, which is a hormone that causes cheerfulness, and increased melatonin, which is a hormone that causes sleepiness.

SPEAKING POST-TEST
Sample Notes
Question 3

TOPIC OF READING PASSAGE: problem at the university's main cafeteria

details about problem:
- main cafeteria closed from October 24 to November 1
- students with meal cards can use them at 3 snack bars on campus

TOPIC OF LISTENING PASSAGE: student discussion of the problem at the cafeteria

details of discussion:
- both man and woman are going to snack bar for lunch
- man saw the notice and woman heard about it
- man can't believe cafeteria is closed during the semester
- woman heard cafeteria is closed because of a fire

Question 4

TOPIC OF READING PASSAGE: importance for a teacher to choose appropriate social environment in the classroom

types of social environments:
- cooperative = students work together to come up with best answers together
- competitive = students work alone to come up with better answers than other students
- individualistic = students work alone to come up with best answers individually

TOPIC OF LISTENING PASSAGE: how a teacher can establish different social environments

ways to establish social environments:
- cooperative (by putting students in pairs or groups and accepting only answers that have been agreed upon by group)
- competitive (by having students work individually and evaluating responses in comparison with answers from other students)
- individualistic (by having students work individually and evaluating responses based upon a predetermined scale)

Question 5

TOPIC OF LISTENING PASSAGE: student conversation about woman's class schedule

main points of discussion:
- woman scheduled four classes in a row in different corners of university and cannot get to her classes on time
- man suggests thinking about where classes meet, not just when

Question 6

TOPIC OF LISTENING PASSAGE: one reason people thought there were living beings on Mars

a linguistic error:
- Italian astronomer saw *canali* on Mars in 1877
- *canali* in Italian can be natural or man-made
- in English canals are man-made and channels are natural
- *canali* was translated into English as *canals* (man-made)
- conclusion was that astronomer said there were living beings on Mars

WRITING ANSWER KEY

WRITING DIAGNOSTIC PRE-TEST

Sample Notes

Question 1

TOPIC OF READING PASSAGE: childhood amnesia, a phenomenon of human memory (inability to remember early years)

studies of childhood amnesia:
- difficult to test whether memories are accurate
- still show that people do not remember first 3 to 5 years

TOPIC OF LISTENING PASSAGE: why childhood amnesia occurs

possible cause of childhood amnesia:
- young children encode randomly (before hippocampus matures and helps to organize memories)
- adults encode in organized patterns (after hippocampus matures)

TOPIC STATEMENT: In this set of materials, the reading passage discusses a certain phenomenon in human memory, and the listening passage discusses a possible explanation for this phenomenon.

WRITING EXERCISE 1

Sample Notes

1. TOPIC OF READING PASSAGE: the Sahara Desert today

   characteristics of the Sahara today:
   - world's largest desert (equal in size to the U.S.)
   - very dry climate (average rainfall under 10 cm per year)
   - little surface water (only Nile River and some oases)

2. TOPIC OF READING PASSAGE: polysemy (one word having different meanings)

   examples of polysemy:
   - *sound* (19 noun meanings, 12 adjective meanings, 12 verb meanings, 4 meanings in verb phrases, 2 adverb meanings)
   - *set* (57 noun meanings, 120 verb meanings)

3. TOPIC OF READING PASSAGE: Margaret Mead's research on culture and gender roles

   Mead's studies of three societies in New Guinea:
   - first society = both men and women have "feminine" characteristics
   - second society = both men and women have "masculine" characteristics
   - third society = men have "feminine" characteristics, women have "masculine" characteristics
   - conclusion = gender characteristics come more from society than from biology

WRITING EXERCISE 2

Sample Notes

1. TOPIC OF LISTENING PASSAGE: the Sahara in the past

   characteristics of the Sahara in the past:
   - 10,000 years ago (wet areas, forests, grasslands, rivers, lakes, large animals, prehistoric hunters, fishermen, and farmers)
   - 6,000 years ago (began to dry out)
   - 4,000 years ago (a desert)

2. TOPIC OF LISTENING PASSAGE: special subset of polysemic words (one word with opposite meanings)

   examples of words with opposite meanings:
   - *bolt* and *fast* (meaning "cannot move" or "move quickly")
   - *sanction* (meaning "permit" or "not permit")

3. TOPIC OF LISTENING PASSAGE: criticisms of Mead's research

   criticisms:
   - results "too neat" (research not usually this tidy)
   - results suggest Mead found what she was looking for rather than what was there

WRITING EXERCISE 3

1. reading passage describes *present*; listening passage describes *past*

2. reading passage describes a *category of words*; listening passage describes *subset of category*

3. reading passage describes *research*; listening passage describes *criticisms of the research*

WRITING EXERCISE 4

1. TOPIC STATEMENT: In this set of materials, the reading passage describes some characteristics of the Sahara Desert today, and the listening passage describes what the area was like in the past.

2. TOPIC STATEMENT: In this set of materials, the reading passage describes a certain category of words, and the listening passage describes a special subset of words in this category.

3. TOPIC STATEMENT: In this set of materials, the reading passage describes research by Margaret Mead, and the listening passage describes some criticisms of the research.

WRITING EXERCISE 5

1. 4
2. 4
3. idea
4. 3
5. 3
6. person on trial
7. this kind of error
8. prosecuting attorney
9. 7 (this set, this legal concept, this legal idea, this kind, This example, this situation, this situation)
10. 1 (that procedure)
11. thus
12. In other words

WRITING EXERCISE 6

1. (A)   In this set of materials, the reading passage discusses one type of management **style, and the** listening passage presents the opposite type of management style. Both of the management **styles were** proposed by Douglas McGregor.

   (B)   The reading passage discusses the theory X management style, **which is an** authoritarian managment style. What a theory X manager **believes is** that employees dislike work and will try to avoid it. Since this type of manager believes that employees do not like to **work, he** or she must force employees to **work. A** manager must force employees to work with threats and punishment.

   (C)   The listening passage discusses a very different management **style; it** discusses the theory Y management style, which is a participative style of management. A theory Y manager believes that employees **work** for enjoyment. Employees do not need to be **threatened; they** work for the pleasure of working. The role that this type of manager needs to **follow is** to set objectives and then to reward **employees as** they meet these objectives.

2. (A)   In this set of materials, the reading passage describes the different types of waves that occur during **earthquakes, and** the listening passage explains how much damage each of these types of waves **causes.**

   (B)   According to the reading passage, three different types of **waves occur** during an earthquake: primary (or P) waves, secondary (or S) waves, and surface waves. Primary waves are the fastest-moving **waves, and secondary** waves are not as fast as primary waves. Surface waves resemble the ripples in a pond after a stone has been thrown in **it; they** are very slow-moving waves.

   (C)   According to the listening passage, the types of waves that occur during an **earthquake do** not cause equal amounts of damage to structures. What **causes** most damage to structures during **earthquakes is** surface waves. The really slow-moving surface waves cause most of the differential movement of buildings during earthquakes, **and it is** the differential movement of buildings that causes most of the damage. Because the primary and secondary waves vibrate much faster and with less movement than surface **waves, they** cause little damage to structures.

WRITING EXERCISE 7

1. (A)   In this set of materials, the reading passage discusses **an attempt** to deal with the problem of spelling in **many** words in American English; the listening passage **explains** why this attempt was not a **successful** one.

   (B)   The reading passage explains that there is a problem in spelling a number of **words** in English where the spelling and pronunciation **do** not match; it then goes on to explain that philanthropist Andrew Carnegie made **an effort** to resolve this. He gave **a huge** amount of **money** to establish a board **called** the Simplified Spelling Board. As the name of **the board** indicates, **its** purpose was to simplify the spellings **of words** that are difficult to spell in English. Because of all **of the work** that the board did, spellings like *ax* (instead of *axe*) and *program*

(instead of *programme*) **became** acceptable in American English.

   (C)   The listening passage **explains** why the work of the Simplified Spelling Board **did** not last. According to the listening passage, the main reason for the board's problems **was** that it went too far. **It** tried to establish spellings like *yu* (instead of *you*) and *tuff* (instead of *tough*). There was a **really** negative reaction to the attempt to change spelling too much, and eventually the board was **dissolved.**

2. (A)   In this set of materials, the reading passage describes **a type** of learning, and the listening passage **provides** an **extended** example of this type of learning.

   (B)   The reading passage discusses aversive conditioning, which is **defined** as learning involving an unpleasant stimulus. In this type of learning, an unpleasant stimulus is **applied** every **time** that a certain behavior occurs, in an attempt to stop the behavior. A learner **can behave** in two different **ways** in response to the knowledge that something unpleasant will soon **occur.** Avoidance behavior is **a change** in behavior before the stimulus **is** applied, to avoid the unpleasant stimulus, while escape behavior is the opposite, a change in behavior after the application of the stimulus, to cause **it** to stop.

   (C)   The listening passage provides **a long** example of aversive conditioning. This extended example is about the alarm in **many** cars that **buzzes** if the driver's seat belt is not fastened. In this example, the method of aversive conditioning that is applied to drivers **is** that every time a driver tries to drive with the seat belt unfastened, the buzzer **goes** off. The driver exhibits avoidance behavior if he or she **has fastened** the seat belt before driving, to avoid hearing the buzzer. The driver exhibits escape behavior if he or she **attaches** the seat belt after the alarm **has started** to buzz, to stop the buzzing.

WRITING REVIEW EXERCISE (Skills 1–7)

Sample Notes

TOPIC OF READING PASSAGE: ancient human body (Iceman) in Alps (in Italy close to Austria)

description of body:
- more than 5,000 years old
- short male aged 40 to 50
- wearing lots of clothing (coat, belt, leggings, shoes, cap, cape)
- carrying lots of equipment (dagger, axe, bow, backpack, quiver with arrows)

TOPIC OF LISTENING PASSAGE: importance of discovery of Iceman

importance of discovery:
- fully preserved prehistoric man
- going about normal day when died

how Iceman probably died:
- traveling in mountains
- originally believed he had fallen asleep and froze in snow
- now assumed (from wounds) he was killed in a fight

TOPIC STATEMENT: In this set of materials, the reading passage discusses the discovery of the body of a man from 5,000 years ago, and the listening passage discusses the importance of the discovery.

WRITING EXERCISE 10

1. 3
2. 3
3. mysterious-sounding answer
4. I do not know.
5. amazed
6. English
7. assignment
8. classmate
9. 3 (this language, this expression, this mysterious-sounding answer)
10. 1 (these two examples)
11. For instance
12. an even more interesting example
13. Overall

WRITING EXERCISE 13

(A)   I definitely believe that taking part in organized team sports is beneficial. However, **it is** beneficial for much more than the obvious reasons. Everyone recognizes, of course, that participation in sports provides obvious physical benefits. It **leads** to improved physical **fitness; it** also provides a release from the stresses of life. I spent my youth taking part in a number of organized sports, including football, basketball, and **volleyball; as** a result of this experience I understand that the benefits of **participation are much** greater than the physical benefits.

(B)   One very valuable benefit that children get from taking part in **sports is** that it teaches participants teamwork. What any player in a team sport needs to **learn is** that individual team members must put the team ahead of individual achievement. Individuals on one team who are working for individual glory rather than the good of the **team often** end up working against each other. A team made up of individuals unable to work **together is often** not a very successful **team; it** is usually a complete failure.

(C)   What also makes participation in team sports **valuable is** that it teaches participants to work to achieve goals. Playing **sports involves** setting goals and working toward **them; examples** of such goals are running faster, kicking harder, throwing straighter, or jumping higher. Athletes learn **that they can** set goals and work toward them until the **goals are accomplished. It is** through hard work that goals can be met.

(D)   By taking part in **sports, one can** learn the truly valuable skills of working together on teams and working to accomplish specific goals. These **goals are not** just beneficial in **sports; more** importantly, the skills that are developed through **sports are** the basis of success in many other aspects of life. Mastering these skills **leads** to success not only on the playing field but also in the wider arena of life.

WRITING EXERCISE 14

(A)   In my first semester at the university, I was **overwhelmed** by the differences between university studies and high school studies. In high school, I had easily **been** able to finish the **amount** of work that was assigned, and if **on a certain** occasion I did not complete an assignment, the teacher quickly **told** me to make up the work. The situation in my university classes **was** not at all like the situation in high school.

(B)   I was tremendously **surprised** at the volume of work assigned in the university. Unlike high school courses, which perhaps covered a chapter in two **weeks**, university courses **regularly** covered two or three chapters in one week and two or three other chapters in the next week. I **had** been able to keep up with the workload in high school, but it was difficult for me to finish all the reading in **my** university classes even though I tried **really** hard to finish all of **it**.

(C)   The role that the teacher took in motivating students to get work done **was** also very different in my university. In high school, if an assignment was **unfinished** on **the** date that it was due, my teacher would **immediately** let me know that I had **really made** a mistake and needed to finish **the** assignment right away. In my university classes, however, professors did not **regularly inform** students to make sure that we were **getting** work done on schedule. It was really easy to put off studying in the beginning of each **semester** and really have to work hard later in the semester to catch up on my assignments.

(D)   During my first year in the university, I had to **set a firm** goal to get things done by myself instead of relying on others to watch over me and make sure that I **had** done what I was supposed to do. With so **many** assignments, this was quite a **difficult task**, but I now **regularly** try to do my best because I dislike being very far behind. It seems that I have **turned** into quite a **motivated** student.

WRITING POST-TEST
Sample Notes

TOPIC OF READING PASSAGE: unintended consequences (effects that are unexpected after a decision)

example of parking ban on Main Street:
• positive consequence = some people get more exercise walking
• negative consequence = some people stop shopping in stores on Main Street

TOPIC OF LISTENING PASSAGE: extended example of unintended consequences

example of increased taxes:
• local government raised taxes to increase revenue
• decision ended up decreasing revenue (citizens had less to spend because of increased taxes)

TOPIC STATEMENT: In this set of materials, the reading passage defines a concept and provides a brief example of the concept; the listening passage provides a more extended example of the concept.

MINI-TEST 1

READING

1. A	4. D	7. B	10. A
2. C	5. B	8. A	11. C
3. D	6. C	9. D	12. D

13. | a theory of migration: | (1) (3) (5) (6) |
|---|---|

LISTENING

1. A	4. B	7. B	10. D
2. D	5. D	8. C	11. A
3. C	6. A	9. C, D	

SPEAKING

Sample Notes

Question 2

TOPIC OF READING PASSAGE: part of syllabus on assignment to watch films

main points about assignment:
• given list of 20 films
• must watch at least 12 films
• students write a report summarizing each film they watch
• may turn in extra reports for extra credit

TOPIC OF LISTENING PASSAGE: student conversation about assignment to watch films

how students seem to feel about assignment:
• man initially thinks assignment is too much work
• woman is enthusiastic about assignment
• man finally decides assignment not so bad (summaries not too bad, there are worse assignments than watching films)

Question 3

TOPIC OF LISTENING PASSAGE: formation of glaciers (masses of moving ice)

how glaciers form:
• considerable snow accumulates
• pressure on snow underneath causes change to small ice crystals
• pressure causes small ice crystals to become large ice crystals
• large amount of crystallized ice begins to move

WRITING

TOPIC OF READING PASSAGE: uses of garlic throughout history

how garlic has been used:
• Egyptians (to cure 22 ailments and make workers stronger)
• Greeks and Romans (to cure illnesses, ward off spells and curses, make soldiers courageous)
• Homer, Vikings, Marco Polo (to help during long voyages)
• World War I (to fight infections)

TOPIC OF LISTENING PASSAGE: scientific evidence showing benefits of garlic

evidence of benefits:
• raw garlic (kills 23 kinds of bacteria)
• heated garlic (thins blood)

TOPIC STATEMENT: In this set of materials, the reading passage describes the various uses of garlic over time, and the listening passage describes scientific evidence that proves its benefits.

MINI-TEST 2

READING

1. B	4. A	7. D	10. C
2. D	5. A	8. A	11. B
3. C	6. C	9. D	12. D

13. | first-borns: | (4) (9) |
|---|---|
| second-borns and middle children: | (2) (10) |
| last-borns: | (1) (6) |
| only children: | (3) (7) |

LISTENING

1. B, C	5. D	9. B
2. A	6. A	10. Y, N, Y, Y
3. N, Y, Y, N, N	7. D	11. D
4. C	8. C	

SPEAKING

Sample Notes

Question 2

TOPIC OF READING PASSAGE: group leadership

two types of group leadership:
• instrumental leadership (concern with getting tasks done)
• expressive leadership (concern for the well-being of group)

TOPIC OF LISTENING PASSAGE: examples of group leadership

two situations showing different types of group leadership:
• group 1 had expressive leadership (activities to get to know each other, positive comments about project, e-mail describing feelings)
• group 2 had instrumental leadership (detailed list of work to be done, meetings about what was and was not accomplished, emphasis on getting work done on time)

Question 3

TOPIC OF LISTENING PASSAGE: student conversation about attending an open student council meeting

main points of discussion:
• meeting will be about changing final exam schedule
• proposed change from six to three days
• students who support change want earlier summer vacation
• both oppose change because both have five exams
• both decide to attend meeting to voice opinions

MINI-TEST 3

READING

1. A	4. B	7. C	10. B
2. D	5. B	8. B	11. D
3. C	6. D	9. A	12. A

13. | the history of a sauce known as ketchup: | (1) (3) (4) (6) |

LISTENING

1. B	5. D	9. A
2. C	6. C	10. C
3. B	7. C1, C2, C2, C3	11. D
4. A	8. B, C	

SPEAKING

Sample Notes

Question 2

TOPIC OF READING PASSAGE: notice about rules in the library

library rules:

• reading, working on research, or studying only
• no music, no talking, no sleeping, no eating or drinking

TOPIC OF LISTENING PASSAGE: student conversation about notice

how students feel about notice:

• woman is happy about new rules (she wants to study in peace and quiet)
• man is unhappy about notice (he wants to talk, sleep, eat and drink, play music while studying)

Question 3

TOPIC OF LISTENING PASSAGE: attempt during neoclassic period to make English more like Latin

main points of this attempt:

• during neoclassic period (17th and 18th centuries) high regard for ancient Greeks and Romans
• academics tried to make English more like Latin
• an example = rule in English against split infinitives

WRITING

TOPIC OF READING PASSAGE: unique flowering and seeding cycles of Asian bamboo

unique characteristics of flowering and seeding cycles:

• all members of a species tend to flower and seed at same time
• flowering and seeding tend to occur at long intervals

example of one species of Asian bamboo:

• all members of a species around the world flower and seed at the same time
• flowering and seeding occurs less than once a century

TOPIC OF LISTENING PASSAGE: problem for giant panda caused by flowering and seeding cycles of Asian bamboo

giant panda's problem:

• some giant pandas still live in wild
• bamboo is main source of food
• giant panda loses food source when bamboo flowers and seeds
• dangerous when giant panda has to move

TOPIC STATEMENT: In this set of materials, the reading passage discusses unique characteristics of Asian bamboo, and the listening passage explains how these unique characteristics have an impact on the giant panda.

MINI-TEST 4

READING

1. D	4. C	7. C	10. B
2. A	5. B	8. C	11. C
3. D	6. A	9. D	12. A

13. | estuary systems on flooded coastal plains: | (2) (5) (8) (9) |
| estuary systems on mountainous coasts: | (1) (4) (6) (10) |

LISTENING

1. D	7. A, B
2. A	8. C2, C1, C2, C1, C2
3. B, C	9. C
4. B	10. A, D
5. D	11. B
6. C	

SPEAKING

Sample Notes

Question 2

TOPIC OF READING PASSAGE: issue of nullification

what nullification is:

• doctrine by which states believed they could refuse to accept federal laws
• federal government did not believe states could nullify federal laws

TOPIC OF LISTENING PASSAGE: situation when issue of nullification arose

main points about situation:

• in 1828 federal government authorized tariffs on some imported goods
• one southern state refused to pay tariffs (nullified federal law)
• federal government sent troops to southern state
• compromise lowering tariffs was reached to resolve situation

Question 3

TOPIC OF LISTENING PASSAGE: student conversation about a paper for psychology class

main points about paper:

• man wrote simple, direct answer to question
• man's paper was praised by professor
• woman wrote creative answer to question
• woman's paper was not praised by professor (professor wrote "needs work")
• woman decides to write simple, direct answer instead of creative answer in next paper

MINI-TEST 5

READING

1. C	4. D	7. C	10. B
2. B	5. D	8. A	11. A
3. A	6. A	9. B	12. C

13.

simple schizophrenia:	(3)
hebephrenic schizophrenia:	(5)
paranoid schizophrenia:	(1)
catatonic schizophrenia:	(7)
acute schizophrenia:	(2)

LISTENING

1. D	5. B, C	9. B
2. Y, Y, N, N	6. B	10. C2, C1, C4, C3
3. A	7. A	11. A, D
4. B	8. A, C	

SPEAKING

Sample Notes

Question 2

TOPIC OF READING PASSAGE: announcement of positions for student assistants in Administration Building

requirement for positions:
- full-time with at least 60 units
- 3.0 minimum grade-point average
- mornings or afternoons Monday–Friday
- computer and telephone skills
- application submitted by Friday afternoon

TOPIC OF LISTENING PASSAGE: woman discusses applying for position with man

woman doesn't meet most requirements:
- has only 45 not 60 units
- has a 2.5 grade-point average not 3.0
- not available every morning or afternoon
- has telephone skills but not computer skills
- already submitted application anyway
- man thinks it is a waste of her time

Question 3

TOPIC OF LISTENING PASSAGE: zero-sum game theory and application in economics

theory:
- total points fixed in zero-sum-game
- total points not fixed in non-zero-sum game

application of theory to economics:
- total resources fixed in zero-sum economy
- total resources not fixed in non-zero-sum game

WRITING

TOPIC OF READING PASSAGE: Joseph Heller's novel *Catch-22*

what the novel is about:
- takes place during World War II
- features bombardier who does not want to be in war

how the novel achieved success:
- book was originally not successful
- during later war, book became very successful

TOPIC OF LISTENING PASSAGE: significance of title *Catch-22*

significance of title:
- title refers to situation with no good choice
- phrase now part of American culture
- number 22 has no special meaning (could be different number)

TOPIC STATEMENT: In this set of materials, the reading passage describes the novel *Catch-22*, and the listening passage explains the significance of the title of the novel.

MINI-TEST 6

READING

1. C	4. B	7. A	10. D
2. A	5. D	8. D	11. B
3. B	6. C	9. C	12. A

13.

the tragedy of the *Exxon Valdez*:	(2) (3) (5)

LISTENING

1. C	5. B	9. C
2. C	6. D	10. B
3. A	7. C2, C1, C3	11. A, B
4. D	8. A	

SPEAKING

Sample Notes

Question 2

TOPIC OF READING PASSAGE: how our solar system and our planet were formed

main points of formation of solar system and Earth:
- solar system started as spinning cloud of dust and gas
- dust and gas began clumping together
- majority of dust and gas became Sun
- smaller clumps became planets
- Earth formed globe with layered structure
- heavier material in middle and lighter material on the outside

TOPIC OF LISTENING PASSAGE: how the layered structure of our planet was formed

two categories of theories:
- the core formed first and the lighter layers came later
- material clumped first and layers formed later

Question 3

TOPIC OF LISTENING PASSAGE: student conversation about a guest speaker tonight

main points about the conversation:
- woman saw sign saying guest speaker will appear tonight
- both thought speaker was next week
- both think schedule must have been changed
- both decide to let friends know about change

MINI-TEST 7

READING

1. A	4. A	7. A	10. B
2. D	5. D	8. C	11. A
3. B	6. C	9. B	12. A

13.	divergent boundary:	(3) (8)
	convergent boundary:	(4) (5)
	transcurrent boundary:	(2) (7)

LISTENING

1. B	5. D	9. A, D
2. D	6. B	10. A
3. A	7. N, N, Y, N	11. C3, C2, C1
4. C	8. C	

SPEAKING

Sample Notes

Question 2

TOPIC OF READING PASSAGE: part of syllabus describing professor's policy on preparation for class discussions

professor's policy:
- students must complete assigned reading before class
- must take part in class discussions
- should not come to class if they have not completed the reading
- should not come to class if they are not going to take part in class discussion

TOPIC OF LISTENING PASSAGE: students' reaction to policy on preparation for class discussions

students' reaction:
- woman at first questions policy
- man explains that he knows policy is real from friend who took class
- woman comes to believe that policy is real

Question 3

TOPIC OF LISTENING PASSAGE: problem called NIMBY (not-in-my-backyard)

situation with NIMBY:
- response when government wants to construct facility that will impact community (prison, landfill, mental hospital, power plant)
- citizens want these facilities but somewhere else
- NIMBY takes form of meetings, demonstrations, picketing, letter writing

WRITING

TOPIC OF READING PASSAGE: hemophilia (disease where blood clots slowly or fails to clot)

transmission of hemophilia:
- disease usually passed from mother to son
- daughter can carry gene for disease and pass it to next generation
- son will develop disease

TOPIC OF LISTENING PASSAGE: royal hemophilia (example of hemophilia)

how royal hemophilia has been transmitted:
- Queen Victoria in England became carrier somehow
- Queen Victoria passed gene for disease to 3 of 9 children (1 son and 2 daughters)
- daughter Beatrice carried gene for disease to royal family of Spain
- daughter Alice carried gene for disease to royal families of Austria and Russia

TOPIC STATEMENT: In this set of materials, the reading passage discusses the characteristics of the disease hemophilia, and the listening passage describes a famous situation where this disease exists.

MINI-TEST 8

READING

1. B	4. C	7. D	10. D
2. B	5. A	8. A	11. D
3. D	6. B	9. A	12. A

13.	only the New York limners:	(3) (8)
	only the New England limners:	(1) (5)
	both the New York and New England limners:	(4) (7)

LISTENING

1. D	7. C2, C4, C1, C3
2. C	8. B, C
3. C, D	9. C
4. B	10. D
5. A	11. A
6. A	

SPEAKING

Sample Notes

Question 2

TOPIC OF READING PASSAGE: characteristics of somnambulism (sleepwalking)

characteristics:
- perhaps caused by fatigue, exhaustion, anxiety, drugs
- may result in simple actions (sitting up, getting up, walking around)
- may result in complex actions (dressing, washing dishes, moving furniture, operating machines)
- may be brief or last more than an hour

TOPIC OF LISTENING PASSAGE: common misconceptions about somnambulism (sleepwalking)

two common misconceptions:
- that it is dangerous to awaken a sleepwalker
- that a sleepwalker can't get hurt

Question 3

TOPIC OF LISTENING PASSAGE: student conversation about a problem the woman is having in a class

main points about the conversation:
- woman taking a class that man already took
- man didn't enjoy class at first but did later

- woman just starting class and doesn't like it
- problem is that professor goes so fast
- man says solution is to ask a lot of questions
- professor slows down to answer questions
- woman decides to start asking a lot of questions

COMPLETE TEST 1

READING 1

1. B	4. B	7. A	10. B
2. D	5. D	8. C	11. A
3. C	6. A	9. B	12. D

13.	study of astronomy as it refers to prehistoric cultures:	(3) (4) (6)

READING 2

14. D	17. C	20. B	23. B
15. B	18. A	21. D	24. C
16. A	19. D	22. C	25. A

26.	Truman and organized labor:	(1) (2) (4) (6)

READING 3

27. C	30. A	33. D	36. B
28. A	31. C	34. B	37. D
29. D	32. B	35. A	38. C

39.	quinary system:	(1) (8)
	decimal system:	(2) (10)
	vigesimal system:	(3) (6)
	sexagesimal system:	(4) (9)

LISTENING

1. A	18. B
2. Y, N, Y, N, Y, N	19. C
3. B	20. D
4. D	21. D
5. D	22. C
6. C	23. C
7. C	24. A
8. B	25. D
9. C1, C1, C1, C2	26. D
10. A, D	27. B
11. D	28. C2, C1, C3
12. B	29. A
13. C	30. B
14. C2, C1, C3	31. B
15. A, D	32. N, Y, N, Y
16. A	33. D
17. C3, C2, C1	34. C

SPEAKING

Sample Notes

Question 3

TOPIC OF READING PASSAGE: notice about getting tickets for special show

main points about notice:
- Spring Show is annual event
- tickets go on sale for students on March 1
- remaining tickets go on sale to public on March 8
- tickets always sell out early

TOPIC OF LISTENING PASSAGE: student conversation about getting tickets for Spring Show

what each student thinks:
- woman has not seen notice and does not know about show (because she is new to school)
- man emphasizes that she should see show and should get tickets soon (before they sell out)

Question 4

TOPIC OF READING PASSAGE: communication by great apes (gorillas, chimpanzees, orangutans)

characteristics of ape communication:
- communicate in variety of ways (facial expressions, gestures, calls)
- express wide range of ideas (anger, fear, danger, dominance, acceptance)

TOPIC OF LISTENING PASSAGE: Limitations of ape communication.

Two kinds of limitations:
- lack of displacement (communicate only about things that are present)
- lack of productivity (communicate without manipulating to create new meanings)

Question 5

TOPIC OF LISTENING PASSAGE: student conversation about woman's schedule for next semester

main points about conversation:
- woman must take a science class next semester
- woman is dreading this class
- man says it is not a problem
- man says there are many science classes to choose from
- man says she should have a more positive attitude about the science class
- man says she should choose a science class and maybe they can take it together
- woman is pleased with man's suggestion

Question 6

TOPIC OF LISTENING PASSAGE: mercantilism (economic policy of trading nations from 1580s to 1720s)

main points about mercantilism:
- was based on developing trade between nations
- had as goal to amass national wealth
- created national wealth by receiving payments in gold for exports over imports

WRITING

TOPIC OF READING PASSAGE: characteristics of planet Venus

characteristics:
- shines brightly (so is called morning star and evening star)
- covered with clouds (clouds reflect sunlight)
- extremely hot (around 900 degrees Fahrenheit)

TOPIC OF LISTENING PASSAGE: surprising heat on Venus

what is surprising about heat:

- clouds reflect sunlight away from Venus
- Venus is farther away from Sun than Mercury but is hotter than Mercury

possible explanation for heat:
- dense atmosphere made of carbon dioxide
- heat trapped by dense atmosphere

TOPIC STATEMENT: In this set of materials, the reading passage describes certain characteristics of Venus, and the listening passage provides a possible explanation for one of the surprising characteristics.

COMPLETE TEST 2

READING 1

1. B	4. C	7. A	10. B
2. A	5. B	8. D	11. A
3. D	6. B	9. C	12. C

13.	direction:	(2) (7) (10)
	latitude:	(1) (3) (6) (9)
	longitude:	(5)

READING 2

14. D	17. A	20. D	23. A
15. C	18. B	21. A	24. D
16. B	19. C	22. B	25. C

26.	our understanding of Neanderthals:	(1) (4) (6)

READING 3

27. A	30. C	33. A	36. C
28. C	31. C	34. C	37. D
29. B	32. A	35. B	38. A

39.	primitive era:	(4) (6) (9)
	transitional era:	(1) (5) (8)
	mature era:	(2) (7) (10)

LISTENING

1. D	13. B	25. C1, C3, C2
2. C	14. Y, N, Y, Y	26. C, D
3. A, D	15. A, C	27. C2, C3, C1
4. A	16. B, D	28. D
5. A, D	17. D	29. C
6. D	18. B	30. A, C
7. A	19. D	31. D
8. C	20. A, C	32. Y, N, N, Y
9. B, D	21. C2, C1, C3	33. A
10. Y, N, Y, N	22. A	34. B
11. A, D	23. B	
12. D	24. C	

SPEAKING

Sample Notes

Question 3

TOPIC OF READING PASSAGE: notice from Business Department on internships

main points about notice:
- some internships in local businesses available
- internships require 10 hours per week for 12 weeks
- students with internships sign up for Business 500
- students submit application and three references

TOPIC OF LISTENING PASSAGE: student conversation about notice on internships

what students think about internships:
- woman not interested in internships at first because there is no pay
- man explains that they get units and experience
- woman changes mind about internships

Question 4

TOPIC OF READING PASSAGE: speed of aircraft

main points about speed of aircraft:
- subsonic = slower than speed of sound
- supersonic = faster than speed of sound
- Mach 1 = at speed of sound
- Mach 2 = twice speed of sound

TOPIC OF LISTENING PASSAGE: sound in relation to supersonic aircraft

when sound from supersonic aircraft is heard:
- person on ground will not hear supersonic aircraft before it approaches (it is flying faster than the speed of sound)
- person on ground will hear sonic boom after supersonic aircraft passes (creates a shock wave as it passes)

Question 5

TOPIC OF LISTENING PASSAGE: conversation about a project two students are starting

main points about the conversation:
- man and woman working on project together
- woman's roommate did same project last quarter so woman knows about it
- professor gives a few instructions each week
- roommate says it is best to work on a few steps each week
- roommate did not do the project step by step
- man and woman decide to start now on first steps

Question 6

TOPIC OF LISTENING PASSAGE: multiple personality disorder (one person with two or more personalities)

characteristics of multiple personalities in one person:
- have different names, genders, and ages (young female Mary versus older male Michael)
- have different personalities (shy and quiet versus outgoing)
- have different talents, abilities, knowledge (musical talent, knowledge of card game, ability to speak foreign language)

WRITING

TOPIC OF READING PASSAGE: library at Alexandria (ancient library)

description of library:
- founded by Ptolemy I
- expanded by Ptolemy II
- had 300,000 to 700,000 scrolls

how scrolls obtained:
- borrowed or bought and copied by hand

- from foreign powers in trade
- from citizens in payment of debts
- from ships in port

TOPIC OF LISTENING PASSAGE: how library was destroyed

<u>thought to have been destroyed by Julius Caesar:</u>
- Julius Caesar invaded port of Alexandria (48–47 B.C.)
- Caesar's forces set ships in port on fire
- fire could have spread to library

<u>clues that Julius Caesar did not destroy library:</u>
- library mentioned in literature long after time of Caesar
- movement to destroy temples and libraries in 4th century

TOPIC STATEMENT: In this set of materials, the reading passage discusses the library at Alexandria, and the listening passage discusses the cause of the destruction of the library.

APPENDIX A

APPENDIX EXERCISE A1

1. *pleases; chance*
2. *speaks; energy*
3. *competitor; shocked; outcome*
4. *remarks; brief*
5. *problems; resolved*
6. *acts; positive; determined*
7. *indicated; finish; eventually*
8. *answers; succinct*
9. *complex; explanation*
10. *novel; concept*
11. *appreciates; animated; discussions*
12. *reasons; involved; episode*

APPENDIX EXERCISE A2

1. *this; herself; she; them; her; this*
2. *our; ourselves; your; mine; our; we; it; ourselves; this*
3. *these; they; their; them; themselves; they; themselves*
4. *he; this; he; it; him; his; himself; he; his*

APPENDIX EXERCISE A3

1. *However*
2. *For instance*
3. *Furthermore*
4. *In fact*
5. *Fortunately*
6. *in contrast*
7. *nonetheless*
8. *therefore*
9. *moreover*
10. *in summary*
11. *surprisingly*
12. *on the other hand*
13. *for example*
14. *as a result*
15. *in conclusion*
16. *consequently*
17. *in addition*
18. *nevertheless*
19. *interestingly*
20. *indeed*

APPENDIX EXERCISE (A1–A3)

1. It (B); he (B); His (B); fear (A); act (A)
2. However (C); this (B); main (A); point (A); board (A)
3. her (B); lecture (A); these (B); concepts (A)
4. He (B); objected (A); Nonetheless (C); plan (A)
5. no late (A); assignments (A); In fact (C); assignment (A); submitted (A)

6. Unfortunately (C); this (B); account (A); newspaper (A); these (B); inaccuracies (A)
7. you (B); this (B); decision (A); yourself (B); thesis (A); comprehensive exam (A); decision (A)
8. Indeed (C); outset (A); huge amount of effort (A); project (A); Not surprisingly (A); their (B); effort (A); they (B); project (A)
9. However (C); assignment (A); assignment (A); he (B); These (B); contradictory things (A); students (A); confused (A)
10. these (B); corporations (A); students (A); interviews (A); corporate (A); representatives (A); campus (A); interviews (A); Thus (C); interviews (A)

APPENDIX B

APPENDIX EXERCISE B1

1. I <u>reasons</u>
2. I (When) <u>everyone</u> . . . <u>decided</u>
3. C I <u>found</u>
4. I <u>discusses</u>
5. I <u>preference</u>
6. C <u>piece</u>. . . <u>was found</u>
7. I (As soon as) . . . <u>article</u> . . . <u>appears</u>
8. I <u>is</u>
9. I <u>agreement</u>
10. C It <u>happened</u>
11. I (As) <u>no one</u> . . . <u>would have made</u>
12. I <u>made</u>
13. C <u>agreement</u> . . . <u>has been reached</u>
14. I <u>poem</u>
15. I (Now that) <u>you</u> <u>have told</u>
16. C We <u>forgot</u>
17. I
18. I (If) <u>you</u> <u>think</u>
19. C <u>manager</u> . . . <u>made</u>
20. I (Even though) <u>you</u> <u>gave</u>

APPENDIX EXERCISE B2

1. I <u>matter was</u> . . . (,) <u>I could to decide</u>
2. C <u>children broke</u> . . . (, but) . . . <u>parents did</u> . . . <u>find out</u>
3. I <u>She expected</u> . . . (, however) <u>she did</u> . . . <u>graduate</u>
4. C <u>family moved</u> . . . (; as a result,) <u>I</u> . . . <u>had</u>
5. I <u>I made</u> . . . (and) <u>I</u> <u>vowed</u>
6. C <u>Sam did</u> . . . <u>sign</u> . . . (, so) <u>he</u> <u>signed</u>
7. C <u>students waited</u> . . . (. Finally,) <u>they got</u>
8. I <u>parents advised</u> . . . ( ) <u>he did</u> . . . <u>take</u>
9. I <u>job</u> . . . <u>was</u> . . . (,) . . . <u>I was given</u>
10. C <u>Tom</u> . . . <u>wanted</u> . . . (, yet) <u>he did</u> . . . <u>know</u>
11. I <u>We must return</u> . . . (, otherwise) <u>we will have</u>
12. C <u>She</u> . . . <u>tries</u> . . . (. However,) <u>she</u> . . . <u>loses</u>
13. I (Therefore) <u>she has gotten</u> . . . (,) <u>she can pay</u>
14. C <u>She had</u> . . . (; as a result,) <u>she is</u>
15. I <u>They left</u> . . . (,) <u>it began</u>
16. C <u>I wanted</u> . . . (; unfortunately,) <u>this was</u>
17. C <u>I will have</u> . . . (, or) <u>I will</u> . . . <u>be</u>
18. I <u>accident happened</u> . . . (, afterwards,) . . . <u>police came</u> . . . <u>wrote</u>
19. I <u>plan has</u> . . . ( ) <u>it</u> . . . <u>has</u>
20. C <u>directions must be followed</u> . . . (; otherwise,) . . . <u>outcome will be</u>

APPENDIX EXERCISE B3

1. I   <u>reason</u> (that) <u>he took</u> . . . <u>it was</u>
2. C   (Why) . . . <u>man did</u> . . . <u>will</u> . . . <u>be</u>
3. C   <u>ticket</u> (that) <u>I needed</u> . . . <u>was</u>
4. I   (What) . . . <u>lifeguard did</u> <u>it was</u>
5. I   <u>day</u> (when) <u>I found</u> . . . <u>it was</u>
6. C   <u>teacher</u> (whose) . . . <u>I remember</u> . . . <u>was</u>
7. I   (Where) <u>we went</u> . . . <u>it was</u>
8. I   (That) <u>he</u> . . . <u>said</u> . . . <u>it could</u> . . . <u>be refuted</u>
9. I   <u>man</u> (who) <u>helped</u> . . . <u>he was</u>
10. C   (How) . . . <u>paper got</u> . . . <u>remains</u>
11. I   (What) <u>caused</u> . . . <u>it is</u>
12. C   <u>plans</u> (that) <u>we made</u> . . . <u>were</u>
13. I   <u>process</u> . . . (which) . . . <u>decisions were made it was</u>
14. C   (Whatever) <u>she gets is</u> (what) <u>she deserves</u>
15. C   <u>employee</u> (who) <u>has</u> . . . (that) <u>you need is</u>
16. I   (What) <u>he wrote</u> . . . <u>it could</u> . . . <u>be taken</u>
17. I   <u>officer</u> (who) <u>stopped</u> . . . <u>he gave</u>
18. C   (How) <u>he could believe</u> . . . (that) <u>is</u> . . . <u>is</u>
19. C   <u>reason</u> (that) <u>I applied</u> . . . <u>was</u> (that) . . . <u>tuition was</u>
20. I   (Why) <u>they said</u> (what) <u>they said</u> . . . (who) <u>tried</u> . . . <u>it was</u>

APPENDIX EXERCISE (B1–B3)
(possible corrections)

1. *relationships, the*	should be	*relationships; the*
2. *reached but*	should be	*reached, but*
o'clock, that	should be	*o'clock; that*
3. *morning it was*	should be	*morning was*
Friday it would	should be	*Friday would*
because did	should be	*because I did*
4. *scholarships have*	should be	*scholarship have*
5. *moves, it*	should be	*moves, but it*
career, so we	should be	*career, we*
6. (no errors)		
7. *raised, however*	should be	*raised; however*
8. *confidential, they*	should be	*confidential; they*
If want	should be	*If you want*
do it is	should be	*do is*
9. *trees and*	should be	*trees, and*
heard they would	should be	*heard would*
10. (no errors)		

APPENDIX C

APPENDIX EXERCISE C1

C 1.   <u>rangers</u> (in the eastern section) (of the park) <u>have spotted</u>
I 2.   <u>flowers</u> (on the plum tree) (in the garden) <u>has started</u>
       (flowers . . . have started)
I 3.   <u>cost</u> (of the books) (for all) (of his classes) <u>are</u>
       (cost . . . is)
C 4.   <u>reports</u> . . . (by the staff) (for the manager) <u>contain</u>
I 5.   <u>light</u> (from the candles) (on the end tables) <u>provide</u>
       (light . . . provides)
I 6.   <u>ideas</u> . . . (at the meeting) (of the council) <u>was</u>
       (ideas . . . were)
C 7.   <u>gemstones</u> (in the necklace) . . . (by the actress) <u>were</u>

I 8.   <u>speech</u> (on a variety) (of topics) (of great importance) (to the citizens) <u>are being broadcast</u>
       (speech . . . is being broadcast)
C 9.   <u>tires</u> (for the front) (of the car) <u>are being installed</u>
I 10.   <u>exams</u> . . . (for the last week) (of the semester) <u>is going</u>
       (exams . . . are going)

APPENDIX EXERCISE C2

C 1.   <u>All</u> . . . (experience) <u>has contributed</u>
I 2.   <u>Most</u> . . . (dishes) . . . <u>was</u>
       (Most . . . dishes . . . were)
I 3.   <u>Some</u> . . . (details) . . . <u>requires</u>
       (Some . . . details . . . require)
C 4.   <u>Half</u> . . . (material) <u>needs</u>
I 5.   <u>All</u> . . . (homes) . . . <u>was</u>
       (All . . . homes . . . were)
I 6.   <u>Most</u> . . . (children) . . . <u>has improved</u>
       (Most . . . children . . . have improved)
C 7.   <u>Some</u> . . . (money) . . . <u>has</u>
I 8.   <u>half</u> . . . (eggs) . . . <u>was</u>
       (half . . . eggs . . . were)
C 9.   <u>all</u> . . . (medicine) <u>has</u>
C 10.   <u>most</u> . . . (time) . . . <u>was</u>

APPENDIX EXERCISE C3

I 1.   <u>was really scary</u> (but) <u>was still quite pleasure</u>
       (pleasurable)
C 2.   <u>that he was sorry</u> (and) <u>that he would make amends</u>
I 3.   <u>idealism</u>, <u>integrity</u>, (and) <u>dedicate</u>
       (dedication)
I 4.   <u>tall</u> (yet) . . . <u>athlete</u>
       (athletic)
C 5.   <u>call</u> . . . , <u>write</u> . . . , (or) <u>send</u>
C 6.   <u>in the spring semester</u> (but) <u>not in the fall semester</u>
I 7.   <u>Los Angeles</u> (and) <u>New York</u> . . . <u>pick up</u> . . . (and) <u>delivers</u>
       (deliver)
I 8.   <u>work</u> . . . (or) <u>studies</u>
       (study)
C 9.   <u>pain</u>, <u>anger</u>, <u>resentment</u>, <u>frustration</u>, (and) <u>disbelief</u>
C 10.   <u>well-rehearsed</u> (yet) <u>natural-sounding</u>

APPENDIX EXERCISE C4

I 1.   (not only) <u>plays football</u> (but also) <u>baseball</u>
       (plays baseball)
C 2.   (either) <u>praised</u> (or) <u>scolded</u>
I 3.   (both) <u>in the refrigerator</u> (and) <u>the freezer</u>
       (in the freezer)
I 4.   (neither) <u>what you prefer</u> (or) <u>what I prefer</u>
       (nor)
C 5.   (not only) <u>misplaced</u> . . . (but also) <u>couldn't find</u>
I 6.   (Either) <u>you can work</u> . . . (or) <u>join</u>
       (, or you can join)
C 7.   She was (both) <u>challenged by</u> (and) <u>frustrated with</u>
C 8.   (Neither) <u>the manager</u> (nor) <u>any members</u>
I 9.   (either) <u>register for three courses</u> (or) <u>for four courses</u>
       (register for four courses)
I 10.   (Both) <u>the children</u> (as well as) <u>the baby-sitter</u>
       (and)

APPENDIX EXERCISE C5

I 1. (the unusualest)
    (the most unusual)
C 2. (more expensive than)
C 3. (the angriest)
I 4. (the hotter than)
    (hotter than)
I 5. (more cloudier) today (than)
    (cloudier . . . than)
C 6. (the most ancient)
C 7. (wider than)
I 8. (the most tallest)
    (the tallest)
I 9. (most efficient)
    (the most efficient)
C 10. (stronger) . . . (more flavorful than)

APPENDIX EXERCISE C6

C 1. (the friendliest)
I 2. (the most difficult of)
    (more difficult than)
I 3. (a nicest disposition than)
    (a nicer disposition than)
C 4. (the best party)
I 5. (the most fuel-efficient of)
    (more fuel-efficient than)
I 6. (the drier that)
    (the driest that)
C 7. (the most understanding of)
I 8. (earlier that)
    (the earliest that)
I 9. (the highest of)
    (higher than)
C 10. (more reticent than)

APPENDIX REVIEW EXERCISE (C1–C6)

C 1.
C 2.
I 3. *(the nearest)*
I 4. *(left)*
I 5. *(were)*
I 6. *(the most important)*
C 7.
C 8.
I 9. *(a more honorable)*
C 10.
I 11. *(are)*
I 12. *(the most ridiculous)*
C 13.
I 14. *(were)*
C 15.

APPENDIX EXERCISE C7

I 1. have came
    (have come)
C 2. thought . . . had told
I 3. has wore
    (has worn)
C 4. have blown
I 5. has running
    (has run)
C 6. had struck . . . had knocked
I 7. have drew
    (have drawn)
C 8. has taught

I 9. had . . . knew
    (had . . . known)
C 10. have . . . gotten

APPENDIX EXERCISE C8

I 1. will be inaugurate
    (will be inaugurated)
C 2. were presented . . . are unchanged
I 3. was took
    (was taken)
C 4. has been promoted
I 5. are . . . arguing . . . is happens
    (is happening)
I 6. should . . . have been smoke . . . was
    (should . . . have been smoking)
C 7. was ringing
I 8. were froze
    (were frozen)
C 9. is wondering . . . will be departing
I 10. were take off . . . land
    (were taking off . . . landing)

APPENDIX EXERCISE C9
(possible answers)

C 1. cannot return
I 2. may preferring
    (may prefer)
I 3. will depends
    (will depend)
C 4. might be coming
I 5. must to try
    (must try)
I 6. could taken
    (could take)
C 7. might announce
I 8. must . . . gave
    (must . . . give)
I 9. will going
    (will go or will be going)
C 10. was . . . would not start

APPENDIX EXERCISE C10

I 1. need . . . was
    (need . . . is or needed . . . was)
C 2. has . . . describes . . . happened
I 3. told . . . is pleased . . . heard
    (was)
C 4. is . . . did . . . understand
C 5. had . . . is going
I 6. leaves . . . took
    (leaves . . . takes or left . . . took)
I 7. was landing . . . remain
    (was landing . . . remained or is landing . . . remain)
C 8. are . . . committed
I 9. filled . . . up . . . heads
    (headed)
C 10. understand . . . happened . . . are . . . occurred

APPENDIX EXERCISE C11
(possible answers)

C 1. is . . . has graduated
I 2. had rung . . . leave
    (had rung . . . left or has rung . . . leave)
I 3. have visited . . . traveled
    (travel or have traveled)

C 4. found . . . had made
C 5. are based . . . have done
I 6. had been collected . . . dismisses
(dismissed)
C 7. was . . . growing . . . had . . . been
C 8. knows . . . have . . . tried
C 9. can tell . . . know . . . has transpired
C 10. will be . . . have submitted

APPENDIX EXERCISE C12

I 1. (By 1995) . . . has decided
(had decided)
C 2. was established (in 1900)
I 3. (Since) . . . saw . . . got
(have gotten)
I 4. Mike has applied . . . (a few months ago)
(applied)
C 5. elected . . . (last month)
I 6. experienced . . . (lately)
(have experienced)
C 7. (By the end of the meeting) . . . had reached
I 8. has . . . graduated . . . (in June)
(finally graduated)
I 9. am living . . . (since) I was
(have been living)
C 10. was . . . called . . . tried . . . (a few minutes ago) . . . got

APPENDIX EXERCISE C13

I 1. will be trim
(will be trimmed)
C 2. is made
I 3. robbed
(was robbed)
I 4. were describing
(were described)
C 5. has been changed . . . have been filled
I 6. have given
(have been given)
C 7. was cooked . . . was brought
I 8. was accepted
(was accepted by)
I 9. will . . . be allowed . . . have . . . been pay
(have . . . been paid)
C 10. is being held . . . will be posted

APPENDIX EXERCISE C14

I 1. won
(was won)
C 2. started
I 3. placed
(were placed)
I 4. selected
(were selected)
C 5. opened
I 6. expected
(was expected)
C 7. amused
I 8. announced
(were announced)
I 9. knocked . . . fell off
(were knocked)
C 10. lasted

APPENDIX REVIEW EXERCISE (C7–C14)

I 1. (may have)
C 2.
I 3. (were washed and chopped up)
I 4. (have drunk)
I 5. (has not taken)
I 6. (expected)
I 7. (was founded)
C 8.
C 9.
I 10. (had paid)
I 11. (am trying)
I 12. (had managed)
C 13.
C 14.
I 15. (was interviewed)

APPENDIX EXERCISE C15

I 1. (Each) exhibits
(exhibit)
C 2. (Both) children . . . (various) assignments
C 3. (single) scoop . . . (two) scoops
I 4. (several) pills (every) days
(day)
C 5. (an) . . . time . . . (many) students
I 6. (Various) plans . . . (a) . . . centers
(center)
I 7. (Every) times . . . (several) acquaintances
(time)
I 8. (single) serving . . . (one) people
(person)
C 9. (One) incident . . . (many) misunderstandings
I 10. (several) candidates . . . (each) ones
(one)

APPENDIX EXERCISE C16

C 1. (Many) applicants
I 2. (amount) . . . people
(number)
C 3. (Few) suggestions . . . (little) help
I 4. (more) opportunities . . . (less) restrictions
(fewer)
I 5. (much) . . . assurances
(many)
C 6. (number) . . . facts
I 7. (less) concern . . . (much) . . . bills
(many)
C 8. (fewer) men . . . women
I 9. (many) . . . problems . . . (little)
(few)
C 10. (amount) . . . paper

APPENDIX EXERCISE C17

I 1. (Him) . . . (me)
(He and I)
C 2. (We) . . . (them) . . . (they) . . . (us)
I 3. (you) . . . (I), (I) . . . (they)
(you . . . me)
C 4. (He) . . . (she) . . . (us) . . . (we)
I 5. (You) . . . (I) . . . (he) . . . (her)
(him . . . her)
I 6. (It) . . . (we)
(for us students)
C 7. (She) . . . (I) . . . (it) to (her) . . . (I) . . . (she)

I 8. (They) . . . (you) . . . (I) . . . (I) . . . (we)
(you and me)
C 9. (It) . . . (us) . . . (it) . . . (him) . . . (her)
I 10. (They) . . . (you) . . . (I)
(you and me)

APPENDIX EXERCISE C18

I 1. (our) . . . (ours)
(our teammates)
C 2. (your) . . . (mine)
C 3. (his) . . . (hers)
I 4. (her) . . . (my)
(mine)
C 5. (Your) . . . (my)
I 6. (theirs)
(their offices)
I 7. (my) . . . (your)
(yours)
C 8. (his) . . . (hers)
I 9. (ours) . . . (theirs)
(our keys)
C 10. (your) . . . (hers) . . . (her) . . . (yours)

APPENDIX EXERCISE C19

I 1. <u>Papers</u> . . . (it)
(them)
C 2. <u>party</u> . . . (my) <u>neighbors</u> . . . (they) . . . (it)
I 3. <u>Everyone</u> . . . (you)
(he or she wants)
I 4. <u>concert</u> . . . (we) . . . (our) . . . (them)
(it)
C 5. <u>sunshine</u> . . . (I) . . . (it) . . .(my)
I 6. <u>man</u> . . . <u>problem</u> . . . (he) . . . (it) . . . (herself)
(himself)
I 7. (My) . . . <u>book</u> . . . (she) . . . (I) . . . (her)
(it)
C 8. (Your) <u>brothers</u> . . . <u>money</u> . . . (they) . . . (you) . . . (it) . . . (yourself)
I 9. <u>person</u> . . . (their)
(her or his)
I 10. (Your) <u>classmates</u> . . . (yourselves)
(themselves)

APPENDIX REVIEW EXERCISE (C15–C19)

I 1. *(many times)*
C 2.
C 3.
I 4. *(He and she)*
C 5.
C 6.
I 7. *(them)*
I 8. *(to you and me)*
I 9. *(few of them)*
C 10.
I 11. *(various needs)*
C 12.
I 13. *(theirs)*
I 14. *(fewer calories)*
C.15.

APPENDIX EXERCISE C20

I 1. *extreme* describes *humid*
humid describes *condition*
(extremely)

C 2. *hungry* describes *baby*
quite describes *plaintively*
plaintively describes *wailed*
I 3. *real* describes *exciting*
exciting describes *movie*
unexpected describes *ending*
(really)
C 4. *striking* describes *workers*
slowly and *deliberately* describe *marched*
locked describes *gate*
front describes *gates*
I 5. *complex* describes *issue*
thoroughly describes *studied*
difficultly describes *decision*
(difficult)
C 6. *parking* describes *lot*
recently describes *had . . . been resurfaced*
thick and *black* describe *asphalt*
I 7. *extremely* describes *cautious*
cautious describes *proceeded*
totally describes *acceptable*
acceptable describes *outcome*
(cautiously)
I 8. *rather* describes *suddenly*
suddenly describes *decided*
considerable describes *alter*
(considerably)
C 9. *large* and *white* describe *building*
circular describes *driveway*
main describes *office*
I 10. *brilliantly* describes *idea*
supposed describes *shortcut*
(brilliant)

APPENDIX EXERCISE C21

I 1. *immediately* decribes *return*
(return the necklace immediately)
C 2. *serious* describes *man*
always describes *works*
diligently describes *works*
C 3. *worried* describes *mother*
gently describes *scolded*
little describes *girl*
I 4. *often* describes *uses*
(often uses)
I 5. *attentive* describes *lifeguard*
quickly describes *jumped*
(attentive lifeguard)
C 6. *clearly* describes *explain*
I 7. *carefully* describes *studied*
monthly describes *report*
(carefully studied)
C 8. *skillfully* describes *questioned*
hostile describes *witness*
I 9. *always* describes *cannot remember*
(cannot always remember)
I 10. *suddenly* describes *dropped*
local describes *people*
chilly describes *weather*
(local people)

APPENDIX EXERCISE C22

C 1. (fast-moving)
fast-moving describes *line*

I 2. (satisfying) customers
satisfying describes *customers*
(satisfied)

I 3. people . . . (shocked) . . . (disturbed) news
shocked describes *people*
disturbed describes *news*
(disturbing)

C 4. (delighted) girl . . . (unexpected) gift
delighted describes *girl*
unexpected describes *gift*

I 5. (depressed) situation
depressed describes *situation*
(depressing)

I 6. (snow-capped) mountains . . . (charmed) village
snow-capped describes *mountains*
charmed describes *village*
(charming)

C 7. (annoying) guest . . . (frustrated) host
annoying described *guest*
frustrated describes *host*

I 8. (correcting) papers . . . (waiting) students
correcting describes *papers*
waiting describes *students*
(corrected)

C 9. (unidentified) attacker . . . (strolling) couple
unidentified describes *attacker*
strolling describes *couple*

I 10. (requesting) room . . . (unobstructing) view
requesting describes *room*
unobstructing describes *view*
(requested . . . unobstructed)

APPENDIX EXERCISE C23

I 1. Man . . . hat . . . door
(A man . . . a . . . hat . . . the door)

C 2. (a) . . . task

I 3. job
(a part-time job)

C 4.

I 5. feeling . . . event
(a funny feeling . . . a surprising event)

C 6. (a) van . . . (a) family

I 7. (the) . . . course . . . textbook . . . presentation
(a textbook . . . a presentation)

I 8. (The) family . . . snake . . . dog
(a snake . . . a . . . dog)

C 9. (a) . . . opinion . . . (a) situation

C 10.

APPENDIX EXERCISE C24

C 1. (an) opportunity . . . (a) one-time

I 2. (a) mistake . . . (a) honest
(an honest)

C 3. (a) hotel . . . (a) jacuzzi . . . (a) heated

I 4. (a) honor . . . (a) guest . . . (a) important
(an honor . . . an important)

C 5. (a) once-in-a-lifetime . . . (a) faraway

I 6. (a) usual occurrence . . . (a) unusual
(an unusual)

C 7. (a) colorful . . . (a) hand-painted . . . (a) helium

I 8. (an) euphoric . . . (an) huge
(a euphoric . . . a huge)

I 9. (a) X . . . (a) signature . . . (a) document
(an X)

C 10. (a) traditional . . . (a) unicorn . . . (a) helpless

APPENDIX EXERCISE C25

I 1. (a) . . . uniforms
(a . . . uniform)

C 2. (a) notebook . . . (a) textbook

I 3. (a) . . . house . . . (a) . . . pool . . . (a) . . .
balconies . . . (a) . . . views
*(a . . . balcony . . . a . . . view . . . balcony or balconies
. . . views . . . balconies)*

I 4. (an) . . . theories
(an . . . theory)

C 5. (a) computer, (a) phone, (a) table

I 6. (a) . . . stories
(a . . . story)

I 7. (a) . . . dress, (a) . . . shoes, (a) . . . purse . . . (a) . . .
earrings
(shoes . . . earrings)

C 8. (a) . . . reason

I 9. (a) . . . biscuits
(biscuits)

C 10. (a) secretary

APPENDIX EXERCISE C26

I 1. (a) . . . ride . . . (an) . . . continent
(the African continent)

C 2. (a) movie . . . (a) . . . ending

I 3. (a) . . . cloud . . . (a) sky
(the sky)

I 4. (The) spacecraft . . . (a) planet
(the planet)

I 5. (The) teacher . . . (a) middle . . . (the) classroom . . .
(the) students
(the middle)

C 6. (an) idea . . . (a) topic . . . (an) . . . paper

I 7. (a) . . . hotel . . . (a) . . . time
(the . . . hotel . . . the . . . time)

I 8. (A) hat . . . (a) . . . hat
(The hat)

I 9. (a) prize . . . (a) . . . essay (the) . . . contest
(the . . . essay)

I 10. (the) man . . . (a) nose . . . (a) . . . nose
(the nose)

APPENDIX REVIEW EXERCISE (C20–C26)

I 1. *(an unbelievably)*

C 2.

I 3. *(often misplaces)*

I 4. *(The engine . . . a funny noise or funny noises)*

C 5.

C 6.

I 7. *(substantial benefits)*

C 8.

I 9. *(a nearby university)*

C 10.

I 11. *(a delight)*

I 12. *(unmade beds . . . unwashed dishes)*

C 13.

I 14. *(swiftly collected)*

I 15. *(the . . . principal . . . a speech)*